THE INSIDERS' GUIDE® TO CAPE COD

NANTUCKET & MARTHA'S VINEYARD

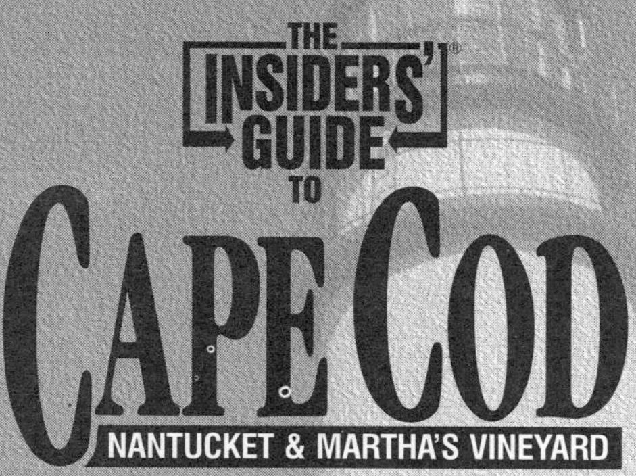

Jack Sheedy
and
Debi Boucher Stetson

Insiders' Publishing Inc.

Co-published and marketed by:
Cape Cod Times
319 Main Street
Hyannis, MA 02601
(508) 775-1200

Co-published and distributed by:
Insiders' Publishing Inc.
105 Budleigh St.
P.O. Box 2057
Manteo, NC 27954
(919) 473-6100

•

SECOND EDITION
1st printing

•

•

Printed in the United States
of America

•

Publications from The Insiders' Guide® series are available at special discounts for bulk purchases for sales promotions, premiums or fundraisings. Special editions, including personalized covers, can be created in large quantities for special needs. For more information, please write to Insiders' Publishing Inc., P.O. Box 2057, Manteo, NC 27954 or call (919) 473-6100 x 233.

ISBN 1-57380-018-X

Cape Cod Times

Strategic Ventures Director
Julie Kaminsky

Sales Executives
Kathleen LeBlanc
Betsy Manning

Researcher
Adriana M. Sheedy

Artist
Martha Flaherty

Insiders' Publishing Inc.

Publisher/Editor-in-Chief
Beth P. Storie

President/General Manager
Michael McOwen

Affiliate Sales and Training Director
Rosanne Cheeseman

Partner Services Director
Giles MacMillan

Sales and Marketing Director
Jennifer Risko

Creative Services Director
Mike Lay

Online Services Director
David Haynes

Managing Editor
Theresa Shea Chavez

Fulfillment Director
Gina Twiford

Project Editor
Molly Perkins

Project Artist
Stephanie Wills

Cover photos courtesy of (clockwise from top left) Cape Cod Chamber of Commerce, Steve Heaslip and Vince DeWitt. Spine photo courtesy of Peter Simon.

Preface

Anyone who has ever visited the Cape knows the thrill of cresting the bridge and getting that first glimpse of this small spit of land that curls its arm out into the Atlantic — or, if they've arrived by air, the excitement of looking down upon a green peninsula dotted with ponds and rimmed with tawny beaches set against a deep blue sea. There's that shudder of anticipation as you look forward to a week, a month or a whole summer of beach walks, lazy afternoons and starlit nights. For those of us who live here, driving back over the bridge after a trip off-Cape triggers an undeniable sense of relief: We are home, we are safe; all is well.

On these shores we can — to paraphrase Henry David Thoreau — leave all of America behind us. You can too. We invite you to come and get to know Cape Cod and the islands, to explore their many facets, to discover what draws thousands of visitors here each year. While the Cape is known as a summer paradise — with some 300 miles of shoreline you're never far from a beach, and the cooling sea breezes make for temperate weather when it's sweltering on the mainland — it is rapidly becoming a popular destination during the shoulder seasons of spring and fall as well. And for those of us who live here, winter is a welcome respite, a time to recharge.

Cape Cod has a large retirement population, but it is also home to many young families. It has more than its share of artists and writers, along with fishermen working to keep alive an age-old industry in the face of modern-day challenges. It is a haven for no small number of celebrities: notables such as Pulitzer Prize-winning author Norman Mailer, acclaimed mystery writer Mary Higgins Clark and actress Julie Harris make their homes here; the Kennedy family's famous summer home is in Hyannisport; and in 1996, Vice President Al Gore and his family vacationed in Truro. It's easy to see why the rich and famous, working folks and creative sorts alike fall in love with Cape Cod. The salt air, sunwashed beaches, the sweet breeze over marsh grass and the honeysuckle scent of dewy evenings conspire to cast their spell, and you'll find yourself returning again and again.

Many people finally decide they can't stay away and move here permanently. When they do, they find there's still much to discover. We've lived here for years, and we're still exploring, still discovering. This book is the perfect companion to take with you on your Cape Cod adventure, whether you are here for a weekend, a month, a season or all year round.

The Insider's Guide® to Cape Cod, Nantucket and Martha's Vineyard is a comprehensive guide to all the Cape has to offer. It is for anyone who plans to visit Cape Cod; anyone who has visited and plans to return; and anyone who has recently moved here, plans to move here or just dreams about it. It is for people who live here and find themselves playing host to an astonishing number of visitors in the summer months — hand your guests this book and send them out exploring and let them choose the restaurant where you'll all meet for dinner. (There's a plethora of dining choices in our Restaurants chapter.) It's for your cousin, who has never been to Nantucket or Martha's Vineyard and is insisting that this year the two of you must hop a ferry and see them together. (Our Nantucket and Martha's Vineyard chapters will show you the way.) It's for your dear friend who lives in the city and won't come with you to the Cape because she fears there's nothing to do. (Highlight the Arts and Entertainment and Nightlife chapters.)

It's for your Uncle Edwin, who keeps talking about retiring to the Cape but won't make a move. (Show him the Real Estate and Retirement chapters — and the Fishing and Golf chapters too!) It's for couples looking for a romantic getaway (you'll find one in the Inns and Bed and Breakfasts chapter), families planning a vacation (flip through our Hotels and Motels chapter, or, for outdoor lovers, our Campgrounds chapter, and don't miss Kidstuff). It's for people who want to know where to go and what to do while they're here and who to call if they need anything — be it a doctor, a kennel or a cottage to rent. It's for people who like to bike, shop, swim, lie in the sun, hunt for antiques, see great plays, go fishing, play tennis, browse in museums, learn about history, eat lobster, attend live concerts, walk on the beach, paint, go to church, sail or watch whales.

This book is for you. Read it, lend it, refer to it, scribble in its margins, use it as a lap desk when you're sitting on the beach writing postcards. Enjoy it, and let us know what you think — you may well end up with some Insider's tips of your own to share!

About the Authors

Jack Sheedy was born in Boston and grew up in Braintree (a suburb of Boston), yet spent nearly every summer of his youth along the beaches of Dennisport. His grandparents' cottage, just a minute's walk from Nantucket Sound, became a second home to him.

So it was only natural, after graduating from college in 1984 with a degree in marketing and with just 32 cents in his pocket, that he would return to Cape Cod to make a life for himself. Within months of his arrival he was engaged to Adriana Rockwell of Centerville and working in the marketing department of a local bank. The happy couple settled in the town of Dennis and today their children, Melissa and Gregory, attend Dennis schools.

Jack began writing while in college. He published his first article in the *Barnstable Patriot* in October 1985 at the age of 23. Since then he has published well over 100 articles and short stories in various Cape Cod newspapers.

Primarily a short story writer, Jack shifted gears in June 1993 to write a series of historical articles for *The Register* newspaper to help commemorate the town of Dennis' bicentennial celebration. That series, which originally was to consist of eight articles over the course of the summer, grew to become a 50-article series spanning a year and a half. Jack later compiled these articles into his first book, *Dennis Journal*.

Meanwhile, he continued as a regular contributor to the *Barnstable Patriot*. Since 1989, he has pitched in each year with articles for the newspaper's annual Cape history supplement, *Summerscape*. The 1995 issue was recognized by the New England Press Association, receiving first place for editorial content at their annual awards ceremony.

In addition to historical articles, Jack's perennial Halloween story in the *Patriot* has been scaring Barnstable residents for the past decade and has provided an outlet for his short story writing.

The success of his first book, now in its second printing, allowed him to publish a second book, a collection of poetry entitled *Autumn Cape Cod*. A third book, a compilation of articles which have appeared in *Summerscape*, is now in the works.

Besides writing, Jack enjoys lecturing on Cape Cod history. His plans include continuing to pursue a writing career while juggling his position at the International Fund for Animal Welfare in Yarmouthport and, of course, his most important role as the father of two very active children.

Originally from northern New Jersey, **Debi Boucher Stetson** first moved to Cape Cod in 1981, moved off-Cape twice but couldn't stay away for long. She has lived in five Cape towns over the years — from Barnstable to Wellfleet — but finally decided on Eastham, helped by the fact that she married a man who had already decided to live there. She has lived in Eastham since 1991.

Her nine-year career as a journalist came on the heels of an earlier career as a graphic artist; in that respect she followed in the footsteps of first her father, a graphic designer, and then her mother, a copy writer and short story writer. In addition to writing features about the Cape's inexhaustible supply of interesting places and people, she has covered news in the towns of Brewster, Harwich, Orleans and Eastham. She has worked as a reporter and editor for Cape Cod Newspapers; a reporter and copy editor for Spotlight Newspapers in upstate New York; and, most recently, a reporter for *The Cape Codder* newspaper in Orleans.

Among the most memorable issues she has covered are the restoration of the Crosby Mansion in Brewster, shoreline erosion and the effort to save Nauset Light in Eastham. Writing about less visible issues such as school expansions, challenges faced by small businesses and help for senior citizens has kept her close to the heartbeat of the Lower Cape.

Debi enjoys community theater and has done play reviews for *The Cape Codder* and the *Cape Cod Times*. She has also done public relations work, including a brochure for the Nauset Light Preservation Society as part of a volunteer stint as public relations coordinator for the nonprofit group.

She switched to part-time reporting soon after the birth of her son, Hunter, on St. Patrick's Day 1993, and last year left her steady job as a reporter in favor of the more precarious, but more flexible role of freelance writer. In between deadlines and keeping up with her preschooler (definitely the hardest but most rewarding job she's ever had), Debi does calligraphy, draws and paints when she has the time, and volunteers for beach cleanups. She works on her novel, reads, attends a writers' group in Yarmouthport and takes walks on the beach. She lives with her husband, Doug, a hotel manager, her son, Hunter, and two red cats on a dirt road in North Eastham, where a car going by is an event and people still leave their doors unlocked.

Though she loves the mountains and enjoys visiting other parts of New England, she would rather be an Insider here than any place else in the world.

Cape Cod

Martha's Vineyard and Nantucket

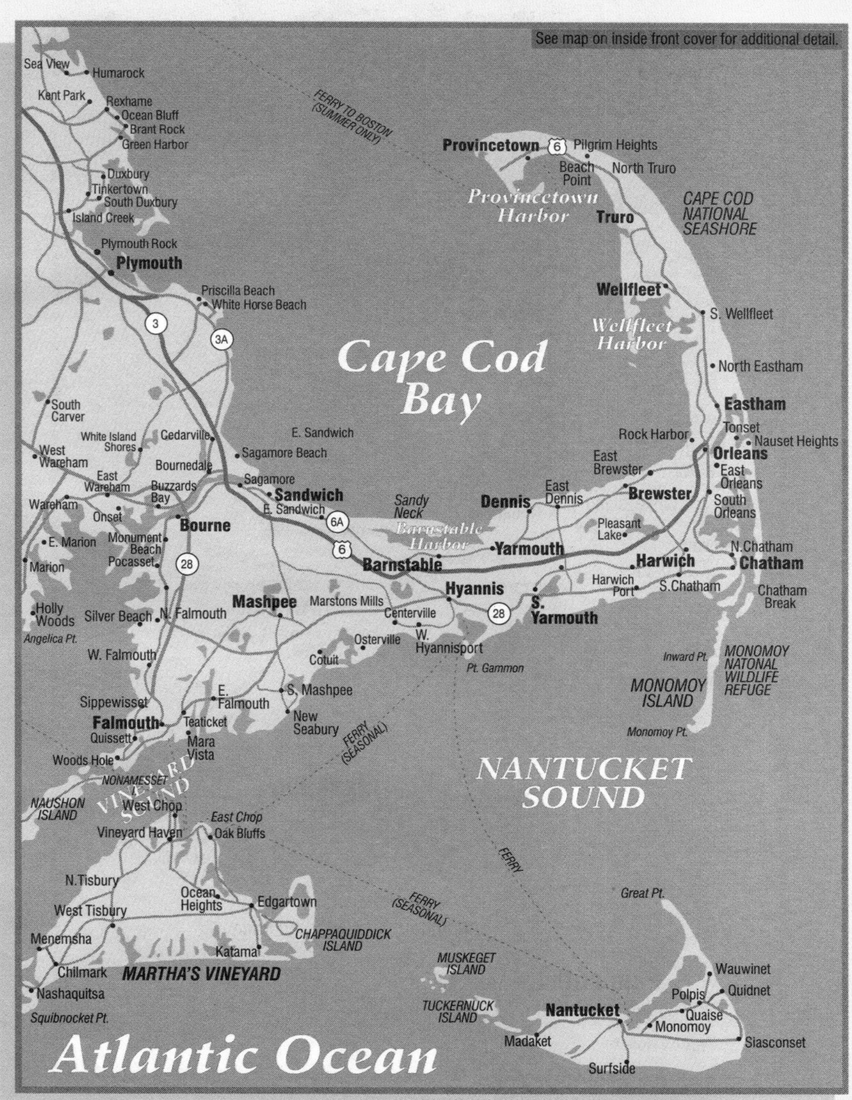

Upper Cape

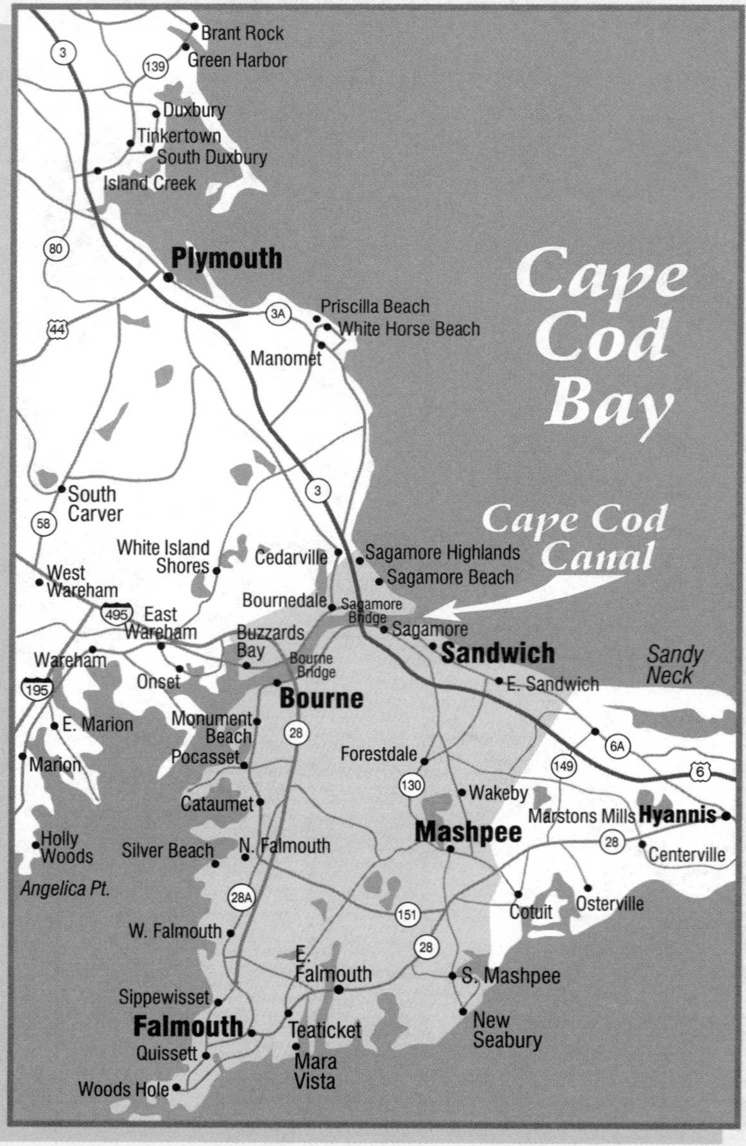

Brant Rock
Green Harbor
Duxbury
Tinkertown
South Duxbury
Island Creek
Plymouth
Cape Cod Bay
Priscilla Beach
White Horse Beach
Manomet
South Carver
White Island Shores
Cedarville
Sagamore Highlands
Sagamore Beach
Cape Cod Canal
West Wareham
Bournedale
Sagamore Bridge
Sagamore
East Wareham
Buzzards Bay
Sandwich
Sandy Neck
Wareham
Bourne Bridge
Onset
E. Sandwich
Bourne
E. Marion
Monument Beach
Marion
Pocasset
Forestdale
Cataumet
Wakeby
Marstons Mills
Hyannis
Mashpee
Holly Woods
Silver Beach
N. Falmouth
Centerville
Angelica Pt.
Osterville
Cotuit
W. Falmouth
E. Falmouth
S. Mashpee
Sippewisset
Falmouth
Teaticket
New Seabury
Quissett
Mara Vista
Woods Hole
3
139
80
3A
44
58
495
195
28
130
149
6A
6
28A
151

Mid-Cape

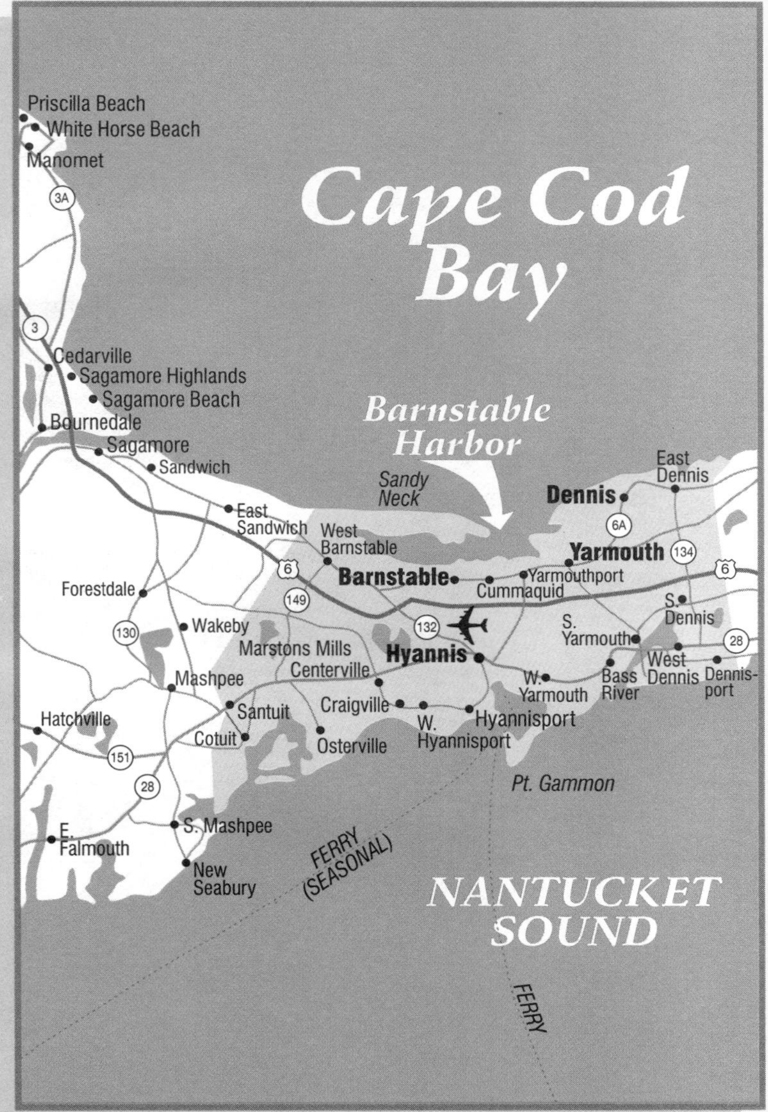

Priscilla Beach
White Horse Beach
Manomet
3A
Cape Cod Bay
3
Cedarville
Sagamore Highlands
Sagamore Beach
Bournedale
Sagamore
Sandwich
Barnstable Harbor
Sandy Neck
East Dennis
Dennis
6A
East Sandwich
West Barnstable
Yarmouth
134
6
Barnstable
Yarmouthport
Cummaquid
Forestdale
149
S. Dennis
130
Wakeby
132
S. Yarmouth
Marstons Mills
Hyannis
28
West Dennis
Mashpee
Centerville
W. Yarmouth
Bass River
Dennisport
Santuit
Craigville
Hatchville
W. Hyannisport
Hyannisport
Cotuit
Osterville
151
Pt. Gammon
28
S. Mashpee
E. Falmouth
New Seabury
FERRY (SEASONAL)
NANTUCKET SOUND
FERRY

Lower Cape

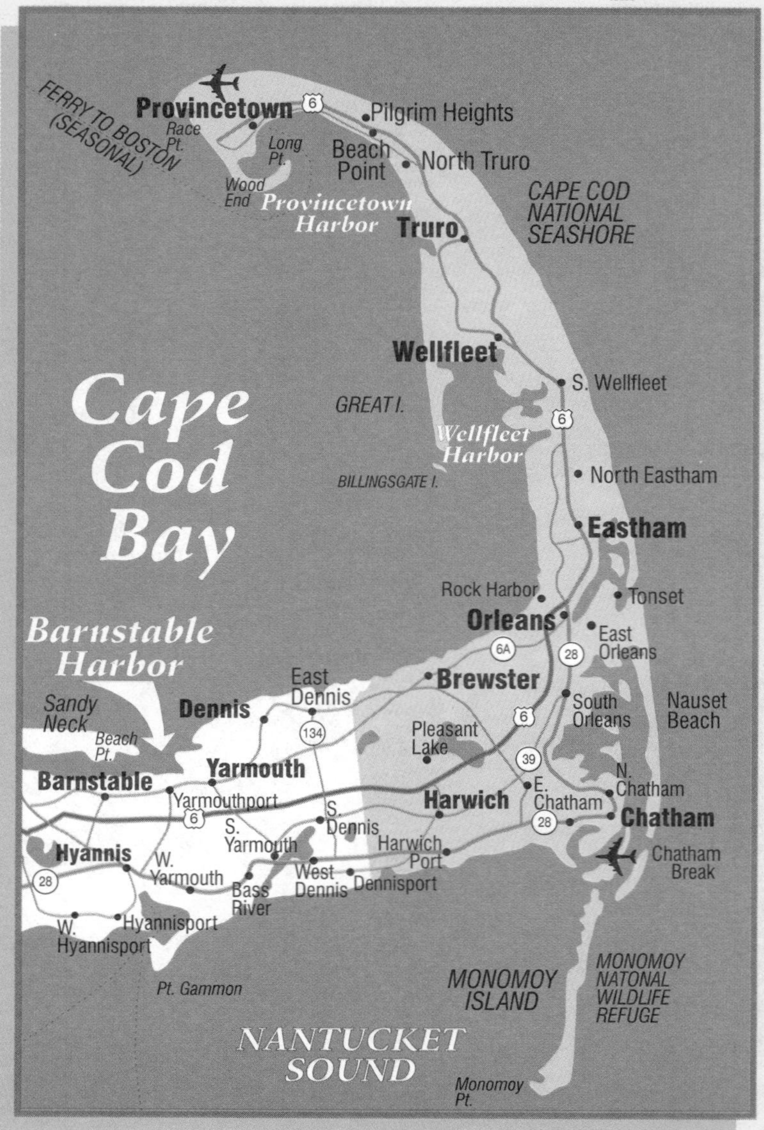

FERRY TO BOSTON (SEASONAL)
Provincetown
Race Pt.
Long Pt.
Wood End
Provincetown Harbor
Pilgrim Heights
Beach Point
North Truro
Truro
CAPE COD NATIONAL SEASHORE
Wellfleet
S. Wellfleet
Cape Cod Bay
GREAT I.
Wellfleet Harbor
BILLINGSGATE I.
North Eastham
Eastham
Rock Harbor
Tonset
Orleans
East Orleans
Barnstable Harbor
Brewster
East Dennis
Dennis
Sandy Neck
Beach Pt.
South Orleans
Nauset Beach
Pleasant Lake
Yarmouth
Barnstable
Yarmouthport
N. Chatham
E. Chatham
Harwich
Chatham
S. Yarmouth
S. Dennis
Hyannis
W. Yarmouth
Harwich Port
Chatham Break
Bass River
West Dennis
Dennisport
W. Hyannisport
Hyannisport
Pt. Gammon
MONOMOY ISLAND
MONOMOY NATONAL WILDLIFE REFUGE
NANTUCKET SOUND
Monomoy Pt.

Eastern Massachusetts

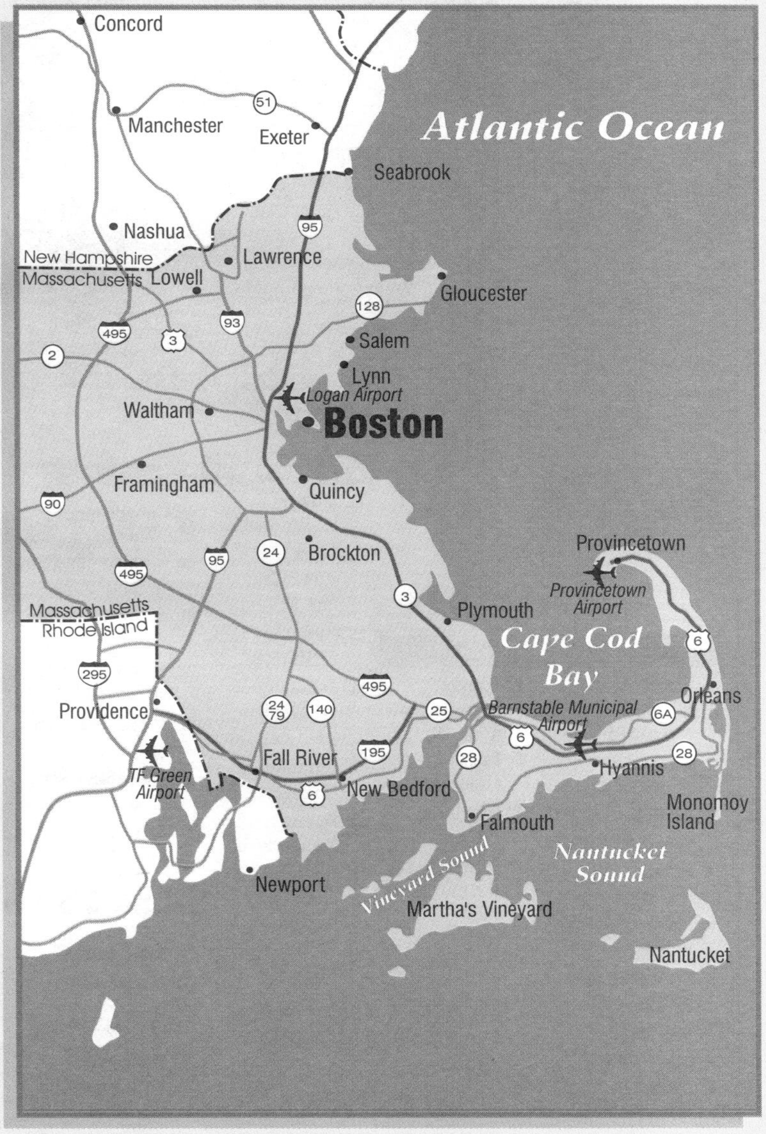

Table of Contents

Directory of Maps

"THE CAPE AND ISLANDS' DAILY NEWSPAPER"

319 Main Street, Hyannis, MA 02601
Telephone (508) 775-1200
Fax (508) 771-8924

BUREAUS: Falmouth, Orleans, Sandwich, Provincetown

On behalf of my colleagues at the *Cape Cod Times*, let me extend to you very best wishes from our wonderful corner of the world — Cape Cod and the islands of Martha's Vineyard and Nantucket.

Whether you are planning to come to our beautiful part of the country for a day or a lifetime, we're sure you will build happy experiences that will stay with you forever. Each season brings something new and special to the Cape and Islands, and we are always pleased to have new friends with which to share them.

Spring breezes are sweetest here, and Summer is quintessential Cape. Fall is the season many believe to be the most beautiful of all. Winter offers its own special pleasures, including unique holiday festivities and glorious walks on pristine beaches. Whatever the time of year, you'll find magic in the air.

We hope this unique guide book, *The Insiders' Guide to Cape Cod, Nantucket and Martha's Vineyard*, will make your time here all the more enjoyable. It is written exclusively by those who live here and know this area best, and so it is the most complete and informative guide of all. It also contains many unique features and advertisements which will allow you to squeeze every ounce of enjoyment and value from your visit.

We are constantly striving to improve the guide and would welcome your comments on the response card found toward the end of this book. You may also wish to visit our internet site for the latest updates at www.CapeCodOnline.com, where you can also send us your suggestions.

Again, we hope your visit to the Cape and Islands provides the stuff of dreams.

JOHN WILCOX
Publisher, *Cape Cod Times*

Acknowledgments

Jack . . .

Any notes of thanks would need to begin with my wife, Adriana. Without her months of research and support I could never have completed my part of this project. All I've written is because of her efforts behind the scenes. Thanks, A.

Besides my wife, I had the chance to work with two special people: co-author Debi Boucher Stetson and editor Molly Perkins. Debi and I became a close-knit team with a common mission — to paint a portrait of Cape Cod from Bourne to P-town. The task was huge and now, as the project winds down, I look back upon our efforts and smile a tired smile of accomplishment. I enjoyed our partnership, and I will continue to enjoy our friendship. Besides being our editor, Molly was also our coach and morale booster. Thank you, Molly, for all your help and patience!

My sincere appreciation goes out to first-edition writers Christie Lowrance and Alan Petrucelli for leading the way. What a job you did!

A heartfelt note of appreciation goes to all the wonderful people I met in my travels across the Cape and Martha's Vineyard. I particularly enjoyed my visits to the island, from Vineyard Haven to Edgartown and from Oak Bluffs to Gay Head and all the places in between. Another thrill was touring the many fine inns and bed and breakfasts from Bourne to Dennis, and meeting the interesting innkeepers who run them. Thank you for making me feel so welcome in your beautiful homes.

My gratitude also goes to the chambers of commerce, especially Randy Vega at the Martha's Vineyard Chamber, and all those at the *Cape Cod Times*, particularly Kathleen LeBlanc, Betsy Manning and Julie Kaminsky.

I applaud WQRC's Night Lights program — until midnight each evening Sinatra, Bennett, Torme, Cole, Holiday and Clooney kept me company as I typed away. As I read over my portions of the book I can almost hear their music playing in the background, accenting my meager words with their melodies.

Daddy would like to thank you, Melissa and Gregory, for sharing me with this project over the past months. I promise to make up any time we've lost along the way.

Which brings me back to my wife, Adriana. I can't thank you enough for all you've done . . . but I think I may know of a great Vineyard bed and breakfast and a restaurant or two where we can go to celebrate!

Debi . . .

It's hard to know where to begin thanking the people who helped make my work on this book possible. In the course of researching and fact-checking I encountered so many friendly, helpful people I'd never be able to list them all here. Special thanks go to my husband, Doug, for being supportive and understanding and for always saying, "Yes, you will," whenever I declared that I would never, ever be able to meet the next deadline.

To my son, Hunter, too young to understand why Mommy is always pounding away at the computer keyboard, thank you for putting up with those interminable phone calls and all that trundling about in the car.

Many thanks to my talented, hardworking co-author, Jack, who listened, commiserated and encouraged, and was always a pleasure to work with — not to mention a challenge to keep up with! And heartfelt thanks to Adriana, for all her thorough, professional research help and for putting up with all my phone calls. We couldn't have done it without you, A. To our editor, Molly, thanks for your careful editing, keen eye and pertinent questions, as well as your friendly, reassuring manner; it was great working with you. Thanks also to Insider's

Guides Publisher Beth Storie, whose professionalism and enthusiasm impressed me from the start.

At the Cape Cod Times, thanks to project manager Julie Kaminsky and our two go-getter ad reps Kathleen and Betsy — I really did appreciate those calls and notes! Really!

I would be remiss not to thank the two people who wrote the first edition of this book, Christie Lowrance and Alan Petrucelli, whom I've never met but highly respect. After seeing how much work is involved in revising and updating such a multifaceted guide book, I can only imagine how much work it was to create one from the ground up. The first edition provided a solid foundation on which to build, and my hat is off to those two fine writers.

I wish I could name all the terrific people I met in my travels on this adventure — all the innkeepers who so graciously led me on tours of their establishments, the restaurant owners and managers who let me take home menus, the antique dealers who took the time to explain things to me, and all the other working folks whom I consider to be the heart of Cape Cod. Many of the people who helped me did so over the phone — thanks to all those who called back in spite of their busy schedules. My thanks to all the staffers at the Cape's museums, theaters, galleries, chambers of commerce, schools, camps, ferry services, tour companies, hospitals, clinics and shops who cheerfully provided me with the information I needed to make my portion of this guide complete and up to date. Many of the people I met on Nantucket were particularly helpful and friendly, reinforcing my impression of that island as a warm and wonderful community. It has always been a magical place for Doug and me (we honeymooned there, and make a yearly pilgrimage) and I look forward to our next visit. Particular thanks to Jonathan Stone and the staff at the Jared Coffin House, and to Judy Kales, who was generous with helpful tips — may your tea business be steeped in success, Judy!

Working on this book has been quite an experience, one that only made me more glad that I live here on this incomparable spit of land called Cape Cod.

How To Use This Book

First, we wish to thank you for selecting *The Insiders' Guide® to Cape Cod, Martha's Vineyard and Nantucket*. We feel you have made a good choice as this book will definitely help you to get the very most out of your time here on the Cape and islands.

No doubt you have already flipped back and forth through the book, thumbing your way quickly from Hotels and Motels to Restaurants to Vacation Rentals, maybe settling briefly on chapters such as Antiques or Arts and Entertainment or some other subject that may have captured your interest. Perhaps you're thinking of planning that perfect Cape Cod vacation and are suddenly indecisive now confronted with a 600-page book chock full of information. Where should you start?

Well, this chapter may be a good beginning. You can consider it an instruction manual for the rest of the book.

We put this book together in a way that will allow you to obtain easy access to all types of valuable information pertinent to Cape Cod and the islands of Martha's Vineyard and Nantucket. It is not necessary to read the chapters in order of appearance, as each chapter stands on its own. It would be helpful, though, to read the Preface, Overview and Getting Here and Getting Around chapters first if you are unfamiliar with the area. Depending upon what you're looking for from your visit, other chapters such as Historic Cape Cod, Worship or even Retirement might be considered a necessary read as you make your plans.

If you plan on visiting Martha's Vineyard or Nantucket, for a day or for an extended period, it would be helpful to read the introduction to those chapters to get a "lay of the land." An island daytrip can be a highly successful one with just a little pre-planning first.

With a book this size and an area as diverse as Cape Cod and the islands, you'll find the Table of Contents and the maps at the front of the book and in the inside cover to be of great help. If you plan on doing a lot of traveling around the Cape you may want to consider picking up a more detailed map — map books are available at most newsstands and bookstores.

Once you get into the individual chapters of your Insiders' Guide you'll be happy to know that we've used a consistent geographical order by town throughout. Whether you're looking for a good place to eat in the Restaurants chapter, that perfect sea captain's house in the Bed and Breakfasts, Inns and Guest Houses chapter or a place to take the children on a rainy afternoon in Kidstuff, all entries are listed by town from west to east (from Bourne to Chatham) and then from south to north along the forearm of the Cape to its fist (from Chatham to Provincetown). Within each town we've also used a consistent order for the individual villages. As you grow accustomed to the town and village order you'll find that locating places within the chapters becomes rather easy.

To help even further, within each chapter we've divided the Cape into three regions: Upper Cape, Mid-Cape and Lower Cape. Upper Cape is the westernmost portion of Cape Cod and includes Bourne, Sandwich, Falmouth and Mashpee. Mid-Cape, located as you've probably already guessed in just about the middle of Cape Cod, consists of the towns of Barnstable, Yarmouth and Dennis.

Photo: Ron Schloerb, Cape Cod Times

Oyster catchers fly in formation over Nauset Marsh in Eastham.

The remaining towns of Brewster, Harwich, Chatham, Orleans, Eastham, Wellfleet, Truro and Provincetown comprise the Lower Cape.

All information concerning the islands (history, accommodations, restaurants, annual events, etc.) is contained within the individual island chapters toward the end of the book. While the island of Nantucket is one town, Martha's Vineyard consists of six individual towns so all establishments on that island are listed within the chapter in the following geographic order by town: Vineyard Haven (Tisbury) first, then Oak Bluffs, Edgartown, West Tisbury, Chilmark and Gay Head.

Though most chapters are arranged in the town-by-town format described above, a couple of chapters do not lend themselves to such a treatment. Annual Events, for example, is arranged by month and is then further broken down by time of month (i.e., early, mid, late).

Each entry in the chapters includes the establishment's address and phone number. It is important to note that since each town has a number of villages — which over the centuries have each acquired and maintained their own individual identities — there exist many cases where towns contain more than one Main Street or a number of other streets within the town with the same name.

For instance, the town of Dennis has a Main Street in both South Dennis and Dennisport. Barnstable has Main Streets in eight villages! Yarmouth contains four streets that answer to the name of Pine. In some towns Route 6A along the north side is also known as Main Street, as is Route 28 running along the south side of other towns. In Yarmouth, both Route 6A and Route 28 are known as Main Street. Some roads magically change names, such as Willow Street in Yarmouth, which becomes Yarmouth Road once it enters the town of Barnstable. Even within a town streets have been known to change names such as Union Street in Yarmouthport, which becomes Station Avenue in South Yarmouth. Other streets just change their spelling slightly, such as Setucket Road of Dennis, which becomes Satucket Road in Brewster.

As for phone numbers, all of Cape Cod, Nantucket and Martha's Vineyard lie within the 508 area code. Now the fun begins — determining which towns constitute a toll call. It all depends upon where you're calling from and which towns abut your town. Typically, you do not need to dial 1-508 if you are calling a town which abuts the town from which you are calling. Yet, it is not entirely that simple. Your best bet is to consult the Local Calling Areas section at the front of your Cape phone book to determine the specifics. By the way, there are three Cape telephone books: Falmouth Area (Upper Cape), Hyannis Area (Mid Cape) and

Orleans Area (Lower Cape). Although all three books contain the same white pages, each possesses its own Yellow Pages.

We have endeavored to be as accurate as possible with the information contained within the chapters to follow. Of course, there will be a mistake from time to time or information will change. If you find any inaccuracies we would appreciate hearing from you so we can make the necessary changes for future editions. Please use the yellow response card toward the end of this book or write to us at the following address: *The Insider's Guide® to Cape Cod, Nantucket and Martha's Vineyard,* P.O. Box 2057, Manteo, NC 27954. You can also visit Insiders' Guides Online™ and make your comments there: www.insiders.com/explore.

We have just two final points to make. If, say, an inn in the Bed and Breakfasts, Inns and Guesthouses chapter has a restaurant on site that is written up in the Restaurants chapter, we'll reference it so you can flip to it for further information (and vice versa). Other types of entries that appear elsewhere in the book will be referenced in a similar fashion. Finally, there are two indexes at the back of the book to make looking up a particular entry very easy; one is an index of advertisers.

Good luck and have fun!

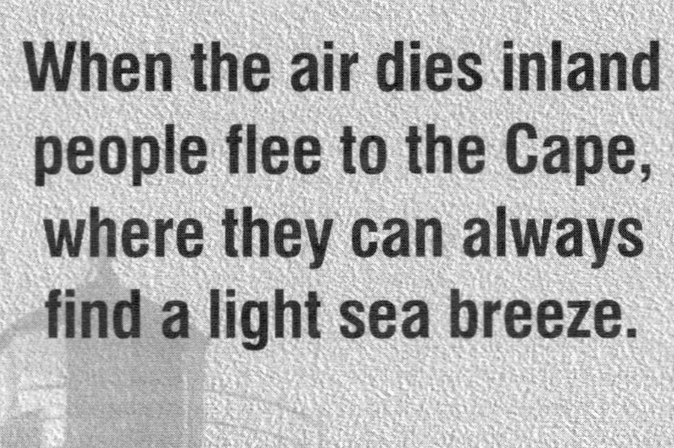

When the air dies inland people flee to the Cape, where they can always find a light sea breeze.

Overview

Cape Cod. The name evokes images of beaches laden with sunbathers and ocean waves racing to greet them; of lighthouses standing watch over the windblown shore, flashing warning and welcome to the vessels that ply its waters; of fishermen hauling in their catches.

Once you've been here, you will never forget the smell of salt breezes scented with pine and marsh, the sound of waves crashing and gulls calling, the taste of salt on your skin as you walk the beach on a quiet morning.

What draws so many people to this peninsula each summer — and, increasingly, spring and fall as well — are the beautiful beaches. But there is much more on our nearly 400 square miles of land — golf courses, museums, art galleries, theater, music and wonderful restaurants.

Cape Cod's population of around 200,000 year-round residents more than triples each summer as visitors flock here from all over the world. That explains the predominance of tourism as the top industry on the Cape, which in generations past relied on fishing, whaling, shipbuilding, salt-making and cranberry cultivation. Two major employers here are the restaurant and lodging industries, which account for nearly 20 percent of the work force. Of the Cape's $1.6 billion economic base, 44 percent of it results from tourism.

Many people who visit here decide to move here, either to retire, raise their children or simply enjoy the slower pace and natural beauty. The Cape's year-round population has increased 5 percent since the 1990 census, making it among the fasting growing counties in Massachusetts. In the decade from 1980 to 1990 Barnstable County ranked second in growth with a 26 percent population growth. Over that same period, Martha's Vineyard (a.k.a. Dukes County) ranked number one with a growth rate exceeding 30 percent!

The most populated town on Cape is Barnstable with about 42,500 year round residents. Truro is the least populated Cape town, home to 1,670 full-time residents. Over the 10-year period from 1980 to 1990, the town of Mashpee experienced 113 percent growth in population, making it the fastest growing town in Massachusetts.

During the popular summer season the Cape population explodes with an influx of tourists, which triples its population to more than a half-million people. The Town of Dennis, for instance, with a year-round population pushing 14,000 sees its summer population swell to more than 60,000. Provincetown, with 3,500 full time residents, is home to nearly 19,000 during the summer. Neighboring Truro's population expands by a factor of 10. In all, it's estimated that more than 17 million people visit the Cape each year, dwarfing the year-round population of less than a quarter million.

Lay of the Land and Waters

A cape is technically a point of land that projects out into a body of water, but Cape Cod is in many ways an island, surrounded as it is by Cape Cod Bay to the north, the Atlantic Ocean to the east, Nantucket and Vineyard Sounds to the south, and Buzzards Bay to the west. The Cape Cod Canal severs the connection with the Massachusetts mainland.

The Cape is prominently hooked northward, and people often use a bent arm as a three-dimensional map to point out the locations of the Cape's towns, with Sandwich at the shoulder, Barnstable at the biceps, Chatham at the elbow, Truro at the wrist and Provincetown at its fingertips. The Cape is divided into three geographic regions: Upper Cape, Mid-Cape and Lower Cape (also known as Outer Cape).

Cape Cod was formed 10 to 20,000 years ago by Ice Age glaciers. Erosion, the tides and the winds have shaped the lands into what they are today. In fact, erosion continues to change the lay of the land— and is a constant worry to owners of shoreline properties. The Cape is cratered with hundreds of ponds and lakes and etched by many rivers and creeks — all products of the very same glacial age.

South of the Cape lie a number of islands, some inhabited, others not. The Elizabeth Islands rest in a straight line running toward the southwest off the southern coast of Falmouth. One of these islands, Cuttyhunk, has a town, Gosnold, named for the 17th-century explorer who discovered the island and Cape Cod. East of Cuttyhunk and just south of Falmouth is Martha's Vineyard, which is home to six towns: Vineyard Haven (also called Tisbury), Oak Bluffs, Edgartown, West Tisbury, Chilmark and Gay Head.

Nantucket island lies slightly southeast of Martha's Vineyard and about 20 miles due south of the Cape. North of Nantucket's Great Point Lighthouse is Monomoy Island — mainly home to birds and seals.

All of the 15 Cape towns comprise the County of Barnstable. Established in 1685, it is one of the oldest counties in the nation along with nearby Plymouth and Bristol counties. Dukes County consists of Martha's Vineyard, a small island off the Vineyard called Noman's Land and Cuttyhunk Island. Meanwhile, Nantucket Island is its own county.

A Brief History

Physical evidence suggests that the earliest inhabitants arrived between 5,000 and 10,000 years ago. A number of European explorers sailed into Cape waters and walked on Cape soil during the early years of the 17th century. In November 1620, the Pilgrims arrived at Cape Cod before finally sailing into Plymouth Harbor one month later.

Within decades after the Pilgrims' arrival the first handful of Cape towns saw settlement: Sandwich, Barnstable, Yarmouth and Eastham. By the end of the 18th century all of the Cape towns with the exception of Brewster, Mashpee and Bourne were incorporated. These three towns would all see incorporation during the 19th century.

Approximately two-thirds of the Cape Cod towns are named for English seaports, and all but two have English names (Orleans is a French word and Mashpee, Wampanoag Indian). The Cape itself was named by English explorer Bartholomew Gosnold who arrived here in May 1602 to discover, among other things, the great number of codfish in Cape waters (see our Historic Cape Cod chapter for a history of the Cape as well as histories of each individual town).

The Cape Towns

Upper Cape

The town closest to the mainland, **Bourne** actually straddles the Cape Cod Canal with nine small villages containing a population of about 16,650 and the Massachusetts Military Reservation in 40 square miles. The village of Gray Gables has the distinction of being home to the first summer White House, where President Grover Cleveland summered in the 1890s. Monument Beach, Cataumet and Pocasset are tranquil, residential seaside villages; Bournedale, nestled between the two bridges on the mainland portion of town, has a country store and a lovely herring pond; Buzzards Bay is a commercial center with pretty views of Buttermilk Bay.

Lying just east of Bourne, historic **Sandwich** is the oldest town on the Cape and is truly charming. Famous for the glass industry that thrived here in the 1800s, Sandwich is still home to a few glass-making studios and the Sandwich Glass Museum. Sandwich has a year-round population of 17,750. The village of Sandwich, with shady lanes dotted with antique shops, a duck pond and working gristmill, is the perfect town for strolling.

Falmouth, resting south of both Bourne and Sandwich, is the second-largest town on the Cape and has more shore and coastline than any other, with 14 harbors and numerous saltwater inlets reaching up like fingers from Vineyard Sound. The town's eight villages include busy Falmouth center, with its village green and historic houses, many of them now bed and breakfasts; residential East Falmouth and Falmouth Heights, popular among sum-

For More Information

Chambers of Commerce

Planning a visit to the Cape? Write or call these chambers of commerce and other organizations for free brochures, travel packs, maps and money-saving coupons. Once you're here, stop by chamber-sponsored information booths set up in many towns and villages for last-minute updates.

We've also listed our town halls below. Beach parking stickers are issued by the town hall in each town. These offices can also provide information about the laws and regulations that are in effect in the town, such as fishing regulations, zoning laws, etc.

A reminder: our area code is 508.

Brewster Chamber of Commerce, 74 Locust Lane, Brewster 02631; 255-7045

Brewster Board of Trade, P.O. Box 1241, Brewster 02631; 896-8088

Cape Cod Canal Region Chamber of Commerce (covering Bourne and Sandwich), 70 Main Street, Buzzards Bay 02532; 759-6000, 759-3122

Cape Cod Chamber of Commerce, Routes 6 and 132, Hyannis 02601; 362-3225

Chatham Chamber of Commerce, Main Street, Chatham 02633; 945-5199, (800) 715-5567

Dennis Chamber of Commerce, Routes 134 and 28, South Dennis 02660; 398-3568, (800) 243-9920

Eastham Chamber of Commerce, Route 6 at Fort Hill Road, Eastham 02651; 255-3444

Falmouth Chamber of Commerce, Academy Lane, Falmouth 02540; 548-8500, (800) 526-8532

Harwich Chamber of Commerce, Main Street, Harwichport 02645; 432-1600, (800) 441-3199

Hyannis Chamber of Commerce, 1481 Route 132, Hyannis 02601; 362-5230

Mashpee Chamber of Commerce, Falmouth Road, Mashpee 02649; 477-0792

Orleans Chamber of Commerce, Post Office Square, Orleans 02653; 255-1386, (800) 865-1386

Provincetown Chamber of Commerce, 307 Commercial Street, Provincetown 02657; 487-3424

Truro Chamber of Commerce, 2 Head of the Meadow Beach Road, North Truro 02652; 487-1288

Wellfleet Chamber of Commerce, off Route 6, South Wellfleet 02663; 349-2510

Yarmouth Chamber of Commerce, 657 Route 28, West Yarmouth 02664; 778-1008

In addition, the **Massachusetts Office of Travel and Tourism**, 100 Cambridge Street, Boston 02202, (617) 727-3201, (800) 447-6277, can provide information about vacationing on the Cape.

Town Halls

Barnstable, 367 Main Street, Hyannis, 790-6200

Bourne, 24 Perry Avenue, Bourne, 759-0600, 759-0613

Brewster, 2198 Main Street (Route 6A), Brewster, 896-3701

Chatham, 549 Main Street, Chatham, 945-5100

Dennis, Main Street, South Dennis, 394-8300

Eastham, 2500 Rt. 6, Eastham, 240-5900

Falmouth, Town Hall Square, Falmouth, 548-7611

Harwich, 732 Main Street, Harwich, 430-7513

Mashpee, Route 130, Mashpee, 539-1400, 539-1416

Orleans, School Street, Orleans, 240-3700

Provincetown, 260 Commercial Street, Provincetown, 487-7000

Sandwich, Main Street, Sandwich, 888-4910, 888-0340

Truro, Town Hall Road, Truro, 349-3635

Wellfleet, 300 Main Street, Wellfleet, 349-0300

Yarmouth, 1146 Main Street (Route 28), South Yarmouth, 398-2231

mer visitors. The village of Woods Hole is home to three important scientific institutions: Woods Hole Oceanographic Institution (WHOI, or "hooey" to locals), the Marine Biological Laboratory and the National Marine Fisheries Service. This quaint village is also a terminus for ferries bound for Martha's Vineyard.

East of Falmouth is **Mashpee**, the town with the strongest ties to the Cape's Native American heritage; in fact, it is administered by the Wampanoag tribe. With a population of only 9,540 in nearly 24 square miles, it has the Cape's highest minority population and has seen dramatic growth in recent years. Its population more than doubled between 1980 and 1990.

Mid-Cape

Moving east to the Mid-Cape, **Barnstable** is the Cape's largest and most populated town, with 42,500 residents in 60 square miles. It serves as the county seat with a complex containing a courthouse and jail located in Barnstable Village, on the north side. Surrounding quiet, historic Route 6A, Barnstable Village is known for its lovely old houses and its harbor. Also on Route 6A is West Barnstable, which enjoys beautiful views of salt marshes and Cape Cod Bay. Barnstable also contains Hyannis, which is the closest thing to a city the Cape has. Many residents of other Cape towns, including the far-flung Lower Cape towns, travel regularly to Hyannis for shopping, medical services or employment. Hyannis Harbor has two docks from which ferries depart for Nantucket and Martha's Vineyard. Hyannisport is famous for the Kennedy Compound, where President John F. Kennedy came to sail and stroll the beach with his family in those Camelot days.

Stretching between Nantucket Sound and Cape Cod Bay, **Yarmouth** is home to historic, tranquil Yarmouthport along Route 6A on the north side, the scenic Bass River and, on the south side, bustling Route 28. If you're looking for a game of minigolf, a quick lunch, shopping or a little nightlife, head for Route 28. If you're into antiquing, putter along Route 6A. Yarmouth's year-round population of 21,000 grows to more than 50,000 in the summer months.

Dennis enjoys a great central location, and, like Yarmouth to the west, stretches from sound to bay. Historic Route 6A wends through the quiet north side, and to the south, Dennisport is very much a family-oriented summer resort with a breezy shoreline dotted with cottages and motels. The 20-square-mile town has a population of 13,950, which includes many young families as well as retirees.

Lower Cape

On the Lower Cape just east of Dennis on Route 6A **Brewster** is often called the sea captains' town, since it was once home to nearly 100 sea captains. Today many of those stately homes have been converted into bed and breakfasts. It's a family town, as evidenced by the high number of elementary school students that required the town to construct a second elementary school, completed in early 1997. Another sign of the town's growth — and its priorities — is the newly expanded Brewster Ladies' Library. Once the north parish of Harwich, Brewster has eight beautiful bay beaches, numerous freshwater ponds and Nickerson State Park. (See our Beaches chapter.)

Over on the south side, **Harwich** boasts 16 saltwater beaches on Nantucket Sound, along with a number of freshwater ponds. Home to 11,000 year-round residents, Harwich sprawls over seven villages, including bustling Harwichport, quiet Pleasant Lake, historic North Harwich and Harwich Center, which is home to an old-fashioned hardware store and a small coffee shop where locals gather each morning to trade news. Harwich has one of the most picturesque harbors you're likely to see anywhere in Wychmere Harbor, and hosts what is probably the biggest fall festival on the Cape, the Harwich Cranberry Harvest Festival in September. (See our Annual Events chapter.)

Tucked away on the elbow of the Cape,

Chatham is almost a world unto itself. One thing that sets it apart is geography: It's not on the way to any other town, so if you wind up there most likely it was by design. With a downtown of upscale shops on brick-lined sidewalks, Chatham exudes gentility and quiet sophistication. It is also home to an active fishing industry, which balances its affluent side. Chatham, with just 6,270 residents, has a higher percentage of senior citizens than any other Cape town and consistently votes Republican in presidential elections.

One of the most scenic drives on the Cape is Route 28 between Chatham and Orleans, a winding stretch of road filled with beautiful vistas of Pleasant Bay. Coming into **Orleans** this way gives you a glimpse of its quietest side, woodsy, residential South Orleans. But even when you reach Orleans center you won't at first understand why this is called the hub of the Lower Cape. It's just a nice little downtown, you think, and then you realize it's got everything you could need. The town has other attractions as well, namely gorgeous Nauset Beach on the ocean side and on the bay side, Rock Harbor, home base to a fleet of charter fishing boats.

The gateway to the Cape Cod National Seashore, **Eastham** enjoys both bay and ocean beaches and a quiet, rural nature. With 4,640 residents, Eastham is home to many young families and has numerous summer cottages clustered along the bay side. Roughly one-third of its 14 square miles are taken up by the National Seashore, which was established in 1961 and comprises Eastham's entire ocean coastline.

Known as a gallery town, **Wellfleet** is an art-lover's haven, a free-spirited-individualist type community of about 2,685 year-round residents. Like Eastham to the south, Wellfleet's ocean side is National Seashore territory, and the Seashore also owns Great Island, a narrow strip of land that juts eight miles into Cape Cod Bay sheltering Wellfleet Harbor. The harbor is home to an active fishing fleet, and the fishing community coexists amicably with the art world.

Vice President Al Gore's visit to **Truro** with his family in the summer of 1996 created a local sensation, but the fact is that Truro, the least populated of all the towns with just 1,670 residents, has quietly established a reputation as a hideaway for those people (some being celebrities) who want to "get away from it all." Wild and woodsy, its a summertime haven for those who crave privacy but want proximity to someplace lively as well — and neighboring Provincetown fills that requirement perfectly. Truro is also home to the National Seashore that stretches up its eastern coastline.

Provincetown explodes on the senses with its fun-loving, artsy, carnival-like flavor that is counterbalanced by a fishing culture and incredible natural beauty. Well-known for its gay community, Provincetown is both colorful and sophisticated with lots of great restaurants, terrific shops and galleries. Many of the town's summer residents are from Manhattan — which perhaps explains its undeniable Greenwich Village flair — and 3,590 people live here year-round. Home to several fine art schools, Provincetown had been attracting artists even before Charles Hawthorne opened

INSIDERS' TIPS

Most of the villages in each town have names which simply take the town name and add a compass direction, such as South Yarmouth and East Harwich. Some village names, though, may leave you scratching your head as to what town it's in. Here is a listing of some of those village names and their corresponding towns: Buzzards Bay, Pocasset, Cataumet, Monument Beach and Sagamore are in Bourne; Forestdale is in Sandwich; Woods Hole and Waquoit are in Falmouth; New Seabury and Poponesset are in Mashpee; Cotuit, Marstons Mills, Osterville, Wianno, Centerville, Craigville, Hyannis, Hyannisport, Cummaquid and Barnstable Village are in Barnstable; and Bass River's in Yarmouth.

Photo: Steve Heaslip, Cape Cod Times

Moving the boom of cranberries to shore is part of the harvesting process.

the Cape Cod School of Art here in 1899, and is still known as an artists colony. Artists say nothing compares to the light here in this Cape-tip paradise that's almost surrounded by salt water. The farthest reaches of the National Seashore end in Provincetown with the dunes of the Province Lands, complete with a visitors center overlooking the Atlantic Ocean beyond.

The Cape's Comfortable Climate

One of the most interesting things about the Cape is its weather. You could be standing on Commercial Street in Provincetown checking out the shops under sunny skies, while a little over a half hour's ride away in Chatham the clouds have rolled in and people are packing up their beach gear to head for happy hour at the local watering hole.

Even within towns it's not uncommon to see a 10-degree or more temperature difference between the north side of town and the south side. A downright sultry summer's day in Marstons Mills can see lifeguards at Craigville beach donning their windbreakers against cool ocean breezes along that south beach.

Even during winter the atmospheric differences are pronounced. One winter's day may see the Lower Cape receiving a half-foot of snow while the Mid- and Upper Cape receive only a dusting. Come the next storm the tables are turned, and Falmouth residents are digging out while in Orleans it's but a light frosting to brush off the windshield in the morning. On Cape Cod, you never know what you're going to get.

Isolation from the land mass of New England and enclosure by ocean waters influences the weather on Cape Cod. The peninsula benefits from warming effects of the ocean in winter and its cooling influences in summer. When the air dies inland, people flee to the Cape, where they can always find a light breeze. On Cape it is physically impossible to be far from water, since the average breadth of the Cape is about 6 miles.

On the whole, the temperature on the Cape is moderate in all seasons. Consider the average monthly temperature range during summer months: June, high 71, low 56; July, 78, 63; and August, 76, 61. In winter the temperature range is fairly constant: January, high 40, low 25; February, 41, 26; and March, 42, 28. The temperatures during the shoulder seasons of spring and fall are comfortable: April, high 53, low 40; May, high 62, low 48; September, high 70, low 56; October, high 59, low 47. The average annual rainfall is about 43 inches, with roughly three inches per month falling during the summer and about four inches of precipitation per month in the winter.

The temperature of marine waters is delightful along the Cape's southern shores, from Bourne along Buzzards Bay down to Chatham on Nantucket Sound. The waters of Cape Cod Bay and especially along the Atlantic are colder than the waters along the south shore — the perfect remedy for a hot summer's day!

Government by the People

A brief discussion of county and town government: While the county operates the jail and courthouse, towns are nearly all run on the town meeting style of government, with the exception of Barnstable, which switched to a town council-based government several years back. The other towns are run by boards of selectmen and, under their direction, town administrators. Each spring, open town meetings are convened to decide budgets, capital expenditures, zoning changes and other significant matters — and most towns have fall meetings as well, along with special town meeting to decide pressing issues. Often called the purest form of democracy, town meetings guarantee that all voting residents have a say in town affairs. There's also a high level of citizens' involvement in the towns' reliance on countless volunteers who serve on a variety of town boards, from financial committees to conservation commissions.

Protecting and Preserving the Cape

Operating at the county level is the Cape Cod Commission, a regional land-use and planning agency located in Barnstable village. Created in 1990, it has one representative from each of the Cape's 15 towns, and, under the Cape Cod Commission Act, has the power to regulate developments of regional impact. It also provides planning assistance to the towns, designates areas of critical concern and maintains a data base of demographic information.

The Cape Cod Commission sprung from a general concern among residents that growth on the Cape needed to be controlled, given the peninsula's sensitive environment and limited land. Land conservation, too, is an important issue on the Cape, where conservation trusts have flourished in every town. With the prevalence of shoreline, ponds and wetlands, conservation commissions in every town hold no small power because they have authority, under state and local laws, to oversee developments that take place near the shoreline and wetlands.

Most residents recognize the need to balance environmental concerns with economic ones, and while the two often appear to be in conflict, the trend is toward somehow finding a middle ground.

Historic preservation is as much of an issue as land preservation, and nowhere is that more evident than on quiet Route 6A, which has maintained its historic charm largely thanks to the jurisdiction of the Old Kings High-

INSIDERS' TIPS

Flotsam is the wreckage of a ship or its cargo found floating on the sea or washed up on shore. Jetsam is the name given to anything thrown overboard to lighten a sailing vessel in distress. Another word for it: litter!

way Historic District from Sandwich to Orleans. While some residents may grumble that they can't even paint their house without approval from the HDC, it's hard to argue with the apparent results: 6A is a lovely stretch of road and tasteful to a fault.

Your Own Piece of Cape Cod

Cape Cod is many things. If you ask those who live here, you're bound to get 200,000 different descriptions of the peninsula. To some, the Cape is a treasure-trove of culture and history, to others it's a saltwater playground, and to some it's just plain home. The population runs the gamut from retirees to families, from year-rounders to second homeowners, from celebrities to those who work two jobs just to make ends meet yet are willing to pay that price to live here. No matter what your situation, you're bound to find that special piece of Cape Cod that you can call your own.

Falmouth was the site of a handful of small battles with the British during both the American Revolutionary War and the War of 1812, and in each case the Falmouth men prevailed.

Historic Cape Cod

An Eden-like peninsula guarded by dangerous shoals, Cape Cod emerged from a half-mile-high glacier and over thousands of years has eroded into a series of rolling hills and outwash plains spilling northward toward Cape Cod Bay and southward toward Nantucket Sound. Seas like relentless bulldozers washed in unfathomable amounts of sands to meet the glacial silt, and waves have smoothed the rough edges of these outermost shores into something that can rightly be called a work of art.

Native Indians arrived upon this newly formed land about 10,000 years ago to settle in areas across the Cape. Members of the Algonquin Indian Nation, the Wampanoag Indians of the Cape were further broken down into five major tribes: Nausets of the Lower Cape; South Sea in the Barnstable and Mashpee areas; Suconessets of Falmouth; Shaumes of Sandwich and the Manamets in the Bourne and Sagamore areas. These tribes were further broken down into sub-tribes, such as the Nobscusset Indians of Dennis who were members of the Nauset tribe.

Indian dominance of the Cape lasted for more than nine and a half millennia. Around A.D. 986, it is believed, Norsemen visited the Cape and islands, though they did not make landfall. Bjarni Herjulfsson was the little-known Norse explorer who made the journey, and if the story is true then he discovered America about 500 years before Columbus. Upon his return to his native Iceland, Herjulfsson told his story and it became incorporated into Norse lore to be retold for years to come. One of those listening to the tales was Leif Ericson, son of Eric the Red. Around the year 1000, Leif borrowed his father's ship and sailed south, past Newfoundland and Nova Scotia to arrive at what some historians believe was Cape Cod. The story goes that he sailed his vessel up a river that flowed in two directions (Bass River?) and made his camp at an inland lake where he could anchor his vessel (Follins Pond at the head of Bass River in Yarmouth/Dennis?).

The Norse conquest of the New World failed as the Native Indians were not yet willing to share their land. America would become a lost discovery, and Cape Cod would revert back to the Indians for another 600 years.

The year 1602 saw a sail on the horizon, growing larger as it approached, a sail to represent the first of many to arrive along these shores over the next decades. It was English explorer Bartholomew Gosnold, who arrived in these parts in the spring of that year to rediscover what the Norse had found six centuries earlier. After landing at a number of spots along the Cape and islands, Gosnold and his crew chose the island of Cuttyhunk to establish their settlement, a settlement that failed shortly thereafter. Four years later, in October 1606, a French expedition arrived at what is now Stage Harbor in Chatham. On board were explorers Samuel De Champlain, Daniel Hay and Jean de Pourtincourt. Unfortunately, a battle commenced between the French and the Monomoyick Indians of the area. The damage done, Champlain and crew departed to explore other parts of North America. For years afterwards, other notable explorers such as Henry Hudson and John Smith avoided these shores as tales of the battle at Stage Harbor no doubt had circulated telling of "hostile" natives.

It was not until November 1620 that European explorers would try again to conquer this virgin outpost. This was the month when the *Mayflower* arrived at Provincetown (the vessel had been blown off course and had landed well-north of its intended destination of Virginia). The Pilgrims spent a little over a month on Cape Cod, at one point journeying to Eastham where they first encountered Native Indians. They then raised anchor and made the short trek across Cape Cod Bay to Plymouth, where they would make their permanent settlement.

Yet the Pilgrims would return to Cape Cod again and again. Many were instrumental in preparing the way for the settlement of a number of the earliest towns. Each of these towns would develop its own independent history, carving out its own niche in the growth of Cape Cod. Meanwhile, the native Indians were a race in decline. Epidemics just three or four years before the coming of the Pilgrims reduced their ranks considerably. Unwise to the white man's law, these Indians unwillingly handed over large tracts of land for a pittance, not realizing their mark on the white man's strange parchment was legal and binding. They did not understand the term "ownership" and thought that they were merely allowing the white settlers use of their land. By the time they began to understand what was happening it was too late.

Religion played a large role in the settlement of the different towns. Though most of the earliest settlers were Congregationalists, there were also Quakers among them and later, Methodists and Baptists. Though these settlers left other places to land here in search of religious freedom, many of them found themselves embroiled in the same old religious arguments. And when the settlers were not arguing about religion, then they were squabbling over land and where one person's boundaries ended and another's began. With the building of a meeting house and the hiring of a minister to preach, a handful of families would form an application for incorporation. The church spurred incorporation, and incorporation spurred more settlers, and thus the towns were born and grew and prospered.

The Cape has more than three and a half centuries of proud history. Each of the 15 towns displays its history like a treasured heirloom. Cemeteries, old churches and houses and museums all help to preserve the stories that will never be forgotten.

Upper Cape

Bourne

Bourne is the place where Cape Cod had its beginnings, both historically and geographically. It is here, in Bourne, where the Pilgrims established their first trading post in 1627, and it is here where present visitors obtain their first glimpses of the Cape and its awesome canal and bridges (two for motor traffic and one for trains). In a paradox of sorts, this township holds the unique position of being both the oldest and yet the newest town on the Cape. Originally settled as part of Sandwich (established 1637), the present town of Bourne was incorporated in 1884 when it broke away from Sandwich after some two and a half centuries of differences. It is named for Jonathan Bourne, a prominent citizen who made his fortune and reputation in the whaling industry.

Bourne was largely an agricultural and fishing community. Its motions for separation from Sandwich never seemed to pass at town meetings so aggrieved citizens in the outlying villages petitioned the state legislature. Since these areas attracted prominent summer people from New York, New Jersey and Boston, there was no lack of advice and perhaps influence. When the town separated, Sandwich lost its warm-water coast, harbors, shellfish beds and a number of industries such as Keith & Ryder, which made stagecoaches and railroad cars.

Thoughts of building a canal at the area now claimed as Bourne first began with Pilgrim Governor William Bradford. He noticed that at this point the Manomet River from the south and Scusset Creek from the north nearly cut through the neck of the peninsula. Indians of the area took advantage of these waterways to transverse the Cape, carrying their canoes the short distance in between the two rivers. In 1627 the Plymouth settlers established Aptucxet Trading Post on the banks of the Manomet River for the purpose of trading with the Dutch from New Amsterdam to the south as well as with Native Americans in the area. The trading post was closed in the late 1650s (see our Attractions chapter). The idea of a canal resurfaced again and again. General Washington inquired about such a waterway during the American Revolution. A number of plans were presented throughout the 19th century, but it was not until the early 20th century that shovel moved dirt and the canal was dug. (See our close-up on the canal in this chapter.)

Like most Cape towns, Bourne supported farmers and fishermen in the early centuries and, in the 19th century, industrial workers, who labored at grist and flour mills, a comb and button factory and in lumbering. Trade necessitated transportation, and the coming of the railroad to Buzzards Bay in the 19th century spawned a tourist industry that thrives today. Bourne villages were popular with wealthy people, who summered here and built handsome estates along the beautiful shore. President Grover Cleveland purchased a summer house called Gray Gables, where he would come to relax and escape the pressures of Washington. Cleveland was an avid sportsman and loved hunting and fishing on the Cape with his good friend, renowned 19th-century actor Joseph Jefferson, who owned a summer home on Buttermilk Bay called the Crow's Nest.

Sandwich

The very first of Cape Cod's 15 towns, Sandwich was settled in 1637 when permission was granted to Edmund Freeman of Saugus to establish a settlement to consist of 60 families. In that year, Freeman and nine other men from Saugus (now Lynn, Massachusetts, a city north of Boston) arrived to tame this area known as Manomet, which was close to the Aptucxet Trading Post in what is now the town of Bourne. These 10 men became known as the "10 men of Saugus" and were joined by some thirty other families from Plymouth, Lynn and Duxbury.

Pilgrims Myles Standish and John Alden journeyed down from Plymouth in 1639 to establish the bounds of this growing settlement. The town became incorporated with the name of Sandwich because a number of its residents originally came from Sandwich, England. At that time, the new township of Sandwich also included all the land that would later become Bourne.

The first settlers were largely Congregationalists, but Quakers came to town shortly afterwards, seeking converts. Some settlers did convert, but the Quakers were persecuted in town and many left for other parts. Pockets of Quakers did remain in Sandwich to take their place in the town's history.

The earliest settlers were chiefly farmers who also raised cattle and sheep. Because Sandwich lacked an adequate harbor, the maritime history of the town was stagnated somewhat and was limited to local fishing and reaping the harvest of the occasional beached whale. Local sailors and ship captains typically sailed from ports of other towns, such as neighboring Barnstable and Falmouth, each of which had decent harbors. Sandwich did contribute with its share of saltworks, but the town remained mainly a farming community, earning its living from the soil rather than from the sea.

The 19th century brought change and unthinkable prosperity to Sandwich. In 1825 Deming Jarves established the Boston and Sandwich Glass Works, which he figured would utilize two of Sandwich's more abundant natural resources: sand and trees. Unfortunately, the sand was found to be the wrong type for producing the glass Jarves had in mind. Sand had to be imported to Sandwich! By 1850 the plant employed 500 workers and was producing a half-ton of glassware each week. Besides standard glassware, the company also created artistic pieces. Jarves had some of the world's greatest glassmakers relocated from Europe to Sandwich to fashion these intricate and decorative works of art.

The same year glassmaking came to Sandwich, Keith & Ryder opened for business to produce wagons, stagecoaches and later, railroad freight trains. This highly successful company remained in business for 102 years, employed many Sandwich residents and produced the vehicles that helped America expand westward.

The decade of the 1880s saw Sandwich's future grow dim. In 1884 Bourne and her six villages separated from Sandwich, taking away residential tax dollars as well as the Keith & Ryder company. Four years later, in 1888, came the major blow as the glass company closed its doors due to competition from elsewhere. People were put out of work and Sandwich's economy crumbled. The ripple effect closed local businesses, which in turn put more people out of work, thus closing more businesses. A number of people moved away to start again elsewhere.

Fortunately, Sandwich has survived intact, carrying along her beauty and historical buildings to the joy of visitors who bring their tourist dollars.

Falmouth

Falmouth was the site of a handful of small battles with the British during both the American Revolutionary War and the War of 1812, and in each case the Falmouth men prevailed. Falmouth was officially settled in 1660 by a dozen families led by Isaac Robinson and John Hatch, both Barnstable Congregationalists fed up with the religious persecutions of the day, particularly the persecution of Quakers. The original name for this area took the Indian term Suckanesset, or Succonessitt, which translated as "black clam" or "the place of the black shells." In 1690 the town was renamed Falmouth after an English seaport.

During the American Revolution, Falmouth was one of the few Cape towns fired on by the British. In 1779 the Brits attempted to loot the town of its supplies and weaponry, but their advances were repelled. Frustrated, the British decided to teach the Falmouth patriots a lesson by burning their town. The marauders were met by 200 members of the Cape militia who prevented an attack. One year earlier, the waters off Falmouth saw perhaps the first naval victory in American history. The British had been off shore capturing Falmouth ships and ransacking them of their supplies. Colonel Joseph Dimmick, who had been training the Falmouth militia on the village green, took three whaleboats out against the British navy and won back a schooner that had earlier been hijacked by the Brits!

During another war, in 1814, the British ship *Nimrod* sailed into the waters off Falmouth. Its captain demanded that the town's cannons, which were positioned in the village square, be handed over. Capt. Weston Jenkins of the Falmouth militia flatly refused to comply, and the pages of history state that his reply to the British was "Come and get 'em!" This, of course, prompted heavy fire, and a number of buildings in town were hit, including the Elm Arch Inn and the Nimrod Inn. Both establishments proudly wear their battle scars today.

The town was ideally suited to fishing and farming. A whaling fleet was based in Woods Hole, where there remains a stone building on Water Street once used to make candles from spermaceti whale oil. Shipbuilding was an important maritime trade, and at one point Falmouth's 300 households included 148 headed by sea captains.

Agriculture thrived here, and cranberries and strawberries were leading crops. In fact, around the turn of the century, the Town of Falmouth was the leading producer of strawberries east of the Mississippi. Many Cape Verde Islanders sought agricultural work here and eventually bought land and settled in the area. Salt harvested from seawater was also an important "crop."

Falmouth set aside its village green in 1749 as common land for the town's 600 residents. Once used for grazing livestock and military training, the expanse now adds charm as well as its proud history to the town.

Across the street from the village green is the First Congregational Church. Built in 1708, its 807-pound bell was made by Paul Revere. Revere charged the town of Falmouth $338.94 for his efforts. Falmouth is also home to Nobska Light, built in 1828; Marine Biological Laboratory, established in 1888; and Woods Hole Oceanographic Institution, established in the 1930s.

Mashpee

The history of Mashpee points to the white man's attempt to allow the Native Indians of the area to "own" their own village and manage their own affairs. Though the intentions were probably good ones, the actual story tells the tale of one race of people trying to decide for themselves what another race wants. The results, though not completely disastrous, were at best off the mark.

Centuries before the Pilgrims set foot on Provincetown, the Wampanoag Federation was well-established in southeastern Massachusetts. The federation consisted of approximately 30 tribes of peaceful people who had a complex social structure. These Native Indians grew crops, hunted, fished, traded amongst themselves and pretty much lived without war, religious persecution, economic and social hardships and the other trappings that infested the European settlers' lives. Among these people, the Massipees of the South Sea tribe lived in the vicinity of the present town of Mashpee.

The town's history is complex and different from the other 15 Cape towns because it is the only one in which native people acquired legal title to their lands. As white settlers and

Photo: Steve Heaslip, Cape Cod Times

A sea gull stands guard in thick fog over a fleet of fishing boats tied up in Hyannis Harbor.

their laws began to hoodwink the Indians out of their treasured lands, three men stepped forward as missionary ministers to level the playing field. Those men were Samuel Treat in Eastham, Thomas Tupper in Bourne and Richard Bourne in Mashpee. Though not an ordained minister, Bourne arrived in Mashpee in 1660 in an attempt to convert the natives to Christianity and to establish a native Indian church. A former member of the General Court, Bourne had the background, contacts and desire to help native people establish the "Kingdome of Marshpee." He realized early on that the only way to gain rights for the Indians was to get them to adopt some of the white man's ways, primarily his church and an understanding of his law.

The year 1684 saw the building of the present Indian Meeting House (see Attractions chapter), now standing as the Cape's oldest church. In 1685, the year of Bourne's death, the General Court voted that no property within the plantation could be sold without the consent of the native residents. Despite this, the Native Americans were not prepared for self-government within an essentially foreign society, and the overseer system imposed by Plymouth virtually made the natives slaves on their own lands. In the 1700s the tribe numbers dropped critically. In 1767 the area had 21 shingled homes, 52 wigwams and 291 people; 100 years later, the population was only 331. During the American Revolution, 70 Mashpee Indians were killed.

Throughout the remainder of the 18th and 19th centuries the town of Mashpee continued to seek its freedom. Assisting in that cause were Indian pastors Blind Joe Amos and William Apes. In 1834 the district of Mashpee was established. The overseer system remained in effect. Immigration in the form of blacks, Cape Verde Islanders and even captured Hessian soldiers added to the bloodlines and began to reduce the numbers of pure breed Indians. Finally, in 1870, Mashpee was incorporated as the Cape's 14th town.

Freedom was still something to be achieved, even with incorporation. Advisory boards continued to meddle in Mashpee's affairs, convinced the Natives could not manage their own town. The last of these advisory councils finally released its grip in 1970 during the year marking the town centennial celebration! Recent decades have seen legal suits by the Wampanoag Tribal Council and unprecedented development, the most of any town in the state for several consecutive years.

Today, its Indian heritage is still solidly a part of Mashpee, and those who want to learn about it can visit the Indian Museum and Tribal Council on Route 130, the Indian church and cemetery on Route 28 and the town archives on Great Neck Road. Or you can attend the Powwow in July (see our Annual Events chapter). Plimoth Plantation in Plymouth is also a good source of information on the culture of the Wampanoag people.

Mid-Cape

Barnstable

Barnstable was one of the first three towns settled on the Cape, incorporated in 1639 along with Sandwich and Yarmouth. Named for Barnstaple, England, (the colonists were not known for their spelling strengths) many place names in the town actually reflect the early presence of Native Indians of various tribes. The villages of Cotuit, Cummaquid and Hyannis can trace their names to Indian roots. Hyannis, for example, is named for Iyannough (also spelled Iyanough, or Iyanno or a number of other ways), the Cummaquid sachem who extended kind hospitality to early settlers. His grave, off Route 6A in Cummaquid along the north shore of Barnstable, is marked (look for the sign), and a bronze statue of him stands in at the Village Green on Main Street in Hyannis as it rightly should.

Another statue in town is of statesman and patriot James Otis Jr. It stands in front of the Barnstable County Courthouse on Route 6A

INSIDERS' TIPS

You can read a gravestone more easily if you look at it through a round tube.

in Barnstable Village, in sharp contrast to the statue of Iyannough in the southern village. Though each man came from the same land, they lived in two entirely different worlds. The relationship between these two cultures was summarized well by local historian Donald Trayser, who observed, "Fear of the Indians was natural, but on the Cape unjustified." How true, for even during the King Philip War of 1676-77, which saw Massachusetts and Rhode Island Indians fighting against white settlers, relations with the Cape Indians remained friendly.

Though the first to settle in the area was a parson, John Hull of Weymouth, Massachusetts, the founding of Barnstable in 1639 is credited to the Rev. John Lothrop, a Congregational minister who had been persecuted and imprisoned in England before emigrating to America with 25 followers. The group originally settled in Scituate, and within five years moved to Barnstable, then known as Mattakeese, where the vast salt marshes at Great Marsh offered unlimited food and bedding for livestock. The settlement originally stretched as far west as to include Falmouth. The southern part of the town was settled in 1660, in the area of the village of Hyannis. In 1685, the county of Barnstable was established with the town of Barnstable serving as the county seat. At the point of the town's bicentennial celebration in 1839 there were 4,000 residents. Imagine, a bicentennial in 1839 when there were 24 states still to be admitted to the Union!

Along Route 6A in Barnstable Village you can view a historic marker at Sacrament Rock, the site of the first communion served by Rev. Lothrop to his congregation. Unfortunately, the historic rock was dynamited to make way for Route 6A (you'd think they could have built the road around it) and has been cemented back together complete with a plaque telling of the history. Not far away is Lothrop Cemetery where the good reverend's remains became one with the earth many years ago.

Another marker on Route 6A identifies the home of Thomas Hinckley, an original settler of Barnstable who was a Colonial governor in 1681. Barnstable is distinguished by a number of individuals and families who influenced the region and in some cases the nation. A marker in West Barnstable shows the home of James Otis, a chief justice during the Revolutionary War. His son, James Otis Jr., was credited with delivering a speech that set the stage for the great rebellion. He participated in many significant events in Colonial history, such as the Stamp Act and the Townshend Acts, and was a good friend of John Adams.

At the intersection of Route 149 and Route 6A in West Barnstable is a cemetery containing the grave of Capt. "Mad Jack" Percival, one of Barnstable's most famous citizens. Percival was captain of the warship *Constitution* ("Old Ironsides") from 1844 to 1847. The famous vessel is now on permanent display in Boston Harbor.

Like the other mid-Cape towns, Barnstable was settled by farmers. In addition to livestock, early farmers raised corn, rye, onions and flax. By the 19th century, fishing, shipping and coastal trading was the foundation of its economy. The town boasted some 800 shipmasters, 104 in the village of Centerville alone. Osterville's Crosby Boatyard is famous for the Cape Cod catboat designed there. The West Barnstable Brick Company was active from 1860 to 1927. The factory produced 100,000 bricks a day.

Cobb's Hill West Cemetery in Barnstable is the burial site of many of the early families in the area, while the West Parish church built in 1717 along Route 149 in West Barnstable stands as a proud monument to the world of 18th-century Cape Codders.

Yarmouth

Next time you're feeling sorry for yourself, think about one of Yarmouth's founding fathers, Anthony Thatcher. Here is a man who lost everything, only to rebuild his life over again and again, and in the process helped to build a town. Before leaving England he lost his first wife and five of his nine children. Remarried, he and his wife and his four remaining children set sail for the New World in 1635. Though they arrived without mishap, a subsequent boat ride from Ipswich to Marblehead ended in the loss of his four children. Of all those on board only he and his wife survived. With everything lost, the Thatchers arrived at Yarmouth in 1639 to found that town along

The Cape Cod Canal

When William Bradford and Myles Standish were exploring the area around Plymouth in 1626, they discovered that two rivers, the Manomet on Buzzards Bay and the Scusset on Cape Cod Bay, were separated by only a short distance of land. The Pilgrims realized the advantages to trade and transportation of digging a canal that would connect the two bodies of water; however, the idea was not acted upon. In 1776 General George Washington, hoping to avoid a British blockade and to enhance security, sent an engineer to conduct the first feasibility study of the area, but still no canal was constructed.

Well into the late 1800s, attempts to organize this mammoth construction project continued to be thwarted until 1904, when New York financier Augustus Belmont considered the project. He purchased the Boston, Cape Cod and New York Canal Company. By July 1907 his newly formed Cape Cod Construction Company moved its first shovelful of dirt and digging was underway. Over the next seven years the men and machinery removed earth. In 1912 two large dredges began digging toward each other from Bourne and Sandwich.

Workers completed the Buzzards Bay Railroad Bridge in September 1910 and finished the two vehicle bridges within the next two years. The finished canal became the world's widest sea-level canal at 480 feet across. It was 17.4 miles long and 34 feet deep. On July 29, 1914, exactly seven years to the day since work first began, the Cape Cod Canal officially opened, heralded by a parade of ships and boats, among them Augustus Belmont's private 80-foot yacht and the U.S. Navy destroyer *McDougall*, which carried Assistant Secretary of the Navy Franklin Delano Roosevelt. The Cape Cod Canal beat the opening of the Panama Canal by 17 days.

In 1915 canal traffic numbered more than 2,600 vessels, but it never achieved the volume of traffic that Belmont had hoped for. When a German submarine attacked and sank the *Perth Amboy* off Nauset Beach in Orleans, President Woodrow Wilson ordered a readily compliant Belmont to permit the government to operate the canal. Eventually, Belmont sold the canal to the American government for $11.5 million, and the Army Corps of Engineers took charge of its operation and maintenance. Although the canal

—continued on next page

Photo: Courtesy of the U.S. Army Corps of Engineers

Survey crew for Cape Cod Canal, c. 1909.

was technically a success, it never brought the commercial prosperity to Upper Cape towns that its planners anticipated.

During the Great Depression, the National Industrial Recovery Act of 1933 provided $4.6 million to build the present three bridges, employing some 700 workers for two years. These modern bridges were completed in 1935. The Bourne and Sagamore Bridges, with a span of 616 feet, became among the longest continuous truss bridges in North America. The railroad bridge, at 544 feet, remains the third longest vertical lift drawbridge on the continent. You can admire the workmanship of the bridges from the 7-mile-long paved service road that lines both sides of the canal.

If you are taking a boat through the Cape Cod Canal, you'll move along at a good clip in the direction of the tide but seem to be fighting an uphill battle when you go against the tide. One reason for this is that Cape Cod Bay waters are about 5 feet higher than Buzzards Bay waters, so a tremendous current is created as they merge and flow through the narrow passageway. Average high tide waters move through the canal at 4 to 5 mph per hour. When high tides are accentuated by a full moon or other conditions, the water's speed can reach more than 7 miles an hour.

If you'd like to learn more about the canal, take a tour of the Corps of Engineers headquarters at Taylors Point in Buzzards Bay, 759-4431, or stop by the visitors center on the Cranberry Highway. If you wish to read about the canal, we recommend *The Cape Cod Canal* by Robert Farson

---

with Thomas Howes and John Crow. John Thatcher, Anthony Thatcher's son born in 1638 at Ipswich, would father 21 children to help populate the new township; his house is directly across the street from the Yarmouthport Post Office on Route 6A.

The lands of Yarmouth had long been settled by Native Indians of the Mattakeese and Nobscusset tribes before Pilgrim Stephen Hopkins came south from Plymouth to build a house here in 1638. The new town, which was most likely named for Great Yarmouth, England, was originally a huge area encompassing the present towns of Yarmouth and Dennis. With its salt marshes, thick woodlands and rich soil, the north side was settled first. Lands were quickly acquired from the Indians and a sturdy community began to grow. The Indians found themselves being boxed in, and areas were set aside for them at Long Pond, Scargo Lake and along the Bass and Parker rivers. Burial grounds at Long Pond and Scargo Lake are marked with plaques; the one at Long Pond reads: "On this slope lie buried the last native Indians of Yarmouth."

Yarmouth was a farming community in the 18th century and was renowned later for its maritime activity until the locomotives came to Cape Cod and the age of steam eclipsed the age of sail. Many ships from Yarmouth were engaged in the Indo-China trade. Secum and Taylor shipbuilders built the legendary *Red Jacket*, which made a record transatlantic crossing in 13 days.

Saltworks and cordage works sprung up on the Bass River. Settled by a Quaker named David Kelly, South Yarmouth became known as Quaker Village or Friends Village, and townsfolk erected a meeting house there around 1809. Though other towns were less tolerant of Quakers, Yarmouth eventually accepted the "heretics," and their settlement played a large part in the development of the town. As early as 1721 an east parish of the Yarmouth Congregational church was established in the area now known as Dennis. In 1793 this east parish, all of Yarmouth east of the Bass River, separated from the town to become the town of Dennis.

Yarmouth is an architectural historian's dream, for it has two historic districts that contain a total of 650 buildings, many of which are on the National Register of Historic Places. The age of the area and the sophistication of its residents is reflected in its varied architectural styles: Federal, Gothic, Greek Revival and Victorian. Of course, the traditional Cape house, full, three quarters and half, is well-represented along the historic routes.

A final note on Yarmouth: It seems it also

has a chapter in the Norse sagas. Leif Ericson's brother Thorvald visited these shores at the beginning of the 11th century and met up with Native Indians at Bass Hole in the northern part of Yarmouth. In a battle with the Indians Thorvald was killed and buried at the beach. Thorvald's grave has never been found.

Dennis

To understand the early history of the town of Dennis you must first study the history of Yarmouth, for Dennis was settled as part of Yarmouth in 1639. Of Old Yarmouth's three earliest settlers: Anthony Thatcher, Thomas Howes and John Crow, two of the three — Howes and Crow — settled in what would later become Dennis. In 1721 the east parish of Yarmouth was established in the area now known as Dennis village and four years later a minister came to this east precinct of Yarmouth to become the church's preacher. That young minister was Rev. Josiah Dennis, a Harvard graduate who was born in Northern Ireland and arrived in Massachusetts around the year 1700 at the age of seven. Josiah Dennis would preach at the east church until his death in 1763. His successor, Nathan Stone, was the minister at the time of the separation from Yarmouth and the town's incorporation in 1793. It was suggested that the new township be named Dennis in honor of its first minister (rather than Nobscusset for the Indians of the area; coincidentally, the last Nobscusset Indian died in 1793, the year of incorporation).

Many of the early residents had been farmers in England and were attracted to the area by the abundance of salt marsh hay for their cattle. Early settlers practiced shore whaling and utilized "drift whales" that floated ashore. As oil became more valuable, whales were more methodically pursued. Watch houses were built at Sesuit and Nobscusset harbors to provide an alert when the great creatures were in the bay. Long boats were sent out, and the whales were herded into shallow water, where they became stranded. As whaling grew into an industry, harpooning, a skill developed in Scandinavia, was employed from boats offshore.

Around the time of the American Revolution, large-scale farming dropped off for lack of land, and many people moved to western Massachusetts. As the deepwater harbors of Nantucket and New Bedford began to dominate the whaling industry, Dennis turned to fishing, coastal trading and shipbuilding. Fishing wharves lined the southern coastline, and Dennisport basked in the sweet aroma of fish drying on fish flakes. Some 400 shipmasters hailed from the town. Shiverick Shipyards in East Dennis produced eight magnificent clipper ships, all of which were recognized in the Golden Age of Sail. Mastered and crewed largely by Dennis men, these vessels helped to open up routes to the Orient and brought much fame and fortune to the town and its residents. Critical as a fast means of transportation, particularly around Cape Horn during the California Gold Rush, these hardworking vessels were often in service for 25 to 30 years. A marker on Sesuit Road denotes the site of the shipyard.

Two major Cape industries, cranberry cultivation and saltworks, were both pioneered in Dennis. During the time the British were blockading American ports, the Continental Congress offered a reward to anyone who could invent an efficient means of producing salt. Capt. John Sears of East Dennis stepped forward in the latter quarter of the 18th century to invent and eventually patent a solar evaporation vat that actually distilled salt from seawater. Though the brunt of many a joke, his "odd" experiments worked and a profitable industry grew from his backyard hobby. Very soon saltworks were everywhere, lining every available beachfront acre around the Cape. Meanwhile, in 1816, Henry Hall of North Dennis observed that wild cranberries flourished in areas where sand blew over them. He replicated the conditions and is considered to be the first person to cultivate cranberries.

Lower Cape

Brewster

Much of the history of Brewster was made beyond the boundaries of the town on the oceans of the world. Brewster raised more deepwater ship captains per capita than all other 19th-century American towns. Many of these ship captains operated slightly outside the law of the day. For instance, during the War of 1812 Brewster's seafaring men defied President Thomas Jefferson's embargo against Britain. There were fortunes to be made crossing the Atlantic, and these men of Brewster were not about to let a Presidential decree stand in the way!

Brewster was originally settled as part of Harwich in 1656 by John Wing, formerly of Sandwich. Early settlement was in West Brewster, around Route 124 and the Brewster Store. A church founded here in 1700 has pews still marked with the names of original members. By the mid-1700s bad feelings existed between the north and south precincts of Harwich as each end of the town was so different in its makeup. The ship captains and the fortunes they made were on the north side while the working class including fishermen and farmers were on the south side. By 1803 each town went in its own direction, the southern part keeping the name Harwich, the northern part opting for the name Brewster to honor Mayflower Pilgrim William Brewster.

In Brewster Center, an old cemetery behind the Unitarian Church is the final resting place of many notable historic figures, including Capt. David Nickerson, who was in Paris during the French Revolution. According to local legend, he was handed a baby — supposedly the Lost Dauphin of France, the son of Marie Antoinette and Louis XVI. He was begged to bring the child to America and asked to name the child Rene Rousseau, which he did. The child grew up to be a sea captain and at the age of 25 he was lost at sea. It is Cape custom for a young man lost at sea to have his name inscribed on his father's headstone, so upon Capt. Nickerson's stone (who was lost at sea a few years later) is also the name Rene Rousseau.

Brewster has more than one connection with France. During the French Revolution, 1794 to be more exact, Capt. Elijah Cobb's ship was seized. Cobb obtained an audience with Robespierre to plead his case for the release of his ship. Robespierre saw Cobb's side of the argument and released the ship just days before he himself was executed. Cobb would later become a prisoner of war during the War of 1812, released in a prisoner exchange. In 1815, Brewster Capt. Jeremiah Mayo had orchestrated plans to take Napoleon to America, but the plans fell apart when the former emperor was captured.

Although Brewster has a strong maritime history, its renowned Cape Cod Museum of Natural History permits an unusual glimpse of prehistoric life in this town. The first people in what is now Brewster would have seen a vast plain covered with pine forests, grasslands, rivers and bogs where Cape Cod Bay is now, for the shoreline was miles away from its present location, nearly out to Georges Bank. As glaciers melted, the sea level rose and covered the land area, now the Continental Shelf. Prehistoric people settled around river mouths such as Stony Brook in Brewster. Stone tools, spears, knives and hide scrapers have been found at the town's Upper Mill Pond. In 1619 a plague killed as much as 90 percent of the native people. Written history kept by the Pilgrims and early Colonists in Plymouth and on Cape Cod reflects a decimated and vulnerable native culture; European settlers, on the other hand, were strong in numbers but considerably divided by economic and religious differences.

Brewster was the birthplace of prolific Cape writer Joe Lincoln who was born in 1870. Through his novels many people were first introduced to Cape Cod and its history.

Harwich

Like all of Cape Cod, Harwich was home to Native Indians, in this case the Nauset Indians of Harwich consisting of the Sauquatuckett tribe to the north and the Monomoyick tribe to

INSIDERS' TIPS

An entry from the diary of English explorer Bartholomew Gosnold, who named Cape Cod, sheds light on his choice: "It's a harbour wherein may anchor a thousand ships, and there we tooke great stoare of codfysshes."

the south. In unspoiled beauty these Native Indians lived, undisturbed for many centuries and even for the couple of decades after the settlements of Yarmouth to the west and Eastham to the east. A last wilderness was this land up until white settlers began to arrive toward the end of the 1650s.

In 1656, John Wing became the first settler to tame these wilds. He was a converted Quaker from Sandwich who apparently tired of the persecutions in that town and left to build a life elsewhere. He settled in the part of old Harwich that would eventually become what is today Brewster. Wing was followed by John Dillingham and later, Gersham Hall, who in the 1660s became the first to settle in the southern area of old Harwich (the section that would remain the Harwich of today). More families followed and by 1690 there were enough living in the area to establish a church. In 1694 this area became incorporated as Harwich and contained the present towns of Harwich and Brewster as well as parts of Eastham and Orleans.

Harwich of the 18th century was a town in separation. Residents in the southern part of town grew weary of traveling to the parish in the north so in 1744 they appealed for the building of a southern parish. Two years later permission was granted and a church was built. This southern parish later saw itself being split into some 15 splinter churches as a religious revolution of sorts took place in town. These religious groups included Congregationalists, Baptists, New Lighters, Come Outers (those who "came out" against slavery) and Standpatters (those who were not abolitionists).

In the 18th century the town itself began to come apart as well. The areas known as Portonumecot and Namecoyick became parts of Eastham in 1772, later becoming South Orleans. About a quarter of a century later the remaining part of Harwich split in two, the northern part becoming Brewster in 1803.

The earliest settlers were farmers, who occasionally shored a whale. Harwich would later become one of the Cape's major fishing ports, reaping huge harvests of cod and mackerel. Other industries included the harvesting of alewives from a number of rich streams as well as the harvesting of cranberries from the many bogs. This latter industry was developed in town by Alvin Cahoon who was instrumental in making cranberries a harvestable crop. Meanwhile, Harwich's Major Nathaniel Freeman gave the saltworks industry on Cape a big boost by utilizing windmills to pump seawater into the salt vats. In fact, so profound was Harwich's contributions to the industry that it became home of the Massachusetts Salt Works Company established in 1797. The industry peaked during the 1830s only to see its decline a decade later when salt mining in the mid-west provided a more cost effective alternative.

Two structures in Harwich on the National Register of Historic Places are the South Harwich Methodist Church on Chatham Road and the Capt. James Berry House on Main Street. You can see other historic sites at the Herring River in West Harwich and Muddy Creek between Harwich and Chatham.

Chatham

If the 13th-century *Flateyjarbok* (Flat Land Book) does in fact provide an accurate account of Norse expeditions around A.D. 1000, then the first visitors to Chatham could most likely have been Vikings from Iceland. If these Norse sagas hold up, then Bjarni Herulfsson sailed right past these shores just over a thousand years ago. The earliest accepted historic record, though, indicates that Samuel De Champlain anchored in Stage Harbor in 1606 to repair a broken rudder and named the site Port Fortune. Though Champlain and his crew

INSIDERS' TIPS

The names of two Cape towns resulted from misspellings. Barnstable is named after Barnstaple, England, while Wellfleet is for Wallfleet, England. Also, many of the village names taken from Indian words are the result of the white settlers interpretation of the Indian dialect, and as a result, their spelling varies greatly depending upon what history book you're reading.

were only able to navigate the treacherous shoals with the aid of Monomoyick Indians of the area, bloodshed between the two groups resulted during a skirmish. The French keel-hauled a few natives, beheaded a few others and then continued on their way to explore Canada (Good riddance!).

Fourteen years later, Chatham provided the Pilgrims with their first glimpse of land since leaving England. Shoals off Monomoy Island drove the ship to the north, however, rather than to their intended southern route to Virginia. Chatham remained unsettled until 1664 when William Nickerson of Yarmouth arrived in the area to stay. Since 1656 Nickerson had been acquiring land from the Monomyicks, though it wasn't until 1672 that he actually received a deed of any kind. By 1682 he was in possession of about 4,000 acres of land — nearly all of Chatham!

In Nickerson's time the area was known as Monomoit and had a difficult time attracting settlers to this remote area of the Cape. Besides the Indians, there was also the threat of attack by pirates. The Monomoyicks turned out to be nonthreatening and were friendly neighbors to the white settlers who did decide to "brave the wilds." At one time it was considered under Yarmouth's jurisdiction, and later under that of Eastham. Though not a town, this area of Monomoit was allowed to separate from Eastham in 1679 to become what was termed a constablewich, meaning Monomoit could collect its own taxes but had no representation in the Colony Court. Monomoit's only chance at incorporation was in establishing a church and then in attracting a minister to this wilderness outpost. After a number of preachers came and went (no less than eight including one who drowned), Rev. Hugh Adams arrived in 1711 and in June 1712 the town was incorporated. The stipulation was that the town had to be incorporated with an English name so Chatham was chosen.

Chatham was the site of one of the worst smallpox epidemics on Cape. During the winter of 1765/66 some 60 people, 10 percent of the population, contracted the disease. Thirty-seven people died, including the town doctor. Chatham is also the site of one of the most dangerous coastlines along the northeast. As Champlain learned in 1606, Chatham is guarded by treacherous shoals that have caused many a shipwreck over the centuries. In 1808 two wooden lighthouses were constructed at the mouth of the harbor to warn approaching ships. They crumbled over the eroded cliff and were replaced in 1841 and again in 1879 and 1881. Today, one of the towers, the Chatham Light, still serves as a navigational aid. The other tower was moved north to Eastham to become Nauset Light. The terrible Monomoy Disaster of 1902 took place just south of Chatham Light. Twelve men lost their lives on Shovelful Shoals that March morning. Sole survivors Capt. Elmer Mayo and Capt. Seth Ellis become heroes, each man putting his own life in harm's way with the slightest hope of saving the life of another. Their tale of heroism is told on a monument out in front of Chatham Light. Their names are forever woven into the fabric of Cape history.

Orleans

The history of the Cape town of Orleans is sprinkled with French seasoning. Though not known for sure, the origin of the town's name seems to point to Louis Philippe de Bourbon, the Duke of Orleans in France. The Duke was in exile during the French Revolution and had visited America one month before the Cape town was incorporated. Thirty-three years later he would become the king of France.

Originally settled as the south precinct of Eastham in 1710, the area was known as Pochet. The first meeting house was built in 1718 to become the South Parish of Eastham. Graves in the nearby cemetery date back to 1719. Orleans broke away from Eastham and was incorporated in 1797 to become one of only two towns on Cape not to bear an English name (the other town is Mashpee). Prior to the white settlers, this land belonged to the Nauset Indians, more specifically the subtribes known as the Monomoyick and the Potonamiquoit (there are numerous spellings for this second tribe). Leif Ericson of the Norse sagas visited Nauset Beach along Orleans' Atlantic coast around the year 1000, Bartholomew Gosnold stopped here in 1602 and named this place Cape Cod for the many codfish he found, and French explorer Samuel De Champlain visited these outer shores in

1606. The first recorded European shipwreck on the East Coast occurred off Nauset Beach in December 1626 when the ketch Sparrowhawk wrecked in a storm. During the 19th century the remains of the historic vessel emerged from the dunes and are now housed in a museum in Plymouth.

One of the smallest towns on Cape, Orleans borders Cape Cod Bay to the northwest, the Atlantic Ocean to the east and the waters of Pleasant Bay to the south. The land itself is marked by many bays, ponds and creeks. The town is also the site of the Cape's first canal, Jeremiah's Gutter, a hand-dug trench that connected Boatmeadow River and Town Cove. Extremely high tides would flood the low-lying lands between the two bodies of water, in fact, Gosnold mistakenly concluded that the Cape north of this spot was actually an island cut off from the rest of the peninsula by this gulf of water. Dug in 1804, Jeremiah's Gutter (named for resident Jeremiah Smith who owned land through which it traveled) was useful during the War of 1812 when British ships were blockading Cape ports. After the war its use diminished and the canal was left to fill in with silt. In 1873, the Cummings-Howes clothing factory was established in Orleans; within 20 years it employed 200 people and operated 125 sewing machines, primarily in the manufacture of trousers.

The French returned to Orleans in 1898 in the form of the French Cable Company. The company managed an undersea cable that connected the Cape town with Brest, France. A second cable then ran from Orleans to New York. Many important news items were received at Orleans first before being referred on to New York and the rest of the country, such as the loss of the steamer *Portland* in 1898, Lindbergh's flight across the Atlantic in 1927 and Germany's invasion of France in 1940. Along with the cable came workers from France to man the company's building. Many of these French remained on in Orleans and raised families here.

Orleans has two extraordinary distinctions: It was attacked by both the British and the Germans. During the War of 1812, the H.M.S. *Newcastle* anchored off Rock Harbor; its captain demanded payment of $1,000 to spare the town's saltworks. The offer was refused and so commenced the Battle of Rock Harbor. British sailors attempted a landing but were driven away by the town's militia. The ransom was never paid.

On July 22, 1918, a German U-boat surfaced off Nauset Beach to fire on and sink three barges and a tugboat, the *Perth Amboy*. An estimated 146 rounds were fired in the one-sided exchange. At least one of the submarine's shells landed on the beach, the only assault of American soil during the war. When word of the attack was received at the Chatham Air Station, three planes were sent up to launch a counterattack. Without weaponry, the best the Yanks could do was toss a monkey wrench at the fleeing sub. You have to admire their moxie!

In 1984 the 470-foot Maltese freighter *Eldia* grounded on Nauset Beach. It had unloaded its cargo of sugar in New Brunswick and was riding light off Cape Cod when high winds and heavy seas hit it. Although the 23-member crew was evacuated with no loss of life, few will forget the bizarre sight of a giant ship on Nauset Beach, a sight that hearkened back to the old days when this coastline snatched many a passing ship to wreck upon her shoals.

Eastham

The decade of the 1640s saw the Pilgrims in Plymouth considering their future, and whether or not they wanted that future to take place in Plymouth. Some thought of relocating their settlement to the outer lands of Cape Cod. In 1643 a committee was formed to investigate that very possibility. Among those in the party who journeyed to the outer Cape was Thomas Prence who came across to the New World on board the vessel *Fortune* in 1621. Upon their return to Plymouth the committee decided to pack up their belongings and take their chances in the land known as Nauset, now known as Eastham.

Settlement commenced in 1644. The boundaries were vague at best, at first consisting of everything east of Old Yarmouth and including the towns of Brewster, Harwich, Chatham, Orleans, Wellfleet, Truro and, of course, Eastham. The township was known as Nauset until 1651 when it was renamed Eastham. This land was reserved for the Old

While traveling down Route 6A, watch for the historic Barnstable Superior Courthouse.

Comers, those Pilgrims who came across on the first three ships — the *Mayflower*, *Fortune* and *Anne*. Joining Prence were John Doane, Nicholas Snow and Josias Cook as well as Higgins, Smalley and Bangs. Eastham is the only Cape Cod town founded entirely by people from Plymouth Colony. It's interesting that Pilgrims should return to Eastham as it was the site of their first contact with Native Indians, at First Encounter Beach, in December 1620 just before they sailed the *Mayflower* across the Bay to settle at Plymouth. Founding father Thomas Prence would later become Governor of Plymouth Colony from 1655 until his death in 1673.

The first meeting house was erected in 1646 on the north side of Town Cove. The much-loved Rev. Samuel Treat came to Eastham in 1693 and his ministry would span the next 45 years. Besides preaching to the white settlers, Treat also ministered to more than 500 Native Americans, or "Praying Indians," and wrote services in their language. He enlisted Native preachers and lived up to his name by treating the Indians with the respect they were owed.

Harwich, which at the time included Brewster, separated from Eastham very early on with its settlement in 1656. Chatham departed next when that area became a constablewich in control of its own destiny in 1679. Truro broke away from Eastham in 1709. Around 1720 a north parish was established in the area of Wellfleet and a south parish at what was later to become Orleans. The divisions were made official in 1763 when Wellfleet became its own town and in 1797 when Orleans followed suit. Eastham, once the most populated town on Cape, became the least populated. Over the century since its settlement, so many trees were cut that the once rich Eastham topsoil was stripped away by the savage ocean winds. Scrub pine took hold where vast forests of oak once stood. Farmers turned from their barren soils to the seas and became fishermen. Those who did remain behind on shore became dairy farmers.

Old Cove Cemetery, started in 1829, is Eastham's oldest cemetery. Three Pilgrims are buried here. In the mid-1800s a small plot was added nearby for the graves of many children who died when a terrible epidemic of small pox struck the town. The small cemetery was so deeply associated with grief and tragedy that people shunned it, and it became overgrown with weeds and briars, forgotten. Only recently have the 22 headstones dating from 1836 to 1892 been rediscovered.

Henry Beston's famous book, *The Outermost House* published in 1928, relates the year he spent in his beach cottage on the Great Dune of Eastham. Although the cottage was destroyed by the Blizzard of 1978, its place in literary history is commemorated by a placard at Coast Guard Beach.

Wellfleet

When the white settlers arrived at Nauset in 1644 to purchase the lands from the Native Indians of the area, they asked the Indians who owned the northern lands from Wellfleet toward Provincetown. The Indians, perhaps not understanding the question and certainly not identifying with this European notion of ownership, answered "nobody." So the white settlers announced in true manifest destiny mentality, "Then, we own it!" And so began the settlement of Wellfleet, known then as Billingsgate, at that time merely the north precinct of the town of Eastham.

The lay of the land at Wellfleet was much different than it is today. Land masses that are now attached to the mainland were actually islands back then. Meanwhile, other 17th and 18th century islands that supported homes and communities are now gone, swept away by the tides. Such was the case with the Island of Billingsgate, which over the years was devoured by the waves. Strangely, much of the settlement of the area occurred on the islands rather than on the mainland. A north parish meeting house was erected in the area in 1723. As early as 1734 the residents here applied for town status, but it would be another three decades before their application was approved. In 1763 the town was incorporated, briefly as the town of Poole, later changed to Wellfleet. Because of its wonderful oyster beds, the town was named after Wallfleet, England, which also was known for its oysters. Unfortunately, the Capers got the spelling wrong. Champlain, who visited these Wellfleet shores back in the early 17th century, named the harbor Port aux Huitres (no need to look for your French dictionary, huitres does in fact translate as oysters).

It is only a mile between Wellfleet shores on the Atlantic Ocean and on Cape Cod Bay. Wellfleet Harbor was once known as Grampus Bay for the blackfish, or pilot whales, that stranded themselves there. When the oyster beds died off in 1770 due to an epidemic of some sort, Wellfleet men became commercial fishermen, lobstermen and whalers. Seed oyster were imported after the Revolutionary War and the beds thrived as they had before to make Wellfleet the largest producer of oysters in the state. During the early 19th century, salt vats were big business, and the town had some 40 saltworks during the 1830s producing roughly 18,000 bushels of salt on an annual basis. The Wellfleet wharf business grew during the mid-1800s, catering to the fishing industry.

In 1717 off the shores of Wellfleet, the pirate known as Black Sam Bellamy was returning to the Cape on board his vessel *Whydah* when the ship was caught in a storm and sank. The location of the wreck baffled salvors and historians until, in 1982, a treasure salvor located the wreck of the infamous ship. Skeptics were silenced when a bronze ship's bell with "The Whydah Galley 1716" inscribed on it was brought to the surface, as well as hundreds of pieces of gold and other treasures.

Wellfleet is the site from which one of the first transatlantic wireless telegraph messages was sent in 1903. The year before a huge station was built on the cliff overlooking the ocean. This miracle of science that allowed messages to travel across the invisible airwaves was the invention of Italian physicist Guglielmo Marconi, who began experimenting with sending wireless messages in his teenage years. Besides that first telegraph message of 1903 (from President Theodore Roosevelt to King Edward VII of England) the Wellfleet wireless station also received a distress message from a sinking liner *Titanic* in April 1912.

The steeple of the Wellfleet First Congregational Church is the only town clock in the world that keeps ship's time (see our Attractions chapter). In the 1870s Captain Lorenzo Dow Baker of Wellfleet introduced bananas to the United States and established the L.D. Baker Company in 1881, which later became United Fruit Company. Wellfleet resident Luther Crowell invented the square-bottom paper bag.

Truro

The history of Truro can be traced to three hills: Corn Hill, the Hill of Storms and the Hill of Churches. In November 1620 the *Mayflower,* with its passengers and crew, wandered up the backside of the Cape to anchor at Provincetown Harbor. An expedition including Capt. Myles Standish and William Bradford explored the lands of this lonely outpost in search of food, water and possibly a good place to settle. In the area of Truro, upon a hill now known as Corn Hill, the Pilgrims stumbled across what appeared to be an abandoned Indian encampment. Here they found Indian gravesites and unearthed buried baskets filled with ears of corn. They took this corn and it become the seeds of the Pilgrims' first planting. Also in Truro, the Pilgrim expedition located their first fresh water supply since leaving England.

Truro was originally settled as part of the Nauset tract in the mid-17th century, later incorporated as Eastham. A group known as the Pamet Proprietors bought the land from the Natives in 1689, and by 1697 farms were established in this remote area of the Cape first called Pamet after the Native American tribe there. Pamet was soon granted municipal privileges in 1705 and called Dangerfield because of the treacherous coastline. When Dangerfield officially separated from Eastham in 1709, the township was renamed Truro for the English town in Cornwall, which, with its rolling hills and lonely moors, resembled this area. The first meeting house was built in 1710 on the Hill of Storms. This meeting house was dismantled in 1840. The hill is also the site of North Cemetery, where the town's oldest stones can be found.

Truro was primarily a fishing and whaling town. At first, whaling was done from shore and later in boats. In the 18th century Truro was a leader in this industry with vessels already visiting the African coast and the whaling grounds of the Pacific. One particular Truro whaler, Icabod Paddock, was even recruited to teach Nantucketers his techniques. (He must have been a good teacher!) Truro's history has always reflected a relationship with the sea. It had two good harbors, Pamet River Harbor and East Harbor (which is now the fresh water Pilgrim Lake). Pamet River Harbor was the site of a thriving wharf business that grew from Union Wharf built in 1829. The town had a sail loft and a shipbuilding yard built in 1830 on the Pamet River where brigs and many Grand Banks schooners were built. The successful Union Company Store, which specialized in ship chandlering and general merchandise, epitomized the flavor of this fishing haven, and many townsfolk owned shares in the store and thereby shared in the town's victories.

Yet a series of events would send the town into a downward spiral. First was the terrible gale of October 2, 1841, which would see the loss of 57 Truro men (10 percent of the town's able seamen) and seven of the town's eight fishing vessels. In the 1850s erosion began to claim the harbor. There was even the realization that erosion could eventually allow the mighty Atlantic to cut through Truro, creating an island of North Truro and Provincetown. To avoid this, the entrance of East Harbor was

INSIDERS' TIPS

The story of the 13 United States Lifesaving Stations (USLSS) that lined Cape Cod's easternmost shore from 1872 to 1914 is a powerful chapter of Cape history. Heroism and tragedy were part of everyday life for the men who watched for ships in trouble along the Cape's treacherous shore. Many Lower Cape museums have displays and records that document this era (see our Attractions chapter). *The Life Savers of Cape Cod*, written in 1902 by J.W. Dalton, is a very accurate account of the USLSS.

blocked to become a lake. Then came the big blow when the Union Store went out of business in 1860. A growing 1840 population of about 2,000 had been cut in half by 1880. Migration cut that number in half again to about 500 people by 1930 as residents moved away to earn a living elsewhere.

The Hill of Churches is the spot where the Methodists of Truro built their meeting house in 1826. Methodists had first arrived here in the 1790s. The Congregationalists then decided to build their new church on the very same hill in 1827. It was built on this high ground to serve as both a worship center and as a beacon for ships. Its bell was cast by Paul Revere's son and cost $320, and the windows were made of Sandwich glass. In 1830, the town hall (Union Hall) was constructed on the same hill and its architecture resembles that of a church.

Highland Light (also known as Cape Cod Light) in North Truro is Cape Cod's oldest lighthouse. The 80-foot tower, which sits atop a 120-foot cliff, was built in 1797 and rebuilt in 1857. Cliff erosion threatened the structure's future so in 1996 the historic lighthouse was moved to its present location. In November 1778, during the days of the American Revolution, the British man-of-war *Somerset* wrecked along the Truro coast at Dead Man's Hollow in a gale. Some 480 Brits were saved as the vessel cleared the outer bars and wrecked along the beach. The people of Truro and Provincetown divided up the spoils of the wreck, stripping the vessel of all its cargo and equipment. Though the British were eventually marched to Boston, the *Somerset*'s doctor stayed on in Truro, married a Truro woman and together they raised a family to become the future generations of the town.

Provincetown

At the very end of the Cape is where all the history of Massachusetts began. Though English explorer John Smith sailed past this spot in 1614 without a thought of making landfall, Provincetown has the historic distinction of being the landing place of the Mayflower's Pilgrims on November 21, 1620. Perhaps even more historically significant, while the vessel was moored in the harbor the Pilgrims drafted and signed the Mayflower Compact, a piece of parchment that became the foundation of democratic government in America. It spelled out the Pilgrim's plans for self-government — a government of, by and for the people (sound familiar?). The Pilgrims spent five weeks in the Provincetown, Truro, Wellfleet and Eastham area before they realized that the Cape's tip did not offer all they needed for settlement. Though some members wished to stay put along this narrow strip of the Cape, eventually all the Pilgrims got back on board the *Mayflower*, raised anchor and continued along the coast to eventually land in Plymouth. Incidentally, a handful of Pilgrims who had died on the crossing were buried in Provincetown.

Long before the Pilgrims came, however, the Provincetown area had attracted native peoples and foreign visitors. Provincetown is not immune to the Norse sagas, which place Vikings as the first discoverers of the New World. Leif Ericson's brother, Thorwald, may or may not have landed here during the first years of the 11th century to repair a damaged keel, naming the place Keelness. Remote as it was, the tip of the Cape was one of the last parts to be settled. The area earned a somewhat unsavory reputation because of the smugglers, looters and gamblers who came here before its actual settlement. Much carousing was done here! No civil order was in place, and anyone who docked here to participate in whatever illegalities took place in the few coastal shacks did so in a land where laws simply did not exist. When nearby Truro was incorporated in 1709, this land to the north termed "Cape Cod" was thrown into the package in an attempt to bring some order to this faraway land. Eventually a permanent though undisciplined settlement did take hold. Law and order took hold as well, and this port town would quickly get down to business.

The township of Provincetown was incorporated in 1727, and the people immediately turned their attention to the sea in the manner of fishing and whaling. By 1760 a dozen whaling ships called Provincetown Harbor home port. These whaling boats, always in search of good crews, found them in the Azores, Canary Islands and Cape Verdes. Experienced Portuguese fishermen and whalers began to make Provincetown their home in the 1800s, and very soon the port town evolved into a highly successful Portuguese fishing village. By the middle part of the century, Provincetown had a tremendous fishing and whaling fleet and was considered one of the most prosperous ports in the country. Seventy-five wharves sprouted up along Commercial Street in this Cape Cod seaport, which was third behind only New Bedford and Nantucket in terms of whaling. The famous whaler, *Charles W. Morgan*, now a prominent display at Mystic Seaport, Connecticut, was a Provincetown whaler that worked up until 1921, well after the quest for the leviathan had ended in the other ports.

Fishing has always been Provincetown's strong suit. Even today, the descendants of 19th-century Portuguese fishermen still carry on the proud tradition. In the mid-19th century the Portuguese here helped to make P-town the Cape's largest and most successful fishing fleet. Hundreds of vessels hailed from this port, which boasted an excellent harbor and was nearby the rich fishing grounds. Even today, the annual blessing of the fishing fleet in June points to the town's proud fishing tradition.

Yet Provincetown is a town of many faces. In 1899 it became the site of America's first art colony. Art schools and galleries sprung up in this salty yet beautiful fishing village. That art legacy lives on with the many shops and galleries still present in Provincetown today. Also, this harbor community attracted playwrights such as Eugene O'Neill, Sinclair Lewis and John Dos Passos. O'Neill, who in his early years worked on fishing boats, joined the Provincetown Players in 1916. The group presented plays at the Playhouse on the Wharf. O'Neill went on to earn three Pulitzer Prizes and a Nobel Prize in 1936.

As you would expect, historic sites include a bronze plaque at the western end of Commercial Street that commemorates the landing site of the Mayflower's Pilgrims in 1620, and the Pilgrim Bas Relief on Bradford Street behind the town hall, which depicts the signing of the Mayflower Compact in Provincetown Harbor. Also honoring the Pilgrims is the 252-foot Pilgrim monument that was constructed between 1907 and 1910. President Theodore Roosevelt oversaw the placement of the first stone, and its dedication ceremony was attended by President William Howard Taft.

Today Provincetown survives off tourism. Commercial Street attracts hundreds of thousands of visitors each year to its many shops. Provincetown is also home to a gay and lesbian population, both full-time residents and seasonal visitors. Many tourists who make the trek to Provincetown tend to associate Provincetown's gay side with their visit. Yes, gay pride is a part of Provincetown, but it is only one face. Provincetown continues to be a fishing community boasting a proud Portuguese heritage. The Portuguese are as large a part of the town's history as the gay community of today, the artists and playwrights of the early 20th century, the looters and smugglers and gamblers of the 17th century, the Pilgrims of 1620 and the Norse who may or may not have landed along these barren shores nearly 1,000 years ago.

The most convenient
way to get here, and
around Cape Cod once
you've arrived here,
is by car.

Getting Here and Getting Around

There is a special sense of anticipation that accompanies a journey to this land set off in the ocean, taking what could be a typical car or bus ride and elevating it into a pilgrimage to some hallowed land.

As children, our excitement grew as we journeyed along the fabled route to the Cape (for us, it was south along Route 3 from Boston), and we recalled every landmark along the way. Entering Plymouth we knew we were in the land of the Pilgrims and that Cape Cod was not much farther. Crossing the Cape Cod Canal atop the Sagamore Bridge we always peered down below in wonderment into the waters of the Canal, seemingly miles below, to see boats and ships going along this man-made waterway. Coming down off the bridge and onto Route 6 on the other side we were officially on Cape — our vacation was just beginning.

It's still hard to resist looking down as you go over the Sagamore or Bourne Bridge. The bridges, and the Canal across which they span, are still as impressive as when we were children . . . perhaps even more so as we have grown to fully appreciate the truly special place that lies just beyond.

Of course, by car and by bus are not the only methods of arriving here on Cape Cod. People also come here by plane, train and boat. We, personally, have arrived to the sandy peninsula via all of the above modes of transportation, and each offers the vacationer with an equally wonderful first impression.

By sea, the Cape emerges from a lush green horizon into a coastline cratered with harbors and accented by quaint villages of sea captains' homes and the soaring spires of old churches. These spires provided mariners of centuries past with visible landmarks as they made their way along the coast.

By rail, the traveler arrives on Cape Cod over a beautiful vertical lift railroad drawbridge — among the three longest such bridges in this hemisphere — which provides a close encounter with the wondrous Cape Cod Canal.

And by air, from Boston, a night traveler sees the awesome beams of Highland Light in Truro and Chatham Light commanding the backside of the Cape. A day flyer can clearly see the artistic movements of the shifting sands beneath the Cape Cod Bay waters as the plane descends for landing.

It is estimated that more than 17 million people visit Cape Cod each year. During the summer, the average daily population is triple that of the usual year-round population of 200,000. With all those visitors, people often joke that the Cape will sink. Well, we're happy to report that it hasn't sunk yet, so come on down, whether by car, bus, boat, train or plane. Below, we've listed your various transportation options.

By Car

People flock to the Cape not only because of its beauty but also because of its proximity to several states and Canada. Tourism specialists estimate that three out of every four visitors to the Cape travel here from either one of the six New England states or from one of the Mid-Atlantic states (i.e., New York, New Jersey, Pennsylvania) — all within easy driving distance. Even closer to home, it is estimated that one of three visitors is from Massachusetts.

The most convenient way to get here, and around Cape Cod once you've arrived here, is by car. Most people do, in fact, come to the Cape by automobile . . . to the tune of more than 50,000 vehicles per day during the popular summer months. As such, during the summer months the major routes can be busy. The Saturday morning approach to the Cape toward both Sagamore and Bourne bridges is usually quite busy, and often traffic will be brought to a crawl for the last mile or two until you cross the bridge. Also, Sunday afternoons see heavy traffic going the other way off-Cape, and again, there can be a backup waiting to get over the bridges.

If you are coming from Boston or northern coastal New England, take Interstate 93 to Route 3 South across the Sagamore Bridge. From Western Massachusetts, Northern Connecticut and Northeastern New York State, follow Interstate 84 East to the Massachusetts Turnpike (Interstate 90) and take Interstate 495 to the Bourne Bridge, the other access point. From New York City, Delaware, Southern Pennsylvania, Southern Connecticut, New Jersey, Washington, D.C., Virginia and all other points south and west, take the appropriate interstate highway to Interstate 95 North and head toward Providence, Rhode Island.

FYI

Unless otherwise noted, the area code for all phone numbers in this guide is 508.

Providence is where the highway divides: Interstate 95 North continues to Boston while Interstate 195 heads east to the Cape. I-195 ends in East Wareham, and there you will pick up Route 25 East, which is the road that will take you to either the Bourne or Sagamore bridge. The Bourne Bridge is at the southwest end of the Cape Cod Canal and also marks the beginning of the Bourne rotary, or traffic circle; look for the topiary that spells out "Cape Cod." At this rotary you can connect with Route 28, which hugs Buzzards Bay and the southern coast of the Cape and temporarily joins with Route 28A before branching out to Orleans. You can also go three-quarters around the rotary and pick up Route 6A, a scenic rural route that skirts the Cape Cod Bay as it runs parallel to Route 6, also accessible here.

Massachusetts is the rotary capital of the world. The Cape has some notable rotary traffic circles (Bourne alone has five, Barnstable has two). The traffic in a rotary travels counterclockwise so when you enter the rotary bear right. Vehicles already in the rotary have the right of way. All along the 360 degrees of the rotary are roads shooting off, sometimes four or five, each one providing you an opportunity to exit the rotary. Usually the signs are pretty good and you can read each sign quickly as you enter the rotary so you'll know which road you need to take. If you do get confused and miss

your turnoff, don't panic! Instead of slamming on your brakes (the last thing you want to do in a rotary!), simply drive around again, making the proper lane switch as you go.

Route 6A ends at the Eastham-Orleans rotary, though it resurfaces for a 10.5-mile stretch from Truro to Provincetown. Route 6, which meets Route 3 at the entrance to the Sagamore Bridge, is designed to be the fastest east-west route across Cape. Known as the Mid-Cape Highway, it runs the length of the Cape, from Sagamore to Provincetown. You'll have the pleasure of driving two lanes in either direction until you reach Dennis (Exit 9), where the road becomes, for a 13-mile stretch, a two-lane highway (one lane going west, one going east). Of course, two eastbound lanes merging into one means a bit of congestion on a busy Saturday morning as vacationers head for their cottages. Remember, patience is a virtue. State law requires that you use your headlights as you travel this 13-mile, 50-mph stretch, even during daylight hours, to increase visibility. This stretch of Route 6 empties into what is known locally as the Orleans rotary (although it is technically just over the town line in Eastham). Beyond this rotary Route 6 once again widens, yet then narrows again from time to time during the stretch from Orleans to Provincetown.

To sum up, there are three major routes across the Cape going from east to west: Route 6A to the north running from Falmouth and Sandwich to Orleans, Route 6 (Mid-Cape Highway) in the middle and Route 28 to the south. At Orleans all three routes merge via the Orleans rotary with Route 6 alone carrying you northward to Provincetown.

Many side roads intercept routes 6, 6A and 28; consult a good map to find shortcuts. Locals use several principal north-south Cape routes to travel between the east-west routes of 6, 6A and 28. Here are a few of those routes:

• Route 151 which runs from Route 28 in Mashpee (at the Mashpee rotary) to Route 28 in North Falmouth

• Route 130 from Route 6A in Sandwich to Route 28 in Mashpee (Route 130 connects with Route 6 at Exit 2)

• Route 149 from Route 6A in West Barnstable to Route 28 in Cotuit (Route 149 connects with Route 6 at Exit 5)

• Route 132 from Route 6A in Barnstable to Route 28 in Hyannis (Route 132 connects with Route 6 at Exit 6)

• Route 134 from Route 6A in Dennis to Route 28 in Dennisport (Route 134 connects with Route 6 at Exit 9)

• Route 124 from Route 6A in Brewster to Route 39 in Harwich (Route 124 connects with Route 6 at Exit 10)

• Route 137 from Route 6A in Brewster to Route 39 in East Harwich and continuing to Route 28 in Chatham (Route 137 connects with Route 6 at Exit 11)

• Route 39 from Harwich center to Route 28 in Orleans.

By Air

Perhaps the best way to get a real feel for the Cape is to approach it by air. On a clear day you can see it all. You'll notice the relationships between the Cape peninsula and the two islands to the south, Martha's Vineyard and Nantucket. You'll also note Monomoy Island off Chatham and the Elizabeth Islands chain off Falmouth.

From this lofty height you feel as if you can get your arms around the whole Cape. You'll have a quick visual tour of everything between the dunes of Provincetown and the gleaming, handcarved waterway that is the Cape Cod Canal. From this height you can see it all.

Barnstable Municipal Airport is the Cape's main airport. The Cape also has several other smaller airports, sometimes just a runway or two, which, with the exception of the Provincetown Airport, only serve private planes. Once you arrive there are plenty of car rental options right at the airport. For all of

INSIDERS' TIPS

When you're driving on the Cape, please remember to take it slow, especially on narrow, winding back roads where children play and pets wander. Slow down and take in the sights; you won't see anything if you go too fast and you'll also upset the locals.

these you should call ahead to make reservations, determine any landing fees and find out what fuels are available.

Barnstable Municipal Airport
Hyannis Rotary, Hyannis • 775-2020

Barnstable Municipal Airport, the Cape's major airport, is situated right in the middle of the peninsula in Hyannis (town of Barnstable). With two 1-mile runways, it is certainly not the largest airport you'll ever land at, but it is far from the smallest. President Kennedy's plane would land here when he was arriving for a Hyannisport vacation. More recently, Vice President Al Gore landed here with his family to begin a Cape Cod vacation back in the summer of 1996.

Four airlines service the airport, three on a full-time basis and one seasonally. Also, two local airlines, Island Airlines and Nantucket Airlines, provide service from Hyannis to Nantucket (Nantucket chapter for details).

Cape Air, (800) 352-0714, offers the most daily flights into Hyannis from Boston and to the Cape and islands in the summer. On average there are about 10 flights a day year round between Boston's Logan International Airport and Barnstable Municipal Airport. These flights take about 20 minutes; it seems once the plane reaches its cruising height it's time to prepare for landing. The airline has 13 flights each day to Nantucket and five flights to Martha's Vineyard. In 1997 a one-way ticket to Nantucket cost around $39; round-trip $62. Martha's Vineyard was a little less expensive — $33 and $66, respectively. Cape Air was the first area airline to offer frequent-flier discounts; at this writing, a book of 10 unrestricted one-way commuter tickets will save you up to 25 percent off tickets bought separately.

USAirways Express, (800) 428-4322, offers three nonstop flights a day from Boston to Hyannis and two nonstop flights from New York to Hyannis. With a Saturday overnight and 14 days advance notice ticket prices drop. The airline also offers service from Newark,

INSIDERS' TIPS

A great way to avoid traffic before you leave the house is to call SmartTraveler at (617) 374-1234. This service employs remote cameras and airplanes to determine up-to-the-minute traffic and parking problems on the Cape and at ferry terminals. For cellular phone users, the numbers are: *ST1 on Cellular One and *1 on NYNEX. Once connected, press 7* to get information on the Cape and islands.

New Jersey, White Plains and Long Island, New York, and Providence, Rhode Island to Boston and then on to Hyannis.

Continental Express, (800) 525-0280, offers flights from Newark, New Jersey, to Boston's Logan International Airport and then on to Hyannis for the last leg of the journey. Six flights a day are flown from May through October.

Colgan Air, (800) 272-5488, offers year-round service between New York and Hyannis with four daily flights each way Monday through Friday, one on Saturdays and two on Sundays. From Memorial Day to mid-October Colgan also flies from Newark, New Jersey, to Hyannis.

Outside the main terminal there are normally a number of taxis waiting. If you plan on leaving your car at the airport overnight, the daily parking rate is $10.

If you need to rent a car you're in luck; there are four car rental companies located in the main terminal.

Avis, 775-2888
Budget, 790-0163
Hertz, 775-5895
National Car Rental, 771-4353

Falmouth Airpark

Fresh Pond Rd., East Falmouth • 548-9617

This one-runway airport is owned by people who live around it — in fact, all the homes have hangars for their planes the way the rest of us have garages for our cars. The 2,400-foot paved airstrip is open to the public and charters. There is a washdown station available.

Cape Cod Airport

1000 Race Ln., Marstons Mills • 428-8732

Cape Cod Airport has three grass runways, the longest being 2,700 feet. It caters to private planes, but there are also sightseeing planes, biplanes and glider rides operating out of this Mid-Cape airport.

Chatham Municipal Airport

George Ryder Rd., West Chatham • 945-9000

Chatham Municipal Airport has a 3,000-foot long, 100-foot-wide paved runway with a grass strip running alongside. The airport is open to the public and offers sight-seeing and biplane rides. There's a restaurant on site as well as a full maintenance facility.

Provincetown Airport

Race Point Rd., Provincetown • 487-0241

Located at the Province Lands, Provincetown Airport has one 3,500-foot paved runway just down the road from Race Point Beach. Cape Air flies into P-town from Boston on a daily basis. During the summer there are sightseeing flights. You can rent a car at Provincetown Airport through U-Save Auto Rental, 487-6343, or Budget, 771-2744.

By Bus

As you go about your business day after day after day, perhaps working in some city high-rise, perhaps daydreaming about a beach vacation, there are buses running nearly every hour to Cape Cod. Perhaps you should make plans to hop on one of them! Like clockwork these buses run, transporting people to the land of surf and sand. And the rates these bus lines charge are quite affordable when you consider what's waiting for you on the other end.

Greyhound

105 Trowbridge Rd. • (800) 231-2222

Greyhound offers service from New York and Boston to Bourne, with connecting service to Hyannis, 17 Elm Avenue, and Woods Hole at the Steamship Authority Wharf. The bus line of-

INSIDERS' TIPS

If you're staying for more than five days and plan to rent a car, here's a way to avoid traffic hassles: Fly into the Provincetown Airport and pick up the rental there. (Budget car rental services the airport.) Driving up Cape (west) is much easier than driving down Cape (east) since you will be going against traffic the majority of the time.

fers some nine buses a day departing both cities for Cape Cod, seven days a week year round. A one-way ticket from Boston to Bourne costs about $15; round-trip is about $29. From New York, one-way is about $40; round-trip, $75.

Bonanza

1 Bonanza Way, Providence, R.I. • (800) 556-3815

Bonanza offers six daily trips from Boston to Bourne, Falmouth and Woods Hole (you can hop a ferry from here to the islands). Connecting service to other points on the Cape is provided via the Plymouth & Brockton line, known locally as the P&B (see below). Bonanza runs seven days a week, 365 days a year, with some eight trips a day from Boston's Logan International Airport and another three a day from South Station (downtown Boston). Tickets from Logan Airport to Bourne run $14 for one-way and $24 for round-trip. From South Station, ticket prices are $10 for one-way and $19 for round-trip. Bonanza has local terminals at the following locations: Tedeschi Food Shop, 105 Trowbridge Road, Bourne, 759-7715; Steamship Authority, Woods Hole Wharf, Woods Hole, (800) 556-3815; Bonanza Terminal, 59 Depot Avenue, Falmouth, 548-7588; and Plymouth & Brockton Terminal, 17 Elm Avenue, Hyannis, (800) 556-3815.

Plymouth & Brockton

Plymouth & Brockton Bus Terminal, 17 Elm Ave., Hyannis • 775-5524 on Cape, (617) 773-9401 elsewhere

Plymouth & Brockton offers regularly scheduled direct service from downtown Boston (South Station) and Boston's Logan International Airport to Hyannis, Sagamore and Barnstable. Connecting service continues on other P&B buses to other points on the Cape, all the way to Provincetown, year round. From Logan Airport a one-way ticket runs $15 while round-trip is $27; from South Station the prices are $11 and $20, respectively. More than 35 P&B buses a day head south to the Cape, with six continuing on to Provincetown. There are also bus stops in many of the Cape towns in between Hyannis and Provincetown.

SeaLine

222 Old Chatham Rd., Dennis • 385-8336, (800) 352-7155

Initiated in 1985, SeaLine offers year-round regularly scheduled bus service on the Cape between Woods Hole and Plymouth & Brockton's downtown Hyannis terminal. Run by the Cape Cod Regional Transit Authority, the bus line makes six round trips during the week and four on Saturday (no service on Sunday). The cost is a mere $3.25 one way; half-price for seniors, the disabled and children younger than age 5. Around the last week in June through Labor Day, SeaLine hooks up with local trolley shuttles in various towns (Falmouth, Hyannis, Yarmouth, Dennis and Mashpee). One-way trolley trips within an area can cost as little as 50¢, half that amount for handicapped; children ages 5 and younger travel free with a paying adult.

B-Bus

222 Old Chatham Rd., Dennis • 385-8326, (800) 352-7155

Unique to the Cape is the B-Bus, a fleet of 30 minivans that will transport you door-to-door between any towns on the Cape Monday through Friday (and on weekends in some towns). Appointments for rides must be made in advance. Adults and children 5 years of age and older ride for $2 (plus 10¢ per mile if traveling between towns) while seniors and the handicapped pay $1.25 (plus 6¢ a mile if traveling between towns). Frequent users may want to consider the economical, no-mileage-fee, three-month Gold Pass, which costs $75; $45 for seniors and the handicapped. Some of the vehicles are wheelchair-accessible. B-Bus is run by the Cape Cod Regional Transit Authority.

INSIDERS' TIPS

Unless otherwise indicated, you can make a right on red after stopping. Also remember: Drivers must stop at pedestrian crosswalks, which are designated by stripes running curb-to-curb. It's a state law.

By Rail

Years ago rail was the most common way to get to the Cape and to the town you were heading for. Today, sadly, rail service is limited; you can get to the Cape by rail in summer only (see Amtrak listing below) and even then only on weekends. The only rail service that goes beyond Hyannis is the Cape Cod Scenic Railroad (see listing below), and that's strictly sightseeing. On the bright side, the old rail beds from Dennis to Orleans have been converted into a great bike trail! (See our Parks and Recreation chapter.)

Amtrak

352 Main St., Hyannis • (800) 872-7245

Every Friday from mid-June through Labor Day weekends only, The Cape Codder runs to Hyannis from Washington, D.C., Baltimore, Philadelphia, New York City, Stamford and New Haven, Connecticut, and Providence, Rhode Island. The entire trip takes approximately seven hours, and return trips are on Sunday. After Labor Day, those traveling by rail can only go as far as Boston and have to take advantage of any other means of transportation to get on Cape.

Cape Cod Scenic Railroad

252 Main St., Hyannis • 771-3788, (800) 872-4508 (Mass. only)

Once you're on Cape, check out the two-hour scenic excursions offered by Cape Cod Scenic Railroad or splurge and take the dinner train. It will give you a taste of what life was like back in the days when everyone traveled by rail, plus you'll see parts of the Cape you wouldn't see otherwise (see our Tours and Excursions chapter for more information).

By Trolley

In the summertime, when tourism is at its peak and the roads are congested, several Cape towns offer trolley rides to attractions and shopping areas. Trolleys, which have really caught on in the past several years, are a hybrid form of transportation that blend function and fun. Passengers use them for plain old transportation and for sightseeing. Also see our Tours and Excursions chapter for more details.

Photo: Cape Cod Chamber of Commerce

A Nantucket ferry returns to Lewis Bay in Hyannis.

Glasstown Trolley
Jarves St. at Railway Station • Sandwich • 428-9973

Run by Aitchison Bus Co., the Glasstown Trolley has a regular route starting at the train station on Jarves Street and extending to the Heritage Plantation, Cape Cod Glassworks, through Market Square and past the harbor. The trolley runs weekends only from Memorial Day through late June, then daily except Monday from late June through Columbus Day. You can get off anywhere you like along the route; the ride costs $5.

Cape Cod Regional Transit Authority
Many locations • 385-8326, (800) 352-7155

The CCRTA operates a number of trolleys in various towns, including Falmouth, Mashpee, Hyannis, Yarmouth and Dennis. Fares are 50¢ for adults and 25¢ for senior citizens and physically challenged people, unless otherwise noted. While most of the trolleys are seasonal, two are year round: the SeaLine between Hyannis and Falmouth, ($3.25 for the entire route, with a minimum fare of 75¢ for shorter routes) and the Villager in Hyannis, which goes to Barnstable Village and the Barnstable County Complex, and in the off-season makes stops at shopping areas on Route 132.

New in 1996, the CCRTA's H2O mini-bus runs down Route 28 from Hyannis to Orleans, making six trips a day all year and increasing to hourly trips in summer. You can get on at regular stops or just flag the driver down. The entire ride takes an hour or so one way. The fare is $3.30 for the full ride, $1 minimum increasing by increments of 50¢ per town. Discount commuting passes are available.

By Bicycle

Cycling is a popular way to get around Cape, especially in summer. You can pedal through villages and towns or get away from vehicular traffic by taking one of the Cape's pretty bike trails (see our Parks and Recreation chapter for details). The 25-mile Cape Cod Rail Trail, which follows the old rail beds, runs from Dennis to Wellfleet and goes through Nickerson State Park. The Cape has dozens of bicycle rental businesses that can put you on two wheels; you can get mountain bikes, kid trailers, even bicycles built for two. See our Parks and Recreation chapter for listings. Most bike rental places also sell bicycles, accessories and parts in addition to renting equipment such as helmets and child passenger seats.

By Sea

Sailing to the Cape may be the most relaxing, some even say the loveliest, way to get here. Several ferry companies offer fast, reliable transportation between various ports to the Cape and islands. It is important to make a reservation, especially if you plan on crossing with your car, since ferries get booked during peak season months in advance. Summer reservations, for example, are often booked by early winter of the preceding year. There are last-minute cancellations, but be prepared to wait for hours. (Don't forget to book your return reservation as well.) All island-bound ferries offer sufficient pay-per-day parking.

The Steamship Authority

Woods Hole Wharf, Woods Hole • 477-8600

The Steamship Authority is the only company offering year-round ferry service from Woods Hole to points on Martha's Vineyard and from Hyannis to Nantucket. It's also the only ferry that transports cars. Keep in mind that taking your car to the islands can be very expensive, and it's usually not necessary since you can rent one upon your arrival. Better yet, rent a bicycle or moped (see our Martha's Vineyard and Nantucket chapters).

Hy-Line

Ocean Street Dock, Hyannis • 778-2600

Hy-Line offers the only service between Hyannis and Martha's Vineyard from early May through late October. The company also services the Hyannis to Nantucket route and offers interisland service between Nantucket and Martha's Vineyard. Ferries leave from Dock One, Ocean Street, Hyannis. Since the fall of 1995, Hy-Line has operated the 40-passenger catamaran *Grey Lady* between Hyannis and Nantucket with a speedy travel time of just one hour.

Bay State Cruises

MacMillian Pier, Provincetown • 487-9284, (617) 457-1428

This is the only company offering daily service between Provincetown's MacMillian Pier and Commonwealth Pier in Boston. The ferry starts up Memorial Day weekend, running five days beginning the Friday of that weekend, then runs Friday to Monday until June 20, when it begins daily service through Labor Day. After that, the service is offered weekends only through September. The trip takes about three hours; adult fares are $30 round trip or $18 one way.

The Island Queen

Falmouth • 548-4800

For $10 round trip ($5 for children), you can take the 500-passenger *Island Queen* from Falmouth Harbor to Martha's Vineyard from Memorial Day weekend to Columbus Day. The trip is a leisurely 35 minutes each way, and food service is available on board, along with a full bar. The passenger-only vessel makes seven trips each day in summer, and reservations are not needed. The *Island Queen* is also available for charters.

Hotels, Motels and Resorts

A Cape Cod vacation. It brings memories of childhood to mind, memories of soft sandy beaches and playful ocean waves, memories of the long days of summer you thought would never end and warm starlit nights in the company of family and friends. A Cape Cod vacation, whether you're an adult or a child, is a treasure of sand and water during the day and of moonbeams dancing off waves at night.

Beginning that perfect Cape Cod vacation begins with finding the perfect Cape Cod accommodation. It has to be the right spot, a perfect mix of location and amenities, a place with the right personality, perhaps close to the beach or close to restaurants or maybe even close to golf courses. On this narrow peninsula you'll find that there's something here to cater to everybody's particular needs, and this chapter is a good place to start the search.

Cape Cod offers hundreds of accommodations — motels, hotels, resorts, hostels, guest houses, inns, bed and breakfasts and even campgrounds. In this chapter we present hotels, motels, resorts and hostels for your consideration. (See our Bed and Breakfasts, Inns and Guesthouses chapter or our Campgrounds chapter for other options.) We've narrowed your search a bit (as we said, there are hundreds to choose from). Your best bet is to begin by deciding how you want to spend your time while you're here, then pick the area that offers the activities you desire. Of course, price is a consideration as well, so we've provided a price code with each accommodation.

It is best to make reservations before coming over the bridge. The Cape fills up quickly, not only during the summer season but also during the so-called shoulder seasons of spring and fall. September and October are surprisingly busy months, and there are weekends during the peak foliage season of October when some towns are completely booked. So we advise that you call well in advance to secure that special place you want.

As you can well imagine, the Cape's summer season is not only its busiest season but also its costliest as far as accommodation rates go. It's the law of supply and demand. Many of the Cape's hotel and motel facilities are only open during a handful of months (typically Memorial Day to Columbus Day) and have to reap a year's worth of income in less than a half-year's time. Therefore, expect to pay more during the peak summer tourist season when demand for rooms is at its height. This peak season typically runs from June to Labor Day. July tends to be the Cape's busiest month, and Labor Day weekend is busy as well. Most places have a basic price that varies according to water view, location, size and amenities, so be sure you ask about the options.

The autumn season in all its glory is quickly becoming a popular season on the Cape. Visitors enjoy all the Cape's beauty at substantially lower prices, and there are plenty of packages available to make the Cape even more attractive. Rates at some accommodations can be as much as 50 percent less than summer rates, and the indoor pool is just as refreshing and the outside sights are just as breathtaking.

Cape Cod is a resort area and as such, many of its hotels, motels and resorts do close after Columbus Day. A good many, though, remain open throughout the year and cater to bus tours, business travelers and winter guests who quickly realize that Cape Cod is just as beautiful with a little frosting on her marshes. Roughly a quarter of the facilities on Cape Cod remain open year round.

In the descriptions that follow, we'll let you know if a place is a year-round facility or whether it's only open during certain times of the year. Children are welcome at all facilities unless we mention otherwise. You can nearly always expect to pay your bill with a major credit card; we'll let you know if an accommodation does not accept credit cards. Most facilities have in-room televisions, telephones and air-conditioning, so we won't normally mention those in our descriptions. Also, most accommodations do not allow pets, but we'll make reference to the ones that do welcome our furry friends. At the end of the chapter we list a few kennels.

FYI

Unless otherwise noted, the area code for all phone numbers in this guide is 508.

Most motels and hotels try to meet the needs of smokers and nonsmokers with restricted areas and/or rooms, while others have a comprehensive nonsmoking policy. You'll want to ask what the smoking policy is at the accommodation you're considering. A number of places also have handicapped-accessible facilities; inquire when you call for reservations.

Price Information

To help you select a hotel, motel or resort in your price range, we have established the following key, based on the average cost of a night's stay in a double-occupancy room during the season, minus tax and special charges. Massachusetts charges a state tax, as do the individual Cape towns, which equates to about 9.7 percent added to your bill.

$	**Less than $75**
$$	**$76 to $110**
$$$	**$111 to $175**
$$$$	**$176 or more**

At the end of the chapter we have included resorts, which offer a combination of townhouse accommodations with amenities not normally found at most hotels and motels. For the budget-conscious vacationer we've also listed hostels at the end of this chapter.

Reservation Services

First, here are some resources that can make planning your vacation much easier. Instead of calling around to see which establishments have openings — especially if you haven't started planning way in advance — enlist the help of one of the Cape's reservation services. Most deal with hotels, inns and bed and breakfasts, though some specialize in the latter. (For details on bed and breakfast facilities, turn to our Bed and Breakfasts, Inns and Guesthouses chapter.) The following reservation services are among the best around.

Bed and Breakfast Cape Cod
P.O. Box 341, West Hyannisport • 775-2772, (800) 686-5252

This 15-year-old reservation service lists 100 bed and breakfast host homes, inns and sea captains' homes throughout Cape Cod, Martha's Vineyard and Nantucket. Properties, which are all inspected and approved annually, range from modest to luxurious. Some have fireplaces, Jacuzzis and beach settings.

Coastal Innkeepers Limited
30 Earle Rd., West Harwich • 430-3103, (800) 368-1180

This organization handles more than 25 properties — inns, bed and breakfasts, cottages, motels and condos — in Yarmouth, Dennis, Harwich, Chatham and Orleans. All sites are inspected annually. The customers pays no fee. The business is closed in January and February.

Destinnations
P.O. Box 1173, Osterville • 420-3430, (800) 333-4667

Handpicked properties on Cape Cod, Nantucket and Martha's Vineyard are described in a detailed full-color catalogue. Award-winning listings range from historic village homes to full-service inns.

In Town Reservations

4 Standish St., Provincetown • 487-1883, (800) 67-PTOWN

In Town handles house rentals by the week, month or season, handling a huge number of annually inspected properties in Provincetown and North Truro. The firm also books reservations at inns, bed and breakfasts, guest houses, motels and condominiums — all for no fee!

Orleans Bed & Breakfast Associates

P.O. Box 1312, Orleans • 255-3824, (800) 541-6226

This well-regarded organization represents the kind of traditional inns that popularized the term bed and breakfast — most are small and homey. Most of the establishments covered here offer three rooms or fewer, which means they are exempt from state lodging tax — a nice bonus. For a $10 reservation fee, Orleans Bed & Breakfast Associates will set you up with one that's right for you. Choose from more than 60 properties (all nonsmoking) from Chatham to Truro, all inspected annually.

Provincetown Reservations System

293 Commercial St., Provincetown • 487-2400, (800) 648-0364

This full-service travel agency handles rooms in more than 85 percent of the properties and more than 100 condos in Provincetown and the Beach Point section of North Truro. All properties are inspected every spring. PRS also handles restaurant and show reservations. You pay no reservation fee.

Hotels and Motels

Upper Cape

Bay Motor Inn

$ • 223 Main St., Buzzards Bay • 759-3989

For 32 seasons this family-owned and -operated motor inn has been providing vacationers with affordable accommodations located just across the street from the Cape Cod Canal. Friendly owners Fred and Irene Carbone dress their air-conditioned rooms with fresh flowers and the kind of down-home feel that only a family-run inn can provide. Popular with families, retirees and even fishermen, the Bay Motor Inn is a short walk to numerous restaurants, a small movie theater and a bowling alley. Spend the day lounging by the handicapped-accessible pool, playing tennis at the nearby courts or just watching the boat traffic on the canal.

The inn's 17 clean units, including singles, doubles, efficiencies and three housekeeping units, are in separate cottages and a motel building. Pets are allowed; in fact, Fred refers to the inn as "pet friendly." The Bay Motor Inn is open from April 1 to Veterans Day.

Best Western Bridge-Bourne Hotel

$$ • 100 Trowbridge Rd., Bourne • 759-0800, (800) 675-0008

You'll enjoy absolutely incredible views of the gracefully arched Bourne Bridge from this appropriately named hotel. Beyond the bridge lie the thick woodlands of southeastern Massachusetts, a patchwork of pines and oaks as far as the eye can see. This 42-room hotel sits high above the Cape Cod Canal and features an indoor heated pool, hot tub and eight deluxe suites with Jacuzzis and kitchenettes. The hotel also features a location that makes it convenient to the many sites of Cape Cod as well as nearby Plymouth and, about an hour to the north, Boston.

Two of the hotel's rooms are handicapped-accessible, a number of other rooms have balconies overlooking the Canal. Function rooms are available for weddings and other events, while the on-site Trowbridge Tavern can chase away any hunger or thirst. Children 12 and younger stay at the hotel free with an adult. It is open year round.

Yankee Thrift Motel

$ • Rt. 28 at the Bourne Rotary, Bourne • 759-3883

The Yankee Thrift Motel lives up to its name, offering downright affordable accommodations just over the Cape Cod Canal. In fact, it's right there as you come down off the Bourne Bridge to start your Cape Cod vacation. The motel has 56 rooms, 20 of which are efficiency units that accommodate as many as six people. Yankee Thrift has an indoor pool, an outdoor pool and a Jacuzzi. There are also a few handicapped-accessible rooms available, a huge sundeck to lounge on and grills. Small pets are permitted at this year round motel.

Dan'l Webster Inn

$$$-$$$$ • 149 Main St., Sandwich • 888-3622, (800) 444-3566

One of the Upper Cape's most distinguished facilities, the Dan'l Webster Inn offers four dining rooms — the Webster Room, the Heritage Room, the Morgan Room and the Conservatory (see our Restaurants chapter) — a devilish English tavern, a gift shop and an outdoor swimming pool, all set in the midst of the historic and beautiful Sandwich Village. This colonial inn is a reproduction of the original tavern, built in 1692, that served as a parsonage and Patriot headquarters during the Revolutionary War. It was patronized by statesman Daniel Webster during the town's mid-19th century heyday, hence its name.

Guests have their choice of 37 guest rooms and 9 suites at the inn or in two older homes, the Fessenden House on the property and the Quince Tree Inn one block away. Furnishings throughout are antiques or period reproductions. Dan'l Webster Inn offers many types of accommodations ranging in style from the formally elegant Daniel Webster Suite with a fireplace and massive canopied bed to double-bed rooms in the Jarves Wing, which are clean and tastefully furnished. All guest rooms are individually decorated and feature private baths; some have a Jacuzzi. Pampering includes fresh flowers, chocolates, turned-down beds and bottled water in the rooms.

While staying here, you are within strolling distance of Sandwich's many museums and other historic attractions, including the Hoxie House and the Grist Mill on Shawme Pond. The Dan'l Webster Inn is open year round.

Sandwich Lodge & Resort

$$ • 54 Rt. 6A, Sandwich • 888-2255, (800) 282-5353

This affordable full-service hotel along beautiful Route 6A has 68 rooms including five efficiencies, 15 two-room suites and two honeymoon suites. Set on 9½ acres, the Sandwich Lodge & Resort offers both indoor and outdoor pools, a laundry, a game room for the kids, a whirlpool and meeting rooms if you plan on mixing business with pleasure. Table tennis, billiards, badminton, volleyball, horseshoes and shuffleboard fill the void between dips in the pools.

In the morning, fresh bakery items await you in the main lobby adjacent to the indoor pool. Artwork by local artists hangs on the walls in the lobby and is for sale if you see anything that sparks your interest. Just down the road is the historic district of Sandwich with its many museums as well as the 76-acre Heritage Plantation. On the grounds of the Sandwich Lodge & Resort is Barney's Restaurant (formerly the Old Kings Highway Publick House), which serves lunch and dinner. Sandwich Lodge & Resort is open all 12 months of the year.

Shady Nook Inn

$$ • 14 Rt. 6A, Sandwich • 888-0409, (800) 338-5208

The immaculate Shady Nook Inn, run by Jim and Sharon Rinaldi, showcases colorful flower beds, well-manicured lawns and a lovely pool area. The 30 attractive rooms, including seven efficiencies, offer king- and queen-size beds and doubles. Most rooms have refrigerators. Laundry service is available, and the office has a coffee bar for guests (available between Memorial Day and Columbus Day). While you are in the office you will want to take a look at Jim's impressive display of Coca-Cola memorabilia.

Convenient to historic Sandwich village and nearby beaches, the Shady Nook Inn is open year round.

INSIDERS' TIPS

The first tourist visited Cape Cod about 997 years ago. Norse explorer Leif Erikson, it is believed, arrived at Bass River about A.D. 1000 and stayed for a half-year at Follins Pond in Dennis/ Yarmouth before departing for his home in Greenland.

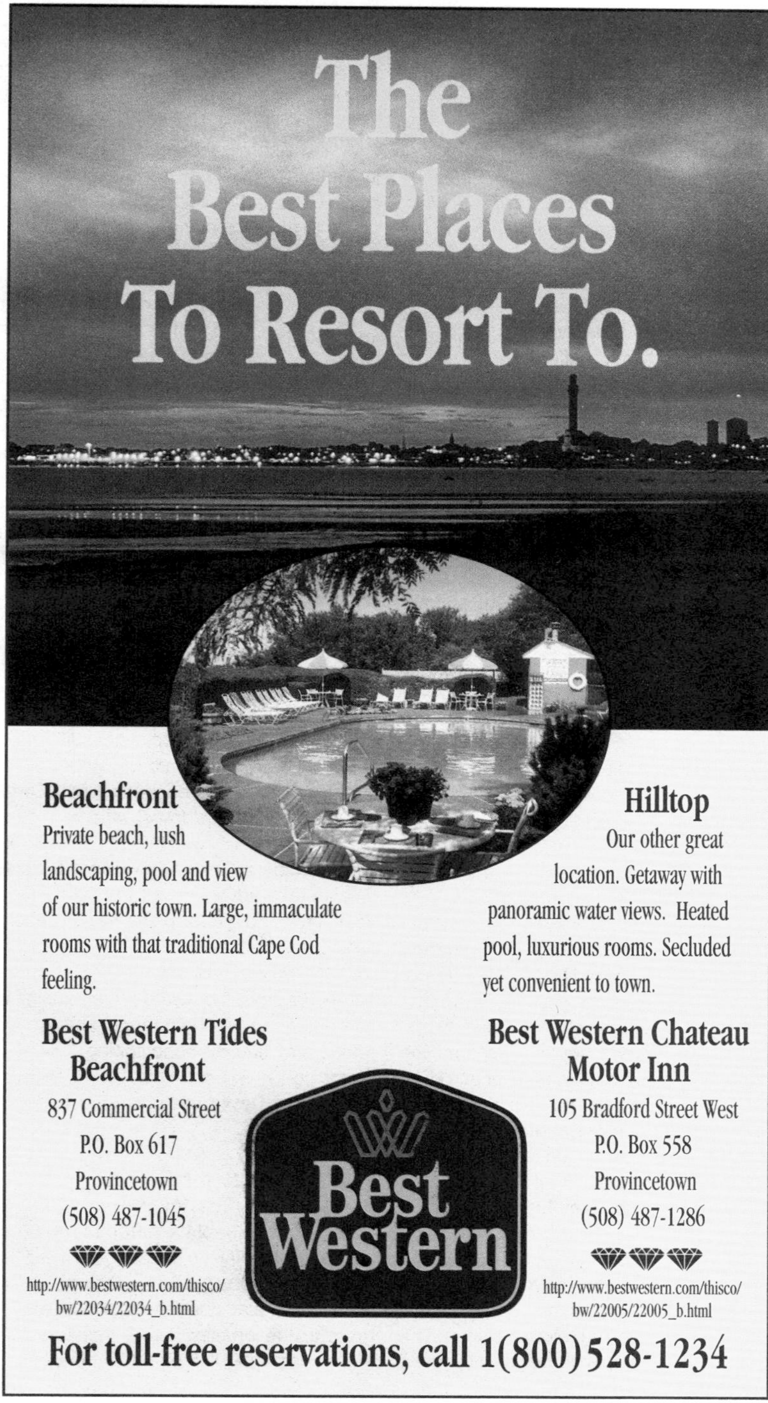
The Best Places To Resort To.
Beachfront
Private beach, lush landscaping, pool and view of our historic town. Large, immaculate rooms with that traditional Cape Cod feeling.
Hilltop
Our other great location. Getaway with panoramic water views. Heated pool, luxurious rooms. Secluded yet convenient to town.
Best Western Tides Beachfront
837 Commercial Street
P.O. Box 617
Provincetown
(508) 487-1045
http://www.bestwestern.com/thisco/bw/22034/22034_b.html
Best Western
Best Western Chateau Motor Inn
105 Bradford Street West
P.O. Box 558
Provincetown
(508) 487-1286
http://www.bestwestern.com/thisco/bw/22005/22005_b.html
For toll-free reservations, call 1(800)528-1234

The Earl of Sandwich

$-$$ • 378 Rt. 6A, East Sandwich • 888-1415, (800) 442-EARL

With walls sporting dark paneling and ceilings featuring exposed beams, you'll think you are staying at a manor in Sandwich, England, rather than a vacation motel along Route 6A in Sandwich, Massachusetts. Nestled 'neath tall trees encircling a peaceful duck pond, the Earl of Sandwich is a favorite spot for Cape visitors in search of serenity and relaxation. Owners Brian and Kathy Clifford provide this tranquility just a short ride from beaches, shopping and the many historical sites in nearby Sandwich village. Many of the 24 rooms here are air conditioned. Rooms are comfortably furnished with two doubles or a queen-size bed. Guests roll out of bed each morning to a self-serve continental breakfast (coffee, juice and Kathy's homemade muffins), which many enjoy at the picnic table outside the kitchenette.

FYI

Unless otherwise noted, the area code for all phone numbers in this guide is 508.

A motel for all seasons, the rates are very reasonable, especially during the off-season. (The Bay waters may be a bit cooler in the fall, but the foliage is outstanding!) Pets are welcome. Golf packages are available, as are handicapped accommodations.

Old Colony Motel

$ • 436 Rt. 6A, East Sandwich • 888-9716, (800) 786-9716

The picturesque Route 6A borders vast salt marshes as it winds its way toward Sandwich, and the Old Colony Motel rests along this ancient carriage route. The property lies adjacent to conservation lands and cranberry bogs. Presented in an early American charm, the rooms here offer two double beds or one king-size bed, air conditioning (heat for the off-season), private baths and refrigerators.

A generous complimentary continental breakfast gets you started for the day at the beach or visiting the many historic sites and museums of Sandwich village. Or if you plan on staying put, the Old Colony has a pool and barbecue area available. The off-season rates are a deal for those wishing to steal some Indian summer days from Mother Nature. The Old Colony Motel is open throughout the year.

Spring Garden Motel

$ • 578 Rt. 6A, East Sandwich • 888-0710

Marvelous marsh views await you at the 11-room Spring Garden Motel located on meandering Scornton Creek. At a price that is just as marvelous, you can have two double beds, or for just an additional $5 you can upgrade to an efficiency unit with a kitchenette that sleeps as many as six. Families will enjoy the swimming pool and a spacious backyard for the children. Scornton Creek is a great spot for canoeing, fishing and swimming. Awake each morning to a complimentary continental breakfast. Flower beds accent the grounds and window boxes spill forth with red geraniums and white petunias. Summer rates are very reasonable, and autumn rates are about $20 less. The motel is open from the beginning of April to the end of November.

Spring Hill Motor Lodge

$$ • 351 Rt. 6A, East Sandwich • 888-1456

An exceptionally well-maintained property with pretty grounds, this East Sandwich facility with a white and Colonial blue decor has a lighted tennis court, heated outdoor pool with a large deck and a basketball net. Owners Trevor and Regina Aldhurst, who have owned the 22-room facility with two efficiencies for 11 years, enjoy an excellent repeat business. Guests take advantage of the Route 6A antique, craft and gift shops as well as beaches, fishing and golfing.

Children are most welcome. All rooms have a queen-size bed or two double beds as well as a color cable TV, telephone, coffee maker, refrigerator and air conditioning. Spring Hill Motor Lodge is open year round, with their after-Labor Day rates dropping into the $ range.

The Admiralty Inn

$$-$$$ • 51 Teaticket Hwy. (Rt. 28), Falmouth • 548-4240, (800) 341-5700

The Admiralty Inn of Falmouth has it all — an outdoor pool with a bar and barbecue area, an indoor heated pool, a whirlpool spa, a playground, the on-site Harry's restaurant and lounge featuring live entertainment (see our

Cape Cod Cooking™
Hearth 'n Kettle
RESTAURANTS

Restaurants chapter), and function rooms. Its central location makes it convenient to the beaches of Falmouth and the various island ferries that leave from Falmouth Harbor and Woods Hole.

Open year round, the Admiralty has 98 air-conditioned rooms including 28 townhouse suites. Eight of the rooms are handicapped accessible. Rooms and suites feature private baths and include a wet bar, refrigerator and coffee maker, while the two-story townhouse suites offer two bathrooms, two TVs, a VCR and a Jacuzzi. The Admiralty is a member of Vacation Inn Properties (V.I.P.), which manages three other facilities in Falmouth (Marina Tradewinds, Park Beach Motel and Surfside Holiday) as well as the Ambassador Motor Inn in South Yarmouth; the five facilities together total some 400 rooms.

Falmouth Inn

$$ • 824 Main St., Falmouth • 540-2500, (800) 255-4157

One of Falmouth's larger hotels, the Falmouth Inn is a single-floor facility with 123 rooms catering to those people who seek value as well as convenience. Rooms include two double beds and color TV. On site is a restaurant (open May to October), a large heated indoor-outdoor pool with a retractable roof and a game room.

Falmouth Inn is near all of Falmouth's marvelous assets, including Main Street shops and restaurants, beaches, Falmouth Harbor and the *Island Queen* ferry. In the fall and spring the hotel offers rates that are nearly half that of summer rates as well as special rate packages that include two meals. The inn is open year round and welcomes pets.

Falmouth Marina Tradewinds

$$ • 26 Robbins Rd., Falmouth • 548-4575, (800) 341-5700

The views you'll have of Falmouth Harbor are outstanding. From your room you can watch sailboats darting their way in and out of the busy harbor and the big, white *Island Queen* ferry pulling away from her slip with another full load of passengers bound for Martha's Vineyard (lucky ducks!). Harbor views, two swimming pools, proximity to restaurants and attractions all make this large facility a popular one with visitors to the grand ol' town of Falmouth.

From its 63 rooms, choose a double room or suite, with a living room, kitchen, bedroom and bath. Rooms are spacious and comfortable and have coffee makers. The facility is open weekends from March 1 to March 31 and then full time from April 1 to mid-October. During the off-season in September and October, room rates are about half-price compared to summer. The world-renowned Falmouth Road Race in August passes right by this property (see our Spectator Sports chapter).

Ramada on the Square

$$-$$$ • 40 N. Main St. (Rt. 28), Falmouth • 457-0606, (800) 676-0000

In a town with so many long-established accommodations, this relative newcomer has a lot to offer, including an indoor heated pool and a dining room and lounge area (Captain Scott's, which is open to the public). The dining room is open for breakfast, lunch and dinner. This Ramada is close to the Bonanza Bus Line terminal and the Shining Sea Bikepath as well as the many shops, museums and restaurants of Falmouth. A nice plus is van transport to local beaches and to the island ferries at Falmouth Harbor and Woods Hole.

The handicapped-accessible inn has 72 attractive rooms and suites. Most rooms have double beds and some of the suites have a Jacuzzi. Housed in two buildings, the Ramada on the Square is open year round.

Red Horse Inn

$$ • 28 Falmouth Heights Rd., Falmouth • 548-0053, (800) 628-3811

The handsome Red Horse Inn is an immaculate 22-room facility that is convenient to Falmouth center and harbor, the ferry boats to the islands and the area beaches. The inn is both attractive and homey with its award-winning flower gardens and a pretty outdoor swimming pool. Rooms are beautifully decorated and include queen-size beds, private baths and air conditioning, and some have refrigerators and paddle ceiling fans.

Personal attention is a priority here. Charming owners Grace and Bob Cashman are always happy to assist guests in developing a daily itinerary. That itinerary could include whale watching, golfing, museum visits, fishing, sailing or biking. Red Horse Inn is open from early May to the end of October. Children are welcome.

Shoreway Acres Inn

$$-$$$ • 59 Shore St., Falmouth • 540-3000, (800) 352-7100

Along Shore Street, with its colonial homes and centuries-old elm trees, rests Shoreway Acres Inn. One end of the street ends with a town beach peering out across Vineyard Sound to Martha's Vineyard, the other end empties onto Main Street where you will find, well, everything. The facility, made up of remodeled sea captain's homes and a conven-

INSIDERS' TIPS

The hurricane season on the Cape and islands begins June 1 and lasts until November 30. The height of activity usually occurs between August and October.

tional motel totaling 85 units, has double rooms, efficiencies and king leisure units.

There's a lot here to keep you busy. Besides a sauna, an outdoor and an indoor pool (enclosed with large windows overlooking the beautiful grounds), there are also badminton, croquet and volleyball courts on site as well as tennis courts, golf courses, horseback riding, fishing and bike-riding facilities located nearby. You can get discounted ferry tickets in the lobby, and the desk staff will help you make arrangements for group activities. Shoreway Acres also offers attractive package deals with meals provided. The inn is open year round.

Surfside Holiday

$$-$$$ • 134 Menauhant Rd., Falmouth • 548-0313, (800) 341-5700

This popular beachfront resort on Maravista Beach is nearly surrounded by water and offers views, views and more views. This place is what summer is all about! The 89 rooms here are all air conditioned and range from waterview rooms to beachfront rooms and from deluxe waterview rooms to beachfront efficiencies. Guests receive a complimentary continental breakfast.

Amenities are numerous: private beach, two outdoor pools, sun decks, private tennis court, volleyball, shuffleboard, an enclosed children's playground, barbecue grills and even jetties along the beach for fishing. Nearby are watersports, boat rentals and parasailing. This is a motel for active vacationers who want to mix a little sport with their relaxation. It's also a great place to bring the kids. They'll never run out of things to do, and, besides, up to two of the little darlings stay free with two adults. The Surfside is open from the week before Memorial Day to Columbus Day.

Green Harbor Waterfront Motor Lodge

$$ • 134 Acapesket Rd., East Falmouth • 548-4747, (800) 548-5556

For 35 years this East Falmouth fixture has rested on the Green Pond inlet, which eventually empties into Vineyard Sound. Green Harbor has 40 units, most of which offer queen and double beds; about half have kitchens.

INSIDERS' TIPS

Nantucket Sound has entertained many a summer guest. Its waters are warmer than the waters of Cape Cod Bay, and much warmer than the Atlantic waves on the outer Cape. The waters of the sound are relatively shallow, partially accounting for its warmer temperatures.

The facility, which caters to families looking to create summer memories, has an outdoor pool as well as a 1.5-foot-deep kiddie pool. There are docking facilities available for your use if you plan on arriving via your own boat. Other on-site amenities include volleyball and shuffleboard courts, charcoal grills and a boating beach. Rowboats and paddleboats are also available for guest use. Open from April to November, pets are allowed as long as they are not left unattended in the room.

Sea Crest Oceanfront Resort & Conference Center

$$$-$$$$ • 350 Quaker Rd., North Falmouth • 540-9400, (800) 225-3110

With a view lovely as an artist's canvas come to life, this exceptional resort/conference center has 684 feet of waterfront on sparkling Buzzards Bay. It offers a plush waterfront dining room, a heated indoor pool, an outdoor pool, an exercise room, a game room, whirlpool, sauna and two all-weather tennis courts. During July and August, the day-camp staff holds activities for children.

This 266-room resort has very nice rooms with two double beds; some have water views and balconies. Available space is sometimes limited by conferences. Guests may wish to take advantage of special programs that include meals in the cost of their stay. On site is the Oceanfront Dinner Room and the Surf Lounge and Piano Bar.

The resort has six conference rooms for those who have to work for a living. For those who can tear themselves away from the meetings and the gorgeous beachfront, Falmouth's downtown and harbor are about a 10- to 15-minute drive away. Sea Crest is a year-round facility.

Park Beach Motel

$$ • 241 Grand Ave., Falmouth Heights • 548-1010, (800) 341-5700

Right across the street from the spectacular Falmouth Heights Beach rests the Park Beach Motel, a Vacation Inn Property (V.I.P.). This motel has 50 rooms just a hop, skip and a jump from Vineyard Sound and even closer to the finish line of the world-renowned Falmouth Road Race. Two of those rooms are penthouses with two queen beds, a wet bar, refrigerator, coffee maker, microwave and stellar views of the sound. Some of the other rooms offer kitchenettes and all rooms have air conditioning, TVs and direct-dial telephones.

A complimentary continental breakfast is served daily. Overlooking the beach is a large outdoor pool and a large sun patio. A courtesy van is available to take you to the three other V.I.P motels in Falmouth (The Admiralty Inn, Falmouth Marina Tradewinds and Surfside Holiday) where the amenities of each are open to you. The van will also take you to various Falmouth area locations, such as the ferry docks, so inquire at the front desk for its schedule. It's open from Memorial Day until Columbus Day. Two children stay free with two adults.

Nautilus Motor Inn

$$-$$$ • 539 Woods Hole Rd., Woods Hole • 548-1525, (800) 654-2333

This motor inn rests atop a hill overlooking Woods Hole Harbor where ferries and oceanographic research vessels motor in and out. The views here are spectacular (yes, that's Martha's Vineyard you see across the water). You may even catch sight, as we did, of a cruise ship heading for the Cape Cod Canal.

Situated close to Falmouth and to the village of Woods Hole, which has great restaurants and marine science attractions, this 54-room facility has a nice outdoor pool, a spacious sundeck and tennis courts. All rooms have balconies or patios, some with lovely views of Vineyard Sound. The geodesic Dome Restaurant and Lounge (see our Restaurants chapter) is on the grounds. Your morning coffee at the Nautilus is complimentary. The Inn is open from April 1 through the end of October.

Sands of Time Motor Inn & Harbor House

$$-$$$ • 549 Woods Hole Rd., Woods Hole • 548-6300, (800) 841-0114

The Sands of Time Motor Inn & Harbor House is so close to Woods Hole village and its oceanographic institute (WHOI) that to be any closer you'd have to spend the night aboard one of the WHOI research vessels docked at the harbor. As for the Martha's Vineyard ferry, it departs just a short three to five minute's stroll away. This traditional motel offers incredible balcony views of Martha's Vineyard across the waters of Little Harbor and Vineyard Sound beyond. Also on the grounds is the delightful Victorian Harbor House, which has four-poster, brass and wrought-iron beds and working fireplaces.

The 33-room motel also has a pool, in-room computer jacks and a fax machine in the office (marine researchers visiting Woods Hole Oceanographic Institute are frequent guests). Complimentary coffee and doughnuts are served in the morning. The Sands of Time is open from April to the end of October.

Mid-Cape

Trade Winds Inn

$$-$$$ • Craigville Beach Rd., Craigville • 775-0365

Set upon a hill that runs down to Craigville Beach on one side and Lake Elizabeth on the other, this inn on 6 acres provides some of the very best views of Nantucket Sound. You can choose from three buildings housing 35 rooms — the Ocean View in the main building offering (you guessed it) spectacular ocean views,

Kennels

If you need a place for your dog or cat to stay — perhaps you got your signals crossed on whether your chosen accommodation allows pets, or maybe you'd like to take a couple of days and visit the islands, sans pooch — the Cape has a number of kennels. Here are a few of the best.

The Animal Inn

Rt. 130, Sandwich • 477-0990

This veterinarian-owned facility has heated individual kennels, sheltered outdoor runs and a separate kitty quarters. It offers grooming, obedience training, an on-premise vet clinic and even a soothing sound system. The manager lives on the property, so your pets are always watched over.

Close-up

Peasant Bay Animal Hospital

Rt. 137 and Queen Ann Road, East Harwich • 432-5500

This facility offers boarding and grooming as well as medical services, from vaccinations to surgery. In business as an animal hospital for 25 years under the ownership of Dr. Christopher Donner, Pleasant Bay began offering boarding two years ago. It has separate, air-conditioned accommodations for dogs and cats, runs for larger dogs and an outdoor play yard for cats. Dogs are walked three times a day or more if an owner chooses.

Derbyfield Country Kennel

556 Depot St., North Harwich • 432-2510

The owners reside at this kennel, which offers separate heated accommodations for dogs and cats and outdoor runs. Grooming and pickup and delivery are also available.

Nauset Kennels

2685 Nauset Rd., North Eastham • 255-0081

In business since 1972, this reputable facility offers indoor and outdoor runs, three outdoor play yards and separate quarters for dogs and cats, with insulated floors and even air-conditioning. Nauset Kennels also does grooming and offers pickup and delivery. The owners live on premises.

Photo: Nauset Kennels

You're not leaving without us, are you?

and the Sea Breeze and Sea Shore buildings without ocean views. All the rooms at this motel-with-a-bed-and-breakfast-feel have air conditioning, and a good many of them come with a patio or balcony.

Tucked away along the east end of Craigville Beach, it is just a five- to 10-minute drive to the fine restaurants of Hyannis, the Cape Cod Melody Tent, the ferries to the islands and Hyannis' Main Street shops. The inn serves a continental breakfast in season and has a lobby bar, Vital Spirits, and a patio with umbrella tables. Tradewinds has its own private beach on Nantucket Sound just a short stroll away, and complimentary chairs are provided. Open from April to the end of October, the inn's off-season rates are nearly half of those during the summer.

The Anchor-In

$$ • 1 South St., Hyannis • 775-0357

You can't get much closer to Hyannis Harbor than this! The Anchor-In offers a great location with outstanding views, super rooms, immaculate grounds and a delightful staff who go out of their way to make you feel welcome. Just 60 feet from the water's edge in downtown Hyannis, the Anchor-In is within walking distance of excellent restaurants, island ferries and excursion boats and shopping. Hyannis Marina, many boats and a public boat launch are within sight.

Most of the 43 rooms, whether economy, deluxe or executive, have a private deck and with it, a harbor view. All rooms are flawlessly clean, comfortable and attractively furnished; two rooms are fully handicapped-accessible. A large private pool and lawn, complete with a huge grounded anchor to support the inn's name, overlook the harbor.

Owners Rex and Pat Arnett have operated the inn for the past 15 years (Pat's parents built the motel back in the 1950s). Open year round, the Anchor-In caters to international guests from around the world (primarily the UK, Germany, France and Canada) who are often surprised and delighted to see their country's flag flying from the Anchor-In poolside flagpole upon their arrival, just one more added touch of hospitality.

Cascade Motor Lodge

$ • 201 Main St., Hyannis • 775-9717

Even in Hyannis, you won't find many other hotels so close to the ferries (one block away), train and bus stations (across the street), restaurants and shops (nearby). Perfect for shoestring budgets, the Cascade saves you the expense of parking at the ferry terminal because you can leave your car in the hotel lot. The hotel also has bike rentals so you can pedal around the islands when you cross over to the Vineyard and Nantucket. This year-round hotel has 28 rooms with private baths and VCRs, an outdoor pool and smoking and nonsmoking rooms.

Days Inn

$$-$$$ • 867 Route 132, Hyannis • 771-6100, (800) 368-4667

Open from mid-February to December 1, this 99-room Days Inn offers a central location convenient to shopping, restaurants and the airport. Just down the road in one direction is the Hyannis Golf Course, in the other direction is downtown Hyannis with its Kennedy Museum and Memorial. On site are two pools (indoor and outdoor), a whirlpool and an exercise room featuring treadmill and nautilus.

Of the rooms here, five are handicapped-accessible. An on-site coffee shop serves complimentary coffee from 7 to 10 AM. A complimentary continental breakfast is also served. The inn is adjacent to the Cape Cod Mall and is a favorite accommodation for families as well as business travelers.

Hyannis Harborview

$$-$$$ • 213 Ocean St., Hyannis • 775-4420, (800) 676-0000

A member of the Cape Cod Remington Hotels, which also include the Ramada Inns in Hyannis and Falmouth as well as the Flagship Inn and Gull Wing Suites in Yarmouth, the Hyannis Harborview offers views of Hyannis Harbor, which lies right across the street. From the docks at the harbor you can catch a boat to the islands. Hyannis Harborview has 136 rooms, outdoor and heated indoor pools, a Jacuzzi and a location convenient to all of downtown Hyannis with its many shops and restaurants. Three nearby restaurants are within a minute or two walk. Open from early May to late October, the hotel allows children 18 years and younger to stay free when accompanied by an adult.

HoJo Inn

$$-$$$ • 447 Main St., Hyannis • 775-3000, (800) I-GO-HOJO

This year-round 39-room inn is about halfway down Main Street, Hyannis where restaurants, entertainment and shopping opportunities are just footsteps away. The harbor, and subsequently the ferry to the islands of Nantucket and Martha's Vineyard, is perhaps no more than a leisurely half-mile stroll (and there's plenty to do and see along the way). In the other direction is the Cape Cod Melody Tent, perhaps a 15-minute walk.

Ideal for families and couples, the inn has an indoor heated swimming pool and a whirlpool to relieve all the tension built up after a relaxing day on the golf course or at any of a number of nearby beaches. The rooms have one or two double beds. Meals are available until early evening at the on-site Duck Inn Pub cocktail bar. Business guests will make use of meeting facilities while families will enjoy the savings as children younger than 18 stay free in an adult's room.

Hyannis Inn Motel

$$ • 473 Main St., Hyannis • 775-0255, (800) 922-8993

Convenient to most everything in downtown Hyannis, the Hyannis Inn Motel offers its guests reasonable rates and comfortable accommodations for those who are looking for an inexpensive Cape Cod vacation. Everything you will need is within walking distance — shops, attractions, island ferries, excursion tours and whale watching — while beaches are but a few miles away.

Family-run for more than 40 years, this motel is clean and well-maintained and offers a heated indoor pool, saunas, a sun deck, Bluebird's Restaurant serving breakfast and the Elbow Room Cocktail Lounge serving good cheer. The inn has 76 standard, deluxe and whirlpool rooms; of these 29 are nonsmoking rooms and one is handicapped-accessible. Deluxe rooms include a choice of king- or queen-size beds, refrigerator and sleeper sofa while the whirlpool room features an in-room whirlpool (but you could have guessed that!). Children younger than 14 stay free. The motel is open from the beginning of February to mid-November.

Hyannis Travel Inn

$-$$ • 18 North St., Hyannis • 775-8200, (800) 352-7190

With 83 rooms, indoor and outdoor pools, saunas and an oversized whirlpool (large enough for all your friends and then some), this well-maintained 31-year-old Hyannis facility is a good value for couples and families who want to be close to the many Hyannis attractions. Minigolf, the Cape Cod and Hyannis Railroad, shops, restaurants, beaches and the John F. Kennedy Museum are all within a five-minute walk. Slightly longer walks will get you to the island ferries, the Hyannis waterfront district and the Cape Cod Melody Tent with performances nearly every summer evening featuring some of the country's most distinguished acts (the great Tony Bennett has performed here!).

Amenities include a continental breakfast with coffee, muffins, bagels and juice plus discount coupons for area restaurants. The motel is closed for 10 weeks between Thanksgiving and February. Off-season rates are incredibly reasonable.

International Inn

$$$ • 662 Main Street, Hyannis • 775-5600

How does a cuddle and bubble sound to you? We suppose that would depend upon who's asking the question. Perhaps the most romantically marketed accommodation in the Hyannis area, the International Inn is as centrally located as it is romantic, resting toward the west end of Main Street just a short stroll to the Cape Cod Melody Tent and all the shops and sites along the popular main drag of Hyannis.

A favorite spot for couples celebrating wedding anniversaries, the Inn's Cuddle and Bubble Plaza Suite is a sought-after getaway around Valentine's Day. This three-room suite includes a romantic king-size canopy bed, a wet bar and an even wetter 5-by-7 foot sunken Jacuzzi. Meanwhile, the 6-by-6 foot Jacuzzi in the Princess Suite features more bubbles than Lawrence Welk ever dreamt of (although Lawrence Welk will be about the furthest thing from your mind as you frolic amidst the suds).

Besides bubble-laden Jacuzzis, the International Inn boasts the Gazebo Garden Room Restaurant, indoor and outdoor swimming pools and saunas for men and women.

Ramada Inn Regency

$$-$$$$ • 1127 Rt. 132, Hyannis • 775-1153, (800) 676-0000

A member of the Cape Cod Remington Hotels (which include five hotels in Hyannis, Falmouth and Yarmouth) this 196-room Ramada features a lovely glass-walled indoor pool area visible from the front lobby. Right off the pool is an inviting lawn with lounge chairs and an attractive dining room that hosts dinner theater and live entertainment. Centrally located along Route 132, shoppers can hit the nearby Cape Cod Mall and the numerous other plazas and shops along this route. Those not in the shopping mood will enjoy the Ramada's convenient location to just about everything else in Hyannis.

The Ramada, which is open year round, offers 16 efficiency units and 20 townhouse loft suites. Rooms have double or king-size beds. Saunas and a steam room are available for guests, and there's a game room for the kiddies. There are a restaurant and lounge on the premises and a large number of restaurants within a mile radius. The Ramada Inn's prices are based on occupancy, therefore the price of a room can vary by greater than $100 depending on demand.

Tara's Cape Codder Hotel

$$$ • Rt. 132 and Bearse's Way, Hyannis • 771-3000, (800) 843-8272

With 261 rooms, all with private baths, this is one of the Cape's largest (if not *the* largest) hotels and a luxurious one at that. On the outskirts of Hyannis along the well-traveled Route 132, it is in perhaps the very heart of Cape Cod with convenient access to the Mid-Cape Highway (Route 6), Old King's Highway (Route 6A) and downtown Hyannis. It's the perfect jumping-off point to begin your Cape Cod holiday, or if here on business, the perfect home base from which to begin your work day.

This place has everything. During the day enjoy such recreational activities as volleyball, tennis and swimming in either the outdoor or indoor pool. During the summer months, recreation directors plan special fun for children, including arts and crafts projects and swimming games. Meanwhile, for the adults the Cape Codder offers mixers and outdoor barbecues and has the fine-dining Sandcastles Restaurant and an English tavern, the Toby Jug Tavern, with live entertainment. Heck, the Codder even has a shuttle service to take you around Hyannis. The only thing it doesn't have is its own airport (although the Barnstable Airport is just a five-minute ride away . . . three minutes if you hit all the lights right).

Choose from attractive double, king and loft suites with two full bathrooms and queen- and king-size beds. Of the 261 rooms, four are fully handicapped accessible. There are a number of function rooms. The Cape Codder is the sister hotel of the Tara Hyannis Hotel & Resort.

FYI

Unless otherwise noted, the area code for all phone numbers in this guide is 508.

INSIDERS' TIPS

Perhaps the most famous cottage on Cape Cod was the Outermost House. It was owned by the writer Henry Beston who penned the book *The Outermost House* about a year he spent at the house in 1927. The house was destroyed by the great Blizzard of '78.

Tara Hyannis Hotel & Resort

$$$ • West End Rotary, Hyannis
• 775-7775, (800) 843-8272

It is safe to suggest that the Tara Hyannis Hotel & Resort is the premier hotel accommodation in Hyannis. Directly across the street from the Cape Cod Melody Tent, it is a convenient accommodation for the Tent's star performers. This top-notch resort is considered one of Massachusetts' premier golf resorts featuring an 18-hole par 3 executive golf course — the Tara Woods (a spectacular 2600 yard course). Tara Woods often hosts golf tournaments. If you're a golfer, look into their golf packages featuring unlimited use of the course.

A full-service hotel/conference center, Tara Hyannis offers everything from concierge and shuttle service to a beautiful 60-foot indoor pool and Seafood Cabana serving lunch and refreshments. Most of the Tara's 224 rooms have views of the golf course or an attractive courtyard and offer double, king or suite units. On premises you'll enjoy the Silver Shell Restaurant as well as the Yacht Club lounge featuring entertainment on the weekends.

On site is a health club, which has free weights, Nautilus equipment, step and pool aerobics classes, a sauna and massage. Off season midweek rates are about half the in-season amount. Ask about their holiday and weekend packages.

Americana Holiday Motel

$ • 99 Main St. (Rt. 28), West Yarmouth
• 775-5511, (800) 445-4497

Conveniently located along Route 28 in West Yarmouth, almost before you enter Hyannis, is the Americana Holiday Motel. This completely renovated motel has 153 rooms, all newly decorated, each with a full-size private bath and air conditioning. A dozen or more beaches are close-by, yet the Americana boasts three swimming pools (yes, three!) — one indoor and two outdoor. The motel also has a sauna, steam room and whirlpool bath to help you unwind. There's an on-site putting green and shuffleboard court for the adults and a game room and playground to keep the kiddies entertained. This family owned and operated establishment also has a coffee shop on site serving free coffee all day and a continental breakfast each morning (which, during the off-season, is free with your stay). The Americana's attractive rates become incredible during the off-season (from the beginning of April to mid-June and from early September to mid-November) when these rates dip down into the high $20s and low $30s! Dinner discounts are offered at select local restaurants and the first two children in your party younger than 12 stay free. The Americana is open from the beginning of April to mid-November.

Cape Point

$$ • 476 Main St. (Rt. 28), West Yarmouth • 778-1500, (800) 323-9505

Centrally located along West Yarmouth's popular Route 28, the Cape Point is an attractive accommodation with pretty flower gardens and reasonably priced rooms for families and budget-conscious travelers. A waterfall in the lobby greets you upon your arrival. The facility includes a lovely outdoor pool, a regal indoor pool with a balcony overhead, a children's pool, Jacuzzi, exercise room and video game rooms to keep the kiddies entertained.

This family-oriented facility offers discounts if you're traveling with children. Standard rooms in the $$ category can be upgraded to deluxe rooms accommodating two adults and three children in the lower $$$ category, and two bedroom suites in the mid $$$ category. Handicapped-accessible accommodations are available. Open year round, the inn also has a coffee shop and a lounge, the Sports Loft, on site.

The Cove at Yarmouth

$$$ • 183 Rt. 28, West Yarmouth • 771-3666, (800) 228-2968

This spectacular Yarmouth resort motel offers 229 beautiful and spacious suites and townhouses with plenty of extras such as refrigerator, wet bar, separate living room, two color TVs, VCR and coffee maker. A sprawling, well-regarded timeshare facility overlooking a conservation area and cove that empties into Nantucket Sound, The Cove is known for its cleanliness and for its many amenities: indoor and outdoor Olympic-size pools, a whirlpool, sauna, indoor and outdoor tennis courts, racquetball and squash courts and a complete fitness center. As you can imagine, there isn't time to get bored!

Treatment here is top-notch and includes concierge. Restaurants and shops are nearby, and Hyannis beaches are just a mile away while Yarmouth beaches are just a couple of miles in the opposite direction. Many restaurants and shops are nearby, but there's no need to go off site as the resort has its own restaurant, Ristorante Pescara, and lounge, The Atrium, which are available to guests and the public (see our Restaurants chapter). *Cape Cod Life* magazine has voted The Cove the best Mid-Cape resort for the past four years (1992-1996). No wonder!

Flagship Motor Inn

$-$$ • 343 Main St. (Rt. 28), West Yarmouth • 775-5155, (800) 676-0000

The Flagship Motor Inn is one of five Cape Cod Remington Hotels, the others being the Hyannis and Falmouth Ramada Inns, the Hyannis Harborview across from the docks at Hyannis Harbor and Gull Wing Suites in South Yarmouth. Flagship has 138 rooms (some handicapped accessible), a heated indoor pool, sauna, Jacuzzi, an outdoor pool and a game room and playground for the kiddies. Its location makes it convenient to the beaches of Yarmouth as well as the many shops, restaurants and attractions of neighboring Hyannis. Flagship Motor Inn is open from early May to late October; children 18 years and younger stay free when accompanied by an adult.

Green Harbor

$$$$ • 182 Baxter Ave., West Yarmouth • 771-1126, (800) 547-4733

Since it is surrounded by saltwater on three sides there's really no sense in mentioning the wonderful water views (oops! we just did). Almost as beautiful as the water views are the lovely grounds of grass and sand and gardens bursting with flowers, some 8 acres worth of land. As for the accommodations, the 50 units here range widely in style from a single room with a kitchenette to a four-bedroom suite with a fireplace and full kitchen. Some units are in separate cottages, others are in the main motel building. Some rooms have decks and patios while villas have decks overlooking the ocean.

An oversize outdoor pool and deck offer a change of scenery for those who have been spending time down on the private beach. An on site minigolf course keeps the kiddies in the swing of things, while bikes, canoes and rowboats are all available. The angler in you will enjoy the jetties off the beaches. Or just pull up a chair and relax watching the tide rise and fall. Green Harbor is open May to mid-October.

The Holly Tree

$$ • 412 Main St., (Rt. 28) West Yarmouth • 771-6677, (800) 452-5202 (in Mass.), (800) 356-4564

This attractive resort hotel offers many amenities at surprisingly reasonable rates. What you get for the cost is no less than a large outdoor pool, an attractive indoor pool area dressed in nautical flags flying overhead, a wading pool for the kiddies, an exercise room, racquetball and squash courts, a game room and even an area where you can have a cookout.

Of the 84 units, 54 are studios with a double bed and sleeper sofa and 30 are one-bedroom suites with a king-size bed and a sleeper sofa. The Holly Tree is convenient to the beaches of Yarmouth, the shops of Main Street in Hyannis, area golf courses and lots of activities to keep the kids amused. The Holly Tree is open year round.

The Mariner

$-$$ • 573 Main St. (Rt. 28), West Yarmouth • 771-7887, (800) 445-4050

This is a Cape golf resort of the most unique kind. You see, the golf portion of the package includes a challenging nine-hole minigolf course. A putter is all you need, and that's provided. So are the golf balls. And the cost for a round is minimal, much less than the other miniature golf courses in the area.

As for the motel itself, it has 100 clean, air-conditioned rooms with in-room refrigerators and safes for all the valuable sand dollars you'll find combing the beaches of Nantucket Sound. At the Mariner you'll also find a 50-foot heated indoor pool, a 55-foot heated outdoor swimming pool, whirlpool, saunas and a barbecue area. Yarmouth's Sea Gull Beach is only a five-minute drive away, and Hyannis (and the island ferries) is no more than 10 minutes down Route 28. There are numerous dining opportunities within a couple of miles radius, from casual to fine dining. Open from early February to early December, off-season rates at the Mariner are incredibly low!

Tidewater

$$ • 135 Main St. (Rt. 28), W. Yarmouth • 775-6322, (800) 338-6322

A well-respected 101-room motel, the Tidewater is situated on 4 acres bordering marshland and a tidal creek. It is ideal for families and couples, providing a location central to the many attractions of Yarmouth and nearby Hyannis. Amenities include a large indoor pool as well as an outdoor pool, spa, sauna, coffee shop and a game room that has table tennis, darts and board games. Beaches are a short drive away, as is just about everything else, from movies, minigolf, and restaurants to outlets and shops.

Outdoor extras include picnic tables, a volleyball net, sandbox, swings and play equipment for kiddies. The rooms, which have double and king-size beds, are clean, nicely furnished, air conditioned and have refrigerators. Half the property is nonsmoking. Handicapped-accessible rooms as well as bed and breakfast packages are available. There is no charge for children younger than 12 staying with an adult. Tidewater is closed December and January.

All Seasons Motor Inn

$$ • 1199 Main St. (Rt. 28), South Yarmouth • 394-7600, (800) 527-0359

The readers of *Cape Cod Life* magazine have voted the All Seasons Motor Inn best Mid-Cape Motel for four years running and for good reason. On site can be found a large outdoor pool, a beautiful indoor pool, whirlpool, saunas, a greenhouse solarium, an exercise room and a restaurant. There is even a game room for the kids and private balconies and patios for adults to relax after a full day of Cape Cod vacationing.

This high-quality facility has earned its reputation for excellent service. The All Seasons Motor Inn has a spacious 3-acre setting with

Photo: Ron Schloerb, Cape Cod Times

A sanderling preens in the shallows of South Monomy.

gorgeous gardens and well-manicured lawns. One hundred and fourteen clean, air-conditioned rooms offer a choice of either one king-size or two queen-size beds. Each room includes a refrigerator and a VCR. Six handicapped-accessible rooms are available. A year-round facility, the inn offers incredibly low off-season rates.

The Ambassador Motor Inn

$-$$ • Rt. 28, South Yarmouth • 394-4000, (800) 341-5700

Just sneaking into the $ range is the Ambassador Motor Inn close to Bass River in South Yarmouth. This inn is part of the Vacation Inn Properties (V.I.P.) group which runs four Falmouth motels including The Admiralty Inn and the Surfside Holiday. The Ambassador offers 89 rooms including standard and poolside rooms with two double beds and king rooms with one king-size bed.

Large indoor and outdoor pools, a sauna and whirlpool are the amenities you'll find at the Ambassador. There is even an on premises restaurant and lounge, Orchids, with live entertainment on Friday and Saturday nights. All rooms here have air conditioning and color cable TV. Three public golf courses are just a five-minute drive away — Bass River, Bayberry and the par 3 Blue Rock. A slightly longer drive (perhaps 10 minutes) will get you to two Dennis courses — Dennis Pines and Dennis Highlands. Public beaches are close by. From November to the end of April the inn is open on weekends only; during the rest of the year it is open full-time.

Best Western Blue Rock Motor Inn and Golf Course

$$-$$$ • Off Highbank Rd., South Yarmouth • 398-6962, (800) 237-8887

This is like dying and going to golfers' heaven. We've golfed here dozens of times and still we've yet to master this devilishly tricky par 3 course with a number of water holes. The Blue Rock Golf Resort has 18 holes, a pro shop, golf school, driving range and putting green as well as a 40-room motel with either double or deluxe king accommodations.

Rooms have temperature control and panoramic views of the golf course. After you've hit the course you can hit the heated outdoor pool, Jacuzzi, Grille Room restaurant or on-site lounge to recount the birdies and pars. While you're waiting for your tee time, enjoy some tennis or a good book on your private patio or deck. Off site you have access to a nearby private beach and biking paths. The inn is open from April to the end of October. There are golf packages (and other packages) available, so you'll want to ask for all the details.

Blue Water

$$$-$$$$ • S. Shore Dr., South Yarmouth • 398-2288, (800) 367-9393

At this oceanfront hotel you can choose from among two swimming pools, a putting green, a tennis court and, of course, the comfortably warm waters of Nantucket Sound. This facility has a dining room lounge that serves breakfast and lunch and offers entertainment. Rugosa roses and sand dunes enhance the attractive well-kept grounds.

The 83 units include clean, attractive rooms with two double beds, some efficiencies, three cottages and a house with an in-room whirlpool. Some units are handicapped-accessible. During the summer Blue Water offers children's activities. Ask about the Blue Water's terrific package deals throughout the year.

The Dunes Motor Inn

$-$$ • 170 Seaview Ave., South Yarmouth • 398-3062, (800) 237-5070

Newly renovated, freshly decorated and resting just 300 yards from the beach, The Dunes is a hidden Cape Cod secret. The facility has 34 guests rooms, all decorated in Cape Cod scenes, and two cottages. The rooms all have two double, king- or queen-size beds, private baths, air conditioning, cable television and in-room phones. Efficiency units have two double beds along with a full kitchen set-up and there's even a two-bedroom family suite.

An on-site coffee shop serves a continental breakfast for a minimal charge. There's a heated outdoor pool available and if that's not enough, the refreshing waters of Nantucket Sound are just a short walk away (location, location, location). The Dunes enjoys a high volume of repeat clientele during the summer and off-season. Speaking of the off-season, they offer a three-night package including breakfast for only $99 . . . that's a tough one to beat! The Dunes Motor Inn is open from May to Columbus Day.

Gull Wing Suites

$$ • 822 Main St. (Rt. 28), South Yarmouth • 394-9300, (800) 676-0000

Offering a heated indoor pool, whirlpool, saunas and an outdoor pool is the Gull Wing Suites, one of five Cape Cod Remington Hotels. Gull Wing has 136 rooms, one of which has been modified to accommodate physically handicapped and sight-challenged individuals. There is a seasonal coffee shop on-site and a game room for the kiddies. For the adults, the mini-suites are equipped with a refrigerator and wet bar. A dinner package is available that, with a two-night stay, allows you a $30 dinner discount at one of three local restaurants (Christine's, Yarmouth House, Roadhouse Cafe). Open year round, Gull Wing Suites welcomes children age 18 and younger free when they accompany an adult.

Ocean Mist

$$$-$$$$ • 97 S. Shore Dr., South Yarmouth • 398-2633, (800) 248-MIST

The warm waves of Nantucket Sound lap at the shore outside your door as you awake in the morning to another fun-filled day at the Ocean Mist on ol' Cape Cod. The beautiful view is perfectly complemented by the quality of this clean, attractive motel where summer memories are made. Its 63 rooms are either deluxe or loft suites. Deluxe rooms have either wet bars or efficiencies while loft suites have wet bars, cathedral ceilings, private balconies overlooking the water and some units have sky lights.

Ocean Mist has a heated indoor pool and a coffee shop. Restaurants are close by, and Hyannis shopping and dining, golf courses and historic sights are within a few miles.

Red Jacket Beach Motor Inn

$$$-$$$$ • S. Shore Dr., South Yarmouth • 398-6941, (800) 672-0500

Red Jacket takes its place among a select group of the Cape's premier resorts. The Red Jacket has everything, including a 1,000-foot sandy waterfront beach as well as frontage on

Parker's River salt marsh. Water views are everywhere: from the dining room, outside swimming pool, putting green, gazebo and, of course, the rooms, some of which are practically on the beach.

A great place for families, the resort offers basketball, shuffleboard, tennis, minigolf, indoor pool and whirlpool, badminton and a playground. You can work out in the exercise room or relax in the lounge while the children enjoy daily supervised activities. There's even a dock where you can try your hand at sailing or parasailing. We told you this place has everything.

Surfcomber

$$$ • 107 S. Shore Dr., South Yarmouth • 398-9228

There's nothing better than taking your vacation right on Nantucket Sound. The Surfcomber provides just that, peace and quiet right by the water's edge. Sunbathing and swimming will be your occupation for the week, yet if you ever tire of saltwater swimming (which we doubt you will), there is a heated outdoor swimming pool within earshot of the ocean waves.

Four rooms look right out over the water. Many rooms offer private balconies overlooking the well-maintained grounds and pool, and approximately half of the rooms are efficiencies with a sink, fridge and four-burner stove. The staff is friendly and often know the guests by name since so many visitors return year after year. Surfcomber is open from May to Columbus Day.

Briarcliffe Motel

$$ • 203 Rt. 6A, Dennis • 385-3464, (800)424-3529

This is a motel that has the feel of an inn. Resting along the beautiful and historic Route 6A, near the Dennis and Yarmouth town line, is the 26-room Briarcliffe Motel. Of these 26 rooms, 12 are single rooms that feature such added touches as four-poster beds, sleigh beds and cherry furniture. All the rooms are different, and two are efficiency units. A two-room efficiency with two double beds and a pullout double couch sleeps a total of six, and a three-room efficiency with a private deck, living room and two separate bedrooms also sleeps six. The efficiencies run into the $$$ range. A continental breakfast is served during the summer months. To cool you off there is an outdoor pool, although many fine Dennis beaches are just a five-minute ride away. Also on-site is a barbecue area, a picnic area, horseshoes and a play area for the kids. Briarcliffe is open from early May to late October.

Colony Beach Motel

$$-$$$, no credit cards • 413 Old Wharf Rd., Dennisport • 398-2217

With its charming Colonial architecture and Cape Cod allure, this motel located right on the Sound is a perfect place to start the summer.

You can choose from 47 rooms including oceanfront and oceanview efficiency units with a fully-equipped kitchen and dining area, motel units or non-efficiency suites with a living room. Among the amenities are a private beach and a heated outdoor swimming pool. Children 3 years of age and older are welcome.

The Corsair and Cross Rip

$$$ • 41 Chase Ave., Dennisport • 398-2279

These two Dennisport motels, resting side by side on Nantucket Sound, form a family-owned and operated oceanfront resort on 3 acres of prime real estate. Together, they offer an abundance of amenities including two outdoor pools (one at each facility) and two large sun decks overlooking the ocean. Recreation buildings across the street feature an indoor pool, a game room, a toddler area chock-full of toys, a barbecue area and an outdoor play area for the kids.

There are many types of rooms to choose from. All rooms at the Cross Rip, except for the economy units, have kitchenettes. You may want to go for a two-room oceanfront suite. Meanwhile, The Corsair offers mini-suites with two double beds and a galley kitchen and oceanview suites featuring two rooms, a galley kitchen and two baths (in the Captain's Suite). Open from late March to December 1, the complex also offers a pair of four-bedroom houses for rent across the street with access to all the amenities.

The Edgewater Beach Resort

$$$ • 95 Chase Ave., Dennisport • 398-6922

You can't help but hum Patti Page's ode to Cape Cod as you stroll along the sandy path through swaying beach grass to the warm waters of Nantucket Sound. Memories of summer vacations past come rushing to mind, bringing a smile to your face and telling you that more memories are about to be made.

Situated on more than 5 acres of waterfront at the farthest reaches of Dennisport, The Edgewater offers 89 units, all with balconies and views of either the ocean in all its glory or the attractive central courtyard and putting green. Sixteen of the units have kitchenettes, but for those staying in the other 73 units there are many fine restaurants within a 10 to 15-minute drive. The Edgewater has, arguably, the finest pool in the area, a magnificent oversized indoor-outdoor pool, complete with a whirlpool and sauna. A note on the pool: half of it is glass contained with a sliding glass door that cuts the inside portion off from the outside portion in the event of inclement weather. Also on site are a fitness center and two shuffleboard courts. Ask about their Indian summer packages. The Edgewater Beach Resort is open from early March to mid-November.

The Garlands

$$-$$$, no credit cards • 117 Old Wharf Rd., Dennisport • 398-6987

At The Garlands along the popular Old Wharf Road in Dennisport, the waves of Nantucket Sound curl and crash right below you. In fact, the front-facing units are a few feet away from the water, and as you stand upon the private wooden deck of your VIP unit it is not too difficult to imagine yourself upon a ship at sea.

The Garlands offers just 16 rooms, but it's not quantity that matters here. The dozen regular units come complete with color cable TV, fully equipped kitchens and daily maid service — all at very reasonable rates considering the proximity to the ocean. There are also four VIP suites, all on the ocean. Units A and B have two bedrooms and full kitchens; Units C and D have one bedroom. The living rooms of all four offer unsurpassed views of Nantucket Sound. After Labor Day these waterfront units drop into the low- to mid-$$ range! Amazing! Children 6 years of age and older are welcome. The Garlands is open from mid-April to mid-October.

Pelham House Resort Motel

$$$ • 14 Sea St., Dennisport • 398-6076, (800) 497-3542

For more than 30 years the Pelham House has been a fixture at the end of Sea Street. A century or more ago the beach at Sea Street was lined with wharves supporting the thriving Dennisport fishing industry. Today, the only fishermen we see are those casting off the jetties, and the only things lining the beach are towels.

Three tiers of balconies encircle the oversized outdoor pool and provide guests with sensational views of Nantucket Sound. There are 35 guest rooms here, each offering comfort as well as a slightly different view of the ocean. A private tennis court helps you work up an appetite for the many local restaurants. The Pelham House is open from Memorial Day to the end of October.

The Soundings

$$$ • 79 Chase Ave., Dennisport • 394-6561

A huge complex right on the water, the front section of its main building is distinguished by Colonial architecture accented with four Greek Revival Doric columns. The Soundings has two swimming pools to compliment its 360 feet of waterfront, one a heated indoor pool and the other one actually situated on the beach with a poolside snack bar to boot (boy, life is tough!). Other amenities include sauna, Jacuzzi, a putting green to loosen up for Dennis' two 18-hole golf courses and an on-site coffee shop serving breakfast to start the day off right.

This oceanside facility has 100 rooms, each with individually controlled air conditioning. Room options range from pavilion rooms at the inner courtyard, deluxe oceanview and deluxe on the ocean rooms, efficiency units to a penthouse with a fully equipped kitchen. The Soundings' season runs from May 1 to mid-October and families are, of course, most welcome. During May, June, September and October, customized golf packages are offered.

Lower Cape

Moby Dick Motel

$$ • 767 Main St., Harwichport • 432-1434, (800) 432-1434

A great place for a family getaway, the Moby Dick offers a whale of a good time without breaking the budget. Its 24 units are surrounded by 3 acres of pine groves and gardens. The motel features a spacious sun deck, picnic area with a charcoal grill, badminton and shuffleboard courts — the list of amenities goes on and on. The beaches are two minutes away, and Saquatucket Harbor, with its boats, ducks and geese, is a mere 200-yard jaunt. The efficiencies and one- and two-bedroom units offer a choice of country decor that owner Judy Parker describes as "Cape Coddy." Nonsmoking units are available. The Moby Dick is open from early April to mid-October.

Handkerchief Shoals Motel

$ • 888 Main St., South Harwich • 432-2200

This motel with the curious name (taken from shoals found on nearby Monomoy Island) offers 26 up-to-date accommodations, clean and furnished with such amenities as cable TV, a refrigerator, microwave oven and courtesy phone. Cribs are free for children 2 and younger. Lawn games and a sparkling outdoor pool will keep the young and young-at-heart busy for hours. This isn't the Ritz, but you'll get more than your money's worth from this single-story property set back from the noisy highway on well-maintained grounds. It's close to shopping, sporting activities and the beach. Handkerchief Shoals is open from late May through October.

Chatham Wayside Inn

$$$-$$$$ • 512 Main St., Chatham • 945-5550, (800) 391-5734

Completely renovated and expanded three

years ago, the Wayside is smack-dab in the heart of Chatham's picturesque historic district. Even better, it's directly next to Kate Gould Park, where concerts are held every Friday evening during July and August. Book a room in the park-side rear building, where you'll have a patio view of the concert — but book early, it's a popular idea. The 56 guest rooms all have private baths, and some have extras such as balconies or patios, fireplaces and spa-jet tubs. Rooms are beautifully decorated, many with four-poster or canopy beds. Four of the rooms are handicapped-accessible, and children are welcome — cribs are available at no extra charge. You'll have use of an on-site outdoor heated pool and little conveniences such as ice machines. The on-site restaurant serves three meals a day, plus brunch on Sunday (see our Restaurants chapter for details). You can have food and drinks in the pub, and in the winter be warmed by a fireplace. The Chatham Wayside Inn is open year round, except January.

Pleasant Bay Village Resort Motel

$$$$ • 1191 Orleans Rd., Chatham • 945-1133, (800) 547-1011

Innkeeper Howard Gamsey spent more than $1 million renovating this 58-room wonder over the last decade — and what a job he's done! You'll discover a delightful surprise at every twist and turn of the 6 acres, most notably in the Japanese gardens. Marking the center of the grounds is a visual delight: Cascading waterfalls feed into a ornamental pond of koi fish. But since you can't sleep amidst such lush greenery, you'll have to opt for one of the cleanest (and most spacious) rooms in Chatham. Pleasant Bay Village Resorts has 58 rooms, one of which is handicapped-accessible. Children are welcome, and the facility, open from mid-April through October, is nonsmoking.

The Seafarer of Chatham

$$$ • Rt. 28 and Ridgevale Rd., Chatham • 432-1739

"We offer the privacy and comfort of a modern motel with the charm of a country inn," says owner John Houhoulis. How true! The Seafarer, situated along Chatham's historic district, has one of the Cape's loveliest (and quietest) settings, where welcoming lounge chairs and old-fashioned Adirondack chairs nestle among lavish flower gardens.

Each of the 20 ground-level rooms have been hand-stenciled in the authentic Colonial manner with decorative borders. Tiled baths and coffee and tea service are offered. Children are welcome at the Seafarer, which is open April through November.

The Cove

$$$ • 13 Rt. 28, Orleans • 255-1203, (800) 343-2233

The sparkling waters of Town Cove lap at the shore of this attractive year-round complex, which features beautifully landscaped gardens and patios, a heated outdoor pool and, of course, terrific water views. Many of the 47 rooms have views of Town Cove, and many have private decks. All are equipped with heat and air conditioning, queen- or king-size beds, private baths, phones, TVs, refrigerators and coffee makers. Nonsmoking rooms are available, and children are welcome. Book a waterfront room or, for an extra special stay, a room at the Inn at the Cove. It has 10 rooms and suites (eight with fireplaces, some with full kitchens), all warm and cozy with Shaker-style furnishings. Don't forget to visit the waterfront gazebo, where you can commune with the terns and gulls and watch sailboats tack by. And while you're here, don't miss taking a cruise around Town Cove.

Nauset Knoll Motor Lodge

$$$ • 237 Beach Rd., East Orleans • 255-2364

This delightful complex, which is owned by the U.S. government and operated under the supervision of the National Park Service, is the only motel on the Atlantic Ocean within the Cape Cod National Seashore. What more could you want? Each of the 12 rooms features a 6-foot picture window offering a breathtaking view of the surf. No need for air conditioning here — the ocean breezes will refresh and renew you. Four acres of manicured grounds assure privacy. Children are welcome at Nauset Knoll, which is open from mid-April to mid-October.

Ridgewood Motel and Cottages

$$$ • 10 Quanset Rd., South Orleans • 255-0473

Snugly tucked away between acres of pine woods, Ridgewood offers some of the finest cottages in the area — especially for those traveling with kids. You can choose from among three sizes of cottages. The efficiency holds three people; the one-bedroom, five; and the two-bedroom, six. Each cottage is spotless and has a fully equipped kitchen, free cribs and foldaway beds and fans to cool the warm summer air. Children will never tire of the myriad of lawn games. The Ridgewood even has a play area and large outdoor swimming pool!

Captain's Quarters Motel and Conference Center

$$ • Rt. 6, North Eastham • 255-5686, (800) 327-7769

With 70 rooms, tennis courts, an outdoor heated pool and access to the bike path, this family-run facility has a lot to offer. Rooms all have wall-to-wall carpeting, air conditioning and heat, refrigerators, phones, color cable TVs and queen-size or double beds. Guests get a complimentary breakfast in the cozy lounge area, which features a delightful hand-painted mural of nearby Nauset Light Beach, and can also help themselves to fresh popcorn later in the day. A great place for families to make their home base as they explore the Outer Cape, Captain's Quarters lets children

INSIDERS' TIPS

Thousands of Cape Cod residents and seasonal college students are employed each year to work in the various hotels and motels around the Cape. Many work as chambermaids and housekeepers, cleaning up after the guests leave. In case you're wondering, it's proper to leave a tip for each night of your stay.

younger than 12 stay free. It's also good for businesspeople, as it has conference facilities and handles groups well. Captain's Quarters is open from April to November.

Eagle Wing Motel

$$ • 960 Rt. 6, Eastham • 240-5656

When Mary and Gerry Orris bought this property in 1995, they saw a diamond in the rough and set to work transforming it into a very desirable property. All 19 rooms have been completely redone, and all have private baths, air conditioning and heat, cable TV and phones. The Orrises also added a back deck that stretches the length of the building so that guests can enjoy the quiet backyard, which borders a wetland sweet with birdsong in spring and summer. Eleven of the rooms have queen or king beds, the rest have two doubles. Best for couples or small families, the Eagle Wing offers suites with connecting rooms, a pool and morning coffee in the lobby, along with special discounts at local restaurants and businesses. The motel, which is all nonsmoking, is open May 1 through the end of October.

Four Points Hotel

$$$ • Rt. 6, Eastham • 255-5000

The Four Points Hotel, part of the Sheraton chain, gets lots of points from us. Its 107 guest rooms and suites are beautifully appointed yet downright relaxing. The indoor atrium and pool are a soothing, steamy balm at the end of a long day (there are also men's and women's saunas and an outdoor pool). The fitness room is stocked with so much up-to-date equipment that even Arnold and Sly would be impressed. Don't miss Blossom's (see our Restaurants chapter) for dinner or the Regency Lounge for late-night cocktails and chatter (see our Nightlife chapter). Four Points is open year round and is great for families or business travelers.

Midway Motel & Cottages

$$ • 5460 Rt. 6, North Eastham • 255-3177

This homey complex is right on the scenic 25-mile Cape Cod Rail Trail bike path, right in the heart of the Cape Cod National Seashore and very close to the glorious Wellfleet Bay Wildlife Sanctuary. The nine modern, well-furnished one and two-bedroom motel rooms are situated on 3 acres in separate buildings; their location from the road (and each other) assures the utmost in privacy. Or you can choose from one of three charming cottages that can accommodate anywhere from two to six people. And while you're catching up on the morning news in the cozy common room, the kids can enjoy the swings and climbing tower.

The Even'Tide

$ • 650 Rt. 6, South Wellfleet • 349-3410, (800) 368-0007 (Mass. only)

This family-owned motel is set so far back

among the woods that you may feel like you're vacationing in the middle of a forest — if forests came complete with a 30-by 60-foot indoor pool, one of the Cape's largest and one of the few in the area that is open year round. All the rooms at this year-round facility come with a refrigerator, 30-channel cable TV, clock radio, coffee maker and heat and air-conditioning controls. The most popular units are the queen-size rooms with their pretty custom-made oak furnishings. Eight cottages, five of them A-frames with wood stoves, are also available and most have decks. Biking enthusiasts take note: The Cape Cod Rail Trail runs right through the back yard. An outdoor play area beckons children, while adults will appreciate the sundeck.

Mainstay Motor Inn

$ • 2068 Rt. 6, South Wellfleet • 349-2350, (800) 346-2350

The Mainstay is convenient to everything. Tennis courts are within walking distance, the Cape Cod National Seashore is a scallop shell's throw away, Wellfleet Harbor's marina is practically in the front yard and whale-watching boats in Provincetown are a few miles away. Each of the 30 rooms here has a king- or queen-size bed or two double beds with a full bath, refrigerator and outdoor deck. A complimentary continental breakfast is served daily in the coffee room, which also houses the Mainstay's free lending library. It's open year round.

Wellfleet Motel & Lodge

$$ • Rt. 6, Wellfleet • 349-3535, (800) 852-2900

What at first seems like a typical '60s strip motel is actually a quite charming getaway and an ideal (and inexpensive) choice for families. The 65 rooms are comfortably furnished with all the basics. The rooms in the adjacent lodge, built in 1986, are much more spacious. But let's face it: Most of your time will be spent out of the room, exploring the nearby beaches and attractions. The must-see Wellfleet Bay Wildlife Sanctuary (see our Parks and Recreation chapter) is just across the street. There are two pools as well as an indoor hot tub.

Topmast Motel

$$ • 209 Shore Rd., North Truro • 487-1189

There are several reasons why this two-story motel, open May 1 to mid-October, is tops on our list. We'll name three: the small, refreshing and sparkling-clean pool; the bayfront rooms with large porches and lawn chairs; and the hearty breakfasts and lunches served at the poolside eatery Harbor Lights, which is the town's only nonsmoking restaurant (see our Restaurants chapter). Run for 25 years by the Silva family, this well-kept facility is the only beachfront motel in the area with its own restaurant. The 33 units include newly renovated efficiencies with microwave ovens.

Best Western Tides Beachfront

$$$ • 837 Commercial St., Provincetown • 487-1045, (800) 528-1234

The Gordon family, which has owned this two-story chain motel for many years, devotes their considerable experience and energies to the care of the tidy, comfy oceanfront motel and its guests. (The lawns alone — greener than we've ever seen — will be your first clue to the staff's special handling.)

The 64 rooms are several notches above your standard motel fare, clean and comfortable, with 27 of them literally sitting at the water's edge. You'll wake up in the morning and walk through the sliders to the surf. The motel also has a fenced-in pool, badminton courts, plenty of free parking and an on-site restaurant (open to the public) that serves breakfast and lunch only. A boon for families: Children younger than 18 stay free!

The Gordons also run, with the same efficiency and service, the 54-room Best Western Chateau Motor Inn, high atop a hill at the opposite end of town (105 Bradford Street West, 487-1286, same toll-free numbers as above). Again, kids stay free. Both facilities are open early May to mid-October.

Resorts

If you're looking for the ultimate in accommodations combined with on-site recreational activities, the utmost in service and a wide range of amenities, opt for one of the Cape's resorts. Practically worlds unto themselves, these destinations can meet all your needs.

INSIDERS' TIPS

A knot is a nautical measure of speed that equals 1.16 miles per hour. It is used as a reference to the speed of water, wind and boats.

Upper Cape

New Seabury Resort

$$$$ • Rock Landing Rd. (off Great Neck Rd. S.), Mashpee • 477-9111, (800) 999-9033

Established in 1962, this exclusive oceanfront resort with 3 miles of beach frontage takes its place as the premier resort on Cape Cod. More than 100 lovely one bedroom/one bath or two bedroom/two bath condo villas are available, some offering fantastic ocean views. New Seabury is an adults' playground with two championship golf courses, two outdoor pools, numerous tennis courts, bike and hiking trails, a restaurant, a lounge and the on-site marketplace dressed in crushed clam shells. There are also programs for the children. Open from March to the end of October, New Seabury offers one handicapped-accessible unit.

Sea Mist Resort

$$-$$$ • 141 Great Neck Rd. S., Mashpee • 477-0549, (800) 228-2968

This family resort is just south of the Mashpee Rotary and the sprawling Mashpee Commons with its many shops. Sea Mist offers 90 suites and townhouses just a few miles from South Cape Beach. The facility has an indoor heated pool as well as an outdoor pool, tennis courts, a Jacuzzi, sauna, miniature golf, volleyball courts, pool and Ping Pong tables and a game room for the kiddies. Every Tuesday evening a movie is shown on a large screen TV in the common room. Grills and picnic areas are also available at this year-round resort. A number of golf courses are close by.

Southcape Resort

$$$ • 950 Falmouth Rd. (Rt. 28), Mashpee • 477-4700, (800) 527-3336 (Mass. only)

Both indoor and outdoor tennis courts are available to you at the Southcape Resort, day and night. This facility offers 55 condominium units featuring two baths, air conditioning, full kitchens, cable TV and private terraces with grills. These units sleep a maximum of six people and are available year round. Southcape has an indoor heated pool, though beaches are just a few miles away. There is a four-night minimum during the summer season (two-night minimum during the off season). Children of all ages are welcome.

Lower Cape

Ocean Edge Resort

$$$$ • 2660 Rt. 6A, Brewster • 896-9000, (800) 343-6074

Truly a landmark, Ocean Edge is distinguished by the impressive Gothic and Renaissance Revival stucco mansion and stone carriage house standing tall and stately beyond a beautifully manicured lawn. Once part of the vast Roland Nickerson estate, the main 400-foot-long building is the Ocean Edge Conference Center, and is every bit as grand inside as out, with carved wood-paneled walls and oriental rugs. The resort takes up 380 acres on both the north side (where the mansion is) and the south side of Route 6A. Attached to the main building by enclosed walkways is a 90-room hotel that offers room service among other amenities. Behind the main building, beyond the tennis courts and pool, are condominiums, some of which have ocean views. Across the road the Villages is a huge residential and rental condominium community with a golf course, pool and Mulligan's Restaurant (see our Restaurants chapter) at its center. You can book anything from suites to three-bedroom condos; some rooms have fireplaces and all have cable TV and phones.

People flock here for the world-class golf (see our Golf chapter), tennis schools and clinics (fees are in addition to room rates) and for the abundance of other recreational activities. The resort has six pools, four outdoor and two indoor, and a 1,000-foot private beach for guests to use. Ocean Edge also offers children's activities in summer, and year-round concierge services to help you plan activities. The mansion is home to the comfortable, wood-paneled downstairs Bayzo's Pub, which serves light fare, and the adjacent Ocean Grill for fine dining.

Chatham Bars Inn

$$$-$$$$ • 297 Shore Rd., Chatham • 945-0096, (800) 527-4884

Call it the last of the Cape's grande dames. Built in 1914 as a hunting lodge by a wealthy Boston family, the inn still maintains its elegance and grandeur but with a much more casual, quiet feel. The inn's main house has 43 rooms, with another 111 in buildings just outside the main house and across the street along the shore. All the rooms are inviting and purposely understated — lots of wicker and floral prints and fabrics — and nearly all of them have a balcony from which to ogle the breathtaking views of the Atlantic Ocean and Pleasant Bay. The 80 acres of grounds boast every conceivable sport from tennis to shuffleboard, along with a private beach and a heated outdoor pool. How about a game of volleyball? There's a concierge available daily in summer and on weekends in the off-season to help you plan excursions and other activities. Three restaurants complete the idyllic picture (see our Restaurants chapter). The Chatham Bars Inn offers a number of off-season packages, including a Romantic Getaway and spa packages.

Wequassett Inn

$$$$ • Rt. 28, Chatham • 432-5400, (800) 225-7125

This inn is so large, some people call it Wequassett Town. The 22-acre estate, which takes its name from a Native American word that means "crescent on the water," is actually comprised of 20 buildings, including one built in 1740. Each of the 104 rooms and suites has views of Pleasant Bay, Round Cove or the woods and is furnished in Early American or country pine. So exquisite is the decor that many rooms have won national design awards.

Tennis buffs can stay in one of three villas, just steps away from four all-weather tennis courts. The inn also has its own dock and offers a sailing program for novice to salty-dog sailors. (The inn even has a rental fleet of Hobie Cats and Sunfish.) If you're not in the mood for saltwater, take a dip in the awesome 68-foot heated pool.

The staff here is attentive but far from stuffy, and a concierge is available to help you with everything from dinner reservations to fishing excursions. One of the area's best restaurants, the pricey Eben Ryder House, is on the premises (see our Restaurants chapter).

Hostels

If you're a back-to-basics type of person who would rather spend money on, say, a nice dinner or some pricey souvenirs than empty your wallet at a fancy hotel, a hostel may be for you. And you won't be alone. What was once the primary lodging choice of the young and the broke has become a frugal favorite among all generations.

Beds are simple and often in dorm-like settings, and lockouts (those times when you must vacate your room) and curfews are strictly enforced. The American Youth Hostels have lockouts timed between 9 AM and 5 PM; nightly curfew is 11 PM. Reservations are only accepted up to 48 hours before your arrival. Check-in is between 5 and 10 PM. All AYHs offer free on-site parking and bike storage.

The cost of a night's lodging is around $15 — a far cry from the usual motel room rate of $60 to $100 or more.

The area has four AYHs — in Eastham, North Truro, Martha's Vineyard and Nantucket — and non-AYH members can stay at them by simply paying the modest additional fee for an introductory membership (also see our Martha's Vineyard and Nantucket chapters). AYH accepts Visa and MasterCard and offers discounts to area attractions. There's also a privately owned hostel in Provincetown.

Hostelling International

$ • 75 Goody Hallet Dr., Eastham • 255-2785

The first things you'll notice as you drive through the 3 acres of grounds are the handmade wooden signs welcoming visitors in different languages. A nice touch, for hostels do attract a number of international travelers. This hostel offers 50 beds in eight rustic red cabins ($12 members; $15 nonmembers). Two family cabins, which offer two double beds and two bunk beds and sleep six, are also available.

Guests can also use the screened-in porch common room, picnic tables, grills, communal kitchen, volleyball and basketball courts and game room. The grounds, just off Bridge Road, are lovely and wild, with birds singing in the trees and a gentle breeze blowing across the patio. The hostel is open mid-May through mid-September.

Hostelling International

$ • N. Pamet Rd., North Truro • 349-3889

There's a reason this hostel is perched high atop the sand dunes: It was once a Coast Guard Station known as Little America — a name for which this hostel is now known. The location within the Cape Cod National Seashore cannot be beat, and the views — the coastline, the cranberry bogs, the beaches, the sunrises — cannot be duplicated. The 42 beds are set up in a multilevel house. Rates are $12 for members and $15 for nonmem-

INSIDERS' TIPS

Cape-bound commuters should expect traffic during the peak season (mid-May through mid-October) on Friday from 3 to 10 PM. Leaving the Cape, traffic builds about noon on Sunday and extends into early evening.

bers. It's open from late June through Labor Day.

Outermost Hostel

$ • 28 Winslow St., Provincetown • 487-4378

This privately owned hostel has 30 beds in five white-washed cabins — nothing to write home about but a steal at $14 per night. The hostel has a common living room and kitchen in one cabin. The expansive yard offers grills and picnic tables. The Outermost has no lock-outs and no curfew. It's open mid-May to mid-October.

Some inns have modern amenities while others pride themselves in being places where guests can escape ringing phones and the ubiquitous tube.

Bed & Breakfasts, Inns and Guesthouses

If you prefer a homier setting for your stay, settle in at one of the Cape's many bed and breakfasts, inns or guesthouses. These accommodations are smaller, more intimate and more individualized than hotels. And, because they are often housed in older buildings, you get a firsthand taste of Cape history.

Bed and breakfasts are usually private residences where the owners rent spare bedrooms (and sometimes suites) and offer breakfast; inns are generally larger and serve meals to the public as well as to guests; and guesthouses offer rooms but not necessarily meals. On the Cape we have another option, cottage colonies, which are clusters of small, individual cottages or cabins that may share a common kitchen and gathering space, or may be self-contained with private bathrooms and small kitchens. Most are housekeeping cottages, meaning you clean up after yourself, and many require that you bring your own linens; be sure to ask exactly what the cottage is supplied with when you make your reservations.

Historic houses with antique furnishings and civilized amenities such as crystal wine glasses and handstitched quilts don't mix well with boisterous children, so most inns and bed and breakfasts have age restrictions for children or don't allow them at all. Families with young children may find that cottage colonies are the best options. Because age restrictions vary (we've heard every age cutoff from 6 to 14), we try to mention them in the writeup for each establishment, but always ask. If you are traveling with children and really prefer inns and bed and breakfasts to hotels and motels, don't despair — there are inns that accept children. They do, however, expect children to be well-behaved and supervised.

As you will see from the listings that follow, the Cape offers a variety of accommodations beyond the conventional. In most cases, the rates include either a full or continental breakfast. Some establishments offer what they call "hearty" or "extended" continental breakfasts, which usually means cereals, fruits and juices in addition to baked goods.

Some rooms have a shared bath — which is one way to get a more economical rate. Some have in-room phones and/or televisions, while others pride themselves on being places where guests can escape ringing phones and the otherwise ubiquitous tube. Often, inns and bed and breakfasts compromise by offering TV and phones only in their common areas. Most establishments do not allow pets ("We provide pets," says the brochure of one lovely inn that is home to a couple of languid cats. "Yours are much happier at home."), but we'll let you know if they do.

About smoking: Most inns and bed and breakfasts do not allow it. More and more patrons are demanding a smoke-free atmosphere, and the small, intimate nature of most inns makes it difficult, if not impossible, to set aside indoor smoking areas. Since there is no lack of patios, decks, lawns and porches at such establishments, in most cases smokers will find some outdoor area where they can light up. If a smoking policy is not mentioned in our writeup, assume it's outdoor smoking only. In rare cases, smoking may be prohibited anywhere on the property, and we'll mention it if the policy is that strict.

Remember that each establishment is as

personal and unique as its innkeeper — someone who wants to share his or her expertise and knowledge with you to make your visit more memorable. So ask for recommendations about things to do in the area, places to visit and restaurants. One good tack: Ask your innkeepers where they go when they want to eat out and where they take friends who are visiting from off Cape. And don't be surprised if you find yourself developing a friendship with your host; many such relationships have been formed over long chats. It is not uncommon, however, for inns and bed and breakfasts to change hands. One innkeeper we know explained that the business is much more labor-intensive than people realize and has a high burnout rate. If your favorite innkeepers decide to retire, give their successors a chance. In most cases, new owners will not significantly change a successful operation. But if you find yourself dealing with a new innkeeper of a familiar establishment, ask before you make reservations if they have made any changes.

A few Insiders' insights: Most establishments have cancellation penalties and restrictions. Calling to cancel less than two weeks before your arrival (especially in season) will almost guarantee that you won't get your deposit back (or that it will be applied to a future stay). Some establishments will give refunds in the event of cancellations only if they are able to re-rent the room you had booked. Most accommodations require a two-night minimum stay during the peak season, three nights on holiday weekends. Some, however, have minimum stays as long as five nights in July and August. Cottages are generally rented by the week in season. Innkeepers are much more flexible in the off-season — before June and after September, or anytime besides July and August, depending on the establishment — and off-season rates are usually drastically reduced.

If you'd like help booking accommodations, check out the reservation services listed at the beginning of our Hotels, Motels and Resorts chapter. Many of them specialize in inns and bed and breakfasts.

FYI

Unless otherwise noted, the area code for all phone numbers in this guide is 508.

Price Code

The following key to room rates should help you get a quick fix on the range of prices available. The key is based on the average cost of a night's stay in a double-occupancy room during the peak summer season, minus tax and special charges, if any. State and local room tax combined is generally 9.7 percent.

$	**Less than $75**
$$	**$76 to $110**
$$$	**$111 to $175**
$$$$	**$176 or more**

Most innkeepers accept major credit cards, but we'll let you know if a specific lodging does not. We'll also let you know when an inn is open year round, or, if not, what months it is open. Many old inns find it difficult to meet handicapped-access codes because of the historic nature of their buildings, but if an inn has handicapped-accessible features, we'll let you know.

If you're planning to stay on Martha's Vineyard or Nantucket, see our special chapters on those islands later in the book for information on their accommodations.

And, please, respect the house rules. Your host isn't on vacation — you are!

Upper Cape

Canalside Bed and Breakfast

$-$$, no credit cards • 7 Coastal Way, Bourne • 759-6564

Situated right on the Cape Cod Canal in a residential neighborhood, this modern-contemporary 9-year-old bed and breakfast has two guest rooms with a shared bath and a suite with a sitting room that features a fireplace and a unique view of the passing tugboats, sailboats and tankers. A private entrance enables guests to go and come as they please. The owner serves a continental breakfast in the common room, which is warmed by a fireplace.

Guests can borrow bicycles to use on the popular canal bike path only a few yards from

the house. Children older than 10 are welcome. The Canalside, which features beautiful grounds and a picnic area, is open year round. Personal checks are accepted.

Wood Duck Inn

$$, no credit cards • 1050 County Rd., Cataumet (Bourne) • 564-6404

Along a peaceful country road meandering past fields and cranberry bogs rests the Wood Duck Inn. Built in 1848, this lovely bed and breakfast offers two suites, each with a private entrance, full bath and sitting room. Interior decor includes charming country antiques, handmade quilts, stenciling and wooden decoys, and outside behind the house are picturesque views of working cranberry bogs. Hosts Maureen and Dick Jason serve up a complimentary breakfast delivered to your suite each morning.

The Wood Duck also has a two-bedroom cottage with its own kitchen, living room and deck. Cataumet's country setting offers relaxing walks along the bog, the adjacent Bourne Conservation Trust lands and nearby Red Brook Harbor. Though out in the country, the inn is 10 minutes from bustling Falmouth center and the island ferries. The Wood Duck welcomes "peaceful" children. The Jasons have operated the Wood Duck for eight years, and Dick crafts the many handcarved decoys throughout the house (accounting for the name of the inn). Open year round, the inn accepts personal checks.

Bay Beach

$$$-$$$$ • 1-3 Bay Beach Ln., Sandwich • 888-8813, (800) 475-6398

Now in its seventh year, Bay Beach has earned some very impressive accolades. This bed and breakfast has been cited by the American Bed and Breakfast Association as one of the top 16 inns in North America. One of the keys to its success is the professionalism, hospitality and superb taste of owners Emily and Reale Lemieux, who have a quarter-century of experience in the travel and leisure industry. The views from this oceanfront bed and breakfast are incredible — on a clean day you can see Pilgrim's Monument across the bay at Provincetown. All six spacious rooms are exquisitely decorated for elegant comfort in wicker, rattan and rich color. Each room has a private bath, air conditioning, a stereo with CD player, refrigerator; three have a Jacuzzi and five have private decks. One room is handicapped accessible. An extensive continental breakfast is served featuring homemade breads and fresh fruits. Children 16 years of age and older are welcome at the Bay Beach, which is open from mid-May to the end of October.

The Belfry Inne and Bistro

$$-$$$ • 8 Jarves St., Sandwich • 888-8550

This Victorian beauty, now known as the Belfry Inne and Bistro, was built c.1879 when Sandwich was still riding the successes of the in-town glass industry. A picture-postcard property in the heart of the Village, The Belfry is newly restored, featuring lofty ceilings and Eastlake details. The eight guest rooms are light and colorful. Some rooms have brass beds, fireplaces and in-room footed tubs (one is an 1887 Demarest tub from England), while other rooms have private balconies and private baths. A ninth room, a three person suite, will be added by the 1997 season.

The Belfry is all beauty and elegance, from the tip of its bell tower on the fourth floor to its cozy, inviting lounge with fireplace on the first floor. Dine on the patio and porch of the Bistro, which serves breakfast and a four-course prix fixe dinner. Though the menu changes regularly, delectable entrees may include roasted breast of duck with spinach, lentil and white bean tian, and baby vegetables served with Madeira wine sauce and choice of dessert. Let's talk about dessert: How does triple chocolate truffle cake served on a bed of creme anglaise and chocolate sauce sound? The Belfry is open year round. Children 6 and older and small kenneled dogs are welcome.

The Captain Ezra Nye House

$$ • 152 Main St., Sandwich • 888-6142, (800) 388-2278

At the Captain Ezra Nye House you can feel yourself being transported to a simpler time when America was new, and clipper ships mastered by Cape men opened up corridors to the Orient. This homey bed and breakfast, built in 1829, displays the international flavor of a traveled sea captain's home: china collections, original art, Sandwich glass (of course) and a prominent painting of *Independence*, Capt. Nye's ship. Resident owners Harry and Elaine Dickson take special pleasure in sharing the history of their house and its namesake.

The inn has two common rooms, one with a 1918 piano once belonging to Nellie Nye — in fact, you can play from some of her original sheet music — and a lovely formal dining room where a large breakfast is served at 8 and 9 AM. Guests rave about Elaine's cheese blintzes, grilled banana bread and apple cinnamon quiche. This bed and breakfast has six very clean, antique-furnished rooms with private baths, some with hand-stenciling and four-poster beds. One room has a working fireplace. A suite with a private entrance has a queen-size bed, two rooms and a private bath. Children age 6 and older are welcome at this year-round inn along historic Main Street, just a pleasant, leisurely stroll to all sights.

Inn at Sandwich Center

$$ • 118 Tupper Rd., Sandwich • 888-6958, (800) 249-6949

At this appropriately named inn you will experience a perfect blend of history and hospitality. The Inn at Sandwich Center is a handsome 18th-century saltbox with hardwood floors and an c.1750 fireplace with a beehive oven. The five spacious and immaculate guest rooms are decorated with antiques and oil paintings. Most rooms have fireplaces and four-poster beds, and all rooms have private baths.

An extensive continental breakfast with homemade muffins, scones, jams and French crepes is served in the charming keeping room by the original fireplace. This comfortably elegant inn, directly across the street from the Sandwich Glass Museum, is centrally located and is within easy walking distance of restaurants, antiques shops, gift shops and the numerous historical attractions of Sandwich village such as Hoxie House and the grist mill. We recommend a walk along Shawme Pond, especially in October when the leaves dazzle the water with yellows, reds and oranges. Heritage Plantation with its 76 acres of rhododendrons is a short walk away.

Innkeeper Elaine Thomas speaks fluent French and Italian and even some Spanish. Eliane's family has managed hotels throughout the world, and she operates the inn with her husband, Al. Children older than 13 are welcome. The inn is open year round.

Isaiah Jones Homestead

$$-$$$ • 165 Main St., Sandwich • 888-9115, (800) 526-1625

The rooms inside the Isaiah Jones Homestead are as beautiful as the eye-catching exterior of this flawlessly maintained 1849 home. Outside, the trim is accented with blues and pinks, which, whether by chance or design, coordinate with the pink rhododendrons out front. The interior is full of rich Oriental items, antiques and all the decorative drama of the Victorian era including a curved main stairway and 11-foot ceilings. Built at the height of Sandwich's 19th-century prosperity, the rooms here are named for important Sandwich citizens such as Thomas Dexter who built the 1654 grist mill in the center of town and Deming Jarves who was the founder of the Sandwich Glass Factory.

All five rooms are elaborately appointed, some with canopied and four-poster beds, two with a whirlpool and one with a working fireplace. Each has a private bath. Owners Bud and Shirley Lamson serve a hearty breakfast that may include fresh scones, hot breads, low-cholesterol egg strata, fresh fruit and juices. After breakfast, retire to a chair on the front porch overlooking Main Street to make plans for the day. There's much to do and see within walking distance. Tea, iced tea and lemonade are served in the afternoon. Children age 12 and older are welcome at this year-round inn.

The Village Inn at Sandwich

$$ • 4 Jarves St., Sandwich • 833-0363, (800) 922-9989

After a busy day of shopping and sightseeing along Sandwich's proud streets, what could be better than kicking your feet up on the long porch at the Village Inn to listen to the village wind down as evening settles in. This inn at the corner of Main and Jarves streets, points to an earlier time, from the pretty front flower gardens to the wonderful wraparound porches with rockers to the rooms with handpainted furniture.

Built in the 1830s during Sandwich's industrial boom, which rendered it among the Cape's wealthiest towns, this home was restored about nine years ago as an inn with eight guest rooms, two sitting rooms and a dining room with a small wet bar for guests. Six rooms have queen-size beds and private baths, and two rooms have twin beds and a shared bath. Complimentary breakfast of French toast with strawberries, juice frappés or puffed pancakes is served at 9 AM. The inn, which welcomes children 12 and older, is closed November through March (though it will open during those months for special occasions).

Pine Grove Cottages

$$ • 358 Rt. 6A, East Sandwich • 888-8179

Ten heated cottages set, not surprisingly, in a pretty 3-acre pine grove offer very clean accommodations for as many as six people. Each of the deluxe cottages has two bedrooms, a sitting room with a sleep sofa and TV and a fully equipped kitchen. The popular cottages rent by the night or the week, and for $38 (yes, that's $38) you can rent a rustic cottage with color TV but no kitchen.

The complex has a swimming pool and a play area for young children. Manager Kathy Bumstead, who runs the cottages with her husband, Roger, says they cater to young marrieds with children during the summer months and retirees during the off-season. They provide cribs, baby baths, barbecue grills and linens and towels. In a party of more than four, the inn charges $7 daily ($25 per week) for each additional person. Pets are allowed. Pine Grove Cottages are available from May 1 through November 1.

The Elm Arch Inn

$-$$, no credit cards • 26 Elm Arch Way, Falmouth • 548-0133

Not only is the Elm Arch a gem of an inn, but it's also a true historic landmark. Built by Falmouth whaling captain Silas Jones in 1810, four years later it was a casualty of the War of 1812. On January 28, 1814, the British brig *Nimrod* was positioned off Falmouth lobbing cannonballs towards the village green in an attempt to knock out two small cannon positioned there. One of the *Nimrod*'s volleys struck this historic home. The story goes that a local woman, Anne Freeman, was in the house at the time cooking a kettle of beans for the Falmouth soldiers and despite the bombardment went on with her cooking. The wall that took the hit still proudly bears its wound where the British cannonball came through.

This delightful 24-room inn, run since 1926 by the Richardson family, offers great rates for immaculate attractive rooms with braided rugs, four-poster canopy beds and Colonial furnishings. The inn has a pool and offers quiet seclusion at an in-town location convenient to shops, museums, restaurants, the beach and harbor. The Elm Arch Inn is open from the end of March to the end of October. Children are welcome.

Mostly Hall

$$$ • 27 Main St., Falmouth • 548-3786, (800) 682-0565

Leave it to a child to give Falmouth's most elegant inn its name. In the 19th century a young boy visiting the house immediately noticed the large central hallway that runs the length of the house and announced, "Mama, it's mostly hall." The name stuck. Today, Mostly Hall is a classic among classics — the type of place you immediately fall head over heels in love with. Built in 1849 by Capt. Albert Nye for his Southern bride, the house is truly elegance personified, featuring 13-foot ceilings, a 360 degree wraparound porch and an acre of pretty lawns and gardens featuring a gazebo. The wraparound porch alone could set this place apart from all others, but there's so much more.

The inn is filled with antiques, personal touches and intriguing spaces, such as the enclosed widow's walk atop the house sporting 10 windows (that's right, 10!) that's now a reading room for guests. From this impres-

INSIDERS' TIP

The shoulder seasons — March and April, and September and October — are good times for a visit to Cape Cod. It's quieter then, but there's still plenty to do.

sive perch you can view the village green below. Meanwhile, all six immaculate guest rooms are equally impressive and feature private baths, queen-size four-poster canopy beds, central air conditioning, soaring 13-foot ceilings and nearly floor to ceiling windows. Imagine for a moment how long the staircases are in a home with 13-foot ceilings, and there are two sets of them to reach the widow's walk on the third level. Incredible!

Resident innkeepers Caroline and Jim Lloyd, whose genuine warmth make them cordial hosts, serve a full breakfast of such scrumptious dishes as cheese blintz muffins and eggs Benedict soufflé in the dining room or out on the porch. In the afternoon, sherry and tea are served. Located along the quiet west end of Falmouth's Main Street, near the green, Mostly Hall is convenient to everything including the island ferries and the Shining Sea Bikepath. The Lloyds have bicycles on hand for guest use. Open every month except January, the inn hosts flute workshops in February and March because the high ceilings provide perfect acoustics. Children 16 and older are welcome.

Palmer House Inn

$$-$$$ • 81 Palmer Ave., Falmouth • 548-1230, (800) 472-2632

Escape to Victorian charm along one of Falmouth center's more secluded tree-lined streets. Experience lace curtains at the windows, a grandfather clock striking the hour and gleaming hardwood floors and stairway. This large and immaculate facility has delightful touches pointing to a time of class and elegance, and yet the inn also provides such modern-day amenities as bubbling whirlpool tubs.

The inn has 12 guest rooms: eight in the Queen Anne-style main house and four in the guesthouse. All rooms have a private bath and ceiling fan, some rooms have air conditioning. There is also a charming honeymoon cottage suite available with a sitting room, large bedroom (with a Jacuzzi), kitchenette and a full bath. One guest room is fully handicapped-accessible. The tasteful touches provided by innkeepers Joanne and Ken Baker are numerous. The gourmet breakfast gives you a taste of what to expect — served by candlelight in the dining room, a full sit-down meal may include Belgian waffles and apricot sauce, Swiss eggs with pastry or chocolate-stuffed French toast. An elegant afternoon tea is available to guests and the public from December through April. In summer, iced tea is served, while in winter mulled cider and hot chocolate are served. Children 10 years and older are welcome.

The Village Green Inn

$$-$$$ • 40 Main St., Falmouth • 548-5621, (800) 237-1119

What a nice place run by nice people! This handsome inn was originally built in 1804 and in 1894 was remodeled in the Victorian style. Friendly innkeepers Don and Diane Crosby have been the charming hosts here for two years now, greeting you with a warm smile and instantly making you feel at home. They'll even loan you their bikes so you can explore the Shining Sea Bikepath just a half-mile away.

From the front porch you can hear the chiming of the Paul Revere bell from the church tower across the green, a daily reminder of the role Falmouth patriots played in the birth of this nation.

At the Village Green Inn you have your choice of five guest rooms, including a fabulous, spacious, sunny suite. All rooms have air conditioning and a private bath, and two rooms have working fireplaces. Rosewood wainscoting and lace at the windows add to the historic flavor here. A full complimentary breakfast in the dining room includes fruit, eggs and baked goods while afternoon sherry or lemonade is served out on the porch. Closed in January, the inn welcomes children 12 and older.

The Wildflower Inn

$$-$$$ • 167 Palmer Ave., Falmouth • 548-9524, (800) 294-LILY

The five rooms here at the Victorian-style The Wildflower Inn are all named after flowers (Jasmine, Moonflower and Beach Rose to name a few). Each room is different — a white wrought-iron bed in one room, a four-poster canopy in another. Some have antiques; all are filled with flowers. Each room has a private bath, and two rooms have a whirlpool. Also on-site is a cottage fashioned from the old stable with a full kitchen, living room and loft bedroom along with a full bathroom complete with tub. The cottage, which is perfect for families with children (the sofa in the living room pulls out), runs $600 for a week's stay. A full five-course breakfast featuring granola, blended frozen juice, baked goods and a hot entree of, say, wildflower crepes or flower-stuffed pancakes (stuffed with real edible flowers!) is served to those staying in the five guest rooms only. Open year round, the inn welcomes children in some of the guest rooms.

Woods Hole Passage

$$-$$$ • 186 Woods Hole Rd., Falmouth • 548-9575, (800) 790-8976

Located along a country road that connects Falmouth center with Woods Hole, this century-old carriage house on 1˘ acres is an ideal place to relax with a good book by the fireplace in the large gathering room or outside on the spacious lawn. New owners Todd and Robin Norman hail from Phoenix, so you'll find a contemporary Southwestern flavor to this bed and breakfast, which has five guest rooms furnished with queen-size and double beds. Todd refers to the style as "country modern." All rooms have private baths, two have cathedral ceilings. Of the five rooms, one is in the main house and the other four are in the carriage house.

The inn serves a hearty homemade breakfast with a Southwestern theme and featuring quiche and soufflé along with homebaked breads and fresh fruits. Woods Hole Passage is within walking distance of picturesque Quisset Harbor and within 2 miles of Woods Hole, Falmouth and the bike path. The inn is open year round and welcomes children age 12 and older.

The Elms

$$ • 495 Rt. 28A, West Falmouth • 540-7232

When you picture a country bed and breakfast, you probably have something like The Elms in mind: A 250-year-old house on 4 acres with gardens, nine spotless bedrooms (seven with private baths), five woodchucks, two foxes and a gregarious innkeeper, Joe Mazzucchelli, who speaks "a little German, a little Gaelic, a little Spanish and a little Italian."

The old-fashioned parlor is inviting, as is the sherry set out for guests. A full continental

INSIDERS' TIP

Many of the bed and breakfasts in the mid-Cape towns of Barnstable, Yarmouth and Dennis lie along Route 6A, also known as Old King's Highway, which centuries ago was an old carriage route.

breakfast with scones, cranberry muffins, cereals, fresh fruit in season and custom-blended coffee is served in the dining room or on the patio. Crisply clean and inviting rooms, some with four-poster beds, have lace curtains and views of Oyster Pond. "People say it's just like staying at your grandmother's," says Mazzucchelli, who operates this gem with his wife, Betty, whose parents ran a bed and breakfast in Ireland.

Guests from all over the world enjoy the spectacular sunsets at nearby Chapaquoit Beach. They also enjoy being close to good restaurants, shops and tennis facilities. The inn is open year round and welcomes children 14 and older. One room is handicapped-accessible.

Sjoholm Bed and Breakfast

$-$$ • 17 Chase Rd., West Falmouth • 540-5706, (800) 498-5706

People disagree over the pronunciation of this 15-room bed and breakfast. Some say the Swedish word is pronounced SHA-holm while others say SO-holm. Regardless of pronunciation, the inn has recently changed hands, the new owners being Bob and Barbara White, who purchased it in 1996. Guests, many of whom have been coming here for years, value the peaceful country setting, where walks and bike rides are popular activities, and beaches, good restaurants and shops are nearby.

The year-round inn is well-suited to bicycle touring and retreat groups of as many as 30 people. The facility includes a 150-year-old house, a carriage house and a two bedroom cottage for four that has a separate deck and kitchen. Of the 15 rooms, eight are in the carriage house (four in the Sail Loft upstairs and four with private entrances located downstairs). About half of all the rooms have private baths. Country decor is present throughout the large inn. The Whites serve a complimentary breakfast. Children are welcome at this year-round inn.

The Beach House at Falmouth Heights

$$$ • 10 Worcester Ct., Falmouth Heights • 457-0310, (800) 351-3426

The Beach House at Falmouth Heights is a breath of fresh air. Seven special rooms and a cottage are decorated with handpainted murals. Each room of this bed and breakfast inn has a seaside theme (i.e., the Wave Room, the Fish Room, the Lighthouse Room, the Floral Room). Each room also has a private bath. Full of color and personality, each room except one has a queen-size bed (the one without has a king). You'll enjoy your full continental buffet breakfast of homebaked goodies on the front deck or outside near the pool, courtesy of innkeepers John and Betty Kearney.

Have we mentioned the beach? Well the beach is right there; you can hear the waves of Vineyard Sound curl and break on the sand.

Besides being close to the beach, The Beach House is also within walking distance of the island ferry, Falmouth Harbor, shopping and restaurants. Truly different from most B&Bs, The Beach House regularly entertains international travelers and is open from the beginning of May to Columbus Day (and on other special weekends and occasions before and after). Children 13 and older are welcome.

Gladstone Inn

$-$$ • 219 Grand Ave. S., Falmouth Heights • 548-9851

The Gladstone Inn provides the kind of Cape Cod getaway you dream about. Overlooking the ocean with Martha's Vineyard off on the horizon, this 1910 inn offers 16 rooms. Its newest accommodation is a studio apartment situated on the second floor of the carriage house. Besides providing a full kitchen and private bath, this studio also provides outstanding ocean views from its private deck.

Period furnishings, including four-poster beds, make this well-established, clean and neat inn a favorite with travelers. Many rooms have private baths; those that share a bath have a sink in the room. A double with private bath runs in the mid $$ price range (a heck of a bargain given the proximity to the water). By the way, the carriage house with its privacy and stellar views is only uper $$. Hosts Jim and Gayle Carroll serve a full breakfast of quiche, cheese casserole, breakfast pizza, muffins and fresh fruit and even provide bicycles if you want to check out the many local sights. The Gladstone Inn is open from mid-May to mid-October and welcomes children 14 years of age and older.

Grafton Inn

$$-$$$ • 261 Grand Ave. S., Falmouth Heights • 540-8688, (800) 642-4069

This beautiful 19th-century Victorian inn sits right on the oceanfront at Falmouth Heights, providing incredible views of Martha's Vineyard across the water. The 11 guest rooms, 10 of which have water views, are furnished with king- or queen-size beds, and owners Rudy and Liz Cvitan have dressed their inn with period antiques. Private baths are available in each room as is air conditioning and individual heat controls for those chilly fall evenings.

Morning arrives with a hearty breakfast of eggs Benedict, Belgian waffles, pecan and cinnamon buns, gourmet coffee and other morning wonders (the Grafton is known for its scrumptious full breakfasts). Afternoon saunters by with wine and cheese, a good book on the sun-filled porch or perhaps a walk along the beach. Evening might find you at one of the many area restaurants, at the theater, perhaps lounging back at the inn talking with new or old friends or maybe playing a board game. Open from mid-February to mid-December, the inn welcomes children 16 and older.

Hawthorne Lodge

$$-$$$ • 211 Grand Ave. S., Falmouth Heights • 548-0389

Located right across the street from Vineyard Sound is the Hawthorne Lodge, a charming bed and breakfast now under new ownership. The inn has eight large bedrooms, three of which offer private baths and water views. The other five rooms share bathrooms. All rooms now have television sets, and a telephone is available on each floor for guest use. All guest rooms are on the second and third floors . . . imagine the views of Martha's Vineyard across the water! New owner Herbert Pendleton serves a full breakfast on the enclosed front porch overlooking the ocean. The Hawthorne's living room and small library are available to guests, as are several bicycles and a refrigerator on the porch. Ceiling fans are one of the new items added with the recent redecoration. The Hawthorne Lodge is open from early May to mid-October. Children are welcome.

INSIDERS' TIP

When packing for a visit to the Cape, be sure to include a sweater or light jacket, even in summer. The nights can get cool — refreshingly so after a hot day — and if you get out on the water for a whale watch or a harbor tour, you'll welcome the extra layer of clothing.

Inn on the Sound

$$-$$$ • 313 Grand Ave., Falmouth Heights • 457-9666, (800) 564-9668

Sitting high on a bluff overlooking Vineyard Sound, and Martha's Vineyard off in the distance, this romantic inn features private baths and magnificent water views from nine of its 10 guest rooms. Each of the rooms has a queen-size bed, and one has a working fireplace. The decor is casual contemporary with natural oak features and ceiling fans. Resident owner Renee Ross, a commercial interior designer, had a grand time redecorating the guesthouse over the past couple of years.

The public areas include a fireplace-warmed living room, a 40-foot deck offering water views and a dining room in which guests enjoy a complete sit-down gourmet breakfast including spinach soufflé, herb eggs, quiche, pastries and fresh fruit. Hot coffee and tea are always available. Falmouth center and the island ferries are close by, as are many fine restaurants and attractions. At the year-round inn rates fall into the $-$$ range in November. Children 16 and older can be accommodated.

The Moorings

$$ • 207 Grand Ave. S., Falmouth Heights • 540-2370

This is what the gods intended when they invented the summer vacation. The sun, the surf, the beach, it's all here at the Moorings along Grand Avenue S. in Falmouth Heights. Water views abound; you can sit on the 40-foot front porch for hours and just stare at Vineyard Sound. At night you can watch Martha's Vineyard sparkle across the dark water, or watch the twinkling island ferries go to and fro in their graceful parade across the waves. Talk about relaxation!

The Moorings is within walking distance of the harbor and nearby restaurants. The famed Falmouth Road Race ends just a couple of hundred feet short of its front door, and the beach is directly across the street. The inn, which has an antiques-filled Victorian decor, is well-suited to families and couples. It has eight charming guest rooms each with a private bath. You can choose between a room with a double bed, or a king, or a double and a twin, or even a double and two twins. Innkeepers Ernie and Shirley Benard, who have owned the inn for 17 years, serve a grand complimentary breakfast buffet that may include fresh fruit with vanilla yogurt, homemade bread and granola, French toast and omelets. Built in 1905, The Moorings is open mid-May to the end of October, and children are most welcome.

The Marlborough Bed and Breakfast

$$ • 320 Woods Hole Rd., Woods Hole • 548-6218, (800) 320-2322

Quality and comfort are served at this delightful facility with five clean and pretty rooms and attractive grounds with an inviting pool and herb gardens. There's even a poolside cottage, the Garden room, with (you guessed it) its own gardens. The decor at the Marlborough is country fresh, the rooms decorated with handmade quilts and the beds dressed with scented linens. All rooms have air conditioning (and a space heater for the chilly evenings of autumn).

A full gourmet breakfast is served from 7:30 to 9:30 AM. After breakfast your plans could include touring Falmouth or hopping a ferry at the Woods Hole dock bound for Martha's Vineyard. Guests, many of whom are from outside the United States, enjoy playing English paddle tennis on the Marlborough's court or golf at a number of nearby courses. The year-round inn serves an informal afternoon tea. Rates for a couple of rooms drop into the $ range during the winter season. Children age 2 and older are welcome.

Mid-Cape

The Inn at Fernbrook

$$$ • 481 Main St., Centerville • 775-4334

A premier Cape Cod inn situated along Centerville village's Main Street, The Inn at Fernbrook was built in 1881 by Howard Marston and was owned in the 1930s by Dr. Herbert Kalmus, who invented Technicolor (and who played host to such Hollywood legends at Cecile B. DeMille and Walt Disney). Donated to the Diocese of New York, the estate was often visited by Cardinal Spellman. It has been a bed and breakfast inn since 1986.

From the neatly trimmed privet hedge and the gardens designed by Frederick Law

Olmsted (the landscape architect who created Central Park and the gardens at the Biltmore Estate in Asheville, North Carolina) to the formal antiques-furnished parlor and dining rooms, this six-suite bed and breakfast bespeaks elegance and grandeur in addition to warmth and hospitality. Sit-down breakfasts may include Dutch babies (German oven pancakes with nutmeg, lemon and powdered sugar served with kiwi fruit and orange marmalade) or Eggs Linden (whole eggs cooked with white pepper, Parmesan and cheddar cheeses and cream) and other delights.

The suites, light, lovely and laden with antiques, are named for the inn's three previous owners and the landscape architect Olmstead. The third-floor Olmstead Suite has a library sitting room, Oriental rugs, 18 windows, a large bathroom, a loft and a sun deck. The Kalmus Suite has an alcove sitting area while the Garden Cottage features cathedral ceilings and a wraparound porch. The inn offers Centerville's quiet historic ambiance yet is within a 10 minute's ride to Hyannis' many activities. Children age 14 and older are welcome. The inn is open year round.

The Long Dell Inn

$$, no credit cards • 436 S. Main St., Centerville • 775-2750

The Long Dell Inn is a clean and bright Greek Revival house built in the 1850s by sea captain Reuben Jones. It lies on S. Main Street in Centerville Village, a road that leads down to the village of Osterville to the west and that rests within walking distance of Centerville's restaurants, antiques shops and Craigville Beach. Each of The Long Dell Inn's five rooms feature a private bath, a double, queen or king-size bed, and color TV. There is also an efficiency apartment available.

Your hosts serve a full homemade breakfast of inn specialties, fresh fruit and coffee, tea and juice in the two breakfast rooms, including one nice sunroom with a painted wood floor. Innkeepers Joy and Roy Swayze set a

Photo: Cape Cod Times

Decisions, decisions . . . all the seasons bring an opportunity for memories that can last a lifetime.

personable tone that has earned them a solid repeat business. Children 14 years of age and older are welcome at The Long Dell, which is open from May until Columbus Day. The inn does accept personal checks.

The Inn on Sea Street

$$ • 358 Sea St., Hyannis • 775-8030

The Inn on Sea Street has the distinction of being the very first bed and breakfast in Hyannis. It is also an inn comprised of two houses — one was built in 1849 with 5 guest rooms and the second was built across the street in 1860 with 4 rooms and a cottage. Eight of the 10 units have private baths, six rooms have air conditioning and seven have a TV. All are lovely. Some guest rooms have claw-foot tubs, four-poster beds with lace canopies and antiques. Window fans are provided.

Oriental rugs, lace curtains, runners and a pitcher of gladiolus on the front hall table contribute to a comfortable, welcoming atmosphere as does a little needlepoint sampler reading "Home Sweet Home." A full complimentary breakfast featuring homemade granola, a hot egg dish, coffee cake, fresh fruit and homemade breads is served in the dining room or on the sun porch. From the inn it is a short walk to the beach in one direction and downtown Hyannis' many shops and restaurants in the other. Evening can be spent before a fire in the living room. The Inn on Sea Street is open from May to November, and children age 7 and older are welcome.

Sea Beach Inn

$ • 388 Sea St., Hyannis • 775-4612

What nice people! When you meet Sea Street Inn owners Neil and Elizabeth Carr you'll think you've known them for years. They make you feel right at home in their comfortable inn, which was once an 1860 sea captain's home. Located close to Sea Street Beach, the inn has five guest rooms in the main house and another four in the carriage barn. Three of the five rooms in the main house have private baths. The rooms in the rustic carriage barn are perfect for families. Visitors from all over the world find their way to the Sea Beach Inn, many are repeat customers who enjoy the inn's down to earth, comfortable atmosphere. Sea Beach offers tin ceilings, air conditioning, pickup service at the train station, bus station or airport, and a lovable pooch named Tyler, who the kids love (yes, children are welcome here). Open from April to the end of October, the Carrs serve a continental breakfast in their breakfast room, or you can take your breakfast outside and watch as the day ahead unfolds.

Sea Breeze Inn

$-$$$ • 397 Sea St., Hyannis • 771-7213

The Sea Breeze Inn displays a nautical flair, and with its superb location so close to the beach you'll really feel the sea breezes firsthand. Besides the proximity to the beaches of Hyannis, the inn is also nearby all Hyannis activities including the Cape Cod Melody Tent, restaurants, golf and island ferries. Formerly from Dublin, innkeeper Patricia Battle has owned the bed and breakfast for the past 11 years.

The 14 bright and airy rooms in the main building feature antique canopy beds, private baths and air conditioning. The inn also has three cottages; all are neat, individually decorated and air-conditioned. One cottage has three bedrooms, two baths and a kitchen, another is an efficiency unit and the third has a Jacuzzi. A generous continental breakfast of muffins, bagels, cereals and fresh fruit is served in the large, pleasant dining room of the main house. The inn is open year round and children are welcome.

FYI

Unless otherwise noted, the area code for all phone numbers in this guide is 508.

Simmons Homestead Inn

$$$ • 288 Scudder Ave., Hyannisport • 778-4999, (800) 637-1649

Hyannisport was the home of President Kennedy's summer White House. Today it is home to the Simmons Homestead Inn, an historic sea captain's home that was built in 1820 by Lemuel Simmons and converted into a country inn by Bill Putman in 1987. Ten years later it remains the only inn in Hyannisport and is the perfect setting for a Hyannis-based stay that will include shopping, dining, entertainment, beaches and boat excursions, all within a short drive.

The property is attractive, with a great rolling backyard and a sitting porch. The interior decor is eclectic, reflecting the personality of its fun-loving innkeeper. The inn has 10 rooms, some furnished with canopied four-poster beds, brass beds or white wicker. Each room has a private bath, one has a private deck and two contain working fireplaces. In 1997 there will be a suite available.

The rooms each have their own animal theme (as in giraffe, elephant, cat, etc). The place is just . . . fun! There's even a spacious billiards room — and a sharp one at that! There are a dozen 10-speed mountain bikes available for guests to use. In the morning guests will find a full country breakfast in the dining room (once the late Dinah Shore cooked breakfast for the guests). Wine is served at 6 PM to get the guests into the evening mood, and a malt tasting is held on Thursday and Sunday evenings during the winter months (we told you this place is fun). Open year round, children and pets are welcome.

Ashley Manor

$$$ • 3660 Rt. 6A, Barnstable • 362-8044

Built in 1699, Ashley Manor is an elegant Cape Cod inn offering warm hospitality and distinctive surroundings. Behind huge privet hedges rests a 2-acre estate featuring beautiful gardens, an enchanting gazebo and at the far end of the property, a regulation tennis court. Inside, the inn offers antique wainscoting, an original beehive oven, a secret passageway (what old country manor doesn't have one?) and six guest rooms, including two double-bed rooms and four suites. One of the suites is the Garden Cottage, which has a fireplace, kitchenette and private terrace.

The intimate guest rooms are furnished with antiques, and all except one offer working fireplaces — a delightful touch on a cool September evening. All the rooms have private baths and air conditioning. Charming innkeeper Donald Bain serves a gourmet breakfast of freshly squeezed juice and homemade hot breads followed by crepes or quiche either in the dining room or out on the terrace. Within walking distance of Barnstable Village center and the harbor, the Ashley Manor is a gem of an inn and is open year round. Children 14 years of age and older are welcome.

Beechwood

$$$ • 2839 Main St. (Rt. 6A), Barnstable • 362-6618, (800) 609-6618

Victorian Cape Cod comes alive at the Beechwood Inn in historic Barnstable. This Queen Anne-style home and its seven guest rooms have been fully and authentically restored, hearkening to a time of grace and elegance when there was time to sit, relax and rejoice in the simple wonders of life. Guests from around the world delight in the century-old weeping beech tree that lent the inn its name, the sprawling lawn, the 10-foot privet hedge and wraparound veranda with comfortable rockers, antiques-filled rooms and huge canopied beds.

Built in 1853, this Victorian home has fireplaces in the dining room and parlor, where afternoon tea, cocoa and coffee are served. Some rooms also have fireplaces, and some have views of Cape Cod Bay. All rooms have private baths. The rich tones of natural wood throughout the inn are set off beautifully by Oriental rugs, armoires and antique furnishings.

Innkeepers Ken and Debbie Traugot serve a three-course gourmet breakfast that draws rave reviews for such items as raspberry bread, banana-chocolate chip muffins and more than 30 different entrees, including tomato pastry puff eggs and apple harvest pancakes. The Beechwood, which is just down the road from Barnstable village, its harbor and area beaches, is open year round. The inn cannot accommodate children.

The Lamb and Lion Inn

$$-$$$ • 2504 Main St. (Rt. 6A), Barnstable • 362-6823

Innkeeper Donald McKeag purchased this inn in 1996 and has been busy renovating and redecorating, with truly special results. Originally built in 1740, the 10 guest rooms provide all the modern comforts in a relaxed atmosphere where you can either relax by the lovely outdoor swimming pool or go for a leisurely walk along historic Route 6A.

Set on 3½ acres of land, this cozy complex contains the 240-year-old house, an antique barn (the "Barn-Stable" housing a three-bedroom suite with a living room, kitchen and deck) and inn rooms surrounding the pool. All rooms have private baths. The Sweets are two-bedroom suites with a kitchen, the Lion's Den has a fireplace as well as kitchen, the Lamb's Retreat is a cottage with two bedrooms, living room and kitchen, while the Innkeeper's Pride offers a fireplace, sunken tub and kitchen. A continental breakfast of homemade breads and muffins, fresh fruit, coffee and tea is served. The Lamb and Lion welcomes children age 12 and older and is open year round. The inn also hosts family celebrations, catered luncheons, small wedding parties and small group meetings.

The Acworth Inn

$$ • 4352 Rt. 6A, Cummaquid • 362-3330, (800) 362-6363

Wonderfully charming best describes the Acworth Inn and its pair of innkeepers, Jack and Cheryl Ferrell. The Ferrells instantly make you feel welcome and make you want to return to visit with them again and again. As for the inn itself, the six guest rooms in this 1860 house are bright and airy, each room offering a private bath and triple-sheeted beds (a sheet above and below the blanket as well as on the mattress). Each evening at bedtime guests are met with miniature roses and chocolates. In the morning guests awake to a bountiful continental breakfast of cinnamon rolls, granola and handground buckwheat pancakes.

A clean, uncluttered inn along historic Route 6A with its large trees overhanging the street, the rooms here feature floral bedspreads and lace curtains. The inn attracts visitors from Europe, which helps to lend an international flair to the morning breakfast conversations. Open year round, the inn's central location makes it convenient to the many shops, galleries and restaurants along the winding and picturesque 6A. The Ferrells will lend you their bikes if you wish to pedal the route. Named for the town of Acworth, New Hampshire, the inn welcomes children 12 years and older.

Fox Glen Manor Bed and Breakfast

$$-$$$ • 4011 Main St. (Rt. 6A), Cummaquid • 362-4657

Situated in a private, pastoral setting, the Fox Glen Manor Bed and Breakfast offers a totally unique vacation experience. Upon the grounds of this fabulous 5-acre estate graze some 14 horses. Many celebrities have stayed at the inn to take advantage of its privacy and its beauty.

Fox Glen Manor offers three of the most elegantly eclectic guest rooms you'll ever come across, seemingly a sharp contrast to the rural setting outside where horses run free. Each room has a private bath, while one of the three rooms has a working fireplace. Marble, antique porcelain, Oriental rugs and classic artwork abound throughout the Manor, set off against salmon-colored walls (innkeeper Doug Kelly mixes his own colors).

The handsomely appointed accommodations include a honeymoon suite with a private entrance and deck. Kelly serves a continental breakfast of fresh juice, breads and delicious Belgian waffles. Have your morning meal while you watch the horses out on the lawn eating apples. The Fox Glen Manor is open from May 1 to November 1 and can't accommodate children.

Captain Farris House

$$$ • 308 Old Main St., South Yarmouth • 760-2818, (800) 350-9477

There is a point where a house approaches a piece of art, and the Captain Farris House is such a case. Located in an historic section of South Yarmouth known as Bass River, the house was built in 1845. This former sea captain's house was purchased last year by Stephen and Patty Bronstein, and what a jewel it is. A perfect blend of antique and contemporary, the inn has eight magnificent rooms, all with private baths, six with Jacuzzis.

Two suites upstairs feature sunken bathrooms, queen-size beds, a living room and upscale European flair. One room offers a king-size bed, double Jacuzzi and a private entrance, while the least expensive room in the house (in the mid-$$ range) has a private entrance, antiques and absolutely gorgeous draperies. Two large rooms upstairs have large four-poster canopy beds and fireplaces. The Captain Farris House is on the National Register of Historic Places and exudes all the warmth and color you expect in a top-notch bed and breakfast. Full gourmet three-course breakfasts are served either in the dining room

INSIDERS' TIP

If staying at a bed and breakfast or inn makes you think you'd like to be an innkeeper yourself, do your homework before you jump into anything. Several people on the Cape offer seminars on innkeeping designed to help you decide if the innkeeping lifestyle is for you and, if you decide it is, how to go about getting into it. One resource is "Innkeeping From the Innside," a seminar offered four times a year by Carol and Tom Edmondson, owners of The Captain Freeman Inn in Brewster, (800) 843-4664. Another is Liberty Hill Inn in Yarmouthport, (800) 821-3977, where innkeepers Beth and Jack Flanigan bring in legal and financial experts to round out the innkeeping seminars they offer three times a year in the spring and fall.

or outside in the courtyard or on the veranda. Candlelight dinners are served to guests during the off-season with advance notice. Afternoon refreshments are also served. Next door is the Elisha Jenkins House, which has a huge suite. The inn is open year round, and children age 11 and older are welcome.

Seaside

$$-$$$ • 135 S. Shore Dr., South Yarmouth • 398-2533

Seaside's rental cottages have been a part of Cape Cod summers for more than three decades. All individually owned condominium units, each reflects the personality of its owner. All units benefit from full housekeeping service providing clean linens, towels and even beach towels. Seaside has 45 units available, 43 of which are one- or two-room efficiencies with the remaining two being efficiency motel units. Like a little village on Nantucket Sound, Seaside has some 475 feet of beach. Open from early May to late October, Seaside welcomes children.

Liberty Hill Inn

$$-$$$ • 77 Main St. (Rt. 6A), Yarmouthport • 362-3976, (888) 821-3977

Yarmouthport is a tranquil Cape Cod village with history dating back to 1638, when the first settlers attempted to conquer the vast wilderness (the town was incorporated in 1639). Part of that tranquility can be found at the Liberty Hill Inn. Located in the heart of the village, the inn is just a short, leisurely stroll away from picturesque country lanes, outstanding restaurants, interesting antiques and gift shops and a number of historical attractions. Built by a shipbuilder in 1825, this handsome Greek Revival with five lovely guest rooms evokes the romance and elegance of the past centuries with its wide floorboards, chandeliers and antiques. Some rooms have four-poster beds, one has twin beds, and all have private bathrooms and air conditioning. Rooms range from the Roscommon Room, with a queen-size bed, white wicker chairs and white eyelet and lace, to the Waterford Room with a grand king-size bed, an extra large bath and views of Cape Cod Bay.

Innkeepers Beth and Jack Flanagan are accomplished cooks, so breakfast is a popular part of day, particularly when Irish apple pastry or Jack's special French toast are on the menu. Some of Beth's favorite recipes are included in her book, *Cape Cod Bed and Breakfast Guide and Innkeepers Recipes*, now in its third printing. The inn is open year round, and children are welcome.

The Village Inn

$$ • 92 Main St. (Rt. 6A), Yarmouthport • 362-3182

Esther Hickey has been the innkeeper here for more than 40 years. Her wonderfully authentic home, built about 20 years after the start of the American Revolution, has wide floorboards, claw-foot tubs, original fireplaces and a great screened-in porch with a nice private backyard. The inn is listed on the National Register of Historic Places.

The 10 rooms here, all doubles (eight with private baths, two with shared), are spacious and comfortable. One bathroom even has a fireplace. The inn also has two sitting rooms available to guests. Children and pets are welcome. Esther serves a traditional full breakfast, complete with oatmeal, eggs and bacon.

The inn is convenient to all of the Mid-Cape attractions. Guests go antiquing, shopping and to the beach and theater. There's much to see within walking distance. Many of the inn's guests come back season after season, a testament to Esther's congenial approach to innkeeping. The Village Inn is open year round.

Wedgewood Inn

$$$ • 83 Main St. (Rt. 6A), Yarmouthport • 362-5157

Built c.1812, this elegant inn located on a knoll overlooking Yarmouthport village is a gem among gems. The guest rooms here are warm and romantic, seven of the nine rooms have working fireplaces. The house is a proud representative from the 19th-century world of our Cape Cod ancestors. The grounds are beautiful — tiered lawns traced with Yankee stone walls and large old maple trees. "Distinctive Lodging" reads the gold beveled lettering on the Wedgewood blue sign out front, and distinctive lodging is what you will receive.

The guest rooms are breathtaking and feature handmade quilts, shuttered windows, and authentic and reproduction antiques throughout. The deluxe accommodations in double rooms and suites offer comfort, privacy and air-conditioning. One east-facing suite has a large bedroom, sitting room, private bath and porch with a view of the gardens and gazebo. In 1997 owners Milt and Gerrie Graham will be opening the renovated barn behind the inn. This will include three of the inn's nine guest rooms. These new rooms will include a private porch.

Wonderful full breakfasts featuring Belgian waffles and blueberry muffins begin the day on the right foot for a full agenda of antiquing, bike riding and sightseeing. The Wedgewood Inn, which is open year round, welcomes children age 10 and older.

The Four Chimneys Inn

$$ • 946 Main St. (Rt. 6A), Dennis • 385-6317, (800) 874-5502

Built in the late 1870s, the Four Chimney Inn is a lovely bed and breakfast along the beautiful and historic Route 6A. A few years ago, Russell and Kathy Tomasetti bought this three-story Victorian house and turned it into one of the Cape's loveliest inns.

Each of the eight guest room's doors bears a hand-embroidered plaque featuring such names as Bayberry, Teaberry, Blueberry and Rosehip. Each room is as different as its name: Some have cherry four-poster beds; others have wicker beds; and still others have antique oak or pine beds. Two rooms have canopy beds. Four rooms have views of Scargo Lake just across the street. All rooms have a private bath. You can read up on the house's history in the detailed account Kathy has put together and keeps in the common room.

An expanded continental breakfast is served on the screen porch or in the dining room if the weather is cool. Lush grounds surround the property, which is just a couple of minutes' ride away from area beaches and a leisurely stroll to Dennis village and its many antiques shops. The Four Chimneys Inn is open from May to the end of October. Children 10 and older are welcome.

Isaiah Hall Bed and Breakfast

$$ • 152 Whig St., Dennis • 385-9928, (800) 736-0160

Along the quiet, less traveled Whig Street is where you'll find the wonderful Isaiah Hall Bed and Breakfast, named for a 19th-century cooper. Hall's brother Henry is credited with developing cranberry cultivation on Cape Cod back in 1814. Isaiah, realizing how successful these cultivated cranberries would become, began producing barrels in large volume. In fact, Isaiah Hall's barrel size is still the accepted unit of measure for the cranberries that are bought and sold today on the open market.

This 1857 Greek Revival farmhouse has 10 rooms, all with private baths. One room is a suite. These rooms are in the main and carriage houses, the latter featuring stenciled walls, white wicker and knotty pine furniture, and some have small balconies.

Friendly innkeeper Marie Brophy serves a delightful extended continental breakfast featuring home-baked breads, muffins and local jams at the dining room's gorgeous 12-foot cherry table. After breakfast, take a stroll through the wonderful gardens or perhaps down to Corporation Beach for a day of sun, sand and surf. Also within walking distance is America's oldest summer theater, the Cape Playhouse as well as all of Dennis village. It's open from mid-April to mid-October, and children 7 and older are welcome.

Captain Nickerson Inn

$-$$ • 333 Main St., South Dennis • 398-5966, (800) 282-1619

The Old South Dennis Historical District with its many beautifully restored sea captains homes and village green, small gingerbread cottage library and magnificent Congregational Church are all yours when you stay at the Captain Nickerson Inn. Built as a Cape half house in 1828, it was redesigned to its current Queen Anne style in 1879 courtesy of Captain Miller Whelden Nickerson. In fact, so complete were these renovations that the original ground-floor keeping room of the half house is now a bedroom on the second floor.

Located just five minutes from all the attractions of Dennis including area beaches, two golf courses and the beginning of the Cape Cod Rail Trail bike path, this wonderful inn features parquet floors, stained-glass windows and fireplaces. The five guest rooms, all on the second floor, are brimming with antiques and period reproductions. Four rooms are named for Nickerson's vessels, the sloops *Elizabeth*, *Hope* and *Susan*, and the schooner *Superior*. The fifth room is the Bridal room which has a queen-size four-poster bed and stained-glass windows. The Hope and Susan rooms share a bath, but the other three rooms have private baths. Guests also have use of the first-floor living room, which is warmed by a fireplace.

Pleasant innkeepers Pat and Dave York, who serve a full complimentary breakfast in their charming dining room, open their beautiful home to guests from the beginning of March to mid December. Children are most welcome

The Lighthouse Inn

$$ • 1 Lighthouse Inn Rd., West Dennis • 398-2244

When we think of summer, we think of West Dennis and the Lighthouse Inn. It is a compound of sorts situated all by itself down at West Dennis Beach, but let's first talk about its history and then discuss its many amenities. The Lighthouse Inn began life in May 1855 as the Bass River Light, the Cape's 15th lighthouse. At that time it consisted of only the very center section of the inn. Though it closed briefly from 1880 to 1881, it remained an important southside lighthouse until 1914 when the opening of the Cape Cod Canal made it obsolete. In 1989, it was recommissioned and is today a working lighthouse from May to October each year. We were given a tour of its tower once, and the view from the top is pretty spectacular.

Accommodations run the gamut from basic rooms and suites in the Main House to oceanfront cottages with decks, fireplaces and comfortable furnishings that sleep as many as six people. All rooms and cottages have a TV, telephone, refrigerator, in-room safe, hair dryer and private bath. Weekly cottage rentals also include daily breakfast and dinner.

On site you will find a tennis court, an outdoor heated swimming pool, a restaurant (known as the Lighthouse Inn, see our Restaurants chapter), a nightclub (the Sand Bar, see our Nightlife chapter) and a private beach with a network of private jetties off which you can cast your line for the blues that run these waters in June. There are arts and crafts classes and sandcastle-building contests and other daily supervised activities for children 3 and older. The Stone family operate the inn from mid-May to mid-October.

By the Sea Guests Bed & Breakfast

$-$$$ • 57 Chase Ave. (also Inman Rd. Ext.), Dennisport • 398-8685, (800) 447-9202

This is certainly a bed and breakfast that lives up to its name. The inn is situated along the coastline of Dennisport, where it has provided guests with seaside accommodations for the past 33 years. Innkeeper Helen Kossifos provides refreshments throughout the day in the form of tea, cocoa, hot coffee, cookies and fruit. A complimentary breakfast of hot and cold cereals, homebaked rolls and pastries is served on the veranda, where salty sea breezes help to awaken you to another fun-filled day on old Cape Cod.

Of the 12 rooms, four are oceanfront and four have ocean views. All rooms have private baths. Larger families can rent the spacious two-room oceanview cottage on a weekly basis. This unit, which accommodates as many as five people, comes with a fully furnished kitchenette. Guests get 10 percent off breakfast and lunch at the on-premises restaurant, Dino's By the Sea. The bed and breakfast is open from the beginning of May to the beginning of December and welcomes children.

The Rose Petal Bed & Breakfast

$$ • 152 Sea St., Dennisport • 398-8470

One end of Sea Street in Dennisport leads to the waters of Nantucket Sound, and the other leads to The Rose Petal Bed & Breakfast tucked away in a neighborhood of century-old houses. The Rose Petal was built in 1872 as the residence of Almond Wixon, whose family was among the original settlers of Dennisport. Wixon himself was among those lost aboard the *Cross Rip* lightship in February 1918, which drifted away on an ice floe, never to be seen again.

Innkeepers Dan and Gayle Kelly completely restored the house in 1986. The Kellys offer guests a choice of three cozy second-floor rooms. Two rooms feature queen-size brass beds (covered with handstitched quilts), antiques and private baths. The third has a private entrance off a large deck and an antique queen-size iron bed and shares a first-floor bath. The elegant dining room is the setting for a full homemade complimentary breakfast featuring homebaked pastries along with your entree. Complimentary beverages are available in the guest refrigerator. The many beaches of Dennisport are close by, and two Dennis golf courses are just a five to 10 minute ride away. It's open year round, and children of all ages are welcome.

The Willows

$-$$$ • 286 Old Wharf Rd., Dennisport • 428-0909

If you're looking for cozy, look no further. This cottage colony consists of two Cape-style cottages and one studio efficiency and is just one-tenth of a mile to private Oak Street Beach. Each of the cottages has either two or four bedrooms, a fully equipped kitchen and fully tiled bathrooms. Other amenities include picnic areas, lawn furniture and even outdoor hot-water showers so you don't track sand into your room. Bring your own linens. The Willows is open from mid-May to mid-September.

Lower Cape

Beechcroft Inn

$$$$ •1360 Main St., Brewster • 896-9534

This old inn oozes character. The 10 rooms are nicely but simply done, with antique furnishings, quilts and tasteful artwork — mostly vintage prints and needlepoint. All the rooms are named after wildflowers indigenous to the Cape; our favorite is the third-floor Queen Anne's Lace, which has a small, private deck and a breathtaking view of Cape Cod Bay.

The 1828 building was Brewster's first Universalist meeting house and was converted to an inn 140 years ago. Innkeepers Celeste and Bob Hunt, who bought the inn two years ago, keep up the tradition with warm New England hospitality, full breakfasts — "I believe in breakfast," Celeste asserts — and extras such as afternoon tea and summer weekend wine tastings on the lawn. The cozy, dark-paneled pub is a popular gathering spot, and in the cooler months you'll find a fire crackling in the hearth. Guests also have use of two sitting rooms. The inn is open year round, and children are welcome. If you feel like dining in, or rather, inn, the intimate dining room is a great option. Open to the public six nights a week in season, and on weekends in winter, the restaurant offers bistro fare, full dinners and an ample wine list.

The Brewster Farmhouse Inn

$$$ • 716 Main St., Brewster • 896-3910, (800) 892-3910

Here you'll experience the best of both worlds: The charm of an old farmhouse with all modern amenities. All five beautifully decorated rooms have air conditioners and private bathrooms with hair dryers, toiletries and thick terrycloth robes. The Shaker Room has a working fireplace, and the Garden Room has a private deck. Outside, beyond the spacious rear deck surrounded by hedges, hydrangeas and gardens, there's a heated pool and a hot tub that can be used year round. The 2-acre property has an apple orchard and is right across the road from a historic windmill and the park-like Drummer Boy property that's the site of Sunday evening band concerts in summer.

Carol and Gary Concors, who bought the inn in 1996 both love to cook, so you can look forward to a full, gourmet breakfast every morning. It's served in the cathedral-ceiling common room or outside on the deck. Children older than 14 are welcome. The inn is open year round.

The Captain Freeman Inn

$$$ • 15 Breakwater Rd., Brewster • 896-7481, (800) 843-4664

This inn has it all: a great location, historic ambiance and incredible food. The former sea captain's mansion has 12 guest rooms, all furnished with canopy beds and antiques. Luxury suites feature small enclosed porches with private whirlpools and fireplaces. Nine rooms have private baths, three share baths. Built in the 1860s, the house features wonderful architectural details such as ornate plaster moldings and ceiling medallions imported from Italy, wood floors showcasing a herringbone pattern and 12-foot ceilings and windows.

Breakwater Beach on Cape Cod Bay is a short walk away, but if you're not in the mood for salt water, take a dip in the pool. Play badminton or croquet on the lawn, take a spin on one of the inn's bicycles or just sit in a rocker on the front porch. Innkeepers Carol and Tom Edmondson offer special weekend cooking classes in winter — Carol is a graduate of the Grand Master Chef program and has written two cookbooks. Ask about specially priced packages that combine classes and accommodations. Open year round, this is a totally nonsmoking property and accepts children 10 and older.

The Inn at the Egg

$$$ • 1944 Main St., Brewster • 896-3123

Opened in 1990, this is one of Brewster's newest "oldest" inns. Formerly the site of the First Parish Church Parsonage, it was home to famous author and parish preacher Horatio Alger Jr. in the late 1800s. Our favorite room here (actually, a suite) is the one named for him that boasts a four-poster pine bed. Each of the inn's other four rooms is named for a town building — the Brewster Ladies' Library room, for instance, is brimming with books. Linger over one of innkeeper Joan Vergnani's homemade candlelit breakfasts, then stroll through town and soak in the charm that has made Brewster one of the Cape's most cherished experiences. The inn is open year round. The inn takes its name from the triangular, grassy park just across the road whose oval, concave contours make it appear as if a giant egg had been resting there. Now you don't have to wonder what on earth the locals are talking about when they refer to the Egg!

Linger Longer By The Sea

$$$ • 261 Linnell Landing Rd., Brewster • 896-3451, 240-2211

The 1907 main building, whose lawn is ringed by a moss-covered stone wall at the edge of Cape Cod bay, conjures up visions of turn-of-the-century seaside grandeur. It now houses six apartments and is flanked by 10 cottages, seven of which also sit directly on the bay. Relax on your private deck and watch the sun set over the shimmering flats at low tide, go to sleep to the calming sound of water lapping the beach outside your door and step out for a morning swim. You'll definitely want to linger here.

All units have fully equipped kitchens, color TV, living rooms, bedrooms and bathrooms with tubs and showers. Cribs and high chairs are provided free on request. You'll have the benefit of a private beach, and the cottages have picnics tables and charcoal grills. Tired of the beach? Use the newly installed professional putting green, take a walk at nearby Nickerson State Park or ride the Cape Cod Rail Trail bike path. Also close by are shops and restaurants. Linger Longer is open from late April to early December. Most of the units are winterized, so you'll be cozy and warm during off-season visits. Cottages 8 and 9 have fireplaces.

Old Sea Pines Inn

$-$$ • 2553 Main St., Brewster • 896-6114

This is the kind of place you'd imagine in a grainy black-and-white movie with Joan Crawford driving up to drop off her rebellious daughter on the wraparound veranda. And you wouldn't be all that far off. In 1907 the inn was

INSIDERS' TIP

One of the advantages of staying at a small inn or bed and breakfast is a proximity to at least one Insider and in most cases two. Innkeepers are usually happy to answer questions and give advice about where to shop, dine and sightsee. Not only do they live here, but they've also had the benefit of reports from other guests. Take advantage of their knowledge and experience.

founded as the Sea Pines School of Charm and Personality for Young Women.

Today, all the charm and personality remains. Just witness the Priscilla curtains, rocking chairs, green wicker furniture, brass and iron beds and framed old photographs dotting the wallpapered walls. And as would befit a former girls' charm school, the TVs have all been painted pink. Some of the inn's 22 rooms, especially the five with shared baths, are small, but at this price, who's complaining? You can also opt for one of the more modern rooms in the adjacent North Cottage.

Don't forget to sample innkeeper Steve Rowan's grandmother-style cooking — full breakfasts are served every morning. The inn, open year-round, also does rehearsal dinners and weddings. Good news for families: Young children are welcome in the inn's two family suites. And good news for culture-craving adults: The inn stages wonderful Sunday evening dinner theater all summer, beginning in June, in conjunction with Cape Rep Theatre Company.

Pepper House Inn

$$$ • 2026 Main St., Brewster • 896-4389

Built in 1793, this Federal Colonial-style sea captain's home is right near the center of town, so you can stroll down lovely Route 6A and visit antiques shops, galleries and craft studios. Beaches and other attractions are just a short drive away. But you may be tempted to just sit out on the back deck listening to the church bell toll the hour and letting the breeze, fragrant with roses and honeysuckle, lull you to sleep.

All four guest rooms have private baths, decorative fireplaces, television and air conditioning, and are furnished with antiques and reproductions. The four-poster and canopied beds are covered with soft quilts and pillows, and the decor is understated and tasteful. A full, homemade breakfast is served on the deck or in the common room, as are afternoon refreshments. The Pepper House is open year round.

The Ruddy Turnstone

$$$ • 463 Main St., Brewster • 385-9871, (800) 654-1995

Set back from the road on 3 acres of land, this lovingly restored 200-year-old house offers a tranquil respite from the rest of the world, yet is centrally located. Shops, attractions and beaches are only a short drive away, but as innkeeper Sally Swanson puts it, "It's really quiet here." The Ruddy Turnstone has five guest rooms, all with private baths and queen beds. Three rooms are in the main house and two are in the carriage house, where Sally and her husband Gordon formerly ran an antiques shop. There are still plenty of antiques furnishing the rooms and common areas. The common room has a television along with a fireplace, board games and books, but the rooms are TV-free. Guests are treated to a full breakfast. The property enjoys marsh views and glimpses of Cape Cod Bay. The hammocks out back are popular spots for relaxation. The Ruddy Turnstone is open most of the year, but closes in January and February.

Augustus Snow House

$$$ • 528 Main St., Harwichport • 430-0528

This inn is as Victorian as they come: One look at the wraparound veranda, gazebo and round turrets and you'll wish you packed your parasol and top hat. Not to worry, this turn-of-the-century house is equipped with modern comforts along with Victorian charm. Each of the five beautifully decorated rooms has a television and ceiling fan; three have air conditioners. Belle's Room (all the rooms have fittingly feminine names) is actually a suite with its own entrance and Jacuzzi tub. Two other rooms have Jacuzzi tubs, and all have spectacular bathrooms with unusual features such as marble or tin sinks, a clawfoot tub and in one, a marble commode!

Guests are treated to a full breakfast, served in the sunny porch or outside on the brick patio. Afternoon tea is a local tradition here, and the downstairs with its brick walls and charmingly mismatched tea cups, is open to the public for tea on Wednesday, Thursday and Saturday all year, with special evening Victorian presentation teas scheduled periodically. Open year round, the inn is within walking distance of the beach and Main Street shops.

Cape Cod Claddagh

$$ • 77 Main St., West Harwich • 432-9628, (800) 356-9628

You don't need the luck of the Irish to find this conveniently located inn, which is reminiscent of a small Irish manor, complete with antiques, Oriental rugs and lace curtains. The main house contains six guest rooms, each with a private bath. A small cottage set in the pines features two rooms with king-size beds. All the rooms have televisions, air-conditioning and heat. The inn is open April through December. Beaches are not far, and if you're in the mood for a non-saltwater swim, the Claddagh has a pool. The inn has a three separate dining areas, including a pub — stop in for what innkeeper Eileen Connell promises is "the best Guinness on Cape Cod" — the romantic art gallery Blarney Room and the more formal, nonsmoking Kerry Room, where an Irish breakfast is served each morning.

The Commodore Inn

$$$ • 30 Earle Rd., West Harwich • 432-1180, (800) 368-1180

White sandy beaches, with lifeguards on duty, are just yards away from this delightful little complex. All 27 rooms have been recently redone in crisp white and blue florals, and have private baths, refrigerators, air-conditioning and private patios overlooking the heated pool. Some rooms also have Jacuzzi tubs, gas fireplaces and wet bars. All rooms can adjoin, so it's easy to create a family suite. The grounds bloom with purple and white impatiens, hydrangeas and other flowers. Inside, the summer-fresh feeling continues with a lobby that's a study in green, red and blue wicker. Guests are treated to an unbeatable all-you-can-eat breakfast buffet — and brunch on Sundays — at the on-site eatery Raspberries, which is also open to the public for its famous breakfasts. The Commodore Inn is open April through Thanksgiving and welcomes children.

Dunscroft Inn

$$$ • 24 Pilgrim Rd., Harwichport • 432-0810, (800) 432-4345

Ah, romance! You'll find it here in bright rooms furnished with canopy beds, plump pillows and lace curtains. Framed love poems adorn the walls, and books of poetry are set by each bed. Information about checkout times, breakfast and the like is presented in the form of a framed letter in each room addressed to a pair of famous lovers ("Dear Robert and Elizabeth," begins the note in our favorite room). Built as a private estate in 1920, the inn has eight beautiful guest rooms in the main house, two of which have private entrances, and a separate suite with a fireplace just beyond the brick patio and garden. Guests enjoy a full breakfast in the dining room and can relax in the comfortable common room with French doors that open onto an enclosed sun porch. There's a lovely ocean breeze here, as the inn is only a stroll away from a mile-long private beach on Nantucket Sound. Open year round, it is also close to Main Street shops.

Resident innkeepers Alyce and Wally Cunningham also run the Wishing Well Motel, 212 Main Street, West Harwich, 432-2150. The 20-unit motel offers full or queen-size beds, private baths and color TV. The grounds have picnic tables, charcoal grills and a large swimming pool.

The Gingerbread House

$$ • 141 Division St., West Harwich • 432-1901, (800) 788-1901

This grand old house, built in 1883, is a classic example of Victorian architecture. Surrounded by country gardens, the gingerbread-trimmed house has five roomy guest rooms, including several suites suitable for families. Proprietors Stacia and Les Kostecki meld Victorian charm with the decor of their native Poland — woodcrafts, crystal and various objets d'art enhance the rooms. The breakfast room features carved wood walls and antiques, but you may be more riveted by the food. Stacia, who is such a good cook she opened a tea room in the adjacent barn, serves up full breakfasts and afternoon tea. In 1997 the tea room was set to begin serving dinners as well. Stacia and her mother whip up incredibly light scones and serve them with real imported Devon clotted cream. The inn, open year round, is close to town and convenient to area attractions. Children are welcome.

Harbor Breezes

$$-$$$ • 326 Lower County Rd., Harwichport • 432-0337, (800) 272-4343

Right near Allen Harbor and a short stroll from a town beach, this relaxing little hideaway has a cottage-like feel, with a series of cedar-shake additions behind the main Cape Cod house forming the guest wing. In a quiet, residential neighborhood, it's just a half-mile away from shops and family activities. All nine guest rooms have private decks and entrances, private baths, small refrigerators and color televisions. A few have air-conditioning, but it isn't really needed here where the ocean breeze blows in across the harbor. The grounds are pretty, with ivy, lilacs, perennial beds and shady pines complemented by hanging baskets of flowers.

Innkeepers Kathleen and David VanGelder, who completely renovated the property when they bought it 12 years ago, offer friendly hospitality and are happy to help guests plan day trips and activities. A charming breakfast room, which overlooks the pool, is open every morning for a hearty continental breakfast that always includes something homebaked. Guests are welcome to borrow beach towels, beach blankets and small coolers. Children of all ages are welcome here, and double suites for families are available — but couples without children will have plenty of privacy since the unique layout allows for it. Open year-round, Harbor Breeze offers special packages in the off-season, and some good deals in summer as well.

West Pines Cottages

$ • 207 Division St., West Harwich • 432-1931

Owners Harold and Lois Schiorring like to say their eight cottages are "exclusive, but not expensive." At $250 a week in-season for a three-bedroom cottage, we think it's a steal! Three cottages have two bedrooms, the rest have three and all come with private baths. Kids will love this place. Scattered across 5 acres of pine groves and apple trees, you'll discover every imaginable activity, from badminton to horseshoes and hammock swinging to hammock snoozing. The Schiorrings, who have been renting the cottages 42 years, get a lot of returning guests. The inn closes during the winter months.

Bradford Inn and Motel

$$$$ • 26 Cross St., Chatham • 945-1030, (800) 242-8426

This property is almost a village unto itself. With 32 guest rooms in seven buildings, there are accommodations to suit just about anyone's needs and tastes. Choose a suite in the Bradford House, Mulberry Inn, Jonathon Gray House or the motel-style Captain's Row, which resembles a motel from the outside but has lovely, inn-like rooms. Or stay down the street at the Azubah Atwood Inn, a 1789 sea captain's house with a screened porch and cozy parlor. Just steps away from tempting Main Street shops, The Bradford House has a quiet church for its closest neighbor — in fact, you can see three church steeples from the property. All of the rooms have private baths, phones, televisions, radios, small refrigerators and air-conditioning.

We favor the luxurious second-floor suite in the Captain Elijah Smith House, which has a sitting room, fireplace, Jacuzzi, private deck and a roomy bedroom overlooking the pool. On the main floor of the historic house, which once stood near Chatham Light, is Champlain's restaurant, serving dinner to the public May through October. Guests are treated to a full, gourmet breakfast in the restaurant that is also open to the public and is a real favorite among locals. In summer, you can enjoy breakfast on the patio, which is also a nice place to enjoy a cocktail in the evening. When the air is nippy, relax by the fireplace in the Lion's Den. More than half the rooms are nonsmoking, as are the dining areas. The inn is open year round, and children 7 and older are welcome.

The Cranberry Inn

$$$$ • 359 Main St., Chatham • 945-9232

Live in the lap of luxury during your stay at Chatham's oldest inn, a grand 1830s building updated with modern comforts such as private baths, air conditioning, telephones and remote-control televisions in every room. Many of the 18 rooms also have working fireplaces, private balconies and wet bars, and all are tastefully decorated and furnished with antiques and reproductions. Guests are pampered with triple sheeting on the beds, feather and foam pillows, cotton towels and cut glassware. You'll want to spend time in the common rooms, decorated with Oriental rugs and fine art from all corners of the world, but the wood-paneled pub is especially inviting, with elegant wooden chess and Monopoly sets.

A full buffet-style breakfast is served in the bright dining room, and afternoon tea is a tradition here. You can sit in a rocker on the wide front porch, stroll to the beach or shops — both within walking distance — or, if you're feeling ambitious, walk the nature trail behind the inn, which circles an old cranberry bog and Mill Pond and eventually leads to the ocean. The Cranberry Inn is open year round and welcomes children older than 8.

Cyrus Kent House

$$$ • 63 Cross St., Chatham • 945-9104

Tasteful, classy and historic, the Cyrus Kent House enjoys a wonderful location tucked away on a quiet street yet within walking distance of town. This stately 1877 home has 11 rooms, all with private baths, televisions and phones; some have air-conditioning and three have fireplaces. With tall windows that let in lots of light, the rooms are beautifully done in muted tones that enhance the historic ambiance. Framed wildflower prints hang on the walls above four-poster beds, and fresh flowers grace each room. Two suites contained in the adjacent carriage house make perfect honeymoon hideaways. We especially like Room 5 in the main house, with its private entrance, slanting beams and unique gingerbread trim.

Innkeeper Sharon Mitchell Swan is as gracious as the inn itself and encourages guests to mingle. In summer, iced tea is served on the porch, and in winter, there are evening wine and cheese gatherings in the large living room, with its marble fireplace and piano. A continental-plus breakfast is served each morning in the dining room or, in warm weather, on the deck that overlooks a meticulous lawn edged with gardens. The inn is open year round and welcomes children 10 and older.

J.B. Horne Cottages

$$$ • Morris Island Rd., Chatham • 945-0734, in winter (803) 837-7477

Muriel Horne describes this retreat launched by her husband's family in 1927 as one of the nicest beach colonies on one of the best beaches on the Cape — and who would argue? Each of the cozy cottages features pine-paneled interiors, a living room with a fireplace, dinette, kitchen, bath and shower and between two and four bedrooms. The cottages are fully furnished except for linens and towels, and are scrupulously clean. Six of the eight cottages are right on the beach, and one of the two on higher ground is more house than cottage. In season, there's a two-week minimum, and the Hornes start booking in January, so call early. Rates include gas, electricity, rubbish collection and use of a gorgeous private beach. The cottages are open from early May to mid-October.

The Moorings

$$$ • 326 Main St., Chatham • 945-0848, (800) 320-0848

Welcome to the home of Admiral Charles Rockwell — well, former home — but the spirit of the 19th-century seafarer lives on in this grand old house, built in 1860. The living room, which the Admiral designed to resemble the interior of a ship, features gorgeous wood paneling, a carved mantelpiece and arched doorways. It's the perfect place to curl up with a book or play cards at the table by the bay window. The main house has five guest rooms, each charming in its own way. We especially like the second-floor Admiral's Room, which has a working fireplace framed by a beautiful handcarved mantel with built-in mirror.

Behind the house are one-, two- and three-bedroom efficiency units and a private cottage (rented by the week) with its own deck, full kitchen and a washer/dryer. Guests in all the rooms gather each morning for a generous continental breakfast in the dining room, and guests are welcome to use one of the inn's bicycles or borrow a beach chair. All this is in easy walking distance of both shops and beaches! The main house is open year round. Children cannot be accommodated in the main house, but they are welcome in some of the other units.

Old Harbor Inn

$$$ • 22 Old Harbor Rd., Chatham
• 945-4434

Sunshine streams through the windows, and the smell of fresh-baked muffins wafts from the kitchen of this 1930 doctor's home/office turned bed and breakfast. Homey as can be, the Old Harbor Inn has a lovely living room complete with a baby grand piano where guests can gather. But new innkeeper Judy Braz, who bought the place with her husband, Ray, in 1996, confesses that many guests like to pull up a tall chair at the huge island-table in the kitchen, have a cup of coffee and chat. The Brazes don't mind a bit; they're friendly people who have a way of making you feel comfortable right away.

The rooms are comfortable and beautifully decorated, à la Laura Ashley. Rich florals, white wicker and English country furnishings prevail in the eight guest rooms, each with a private bath. Our favorite room is Port Fortune, named for Chatham's original moniker and featuring low, white-painted beams, a skylit bath and a secret-room feeling. Some rooms have gas fireplaces and all are air-conditioned. A continental buffet breakfast (don't miss Mrs. Braz's banana bread!) is served in a lovely sunroom, or you can eat outside on the deck, which is partially shaded by a great old cherry tree whose blossoms alone make a springtime visit worthwhile. On a quiet street close to town, the inn is open year round and welcomes children 14 and older.

The Queen Anne Inn

$$$ • 70 Queen Anne Rd., Chatham
• 945-0394, (800) 545-INNS

If you're looking for a historic landmark with the recreational amenities of a resort, look no further. The Queen Anne Inn, built in the 1840s by a sea captain for his daughter, has been an inn since 1874 and is one of Chatham's — even the Cape's — loveliest treasures. Though it's part of the Romantik Hotel chain, innkeeper Gunther Weinkopf offers nothing but personal, classy touches. Each of the 30 rooms features a private bath and varies in size, decor and price. For instance, the Duplex Suite (our favorite) has a staircase leading to a Jacuzzi on the upper level. The inn has three tennis courts and a lovely outdoor pool, not to mention an indoor whirlpool and a fine restaurant. Children are welcome. The inn is open full-time April through November, and for weekends only February through March.

Hillbourne House

$$$ • 654 Chatham Rd., South Orleans
• 255-0780

Stay here and the history lesson's free. This 1798 home was used during the Civil War as one of the several stops of the Underground Railroad. A circular stone hiding place, used by slaves on their way to freedom in Canada, is still visible beneath a trap door in the common room.

INSIDERS' TIP

For the best of both worlds — warm weather and no crowds — schedule a Cape Cod vacation in early June. It's often warm enough for sunbathing, and it's still relatively quiet because families with children don't arrive until after school lets out. Plus, everything is open for business — minus the crowds!

The common room and three of the guest rooms have gorgeous views of Pleasant Bay, which is just across the road. In addition to five guest rooms in the main house, the adjacent Paddock has three rooms, each just as cozy and comfortable. Open year round, Hillbourne House offers a complimentary deluxe continental breakfast. If you wish hard enough, perhaps innkeeper Barbara Hayes will make her special Dutch oven pancakes with cinnamon syrup.

Morgan's Way

$$, no credit cards • 9 Morgan's Way, Orleans • 255-0831

Drive up the winding road from Route 28 and you're suddenly in a quiet, rural world, where sheep graze on neighboring pastures and rolling hills overlook acres of woods. This small, secluded bed and breakfast offers casual luxury in a beautiful setting and heavenly quiet. Isolated as it seems, Morgan's Way is only a short drive to downtown Orleans, beaches and other attractions. But you may not want to leave at all. The two lovely guest rooms in the main house, a sprawling contemporary furnished with antiques, both have private baths. The Greenhouse Room, in green and rose floral, connects to a small greenhouse that opens onto the pool and deck area. The periwinkle and white Blue Room, on the second floor (accessible by a wooden spiral staircase), overlooks the pool and garden. Then there's the poolside guesthouse, a private oasis with glass walls, a full kitchen (with dishwasher!), loft bedroom and private deck.

Guests have use of two common rooms — one upstairs and one down — as well as a spacious deck that offers panoramic views of wetlands and woods of the 5-acre grounds. Innkeeper Page MacMahan serves up a full gourmet breakfast and is happy to accommodate special diets. Morgan's Way is open year round.

The Nauset House Inn

$$-$$$ • 143 Beach Rd., East Orleans • 255-2195

One of the nicest inns we've seen, the Nauset House has 14 charming guest rooms, imaginatively yet simply done, furnished with antique and handpainted furniture. Rich shades of antique blue, green and berry coat the wide floor boards, and wood paneling and antique quilts hang beneath hand-stenciled wall borders. Four-poster beds are invitingly covered with quilts and pillows. The large common room in this 1810 house is set up with several intimate sitting areas for sociable conversation or solitary reading by the fireplace. Past the brick-floored breakfast room is an enchanting greenhouse conservatory, where ivy climbs the glass walls, fragrant camellias hover near wicker chairs and grapes ripen on the arbor above the entrance.

Innkeeper Diane Johnson's breakfasts are well-worth the extra charge and so popular that she has compiled several cookbooks for those who want to try her ginger pancakes, Portugese omelets, fruit torte and oatmeal butterscotch muffins at home. The inn is open April through October and welcomes children 12 and older.

The Parsonage Inn

$$ • 202 Main St., East Orleans • 255-8217

Built around 1770, this house still has its original wide floorboards and the tranquility of the 19th-century parsonage it once was. The eight guest rooms, each with a private bath, are furnished with country antiques and decorated simply with hand-stenciling, quilts and fresh flowers. Each room is a bit different, but all are quietly pretty. We especially like the room called the Barn, in the adjacent outbuilding, which features old, rough-hewn beams and a fencepost bed, along with its own refrigerator and sitting area.

Innkeepers Ian and Elizabeth Browne serve a hearty morning meal in the charming little breakfast room or outside on the brick patio. You can also opt to breakfast in your room. The offerings usually include pancakes, waffles or French toast. Later in the day, enjoy refreshments in the parlor, play the piano or relax in front of the fire. Just a mile and a half from Nauset Beach, the Parsonage is also close to shops, restaurants and galleries, and is open year round. Children older than 6 are welcome.

FYI

Unless otherwise noted, the area code for all phone numbers in this guide is 508.

Ship's Knees Inn

$$ • 186 Beach Rd., East Orleans • 255-1312

This restored 1820 sea captain's home is just steps away from Nauset Beach and enjoys beautiful ocean views and ocean air. The rooms are cozy and comfortable, with a homey, old-fashioned feel and no pretenses. Most rooms have TVs, air-conditioning and refrigerators. You can also opt for a one-bedroom apartment with its own deck and water view or one of two heated cottages with decks, fireplaces, kitchens and living rooms.

A continental breakfast is served on the patio, which gets a lovely sea breeze, or in the common room. The inn has a pool and tennis courts, is open year round and welcomes children 12 and older. Ship's Knees also operates the Cove House, 3 miles away on Town Cove in Orleans, with three guest rooms, a one-bedroom efficiency and two cottages with fireplaces.

The Green Heron

$$, no credit cards • 45 Wild Goose Ln., North Eastham • 255-5753

A truly private getaway, the Green Heron offers just one guest room, a second-floor suite with its own entrance and private deck overlooking a heated pool and lush gardens. Crisp and bright, with cathedral ceilings, skylights and ceiling fans, the suite has a television and its own kitchenette, complete with refrigerator and coffee maker, that is stocked every day by your hosts, Suzanne and Carl Goodrich. Have breakfast out by the pool, on the deck or in your room. In the early evening, the Goodriches serve wine or the cocktail of your choice — a nice personal touch that will make you feel even more at home.

Just a short walk away from the Cape Cod National Seashore Visitor Center, the Green Heron is right near the bike trail and provides two bicycles for guests to use. Open June 15 to October 12, the Green Heron also has a cottage beyond the pool that is rented by the week. The Green Heron cannot accommodate children.

The Over Look Inn

$$-$$$ • 3085 Rt. 6, Eastham • 255-1886

Combine a gorgeous Victorian building, artistic taste and Scottish charm, and you have the Over Look Inn. Nestled in a wood across from the entrance to the Cape Cod National Seashore, this 1869 place is beautifully decorated, with imaginative colors blending nicely with antique furnishings. The front parlor, for instance, is a rich berry color that complements the mahogany furniture. Lace curtains let in plenty of sun. Or sit in the Churchill room, which innkeeper Nan Aitchison says is the most popular of the inn's several common rooms.

The inn has 11 guest rooms, each with private bath, including a handicapped-accessible suite. Out back is a renovated 18th-century barn that houses three lovely suites. There's even a gift shop, the Wee Hebridean Shop, that sells the finest Scottish woolens. The Aitchisons are proud to say theirs is a TV-free inn — and there's no need for it in this lovely inn, which is filled with art and books and even has a billiard room. (Even if you don't play, visit this room to peruse the Aitchison's collection of Nigerian art.) The Over Look Inn is right next to the bike trail — around the corner is a friendly bike shop where you can rent bikes — and a short pedal away from beaches and area attractions such as the Eastham windmill. The inn is open year round.

Whalewalk Inn

$$$ • 220 Bridge Rd., Eastham • 255-0617

Elegant and accommodating, the Whalewalk offers 12 guest rooms, all beautifully done in pastel colors and furnished with antique reproductions, original art, baskets, throw pillows and fresh flowers. Everything is perfect, and you'll feel perfectly at home with innkeepers Dick and Carolyn Smith and their staff going out of their way to please you. Brownies, shortbread or gingerbread await you in the afternoon when you come in from a day of sightseeing, shopping or beaching it at the nearby National Seashore. Bring your own bottle and stash it in the inn's bar area (equipped with name tags for bottles) to imbibe during the evening social hour, when guests mingle and browse through the inn's library of books, menus from area restaurants and other resources. In the morning, help yourself to coffee and then sit down to a full breakfast in the sunny dining room. Relax in one of several common areas. There is a television available if you really need it, but the rooms are TV-free. Some rooms have sitting rooms and private entrances and some have fireplaces; all have air-conditioning.

To the rear of the main 1830s house is the Guest House, with two suites and a main room (families traveling together often rent the whole building) and the Saltbox, a charming cottage with a fireplace and private patio. The 3½-acre grounds feature impeccable lawns with comfortable Adirondack chairs. The Whalewalk is open from April through November and welcomes children 12 and older.

The Penny House Bed and Breakfast

$$$ • 4885 Rt. 6, North Eastham • 255-6632, (800) 554-1751

Bright as a shiny penny, this welcoming house, set on 2 acres of land, offers 11 comfortable rooms, each with a private bath. In fine weather, sit outside on the roomy brick terrace and watch birds alight in the trees. Don't miss the full breakfast in the dining room, which features the home's original 1690 wide-wood floorboards. "We have people come and ask if they can buy our floorboards," laughs innkeeper Margaret Keith. She points out that the house actually has two sections — the old 1690 portion and what she calls the new section, which dates to 1750.

The rooms, which all have cute names like A Penny Earned and A Pretty Penny, are of varying sizes and rates. Most rooms have air-conditioning or ceiling fans, and one, the Penny Serenade has a fireplace, private entrance and private deck overlooking the terrace — a perfect honeymoon suite! Guests enjoy a small sitting room with refrigerator and wet bar and the Great Room that was added three years ago. Open year round, this inn offers guests afternoon tea in winter and cookies and lemonade in summer. The Penny house is nonsmoking, and children older than 8 are welcome.

Oak Grove Cottages

$$$ • 35 Old County Rd., North Eastham • 255-3284

The name sets the scene for these nine cottages, huddled among groves of towering oaks. It's a relaxing, rural setting, and yet close to shops, restaurants and attractions. A short drive or bike ride away is Nauset Light Beach, part of the Cape Cod National Seashore, and the Cape Cod Rail Trail bike path is also close by. Walk to coffee shops, restaurants and ice cream shops and visit the nearby Wellfleet Flea Market (see our Shopping chapter) and Wellfleet Drive-In (see our Arts and Entertainment chapter). All the cottages are heated, and some have air conditioning. All feature color TVs, fully equipped kitchens, sun decks and patios furnished with chairs, tables and kettle grills. Some cottages even have dishwashers, fireplaces and convertible sofas. There's a laundry facility on the grounds — a big plus! Oak Grove Cottages are open year round.

Cranberry Cottages

$$ • 785 Rt. 6, Eastham • 255-0602

Owners Lisa and Guy Grant are sticklers about offering their guests the best in carefree and comfortable accommodations. Snugly tucked away among locust trees, these two-bedroom cottages are so far apart that privacy is never an issue. Though all cottages offer cooking facilities, we prefer the larger ones (numbers 11, 12, 13 and 14) with their separate kitchen areas. The innkeepers provide daily maid service for some of the units, and others are housekeeping cottages. If you visit during the off-season, you'll be glad to know that the cottages are individually heated for nippy autumn and winter nights. The cottages are open year round, and in season they're rented by the week only.

Cahoon Hollow Bed & Breakfast

$$ • 56 Cahoon Hollow Rd., Wellfleet • 349-6372

This 1842 sea captain's home has only two suites, but what gems they are! Each is spacious and elegantly (yet comfortably) furnished and contains a queen- or king-size bed, private bath and sitting room. Owners Wally and Bailey Ruckert will go out of their way to assure that your visit is care- and stress-free. They'll help you plan a full day of activities (Wellfleet's great galleries and beaches are but 2 miles away) if you'll want to leave the breakfast table. Bailey's talents in the kitchen produce such tasty fare as pecan coffeecake, sherried eggs and ham, four-grain pancakes, popovers with honey butter, deep-dish custard, French toast with beach plum jelly . . . you'll beg her for the recipes! Bailey will also accommodate special dietary requests. The common room, with its fireplace and comfy furnishings, is a good place to get to know your hosts better. Cahoon Hollow, which is open year round, also provides bicycles for guests.

The Colony

$$$ • Chequessett Neck Rd., Wellfleet • 349-3761

Welcome to the simple life. Built as a private club in 1949 by one of the founders of Boston's Institute for Contemporary Arts, this collection of masonry and wood-frame duplexes, scattered along a wooded hillside overlooking the water, has been run as a cottage colony since 1963. With bedrooms that double as sitting rooms during the day, the cottages have fireplaces, galley kitchens, glass- and screen-enclosed dining porches and patios or decks. Some of the original furnishings in the cottages, available as one- or two-bedroom units, were designed by well-known artists and have counterparts in museums. You'll find fresh flowers in your room and have the benefit of daily maid service, but you won't find a television or telephone. If you insist, owner Eleanor Stephani will let you bring your own, but she'll probably talk you out of it and convince you to "let go and relax." And who needs TV in this tranquil setting? Instead, commune with nature, read a book, stroll down the road to the harbor or go to the beach.

The Colony is open from late May through September; units are rented by the week. Children are welcome provided they are well-behaved, but remember, this is a quiet retreat — you might just want to leave them at home.

The Holden Inn

$, no credit cards • Commercial St., Wellfleet • 349-3450

This 1840 sea captain's house, in the same family since 1924, has to be the best bargain on the Lower Cape. If you can deal with rooms that are somewhat oddly and old-fashionedly appointed, then you can deal with the budget-stretching Holden Inn.

The main house has 14 rooms; all share a bath with another room and are simply furnished with a sprinkling of antiques, wicker and whatnots, including iron and spindle beds. The adjacent buildings house 12 more rooms; these have private baths with old porcelain sinks just like the ones at Grandma's. Long screened porches have rockers. Picnic tables and gardens beckon along with singing birds. The inn, a short walk from the harbor, is open seasonally.

The Inn at Duck Creeke

$$ • 70 Main St., Wellfleet • 349-9333

The rooms are snug but comfy, and the location (a short walk into Wellfleet center) and views among the 5 acres (of a duck pond, salt marsh and tidal creek) are priceless. Most of the 25 rooms in the main 1810 sea captain's house offer touches of country charm such as rag rugs, lace curtains and claw-foot tubs. You also have a choice of guest rooms in the adjacent saltworks cottage and carriage house. Two fine restaurants, Sweet Seasons and the Tavern Room, will leave you hungry for a return visit (see our Restaurants chapter). The inn closes for the winter in October.

Surf Side Colony

$$$ • 350 Wilson Ave., South Wellfleet • 349-3959

Talk about location! Scattered along the sand dunes and fragrant pines of the Cape Cod National Seashore, Surf Side is part of an idyllic summer community, where children run free down sandy dirt roads and the only sound late at night is the roar of the tide. This is quintessential Outer Cape, where the sharp beach grass blows on high dunes overlooking white beaches. With knotty pine interiors, screened porches, fireplaces, kitchens, bathrooms, barbecues and heat, these 17 cottages are equipped with everything you need — there's even a laundry facility! These are some of the only oceanside accommodations in this area, perfect for families, and they book fast. Try for the Ocean Breeze or Surf View cottages, the two closest to the water. Pets are permitted off-season (before Memorial Day and after Columbus Day), for an additional charge. Surf Side is open from early March through October.

Days Cottages

$$$ • 271 Shore Rd., North Truro • 487-1062

If these pretty-as-a-picture waterfront cottages look familiar, it's because they have been immortalized through the years by dozens of artists in countless paintings and postcards.

What began with nine cottages in 1931 has grown to 23 — all exactly alike. In the summer of 1996, they were white with aquamarine shutters, though the colors are likely to change depending on the whim of the owner. Each blooms with the name of a different flower (such as larkspur and dahlia) and offers comfy living rooms with stunning water views. Remember, however, that these cottages are so popular with returning guests that it's nearly impossible to book one for less than a week during the season. The on-site self-service market stocks everything you'll need, from postcards to pomegranates. The cottages are open May through October.

Kalmar Village

$$$ • 674 Shore Rd., North Truro • 487-0585, off-season (617) 247-0211

Kalmar is a perfect family retreat — truly a little village — that's been in the same family since the 1960s. It features a 400-foot private beach, a pool, barbecue and well-maintained grounds awash in fragrant lilac and rose rugosa. The location can't be beat: Kalmar is just steps away from the Provincetown border and close to the National Seashore. Rates include maid service and cable TV, and there's even a laundry on the premises.

Kalmar has a total of 55 units but is extremely popular and usually gets booked at least a year in advance. If you can't finagle getting one of the cottages — the epitome of Cape Cod charm — consider one of the efficiency units. Kalmar Village is open March through October.

The Moorlands

$$ • 11 Hughes Rd., North Truro • 487-0663

It's off the beaten track, but once you find The Moorlands, we promise you'll have no problem returning again and again. Built by Capt. Atkin Hughes about 200 years ago, the house has been lovingly restored to Victorian splendor, updated to include such modern amenities (and conveniences) as in-room phones, ceiling fans and TVs.

The hosts serve a continental breakfast daily in the dining room (wait 'til you see the green faux-marble table top!), and you may play the antique pump organ, chat with newfound friends or curl up with a book in the parlor. Accommodations at this year-round inn vary: Choose from one of five guest rooms (three with private baths), a two-room suite, three-room apartment or the 18th-century restored carriage house, which has a fully equipped kitchen, TV and VCR, private bath and even a five-person hot tub!

South Hollow Vineyards

$$ • 11 Shore Rd., North Truro • 487-6200

Close your eyes and breathe deep the scent of plump grapes spilling from vines on the hillside, the smell of oak casks. If you love wine, this is a great place to stay, for it's made right here on the 5-acre grounds. Owners Kathleen Gregrow and Judy Wimer celebrated their first release in 1996, a barrel-fermented Chardonnay that has received favorable reviews. A Cabernet was scheduled for release in May '97. Guests are treated to a full breakfast and afternoon wine tastings in the sunny dining room of this 1836 Federal-style farmhouse, which has five lovely guest rooms, all nonsmoking. As you might expect, the predominant color is wine. You'll appreciate nice touches such as antique light fixtures and cozy comforters on the four-poster beds. Our favorite room is the Chardonnay with its intoxicating views of the vineyard, though we also savor the Vintage's two-person Jacuzzi. Cheers! The inn is open year round.

The charms of Chatham year-round

Welcome to the Quaint Seaside Community that knowledgeable travelers consider the most desirable on Cape Cod

Chatham Chamber of Commerce
Box 793, Dept. Z
Chatham, MA 02633

508-945-5199
800-715-5567

Come begin an old tradition.

Since 1860, the Chatham Wayside Inn has been host to many a weary traveller. Open year 'round, the Inn now offers 56 beautifully appointed rooms, a full service restaurant, and a heated pool, all just steps from golf, galleries, boutiques, and the beaches.

512 MAIN STREET CHATHAM, CAPE COD 800.391.5734

Distinctive lodging and timeless elegance in Chatham's oldest inn and true Cape Cod landmark.

Meticulously restored and ideally located, a visit here is filled with all the charm of yesteryear and all the comforts of home.

359 Main Street, Chatham, MA 02633
Phone 508 945-9232
800 332-4667 • Fax 508 945-3769

The charms of Chatham *year-round*

A 19th Century Sea Captain's House Reborn ...

Now a Gracious Inn!

Enjoy the subtle mingling of past and present, found within our quiet informal Inn. A fireplaced suite makes a restful retreat. Our special getaway packages are available through April, 1997. Call us for information.

The Cyrus Kent House Inn

63 Cross Street, Chatham, MA 02633 508.945.9104 • 1.800.338.5368

THE MOORINGS

Relax in the charm and hospitality of a Bed & Breakfast with a choice of accommodations.

A Short Walk to the Beach & Chatham Restaurants & Shops

Innkeepers: Roberta & Frank Schultz

508.945.0848 or 800.320.0848
326 Main Street, Chatham, MA 02633

Explore ~ Discover Be Pampered

THE OLD HARBOR INN

'Best B&B-Lower Cape' ~ **Cape Cod Life Magazine 1996**

English Country Decor Private Baths
Delectable Buffet Breakfast Sunroom Deck Fireplaces
Antiques Gardens Afternoon Teas
Easy Walk to Historic Seaside Village

AAA 3 diamonds ABBA 3 Crowns *Innkeepers Judy and Ray Braz*

22 OLD HARBOR ROAD CHATHAM, MA 02633 **1-800-942-4434**

Bradford Gardens Inn

$$$ • 178 Bradford St., Provincetown • 487-1616, (800) 432-2334

This charming year-round retreat, just a short walk from town, is larger than it appears at first glance. With 13 rooms in five buildings — including two historic houses that were floated across the harbor from the Point — the inn retains a homey feel. Guests gather in the quaint, fireplaced Morning Room in the 1860 main house for country breakfasts or just to chat and gaze out at the lovely gardens. The rooms are all different, but all cozy and charming; most have fireplaces and all have private baths. We love the Honeymoon Suite, with its Franklin stove, canopy bed and view of the gardens. The Jenny Lind Salon has a window seat, and the Cherry Tree Room is especially popular in May, when the tree is in glorious bloom just outside the window. For true luxury, reserve the Penthouse across the street, which has a rooftop harbor view, private deck, wood stove, stereo, TV and kitchen. This, we are told, is one of the places celebs favor when they come to Provincetown.

The Brass Key

$$$ • 9 Court St., Provincetown • 487-9005, (800) 842-9858

You can't help but fall in love with this glorious guesthouse, from its beckoning yellow and black shutter facade to host Michael MacIntyre's one-of-a-kind touches — vaulted skylights, a teddy loft, a rooftop widow's walk, tasteful antiques, wrought-iron lamps, a collection of decoys and, you guessed it, brass keys.

The main house has 10 guest rooms, or you can opt for one of the two poolside cottages. The property has been expanded to include four new buildings expected to be open by the summer of 1997, bringing the number of available rooms up to 34. All rooms feature private baths, telephones, TV/VCRs, refrigerators, even terry cloth robes and hair dryers. Some rooms have private Jacuzzis and fireplaces. Room 11 is our favorite; it has a fireplace, and the bathroom features a stand-up Jacuzzi with six horizontal jets.

The Brass Key also has a large, in-ground hot tub set in a brick-lined courtyard. A five-night minimum is required during the busy season (early June through mid-September). The inn is open most of the year, but generally closes for a couple of months in the dead of winter.

Captain Jack's Wharf

$$, no credit cards • 73A Commercial St., Provincetown • 487-1450

What could personify Provincetown more than 13 rustic apartments sitting on an old fishing wharf? Some of the units here are really rustic. For instance, there are cracks in the floorboard of Hesperus, in which the waters of Cape Cod Bay are visible below! Most are less Bohemian, but they're all charming. The Spindrift is a spacious wharf-end apart-

Photo: Steve Heaslip, Cape Cod Times

Chatham fishing boats rest on their moorings.

ment with spectacular wraparound views and a unique transom window that opens on a pulley (it was once used to haul boating equipment on and off the wharf). The upper-deck Neptune, all snug and cozy and, with its decor and feel, is a throwback to the 1940s. Modern mavens might want to opt for the more-expensive Australis, a two-story townhouse with a high-tech kitchen, spiral staircase, skylights, microwave, two TVs and lots of windows and beds. During the season, apartments rent by the week only; off-season, by the week or day. Well-behaved pets are welcome.

The Inn at Cook Street

$$ • 7 Cook St., Provincetown • 487-3894, (888) COOK-655

This cozy little inn, opened in 1996, offers three guest rooms, two suites and an adjacent cottage, all with private baths and nice touches such as stuffed animals, flowers and framed photographs taken by one of the innkeepers. Most have TVs and some have decks, either private or shared. Our favorite is the Hobbit Suite with its sloping ceilings and private deck overlooking the lush back yard, where Adirondack chairs beckon. Sit for a while and watch the carp in the small fish pond. Innkeepers Paul Church and Dana Mitton serve up a hearty continental breakfast and genuine hospitality. Molly, the resident Golden Retriever, will greet you with a friendly, gentle nuzzle. The inn is open year round.

Land's End Inn

$$$-$$$$ • 22 Commercial St., Provincetown • 487-0706, (800) 276-7088

Land's End is a celebration of art. With sweeping water views as a backdrop, the interior is filled with an incredible collection of vases, lamps, wood carvings and Tiffany lamps. Oriental rugs and unusual antique furniture abound, and each of the 16 guest rooms — all with a private bath — is unique. Perched on top of Gull Hill at the far end of Commercial Street and reached by climbing an enchanting brick path that twists and turns, the inn is a remarkable piece of architecture — sort of Victorian contemporary. The main building dates to 1904, and a wraparound porch and rear addition are recent but in keeping with the turn-of-the-century feel of the place, as are the terraced gardens on the 2-acre grounds. Even more unique is the fact that the year-round inn helps support the arts in Provincetown, through the David Adam Schoolman trust, named for and established by the inn's founder.

ShireMax Inn

$$$ • 5 Tremont St., Provincetown • 487-1233

Innkeeper Jack Barnett named his inn after his two Samoyed huskies, Shire and Max. Jack is such a dog lover that his inn in the quiet west end of town is one of only a handful of places that welcomes — actually encourages — guests to bring their pets. (The inn charges an additional $5 per night per room for pets.)

The seven rooms are large and homey and are stocked with everything from irons and ironing boards to beach chairs and towels. Four have private baths, three share. The room in the far back of the main house offers a private bath, private entrance and sun deck. Two separate apartments are also available; each has a VCR and TV (you can select from more than 750 movies), telephone, double bed and fully equipped kitchen. Each apartment has its own sun deck. A minimum stay of five nights is required in July and August; the apartments are rented by the week. The ShireMax is open year round.

Six Webster Place

$$$ • 6 Webster Pl., Provincetown
• 487-2266, 487-9242, (800) 6-WEBSTER

Why shop for antiques? Sleep in one! The main three-quarter Cape residence dates back to the 1750s, making this one of the six oldest houses in Provincetown. Indoor plumbing wasn't even installed until 1986!

Innkeeper Gary Reinhardt has restored the original Colonial charm to the five guest rooms (two share a bath), one luxury suite and three apartments. With the addition of a new nine-person Jacuzzi and tanning area, the inn is a wonderful blend of historic ambience and modern luxury. Although it is in the center of town, within easy walking distance of shops and restaurants, the inn is on a quiet lane, with lush gardens and sunny alcoves. Most rooms have fireplaces that make staying here in the off-season especially cozy. The inn is open year-round.

Three Peaks

$$ • 210 Bradford St., Provincetown
• 487-1717, (800) 286-1715

Named for its unusual architectural detail, Three Peaks was built in the 1870s for a prominent Midwestern family. Today it's a lovely smoke-free respite from the stress and confusion of everyday life — and from Provincetown's bustling town center. Situated in the quiet East End, Three Peaks offers five guest rooms, each with a private bath, cable TV, a refrigerator and either ceiling fans or in-room air conditioning. Opt for the converted front parlor room that features a bay window, the second-floor former master bedroom with art deco furnishings and an original claw-foot bathtub, or the former nursery, now a cozy study in wicker with a private outdoor porch. Three Peaks also has two fully furnished apartments. Guests enjoy a continental breakfast each morning and have use of the inn's comfortable common room and deck. Three Peaks is open year round; ask about the money-saving off-season rates.

Windamar House

$$ • 568 Commercial St., Provincetown
• 487-0599

This elegant former sea captain's house, c.1840, sits behind a white picket fence that encompasses manicured lawns and lush English gardens. Inside, antiques and original artwork mesh perfectly with fine wallpapers and coordinating fabrics.

This is one of the finest accommodations in Provincetown, just a 15-minute walk to the center of town yet so far removed that you'll swear you're alone in paradise. The inn has six guest rooms, each with its own special motif. Two rooms have private baths. Our favorite is The Studio, with its cathedral ceiling and an entire wall of glass overlooking the gardens and grape arbor. The Windamar also has two furnished apartments, including a penthouse with its stunning panoramic views of Cape Cod Bay and Provincetown Harbor. Located in Provincetown's quiet East End, the inn is open year-round and provides free onsite parking.

Almost all weekly rental units of any kind rent from Saturday to Saturday.

Vacation Rentals

Cape Cod, with its miles and miles of beaches, quaint villages, delicious restaurants, numerous attractions, challenging golf courses and thousands and thousands of rental properties, is especially well-positioned to create the quintessential summer vacation. Summer gatherings with family and friends, outdoor picnics, oceanside clambakes, after-dark cocktails by the flickering July candlelight . . . these memories and many more can be harvested from a vacation spent at a cottage or home located down near the ocean's edge.

Though the Cape is probably best known for its summer season when the beaches become the most popular attractions, Cape Cod is also an excellent place to spend a week or two during the shoulder seasons of spring and autumn when the air is cooler and the rents are lighter. We year-rounders even enjoy the snows of January and February, especially when it graces the marshes of meandering icy streams and accents the climbing dune cliffs. For us, Cape Cod is a treasure in all seasons.

The warm summer months provide a variety of rental properties from cottages to houses to condominium units. A rental cottage is usually a three-season small house with a yard and is typically on or nearby the ocean. Though many cottages are freestanding, almost all but the most deserted ones are found in colonies, that is, a community of similar structures of about the same size. Many cottage rentals, even long-term ones, do not supply linens (such as sheets or towels), paper goods or toiletries. Some offer housekeeping and laundry services for an extra fee. Almost all weekly rental units of any kind rent from Saturday to Saturday.

When you think of condominiums and timeshares, think upscale apartments, almost always fully furnished and usually part of a waterfront or waterview complex. Timeshare units are owned by a person or company who then rents out the unit for various periods of time. Timeshares should only concern you if you plan on buying into one.

To make your vacation run more smoothly, remember that the price you'll pay is based on several factors, including location (those near or on the water are, of course, the most expensive), length of stay, how long in advance your reservation was made and the time of year of your visit. July is the Cape's busiest month in terms of rentals. August, September and especially October are also very busy months on Cape Cod. Columbus Day weekend can find almost every hotel room filled as visitors enjoy the Cape's more colorful shades.

If you do want to rent a cottage for a week, especially during July, plan on calling well in advance. Many rental offices are busy in January and February booking rentals for the coming summer season. In-season rates are the priciest; those in shoulder seasons (right before or immediately following the busy summer season) can drop as much as 30 percent; off-season rates (if the accommodations are available) can be as much as 50 percent off seasonal prices.

While it would be impossible to mention all the resorts and rental agencies on the Cape, we've put together a list of those that offer the finest in vacation rentals. Keep in mind that many of these agencies are also full-service real estate companies (see our Real Estate chapter) and will be more than happy to answer any questions — and perhaps sell you a property once you've acquired a taste for Cape Cod. Many of those who join the ranks of the year-rounders begin as summer renters who get hooked and later buy a cottage. Once you begin to spend some time here you'll find leaving the Cape increasingly difficult.

The typical Cape Cod vacation lasts a week, but a good number rent for two weeks, sometimes a month, and some even rent for the entire summer season. Usually the rental properties contain a fully equipped kitchen, but it is important to remember that the Cape includes such a range of properties — from year-round homes to three-season cottages — that "fully equipped" can mean different things depending upon the situation. For instance, where a dishwasher may be considered standard issue for a year-round house it is not always available in a small cottage that may have been built 50 years ago before dishwashers were an option. A microwave oven may or may not be available. Blenders, electric can openers and the like should all be determined up front if such items are considered a must. Also, you may want to inquire as to whether the stove and oven are electric or gas.

Televisions, VCRs, telephones, whether or not the cottage has a tub or just a shower (families with small children who are used to taking baths will want to know) are all items to be questioned before you send in your deposit. By the way, the typical deposit on a vacation rental is 50 percent due upon making reservations, with the balance due prior to your arrival. Before you book, always ask about cancellation policies and whether pets, visiting guests and/or smoking are allowed. If a particular item is important to you, or when in doubt, it's better to ask than to run the risk of being disappointed when you arrive (although we seriously doubt you'll suffer any disappointments on good ol' Cape Cod).

Finally, if you cannot find what you're looking for in this chapter, call the chamber of commerce in the town in which you're interested (chamber of commerce phone numbers are listed in the Overview chapter). The local chambers are more than happy to offer you more information so you can plan that perfect summer vacation.

FYI

Unless otherwise noted, the area code for all phone numbers in this guide is 508.

Upper Cape

Cape Coast Realty

18-B MacArthur Blvd., Bourne • 759-9517

You can choose from approximately 50 waterfront and waterview homes for rent in Bourne, Sandwich, Falmouth and South Plymouth. The rate for a small cottage is about $750 per week; a private luxury home rents for around $2,000 per week.

Beach Realty

133 North Shore Blvd., East Sandwich • 888-4998

This office carries approximately 150 property listings in five beach areas from Sagamore to Sandy Neck. Properties differ in size, and most of them rent by the week though season rentals are also available.

Barrett Real Estate

178 Rt. 28, Falmouth • 548-2000

With an inventory of 500 vacation rentals from cottages to waterfront homes, this office has listings in Falmouth, Bourne and Mashpee, including Popponnessett. Homes and condos are rented by the week or full season.

Harriet Dugan Realtors

598 Main St., Falmouth • 548-4093

This office has about 200 summer rental properties in the Falmouth area, including Woods Hole. Choose from in-town, waterfront, waterview and walk-to-beach locations in two- to five-bedroom houses.

Donahue Real Estate

850 Main St., Falmouth • 548-5412

This active rental office lists approximately

INSIDERS' TIP

If you're vacationing in Dennisport or along many of the southern town beaches, you'll be interested to learn that the shoreline rested further south than it rests today. Hurricanes and storms over the past century have robbed Cape Cod of much of its former coastline and have taken a number of cottages along with it.

150 rental properties, including houses, condominiums, duplexes and apartments, many with three and four bedrooms. Most of these properties are in Falmouth, and they are available for one week to a full season.

Ermine Lovell

881 Palmer Ave., Falmouth • 548-0711

With many inland and waterfront properties, including eight- or 11-bedroom houses, this 60-plus-year-old real estate office offers vacation rentals exclusively in the Falmouth and Woods Hole areas.

Great Bay Associates

77 Cypress St., East Falmouth • 540-3775

Great Bay Associates carries about 50 vacation rentals that range in cost from $700 to $2,500 per week for two- to five-bedroom facilities. Some have ocean or bay views, and a few are oceanfront. Properties are available for the week or the summer season.

Real Estate Associates

563 Rt. 28A (At Rt. 151), North Falmouth • 563-7173

This office had more than 100 houses, condos and cottages in waterfront, waterview and beach locations. Within Falmouth, Bourne and Mashpee (many along Buzzards Bay and Vineyard Sound), properties range from one- to 10-bedroom homes. This 25-plus-year-old business also has offices in West Falmouth, Pocasset and Falmouth.

Popponesset Real Estate

Shore Rd., Popponesset Beach (Mashpee) • 477-1143

This agency handles approximately 100 properties in the long-established beachfront community of Popponesset in Mashpee, where Popponesset Marketplace offers shops, eateries, live entertainment and children's activities. The Popponesset Beach Associations's community building is often the setting for such family activities as softball, card games and square-dancing. Properties run from $650 to $3,500 a week.

Sound Realty

Rt. 28 at Mashpee Rotary, Mashpee • 477-8300, (800) 388-7686

Nearly all Sound Realty's rental properties lie within the 2,000-acre New Seabury Resort. The number of available homes and condominiums varies year by year but averages about 200 a season. Some are waterfront and range from two- to four-bedroom units. Country club, golf, tennis and beach memberships are available. Membership fees allow you to utilize the pool and health club. Weekly rates average $1,600 and range from $1,000 to $3,500.

Cape Cod Holiday Estates

97 Four Seasons Dr., Mashpee • 477-3377, (800) 228-2968

This facility has 33 weathered-shingle two-bedroom houses, each sitting on a one-third acre of land. The property is about 2 miles from beautiful South Cape Beach and offers an indoor pool, shuffleboard, tennis, basketball courts and a putting green.

Mid-Cape

Craigville Realty
648 Craigville Beach Rd., Craigville • 775-3174

In business since 1951, Craigville Realty has more than 200 rental properties, mostly homes and cottages in Hyannisport, West Hyannisport and Craigville. They range from modest to exclusive, from $600 to $3,600 per week, including some waterfront. Craigville also rents properties for two weeks and has some properties available for the full summer season.

Walsh Realty
610 W. Main St., Hyannis • 775-7330

Rentals by the week, for two weeks or a month in Hyannis, Hyannisport and Craigville are available through Walsh Realty. The company handles the summer rental of some 90 two- and three-bedroom properties ranging in price from $600 to $2,500 (waterfront) per week.

Shoreland Real Estate
724 Main St., Hyannis • 771-2008

Shoreland deals primarily with Mid-Cape (Mashpee to Harwich) rentals on a year-round basis and the Barnstable villages of Osterville, Cotuit and Hyannis for seasonal rentals. The company specializes in short-term corporate relocation rentals and also offers weekly sea-

Photo: Vincent Dewitt, Cape Cod Times

Young visitors splash through the surf at White Crest Beach in Wellfleet.

sonal rates. The properties range from efficiencies to six-bedroom homes. Summer weekly rates range from a low of $700 to upwards of $4,500 for a beachfront house.

Marchildon Associates, Realtor

572 Rt. 28, West Yarmouth • 775-5200

Most of this company's seasonal rental properties are in West Yarmouth although some are also available in South Yarmouth. The price range is about $600 to $2,500 (for waterfront) per week. Marchildon has properties available by the week, for two-week periods or by the season.

Waterfront Rentals

20 Pilgrim Rd., West Yarmouth • 778-1818

You can rent estates, homes and condos from Bourne to Truro through this 16-year-old agency that offers a wide selection of mid-Cape properties. Approximately 150 properties are available for weekly, seasonal or year-round rental and range from one- to nine-bedroom facilities. These rental properties range from $700 a week to $8,000 for a seven-bedroom, seven-bath home on the beach. Videos of properties can be viewed at the office.

Clipper Ship Cove

183 South Shore Dr., South Yarmouth • 394-6044, (800) 439-6044 (Mass. only)

This small, well-maintained complex offers 10 one- and two-bedroom townhouses with full kitchens, fireplaces, cathedral ceilings, air conditioning and a lovely private beach. Rose bushes, weathered shingles and brick patios lend a Cape Cod look to this quaint village setting. The condominiums, which range from $1,400 to $1,700 per week, are open from April 1 to October 31.

Peter McDowell Associates

585 Main St. (Rt. 6A), Dennis • 385-9114, (888) 385-9114

11 Rt. 28, Dennisport • 394-5400

This full-service real estate company has been servicing the Dennis area for more than 30 years. It offers a couple of hundred summer rentals located primarily in the town of Dennis. Rental properties are available for a week, two weeks, a month or for the whole summer season and range from $500 to $3,000 for a waterfront property.

Steele Associates

1372 Rt. 134, East Dennis • 385-7311

This family-owned company, in its 12th year in business, offers more than 50 rental homes in beach areas primarily in the villages of Dennis and East Dennis. Rentals are weekly, monthly or seasonal. Besides a busy summer rental season, Steele Associates also offers rentals during the colorful off-season months of September and October. Summer weekly rentals range from $650 to $3,000 (for waterfront), and houses generally range from two to four bedrooms.

James E. Mischler, Realtors

Intersection of rts. 28 and 134, West Dennis • 394-3330, (800) 863-3330

This mid-Cape office, established by Jim and Rita Mischler in 1979, has some 400 vacation properties in the Dennisport, West Dennis, Brewster and Harwich areas. These quality properties, which include vacation homes as well as cottages, rent for between $395 to $4,000 a week — the former being an efficiency and the latter a five-bedroom home on the water.

Lower Cape

Bay Village Realty Better Homes and Gardens

1990 Main St. (Rt. 6A), Brewster • 896-7004, (800) 338-1851

With five offices handling seasonal rentals, Bay Village is one of the Cape's largest real estate companies. It has an excellent selection of rental properties available by the week, for two weeks, the month or on a seasonal basis. Properties include homes, cottages and condominiums in the lower Cape towns from Brewster to Wellfleet. Rentals range from $400 to $3,500 a week for a waterfront property. A typical Brewster property would run about $800 to $900 for a walk-to-the-beach cottage. Bay Village also has sales/rental offices in Harwichport, Chatham and Wellfleet, a rental office in East Orleans and a real estate sales office in Orleans (see our Real Estate chapter).

Great Vacations Real Estate

2660 Main St. (Rt. 6A), Brewster • 896-2090, (800) 626-9984

Great Vacations offers exceptional vacation rentals including a large selection of condominium rentals at Ocean Edge resort in Brewster. The properties Great Vacations handles are primarily in the Brewster and Orleans areas, are well-equipped and, unlike most rental situations, come with bed clothes and linens as well as a fully stocked kitchen (just bring your own toothbrush). Prices range from $800 to $2,700 per week in season, the latter being a three-bedroom house on the water. Monthly and seasonal rentals are also available through this high-quality vacation rental outfit.

Harold McKenna Realty

947 Main St., South Harwich • 432-9813

More than 200 properties, mostly private homes in Chatham and the Harwiches, are available by the week, two weeks or the month. Weekly rentals range from a low of $550 to an oceanfront or oceanview property at around $2,500.

Thomas H. Peterson Real Estate

255 Main St., West Harwich • 432-1220

Thomas H. Peterson Real Estate offers about 100 rentals ranging from summer cottages to year-round homes in the Harwich, Dennis and Chatham areas. Its vacation rentals are available by the week, month and season.

Sylvan Realty

2469 Rt. 28, South Chatham • 432-2344

Founded in 1939, this family-owned and operated agency specializes in rentals of some 200 individually owned cottages and homes in the Chatham and Harwich areas. Fully furnished beach cottages go for about $650 per week while luxury beachfront houses can run $3,000 per week. The average range is between $800 and $1,500 per week. Monthly and seasonal rentals are also available.

Pine Acres Realty

938 Main St., Chatham • 945-1186

This company truly lives up to its motto,

INSIDERS' TIP

Most people are familiar with John F. Kennedy's connection with Hyannisport. He summered at the family compound there, which became the summer Whitehouse during his administration. Yet before JFK, President Grover Cleveland had a summer place in Bourne called Gray Gables.

"Bringing people and houses together since 1948." Choose from more than 150 Chatham properties rented by the week, season or year. Rentals run from $500 to $5,000 for a waterfront estate.

Connolly Real Estate

894 Main St., Chatham • 945-4663

Marie Connolly has been providing rentals exclusively in Chatham and East Harwich for the past seven years. Rentals range from $600 to $3,000 a week. Biweekly, monthly and seasonal rentals are also available.

Compass Real Estate

2 Academy Pl., Orleans • 240-1307, (800) 724-1307

Compass has been filling the needs of renters for more than 20 years. The two offices (the other is in Wellfleet, 349-1717, (800) 521-1343) focus primarily on private homes, condos and cottages throughout the Lower Cape. The Orleans office has numerous listings, from cottages at $325 a week to exclusive $2,500-a-week waterfront retreats. Compass also has a large international clientele and offers translation services in German and other languages.

Pike Properties

8 Main St., Orleans • 255-5900

Pike Properties handles more than 70 properties, many of which are waterfront and waterview homes, cottages and walk-to-water properties. Rent by the week, month, season or year. Most properties range from $800 a week to a waterfront home for $2,000, although you may be able to get into a two-bedroom cottage for $475.

Anchor Real Estate

Rt. 6, Eastham • 255-4949

A well-respected real estate office on the lower Cape, Anchor Real Estate and its owner Suzanne Goodrich have received a number of awards over the years. In 1993 Goodrich was named Massachusetts Realtor of the Year, while in 1996 Anchor was named the MLS leader in listings sold and number of sales in the town of Eastham. The office has some 200 quality summer vacation rentals ranging from $625 per week to $3,000 per week on the water. An average rental is about $900 for a three-bedroom, two-bath house within a half-mile of the water. Unique services include convenient linen rentals for tenants and bed and breakfast reservations.

Pat Shultz and Associates

406 Commercial St., Provincetown • 487-9550

Pat Shultz and Associates has been handling Provincetown rentals since 1970. Over that time it has established itself as a major player in both residential and commercial rentals. A friendly four-member staff promises to find the perfect place for your needs — weekly, monthly, seasonally or annually. Properties range from $500 studios and $800 one-bedroom properties to $1,000 two-bedroom units and $2,500 waterfront houses.

Harborside Realty

162 Commercial St., Provincetown • 487-4005, (800) 838-4005

Harborside Realty handles 200 Provincetown properties, from basic quaint cottages at $650 a week to the most trendy three-bedroom private homes at about $2,000 a week. Properties are available by the week, month and for the summer season.

Beachfront Realty

151 Commercial St., Provincetown • 487-1397

Beachfront's properties are in Provincetown. The company represents more than 50 accommodations for weekly rental and approximately 25 for seasonal rental. Weekly rates run from $750 to $2,500.

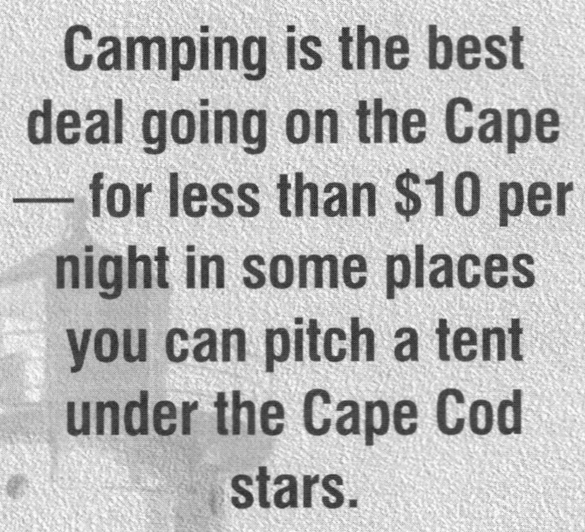

Camping is the best deal going on the Cape — for less than $10 per night in some places you can pitch a tent under the Cape Cod stars.

Campgrounds

The scent of pine needles drifts through the flap of your tent as you wake to the musical call of birds high in the treetops. Outside a mist rises from the pond in the first rays of sunlight, and a fire begins to crackle at a nearby campsite. Aside from the birds and the chatter of squirrels, the silence is palpable. You can't get much closer to nature than this. Nothing beats camping for a truly relaxing, rejuvenating vacation. There's something about going to sleep in the middle of the woods that does wonders for the soul. And nothing tastes as good as a breakfast cooked outside over a camp stove.

Camping, whether it's in a tent or an RV, takes you out of the rhythm of everyday life into a new awareness of your surroundings. It heightens your senses so that colors seem brighter, bird songs sound sweeter, water feels cooler and fresher on your skin when you take that early-morning dip in the pond near your campsite. You'll go home a new person. And you'll save scads of money. Camping is the best deal going on the Cape — for less than $10 per night in some places you can pitch a tent under the Cape Cod stars and still see the same museums, take the same tours and sunbathe on the same beaches as visitors paying 10 times that amount for a place to sleep.

In this chapter, we've included information on public and private campgrounds. For more information on private campgrounds contact Yvonne Drew at the **Massachusetts Association of Campground Owners**, (617) 544-3475. If you'd like more information about the state facilities in Sandwich, Mashpee and Brewster, write to Region I Headquarters, Myles Standish State Park, P.O. Box 66, South Carver, Massachusetts 02366.

Upper Cape

Bay View Campground
260 MacArthur Blvd. (Rt. 28), Bourne • 759-7610

Perched on one of the highest points of land on Cape Cod, this 430-site campground is the perfect spot to enjoy beautiful sunsets and recreational opportunities in the area. Bay View is 20 minutes by car from Falmouth, Sandwich and the Steamship Authority parking lot on Route 28. Walkers, runners and in-line skaters enjoy the nearby canal bike path. Also close by, within a mile, is Adventure Isle, which has miniature golf, amusement rides, batting cages and a go-cart track. Needless to say, Bay View is extremely popular with families!

The campground offers so much leisure activity you may find it hard to fit it all in. Outdoors, Bay View has areas for tennis, basketball, volleyball, shuffleboard and horseshoes, plus two playgrounds, three large in-ground swimming pools and a baby pool. In the recreation hall you can play table tennis, pool and video games. Bay View has a full-time recreation director who organizes daily activities for all ages, from teen dances with pizza to arts and crafts, water volleyball games, magic shows, baseball games and family wagon rides and dances.

Each site has a picnic table, fireplace and hookups for water and electricity (up to 30 amps); most have sewer hookup. A cable TV connection costs $2. Facilities include showers and toilets, ice, gas and wood. You can buy RV supplies such as hoses and awnings at the office.

INSIDERS' TIP

You'll have to get up pretty early to watch the Cape's fishing boats set out: Most of them leave the harbor between 2 and 5 AM.

The campground is open from May to mid-October. Pets are welcome but must be restrained, and you'll need to bring their current rabies shot certificate. In-season rates are $25 per night for two plus $3 for each child age 2 to 18.

Bourne Scenic Park

Bourne Scenic Hwy. (rts. 6 and 28), Buzzards Bay • 759-7873

For location, Bourne Scenic Park rivals the best accommodations on Cape Cod. Situated on the banks of the world's widest sea-level canal, this 475-site facility offers shady woods and proximity to shops and grocery stores. And the scenery? It's extraordinary: Gigantic white cruise ships and tankers glide past your campsite and occasionally give a massive blast on their horns.

FYI

Unless otherwise noted, the area code for all phone numbers in this guide is 508.

From the park, bikers and strollers have several access points to the popular canal service road bike path where people push baby strollers, walk dogs, bike and in-line skate all day long. In the summer, the park offers hayrides and live entertainment including bands and DJs. A new Olympic-size swimming pool replaces the large saltwater pool that for years served the campground.

Operated by the Bourne Recreation Authority, the Scenic Park has electric and water hookups, a dump station, playgrounds, a recreation hall, a volleyball court and activities for children throughout the summer. The country store sells basic supplies, including ice and wood.

In peak season, the rates are $22 per day with electricity hookup and $20 without. In the off-season, a two-weeks' stay costs $134 ($77 per week) with electricity, $124 without.

Peter's Pond Park

185 Cotuit Rd., Sandwich • 477-1775

For campers who return year after year, this facility is as close to owning waterfront property on Cape Cod as you can get without paying taxes. A 100-acre campground situated on a lovely freshwater pond, Peter's Pond Park offers swimming, fishing and boating. It abuts a large conservation area with walking trails and has playgrounds, playing fields for baseball and volleyball, horseshoes, a convenience store, adult and teenager recreation halls and outdoor grills.

The campground, which has been in the DeGraw family for 65 years, offers 500 large sites, one-third of which are for tent camping and the rest are for RVs. Handicapped-accessible facilities are available. You can cook on individual charcoal and gas stoves or central fireplaces. Campers are only a few miles from beaches, museums, the Cape Cod Canal and antique and gift shops in Sandwich and Mashpee.

The park rents tepees, trailers, tents and rowboats by the week (daily off-season). The rates run between $21 and $35 per night. The campground is open from April until mid-October.

Scusset Beach Reservation

Scusset Beach Rd., Sandwich • 888-0859

What a great place to spend a vacation! Barely a few hundred yards from a beautiful sandy beach on Cape Cod Bay, Scusset offers pleasant walking trails and immediate access to the Cape Cod Canal bike path. Deer, fox, upland game birds and rabbits make their homes in the 380-acre preserve.

Bring your bikes and in-line skates to use on the 7-mile-long canal bike path. Fishing enthusiasts cast their lines from the stone jetty at the end of the canal, the banks of the canal and from a wheelchair-accessible fishing pier. Scusset has 97 campsites, most in the open, including three handicapped-accessible sites. Fresh water and dumping stations are nearby.

The reservation is owned by the U.S. Army Corps of Engineers but run by the state. Through interpretive programs, campers here can learn about the origins of the canal, tour the marine traffic controller's office and the World War II embattlements on the Sagamore Hills, and explore the bike path.

The campground is open year round; however, after Columbus Day the water is turned off in the public facilities, and only self-contained vehicles are permitted until early April. The seasonal rate is $9 per night ($7 in winter). Electricity in the off-season is $7. Large groups or clubs with self-contained RVs might be interested in reserving the 3.5-acre field with grills and tables.

No reservations are accepted for the other sites, so first-come, first-served is the rule. Stays are limited to no more than two weeks between June 30 and Labor Day. Slightly out of the way, Scusset sits at the end of Scusset Beach Road, which runs parallel to the canal. To get on this road, make a three-quarter turn around the Sagamore rotary coming from Boston on Route 3.

Shawme-Crowell State Forest

Rt. 130, Sandwich • 888-0351

The cool, wooded setting for Shawme-Crowell offers a summer haven for tent campers and RV owners. Just a half-mile away from scenic Route 6A, it's close to the Sandwich Marina, canal bike path access and Sandwich's museums and restaurants. Campers here have beach privileges at Scusset Beach on the opposite side of the canal.

A 742-acre park with 285 sites, Shawme-Crowell has picnic tables and fireplaces at each site. Scattered throughout are clean restrooms, hot showers and sewage disposal sites. The park has no on-site hookups for water or electric. A convenience store carries firewood, ice and other camping needs.

Overseen by some of the friendliest park rangers you could meet, this quiet, uncongested campground is open year round, but only self-contained vehicles are allowed from December to March. Reservations are not accepted. The nightly fee is $6 for two adults per site; there is no extra charge for children.

Waquoit Bay National Estuarine Research Reserve

Washburn Island, Mashpee/Falmouth • 457-0495, ext. 100

Wilderness camping on 300-acre Washburn Island in Waquoit Bay should be considered a privilege as well as a luxury. This beautiful island is now managed by the state, and campers must have permits (see information below). Ten sites are available, nine for families and one for a group of no more than 25. Facilities consist of composting toilets and outhouses; the island has no electricity or fresh water. Only hibachis and Coleman-type stoves can be used for cooking. Access to the island across a narrow tidal channel is possible only by private boat. Camping ends in mid-October.

"It is a special place, a neighborhood place, and the people here think of it as their own Eden," says Nancy Anderson at the Waquoit Bay National Estuarine Research Reserve. Permits cost $4 a night. For more information, call the number above or write Waquoit Bay Research Reserve, P.O. Box 3092, Waquoit, Massachusetts 02536.

Sippewissett Family Campground

836 Palmer Ave., Falmouth • 548-2542, (800) 957-CAMP

This 35-year-old, family-owned campground offers a home base from which to reach the shops, restaurants and historic sites in Falmouth. In fact, campers can pick from seven great beaches, two windsurfing beaches, fishing, golf, boating and hiking trails that are no more than 15 minutes away by car. A free shuttle service transports campers to nearby beaches and the Martha's Vineyard ferries that depart from Falmouth and Woods Hole.

The campground has an activity center, a playground, a volleyball area and a snack bar. Most of the 120 sites (60 for tents and 60 for RVs) are wooded, and all have picnic tables and firepits. This shady campground offers 24-hour security, emergency assistance and a coin-operated laundry. Dogs are not permitted here from Memorial Day to Labor Day.

Nightly charges include a $10 site fee plus $8 for each adult; the family rate is $26 in season and $18 off-season (no additional charge for children). Electric and water hookups are $2.50 per day. Off-season rates apply at the beginning and end of the season, which runs from mid-May to mid-October.

Mid-Cape

Grindell's Ocean View Park

no credit cards • 61 Old Wharf Rd., Dennisport • 398-2671

This is a RV aficionado's dream come true — a real village within one of the prettiest stretches of the Cape. The park has 160 sites for RVs up to 34 feet long; book early if you want to stay right on the ocean. All sites have three-way hookups and concrete patios.

You can also opt for one of the 11 white and weathered-gray cottages, all with bathrooms, electricity, wooden decks and lots of privacy, on the ocean or nestled among pines. Spend the day relaxing on the private saltwater beach, or try your luck at fishing — cast your line off the breakwater right outside your door.

The park has two pay toilets, hot-water showers and even a fully stocked grocery store. The park is open from mid-May through the end of September; rates are $30 a night ($189 per week), higher for the cottages. Off-season discounts are available, and reservations are a must from mid-June through Labor Day.

Campers Haven Ltd.

184 Old Wharf Rd., Dennisport • 398-2811

Hosts Paul and Elaine Peterson place the emphasis on family fun. The festivities include free movies, sing-alongs, story hours, candy bingo, beach barbecues, minigolf, volleyball, basketball, horseshoes, potluck suppers — even a playground (try getting your kids away from the fire engine-red slide tube!) — all included in the rock-bottom price. Some of the warmest waters on the Cape are just seconds away so hop aboard the free shuttle to the beach.

Choose from among 265 shaded sites; all include water and electricity. Rates are $30 per day ($195 per week); all rates include electric and water hookups. The park is open from April to Columbus Day.

Lower Cape

Nickerson State Park

no credit cards • 3488 Main St. (Rt. 6A), Brewster • 896-3491, reservations 896-4615

This is the granddaddy of them all — Cape Cod's crown jewel. The 1,900-plus wooded acres that make up the bulk of the park (it also has land on the north side of 6A) once belonged to Roland Nickerson, a multimillionaire who founded the First National Bank of Chicago. The Nickersons, who lived in an opulent estate farther west on 6A that is now known as Ocean Edge (see our Hotels, Motels and Resorts chapter), had a hunting lodge on the acreage that is now the state park. The Nickersons hosted private hunts at their "Bungalow Estates," as they referred to their rustic playground. Nickerson's wife, Addie, donated the land to the state in 1934 in honor of their son, a victim of the 1918 influenza epidemic, and in honor of her husband.

The park, one of the state's largest, features eight kettle ponds formed by Ice-Age glaciers. (A kettle pond here today may be gone next season. The ponds are completely dependent on ground water and precipitation, and the water level fluctuates year to year.) You can spot many rare species of plants and wildflowers growing on the edges of kettle ponds; it's against the law to trample or pick them.

You could spend a month here and still have things to do. How about motorboating or swimming in the beach-edged Cliff Pond,

Photo: Cape Cod Times

Pass some afternoon hours looking at boats in the harbors.

the largest in the park? Into bird-watching? Nickerson is a regular stop on the migration route of such feathered friends as larks, woodpeckers, wrens, warblers and thrushes. It's also a watering hole for cormorants, Canada geese, great blue herons, ducks — even the occasional common loon. Or study the owls, osprey, hawks, eagles and such woodland animals as red foxes, skunks, chipmunks, white-tailed deer and nonpoisonous snakes. If you like bicycling, the Cape Cod Rail Trail passes right through the park, with a few loops branching off through different areas of the park. Try your luck at fishing at one of the four ponds that are continually stocked with trout. And that's just in season! Nickerson is open year round, and winter visitors can ice-fish, ice-skate and, when there is snow, cross-country ski on marked trails. The park is an easy walk or drive from bay beaches, and beach walks are among the interpretive activities led by park naturalists in season.

Nickerson offers 420 camping sites at just $6 per night but does not offer electric or RV hookups. Nonprofit organizations can reserve one of the two group camping sites (each cabin holds about 30 people). Reservations are a strongly recommended; 250 of the park's sites are under the reservation system established four years ago. Self-contained camping is permitted in the off-season (mid-October to mid-April) for $6 per night. There are no lifeguards at Cliff Pond.

Shady Knoll Campground

1709 Main St. (Rt. 6A), Brewster
• 896-3002

With 100 wooded sites for tents and RVs, Shady Knoll is close to bay beaches, the bike trail and shops, and is within walking distance of a small grocery store. It offers hot showers, full hookups, fireplaces, laundry facilities, a playground and a game room. Reservations are requested. It's open May 15 to October 15. Rates are $24 to $30 a night, depending on the number of people and whether you need electric or sewer hookup. Pets are allowed, provided you take them with you when you leave your site.

Sweetwater Forest

no credit cards • Rt. 124, Brewster
• 896-3773

Don't let the winding, bumpy dirt driveway fool you: That's as rough as it gets around here. One of the largest and oldest campgrounds on Cape Cod, Sweetwater is a sprawling spread of 250 sites situated lakefront and on 60 acres of thickly-settled woodlands.

You can rent a canoe and paddle around the lake, fish off the dock or play horseshoes, among many other activities — you can even arrange for a pony ride! And in case you forgot to bring enough reading material, Sweetwater offers a free lending library.

Sites are available with partial or full hookups, and there's a separate area just for tents.

Four modern comfort stations assure that you won't have far to go when you have to go. Rates start at $20 per day, and reservations are recommended during the summer and on holiday weekends. Though the grounds officially close from November through April, self-contained camping is allowed during these months.

Atlantic Oaks

3700 Rt. 6, Eastham • 255-1437

Just a half-mile from the visitors center of the Cape Cod National Seashore, this modern campground meets the needs of RVers and tent campers alike (though the emphasis here is on the former). The 135 large wooded sites include 100 drive-throughs with full electric and water hookups and cable TV. Other amenities include metered gas service, free hot showers, laundry facilities, nightly movies during the summer and, to keep the kids entertained, a playground. Unlike many campgrounds, dogs are allowed here, provided that they are taken with you when you're away from the camp. You might want to bring your bicycles, as Atlantic Oaks abuts the Cape Cod Rail Trail.

First time exploring the great outdoors? Displaced city folk need not worry: The grounds are protected (as if they need to be!) by a 24-hour security gate. Rates are $24 to $32 per night at this year-round campground, which offers lower off-season rates as well as discounted rates for monthly rentals. Winter camping (November through May) is by reservation only.

Paine's Campground

175 Rt. 6, South Wellfleet • 349-3007, (800) 479-3017

Who needs Niagara Falls when honeymooners can choose special "couples only" sites — private and with no electricity? This is just one of the special amenities the Paine family has offered dedicated campers since 1958.

Family sites include electric service and will accommodate tents, vans or small tent trailers. Larger group sites, which are perfect for family reunions, are extremely popular and go fast. Several private shaded "lug-in" sites are available for those who want to simply unwind under the fragrant pines. And though Paine's preference is for tents, seven sites have been converted for RVs, with electric and water hookups, for an additional $4 per day.

Charges range from a paltry $7.50 in early to mid-May and September to a reasonable $10.50 for the rest of the season. Children ages 6 through 18 stay for $3 each per night with an adult family member; ages 6 and younger stay free. Reservations are strongly advised.

Maurice's Campground

80 Rt. 6, Wellfleet • 349-2029

This place redefines "rustic." The 200 tent, trailer and RV sites, as well as four cottages and seven cabins, are set in the middle of a large pine grove, so far from the hustle and bustle of Route 6 that even the site closest to the road seems miles away. Each site is spacious and has a picnic table. The general store offers pick-your-own lobster — perfect for a clambake! (State law forbids open fires in any campground, but, hey, a lobster cooked over a camp stove or a charcoal grill is still lobster to us!)

The cottages, always in demand, can sleep two to four people and have insulated walls, fully equipped kitchens and maple furnishings. The cabins, which can accommodate two or three people, are similar in construction to the cottages but do not accommodate cooking. Three utility buildings provide plenty of sanitary facilities, including metered hot water showers (a quarter and a bar of soap will do the job!).

The site fee is $20 per day and $3 extra for electric and water hookups. Cottages start at $375 for a week; cabins, $55 nightly. Reservations are strongly recommended for July and August.

North Truro Camping Ground

no credit cards • 48 Highland Rd., North Truro • 487-1847

This is camping at its finest: 350 tent, trailer and RV sites surrounded by 22 acres of sweet

INSIDERS' TIP

When do you pronounce the "ham"? Chatham is pronounced CHAT-em. Nearby, Eastham is pronounced EAST-ham.

native pines and rambling hills, smack-dab in the middle of the Cape Cod National Seashore. Think of it as your year-round vacation home, replete with flush toilets, metered hot showers, a Laundromat, private picnic tables, ceramic-tile restrooms and even free cable hookups for your portable TV! Saunter over to the ocean or bay beach, both less than a mile away, or hike and bike the nearby trails.

The cost ($15 per day for a 50-foot by 50-foot site; electric and water hookups are an additional $5 per day) will leave you with enough money to splurge on a great dinner in nearby Provincetown.

An added bonus: Stay for a week and deduct 10 percent. Stay for a month, and the discount increases to 15 percent.

Horton's Camping Resort

71 S. Highland Rd., North Truro • 487-1220, (800) 252-7705

Take your pick: The 220 sites here come in one size (large) but in a choice of sunny, shaded or wooded areas. Some tent sites have partial hookups (electricity and water) for a nominal additional fee. RV owners can choose from 74 sites with hookups, most in an open grassy area, though you can opt for a wooded site (the latter does not provide electric, water or sewer connections). Horton's, open from May to Columbus Day, is close to the Cape Cod National Seashore and other Lower Cape attractions.

Site fees start at $16 per night and work their way up to $24 for those with full hookups. For $2 extra, choose site 152, which offers sweeping views of Highland Light and the Pilgrim Monument in Provincetown. There's no charge for the sea breezes. Reservations are strongly recommended from July through Labor Day.

Dune's Edge Camp Ground

no credit cards • 386 Rt. 6, Provincetown • 487-9815

Only in Provincetown would the roads of a campground be named such cute names as Bunny Trail, Blueberry Lane, Cranberry Bowl and Beach Plum Road. And it's true what they say: All roads (and trails and bowls) lead to mecca, for Dune's Edge, nestled beneath the shadow of Horses Head, one of the tallest hills in town, is as idyllic, clean and quaint as you're going to get short of starting your own outdoor hideaway.

Most of the 85 tent sites and 15 trailer spaces offer the utmost in privacy. And the rates are reasonable: $22 per day for one to two people, less in the off-season, plus an additional few dollars for more campers. The limit is six people per site. Your pet — one per site, welcome as long as it's leashed — stays free! Reservations are highly recommended. Personal checks are accepted for the initial deposit only, then only cash or a traveler's check upon arrival.

Waterside Dining

OVERLOOKING OUR MARINA

It's the most relaxing way to enjoy fine dining in a casual atmosphere while watching the sun set over the water. Weather permitting you can dine on our outdoor deck. We have something for everyone on our menu. Enjoy our chef's specialties, as he prepares everything to order using the freshest and finest seafood, steak, pasta, chicken and veal. We cater weddings, luncheons, banquets and tour groups up to 250.

Skippy's Pier 1

Serving Lunch from 11:30 am
Dinner from 4:00 pm

17 Neptune Lane • South Yarmouth • 398-9556
(OFF RT. 28, BEHIND PIER 7 CONDOMINIUMS)

Restaurants

Food, glorious food! There's plenty of it here on the Cape, where the salty air can do wonders for the appetite. You're bound to get hungry doing all there is to do on the Cape, so after you've played on the beach, splashed in the bay, hiked a nature trail, played minigolf, joined an impromptu game of volleyball, visited a museum and shopped 'til you're ready to drop, check out one of the Cape's many eateries. Talk to anyone who has recently — or even not so recently — visited Cape Cod and you're bound to be regaled by descriptions of not only the beautiful beaches and spectacular sunsets but also the wonderful restaurants. Your mouth is sure to start watering as you hear of succulent clams, rich lobster and fresh swordfish, the wood-grilled chicken at The Bistro in Chatham and the incredible tiramisu on the dessert menu at Chillingsworth, the renowned French restaurant in Brewster.

What's remarkable is the incredible variety of eating establishments on this relatively small spit of land. There's a restaurant here to suit every mood, taste, whim and budget. Feel like taking the kids somewhere super casual and cheap? Head to a clam shack for fish and chips, then treat the clan to ice cream for dessert. Celebrating a birthday, anniversary or other special occasion, or do you just want to splurge? The Cape has more than its share of renowned restaurants that serve fabulous fare amid sophisticated ambiance. Have a yen for Chinese, or are you itching for Mexican? How about some Japanese sushi? We've got all that too. And let's not forget lobster — indulge, you're on Cape Cod!

One of the nice things about eating out here is that most restaurants maintain a come-as-you-are dress code. You can dress up at many of the fine dining establishments, but you don't have to. We'll flag the jacket-required establishments, but it's a good idea to double-check for a dress code when you make a reservation.

About reservations: Remember that many restaurants will be packed during the height of the tourist season (Memorial Day to Labor Day) and on weekends and holidays. In summer, reservations are a must at fine restaurants, and waits are common at those that maintain a first-come, first-served policy. You may even have to wait a bit when you've made reservations, as even the most efficient restaurant can get backed up with lingering diners. This is, after all, the Cape, where no one is in a hurry! But remember, if we've recommended the eatery, the wait is worth it.

Most restaurants accept major credit cards (we note the ones that don't) and, unless otherwise stated, all are handicapped accessible. Smokers may want to take note that more and more restaurants are now smoke-free. So, if you prefer to smoke and dine, call ahead to make sure it's allowed.

Price Code

The following price code is meant strictly as a guideline in helping you decide where to dine. The code is based on the average price of dinner for two, excluding appetizers, alcoholic beverages, dessert, tax and tip. (Tipping is customarily 15 to 20 percent.)

$	**Less than $20**
$$	**$21 to $35**
$$$	**$36 to $50**
$$$$	**$51 and more**

Many restaurants offer early bird dinner specials, with discounts ranging anywhere from 10 percent to 30 percent off the regular price. This is especially true in the off-season; don't expect too many bargains in the height of summer.

When we describe a restaurant as being open seasonally, we're referring to that busy tourism time generally falling between Memorial Day and Labor Day. We have arranged the restaurants geographically — Upper Cape to Lower Cape, or Bourne to Provincetown. Bon appetit!

Upper Cape

Lobster Trap Restaurant

$$, no credit cards • 290 Shore Rd., Bourne • 759-3992

For 25 years the Lobster Trap Restaurant has been satisfying tourists and locals alike with its great seafood. Open from Memorial Day to mid-September, the Lobster Trap is a busy lunch spot and is packed at dinner time (it's best to arrive early). On the menu are such popular dishes as fish and chips, broiled haddock, chowders, steamers and, of course, lobster as well as many other kinds of broiled, boiled and fried seafood. Special treats may include such tasty dishes as broiled swordfish tips. Burgers and chicken dishes are also served. The restaurant features a leisurely atmosphere — paper plates, plastic forks and a large deck overlooking scenic Buzzards Bay. Attached to the restaurant is a fish market open year round and featuring the freshest in native New England seafood (cod, lobster, steamers, little necks) as well as specialty items from down south and from as far away as Prince Edward Island up in Canada. The fish market, which can be reached at 759-7600, is open 9 AM to 6 PM Monday through Saturday, 10 AM to 5 PM on Sunday. The restaurant is open for lunch and dinner seven days a week.

FYI

Unless otherwise noted, the area code for all phone numbers in this guide is 508.

Trowbridge Tavern

$$ • 100 Trowbridge Rd., Bourne • 759-0006

Opened in March 1996, the Trowbridge Tavern has already established itself as a popular Cape Cod pub steeped in the English tradition. It has a cheerful, homey atmosphere that makes you feel welcome the moment you walk through the door. In the same building as the Best Western Bridge-Bourne Hotel (see our Hotels, Motels and Resorts chapter), the tavern serves American cuisine ranging from prime rib to local seafood. Also on the menu are chicken and pasta dishes and a variety of appetizers including salads and soups. Trowbridge Tavern has seating for about 100, while an outside deck overlooking the beautiful Cape Cod Canal and Bourne Bridge offers seating for an additional 60 people. Clientele ranges from those in their 20s to families with children to those in their 60s and 70s (and older). Like a traditional English pub, it is a gathering spot where everyone feels welcome. The tavern serves lunch and dinner seven days a week year round.

The Bridge Restaurant

$$ • 21 Rt. 6A, Sagamore • 888-8144

Many travelers pass right by The Bridge Restaurant, which sits at the foot of the Sagamore Bridge. But if you want to prolong your stay or grab a hot meal just before leaving the Cape, get off Route 6 at Exit 1 (the restaurant is right across from the exit ramp) and bring your appetite. Home-style New England and Italian specialities such as Yankee pot roast and eggplant Parmesan have been drawing loyal locals here for the last 36 years. The restaurant is open for lunch and dinner year round, except for Thanksgiving and Christmas Day. The Bridge offers early bird specials from 4 to 6 PM, and small portions are available for seniors and children.

Sagamore Inn

$$ • 1131 Rt. 6A, Sagamore • 888-9707

Locals love the family feel at the Sagamore Inn. There are three main reasons why the parking lot is always jammed: 1) the service is excellent; 2) the staff, mostly native Cape Codders, is fun-loving; and 3) Shirley's mouth-watering pot roast is on the menu. Owners Shirley and Patty Pagliarani both cook at the inn, concocting their wonderful Italian sauces from scratch. Their son operates a commercial fishing vessel, so you know the seafood is the freshest. The shrimp, lobster and home-made lasagna are superb. Equally superb are the freshly made desserts, such as banana cream pie and Grape-Nuts pudding. Sagamore Inn has a real Cape Cod feel mixed with a family-dining atmosphere. It is open for lunch and dinner daily except Tuesday from April through mid-November.

Photo: Cape Cod Times

Catch a beautiful view while dining near the water at the Chatham Bars Inn.

Craigville Pizza and Mexican at Pocasset

$ • 4 Barlows Landing Rd., Pocasset • 564-6306

Burritos and tacos are always popular at this Mexi-pizza place, which also serves salads, subs, calzones, enchiladas, chicken dishes, pastas, soups and, of course, all types of pizza. There is a second location in Craigville. Both facilities have a beer and wine license. The restaurants are open for lunch and dinner daily year round, with later hours on Friday and Saturday.

Stir-Crazy

$ • 626 MacArthur Blvd., Pocasset • 564-6464

Curry lovers, do yourself a big favor and stop off for dinner or take-out at this small restaurant on MacArthur Boulevard (Route 28) for a taste of Bopha Samms' Cambodian cooking. The food is rich with flavor, texture and healthy ingredients such as vegetables, rice and homemade noodles. "Everything is different and everything is prepared from scratch," says Samms. Although the food can be spicy, it is not hot unless you request it. Stir-Crazy started as a tiny place on Main Street in Buzzards Bay, but success necessitated expansion to the present convenient location. It is open for dinner from Tuesday to Sunday and serves lunch only on Friday. Stir Crazy closes in January.

The Chart Room

$$ • 1 Shipyard Ln., Cataumet • 563-5350

The staff at the Chart Room, located at Kingman Marina, is expert at accommodating weary and rumpled mariners looking for a good meal. And that's what they find at this 31-year-old casual-style restaurant with an excellent reputation for consistency and good seafood — baked stuffed lobster, lobster salad, scrod, sole, bluefish, striped bass and halibut — in addition to steaks and chops. The freshly made quahog chowder is just right, not too thick or too watery. Desserts, such as apple pie and ice cream puffs, are made locally.

The Chart Room opens around Memorial Day for weekends only until mid-June, daily through the summer and weekends only after Labor Day until Columbus Day. Call and ask for directions — this one's a little hard to find, but worth the trouble.

Bayberry's Log Cabin Restaurant

$ • 271 Cotuit Rd., South Sandwich • 477-4094

This log-cabin restaurant with homemade New England cooking, comfortable booths and reasonable prices is perfect for families. Breakfast entrees include some pleasant surprises — chocolate chip pancakes, raisin French toast and Belgian cranberry waffles — among the more traditional morning fare. For lunch and dinner you can choose from ham and cheese croissants, prime rib, pizzas, burgers and fried seafood. Bayberry's is open daily all year long for breakfast, lunch and dinner. Reservations are accepted for parties of five or more.

Bobby Byrne's Pub

$ • Tupper Rd., Sandwich • 888-6088

When locals are in a mood to relax, this is one place they'll head. This friendly pub lives up to its billing as "an eating, drinking and talking establishment." Its casual atmosphere, reasonable prices, savory sandwiches, such as the Reuben and chicken fillet, hamburgers and specials will certainly hit the spot. Freshly made soups and lighter fare are always popular. Bobby Byrne's serves lunch and dinner daily year round. The large bar with a wide-screen TV draws fans of the Patriots, Red Sox, Celtics and Bruins and friends who just want to get together to catch up on the latest. You'll find other Bobby Byrne's Pubs at Mashpee Commons in Mashpee and at the corner of Route 28 and Bearses Way in Hyannis.

Captain Scott's

$ • 71 Tupper Rd., Sandwich • 888-1675

If you're into the casual dining thing, then slip into something more comfortable, like per-

INSIDERS' TIP

If you want to order scallops like a Cape Codder, pronounce them "scollups".

haps Captain Scott's, a small, very casual eatery with great food and easy prices. You have your choice of indoor or outdoor seating, or you can order take-out. Captain Scott's, near the town marina, features early bird specials and a daily special. In addition to the fish and chips and fried smelt, the chicken and Italian entrees are very popular. Captain Scott's is open daily year round.

Captain's Table Restaurant

$$ • 14 Gallo Rd., Sandwich • 888-8440

From tables inside or on the screened deck overlooking the Cape Cod Canal, you can watch ships and boats sail through the waterway while you sip something cool or settle down to a bowl of seafood stew. The traditional New England menu focuses on seafood specialties, including swordfish, baked stuffed lobster and shrimp. For dessert try the ice cream truffles with white or dark chocolate. The Captain's Table is open April 1 through the end of December and serves lunch and dinner daily except Monday from Memorial Day to Labor Day. It is open Thursday through Sunday before Memorial Day and from October through December.

The Dan'l Webster Inn

$$$ • 149 Main St., Sandwich • 888-3622

This is a Cape Cod dining encounter of the most wonderful kind. One of the best restaurants in the area, the award-winning Dan'l Webster (see our Hotels, Motels and Resorts chapter and our Nightlife chapter) offers excellent American cuisine, fine service, an exemplary wine list and classy ambiance. We recommend dining in the Conservatory, a glass-walled area that offers a lovely view of a linden tree and gardens. Seafood entrees are always delicious here, but the chicken pot pie has been the consistent top seller through the years. This year-round restaurant offers early evening specials, which include soup or salad and dessert, from 4:30 to 5:45 PM. The 21-page wine list, which has received *Wine Spectator*'s award of excellence, includes superb French, Italian, German and American varieties.

The Dan'l Webster, which is housed in a Colonial inn, serves breakfast, lunch and dinner in four dining rooms (from formal to slightly casual). The menu changes every five weeks. The inn's Devil and Dan Tavern offers lighter fare, including complimentary cheddar cheese and crackers. Sunday brunch features an extensive à la carte menu.

Horizons on Cape Cod Bay

$$ • 98 Town Neck Rd., Sandwich • 888-6166

After seeing Horizons' panoramic view across Cape Cod Bay from Sandwich to Provincetown you can understand why this restaurant is so popular. Sit indoors or out on a deck (bring your sunglasses on a bright day) and order from a menu that's as casual as the atmosphere. The ocean crab sandwich and fried blooming onions are particularly tasty. You'll find the traditional seafood fare you'd expect from a place this close to the water. Horizons serves lunch and dinner daily from April to early November. The downstairs Cape Cod Bay Room is open for special functions, but book it early. Horizons will also arrange traditional clambakes on the beach.

Marshland

$, no credit cards • 109 Rt. 6A, Sandwich • 888-9824

This local favorite might look inconspicuous, but the long bench outside is a tip-off to its popularity — there's often a line here. The wait is seldom long, however, and the food is terrific, especially the breakfasts. Daily specials, quick service and booth seating make this a popular meeting place, so expect friendly hubbub. Everything on the menu is homemade, and the baked stuffed shells, lasagna, meat loaf and broiled scrod with crab sauce sell particularly well. If you are in a rush, grab some coffee and a fresh muffin or cinnamon roll in the coffee shop. Marshland is open daily year round. Breakfast, lunch and dinner are served Tuesday through Saturday, but breakfast is the only meal served on Sunday, and dinner is not served on Monday.

Merchant Square Deli

$, no credit cards • Rt. 6A, Sandwich • 888-7717

For your early morning hazelnut coffee fix or a big sandwich with a free chocolate chip cookie and chips stop by the Merchant Square Deli. Its spacious and sunny indoor seating makes it the meeting place of choice for many locals who gather here year round. It's open daily during breakfast and lunch hours.

Sandwich's Sandwiches

$, no credit cards • 132 Rt. 6A, Sandwich • 888-1221

Situated at the traffic light near the train station, this cute little sandwich shop serves outstanding homemade soups and sandwiches. Don't even look at the brownies unless you're prepared to devour one — or two. The shop is open for lunch only and is closed in January and February.

Sweet Tomatoes

$ • 148 Rt. 6A, Sandwich • 888-5979

This is pizza with pizazz! From the crust to the creative toppings, these Neopolitan pizzas are full of flavor and healthy ingredients, and you can watch them being assembled. How about a white Greek pizza with feta, spinach and garlic, or maybe a white pizza with shrimp, garlic, onion and capers? Whatever you decide, don't wait until you're hungry to call in an order because they often need a half-hour to an hour to fill orders.

Lunch and dinner are served daily during summer. From Labor Day to Columbus Day lunch is served Friday, Saturday and Sunday, while dinner is served Tuesday through Sunday. Sweet Tomatoes is open year round, with midday hours Friday through Sunday; it is closed on Mondays in the off-season. Another eatery is in Osterville at 770 W. Main Street.

The Bee-Hive Tavern

$$ • 406 Rt. 6A, East Sandwich • 833-1184

The day The Bee-Hive opened in 1992, it was so mobbed it ran out of food and had to close two hours early. Credit the business savvy of owners Bob King and Tobin Wert, who have built success around cozy seating, reliably good food and a personable staff. The menu offers a mix of specials, traditional entrees and fresh seafood. The fried oysters are absolutely wonderful! Rolls and desserts are baked on site, and the homemade Bee Sting ice cream with butter crunch bits makes a memorable dessert. The Bee-Hive is open daily for lunch and dinner and serves breakfast on Saturday and Sunday only. The Bee-Hive is usually busy, but it's worth the wait.

Sandy Neck Restaurant

$$ • 679 Rt. 6A, East Sandwich • 362-2943

This cozy, casual restaurant with a bar is a great place to get a bite to eat before or after going to Sandy Neck Beach, or if you're just out sightseeing along Route 6A. The waitresses are friendly, and the daily specials are popular. For $18.95 you can get one of two great meals: the Cape Cod Clambake, which has a lobster, linguiça, steamers, chowder, french fries and cole slaw; or the Cape Cod Barbeque, with chowder, ribs, half a lobster, steamers, fries and coleslaw. Located at the entrance to the road leading to Sandy Neck Beach, the restaurant is open year round. Reservations are accepted.

6A Cafe

$ • 415 Rt. 6A, East Sandwich • 888-5220

What a perfect gem! This cozy, personable diner-style cafe offers personality plus excellent food at unbelievably low prices. For instance you can enjoy swordfish or a Delmonico steak dinner for less than $10! Adding to the fun atmosphere, an electric train circles the dining room overhead, not unlike the train that travels along the tracks crossing Route 6A not far from the cafe. You can order anything from pizza to burgers and prime rib. 6A Cafe offers daily specials. The menu also includes beer and wine. The comfortable, spotless cafe serves breakfast and lunch daily and dinner Thursday through Sunday.

Box Lunch

$ • 781 Main St., Falmouth • 457-ROLS

The menu at Box Lunch boasts more than 50 "rollwiches" — sandwiches built on thin pita-like bread then rolled up for easy eating. These sandwiches have such names as the Monument, which features heaps of turkey, ham, Swiss, Durkee's dressing and either lettuce and tomato or avocado, and Jaws II, which is an oversize monstrosity featuring a half-pound of rare roast beef, horseradish, onions and mayo. (This one bites back!) There are meatless selections as well, such as the Organic Pocket. Other year-round Box Lunch locations can be found in Hyannis, South Yarmouth, South Dennis, Brewster, East Orleans, North Eastham, Wellfleet and Provincetown (each is individually owned). This is great food that won't cost you a lot of bread!

Cape Cod Chicken

$ • 235 Main St., Falmouth • 457-1302

If you like chicken, you'll love Cape Cod Chicken. The price is right, the rotisserie-roasted chicken is tender and tasty, and if you've got to feed four to 20 people in a hurry, Cape Cod Chicken caters. The menu includes roast pork, beef and turkey, chicken pot pies, soups, salads, sandwiches and 21 side dishes.

The restaurant seats about 35; otherwise, you can get your food to go or have it delivered free within 2 miles. Cape Cod Chicken serves lunch and dinner year round.

Chapoquoit Grill

$$ • 410 West Falmouth Hwy., Falmouth • 540-7794

This is a real locals' favorite so you may have to wait to be seated, even on a Tuesday night. Our advice is to head for the bar, which is a delightful place, and start the evening off with a beverage and some savory garlic bread. The menu puts a spin on the concept of eclectic, for everything here is unusual — shrimp diablo pizza, roast chicken sandwiches with sliced apples and mango chutney spread, and seafood Trinidad with lobster, shrimp and scallops in a spiced cream sauce on pasta. The food here is excellent. Cocktails come in huge water glasses with a plastic mermaid and a palm tree stirrer. Open daily year round, the Chapoquoit Grill serves dinner only (pizzas until 11 PM on weekends). Next door, the Chappy Cafe serves breakfast and lunch until 5 PM with mostly take-out and some seating. Specials for both the Grill and Cafe change regularly.

The Coonamessett Inn

$$ • 311 Gifford St., Falmouth • 548-2300

A country showplace with fresh flowers and cozy fireplaces, The Coonamessett Inn has been for decades a Falmouth favorite for weddings, special occasions and dining out. The restaurant has four attractive dining rooms, one with a fireplace and two with views of Jones Pond behind the inn. Look for original works of well-known local primitive artist Ralph Cahoon. Popular menu items include regional favorites such as herb-crusted Chatham cod, the heart-healthy special of the day and freshly made soups — roasted eggplant and tomato or butternut-squash bisque to name two. Some of the soup recipes have been published in *Gourmet Magazine*. You have your choice of vegetarian entrees, and all desserts are freshly made.

Breakfast is served daily from April through October. For lunch and dinner, dine here daily May through December and Friday through Sunday from January to April. Sunday brunch is served from 11 AM to 2 PM. We recommend you make reservations.

Flying Bridge Restaurant

$$$ • 220 Scranton Ave., Falmouth • 548-2700

If you're looking for good food, delightful outdoor seating and a fabulous view of Falmouth's busy inner harbor, you'll find it here. Whether you're seated upstairs, downstairs or on the sun deck, it's always a pleasure to dine at the Flying Bridge. The menu offers a nice mix of native seafood, Italian dishes, steaks, burgers, sandwiches and chef's specialties. Lobster, swordfish and fresh-caught tuna are always popular. About half of the seating is outdoors at this large restaurant, which is heavily booked for weddings and special functions.

You can dine here daily in season for lunch and dinner, with late-night hours on weekends. The restaurant is open on weekends only after October 31 until mid-December. The Flying Bridge reopens for the season on April 15. As they say, the only thing they overlook is Falmouth Harbor.

Golden Swan

$$ • 323 Main St., Falmouth • 540-6580

For a quiet, moderately priced restaurant with a German flavor and a diverse menu, stop in at the Golden Swan. Local customers enjoy the well-prepared veal, shrimp and chicken dishes. Come in before 7 PM on Saturday evenings for the early bird specials. The wine and beer list is ample. Golden Swan is open for dinner daily year round.

INSIDERS' TIP

Pack a picnic lunch and head over to the grounds of the Cape Playhouse in Dennis. Sit on the expansive lawns or opt for the shade of the gazebo. Seeing the show at the Playhouse will enhance the adventure even more.

Grasmere Pub

$$ • 327 Gifford St., Falmouth • 548-9861

Some say you'll get the best fish chowder on Cape Cod here. If you also want a light supper or a quiet spot for good conversation, come to the Grasmere, beside the Woodbriar Golf Course. The pub has a small bar that seats seven. The menu features seafood, lobster, steak and sandwich items, and you get a trip to the salad bar with all entrees. In addition to the day's specials, Tuesday is Italian night, Friday is fish and chips night, and Saturday is prime rib night. The pub is open year round for lunch and dinner Tuesday through Saturday and dinner only on Sunday and Monday.

Hearth and Kettle

$ • Rt. 28 (at Colonial Shopping Center), Falmouth • 548-6111

The family-owned Hearth and Kettle has built a rock-solid reputation among locals for good food and a flexible menu. For instance, early bird entree specials are served from noon to 6 PM . . . talk about giving the people what they want!

The restaurant, which has a rustic Colonial decor, has many faces. It is a great breakfast spot, yet it's also the place for a lunch break from the ardors of shopping or sightseeing. In the evening it becomes the ideal family dinner choice. Parents will feel comfortable here with young children (kids get crayons and a coloring book along with a special menu), and the locals feel just as comfortable meeting friends here after hours for a drink.

The menu ranges from traditional New England dishes such as scrod and Indian pudding to contemporary chicken stir-fry and heart-smart dishes. Cranberry and blueberry muffins and breads are fresh-baked daily, and there is always clam chowder and soup of the day. By the way, the lobster chowder is the same chowder served at the prestigious Dan'l Webster (same owners). Friday is fish-fry night.

Hearth and Kettle also has locations in Centerville (which also has the H&K Bakery), Hyannis, Yarmouth and Orleans as well as in Plymouth at the John Carver Inn. They're open daily year round.

Lawrence's Restaurant

$$ • 24 Nantucket Ave., Falmouth • 540-9600

Tucked away in the Heights, Falmouth's oldest restaurant offers good food and that pleasant neighborhood feel. You can eat inside or outside on the patio. Long a fixture in the area, Lawrence's was overhauled a few years ago. Although you can still get your favorite sandwiches or pizza, the menu now includes such upscale items as grilled oysters and roasted stuffed rack of lamb. Lawrence's serves both lunch (weekends only) and dinner (daily) from mid-April to December. Getting to this restaurant can be a little complicated so we'll give you some directions: Take Falmouth Heights Road to the end of the harbor, turn left onto Grand Avenue and follow Grand to the Park Beach Hotel; turn left and immediately look on the right for Nantucket Avenue, which runs parallel to Grand Avenue.

Peking Palace

$ • 452 Main St., Falmouth • 540-8204

This 11-year-old restaurant is always packed, and it's no wonder. The food is excellent, creative and served in generous portions, even the takeout. The lunch and dinner menus focus on Mandarin Szechwan and Cantonese, with an assortment of chicken dishes such as Paradise Chicken. A recently introduced spicy beef dish served on Chinese greens has also caught on with diners.

Peking Palace, which has an authentic Chinese decor, is one of the few places in town you can go after midnight. The restaurant also offers take-out, catering and special functions. Dishes are prepared exclusively with canola oil. The chef will accommodate special dietary requests and preferences, if possible. The Peking Palace is open daily year round and stays open until 2 AM in the summer; until midnight the rest of the year.

The Quarterdeck

$ • 164 Main St., Falmouth • 548-9900

What a cozy, laid-back place to duck in to for a bite to eat! Right on Main Street, the Quarterdeck has a "Cheers" feel to it. And if you're there when the homemade mushroom soup is on the menu, trust us, you'll never

taste better. Fried calamari, seafood, pasta, vegetarian entrees and the Quarterdeck Sampler, a collection of appetizers are also great, but be on the lookout for something new when the chef is feeling creative. The Quarterdeck has a nautical decor, friendly staff and a large choice of beers. The decent wine list includes Portuguese selections. It is open seven days a week for lunch and dinner year round.

Regatta of Falmouth By the Sea

$$$ • 217 Clinton Ave., Falmouth • 548-5400

This award-winning restaurant has much to offer — a unique waterfront location at the entrance of Falmouth Harbor, absolutely wonderful food and service, and an exceptional wine menu. Simply put, meals here are beautifully cooked and beautifully served. With 21 windows facing Vineyard Sound, the Regatta's outstanding waterfront location complements its contemporary French-inspired decor.

The menu offers all manner of delights, including the freshest seafood and American, European and Asian cuisine creations. Three menus accommodate differing appetites and pocketbooks, but all are top-quality. Early three-course dinners are served from 5 to 6 PM. Lighter fare is served at a lighter price. Dinner entrees are works of art. Desserts are legendary, but the one that soars above them all is the Dessert Trilogy, which combines three of the Regatta's favorite desserts. The restaurant is open nightly for dinner only from May through September.

Seafood Sam's

$ • 356 Palmer Ave., Falmouth • 540-7877

If you're looking for a great place to stop in for seafood at prices that won't break your budget, especially if you have kids, this is it. An immaculate restaurant with outdoor seating, Seafood Sam's is known for its tasty lobster roll, but the fresh fried or broiled seafood is just as good. There's a children's menu, or families can buy a family fish fry for four. Sam's offers luncheon specials all year long. Beer and wine are available. Other Seafood Sam's are in Sandwich, Yarmouth and Harwich.

The Wharf

$$ • Grand Ave., Falmouth Heights • 548-0777

Picture a glass of frigid beer and a plate of fried clams served on an outside deck. You're getting a little sunburn on your nose, the summer breeze is sweet and a guitar player is entertaining the bar crowd. To your left is a beach full of sun worshippers, and straight ahead is lovely Martha's Vineyard. This is no Cape Cod daydream — this is the Wharf. We get a kick out of their slogan: "If our fish were any fresher, you'd have to slap it." The Wharf is open daily during the summer season for lunch and dinner with variable hours during the off-season months.

The Silver Lounge Restaurant

$-$$ • Rt. 28A, North Falmouth • 563-2410

Day after day, year after year, the Silver Lounge is busy. A favorite year-round watering hole for locals and visitors who like to stop in for steaks or a light meal, the restaurant offers a full menu from midday to 1 AM. The menu is casual, with a lot of steaks, sandwiches and reasonably priced seafood. Seating is booth or table, with additional seating in a converted railroad car. Don't worry if there's a line — the wait is usually not long, and if you're really crunched for time, everything on the menu is available for take-out.

Captain Kidd Waterfront Tavern

$ • 77 Water St., Woods Hole • 548-9206

There's the Oceanographic Institution, then there's the other Woods Hole institution, the Captain Kidd, which opened shortly after Prohibition ended. Don't miss it. You can settle down at the bar or lounge complete with a fireplace, in the waterfront dining room or outside on the patio or dock overlooking Eel Pond. The menu features fresh seafood, including scrod, tuna and lobster brought in by local fishermen.

The Kidd starts serving daily at lunch, and the full menu is available until 10 PM. The bar stays open until 1:30 AM. Captain Kidd is open year round.

The Dome

$$ • 539 Woods Hole Rd., Woods Hole • 548-0800

This eye-catching restaurant overlooking Little Harbor is in fact the nation's oldest geodesic dome, whose high-ceiling design gives the restaurant a spacious feeling. The structure was built in 1953 for Gunnar Peterson by the renowned architect Buckminster Fuller. The menu is traditional New England — seafood, duckling and prime rib are the most popular entrees. And don't pass up The Dome's rich fudge cake or the chocolate Nautilus shell filled with mousse for dessert. The Dome has an excellent selection of American, Italian and French wines. The restaurant is open daily for dinner only except on Monday from April to October.

Fishmonger's Cafe

$$ • 56 Water St., Woods Hole • 540-5376

Where else besides Woods Hole could you enjoy a good ol' fisherman's stew beside a drawbridge? Watching the little bridge being raised and lowered for boat traffic passing within a few feet of the restaurant is a fascinating pastime at Fishmonger's. In fact, all of Woods Hole's remarkable sights, marine and otherwise, are part of the view from this restaurant's windows. The casual gourmet menu focuses on natural foods, grains, fresh fish, homemade soups plus a number of vegetarian entrees — all excellent. Daily special dishes are very popular. The Fishmonger is open for breakfast, lunch and dinner from mid-February through mid-December. It is closed on Tuesday except in July and August.

FYI

Unless otherwise noted, the area code for all phone numbers in this guide is 508.

The Landfall

$$$ • 2 Luscombe Ave., Woods Hole • 548-1758

At The Landfall you can enjoy both fresh seafood and a flawless view of the harbor activity, from sailboats and fishing vessels to lumbering ferries pulling into their Woods Hole berth only a few hundred feet away. The restaurant's nautical decor complements its surroundings. Look for a 2,000-year-old Grecian urn among the decorations on the ceiling. It would be a pity not to order fresh seafood here, especially the scallops, lobster or seafood platter. Swordfish with lobster medallions, asparagus and hollandaise sauce is popular, as are the clam chowder and the Key lime pie. Regulars remember the beating The Landfall took from Hurricane Bob in 1991, but after repairs the restaurant was even better than ever. It is open for lunch and dinner daily from April through October.

Shuckers

$$ • 91-A Water St., Woods Hole • 540-3850

This is a super-casual place to meet, eat and order a Nobska Light beer. Shuckers has a raw bar and outdoor seating overlooking Eel Pond. Look for the twin lobster special and the mussel stew. It's a lively place, and everything is prepared on the premises. The bartenders are fun and the seafood is exceptional. It is open for lunch and dinner daily from Memorial Day until two weeks after Labor Day.

Bobby Byrne's Pub

$ • Mashpee Commons, Mashpee • 477-0600

Locals head to this friendly pub for the casual atmosphere, reasonable prices and delicious sandwiches. Bobby Byrne's is open for lunch and dinner year round. Other locations can be found on Tupper Road in Sandwich and at the corner of Route 28 and Bearses Way in Hyannis. (Also see our Sandwich section.)

Cherrystones

$$ • 413 Rt. 151, Mashpee • 477-4481

Warm and inviting with pine paneling, booths and tables, and a rustic Cape Cod decor, Cherrystones is a great family place. The menu is typically Cape Cod, too, featuring hearty home-style cooking. The quahog chowder is delicious, and the sliced leg of lamb is cut-with-a-fork tender and costs considerably less than you'd pay at most places. The lemon cake with raspberry sherbet and the cr ème de menthe parfait are wonderful. This well-run, family-owned place is open for dinner daily year round.

The Flume

$$ • 13 Lake Ave., off Rt. 130, Mashpee • 477-1456

The Flume has an enviable reputation based on countless happy customers who have stuffed themselves with such wonderful traditional dishes as codfish cakes, finan haddie, chicken pie, blueberry pie and apple brown betty. Everything here is homemade and delicious, but seafood gets the rave reviews. Casual and family oriented, the Flume is open from April 1 until the end of November and serves dinner daily from 5 to 9 PM (Sunday is from noon to 8 PM). The restaurant is usually crowded, but it's a pretty spot so you shouldn't mind the wait.

Gone Tomatoes

$$ • Mashpee Commons, intersection of rts. 28 and 151, Mashpee • 477-8100

Gone Tomatoes at Mashpee Commons is the perfect place to meet friends for lunch while shopping, to have dinner before or after seeing a movie next door and to enjoy live music outdoors in the summer (see our Arts and Entertainment chapter). The attractive bistro decor and versatile seating combined with a great Northern Italian menu account for the popularity of this place. We are tempted to say the chicken Parmesan with pasta is the best, but what about the mushroom scampi on an angel hair pancake? The restaurant is open year round for lunch and dinner seven days a week.

Popponesset Inn

$$$ • Shore Dr., Mashpee • 477-1100

One of the loveliest oceanside dining spots on Cape Cod, the award-winning Popponesset Inn has been cited for excellence by *Boston Magazine* and *USAir Magazine*. The 250-seat restaurant is in tremendous demand for weddings and other private functions such as clambakes, oceanside buffets and barbecues, but it's also open to the public. The menu is traditional New England cuisine with a twist. Seafood specialties such as bouillabaisse, scallop-and-shrimp Newburg and shrimp scampi are particularly popular. The Popponesset Inn is open for dinner daily April through mid-October and daily for lunch from June through Labor Day. Lighter fare, including steamers, hamburgers and salads, is served outdoors from Sunday to Friday. Reservations are suggested.

Zuni Cafe

$-$$ • Mashpee Commons, Mashpee • 539-2354

After touring the many shops at Mashpee Commons or perhaps after sampling the warm waters at Mashpee's South Cape Beach, stop in at the Zuni Cafe for the best in Southwestern/Mexican food. Opened in August 1996, this year-round restaurant serves the spicy stuff for lunch and dinner Monday through Friday and for breakfast, lunch and dinner on Saturday and Sunday. Breakfast specialties include both traditional and Mexican-style offerings. How about a beef tortilla along with your eggs and home fries? Dinner choices include a vegetable quesadilla topped with guacamole, refried beans and Mexican rice and all kinds of fajitas: carne con queso (steak), chicken and even shrimp. Of course, burritos and taco salad are on the menu. Speaking of the menu, kids have their own to choose from. Zuni Cafe offers seating for nearly 100; parties of five or greater are asked to make reservations.

Marketplace Raw Bar

$ • off Great Neck Road S., Popponesset Marketplace, New Seabury (Mashpee) • 477-9400, ext. 1572

This hot spot on the grounds of the New Seabury Resort off Great Neck Road S. (see our Hotels, Motels and Resorts chapter) is a great raw bar serving appetizers and drinks. With a little reggae music playing in the background and happy folk in the foreground, this is definitely a happening place. And this is the place to get a great Cape Cod lobster roll with big, tender chunks of lobster. The raw bar is open daily from mid-June to Labor Day; weekends only from Mother's Day to mid-June and from Labor Day until the end of October.

The Players Club at New Seabury Country Club

$$ • off Great Neck Rd., New Seabury (Mashpee) • 477-9111

What better place than the Players Club to unwind after a challenging game of golf or to just watch others working their way around New Seabury's famous Blue Course. The club has indoor and outdoor seating and one of the best views of Vineyard Sound you'll find. Dine here for lunch and dinner. The menu, like the restaurant, is casual: burgers, lobster, clam chowder and steak. The Players Club is open daily in season — mid-April through the end of October — and with limited hours at other times.

Mid-Cape

The Regatta of Cotuit

$$$ • Rt. 28, Cotuit • 428-5715

No wonder the Regatta of Cotuit wins the hearts of diners and food critics alike! Set in an 18th-century inn, this much-awarded restaurant has eight small dining rooms that provide the intimate environment that fosters fine dining. Candlelight, old wood and superb piano music create a warm, romantic tone. The distinguished wine list and exclusive regional American menu with Oriental influences will satisfy the most demanding gourmet. Selections include such items as a wild mushroom strudel appetizer, seared center cut black and white sesame encrusted swordfish steak with a scallop and shrimp farci, and the dessert trilogy, which includes three of the Regatta's favorite desserts all in one. Meat dishes are especially noteworthy; don't be surprised to discover rabbit, pheasant and duck on the menu. Fish choices include native favorites plus seafoods from around the world.

Open daily year round for dinner, the Regatta offers three menus, including one for a three-course meal for $19.97 from 5 to 6 PM, (one of the best fine-dining values around) and another for tavern fare. Brantz and Wendy Bryan own and operate both the Regatta of Cotuit and the Regatta of Falmouth.

Joseph's

$$ • 825 Main St., Osterville • 420-1742

This is one of the few restaurants where people are likely to encounter the owner and the chef. Joseph Murray, who wears both hats, does the cooking and often follows it up with a visit to the table. Although this is essentially an upscale Italian restaurant, Joseph applies his considerable talents to fresh seafood and will do his best to satisfy your special requests. The cozy decor makes use of soft colors, plants and a wall of bookshelves that runs the length of the restaurant. Prices are reasonable, and the food is high quality. Joseph's is open year round. In season it's open daily for breakfast, lunch and dinner, and from November through March it's open Wednesday through Sunday for all meals.

Hearth and Kettle

$ • 23 Richardson Rd., Centerville • 775-8878

Locals and visitors to the Craigville-Centerville area enjoy breakfast, lunch and dinner at Hearth and Kettle's Centerville location. This restaurant has a bakery on location where you can get your morning muffins and pastries or a cake for a special occasion. Other year-round Hearth and Kettles are in Falmouth, Hyannis, Yarmouth and Orleans. There is also a Plymouth restaurant. (See our write-up in the Falmouth section.)

Sprouts Cafe

$ • Bell Tower Mall, 1600 Rt. 28, Centerville • 771-8394

Located inside Cape Cod Natural Foods (see our Shopping chapter), this cafe specializes in vegetarian and organic foods and offers seating for about 15 as well as take-out service. Open from 8 AM to 7 PM year round, Sprouts brews organic coffees, pours fresh-squeezed juices and bakes muffins in the morning. It also offers health-conscious selections for lunch and dinner including sandwiches, salads and hot vegetarian, chicken and fish dishes. All food is prepared using only the freshest ingredients. Besides a hot table, there's also a deli case and a grab-and-go case filled with sandwiches and salads already made, wrapped and ready to go.

Alberto's Ristorante

$$$ • 360 Main St., Hyannis • 778-1770

With Northern Italian cuisine, freshly made pasta, daily and early bird specials, an extensive wine list and a quiet, elegant decor, this restaurant has made its mark on Main Street as a bright and comfortable dining place that is consistent and well-managed. Whether its for stuffed pasta, seafood dishes or sirloin, Alberto's Italian hospitality will have you coming back again and again. Seafood ravioli is filled with lobster, scallops, shrimp and ricotta, Romano and Parmesan cheeses. Alberto's is open daily for lunch and dinner year round. Reservations are suggested.

Baxter's Boathouse Club

$ • 177 Pleasant St., Hyannis • 775-7040

When tourists ask the locals where to find a waterfront restaurant in Hyannis, the answer is often, "Go to Baxter's." It's a perfect choice for cocktails in a waterfront setting — the view of the harbor is fabulous. If you are arriving by boat, you can tie up at the small dock, or you can stay on your boat and be waited on (talk about service!). The *Governor Brann*, a converted Maine ferryboat tied alongside the restaurant, seats more than 200 people. Kids get a kick out of feeding the sea gulls and ducks looking for a snack. Fried clams are the most popular menu item, and in addition to seafood, Baxter's also serves steaks, sandwiches and burgers. Baxter's serves lunch and dinner daily from April through Columbus Day. The bar stays open until the wee hours.

The Benchmark

$-$$ • 11 Ridgewood Ave., Hyannis • 771-2822

"Fresh" is the password here, for everything from the pasta and bread to the salad dressings is made fresh daily. The menu includes wonderful gourmet pizzas that have such tempting additions as fresh herbs and vegetables in season, sun-dried tomatoes and artichoke hearts. Don't overlook the homemade vegetable ravioli with soy and mustard sauce or the tabbouleh, spinach and Greek entree salads served with a choice of four homemade dressings, including lemon oregano and ginger-soy. The restaurant has seating for 75 and offers take-out service and a children's menu. It is open daily for lunch and dinner year round (but there's no lunch on Sunday). The Benchmark is a block behind the Colonial Candle of Cape Cod on Main Street. It can be a little hard to find, but just envision that chocolate bread pudding with vanilla cream sauce waiting for you and you're sure to find it.

Bobby Byrne's Pub

$ • Rt. 28 and Bearses Way, Hyannis • 775-1425

This favorite mid-Cape restaurant is open year round, serving lunch and dinner as well as brunch on Sundays. Specials are offered throughout the week. Bobby Byrne's has two other Cape locations — on Tupper Road in Sandwich and at Mashpee Commons in Mashpee. (See the write-up in the Sandwich section.)

Cape Cod Dinner Train

$$$$ • Main St., Hyannis • 771-3788

If you want to impress or delight someone special, make a reservation on the elegant Cape Cod Dinner Train, certainly the Cape's most unique dining experience. You pick up the tickets at the small station at the east end of Main Street, and from the minute you step onto the train and are seated at your four-person table (you can pay more for a private table) until the second you disembark nearly three hours later, you'll be charmed by this moveable feast. You'll travel about 42 miles from appetizer to dessert, passing by Cape Cod cranberry bogs and salt marshes.

Tables are set with white linen, silverware and a red rose, and classical music plays quietly as servers bring in five well-spaced courses. The entree can be meat, fish, poultry or vegetarian. The menu, which changes monthly, features such items as broiled salmon, swordfish, Chicken Françaises and tenderloin of beef with port wine.

The dress code requires men to wear a jacket or tie; young diners should be 14 or older. The Cape Cod Dinner Train operates on weekends from Valentine's Day through May; Wednesday through Sunday in June; Tuesday through Sunday in July and August; Wednesday through Sunday from September through October and weekends only in November and December. It is closed from January 1 until Valentine's Day. Gratuities are additional, and special functions and group rates are available.

Cooke's

$ • Rt. 132, Hyannis • 775-0450

For locals, the year doesn't begin until Cooke's reopens for business. That first plate of fried clams is like throwing out the first pitch for the start of the new baseball season. This award-winning seasonal restaurant has earned its reputation the hard way — by consistently serving good meals. It offers burgers, but many locals consider Cooke's to be the best value for fresh fried and broiled seafood in the area. Try the fish and chips or scallops, and see if you agree. If there's a line, stick around; the broiled seafood platter is well-worth the wait. Cooke's is open daily for lunch and dinner from mid-March to the end of November. There's another location in Orleans.

The Dragonlite

$ • 620 Main St., Hyannis • 775-9494

Now owned by Sharry and Monte Lui, The Dragonlite was the first Chinese restaurant on Cape Cod about 50 years ago (it started out as a New York-style deli in the late 1800s). Lunch and dinner menus include traditional Szechwan, Cantonese and Mandarin dishes, including steamed whole fish, other seafood and some casual fare. The restaurant has both booths and table seating and a large room for parties. The Dragonlite is open all year and serves lunch and dinner daily except Sunday and holidays, when it serves dinner only from midday to late evening. Summer hours extend into the wee hours.

D'Olympio's New York Deli and Bakery

$ • 55 Iyanough Rd., Hyannis • 771-3220

How long has it been since you had a real New York steak grinder? Or a hot pastrami sandwich? Or perhaps potato pancakes with applesauce? D'Olympio's has an extensive and clever menu, excellent prices and an all-day breakfast, to say nothing of incredible pies and bologna sandwiches with meat piled high and shaved thin. Also, there are plenty of soups, salads and pasta dishes to choose from. Coffee fans can get cafe au lait, espresso and cappuccino. The kids' menu is more than a token gesture toward youthful tastes and appetites, and for children younger than 10, D'Olympio's serves Baby Cakes and French Toast. Everything is available for take-out. This restaurant is open year round for breakfast, lunch and dinner daily.

The Egg and I

$ • 521 Main St., Hyannis • 771-1596

The Egg and I offers distinctive hours of operation — all night long — making it the perfect place to satisfy those late-night munchies. For possibly the most satisfying breakfast you will ever eat, stop by this little restaurant with the big gourmet menu and huge portions. The ingredients are fresh, the wait staff is friendly, and you can linger long over coffee and no one glares at you. Not for the calorically challenged, the Crow's Nest

specialty is a dish of home fries, scrambled eggs, sausage, cheese and sausage gravy. A new favorite is the raspberry cream cheese French toast, which the cook describes with impressive understatement as "a little rich." This unassuming charmer seats 70 and is open for breakfast daily all year long from 11 PM until 1 PM (the next afternoon).

The Gourmet Brunch

$, no credit cards • 517 Main St., Hyannis • 771-2558

Not for the indecisive, this menu has many omelets from which to choose. The variety is made possible by the combination of such tasty additions as sausage, bacon, asparagus, peppers, cheese, bean sprouts and even peanut butter. Or order waffles or a specialty item such as Brunch Supreme, which is made with puff pastry, ham, artichoke hearts, poached egg, cheese sauce and crabmeat. There are Belgian waffles and quiches to round out the breakfast selections. A glass of champagne and strawberries make this a festive brunch indeed.

Don't overlook the lunch menu, however. Soups, clam chowder, hot and cold sandwiches and salads are standouts. The offerings continue beyond the menu with daily blackboard specials. The restaurant is open for breakfast and lunch daily year round.

Hearth and Kettle

$ • 412 Main St., Hyannis • 771-3737

Located along the popular Main Street in Hyannis, Hearth and Kettle is a great place to duck in for breakfast, lunch or dinner year round ... it only closes on Christmas! The restaurant offers a menu steeped in traditional New England dishes with some surprises. There are other Hearth and Kettle locations in Falmouth, Centerville, South Yarmouth, Orleans and even in Plymouth. (See our write-up in the Falmouth section)

Murph's Recession

$ • 12 Thornton Dr., Hyannis • 775-9750

Off the beaten path in a barn-like building in Independence Park, Murph's Recession is one of those places that has a wonderful love-me or leave-me attitude. Locals have been frequenting Murph's for years. If you're in search of excellent food at excellent prices, you've come to the right place. With a menu that offers homemade soups and salads, prime rib, chicken teriyaki and macaroni and cheese, Murph's has built a loyal clientele around consistency, quality and reasonable prices. Murph's is open for lunch and dinner Monday through Saturday and dinner only on Sunday.

The Paddock

$$$ • West End Rotary, Hyannis • 775-7677

Providing affordable excellence in fine dining since 1969 is The Paddock restaurant at West End Rotary in downtown Hyannis (right next to the famous Melody Tent).

Aside from great service and hospitality, The Paddock offers a delicious menu and an extensive wine list that has been recognized by *Wine Spectator*. Owners John and Maxine Zartarian operate the restaurant (they met as college students working at the Flying Bridge in Falmouth) and two sons are also involved in the family business. Appetizers include such treats as baked clams casino, fresh littlenecks, steamed mussels and fresh Cotuit oysters on the half shell. In the entree department, you have your choice of fine meat and poultry dishes such as grilled filet mignon, grilled New York sirloin or Tuscany lemon chicken. Or you may opt for grilled or poached fresh Norwegian salmon or perhaps something closer to home such as Chatham scrod or native two-pound baked, stuffed or boiled lobsters. The Paddock offers four specials each week — two seafood and two poultry or meat. All entrees include a fresh vegetable plate and your choice of tossed garden salad or soup du jour. The Paddock is open April through mid-November for lunch and dinner. Early evening discounts are offered before 5:45 PM.

FYI

Unless otherwise noted, the area code for all phone numbers in this guide is 508.

The Roadhouse Cafe

$$-$$$ • 488 South St., Hyannis • 775-2386

The Roadhouse is always a favorite spot and never disappoints. In fact, you'll be hard-pressed to find a critic of the Roadhouse Cafe. It seems as if everybody loves it, and what's not to love? The lobster bisque has huge chunks of lobster; the chicken homard, rolled with lobster and Swiss cheese, is take-out from heaven; and patrons say the cafe has better Italian cuisine than Italian restaurants. The bistro tavern area looks something like backwoods Maine with its fireplace and beamed ceiling. You can sit at bar stools or booths. The Roadhouse Cafe is open for dinner daily year round; reservations are recommended. Early bird specials are served every night from 4 to 6 PM. Live entertainment adds a perfect touch to an already perfect evening (see our Nightlife chapter).

Penguins Sea Grill

$$-$$$ • 331 Main St., Hyannis • 775-2023

If you have high expectations and a low tolerance for disappointment, make a reservation to eat here. From start to finish, Penguins Sea Grill is predictably wonderful. Appetizers such as the shrimp and escargot are outstanding, and the wood grill imparts a superb flavor to traditional steaks and chops. Seafood, Italian entrees and unusual specials such as swordfish all vie for top honors in a top-flight menu. Early bird specials are available from 5 to 6 PM. The wine selection is especially noteworthy. When people talk about the high quality of this restaurant, they invariably credit the owner, Bobby Gold, a true restaurateur who keeps on top of everything and makes sure that patrons are completely satisfied. Penguins Sea Grill is open daily for dinner from February to December. It closes from New Year's to February 13.

Sam Diego's

$-$$ • 950 Iyanough Rd., Rt. 132, Hyannis • 771-8816

It seems that everyone goes to Sam's. The place has a fiesta atmosphere, and the food is fun, fun, fun! Free chips and salsa arrive shortly after you sit down, giving you something to munch on as you peruse the extensive menu and wait for a golden Margarita. If you ask for the hot stuff, they've got it. We usually opt for the taco salad. Sam Diego's is one of the best Mexican places on the Cape. It's an enjoyable and comfortable dining experience with reasonable prices and a convenient location that offers good parking. One of the nicest things about it is that it's a multigenerational watering hole. Save room for the fried ice cream — it's almost a meal in itself. Sam Diego's is open for lunch and dinner daily year round. Meals are served until midnight.

INSIDERS' TIP

Even if you vow you hate oysters, try one harvested from Wellfleet. Mmmm! And all that potassium!

Up the Creek

$$ • 36 Old Colony Rd., Hyannis • 771-7866

Tucked away from the Hyannis hubbub (Old Colony Road runs parallel to Ocean Street), this casual home-style restaurant is a favorite local hangout. It is well-liked for its tasty specials, good service and festive conversation. It can get a little crowded, but if you like a cozy atmosphere, you'll love Up The Creek. If you see a line, just relax at the bar before getting down to the serious business of ordering. Besides, you'll need the time to decide among the numerous entrees, including a broiled seafood platter, lobster, scrod, stuffed shrimp, veal, chicken, steak, pasta and the delicious seafood strudel. Up The Creek is open for lunch and dinner year round and for Sunday brunch. In the off-season it is closed on Tuesday and Wednesday.

Barnstable Tavern

$$$ • 3176 Main St., Barnstable • 362-2355

This is everybody's idea of what a Cape Cod tavern ought to be: historic, hospitable and cozy. Built in 1799, the tavern has a rustic, Colonial decor with tables and booths complemented by a traditional New England menu of grilled fresh seafood, steaks, chops, meat and chicken pot pie. Lighter fare includes pasta plates and Caesar salad. The waitresses are friendly and gladly accommodate special requests. Portions are generous — don't be surprised if you need a doggie bag for the extras. It's a comfortable place to spend a couple of hours over a leisurely lunch. You can dine here for lunch and dinner daily year round. The patio outside has a fine view of the stately and historic Barnstable County Court House.

The Dolphin Restaurant

$$ • 3250 Main St., Barnstable • 362-6610

The Dolphin is one of many bright spots along Route 6A in Barnstable village. With low ceilings and a cozy fireplace, this good third-generation family restaurant has changed little over the decades. The menu includes seafood, steaks, some veal and duck, sandwiches, burgers and good daily specials. The calamari is also good, and so is the lively conversation at the bar. The Dolphin, which seats about 125, is open daily for dinner and everyday except Sunday for lunch. Reservations are recommended.

Black Rock Grille

$$ • 633 Main St., West Yarmouth • 771-1001

If you're in the mood for beef, then you'll want to get on down to the Black Rock Grille on Route 28 in West Yarmouth. Besides serving 100-percent certified Angus beef, the Black Rock Grille also offers an array of seafood dishes such as baked lobster pie and, of course, native cod. Broiled or baked lobsters, ranging from 1½ to 3 pounds, are also on the menu. But getting back to the beef, there's prime rib, New York sirloin, steak teriyaki, baby back ribs and filet mignon just to name a handful. For those who would rather graze, there's a salad bar and a couple of veggie dinners. Black Rock offers a huge selection of beers — domestic, imports and micro-brewery selections. Dinner is served daily, year round. The bar opens at 3 PM and the restaurant at 4 PM.

Captain Parker's Pub

$ • 668 Rt. 28, West Yarmouth • 771-4266

Locals and visitors alike flock to Captain Parker's. Enormous portions, old-fashioned home-style cooking (including prime rib) and a huge list of specials are a few reasons this place is often crowded. In fact, you're likely to see familiar faces if you come here more than once. Entrees include baked stuffed scrod served with Newburg sauce and London broil. Parker's clam chowder is out of this world. Captain Parker's Pub is open daily year round for lunch and dinner, and the prices are always reasonable. Check out their Sunday brunch.

Molly's Restaurant and Sports Bar

$$ • 585 Main St., (Rt. 28) West Yarmouth • 778-1927

Join the locals at Molly's for the comfortable, casual atmosphere and hearty menu that includes prime rib, lobster and Italian dishes. The seafood selection, which includes baked salmon, is large and varied. Molly's also has a children's menu and serves lighter fare such as club sandwiches. The sports bar has a large-screen TV and five smaller ones and, of course, darts. The draft beer selection is excellent. All dinner items are available in the bar. Occasionally the pub has live entertainment, and sometimes members of the Crusaders, the Cape's own soccer team, stop by. Molly's is open year round and serves breakfast, lunch and dinner in the summer, dinner only in the off-season.

Hearth and Kettle

$ • 1196 Main St., (Rt. 28) South Yarmouth • 394-2252

This mid-Cape Hearth and Kettle location is open year round for breakfast, lunch and dinner. Kids, and adults, will enjoy watching ducks in the pond right behind the restaurant — visible through the many back windows. You can find other Hearth and Kettle locations in Falmouth, Centerville, Hyannis and Orleans as well as off-Cape in Plymouth. (See our write-up in the Falmouth section).

Photo: Cape Cod Times

Opportunities to dine alfresco, like at the Bookstore and Restaurant in Wellfleet, are a nice way to relax.

Skippy's Pier I

$$ • 17 Neptune Ln., South Yarmouth • 398-9556

Why come to Skippy's? For starters, it has a great view of Parker River. It also has seating for 250 people, including deck seating for 120, and is relaxing, comfortable and clean. And it has reasonable prices. All the seats are water view, and the sunsets are gorgeous. Skippy's serves grilled chicken Caesar salad, seafood from the raw bar, scrod, clams, scallops and burgers and pasta dishes — it's not too tough to figure out why this place is so popular! With hanging pots, a contemporary nautical decor expressed in hardwood and glass and a bar in the shape of a boat, Skippy's is attractive and fun. Go ahead and wear your shorts. Skippy's serves lunch and dinner daily. The restaurant is closed in January.

Abbicci

$$$ • 43 Main St., (Rt. 6A) Yarmouthport • 362-3501

This outstanding contemporary Italian restaurant specializes in native seafood, pasta and veal. It has a reputation for consistently high-quality food and service and excellent small-production wines, mostly from Italy and California. A regularly changing menu ensures that Abbicci is never predictable, although regulars would be unlikely to object if it were. The osso bucco, pan-seared halibut with lemon caper and anchovy sauce or mushroom-filled ravioli with caramelized onions are always popular. You may want to start off as we did with mussels and fried calamari. Time-honored methods and recipes are carried through to the desserts, which include mocha Italian trifle and crème brûlée. The restaurant serves lunch, dinner and a popular Sunday brunch. Take advantage of the daily early evening specials. Reservations are suggested. Abbicci is open daily year round.

Inaho

$$ • 157 Rt. 6A, Yarmouthport • 362-5522

Inaho means "ear of rice" in Japanese, and as a symbol of a good harvest or prosperity, the image is apt indeed for this Japanese restaurant. Inaho has been drawing rave reviews from locals and visitors alike for its beautifully prepared food, especially fish. Co-owner Alda Watanabe says the sushi and tempura are popular. Another often-ordered item is shabu-shabu, a beef and vegetable dish that is brought to the table and cooked much like a fondue. The restaurant has a full sushi bar and is open for dinner year round. It is closed on Mondays.

Jack's Outback

$, no credit cards • 161 Hallett St., Yarmouthport • 362-6690

Local flavor abounds at Jack's Outback, giving new meaning to the concept of informal. This is a restaurant with an attitude — the welcome mat reads "Go Away" — reminiscent of Boston's old Durgin Park, where the waitresses always seemed deeply irritated that you showed up. But the tone of friendly surliness has endeared Jack and his establishment to Cape Codders. Part of the charm: The menu is handwritten on the wall complete with deliberate misspellings. At Jack's you'll write your own food slip, pick up your own order and automatically assume responsibility for any problems with the food. Fortunately you won't be asked to wash your own silverware (if you're lucky!). Tips are collected in a bowl earmarked for the staff. You get an endless number of refills on iced tea and other soft drinks, and some regulars aren't shy about making six or seven trips back for more tea, risking — probably to their delight — getting shouted at by Jack, who, perhaps grudgingly, stays open for breakfast and lunch daily year round.

Oliver's Restaurant

$$ • Rt. 6A, Yarmouthport • 362-6062

Generous portions, consistent food quality, minimal turnover in staff (eight people have worked at Oliver's since it opened 12 years ago) and a large, varied and changing menu of 74 items, not including desserts and specials, all contribute to Oliver's popularity. Entrees range from seafood to chops to Italian. In addition to regular offerings, you can order from a seasonal menu that changes four times a year. Veal Oliver is the house specialty, and desserts include cheesecakes, mud pie with fudge sauce and Ben and Jerry's ice cream. Oliver's serves lunch and dinner daily, except Thanksgiving and Christmas Day. They close on Labor Day, too, so owners Glen, Rick and Dale Ormon can throw a big party for the staff — which also sheds considerable light on the key to this restaurant's success.

Gina's By the Sea

$$ • 134 Taunton Ave., Dennis • 385-3213

Garlic with a capital "G" is a main ingredient in many of the scrumptious Northern Italian dishes such as Scampi à la Gina and Chicken Gismonda served at Gina's by the Sea. This intimate family-owned restaurant,

replete with fireplace, knotty pine walls and homespun ambiance, has been serving customers since 1937. Chances are you'll have a bit of a wait, so relax at the laid-back bar or take a stroll on the beach, just steps away, until your table's ready. Gina's is open for dinner from the beginning of April through the end of November and adds lunch service through July and August. It is closed Monday and Wednesday during October and November.

Joe Mac's

$ • 85 Taunton Ave., Dennis • 385-9040

A local favorite, year rounders and visitors come here after a day on the beach in the summer; in the off-season, they come after a day of shopping. It's a good family place. Lunch and dinner blackboard specials feature everything from steamers to prime rib, or try one of Joe Mac's famous cheeseburgers, with equally famous fries and onion rings. Casual is the key word here, and a video room keeps the little ones busy while Mom and Dad are enjoying coffee and dessert. Open daily in season, Joe Mac's is closed Monday and Tuesday in the off-season.

The Red Pheasant

$$-$$$ • 905 Main St. (Rt. 6A), Dennis • 385-2133

Clearly one of the high points along the mid-Cape's fine dining circuit, the rustic and romantic Red Pheasant is considered one of the Cape's finest. The menu is a delectable blend of game, lamb and seafood served in a pleasant setting that reminds you why you came to Cape Cod in the first place. Tables at The Red Pheasant, which is housed in a 200-year-old barn with wide pine floors and two fireplaces, are adorned with locally crafted pottery and glassware and fresh flowers. The service is impeccable, and the food is second to none. Chef Bill Atwood, who runs The Red Pheasant along with his charming wife, Denise, creates such wonderful dishes as cedar planked salmon and boneless roast Long Island duckling. Dessert could include a trio of mousse in petit chocolate cups. The award-winning wine list (it has received the Award of

Excellence since 1987 by *Wine Spectator*) is prodigious — there are more than 300 from which to select.

Situated along historic Route 6A, The Red Pheasant provided us with a picture-perfect setting for a Christmas season dinner, with snow gently falling outside and a blazing fire in the hearth warming us all through our meal. The Red Pheasant serves dinner only, and reservations are strongly suggested. The restaurant is closed Mondays and Tuesdays from January through March. 1997 marks the restaurant's 20th anniversary of serving four-star meals.

Scargo Cafe

$$ • 799 Main St. (Rt. 6A), Dennis • 385-8200

This is one of our favorite spots for lunch or dinner. What was once a sea captain's house (and, with all its wainscoting and wood paneling, quite a lovely one at that) is now home to one of the Mid-Cape's finer casual restaurants. The cafe has two cozy dining rooms and a glassed-in atrium and greenhouse. The menu offers familiar favorites such as pasta marinara, fettuccine Alfredo, baked Cape sea scallops and crab in puff pastry. We usually begin with shrimp seafood stuffed mushrooms or mussels Ferdinand. The dessert pièce de résistance is Grape Nuts custard. Children's and early bird menus are also available. Reservations are accepted for parties of five or more. Scargo serves lunch and dinner daily year round.

The Marshside

$$ • 28 Bridge St., East Dennis • 385-4010

We know of some people from just south of Boston who will make a day trip to Dennis just to have lunch at the Marshside. Located just a stone's throw north of the intersection of routes 6A and 134, this is a restaurant that attracts tourists as well as locals and maintains a passionate following. You may want to start off with a stuffed quahog appetizer — no summer vacation is complete without one. Dine on baked stuffed shrimp or the surf and turf, but save room for an after-dinner slice of pecan, mud or coconut cream pie! Besides seafood entrees, the restaurant also serves lighter fare, such as burgers. Marshside caters to the kids with a special kids' menu and coloring books.

Owner Mary Lou Goodwin will most likely be around to greet and seat you — ask for a table with a view of the marsh full of wildlife and Sesuit Harbor beyond. High tide comes right up the back of the restaurant. The Marshside serves breakfast, lunch and dinner daily and is open year round so you can see the marsh during all four seasons.

Red Cottage

$ • 36 Old Bass River Rd., South Dennis • 394-2923

In a phrase: home-cooking at its best. Open all year for breakfast and lunch, the Red Cottage is famous for its home fries. No simple sliced and fried taters here. Instead, the potatoes are tossed with ham, mushrooms, tomatoes, green peppers and onion then smothered with hollandaise sauce. Equally delicious are the crêpes and Belgian waffles. The Red Cottage also features an extensive "lite side" menu, complete with a listing of fat grams per serving. Open Tuesday through Sunday, it's a busy place on weekend mornings but well-worth the effort.

Christine's

$$ • 581 Rt. 28, West Dennis • 394-7333

Christine's is sure doing something right, as the parking lot is always full. Some people flock here for the food, an eclectic mix of Lebanese and Italian dishes. Others gather for the live music and nightclub (see our Nightlife chapter). And expect to see buses in the parking lot — Christine's is a favorite spot for daytrippers. Everything about the place is pleasant: the etched-glass dining room, the artwork dotting the walls, the Tiffany lamps illuminating the booths. Popular Lebanese dishes include a combination of stuffed grape leaves, spinach pie and rice pilaf. Lovers of Italian cuisine will relish the shrimp scampi. Chicken Christine is an excellent choice, or you might opt for the fried or baked seafood specials. We always go for the baked native scallops. Christine's is also famous for its Sunday brunch, a spectacular array of more than 20 goodies served on a 30-foot cruise ship-style buffet. Reservations are only accepted for parties of six or more. Christine's serves breakfast, lunch and dinner daily except Tuesday year round. Early birds specials are served 4 to 6 PM year round.

The Lighthouse Inn Restaurant

$$$ • 1 Lighthouse Rd., West Dennis • 398-2244

Located within the Lighthouse Inn (see our Bed and Breakfasts, Inns and Guesthouses chapter), this spacious restaurant is reminiscent of the classic Cape Cod restaurants of bygone years. Resting right on the water, the windows along the south-facing wall are many and offer breathtaking views of Nantucket Sound. Peaked ceilings give the restaurant an airy feel. Service is quick and efficient. The food gamut here runs from the traditional (steamed lobster, filet mignon) to such innovative and enticing delectables as almond-encrusted salmon and chicken breast coated with hazelnuts. Did we mention the breathtaking views of Nantucket Sound?

Situated on the site of the current West Dennis Lighthouse (formerly the Old Bass River Light, see our Attractions chapter) the Lighthouse Inn serves breakfast, lunch and dinner daily during the season, mid-May to mid-October. Reservations are suggested.

Bob Briggs' Wee Packet

$$ • 79 Depot St., Dennisport • 398-2181

It may bear an unusual name, but Wee Packet is more like a big package of fun at unbeatable prices. A well-known Cape eatery, think of it as eating in someone's house filled with Formica-topped tables, seashells, driftwood and other Cape Cod items. It has exposed views of the kitchen and blue-plate specials such as broiled scallops and baked stuffed bluefish. Briggs' son, Rob, and daughter, Sheila, now run the place, where the tourists get a chance to mingle with the locals. Wee Packet serves breakfast, lunch and dinner daily from the middle of May through the end of September. It is convenient to all those summering in Dennisport and Harwichport.

Captain William's House

$$ • 106 Depot St., Dennisport • 398-3910

Pressed linen, gleaming silverware, soft candlelight . . . it all adds to the ambiance at the Captain William's House. It is the epitome of elegance without any of the stuffiness or high prices. Begin with an appetizer of crabmeat strudel or creamy New England clam chowder. Move on to grilled marinated shrimp with roasted red peppers coulis or perhaps baked stuffed or broiled lobster priced to catch. Early dinner selections (from 4:30 to 5:45 PM) such as cranberry chicken or a seafood sampler of cod, shrimp and scallops can save you a few bucks on the entree prices. Take time after (or before) dinner to savor the fascinating features of this former sea captain's home, especially the unique nine-over-six doors. It's closed from the end of December through April.

Clancy's

$$ • 8 Upper County Rd., Dennisport • 394-6661

Clancy's is a great "county tavern for ladies and gents" who are looking for a good meal at a decent price in a fun atmosphere. A fixture in Dennisport that was completely renovated a few years back, Clancy's serves plenty of delicious food amid a friendly ambiance by a most congenial staff. Clancy's itself is quite a dish: It sits on the banks of Swan River, and the views are almost as wonderful as the food. (The view of the water is spectacular off the sun deck — no extra charge!) Here, you'll be able to get your fill without breaking the bank, even if you order the popular Steak Lucifer, a meld of sirloin, lobster and asparagus topped with Béarnaise sauce.

Lunch is served Monday through Saturday, and dinner is served nightly (with later hours Saturday and Sunday). Clancy's also serves a Sunday brunch. The restaurant is closed Thanksgiving and Christmas Day. From November through April Clancy's runs specials on Monday, Tuesday and Wednesday nights.

Lower Cape

The Bramble Inn

$$$ • 2019 Main St. (Rt. 6A), Brewster • 896-7644

Celebrating its 13th season in 1997, this well-regarded restaurant offers fine dining in an intimate setting. Each of five small dining rooms is set with linen, antique china, candlelight and fresh flowers, and the food is worthy of the ambiance. The Bramble Inn serves a four-course dinner with a menu that changes every two weeks, always offering about eight different choices. Some of the most popular specialties prepared by chef/owner Ruth Manchester are rack of lamb, assorted seafood curry and roasted boneless chicken breast served with a whole lobster and Champagne sauce. For dessert, indulge in such homemade confections as white chocolate coeur la creme with raspberry sauce and flourless chocolate cake. Although there is no dress code, many patrons do show up in their best clothes, so you might feel more comfortable trading your jeans for something a bit dressier. Reservations are accepted and encouraged in summer. The restaurant is open from May through New Year's Eve, six days a week in summer with a more limited schedule in the off-season.

Brewster Coffee Shop

$, no credit cards • Main St. (Rt. 6A), Brewster • 896-8224

This is a great place to meet a friend for breakfast or lunch any time of the year. Homey and friendly, the shop serves up terrific omelettes, pancakes and other breakfast specialties. Lunchtime features burgers, chowder and fresh fish. Fresh coffee is served all day in big white mugs.

Brewster Fish House

$$$ • 2208 Main St. (Rt. 6A), Brewster • 896-7867

This small, well-established restaurant serves some of the best seafood on the Cape, reasonably priced and delightfully innovative. You'll have a huge menu of wonderful entrees from which to choose, enhanced by an ample wine list. The decor is simple but comfortable. Be forewarned: There is often a wait to get in since the restaurant has limited seating and does not take reservations. The bar is small so many folks must wait outside on the park benches, but they do so willingly — the food is worth the wait! The Fish House serves lunch and dinner daily in season, and Thursday through Sunday from April through May and mid-October to late November. The restaurant is closed December through March.

Brewster Inn and Chowder House

$$ • 1993 Main St. (Rt. 6A), Brewster • 896-7771

As its name suggests, this restaurant serves some of the best chowder you'll ever taste. The home-cooking here is equally superb. Lean, juicy Yankee pot roast and flaky broiled Chatham scrod are two patron favorites, and the burgers can't be beat. Mom's apple pie was almost as good as the one you'll get here. The dining room is small and homey, and the service friendly. The Brewster Inn and Chowder House serves lunch and dinner daily year round.

Chillingsworth

$$$$ • 2449 Main St. (Rt. 6A), Brewster • 896-3640

Long considered the Cape's finest (and most formal) restaurant, Chillingsworth is the pinnacle of French nouvelle. Chef/owner Robert Rabin offers constantly changing, seven-course prix fixe candlelight dinners, served at two seatings in season (one in off-season), amid priceless French antiques. Feast on at least a dozen variations of appetizers and entrees, including roast lobster with spinach and basil sauce and caramelized scallops. The desserts are heavenly; one connoisseur of tiramisu we met insists Chillingsworth's is the best around.

Men are requested to wear jackets, and women will want to wear elegant attire. Dinner is served nightly from mid-May to late November in both the main restaurant and the bistro-like Garden Room. Reservations are preferred.

Cobie's

$ • 3260 Rt. 6A, Brewster • 896-7021

Launched in 1948, Cobie's is a veritable institution around here, and faithful patrons come back year after year for some of the best fried seafood anywhere. With white-clapboard, clam-shack ambiance, this is one of the most comfortable outdoor eateries you'll find. It's open-air, but there is a roof over the picnic tables, which are freshly painted and kept squeaky clean. Right off the Cape Cod Rail Trail near Nickerson State Park, Cobie's is a popular stop for seafood-craving cyclists and campers. Cobie's is open daily for lunch and dinner from late-May through mid-September.

High Brewster

$$$ • 964 Satucket Rd., Brewster • 896-3636, (800) 203-2634

This former farmhouse's three small dining rooms, with their low ceilings, ladder-back chairs, fresh flowers, exposed beams and candlelit ambiance, make for romantic dining. The food is superlative. The menu changes often, but the entrees dreamed up by Chef Kevin Jamieson usually include items such as duck, grilled salmon and rack of lamb. Reservations are requested, and there is not a smoking section. Dinner is served daily from mid-April through mid-October and five days a week (closed Monday and Tuesday) from mid-October through December.

Laurino's

$$ • 3668 Rt. 6A, Brewster • 896-6135

Here's a great place to bring the family. It serves huge portions of such Italian dishes as Chicken Lauro (boneless chicken breast with scallops, sun-dried tomatoes, mushrooms and tarragon cream) and seafood chioppino served by super-friendly servers at penny-pinching prices. Laurino's also has a nice selection of pizza and grinders and a special children's menu. If that's not enough to keep the little ones entertained, Laurino's also has a video room. Laurino's serves dinner daily year round and only accepts reservations for groups of eight or more.

Mulligans

$$ • 832 Villages Dr., Brewster • 896-8251

Overlooking a golf course with lush greens, Mulligans is where you can experience one of the most satisfying and original meals on the Cape. Owner/chef Jake Jacobus constantly challenges himself to come up with new dishes, and he's never failed us. The wild mushroom strudel is a great choice for starters, perhaps followed by lobster thermidor or roast rack of lamb. There's also a full pub menu featuring such goodies as quesadillas and burgers. In season, Mulligans serves brunch every Sunday, and this brunch buffet is something to rave about. In addition to salads, breads, hot dishes and fruits, you get eggs or omelets cooked to order and a huge dessert table. Also in season, Mulligans hosts an outdoor Italian buffet every Monday, traditional Cape Cod clambakes every Tuesday, TexMex night on Wednesday and a seafood buffet on Sunday. Mulligans is open mid-March through Christmas for lunch, dinner and Sunday brunch and will also cater weddings and private parties.

The Country Inn

$$ • 86 Sisson Rd., Harwichport • 432-2769

This year-round inn specializes in classic dishes such as roast prime rib, filet mignon, lamb chops and duck (theirs is semi-boneless and served with an apple-herb stuffing), plus fresh seafood, including a wonderful lobster pie. Romantics can go for the special "Loving Couple" platter of two filet mignons, shrimp scampi, scallops and lobster claws, along with a seafood appetizer, salads and vegetables. This is one of the few places where you'll find desserts such as flambéed strawberries Romanoff and bananas Foster, so indulge!

400 Club

$$ • 429 Main St., Harwichport • 430-0404

Ask anyone where to find the best burger in town, and you'll be pointed to the 400 Club.

The menu bulges with dozens of other choices — the triple-decker clubs and chicken teriyaki are also quite good — but nobody makes a bigger, juicier or tastier burger. The Club is more a pub, chock-full of dark woods, captains chairs and comfy booths, with a super friendly waitstaff. In the summer, opt to sit on the outdoor patio. The 400 Club serves lunch and dinner daily year round. A second location, 400 East, is on Route 39 in Harwich, 432-1800.

The Gingerbread House

$$ • 141 Division St., Harwich • 432-1901

This charming little eatery specializes in Polish fare, making it a refreshing change. Where else can you get stuffed cabbage or pierogi stuffed with mushrooms or potatoes and cheese? Owner Stacia Kostecki also serves a traditional English daily tea, with a special house blend tea alongside assorted finger sandwiches and homemade, melt-in-your-mouth scones with real clotted cream imported from England. Dinners are served by reservation only. It's open April through December for tea and dinner.

Goucho's Mexican Restaurant and Bar

$$ • 403 Lower County Rd., Harwichport • 432-7768

Have you had your fill of fried oysters and clams? Then head south to the border of Harwichport and Dennis for Mexican food so tasty even die-hard gringos would convert. The eatery itself is an unassuming green-shuttered yellow house — hardly the sort of place Pancho Villa would call home. But once inside, olé! The menu is whimsical and eclectic, including your standard baby backs and chimichangas. The Philly Burrito, for instance, pays tribute to the Philadelphia cheese steak with loads of sliced steak, cheese and onions wrapped in a flour tortilla. The restaurant serves lunch and dinner daily from mid-June to mid-October.

Jake Rooney's

$$ • 119 Brooks Rd. (corner of Rt. 28), Harwichport • 430-1100

Talk about an extensive menu — Jake Rooney's has a seven-page one with something for everyone. Along with fresh seafood, chicken, burgers and steaks, the restaurant serves Southwestern, Greek and other international specialties. It's all served in a casual, pub-like atmosphere dressed up with antique paintings — a nice touch. You'll find yourself wanting to come back, and you can any time of year. Jake Rooney's is open daily for lunch and dinner plus brunch on Sundays year round.

L'Alouette

$$$ • 787 Rt. 28, Harwichport • 430-0405

Beloved by regular patrons for more than a decade for its sophisticated French food, L'Alouette also boasts a cozy atmosphere and cordial, attentive staff. The rack of lamb with garlic crust is a particular favorite, along with roast duckling accented with a sweet orange sauce. For dessert try the crème brûlée, for which the restaurant is known, or (if you're a die-hard chocolate addict) the chocolate truffle cake with raspberry sauce. Open year round, the restaurant offers good deals in the winter for those who eat early. Dinner is served Tuesday through Sunday in season and Wednesday through Sunday in winter. Reservations are requested.

Raspberries

$ • 30 Earle Rd., Harwich • 432-3103

This is an ideal place to go for breakfast, especially for hearty appetites. The breakfast buffet here is bountiful and a great deal — all-you-can-eat for less than $5.95, or $9.95 for Sunday brunch. Indulge in pancakes, waffles, scrambled eggs, French toast, home fries, eggs Benedict, ham, muffins, fresh fruit . . . the list goes on and on. Raspberries is open from Memorial Day to mid-October.

INSIDERS' TIP

Eating and drinking establishments hire more people on Cape Cod than any other industry.

The Bistro

$$$ • 595 Main St., Chatham • 945-5033

One of our very favorite restaurants, The Bistro features an unusual, ever-changing menu with an emphasis on wood grilling, which adds incredible flavor to meats, chicken and vegetables. No dish is ordinary here, where specials may include such innovations as baked pumpkin and sage raviolis, wood-grilled chicken breast stuffed with figs, pine nuts and spinach (incredible!) or grilled pork tenderloin with corn bread stuffing and grilled apples. And always, great pastas. Reservations are accepted; ask for a window seat, as the restaurant is on the second floor, and it's fun to look down at the folks out strolling Main Street — or up at the moon! The Bistro is open for dinner April 1 through New Year's Eve.

Champlain's

$ • 20 Cross St., Chatham • 945-1030

Champlain's is inside the Bradford Inn, but you don't have to be staying at the inn to enjoy a meal here. The menu offers something for everyone. The lunch menu alone has more than 30 selections, including old-fashioned chicken pot pie and various Caesar salads. For a simple supper, the shepherd's pie can't be beat, enjoyed in the dark wood-paneled ambiance of the main dining rooms. Breakfasts here are locally famous, served in the sunny dining room overlooking the pool. Champlain's is open from mid-May through Columbus Day.

Chatham Bars Inn's Beach House Grill

$$ • 297 Shore Rd., Chatham • 945-0096

One of three restaurants owned by the plush and pricey Chatham Bars Inn, this is an ideal choice for an alfresco lunch. Sit on a deck that is literally anchored in the sand, or if the wind is too much, opt for the glass-enclosed dining room. Lunch features the typical Cape Cod staples: burgers, salads and fried clams. (To befit the posh Chatham Bars Inn, the fried clams are served with remoulade sauce instead of tartar sauce.) You can dine here for breakfast and lunch daily during the season. The restaurant is open July through early September.

Chatham Bars Inn's Main Dining Room

$$$ • 297 Shore Rd., Chatham • 945-0096

A meal here is more than memorable. With a menu that changes daily, the restaurant offers four-course à la carte dinners and six- to 10-course wonders. With attentive service and a refined, unhurried atmosphere, this is fine dining as it should be. Linger over each course, and save room for a fabulous, homemade dessert. Men are requested to wear jackets and ties. The restaurant is open mid-April to mid-November.

Chatham Bars Inn's Tavern at the Inner Bar

$$ • 297 Shore Rd., Chatham • 945-0096

Less formal than the Chatham Bars Inn's Main Dining Room, the tavern underwent a major renovation in 1994, making the cozy and casual niche even more so. The lunches and dinners here are every bit as good as what's dished out in the more pricey sister eatery, though we know many people who come here to simply savor coffee and dessert. The tavern is open year round.

Chatham Squire

$$ • 487 Main St., Chatham • 945-0945

Home to Chatham's only raw bar, the Squire offers a delightfully eclectic menu (a little Chinese, a little Mexican, a lot of seafood and beef), and the food is out of this world. In addition to the dining room, the Squire has a large pub where you can get munchies. Locals have been eating here since 1968, and the waitstaff knows just about everyone by first name. Add yours to the list! It's open year round for lunch and dinner.

Chatham Wayside Inn

$$$ • 512 Main St., Chatham • 945-5550

This downtown inn, completely redone three years ago, has several dining rooms and serves breakfast, lunch and dinner — and you can't miss with any of them. The breakfast menu lists imaginative creations such as Louisiana corn bread stuffed with sausage, red onions and cheese along with classic items such as French toast, waffles, omelets, fresh fruit and muffins. Lunch might be grilled vegetables on focaccia or the chili maple chicken salad plate, but if you're in the mood for simpler fare, order a burger, sandwich or fish and chips. But save your appetite for dinner here, which might be rack of lamb — hailed by more than one world traveler as the best anywhere — lemon pepper Atlantic salmon or, our favorite, shrimp sauteed with wine, eggplant, garlic, olives and tomatoes served over linguine with a creamy Dijon sauce. The restaurant is closed on Mondays in the off-season.

Christian's

$$ • 443 Main St., Chatham • 945-3362

A choice place to eat for more than 16 years, Christian's is housed in a lovely old building with two levels of distinct personalities. Downstairs, the wood paneling and beams are painted antique blue, and the tables are covered in florals and lace. Upstairs, old books line the walls and a grand piano stands near a mahogany bar and leather sofa and chairs. The restaurant places an emphasis on American and continental dishes with a flair, such as coconut-crusted shrimp with curried pineapple salsa and chicken coated with macadamia nuts. One favorite dish is the Sea of Love, lobster, shrimp and scallops sauteed with basil, artichoke hearts, mushrooms and sun-dried tomatoes, tossed with penne noodles. For dessert, try the People's Choice, a chocolate meltaway pie. Christian's is open for lunch and dinner year round, daily during the season and Thursday through Monday from January through March. Reservations are suggested.

Eben Ryder House at the Wequasett Inn

$$$ • 173 Rt. 28, Chatham • 432-5400

This restaurant is undeniably classy, and patrons are expected to dress for the occasion. (Men are requested to wear jackets.) With low-key decor, candlelight and linen, the dining room enjoys a view of Pleasant Bay, but by no means relies on its prestigious location. Expect not only attentive service, but also excellent food. Award-winning Chef Frank McMullen turns out such delicacies as sauteed veal loin chop with sun-dried cranberries and white-truffle mashed potatoes, baked stuffed prawns with a shrimp and three cheese filling and red Thai soba noodles with Pacific Rim vegetables — all with an emphasis on presentation. This is the kind of restaurant where you absolutely must try an appetizer — if not the Chatham littleneck clams or escargot, then Portabella tarte with wild mushroom and Gruyère cheese filling. The problem is you'll want dessert as well, for who could resist such items as white chocolate cranberry mousse, served in an edible chocolate doily? The Eben Ryder House is open May through October.

Impudent Oyster

$$$ • 15 Chatham Bars Ave., Chatham • 945-3545

With a lively, friendly atmosphere, this restaurant is a favorite among locals. The fun menu offers cleverly-named sandwiches, such as Meat George Jetson (roast beef, sun-dried tomatoes and red onions), and such international fare as Szechwan beef sauté. Everyone orders (and loves) Yesterday's Quahog Chowder, so named because it "ferments" for a day. Exposed beams, plants and skylights make this eatery attractive. And unlike its namesake, the service is anything but impudent. The Impudent Oyster serves lunch and dinner daily year round.

Larry's P.X.

$ • 1591 Main St., Chatham • 945-3964

Very early risers will gravitate here along with local anglers, who often stop by for their first cup of java when Larry's opens at 4 AM. If you're a late riser, take heart — this place serves breakfast all day! You can also get burgers, soup and sandwiches. It's not fancy by any stretch, but it's comfortable, clean and friendly. And if you want to know what's going on around town, this is a good place to come. You can order food until 4 PM. Larry's P.X. is open daily except Thanksgiving, Christmas Day and through January and February.

Pate's

$$ • 1260 Main St., Chatham • 945-9777

In business since 1957, this restaurant still cooks its food in an open hearth, exactly as it's been doing all these years. Most locals will tell you to order the swordfish or prime rib (one patron we know dares you to find anything fresher). Legend has it that this was summer resident Tip O'Neill's favorite restaurant. Pate's is open from early April through January 15.

Two Turtles

$$ • 11 Library Ln., Chatham • 945-1234

If you're in a hurry, don't eat here. All the food is cooked to order — even the soup — but the wait is worth it. You'll never taste sweeter mussels (served in a cast-iron skillet, along with passion fruit batter) or richer lobster risotto with porcini mushrooms and shaved Parmesan. And that's just for starters. For dinner, savor such delicacies as black pepper couscous-encrusted native tuna with wasabi creme and a salad of blood orange and jicama. Two Turtles serves dinner only and is closed mid-October through Memorial Day.

The Arbor

$$ • 20 S. Orleans Rd. (Rt. 28), Orleans • 255-4847

Dinner here is a memorable experience, not just because of the food, which is imaginatively prepared and wonderfully tasty, but because of the atmosphere, which is delightfully different. Each of several cozy dining rooms (we especially like the smallest one, off to the right as you enter) is filled with Victorian lamps, old dolls, antique toy cars, bottles and knickknacks that are just fun to look at. Add lace curtains and mismatched, pretty china, and you have The Arbor, a truly unique place. Ladies must check out the upstairs powder room, which is filled with vintage hats! But enough about the ambiance — we love the food too. The menu features some great pasta dishes, chicken, veal and seafood, all with terrific sauces. The desserts are all tempting, and you'll want to linger over coffee; it's just that kind of place. The Arbor serves dinner daily in season and Thursday through Sunday in winter, except for the month of January, when it is closed.

Barley Neck Inn

$$$, $$ (pub) • 5 Beach Rd., East Orleans • 255-0212

This grand old 1857 sea captain's mansion was lovingly restored by Joe and Kathi Lewis, who run a classy, fine-dining restaurant along with a more casual — but still classy — pub. The fine dining portion of the restaurant has several dining rooms, the most intimate being the Taylor Room, named for the mansion's original owner, Captain Joseph Taylor. The atmosphere is elegant and romantic, the service attentive. The food is superlative, as is the presentation, with each dish appearing as a work of art. Specialties include roasted duck breast with apple and cranberry chutney and broiled salmon medallions. For starters, we recommend the Cape Cod crab cakes, though you can't go wrong with the scallops ravioli. Save room for dessert.

If you're in the mood for something more casual — and much less expensive — check out Joe's Beach Road Bar & Grill, where the menu includes gourmet pizza and Mexican specials, and a huge stone fireplace warms chilly nights. There's also entertainment year round (see our Nightlife chapter).

The Barley Neck Inn is open daily year round. Dining room hours vary in the off-season, so call ahead. Reservations, in any case, are a good idea for the dining room.

The Binnacle Tavern

$ • 20 S. Orleans Rd. (Rt. 28), Orleans • 255-7901

Tucked behind The Arbor (see above), this casual, pub-like eatery, decorated with an impressive assortment of nautical antiques, is popular for its gourmet pizzas and homemade pasta dishes. So popular, in fact, that there is usually a wait to be seated in season. Sidle up to the small bar, if you can, and be patient, the wait is worth it. We highly recommend the pizzas, with toppings as basic as pepperoni and cheese or as adventurous as gorgonzola and currants or shrimp and apples. Our favorite is the vegetarian. The pastas are delicious, too, and we once savored a cup of lobster bisque

INSIDERS' TIP

Even at the height of the Cape's busy tourist season, in July and August, there are ways to avoid the crowds. One is to get up early — very early — for a walk on the beach. Pick up some doughnuts and have a picnic breakfast by the sea, and leave before the first sunbathers arrive. Then, while everyone else is at the beach, visit the shops, which will be mercifully quiet. If it rains, don't go shopping, because everyone else will. Instead, don a raincoat and go see what the beach looks like wet — and empty!

here that was the best we'd ever tasted. The Binnacle is open daily in season, and Thursday through Sunday in winter.

Captain Linnell House

$$$ • 137 Skaket Beach Rd., Orleans • 255-3400

This classic 1854 mansion, which seems to magically appear as you round a curve in the road toward Skaket Beach, is well-worth finding. Since 1988, owner/chef William Conway has been creating award-winning cuisine such as sautéed oysters in Champagne-ginger sauce, and shrimp and scallops sautéed in tarragon lobster butter. The roast pork tenderloin is excellent, and the bourbon lobster bisque is a must! Conway is smart to serve children smaller portions, and he entices patrons with free chowder and dessert if they're seated by 5:30 PM. Open year round, the restaurant serves dinner seven days a week in season, with a reduced schedule in winter; call for hours then.

The Cheese Corner and Deli

$ • 56 Main St., Orleans • 255-1699

A favorite lunch spot among locals, this small shop has only a handful of indoor tables, and in the summer a second handful on the patio. The soups and salads are made from scratch, as are the breads, and the sandwiches are tasty. The shop also carries an array of gourmet and Scandinavian foods and gifts, imported and domestic cheeses and homemade dinner entrees. Call ahead and your lunch will be ready for you. It's open year round.

Ciro di Pasta

$$ • Rt. 6A, Orleans • 240-0747

Launched in 1996 by Ciro Cozzi, of the famed Provincetown restaurant Ciro & Sal's, Ciro di Pasta is aptly named. We doubt there's a pasta made that this place doesn't serve — everything from capellini to cavatelli, prepared in classic and imaginative styles, at great prices! Some tempting specialties include cannelloni verdi, a rolled spinach pasta filled with spinach, cheese and nuts in a bechamel sauce, and pasta di noci, with walnuts, almonds, pine nuts, ricotta, pecorino, herbs and spices. There's plenty of seafood on the menu, too, from local clams on the half shell to scallops and mussels in a light sauce over pasta. The ambiance is sophisticated yet warm, with blond wood beams and tall glass windows that reflect the tiny white lights strung throughout the room. Ciro di Pasta features fresh desserts to go with your cappuccino or espresso and also offers takeout. Reservations are accepted at Ciro's. It's open for lunch and dinner daily in season and dinner only in winter. The restaurant is closed in January.

Cottage St. Bakery

$ • 2 Cottage St., Orleans • 255-2821

Tucked away on a little street off Route 28,

opposite the Christmas Tree Shop, this charming little bakery turns out scrumptious muffins, cookies, coffee cakes and scones, among other specialties. Come here for the perfect birthday cake, or just the perfect muffin. Try the Fly Cemeteries, pockets of puff pastries filled with cheese, walnuts and raisins, so named because, after baking, the raisins resemble flies sitting on a tombstone. The bakery is open daily year round and does catering, wedding cakes and mail order.

Hearth and Kettle

$ • 9 West Rd. (At Skaket Corners), Orleans • 240-0111

One of five Hearth and Kettle restaurants on Cape, this Orleans location serves breakfast, lunch and dinner year round. The Orleans Hearth & Kettle is a favorite among both locals and visitors for good reason. The food is always good, the prices reasonable and the service friendly and prompt. It's also child-friendly: kids not only have their own menu, but get coloring books, crayons and special cups as well! Other H&Ks are in Falmouth, Centerville, Hyannis and South Yarmouth. The restaurant has a full bar and is all nonsmoking. It's open daily year round.

The Hot Chocolate Sparrow

$ • Rt. 6A, Orleans • 240-2230

This is the hot spot in town to go for espresso, cappuccino or just plain coffee. Even those are anything but plain — every day there are a half-dozen flavors from which to choose. In warm weather try one of their frozen coffee-chocolate drinks. The decor is attractive — black marble tables and wood tones splashed with raspberry accents — and there's always good music playing. But the scent — fresh coffee beans mingled with chocolate — is most memorable. Which brings us to the chocolate, as if anyone could stay away from it. Homemade at the Sparrow's mother store in Eastham are incredible truffles, fudge, caramels, toffee and chocolate. All candy is sold by the pound or piece, and gift tins and packages are available as well. And, yes, they do mail orders. Open year round, the Sparrow also serves grilled sandwiches (our favorite is the mozzarella, artichoke and sun-dried tomato) and a mouth-watering array of desserts, along with ice cream and frozen yogurt.

Hunan Gourmet III

$$ • Underground Plaza, 225 Rt. 6A, Orleans • 240-0888

Craving Chinese? You'd be hard-pressed to find better anywhere on the Cape. Hunan Gourmet III is perhaps best-known for its all-you-can-eat buffet, a seemingly endless feast including sesame chicken, garlic noodles, vegetable lo mein, chicken with black bean sauce, shrimp and scallop medley, you-shell shrimp, almond cookies, dumplings, chicken teriyaki, pork fried rice, egg rolls, boneless ribs, fruit salad and the ubiquitous Jell-O. The price? Just $9.95, or $5.95 for kids ages 4 to 12 (free for a child younger than 4 with an adult).

Insiders know to avoid the wait by getting to Hunan Gourmet III at 5 PM, when the buffet first opens. You can order from the menu anytime from lunchtime to closing (later hours on Friday and Saturday). Luncheon specials are also available daily, and the restaurant is open year round.

Land Ho!

$$ • 38 Main St., Orleans • 255-5165

This is a favorite haunt of locals, just as it's been since owner John Murphy took it over in 1969. A comfortable place to sit and chat over a meal, the wood-paneled pub is brightened by red and white checked tablecloths and hundreds of original, wood-carved signs hanging from the ceiling. The blackboard specials are always good, as are the chowder, kale soup and burgers. The stuffed quahogs are terrific, and the crab cakes are always great too. Actually, we've never had a bad meal here, which may explain why we come here again and again. The Ho! is open for lunch and dinner

INSIDERS' TIP

If you're going to eat them — those tasty local clams, that is — you'd better know how to say it. "Quahogs" is pronounced CO-hogs.

daily all year. It's also a cool nightspot (see our Nightlife chapter).

Lo Cicero's

$$ • Rt. 6A, Orleans • 255-7100

Mama mia! Great Italian dinners at great prices — and then some. The stuffed clams, more clam than bread crumbs, are superb, and the clam sauces (red and white) are chock-full of clams and garlic, just the way they should be. The fried seafood platter is enough to feed two, we kid you not. Lo Cicero's also serves an interesting selection of individual-size pizzas (perfect for two as an appetizer). Open for dinner year round, Lo Cicero's also offers vegetarian and macrobiotic specials.

Nauset Beach Club

$$$ • 222 E. Main St., Orleans • 255-8547

The Northern Italian delicacies served here are huge and delicious. Everything is tasty, especially the dishes made with locally caught fish. The risotto is superb, the appetizers terrific and the desserts make a heavenly finish to a great meal. The restaurant, housed in a former duck-hunting cottage on the way to Nauset Beach, has a warm atmosphere, with terra cotta walls, a tiled bar and low lights. A couple of unusual touches: The waitstaff wears sweatshirts emblazoned with the name of the restaurant (sweatshirts are for sale too), and draped over the linen on each table is a sheet of heavy paper for your coloring pleasure, with a jar of crayons provided as well. That way you won't feel too sophisticated amid all that candlelight and fine fare. Dinner is served every evening during the season, and Tuesday through Saturday from late November through mid-May.

Off The Bay Cafe

$$$ • 28 Main St., Orleans • 255-5505

This fine dining establishment offers a sophisticated yet comfortable atmosphere along with superb food and attentive service. In addition to seafood, chicken and steaks, the restaurant offers some unusual specialties such as Barnstable-raised pheasant served with wild mushroom and Madeira cream sauce, and aged prime rib. The lobster and lump crab cake combo is a must for anyone craving a really well-prepared lobster. The menu also includes a yummy assortment of appetizers; try the grilled seafood cakes, each with a different sauce, or the walnut and gorgonzola ravioli. Off the Bay is open daily year round for lunch and dinner.

Old Jailhouse Tavern

$$ • 28 West Rd., Orleans • 255-JAIL

Occupying the former home of Orleans constable Henry Perry (the stone room was actually used as a jail), this jailhouse rocks year round with regulars who find the food, ahem, arresting. (It would have been a crime for us not to have said that.) You'll find all the basics here: spinach and Cobb salads, quiche and burgers, and hardier fare such as steamed-in-beer, you-peel-'em shrimp, flour tortilla pizza and chicken parmigiana. Then there is the menu's most unusual dish: toast Nelson, which is French bread smothered with bacon, onion, shrimp, scallops, crabmeat, Parmesan cheese and Hollandaise sauce. We promise you'll want to visit this jailhouse year round.

Arturo's

$ • 600 Massasoit Rd., Eastham • 240-7828

For the last six years, Arturo's has been easing the hunger pangs of locals. Now the secret's out. It's not the easiest place to find (heading north on Route 6, take a left at the sign for the Catholic church, just past the Elks Lodge), but we promise you'll always find your way back. The super-small take-out-only store offers various fresh-baked hard-crust breads along with a tasty selection of stuffed breads (broccoli, mushroom and cheese, and the ever-popular sausage and pepperoni, crammed with onions, peppers, spices and two kinds of cheese). Sauces are available by the pint and include garlic and oil, black olive and primavera. We won't even get into the soups and sandwiches, pizza and pasta. Arturo's is closed Monday and Tuesday.

Box Lunch

$-Seatoller Shops, Rt. 6, Eastham • 255-0799

Once you try one of the Box Lunch's locally famous "rollwiches" — meats, cheeses, salads and spreads on thin, pita-like bread rolled up for easy eating — you'll be hooked. There's a huge variety, everything from the Ferdinand, a quarter-pound of roast beef, three melted cheeses, onion, tomatoes and mayo, to the Organic Pocket, chock full of cheeses, sprouts, avocado tomatoes, lettuce and creamy Italian dressing. You can call your order in for a fast take-out or eat there; it's open daily all year. The Box Lunch also has locations in Brewster, 896-6682; Wellfleet, 349-2178 and Provincetown, 487-6026.

Ben & Jerry's Ice Cream

Rt. 6 and Brackett Rd., North Eastham • 255-2817

Locals cheer when this cheerful shop reopens in early March and weep when it closes after Thanksgiving. It's a lively place in summer, when there can be people lined up all the way out the door for those yummy 34-plus flavors of ice cream, frozen yogurt and sorbets. In 1997 look for new low-fat ice cream. That's also a landmark year for the North Eastham shop, celebrating its 10th anniversary. All through 1997, once a week — which day of the week will be a surprise — the 10th customer to come into the shop will get a free ice-cream cone. And on Tuesday nights in summer, the place gets even livelier with Theme Night — anything from polka to reggae. There's a sister Ben & Jerry's shop in Chatham at 10 Chatham Bars Avenue, 945-5959.

Eastham Lobster Pool

$$ • 4380 Rt. 6, Eastham • 255-9706

Landlubbers beware: Though you can choose from several dishes, including steaks and burgers, the thing to order here is fish. In fact, the menu offers so many choices that it's seven pages long. Don't want it fried? How about grilled, baked or poached in fat-free, lemon-herb sauce? Or go for lobster — this is a great place to get it. The fish is local, guaranteeing the finest in freshness. If the weather is nice, sit outdoors instead of at the barracks-like communal wooden tables indoors. The entire menu is available daily in season from midday until late night. In business more than 30 years, the Lobster Pool is open April 1 through October.

Eastham Superette

$ • Rt. 6, Eastham • 255-0530

This small grocery/package store sells just about everything you could need, including fresh fruits and vegetables, but the deli counter is what makes it really special. This is a great place to grab a quick lunch — order one of their fabulous overstuffed subs and walk across the street for a picnic on the windmill green.

Fleming's Donut Shack and Bakery

$ • Town Center Plaza, Rt. 6, North Eastham • 255-6551

This unpretentious, old-fashioned coffee shop has terrific donuts and a loyal following, along with a rich history. In business more than 35 years, Fleming's proudly displays a letter of thanks from the late President John F. Kennedy, who enjoyed a gift of doughnuts while still a senator. They still use the same family recipe.

Hole-in-One

$ • Rt. 6, Eastham • 255-9446

The line begins forming outside at about 4:45 every morning — 15 minutes before the store officially opens. That should tell you something. Choose from more than 15 varieties of donuts, all hand-cut and made fresh daily. The sour cream donuts seem to go fastest, perhaps because they are the audience favorite. Hole-in-One is open every day until noon all year long. They also have a location on Route 6A in Orleans that serves a complete lunch menu.

Lori's Family Restaurant/ Mitchel's Bistro

$$ • Main Street Mercantile, Rt. 6, Eastham • 255-4803

Chef Mitchel Rosenbaum and his partner, Laxmi Venkateshwaran, for years ran the successful Cielo Cafe in Wellfleet before taking over Lori's in 1995. They decided to keep the name Lori's for daytime use, continuing and enhancing the popular breakfast and lunch operation, and turn it into Mitchel's Bistro at night. The arrangement works beautifully. After 5, they bring out the linens and candlelight, and the place is transformed into Eastham's only fine dining establishment — one that has won raves from locals and visitors alike. In May 1997 they opened Club Bombay upstairs (see our Nightlife chapter).

Mitchel and Laxmi cook everything from scratch, using locally grown produce and seafood whenever possible. Specialties include curried crab cakes, butterfly grilled leg of lamb and roasted red pepper and goat cheese raviolis. For dessert, there's a different cheesecake every day, along with other homemade concoctions such as double rich chocolate mousse cake. Lori's and the Bistro are open year round, both daily April through November. The breakfast and lunch portion stays open daily in winter, while Mitchel's Bistro is open Friday through Sunday in winter.

Aesop's Tables

$$$ • Main St., Wellfleet • 349-6450

We love the layout of this lovely restaurant, which occupies a big, old house in the center of town. Aesop's has no less than six dining rooms, plus the intimate parlor-style Upstairs Bar, with its comfy window seats, soft couches and armchairs. In summer, you can dine on the terrace. Much of the menu is determined by market availability (no frozen fish here), and some of the herbs are organically grown in Aesop's own herb gardens. In fact, one of the most popular choices here is Monet's Garden Salad, a heaping serving of all kinds of greens and all things natural, including exotic edible flowers, tossed with goat cheese and pine nuts — a true work of art! And the desserts — Aesop's is famous for its Death By Chocolate, a sinfully rich dark Belgian chocolate mousse served in a brownie crust, and other delights including cranberry pecan torte. Aesop's Tables is open daily from mid-May to late October for dinner and late June to the end of September for lunch.

(508) 349-6333

Bayside Lobster Hutt

$$$ • Commercial St., Wellfleet • 349-6055

It's rumored that if you show up wearing a tie, you won't be allowed in. And tipping? Absolutely forbidden! That's how informal this former oyster shack turned lobster pound is. For more than 20 years, Bayside has been serving lobster in the rough; order your grub, sit at one of the large communal tables and join your dining companions as you crack away. (The neighbors at the table may be strangers when you arrive, but there's something about lobster juice running down chins that bonds people.) Feel free to use the wash basin when you're through — those little towelettes just won't do it. For kids who refuse to crack a crustacean, there's a burgers-hot-dogs-and-fries menu. Bring your own booze. Bayside is open for lunch and dinner from late May through Columbus Day.

The Bookstore Restaurant

$$ • Kendrick Ave., Wellfleet • 349-3154

This comfortable eatery, which enjoys spectacular views of Wellfleet Harbor, is so popular

INSIDERS' TIP

A word of caution to the uninitiated: On the Cape, fried clams are usually served whole, with the bellies. If you're used to clam strips, the bellies may come as a surprise (to some, an unpleasant one), so ask before you order.

we can almost guarantee you'll have to wait for a table in summer, and sometimes in the fall as well. But all those people can't be wrong — they know this is the place to go for great food at reasonable prices and water views to boot. Open year round for breakfast, lunch and dinner, The Bookstore really does have a bookstore around back. Stop there if you love hunting for bargains among shelves and shelves (not to mention boxes) of old books. Then bring your appetite to the dining room for baked stuffed lobster, grilled swordfish or fish and chips, to name just a few of the many seafood specialties on the menu. There's even a raw bar, and for landlubber, there are pastas, soups, sandwiches and salads. For lunch, order a sandwich that comes with curly fries — they're terrific! In fine weather, try for a table on the deck and enjoy the gentle breeze off the harbor.

The Duck Creeke Tavern Room

$$ • East Main St., Wellfleet • 349-7369

You need not be staying at the Inn at Duck Creeke to eat in one of its two restaurants. We prefer this one for its simplicity in both food (pizza, chowders and pasta) and decor, if you can call a bar made out of antique doors simple. Stick around after dinner for the live entertainment every night except Monday in season (see our Nightlife chapter). The Tavern serves dinner Tuesday through Sunday during the season; it's closed from mid-October through late May.

Finely J.P.'s

$$ • Rt. 6, Wellfleet • 349-7500

It would be easy to pass right by this tiny restaurant since it almost looks like a cottage, but we recommend you stop. Since it opened six years ago, Finely J.P.'s has received rave reviews for such dishes as oven-poached salmon with ginger and soy sauce, pork medallions with apples and goat cheese and their famous Caesar salad. Vegetarians will like the lasagna, made with pesto, ricotta, zucchini and grilled tomatoes. Finely J.P.'s is open for dinner seven days a week in summer, and Thursday through Sunday the rest of the year.

The Lighthouse

$$ • Main St., Wellfleet • 349-3681

This comfortable restaurant, right in the center of town, is one of those old standbys we return to again and again. The atmosphere is friendly, the food is good — not fancy, just good and reasonably priced — and it's a great place to take kids. The young ones can get hot dogs and be happy as clams, and you can eat clams, fish and chips, burgers, chili or one of the blackboard specials. A great place to meet friends any time of day, The Lighthouse is open year-round for breakfast, lunch and dinner. It also has a bakery, 349-1600.

Painter's

$ • 50 Main St., Wellfleet • 349-7343

Paint this one a winner! Since 1992

Kate Painter has whipped up some of the most imaginative sandwiches and soups to come out of a kitchen. It is hearty fare such as the Rockin' Lobster Roll (chunks of locally caught lobster mixed with red onions and lemon zest) and the Bayou (Cajun turkey, caramelized onions and melted Swiss cheese on French bread). Soups change week by week; one favorite is white bean laced with sour cream. Open daily during the season for breakfast, lunch and dinner, Painter's has varying hours in the off-season.

P.J.'s Family Restaurant

$ • 2616 Rt. 6, Wellfleet • 349-2126

A local institution since 1971, P.J.'s serves up great chowder, homemade kale soup and onion rings along with broiled scallops, fish and chips, hot dogs and lobster. There's nothing like one of their huge fish sandwiches followed by some soft-serve ice cream. The take-out window at P.J.'s is always bustling; place your order and sit outside at a picnic table. Or you can sit inside in the comfortable dining room. The restaurant serves lunch and dinner daily from mid-April through mid-October.

Serena's

$$ • Rt. 6, South Wellfleet • 349-9370

If you're looking for great Italian food in a family-friendly atmosphere, this is the place. In addition to traditional favorites like lasagne (choose from meat or vegetarian) and pastas, the menu offers plenty of seafood — what else would you expect on the Outer Cape? If you like spicy dishes, try the Seafood Fra Diavolo, billed as "hot as the devil" with mussels, littlenecks, Wellfleet oysters, scallops, scrod, squid and jumbo shrimp swimming in a wine and marinara sauce and spiced either regular, hot or very hot. Our preference is the broiled Wellfleet scallops, sweet and done to perfection in butter and lemon wine sauce. Serena's welcomes young diners with a children's menu. Serena's is open for dinner only from mid-April to mid-November.

Van Rensselaer's

$$ • Rt. 6, South Wellfleet • 349-2127

This restaurant has a strong local following, and it's easy to see why. VR's, as most locals call it, serves wholesome food in a casual setting at reasonable prices. Popular breakfast items include the Homegrown, scrambled eggs with fresh basil and tomato, served with fresh fruit. The dinner menu, enhanced by a terrific salad bar, lists specialties such as a mixed seafood grill, seafood fettuccine and steak tenderloin au poivre. The menu also includes a number of vegetarian dishes, and there's a children's menu too. For dessert, don't miss the New Orleans bread pudding with bourbon sauce. Van Rensselaer's is open May 15 through the end of October for breakfast and dinner, daily in season and on weekends in the fall. The restaurant is right across from the National Seashore's Marconi Station.

Adrian's

$$ • 535 Rt. 6, Truro • 487-4360

Perched high atop a bluff overlooking Cape Cod Bay, Adrian's features fantastic views and fantastic food. Owners Adrian and Annette Cyr regularly travel to Italy, where they gather and fine-tune recipes for their loyal following. (The wood-fired brick pizza oven, in fact, was brought over from Italy — brick by brick!) The thin-crust pizzas here are meals in themselves, featuring such enticing combinations as lamb and feta, and shrimp, garlic and artichokes. The homemade pastas are served in two sizes, regular and large, and the Gorgonzola Cappeletti, with a sage, butter and Parmesan sauce, cannot be beat. For dessert, look no further than the liquor-soaked tiramisu. During the season, Adrian's serves wonderful breakfasts, including such yummies as cranberry pancakes with orange butter and a zucchini Provolone and Romano frittata. You can have breakfast and dinner at Adrian's daily from mid-May through Columbus Day weekend.

Harbor Lights

$, no credit cards • Rt. 6A, Truro • 487-3062

Here is a place for bountiful breakfasts. The best of the best is the stack of Big, Fat Blueberry Pancakes, as the menu accurately describes them. The pancakes are indeed big and fat, but they are also extremely light and quite satisfying. (The blueberries, by the way, are fresh.) Are the basics more your style? A

mere $2.25 will get you a plate of eggs, home fries and toast, or opt for any of the numerous daily specials, such as Mexican omelets oozing with cheese and chili. You can have breakfast here daily through the lunch hours. Harbor Lights also has a good lunch menu and offers a fish fry on Friday evenings. It's open from early May to Columbus Day.

Montano's

$$ • 481 Rt. 6, Truro • 487-2026

Have a yen for steak — not just any old steak, but a slab of the finest, freshest, tastiest beef ever? Head over to family-oriented Montano's, where carnivores can indulge in such dishes as Steak Montano (18 ounces of sirloin topped with roasted garlic butter) and the trademark Steak Umbriago, 18 ounces of sirloin smothered with sautéed onions, roasted peppers, garlic, mushrooms and olives and served in a wine sauce. It just doesn't get better than this. Seafood, chicken and veal lovers will also have a field day choosing among the menu's many items. You can also order from among a dozen pasta dishes or create your own pizza. All meals come with a bottomless salad bowl. It's open all year except January and February.

Terra Luna

$$ • 104 Shore Rd., Truro • 487-1019

With its cathedral ceiling, barnboard walls, exposed beams, tin-and-wood roof and whimsical pieces of art (check out the cat painting in the unisex bathroom), this eatery knows the importance of being different. And it shows on the menu and blackboard specials. The steamers prepared in beer are the best. Favorites here include risotto with shrimp, clams and andouille sausage, polenta with grilled Portobello mushroom ragu and spinach tortellini with crabmeat, which is served at room temperature — an interesting taste sensation in more than one way. Breakfasts here are fun too: cornmeal pancakes made with bananas, almonds or chocolate chips and breakfast burritos, soft tortillas filled with black beans, cheese, salsa, sour cream and veggies. Terra Luna serves breakfast and dinner daily from mid-May through October.

Jams

$ • Truro Center, Truro • 349-1616

For many people Memorial Day marks the official start of the season on the Cape. It also marks the day Jams opens its door after months of hibernation. Let's say this right off: The prices are steep — quite steep for sandwiches — but people pay them for the luscious, mouth-watering favorites, all handmade on the premises. The sandwiches are named after Cape Cod sites and sights. The Long Nook, for example, features tarragon chicken salad with lettuce and tomato; the Bikini has provolone, lettuce, tomato, onions, sprouts and creamy Italian dressing. We won't even get into the rotisserie-roasted chickens, ducks and ribs and incredible desserts. Jams offers lunch and take-out and closes its doors in September.

The Whitman House

$$ • Rt. 6, Truro • 487-1740

Great food, great service, homey atmosphere — this is one of those restaurants you'll find yourself returning to again and again. And that's exactly what the Rice family, who's been running The Whitman House since 1962, wants. For starters, cheese and crackers, along with homemade bread, are brought to the table before you order. The menu has something for everyone, including prime rib au jus, baked stuffed shrimp, charbroiled swordfish and, of course, lobster. No particular dish stands above the rest, but everything is delicious and satisfying. Whitman House serves dinner daily during the season; it's closed from January through March.

Cafe Heaven

$, no credit cards • 338 Commercial St., Provincetown • 487-3314

If you're a late riser and don't mind sitting in a storefront (hey, this is P'town!), then here's a slice of heaven just for you. The tiny, noisy eatery serves breakfast, including fresh-squeezed orange and grapefruit juices and their signature custom-made omelets, daily until 3 PM, or you can order lunch. At dinnertime, they move on to burger heaven, featuring such luscious gems as Brie and garlic burgers. Heaven is open from mid-May to late October.

Ciro & Sal's

$$$ • 4 Kiley Ct., Provincetown • 487-0049

Once a coffeehouse for artists back in the '50s, Ciro & Sal's is considered one of the better Italian restaurants on the Lower Cape, especially when it comes to such Northern Italian delicacies as salmone alla Vincenza and spaghetti alla Puttanesca. For desserts, nothing beats the homemade zabaglione. And it would be hard to beat the atmosphere: Nestled in a low-ceilinged plaster and brick-walled cellar off Commercial Street, Ciro & Sal's is filled with raffia-wrapped Chianti bottles hanging from the rafters, and arias fill the air. It's open daily for dinner during the busy season and weekends only from November through May.

Clem and Joe's

$ • 338 Commercial St., Provincetown • 487-8303

This take-out eatery, praised by diners and critics alike, offers good home cooking that you don't have to cook! You can get a whole rotisserie chicken with corn bread, gravy and side dishes, meat loaf, glazed baked ham or Texas chili. Or try one of their specialty sandwiches, like the "Magilla Grilla," grilled chicken breast with red pepper, onion and carrot. For dessert order whole homemade pies, cakes or cookies. During the season, you may find a seat at the one or two outdoor tables. Clem and Joe's will also deliver locally to your home or hotel. It's open daily mid-April through October.

Fortune Cookie

$ • 205 Commercial St., Provincetown • 487-6688

Tucked away in the Aquarium Mall — the restaurant is very easy to miss since it's the size of a postage stamp — this eatery serves terrific take-out at incredible prices. Six bucks will get you a huge portion of boneless spare-ribs. The same money will also buy you a platter of chow mein, egg roll and fried rice or one of several other entrees. If you like your food spicy, skip the prepackaged hot mustard and ask for a sample of the real stuff, kept in a

INSIDERS' TIP

If you make a reservation at one of the Cape's fine dining establishments and then change your plans, be courteous and cancel the reservation. In the off-season, restaurants schedule waitstaff according to how many reservations are on the books, and in summer are most likely turning others away in order to hold your table.

squeeze bottle behind the counter. During the season, eat at one of the outside tables at the end of the mall. Fortune Cookie is open daily from mid-October to mid-May.

Front Street

$$$$ • 230 Commercial St., Provincetown • 487-9715

One of the town's most popular and romantic restaurants — bistro may be a better word — Front Street is hidden in the brick-lined cellar of a Victorian house. Chef Donna Aliperti changes the menu weekly, showing off her culinary craft with such dishes as avocado latkes, curried apple carrot bisque, barbecued spareribs with plum sauce and her famous braised lamb shank. The wine list is quite extensive, and the waitstaff knows just how to serve (they are there, but they never hover). Stargazers will spot comedian Kate Clinton dining here whenever she's in town. Front Street is open daily during the season and is closed January through mid-May.

Georgie Porgie's Bagel Factory

$ • 100 Shank Painter Rd., Provincetown • 487-1610

The Cape has several bagel shops, but no one makes a better bagel than Georgie Porgie's. At least 15 varieties (including garlic, sesame, poppy, cinnamon raisin and vegetable) are hand-rolled, cut and kettle-boiled every morning starting at 4:30. Eat 'em plain, with butter or with one of the yummy cream cheese spreads (light spreads are also available). Georgie Porgie's is open from 5 AM (those anglers get hungry!) through 2 PM daily year round. G.P.'s is closed Saturdays during the off-season. Expect no ambiance and no tables, just the best bagels you've ever eaten.

Governor Bradford

$ • 312 Commercial St., Provincetown • 487-9618

Though most people know it as one of Provincetown's hippest hot spots (see our Nightlife chapter), the Governor Bradford is also a terrific informal restaurant. You can either eat indoors or on the patio; on a warm day, opt for the latter. Order from a variety of burgers and seafood. There's also a separate children's menu. It's open for lunch and dinner daily all year. Look for the great lunch specials in winter.

The Lobster Pot

$$$ • 321 Commercial St., Provincetown • 487-0842

Ask anyone in town where to go for the best seafood, and everyone will tell you The Lobster Pot. The wait can be long in the summer, since the Pot, as everyone calls it, doesn't accept reservations. Wait it out. The seafood is the freshest available, and Tim McNulty's clam chowder (now available frozen for take-out) has won more "best of" awards than anyone can remember. (Some of the awards, if you care, can be spotted in the Top of the Pot, the small bar/dining area overlooking the bay, and a great place to sit.) The menu is extensive, but almost everyone orders lobster. The Pot usually has multiple sizes in stock (check the tank as you enter), and despite popular rumor, the bigger the lobster does not mean the tougher the meat. The Lobster Pot is open daily for lunch and dinner nearly year round (it closes for six weeks beginning January 1).

The Martin House

$$$ • 157 Commercial St., Provincetown • 487-1327

This highly acclaimed restaurant focuses on regional food with an international influence. The menu, which changes four times a year, always offers lots of seafood — Wellfleet oysters are one of the chef's favorite ingredients — along with game, Angus beef and vegetarian dishes. Housed in an 18th-century building by the water's edge, the Martin House has a number of intimate dining rooms, with five fireplaces used in the cooler months and an outdoor garden patio for warm-weather dining. Open year round, the Martin House serves dinner seven days a week May through October, and Thursday through Monday the rest of the year.

Michael Shay's Rib and Seafood House

$$ • 350 Bradford St., Provincetown • 487-3368

This friendly, sparkling restaurant serves great steaks, chicken and seafood in a pretty dining room overlooking Provincetown Harbor. You know it's child-friendly by the small basket of toys near the door, for parents who may have forgotten to bring diversions for their little ones. It's open daily for breakfast, lunch and dinner year round, but the best deal is the Friday night fish and clam fry. For just $7.95, feast on unlimited plates of fish or clams, lightly breaded and fried and served with coleslaw and french fries.

The Moors

$$ • 5 Bradford St. Ext., Provincetown • 487-0840

When The Moors burned to the ground in 1956, locals clamored to the side of owner Maline Costa and worked with him day and night to rebuild the restaurant. In 30 days, the "new" Moors was open for business, once again serving the best Portuguese food in town. This is where Walter Cronkite and Norman Mailer eat — both love the kale soup and Porco em Pau (marinated pork cubes). Artist Franz Kline and Tennessee Williams were also regulars. The Moors has daily blackboard specials, such as the Shrimp Dazzler, a pound of shrimp prepared five ways. While dining, take a look around. The eclectic objets d'art decorating the restaurant all belonged to locals who donated them to help the decor! And don't forget to stop by and catch the grand Lenny Grandchamp, who's been entertaining patrons for the past 20 years (see our Nightlife chapter). A plus: The Moors has a huge (free)

INSIDERS' TIP

Long before supermarkets carried salt in a box, Cape Codders used to make their own salt. They boiled ocean water in iron kettles until it evaporated, scraping the minute amount of salt from the bottom. Salt shakers came much later.

parking lot! It's closed mid-October through mid-April. Lunch is served in July and August only.

Napi's

$$ • 7 Freeman St., Provincetown • 487-1145

In 1973 Helen and Napi Van Dereck built this restaurant, and today, nearly a quarter-century later, its nickname, "Provincetown's most unusual restaurant," still sticks. Napi's is a work of art with walls built from pieces of discarded Boston factories and with decor of salvaged bric-a-brac, artwork and antiques. The menu is nearly novella-length, offering international dishes such as Brazilian shrimp, Szechwan stir-fry, Russian oysters and Thai chicken and shrimp. We love the Syrian falafel melt — in fact, we love this restaurant!

During the season, Napi's serves dinner nightly. In the off-season, Napi's serves lunch and dinner, and on off-season holidays and weekends, they serve brunch. You'll find free, limited parking adjacent to the restaurant, on the corner of Bradford Street.

A day of summer sun
and surf dissolves with
the growing twilight into
something magical.

Nightlife

Most of us who grew up summers on Cape Cod know her sunny side. Her sandy shores and curling waves have filled our days with memories enough to last a lifetime.

After dark Cape Cod puts on a different face. A day of summer sun and surf dissolves with the growing twilight into something magical, enveloped within a playful gown of darkness. Pleasure boats head for their harbors, lighthouse beams come alive to sweep above the dunes and darkening waves of the lower Cape, fireflies twinkle like brief stars in midsummer night back yards, and peepers in the kettle ponds begin their chorus. A Cape Cod summer evening in all its wonder is upon us!

Summer strollers work off their evening meal, parents take their sunburned children out for an after-dinner ice cream at the local parlor, and a gentle silence calms the communities of cottages hugging the coast.

As wonderful as it sounds, a Cape Cod evening is good for more than just strolling down to the local ice cream shop. After the kiddies are tucked into bed and darkness settles down across the beaches and lakes and ponds, Cape Cod's wild side comes out to play. As day becomes night, and dinner crowds become evening crowds, nightclubs and restaurants open their doors to locals and visitors looking to be entertained. Band members tune their instruments. Bartenders mix drinks with jovial conversation, and wait staff serve up appetizers. All across the Cape the night energy is high, and very soon you discover that summer fun does not end when the sun goes down.

In fact, there's so much going on after the sun sets that you may want to extend your Cape Cod stay. Some towns offer a wide variety of hot spots, from relaxing piano bars to hopping clubs playing the latest electronic noises (a.k.a "music" for those of the younger than 30 crowd). Other towns are less nocturnally active, satisfied in offering just a few after-dark spots to keep things interesting. Some of these night spots are clearly geared toward the summer crowd, other places cater to the locals, and most are designed to entice both sets. Yet, only on Cape Cod can you find a crusty fisherman and a suited business professional drinking a pint or two at the same bar . . . and finding something in common to talk about.

This is probably as good a place as any to get serious for a moment and provide you with the legal small print associated with after-dark activities. The legal age in Massachusetts for the sale of alcohol is 21, and the law is strictly enforced. Bars close at 1 AM, but they may have special hours on holidays; the local newspapers usually carry that information. Wine and beer are only sold in package stores (the Cape term for liquor stores) and at selected convenience stores but not in grocery stores as in some other states. Package stores are closed on Sunday (so plan accordingly for any Sunday afternoon clambakes).

As in other parts of the country, drinking and driving is a serious matter on Cape Cod. If you are suspected of driving under the influence of alcohol, you can be pulled over by the police and given a field sobriety test. If you fail it, you can be arrested on the spot, taken to the police station, booked and suffer all the unpleasantries that go along with that. If you refuse the Breathalyzer test, you can lose your driver's license in Massachusetts, which is reciprocal in some other states. Just so you know all the rules.

Legalities now taken care of, there's nothing left to say but, "Go out and have some fun!" Yet, with all the hot spots available, there's still nothing quite like a nice stroll along the beach at night with the sound of the waves crashing. Better yet, drive out to Truro, Eastham or Chatham and stand entranced as you watch a lighthouse beam sweeping through the gloom to take control of the night. Talk about awesome!

For those interested in exploring Cape nightlife, we present here some of the bright spots you'll find from Bourne to P-town. Listings in this chapter predominantly cover bars, clubs and restaurants that offer live entertainment. See our Arts and Entertainment chapter for theater, concerts and other evening activities, and check local newspapers for special events such as dances and dinners sponsored by local churches and fraternal organizations.

Upper Cape

The Courtyard Restaurant

1337 County Rd., Cataumet (Bourne) • 563-1818

The Courtyard Restaurant pushes back the tables in the room off the bar at 9 PM on Friday and Saturday nights to make way for dancing and live entertainment that runs the gamut from contemporary jazz and blues to light rock and Top 40. Entertainment is provided Wednesday through Saturday evenings year round. The crowd, which often ranges in age from late 20s to early 50s, takes in the music of such local groups as Mark Hennesey & Tish who play contemporary Top 40 music and Mark the Shark & the Central Ave Rhythm Section, who specialize in the blues.

FYI

Unless otherwise noted, the area code for all phone numbers in this guide is 508.

The Captain's Table Restaurant

14 Gallo Rd., Sandwich • 888-8440

Overlooking the Cape Cod Canal and the marina, The Captain's Table Restaurant offers a pretty outside deck and comfortable lounge with piano entertainment, dancing, sing-alongs and a joke-cracking puppet named Howie and his human sidekick, Pete. Nick Lombardo performs in the lounge on Friday nights. You can order from either a full or light menu in the lounge, which is open from April through December.

Dan'l Webster Inn

149 Main St., Sandwich • 888-3622

The Dan'l Webster Inn (see our Hotels, Motels and Resorts chapter as well as our Restaurants chapter) has piano music on weekends and special entertainment on occasion. Located in historic Sandwich center, the Dan'l Webster is a beautiful setting for a perfect evening. You can order from the tavern menu until midnight.

Ye Olde Sandwich Tavern

290 Rt. 130, Sandwich • 888-2200

Ye Olde Sandwich Tavern has a down-home flavor as well as karaoke, video games, Keno and a big dance floor where popular local bands such as Catch 22, Glasstown, Spank 'n Sally and the Race Lane Band perform on weekends. The Moonlighters, a fabulous 20-piece swing orchestra, and Freddy and the Maybellines, a terrific '50s group, perform to packed houses once a month throughout the year. Thursday is karaoke night. You can order pizza in the bar until closing, and the downstairs bar has a game room with pool tables, air hockey, darts and shuffle bowling.

Grange Hall

Old County Rd., East Sandwich • No phone

The Grange Hall in East Sandwich features contra dancing on the third Saturday night of every month year round. The Grange is owned by the Nye Family Association. Watch local newspapers for information.

Rof-Mar Diplomat Club

Popplebottom Rd., South Sandwich • 428-8111

Watch for special ballroom dance events at the Rof-Mar Diplomat Club on Popplebottom Road in South Sandwich. Dances are held every Saturday night year round. Reservations are required at this dinner/dance establishment.

Silver Lounge

Rt. 28, North Falmouth • 563-2410

Driving toward Falmouth on Route 28A, you'll come upon the Silver Lounge in North Falmouth. This place has been a favorite hangout for years and is one of the few that serves food until 1 AM. Eat in the railroad car, then join the crowd at the piano bar in the lounge, always a focal point for local gatherings. The pianist plays Thursday through Saturday from 8:30 PM to midnight.

Surf Lounge

350 Quaker Rd., North Falmouth • 540-9400

Falmouth nightlife seems to center around hotels, restaurants and Irish pubs. Surf Lounge at the Sea Crest Resort and Conference Center in North Falmouth (see our Hotels, Motels and Resorts chapter) fits that bill. This ocean-front resort is a great place for an evening out if you want a romantic dinner overlooking Buzzards Bay followed by some music and maybe a little cheek-to-cheek dancing. Live entertainment runs nightly from Memorial Day to the end of September and includes four- to nine-piece bands performing everything from blues and show tunes to Top 40.

Handlebar Harry's

51 Main St. (Rt. 28), Falmouth • 548-4240

In town, popular local bands at Handlebar Harry's at the Admiralty Hotel (see our Hotels, Motels and Resorts chapter) often pack the lounge to capacity from 9 PM to 1 AM on Friday and Saturday to dance to Elvis tunes, reggae, Top 40 and everything in between. The lounge is open from 4:30 PM to 1 AM. Harry's, the restaurant at the Admiralty, is also a great place for dinner (see our Restaurants chapter).

Coonamesset Inn

Jones Rd. and Gifford St., Falmouth • 548-2300

Among the restaurants that offer entertainment, the Coonamesset Inn is one of the oldest places in town. The Ken Leray Duo performs on Thursdays, the John Salerno Trio on Fridays and the Eddie Sheer Trio on Saturdays.

The Flying Bridge

220 Scranton Ave., Falmouth • 548-2700

Definitely one of Falmouth's brightest and best, The Flying Bridge is a large facility that offers harbor-front drinks and dining nightly and live entertainment in the upstairs lounge on weekends (see our Restaurants chapter). The lounge is open from May through September, and live entertainment is provided during the summer months. Local bands perform Top 40s, jazz and requests for dancing and listening until 12:30 AM on Friday and Saturday.

Century Irish Pub

29 Locust St., Falmouth • 548-6631

If the sound of an Irish fiddle and bodhran starts your feet to tapping, then you'll want to lift a few pints at Falmouth's Century Irish Pub. The accents you'll hear have a lilt because the pub, which has a long presence in Falmouth, is owned by two Dubliners and a lad from Galway. You'll enjoy centuries-old traditional Irish music featuring banjo and Uillean pipe, akin to the Scottish bagpipe. Non-Irish nights showcase blues, country and reggae. The pub is open from May through Columbus Day, with live music nearly every night in the peak summer months.

Irish Embassy Pub

734 Rt. 28, East Falmouth • 540-6656

The Irish Embassy Pub in East Falmouth pulls in legendary names like The Chieftains, the Clancy Brothers and Luka Bloom. You might also catch The Commitments, the Irish group depicted in the movie named for them. The 14-year-old pub is open daily from April to November and has a European-style nightclub and an Irish pub for darts and Irish step dancing on Friday nights. And join the crowd for the Irish sporting events brought in by satellite.

Liam Maguire's Irish Pub and Restaurant

273 Main St., Falmouth • 548-0285

At this Irish pub and restaurant you'll get lively entertainment nightly in season when owner Liam Maguire takes the stage with his guitar to perform traditional and current Irish folk music and requests such as "Danny Boy," "Green Fields" and "My Wild Irish Rose." International Irish music greats Tommy Makem and Paddy Reilly usually make a special appearance once a year to the delight of those of us who wear our green and orange with pride. The restaurant is open year round and serves both Irish and non-Irish food until 10 PM. The pub has a number of Irish beers on tap. Every time we come here we have clam chowder and

Guinness, a great combination which satisfies an affinity for two very special places.

The Wharf

Grand Ave., Falmouth Heights • 548-0777

The Wharf in Falmouth Heights has a fun bar and live entertainment on Friday and Saturday nights. Good ol' rock 'n' roll, reggae and 50s bands keeps the crowd grooving from May until the end of the summer.

The Dome Restaurant

539 Woods Hole Rd., Woods Hole • 548-0800

You'll find a crowd gathering around Doc Harvey at the piano bar at The Dome Restaurant in Woods Hole on Fridays and Saturdays. On Sundays in July and August jazz entertainment is the rule from 7:30 to 11:30 PM. The Dome is an unconventional structure shaped like, well, a dome. It is located right down by Little Harbor (see our Restaurants chapter) and is convenient to the ferry to Martha's Vineyard. The restaurant, which is open from April through October, is closed on Mondays.

Woods Hole Community Hall

Water St., Woods Hole • No phone

The Woods Hole Community Hall is a nice place to spend an evening contra dancing, watching theater (see our Arts and Entertainment chapter) or listening to great folk music, including recording artists Ann Muir, Ed Trickett and Gordon Bok of Maine and Cathy Parton of Arkansas, an acclaimed hammered-dulcimer player. The intimacy of the Community Hall permits you to sit within feet of performers. There is dancing every Wednesday night year round. Plays and jazz concerts are also held on occasion. There's really no central phone number to call, so you'll have to watch local papers for upcoming events.

New Seabury's Players Club

off Great Neck Rd. S., New Seabury (Mashpee) • 477-9111

At New Seabury's Players Club, which has a pub-like decor, you can have dinner overlooking the golf course and Vineyard Sound then listen to the piano playing of Jerry Skelley and Michael Critch, who perform a little of everything from blues and jazz to pop and oldies Thursday through Sunday and weekends only November through March.

Mashpee Commons

Mashpee Rotary, Mashpee • 477-5400

Grab your lawn chair and spend a summer evening enjoying free music and entertainment at Mashpee Commons, a retail center that sponsors 35 outdoor concerts and performances a season and has become an important entertainment center on the Cape. The Commons presents a New England Jazz Festival featuring nationally known jazz performers. Call the above number for a schedule of events.

Mid-Cape

Liberty Hall

2150 Main St., Marstons Mills • 428-5662

This is like one of those 1960s coffee houses our parents used to frequent to hear folk music and listen to beat poets and talk about really deep stuff. Liberty Hall in Marstons Mills features such top local, national and international folk singing talent as the superb Canadian singer-songwriter Garnet Rogers and Les Sampou, a local singer-songwriter. Cool, man.

Box Car Willy's

165 Yarmouth Rd., Hyannis • 775-4421

Two converted railroad cars form Box Car Willy's along the railroad tracks in Hyannis. This year-round spot has a popular dining room, sports bar and an outdoor deck featuring local groups for nightly entertainment during the summer months. It is known for its great appetizers.

Emerald Room

Rt. 132, Hyannis • 771-3000

At the Emerald Room in the Tara Cape Codder Hotel (see our Hotels, Motels and Resorts chapter) topnotch Irish entertainment pleases audiences all year long (seven nights a week during the summer and weekends only September through May). A concert series has featured such nationally known performers as Noel Henry's Irish Showband, Andy Healy, Diedre Reilly and Finton Stanley.

The Paddock

West End Rotary, Hyannis • 775-7677

The lounge at The Paddock (see our Restaurants chapter) is packed on Friday and Saturday nights with people who come to hear pianist and organist Ray Rasicot, who makes musical magic on the keyboard as he performs everything from "Georgia on My Mind" to the theme from *The Phantom of the Opera*. A Cape performer for 25 years, Rasicot plays nightly from Tuesday through Saturday during the summer and on weekends in the off-season. The Paddock is open from April to early November.

Pufferbellies

183 Iyanough Rd. (Rt. 28), Hyannis • 778-2515, (800) 233-4301

Looking for a good time? Pufferbellies is your one-stop year-round party center. You can work up a sweat just reading the schedule of events: Country line-dancing instruction is given daily except Tuesday; intermediate and advanced instruction for couples is given Tuesday. The sports bar, with three large-screen TVs, is open daily. A dart league meets on Wednesdays. Outdoors, you'll find patio seating and volleyball. Wait, there's more: Owner John Morgan entertains on 12-string guitar early Saturday evening, and DJs keep the place hopping every night. And you don't need to know all the steps or be young and agile to have a great time here. Pufferbellies also has a 500-seat Top 40s dance club on site.

Roadhouse Cafe

South St., Hyannis • 775-2386

For another guaranteed good time, try the Roadhouse Cafe. Since the owner's dad is Lou Colombo, the highly regarded jazz musician, it's no surprise that the Lou Colombo Jazz Ensemble takes the floor here on a regular basis (every Monday night, as a matter of fact, year round). "He's very outgoing and entertaining," says Dave Colombo of his trumpet-playing father. Dave McKenna and Joe Delaney also play sweet tunes from Gershwin, Armstrong and Carmichael on Friday and Saturday nights year round. During the summer there is entertainment seven nights a week. How old is the crowd? "Twenty-one up to 80," says Dave Colombo.

Tara Hyannis Hotel and Resort

West End Rotary, Hyannis • 775-7775

The Tara Hyannis Hotel and Resort (see our Hotels, Motels and Resorts chapter) at the West End Rotary has a DJ on Fridays and local two- or three-piece bands playing Top 40 or jazz on Saturday.

The Cape Cod Brew House

720 Main St., Hyannis • 775-4110

The Brew House located in the heart of downtown Hyannis makes their own beer to

Ice Cream of the Crop

Perhaps the most popular nightlife activity is the very one that includes the whole family. We ask you, what summer day is complete without a visit to the local ice cream parlor after dinner? It has become a Cape Cod tradition.

Thankfully, there are many ice cream establishments across the Cape providing the very best in frozen desserts. Whether you like your ice cream in a cone or in a cup, alone or with bananas and hot fudge and nuts and whipped cream and cherry on top, here or to go, fat free or devilishly sinful, you're bound to find what you want at any of the following places.

If you're cruising the many shops at Mashpee Commons you may also want to cruise over to the **Inside Scoop**, 6½ Mashpee Commons, 539-0900. They'll certainly satisfy your sweet tooth. A stroll along Main Street in Hyannis after dinner could consume your whole evening with its many shops and hot spots. While you're there you can hit two cool spots to consume the very best in yummy stuff. **Ben & Jerry's Ice Cream** toward the east end of Main Street (352 Main Street), 790-0910 is always a good choice (being Dead Heads, we suggest Cherry Garcia in a cone). About half-way down Main Street at #570 you'll find **Maggies Ice Cream**, which is a perfect place to stop for a rest and dessert before finishing the Main Street walking circuit.

At **Steve & Sue's Par-Tee Freeze**, 455 W. Main Street, Hyannis, 771-3194 you can have your ice cream and play a round of golf all in one fell swoop (or should we say scoop). They also have another establishment, **Steve & Sue's Soft Serve** in West Yarmouth at 37 E. Main Street, 775-4674. **Yarmouthport's Hallet's Store**, Route 6A, 362-3362, hearkens back to the old days with its antique soda fountain counter in an equally old-fashioned building.

—continued on next page

Photo: Jack Sheedy

Enjoying sweet things at one of the Cape's many ice cream parlors.

Perhaps the granddaddy of all Cape ice cream shops is **Four Seas Ice Cream** at 360 S. Main Street in Centerville, 775-1394. It is convenient to those visiting Craigville Beach, Centerville, Osterville and Hyannis. This place is as close as you can get to an ice cream mecca. People talk about it . . . in public. Locals line up at the end of the season to buy pints, quarts and gallons of the homemade stuff in hope that it will last them until Four Seas opens again come next spring. Good luck!

Dennis is blessed with three fine ice cream spots. **Sundae School** at 387 Lower Country Road, Dennisport, 394-9122, is a must-stop for summer visitors. The place has a real soda-fountain atmosphere right down to the player piano (bring your quarters!). Another place with an old time feel is the popular **Ice Cream Smuggler** at 716 Main Street (Route 6A), Dennis, 385-5307, housed in a quaint Cape house with a bowed roof. **Lickety Split JTC's** on Route 134, Dennis, 385-8707, offers a mini-golf course along with great ice cream, as does the **Weatherdeck** at 168 Main Street in West Harwich, 432-8240.

Harwichport is home to the very popular **Nick & Dick's** ice cream parlor at 710 Main Street (Route 28), 430-2444. This place is convenient to Wychmere Harbor, a great spot to watch the boats as twilight settles in. Along Route 6A in Brewster (3260 Main Street to be more exact) is **Cobie's**, which is an ideal spot for those taking a nice leisurely after-dinner drive down the Old King's Highway.

If you're into lighthouse watching then plan to visit **Ben & Jerry's** at the corner of Route 6 and Brackett Road in North Eastham. You can either eat your cone there or else drive down to the end of Brackett Road, take a left onto Nauset Road and then a quick right onto Cable Road and follow it to its end where you'll find Nauset Light. Now that's what we call an after dinner treat!

---

the delight of those who like to sample different types of brew. Popular local groups perform contemporary music five nights a week during the summer months and two to three nights during the off-season.

The 19th Hole

11 Barnstable Rd., Hyannis • 771-1032

The 40-and-younger crowd flocks to The 19th Hole, a happening sports bar with darts, pool and a juke box.

Sophie's Bar and Grill

Main St. and Barnstable Rd., Hyannis • 775-1111

Sophie's is a great place for those in their 20s, 30s and even those youngsters in their 40s. Live music featuring local groups is presented seven nights a week during the hot summer months and 5 nights a week the rest of the year.

Dolphin Restaurant

3250 Main St. (Rt. 6A), Barnstable • 362-6610

The Dolphin in Barnstable Village is a homey place to settle in for an evening of good music and conversation. Enjoy blues on Fridays while on Saturdays Ted Meyers and Dick Nelson offer up popular dance tunes. Occasionally the Lower Cape-based Jerome Howard Blues Band performs.

Harbor Point

Harbor Point Rd., Cummaquid • 362-2231

With an exquisite view of Barnstable Harbor, the Harbor Point off Route 6A in Cummaquid is a beautiful spot for a special evening of dinner and dancing (see our Restaurants chapter). Besides great sunsets (sometimes the patrons actually applaud the sunsets!) Harbor Point also offers live music nightly from June to September; live entertainment is provided on weekends only during the off-season. The bar and restaurant are open April 1 to January 15.

Cape Cod Irish Village

Rt. 28, West Yarmouth • 771-0100

Traditional Irish music performed by Irish-born entertainers delights the guests and visitors at the Cape Cod Irish Village. Entertainment is featured seven nights a week April through October and includes Irish performers who can bring the fiddle and accordion to life as they play jigs, popular songs and requests. The lounge and restaurant have recently been combined so the full restaurant menu is available. You should try to get a seat before the entertainment starts since hotel guests often fill the lounge. Non-guests pay a cover charge during the summer season for selected performances. You can hear entertainment on weekends (Fridays and Saturdays) during the off-season, and on Sundays too during long weekends.

Mill Hill Club

Rt. 28, West Yarmouth • 775-2580

Attention, sports fans: Do 23 televisions tuned into sports 24 hours a day sound like a dream? It's reality at the Mill Hill Club. The diversions here include pool tables, six bars and video games. Regional and local bands perform regularly, and R-rated comic-hypnotist Frank Santos "brings the audience right into it." Men From Heaven, a male revue, struts its stuff in what one observer calls "a certain degree of clothing." If male and female bikini contests and DJ dance parties are more your style, you'll find them here too. The Gordie Milne Happy Hour here has for 15 years highlighted the R-rated singer-comedian in the summer on Saturday and Sunday. Clientele is 18 and older; minors pay a cover charge, and some shows require a cover charge for everyone.

Compass Lounge

976 Rt. 28, South Yarmouth • 394-4450

The spacious Compass Lounge is open year round Wednesday through Saturday and offers a little of everything from DJs to national recording groups such as God Street Wine, Ugly American and Great White. Local groups Cape Fear, Toadhouse (an alternative rock group), Joshua Tree (the U2 clone from Ireland) as well as Stillwater are popular here. During long holiday weekends, Sunday nights are set aside for teenagers.

Jonah's Pub

South Shore Dr., South Yarmouth • 398-2288

Listening to Top 40s and oldies is a popular pastime on weekends at Jonah's Pub at the Blue Water Resort where popular local groups such as Dennis and John and the Troy Williams Group have a following. Geared to older audiences (40s and older), the pub is relaxing and intimate. It's open nightly from April through October 31.

Union Station Restaurant

Station Ave. and White's Path, South Yarmouth • 398-3883

At the Union Station Restaurant the entertainment goes on year round (five nights a week in the summer and two to three nights a week after Columbus Day). The music varies nightly, from karaoke on Friday to country rock on Thursday and Saturday. The popular local group Stillwater performs regularly. The restaurant serves a full menu in the lounge, which has a small dance floor.

Oliver's Eating & Drinking Establishment

Rt. 6A, Yarmouthport • 362-6062

If you're overdue for a good time, get yourself down to Oliver's in Yarmouthport (see our Restaurants chapter), near the town line with Dennis. The lounge seats about 45. During the summer live entertainment can be heard on Friday, Saturday and Sunday night; on Friday and Saturday night only during the rest of the year. The music is 1970s and 80s dance music, and the crowd usually ranges in age from late 30s to 50s. Co-owner Rick Ormon describes his club as a good locals place; it also attracts tourists, who hear about the place from Insiders.

Christine's

581 Rt. 28, West Dennis • 394-7333

By day, Christine's is humming with busloads of hungry tourists looking for good food. At night, it's hopping with locals who cram the 300-seat showroom for concerts by top draws, such as Herb Reed and the Platters, Chubby Checker, Tom Rush, Rick Danko and the Tommy Dorsey Band. There's something happening seven nights a week during the summer. Monday, for instance, is reserved for jazz, and Tuesday and Thursday are comedy stand-up nights. During the off-season,

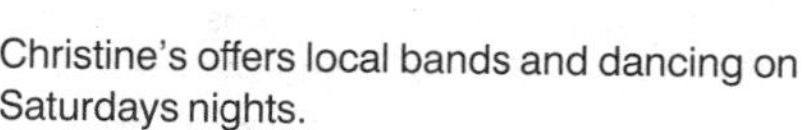

Christine's offers local bands and dancing on Saturdays nights.

Sundancer's

116 Rt. 28, West Dennis • 394-1600

Talk about mass appeal. On Sundays during the summer, Sundancer's showcases reggae music. The rest of the week the club is home to local alternative rock bands and their (mainly) youthful devotees.

Clancy's

8 Upper County Rd., Dennisport • 394-6661

Clancy's on Upper County Road in Dennisport, along the banks of Swan River, caters to those seeking soothing background music while wining and dining. Five nights a week year round a pianist plays everything from jazz to contemporary favorites.

Sand Bar

Lighthouse Rd., West Dennis • 398-2244

No visit to the Cape would be complete without spending an evening with Philo Rockwell King, better known as Rock King, who has been playing to royal (and somewhat older) audiences at the Sand Bar, on the road to West Dennis Beach, for the past 38 years! King does everything from bouts of boogie-woogie to jokes. King holds court Tuesday through Saturday (weekends only Memorial Day through the end of June).

Improper Bostonian

Rt. 28, Dennisport • 394-7416

The entertainment at the classic Improper Bostonian is a meld of jazz, rock, pop and blues — terrific sounds, but only from Memorial Day through Labor Day. The crowd ranges from early 20s to late 30s.

Rum Runner's Cafe

243 Lower County Rd., Dennisport • 398-5673

Rum Runner's Cafe in Dennisport offers some of the finest Boston-based and local blues and classic rock and bands year round. It's open nightly from Memorial Day to Labor Day and Fridays and Saturdays off-season. The crowd runs from 20s to 40s.

Michael Patrick's Publick House

435 Rt. 28, Dennisport • 398-1620

During the summer, Irish music can be found nightly at Michael Patrick's Publick House. When the tourists leave, the jig is up, so to speak, and the live music switches over to contemporary dance favorites from the '50s through the '90s. Yes, there's even a dance floor. Sundays from 4 to 8 PM are reserved for jazz. Michael Patrick's is a place for all ages.

Twenty-Eight Club

Rt. 28, Dennisport • 398-9044

Although the music isn't live (there's a jukebox), the Twenty-Eight Club is always jumping with partygoers willing to pack themselves on the dance floor. With three TVs, it's also a great place to watch the big game — whether its the Sox, the Pats, the Bruins, the Celts or even the Boston College Eagles. Open year round, the Twenty-Eight Club attracts everyone from 21 to 71.

Lower Cape

The Woodshed

1989 Main St., Brewster • 896-7771

Adjacent to The Brewster Inn and Chowder House, The Woodshed is a great place to unwind and take in some local color, along with great acoustic rock. As its name implies, this is a rustic venue and definitely casual. It can get noisy, but the crowd is relaxed and fun-loving.

FYI

Unless otherwise noted, the area code for all phone numbers in this guide is 508.

Longfellows

2377 Main St., Brewster • 896-5413

This pub showcases up-and-coming local bands on Thursday through Saturday nights. Off-season, the fun continues, but only on Fridays and Saturdays.

The Reef Cafe

1 Village Dr., Brewster • 896-7167

Located just off Route 6A within The Villages at Ocean Edge, The Reef features superlative rhythm and blues and Top 40 bands year round on Friday and Saturday nights only.

Lemon Tree Village

1069 Main St., Brewster • 896-3065

This entertainment is free! The grounds of this great little shopping mecca throb to the sounds of a steel drum band every Friday evening during the season.

Bishop's Terrace

Rt. 28, West Harwich • 432-0253

For the finest in classical music, come hear renowned concert pianist Ken Manzer, who holds court at Bishop's terrace every Wednesday through Sunday from Memorial Day to Labor Day. On Saturday evenings, jazz legend Marie Marcus slides and scats supreme — the Cape's very own answer to Ella and Dinah.

Brax Landing

Rt. 28, Harwichport • 432-5515

Top area bands playing everything from rock to jazz to country draw huge crowds all year long to the small dance floor at Brax Landing. This place also does a superb jazz brunch on Sundays in season.

Jake Rooney's

119 Brooks Rd. (corner Rt. 28), Harwichport • 430-1100

This year-round restaurant showcases country and rock bands and karaoke six or seven nights a week in summer and on weekends in the off-season. You can also play Keno and the new interactive trivia game, NTN. Or just tear up the dance floor! Good news for those who like to get out, but hate the smoke so prevalent at most bars: Rooney's has two lounges, one nonsmoking and one smoking.

The Irish Pub

Rt. 28, West Harwich • 432-8808

Traditional Irish music fills the air every evening from 9:30 to 10:30 PM; 30 minutes later, the band changes gears and whips out covers of everything from Paul Simon to the Beach Boys and U2. Irish superstars such as Tommy Makem and The Clancy Brothers often pop by for appearances. The Pub is open from Memorial Day through Columbus Day.

The Country Inn

86 Sisson Rd., Harwichport • 432-2769

This low-key restaurant offers live piano music on Friday nights and Society By the Sea, a piano and bass guitar duo, on Saturday nights year round.

Chatham Bars Inn

Shore Rd., Chatham • 945-0096, (800) 527-4884

If you want to dress to the nines and strut your stuff, head over to the South Lounge at the Chatham Bars Inn, where you can dance in style to live piano music. The Inn's Beach

House Grill, less formal and much more hip, also features live entertainment.

The Chatham Squire

487 Main St., Chatham • 945-0945

The Squire has a split personality: Half of the tavern is a nice restaurant, the other, a casual bar (actually, four bars). During the season, the lively crowd consists of tourists hanging out at the raw bar (the only one in town) or pool tables. Come Labor Day the locals take back the place. Most of the entertainment comes from a jukebox, though a live band makes an appearance every once in a while.

Chatham Wayside Inn

512 Main St., Chatham • 945-5550

In the fall and winter, the Wayside Inn has live entertainment, often a jazz duo, and dancing. In summer they need all the space they can get for serious dining, and in the spring the dance floor is often booked for receptions and special events, so take advantage of the fall and winter dance time.

Photo: Cape Cod Times

It's always hard to drag yourself away from a day at the beach.

Upstairs at Christian's

443 Main St., Chatham • 945-3362

This cozy, book-lined second-floor space is a year-round piano bar, with entertainment until midnight.

Sou'Wester Steak House

1549 Rt. 28, Chatham • 945-4424

Here's a great place to kick up your heels. The Sou'Wester's dance floor is open all year. Thursday through Saturday, bands are usually rock 'n roll or blues, and on Sunday afternoons from 4 to 8 PM, it's country.

Wequassett Inn

Rt. 28, Chatham • 432-5400

The lounge here hosts a jazz duo nightly in season. It's an upscale, civilized place to hear music that accompanies your conversation rather than drowning it out. Men are required to wear jackets.

Joe's Beach Road Bar & Grille at the Barley Neck Inn

5 Beach Rd., East Orleans • 255-0212

The high-ceilinged, barn-like lounge at the Barley Neck has a beautifully redone bar and a great old stone fireplace. Sink into comfortable armchairs and listen to some of the best piano music you'll hear anywhere, tap your feet to the lively sound of local bands or come for the Sunday Jazz Brunch. The schedule of performers varies, but there's entertainment here year round, and it's always good.

Charles Moore Arena

O'Connor Way, Orleans • 255-5902

A cool alternative for kids: Every Friday from mid-September through the end of March, the indoor ice-skating rink features Rock Night from 8 to 10 PM. Kids ages 9 to 14 can skate while a DJ plays their rock favorites.

Off the Bay Cafe

28 Main St., Orleans • 255-5505

Toni Caputo charms the lounge and dining room with piano music every Saturday night in season as well as on New Year's Eve. If your tastes run to show tunes and Gershwin, you'll agree: 'S Wonderful!

Land Ho!

Rt. 6A, Orleans • 255-5165

This popular pub, hung with hundreds of original signs, is one of the few Cape showcases for Cajun and surf music, along with rockabilly and blues. Look for hot bands such as Johnny Hoy and the Bluefish, Mickey Bone, the Beat Poets, Hurricane and the Stoveall Blues Band. The music plays Sunday and Monday nights from Memorial Day through Labor Day. The rest of the year, the Ho, as it is affectionately known by locals, rocks on Thursdays and Saturdays. When there's no live music, the well-stocked jukebox is always playing.

The Nau-Sets Square Dance Club

Willy's Gym, Rt. 6A, Orleans • 255-5079, 394-0257

This group meets every Tuesday from 8 to 10 PM at Willy's Gym at the Orleans Marketplace. There are even live callers. Get yer pardner and promenade!

Orleans Line Dance Club

Willy's Gym, Rt. 6A, Orleans • 255-6826

This club also meets at Willy's Gym (see above). You can take beginner lessons every Wednesday at 7 PM; intermediate lessons begin at 8 PM. Drop-in admission is $6.

Club Bombay at Mitchel's Bistro

Main Street Mercantile, Rt. 6, Eastham • 255-4803

After opening Eastham's only fine dining establishment at Lori's Restaurant (the old name still stands by day, by night it's Mitchel's Bistro), Mitchel Rosenbaum and partner Laxmi Venkateshwaran in May of 1997 opened the upstairs portion of the restaurant as a club with entertainment and a menu of light fare (which, if the restaurant is any indication, will

INSIDERS' TIP

Eighteenth-century settlers changed the name of the town of Pamet to Dangerfield because of its dangerous waters. Today we call it Truro.

be filled with superlative items). The club offers sophisticated entertainment such as jazz, West Indian and folk music — as Mr. Rosenbaum described it, "eclectic, artistic" entertainment. In addition, he is hoping to attract some big names from the 30's through '50s that will appeal to the baby-boom crowd.

First Encounter Coffee House

Samoset Rd., Eastham • 255-5438

Many big names, including Wellfleet's own Patty Larkin and Livingston Taylor (James' brother), got their start and still perform at this well-known coffee house. The building itself is an 1899 yellow clapboard and stained-glass church (the coffeehouse is also a Unitarian church, and its location has earned it the name "Chapel in the Pines"). Concerts are given every Saturday night in the summer and on the third Saturday of every month the rest of the year. If you're late you won't stand a prayer of chance of getting in — the seating is limited to 100 people.

The Regency Lounge

Four Points, Rt. 6, Eastham • 255-5000

This lounge is home to easy-listening and mellow acts that allow for conversation as well as slow dancing. The lounge is open year round.

Rick's Outer Bar

Town Center Plaza, Rt. 6, North Eastham • 255-4959

Every weekend night year round, locals hang out at Rick's to groove on out-of-state and local bands specializing in alternative rock. When they're not listening, they're letting it rip on the dance floor.

The Beachcomber

Cahoon Hollow Rd., Wellfleet • 349-6055

Ask any local person where the best music is on the Lower Cape, and everyone will point you to the Beachcomber. The former 1897 Coast Guard station sits almost at water's edge and attracts a collegiate crowd, especially after a day on the beach. The music here ranges from loud to louder. Mondays are usually set aside for all-age no-alcohol dancing, making The Beachcomber a favorite hip-hop hangout for the not-yet-legal crowd. The Beachcomber charges a modest entertainment fee beginning at 8 PM; get there before then and use the bucks saved for an order of Surfin' Sushi.

The Wellfleet Bookstore and Restaurant

50 Kendrick Ave., Wellfleet • 349-3154

Every Friday through Monday night during season, The Wellfleet Bookstore and Restaurant features the easy-listenin', toe-tappin', harmonica-playin', guitar-strummin' talents of Jac Veronesi. Expect a more reserved — but still fun-seeking — crowd.

The Tavern Room at the Inn at Duck Creek

E. Main St., Wellfleet • 349-7369

Forget rock 'n roll — this 1800s building is a venue for great jazz, pop and Latin ensembles. With its fireplace and authentic beams, the room is a great place to savor live entertainment. It's open spring through October.

Painter's

50 Main St., Wellfleet • 349-3003

This is the place to come if you're looking to brush up on current and cult sounds. The musical menu is as diverse as its culinary counterpart, including rock acts such as Gary Arnold and the G Monster and jazz master Alexander Flamer Quartet. (See our Restaurants chapter.)Painter's is open in the spring through the fall.

Wellfleet Town Pier

Commercial St., Wellfleet

Dancing in the dark? Why not? And throw

INSIDERS' TIP

As you travel the Cape, keep your eyes peeled for quaint — and not so quaint — street names such as Skunknet Road, Goat Field Road, Rascally Rabbit Road, Mouse Hole Lane, Plum Daffy Lane and Nowhere Way. We even have a Yellow Brick Road.

the stars in for good measure! On Wednesday evenings in July and August, the Wellfleet Town Pier becomes a stage for square dancing, complete with a live caller. The fun starts around 7:30 PM and lasts until 11 PM.

Atlantic House

4 to 6 Masonic Pl., Provincetown • 487-3821

Built in 1798, this was once a favorite meeting and drinking place for whaling ship captains. (In subsequent years, the tavern became a custom and court house, and it's now on the National Register of Historic Places.) Time marched on, the crowds still came; even such luminaries as Judy Garland, Billie Holiday, Liz and Dick and Joan Rivers dropped by. Now the rambling green-and-white hot spot is a popular gay men's bar. (Actually, it's three bars in one, including an upstairs in-season "macho" leather bar.) The bar has weekly theme costume parties, and the competition gets tough! When was the last time you saw dozens of beefy studs dressed up like Ann-Margret? The Atlantic House is open seasonally.

The Boatslip

161 Commercial St., Provincetown • 487-1669

Music rarely gets as loud as this, and the dance floor is one hot spot for a mostly male crowd. The club has indoor and outdoor dance floors, with entertainment Thursday through Sunday. There's also a mixed lesbian and gay tea dance most afternoons in season on the outdoor pool deck. It's open April through October.

Cafe Mews

429 Commercial St., Provincetown • 487-1500

In summer, this waterfront restaurant offers live entertainment, usually a cabaret act, on Fridays, Saturdays and Sundays. Some of the best entertainment, however, is in the off-season. October through May, Cafe Mews hosts an open-mike coffee house on Monday nights, broadcast on the hip local radio station, WOMR FM.

Club Euro

258 Commercial St., Provincetown • 487-2505

Once home to a congregational church and movie theater, this restaurant uses the pulpit/stage to host some of the best acts in world music, jazz, blues, funk and reggae. (The room itself is a sight to see: murals of deep-sea denizens, including 3-D mermaids, awash in an ocean of greens and blues.) Repeat performers include such faves as Taj Mahal and Buckwheat Zydeco. There are also frequent classic dance video nights. The crowd is hot and hip. Wednesdays are open mike nights; Thursdays are DJ dance parties. It's open seasonally.

Crown & Anchor

247 Commercial St., Provincetown • 487-1430

One of the few year-round venues in town, the Crown & Anchor specializes in cabaret, with two shows that run all summer, and entertainment throughout the year that often includes various drag acts. There are six bars here so there is plenty of variety. The most mellow is the Lobby Bar, which is more formal and quieter than the others but also has entertainment. The Rooster Bar has a pool table, and the Vault is a dark basement that caters to men in leather.

Governor Bradford

312 Commercial St., Provincetown • 487-2781

Right in the center of town, this local hangout has chess and backgammon sets, and features such acts as the Provincetown Jug Band and One Foundation. Karaoke fever hits a high Tuesday through Thursday nights between 9:30 and 11:30 PM. The Bradford gets smoky, loud and crowded quickly. It's open year round.

Holiday Inn Whaler Lounge

Rt. 6A, Provincetown • 487-1711

The best bargain in town: Every night, the lounge offers free movies! They show recent flicks on a big-screen — actual reel-to-reel 35mm prints, not VCR projection. And the popcorn is free! The lounge is open all year.

Photo: Jon Hamill, Cape Cod Times

Fine food, scenery and company can complete a perfect day on the Cape.

The Moors Smuggler's Lounge
Bradford St. Ext., Provincetown
• 487-0840

Lenny Grandchamp is not called the Grand Champ for nothing: He's been packing them in here for more than 20 years! Grandchamp's schtick is part corn, part camp and totally entertaining. He performs every night except Wednesday from 7:30 to 11 PM Memorial Day through Labor Day.

Pied Piper
193A Commercial St., Provincetown
• 487-1527

Many people consider this the quintessential lesbian dance club. Indeed, even *Time* named it one of the best women's bars in the country! The triangular dance floor is small, noisy and crowded and only gets smaller, noisier and smokier as the evening wears on, though you can cool off on the small bayside deck. Sweating to the oldies is de rigueur — classic disco music has found a second home here. Monday nights are also popular since that's when locals and tourists compete against each other in the "Putting on the Hits" talent show.

Shopping

Friends who live off-Cape have been known to ask, "Only one big mall? Where do you shop?" Our reply: "Everywhere." While the Cape does have only one large mall, the Cape Cod Mall, it is centrally located so that even those of us who live on the outer Cape have no trouble getting there when we need to. But we also enjoy shopping locally, at the scores of small, unique shops in every Cape town.

We do get the latest fashions here, along with (thank heavens) both classic designs and offbeat clothes just right for artistic-minded people. We've got gourmet shops, jewelers, outdoor shops, shoe stores, book shops galore and wonderful gift shops. Many of our gift shops double as galleries, making it easy to find that special, one-of-a-kind wall hanging, basket, vase or planter.

Shopping on the Cape is an adventure. It's also a personal, pleasant experience with friendly shopkeepers and clerks just as likely to strike up a conversation about the weather or current events as the latest fashions or home decor. In a tight-knit economic community, shopkeepers and business people present a united front, so that the lady at the plant shop will recommend the potter down the street, who'll tell you about the stained-glass artist next door, who'll send you to the fabric shop in the next town over.

There are a few sizeable retail centers besides Cape Cod Mall. Busy Route 132 is also home to three shopping plazas right nearby. On the Upper Cape the open-air Mashpee Commons, with more than 50 shops plus four banks and a half-dozen restaurants, is a beautifully designed area that makes shopping a pleasure. In Falmouth, there's the Falmouth Mall with 27 stores and the Cape Cod Children's Museum (see our Kidstuff chapter). While these large centers certainly come in handy — and sometimes you're just in the mood for a mall-type shopping experience — some of our happiest hours have been spent ducking in and out of Main Street shops in towns such as Chatham, Orleans and Sandwich. And don't miss downtown Hyannis, which has some great shops that some people overlook because they're concentrating on the large retail hubs on Route 132. The village of Osterville has its own little downtown. On the north side of the Cape, Barnstable Village, West Barnstable and Sandwich all have some great shops. Sandwich has a lovely Main Street with plenty of shops you can walk to, and Woods Hole is another quaint area you should check out if you're in the Upper Cape area. Yarmouthport has a quiet Main Street on Route 6A, with a cluster of stores and antique shops in one central area.

For a really different shopping experience, spend a day in Provincetown, where Commercial Street is as funky and colorful as Greenwich Village — only with a small-town, seaside flavor. This is the place to go for the offbeat and the outrageous, along with the artistic and spiritual. But don't forget to wear good walking shoes: it can take a good portion of the day just to get from one end of Commercial Street to the other! Wellfleet has a nice downtown, with an emphasis on galleries mixed with a few choice shops. Eastham's shopping scene is a bit scattered geographically, but there are more worthwhile shops there than you might realize. They're just not all in one place, so you do need a car.

Orleans is the real retail hub of the Lower Cape. Many residents of surrounding towns come here regularly to do their grocery shopping, pick up dry cleaning, buy flowers and just shop. It's the kind of town where you're bound to run into someone you know, and even if you don't, you'll get the same warm, comfortable feeling because it's such a friendly town. It has a nice downtown area where you can park your car and stroll down the brick-paved sidewalks.

Chatham is also a great walking town, though there are shops beyond the downtown area you may want to drive to. Main Street Chatham has a genteel, relaxed feel — no hustle-bustle here. In summer, spend a Friday afternoon browsing on Main Street, and hang on to your parking space so you can stay for the outdoor concert on the green! Harwich is sprawling, with shops all along Route 28 and in other areas of town. Harwichport is a good place to start, because much of it is walkable. Brewster, likewise, has a couple of little centers, with a cluster of shops near The Brewster Store (which is itself a must-see), another cluster a mile or so east and, to the west, the Lemon Tree complex of shops (which we recommend you check out).

Shopkeepers accept many forms of payment — cash, personal checks (with proper ID), traveler's checks and credit cards — and the Cape Cod Cooperage in Harwich will even accept regulator clocks, cattle and roll-top desks (or so the sign near the cash register says!). Not all shops take all credit cards, but most accept at least one or two.

About business hours: While most stores are open seven days a week during the season (Memorial Day to Labor Day), many shops — especially those on the Lower Cape — have sporadic off-season hours or are open only on weekends in winter. We'll let you know if that is the case, and, of course, we'll tell you when a shop is closed in the off-season. Otherwise, you can assume the store is open all year. It's always a good idea to call first in the really quiet months such as January, February and March; even shops that are open all year sometimes close for a week or two in the dead of winter to clean house, paint or redecorate so they'll be ready for another busy summer. Happy shopping!

Upper Cape

Tanger Factory Outlet Center
Bourne Bridge Approach, Buzzards Bay • 759-7771

This small collection of outlets has been known to slow us down considerably when we're heading off Cape. There's a great Liz Claiborne outlet plus outlets for other quality names including Levi's, Izod and Barbizon. Look for the sign just before you get onto Route 25 in Buzzards Bay. It's open every day.

Bournedale Country Store
26 Herring Pond Rd., off Scenic Hwy., Bournedale • 833-0700

A delightful little shop where you can get anything from handmade crafts and antiques to a hot sandwich and a good cup of coffee, the Bournedale Country Store is a place to find local foods such as Tugboat Cookies, Kimberley's Fudge Sauce and Crazy Jim's Barbeque Sauce. It also carries custom gift baskets, specialty coffees and marinated stuffed cherry peppers. "We carry a little bit of everything," says co-owner Susan Texiera. "One year we even put out a kitchen sink." You get the point. The store is open March through New Year's Day.

Cape Cod Factory Outlet Mall
1 Factory Outlet Rd., Sagamore • 888-8417

This is a nice collection of 21 well-known manufacturers, including **Bass**, **Boston Bed & Bath**, **London Fog**, **Aileen**, **Oshkosh B'Gosh**, **Buck-A-Book**, **Corning Ware** and **Carter's**. It also has kiosks for leather goods, clothing and jewelry. Look for Bao, a talented pastel artist who can turn a photo into a portrait. The mall is open daily year round and is just off Exit 1 as you're heading on-Cape on Route 6. It's right at the base of the Sagamore Bridge.

Cape Cod Glass Works
845 Sandwich Rd., Sagamore • 888-9262

This unique business, located right next to the Sagamore Bridge, is a studio and gallery all in one, so customers can watch four artisans create beautiful glass pieces. "We tell them, 'Come on in and feel the heat,'" says Mark Burchfield, co-owner of the shop with his father, William Burchfield. "We can answer questions too," he adds. Cape Cod Glass Works specializes in millefiori paperweights, characterized by beautiful floral designs done in glass and encased in more glass, and ranging in price from $300 to $3,000. The shop does a lot of Christmas ornaments — a small glass candy cane goes for $6. The artisans also make lovely functional pieces such as bowls and vases and

CAPE COD'S 1ST AND BEST

BOSTON
BED & BATH
We know where you live.

We've Added Boston To Our Name!
We're Proud Of Our 25 Year New England Heritage!

THE BEST NAMES
Up to the minute home collections from Ralph Lauren, Laura Ashley, Royal Velvet, Martex, Wamsutta, Croscill & more.

THE GREATEST VALUES
From top-of-the-line first quality styles through special purchases of designer closeouts and selected seconds, we offer values that are hard to match.

THE WIDEST ASSORTMENT
Sheets, comforters, towels, rugs, table linens, curtains, draperies, blankets, bedspreads, pillows, mattress pads, quilts, bath and closet organizers, decorative furnishings and accessories in wicker, wrought iron, wood and more - not to mention the largest collection of beach towels on Cape Cod!

FOR EVERY TASTE & BUDGET
Formal to casual, traditional to contemporary, simple to elaborate if you don't find it here, you won't find it anywhere!

BOSTON
BED & BATH
We know where you live.

HYANNIS
Festival Mall at Hyannis
Rte. 132, 778-2877

FALMOUTH
Falmouth Plaza
Rte. 28, 540-7004

ORLEANS
Skaket Corners
Rte. 6A, 240-1455

SAGAMORE
OUTLET STORE
Cape Cod Factory Outlet Mall
833-0550

Vist Us On the World Wide Web @ www.bednbath.com

more whimsical items such as marbles. The studio-gallery is open daily from 10 AM to 6 PM in summer, and in the off-season Monday through Saturday from 10 AM to 6 PM.

Christmas Tree Shop

Rt. 6A, Sagamore • 888-7010

Warning: People have been known to lose track of time in this store and to emerge dazed and happy, carrying bags filled with all kinds of things they didn't know they needed. The bargains here are irresistible! Locally owned and operated, the Christmas Tree shop carries an A-to-Z inventory of gifts and housewares, including lamps, lawn furniture, greeting cards, foods and gourmet items, paper goods, linens and, of course, Christmas items, all at near wholesale prices. The inventory is always fresh and interesting, and the staff pleasant and helpful. The Sagamore shop, with its unusual thatched roof, is a regional attraction; other Christmas Tree Shops are located in Falmouth, Hyannis, West Dennis, Yarmouth and Orleans. The shops are open daily.

The Chocolate House Fudge and Gift Shop

11 Cranberry Hwy., Sagamore • 888-7065

This longtime sweet shop has no less than 14 varieties of homemade fudge, hand-dipped chocolates and specialty candies, including sugar-free chocolate. Gift selections include the Dept. 56 Villages, cranberry glass and soaps. Since this is so near the Sagamore Bridge, why not pick up a box of saltwater taffy before you head home? It's open daily year round.

Pairpoint Crystal

851 Rt. 6A, Sagamore • 888-2344

In keeping with the glassmaking history of the area established in the 1800s by Boston & Sandwich Glass Co., Pairpoint produces and sells beautifully fashioned handblown and pressed glass. Pairpoint makes vases, candlesticks, sun catchers, cup plates and stemware, along with authentic reproductions of early American glass originals found in museums. You can watch glassblowers at work Monday through Friday from 9 AM to 4:30 PM. The shop is open daily.

Angelthreads Folk Art

186 Rt. 6A, Sandwich • 888-4847

This fascinating shop features the considerable talents of owner Susan Strauss and other crafters who produce painted folk art on wood, tin, slate, fabric and found objects. Memory boxes are a specialty, and, of course, anything to do with angels fills the shelves. Strauss carries some tinware, dried flowers, miniatures and small items to use in a type-tray shadowbox or a dollhouse. The shop is open daily except Monday in season and on weekends only in the winter. The shop will special order and ship your purchases.

Carousel Candy

132 Rt. 6A, Sandwich • 888-7000

A sinfully sweet shop, Carousel Candy sells rich handmade chocolates, caramels, saltwater taffy and choco-dipped ginger, pineapple and apricot. Save room for the scones and other baked goods, ice cream cones, gourmet coffees, specialty vinegars and sauces, beach plum jelly and maple syrup. Specialty and holiday baskets are available. The shop is open daily, but the staff often takes a brief well-earned break after the holidays.

Circles and Stems

Merchants Square, Sandwich • No phone

This nice little shop has a pleasing collection of gift items including Catskill wind chimes that sound like a cathedral, gift mirrors, Marion Heath cards and Debbie Blueberry pottery, china and crystal. The shop also has a selection of toys, books and puzzles for children.

INSIDERS' TIP

Stuck without a bottle of wine to go with your Sunday dinner? One way to get around local "blue laws" that prohibit the opening of package stores on Sundays is to visit the Chatham Winery, which can sell wine on Sundays because it is an agricultural business. In the off-season, call ahead to be sure it is open.

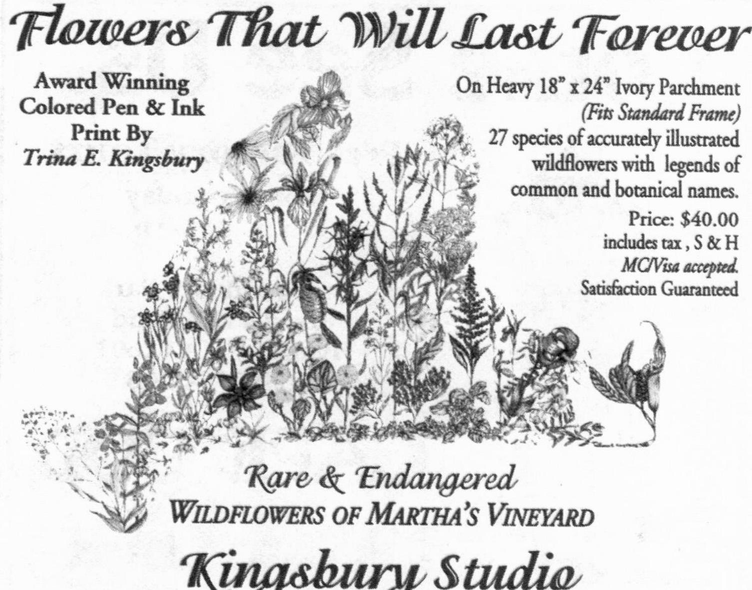

The Cinnamon Stick

450 Rt. 6A, East Sandwich • 833-0006

The Cinnamon Stick is the creator of Cape Cod angels, which are the shop's biggest sellers, along with Sandwich pottery and Sandwich-made woven baskets and throws. Also popular are the shop's Boyd's Bearstones and Folkstones, yellow ware, rag dolls and other country items. The Cinnamon Stick is open daily from May to December.

Home for the Holidays

154 Main St., Sandwich • 888-4388

This shop occupies a beautiful 19th-century home with a classic stairway (always a treat to see decorated at Christmas!). What you'll find here reflects fine and selective tastes that can make gift shopping for weddings or special occasions a genuine pleasure. The shop caters to every holiday and has special gifts for Christmas, Mother's Day and New Year's. Gifts range from one-of-a-kind Christmas tree ornaments to Sandwich mirrors, whimsical or educational children's books, unique toys and miniatures. In winter, the store has shorter hours.

The Jewel Box

Merchants Square, Sandwich • 888-3251

If you want a unique memento of your stay on the Cape, visit The Jewel Box to see the Cape Cod watch for women and men, a Cape Cod map in the form of a pin or charm and a brass Christmas ornament, one of a collection of 15. A full-service jewelry shop, The Jewel Box also creates custom designs, does appraisals, repairs watches and sells jewelry boxes. It's open daily.

Mary's Bookstore

604 Rt. 6A, Sandwich • 833-2986

Owner Mary Wagner opened this family-oriented book shop in 1992 in a portion of her house. Since she lives there, she doesn't mind keeping evening hours; if the light is on, she's open. The shop concentrates largely on fiction, biographies and books for children of all ages. In addition to a children's area, it has a room just for young-adult readers. Mystery lovers, take note: the shop carries the works of more than 230 mystery authors. There's also

a section of poetry, literature and spiritually oriented books. It's open daily.

Picture This

Merchants Square, Sandwich • 888-4600

Open Monday through Saturday all year, this large photography shop has a good selection of prints, frames, albums, gifts, stationery and cards. In addition to film processing and while-you-wait enlargement services, the shop offers printing on T-shirts, mugs, cups and pins. You can also buy cameras and binoculars here. A second location of Picture This is in Pocasset.

Sandwich Lantern Works

17 Jan Sebastian Way, Sandwich Industrial Park • 833-0515

Handmade on the premises, the handsome brass and copper onion lights sold here are replicas of those once carried on whaling vessels. Pre-1800s lanterns, wall sconces and chandeliers to hang indoors or outdoors are also available. The shop is open Monday through Saturday.

Titcomb's Bookshop

432 Rt. 6A, East Sandwich • 888-2331

It would be easy to spend hours in this shop. Its three floors have all manner of cozy places to sit and peruse the large selection of new, used and historical books. Titcomb's is particularly strong in rare books, local authors and regional history, and a wide range of children's selections include the popular American Girl series (you'll find everything from books, trading cards and albums, project books, posters and theater kits). Titcomb's sponsors a number of special events for children throughout the year, such as period tea parties. It also carries greeting cards and orders and ships books. It's open daily.

Toy Chest and Hobby Shop

Merchants Square, Sandwich • 833-8616

This cute shop for children carries popular brands such as Lego, Brio and Playmobile along with Lionel trains, books and hobby pieces, stuffed animals, baby toys and lots of arts-and-crafts items for children. The store also sells educational puzzles, books, model planes, boats and cars. It's open daily.

Youlden's Cranberry Barn

348 Rt. 6A, East Sandwich • 888-7699

If you love lace, don't miss this shop. It stocks 25 styles of imported and domestic curtain and table lace. Parchment paper roses, which are ideal for interior decorating or for special occasions, are prominent here and are complemented by all kinds of country gifts, pottery, baskets, cranberry scoops, clam baskets and wreaths, many of which are locally made. Youlden's also carries the popular Doris Morgan prints. The Cranberry Barn is open daily April 1 to early January.

Bean & Cod

95 Queen's Byway, Falmouth • 548-8840

This shop is both attractive and appetizing: Intriguing gourmet food baskets are custom-filled with cheese, crackers, teas and coffee or regional products, and they can be shipped wherever you want. The New England Bucket contains pancake mix and syrup from Vermont, baked beans, Lake Champlain chocolate and New England clam chowder. The store also carries cookbooks, food mills and other cooking equipment and gift items. The shop is open daily.

The Bird Store

100 Palmer Ave., Falmouth • 540-1701

Need a bat box or a sundial? The Bird Store is a bird-lover's paradise with many styles of feeders, decoys, birdhouses, songbird cassettes, bird videos, assorted bird seeds and suet, thermometers, wind chimes and garden ornaments. Open daily in season, the store's hours are limited in winter.

Boston Bed & Bath

Falmouth Plaza, Rt. 28 • 540-7004

Those who can't resist shelves and shelves of soft, colorful towels, bins and bins of sheets and walls stacked with comforters and blankets will have a hard time getting out of this store. Formerly known as LeeJay Bed & Bath, this chain has developed a reputation for its great selection and reasonable prices. In addition to a huge selection of basics, Boston Bed & Bath carries an amazing assortment of accessories. There are also locations in Sagamore, Hyannis and Orleans.

Eight Cousins Children's Books

189 Main St., Falmouth • 548-5548

With some 14,000 children's titles available, Eight Cousins has an impressive collection of books that children of all ages can explore. New authors such as John Scieszka and Yoko Kawashima Watkins of Brewster are represented along with old favorites such as H.A. Rey, author of the Curious George series, and Robert McCloskey, author of *Make Way for Ducklings*. Several successful Cape writers, including Molly Bang of Falmouth, participate in book signings here. Cassette tapes, educational toys, multimedia products, teacher aids and parenting books are for sale. The bookstore is open daily.

Europa Importers Outlet

628 Rt. 28A, West Falmouth • 540-7814

This well-stocked boutique carries an amazing diversity of items from around the world and the USA. Though it concentrates mainly on women's clothing and jewelry, Europa offers a large variety of accessories such as silk, wool and chiffon scarves. It also carries leather items such as backpacks, brief cases and dress purses, along with children's clothing, cards and unusual items such as Native American drums. Europa is open daily all year.

Falmouth Mall

Rt. 28, Teaticket • 540-8329

This large retail center has 27 stores, including **Bradlees**, **Cherry&Webb**, **T.J. Maxx** and **Perfecta Camera**. In addition to major clothing and food stores, you can also browse through small gift shops. The mall also has a restaurant, Clyde's.

Howlingbird Studio

91 Palmer Ave., Falmouth • 540-3787

A popular silk-screening studio that hand-prints on canvas bags, long- and short-sleeve T-shirts, sweatshirts and hats, Howlingbird is open daily year round. Its retail shop in Woods Hole is open only in season. Items are stocked and ready for printing, some are already printed, or you can bring in your own article. If the screen you select is in use, your order can be printed immediately.

Market Bookshop

15 Depot Ave., Falmouth • 548-5636

Housed in a historic building right off Main Street, the Market Bookshop is celebrating its 27th successful year in 1997. The shop maintains an excellent selection of local authors, geography, travel, fiction, nonfiction and children's books. A second Market Bookshop, in Woods Hole, specializes in science titles. Settle into a comfortable chair by the fireplace to peruse hardcover and paperback books and magazines. The store does a lot of special orders and ships anywhere. It's open daily all year.

Quaker Bonnet

140 Main St., Falmouth • 548-1815

A longtime presence in Falmouth, the Quaker Bonnet has many lovely gift and housewares items, such as glasses, trays, placemats and lamps. If you need a present for a formal or special occasion, you'll find it here. It's open daily.

Soft As A Grape

251 Main St., Falmouth • 548-6159

This well-established business carries T-shirts, shorts and other casual apparel at two shops on Main Street. One carries mostly floral limited-edition designs in dresses, hats, Ts and sweaters; another is a souvenir clothing shop specializing in nautical designs for men. The stores, which carry some jewelry, barrettes and trinkets, are open daily year round. You'll find other Soft As A Grape shops — there are 11 — in Sagamore, Mashpee Commons, Hyannis and Chatham.

Uncle Bill's Country Store

Rt. 28A, North Falmouth • 564-4355

This favorite for Falmouth shoppers carries a little bit of everything — antiques, greeting cards, collectibles, homemade jams, penny candy and jewelry. You can also pick up fresh or silk flowers here. Special collections include Byers Choice carolers, Old World Christmas, Dept. 56 villages and decorations for all holiday seasons, especially Christmas. The store has a huge variety of teddy bears and also stocks a large number of cranberry and cranberry-design products, among them linen, pottery, food, cookbooks and children's toys. The store is open daily.

INSIDERS' TIP

Massachusetts has no sales tax on clothing purchases up to $175 and a 5 percent tax added above that amount.

Under The Sun

22 Water St., Woods Hole • 540-3603

Under The Sun has been in business in Woods Hole for 21 years and has always emphasized locals artists and artisans who make jewelry, glassware, pottery and other functional and artistic pieces, including the works of well-known Cape artisans Rosalie Nadeau and Al Glover. You can take your pick of puzzles, soft toys, educational playthings and some leather items. The shop is open daily in season and Tuesday through Saturday in the winter.

Woods Hole Handworks

Water St., in the Community Hall, Woods Hole • 540-5291

A cooperative that represents the works of a number of excellent local artists who work with clay, wood, metal, wool and other materials, the Handworks shop is an opportunity to learn more about Cape art and is well-worth a visit. The shop is open daily in the summer, with limited hours other times of the year; it's closed January through April.

Dick & Ellie's Flea Market

Rt. 28, Mashpee • 477-3550

Not to be missed. If you can't find it here, it hasn't been invented yet. Allow time to savor the merchandise on display and to get to know the vendors, some of whom have been at Dick & Ellie's for 15 years. Right next to the golf course, the flea market is open Friday through Sunday and Tuesday in season and on weekends through October.

Factory Shoe Mart

Rt. 28, Deer Crossing, Mashpee • 477-0017

Looking for great savings on new shoes and sneakers? Step right up to Factory Shoe Mart for incredible outlet prices on such names as Reebok, Rockport, 9 West and Esprit. Factory Shoe Mart also has a branch in Dennisport. It's open daily.

Mashpee Commons

at the Mashpee Rotary between rts. 28 and 151 • 477-5400

With 62 businesses, including four banks, six restaurants and several nationally known chains, Mashpee Commons has been cited in national design magazines for its attractive, functional and unique retail shopping area. Some of its best known businesses include **The Gap**, **Blockbuster Video**, **Puritan Clothing Store**, **P.A. Company**, **Hoyts Cinema** and **BayBank**. The acclaimed **Gone Tomatoes Restaurant** is a good place to treat yourself to a nice lunch between shopping, or you can recharge at **Starbuck's Coffee House**. Mashpee Commons sponsors 35 annual outdoor concerts and activities throughout the year, including hayrides, Christmas caroling and Pops symphony performances. Mashpee Commons is open daily all year, with longer evening hours in summer. Keep reading for information on some of the other shops in Mashpee Commons.

Homecomings

Mashpee Commons, Mashpee • 477-8519

You'll find everything imaginable for the kitchen, from small appliances to gourmet coffees and utensils. Homecomings has regional food such as New England chowder, corn relish, beach plum jelly and cranberry vinegar in a lobster bottle. The shop also carries cookbooks, jellybeans and contemporary gift items.

Kensington's

Mashpee Commons, Mashpee • 477-4006

Here's a store for the young and restless, or just the restless: Nantucket bags, all kinds of luggage, everything for the beach (from portable chairs to coolers) backpacks, current and historical maps, journals and countless other upscale items related to travel, even a tide clock. Items are priced from very reasonable to expensive.

Lovers For Everyone Ltd.

Mashpee Commons, Mashpee • 477-2221

Do they have every toy imaginable or does it just seem that way? Legos, Gund stuffed animals, European educational toys, great beach toys and instructions on how to make a sand dragon are a mere sampling of the delights inside this shop. Lovers has something for children of all ages, including the wee ones.

Peach Tree Designs

Mashpee Commons, Mashpee • 477-3920

The term "a little bit of everything" should be interpreted literally here, for this shop carries furnishings (beds, sofas and tables), teapots, oil lamps, toiletries (soaps and body creams), chandeliers, picture frames and even a 3-foot-long working model of a sailboat. A classy shop that now displays antique reproduction furniture and all manner of lovely and irresistible gift items, Peach Tree Designs is appreciated for its broad representation of traditional and classic New England designs. A second store can be found in Yarmouthport.

Signature
Mashpee Commons, Mashpee • 539-0045

This is an American Craftsman Gallery, a designation that indicates all goods are American-made. The items are distinctive as well, for nearly every piece of jewelry, artwork and stemware displayed at Signature is one of a kind. Fascinating art objects in glass and metal, unique pieces of jewelry in gold and semiprecious stones and even garden sculpture are displayed here, creating a gallery atmosphere in a unique shop.

Mid-Cape

Artistic Framer & Gallery
843 Main St., Osterville • 428-8802

If you're searching for the perfect frame, this is the place. Camilla and Jim Richman are keeping alive an age-old art by making custom frames for artwork and mirrors the old-fashioned way — by hand. You won't find any ready-made frames in stock here; all frames are done to order with prices starting at $130. The Richmans even do gilding in the traditional method. "There are 20th-century shortcuts, but you don't get the same quality," explains Camilla. The shop also specializes in antique prints, some of which date to the 1600s, as well as some unfinished furniture, textiles, rugs, finials and rods. Open year-round, the shop does a lot of work with decorators, and sends custom orders all over the country. The Richmans' friendly golden retriever, Sierra, is generally on hand to greet customers.

Checkerberry House
857 Main St., Osterville • 428-5533

Your home-decorating prayers have been answered. Checkerberry, housed in a former church, offers two floors of everything you could possibly need or want for your home. In addition to a full decorating service that does everything from window treatment to assisting with new construction, this two-story shop offers rugs, furniture, accessories and gifts. You'll find plant stands, umbrella racks, curtains and tiebacks, wallpaper, silk flowers, ceramics and dinnerware, to name just a few. Among the specialty items in the gift section is a huge assortment of Limoge boxes and lamps. The shop is open daily.

Claire Murray
Main St., Osterville • 428-5816, (800) 252-4733

Claire Murray's handmade rugs are so beautiful you won't want to walk on them. Actually, some of the smaller ones make great wall hangings! The colors are rich and the designs delightful on these are heirloom pieces. You can buy finished rugs — prices range from $99 to $4,000 — or a kit. Some patterns are simple enough for beginners; others are a challenge to accomplished rug makers. Kits average about $130, and classes are offered with a purchase. The year-round shop also carries needlepoint and counted cross-stitch kits, gift items and cotton throws. There's a Claire Murray shop on Nantucket too.

Joan Peters of Osterville

885 Main St., Osterville • 428-3418

Interior designer Joan Peters brings together the elements of her own original paintings, wall coverings, handpainted furniture, sinks and tiles to create a distinctive, coordinated look. She'll even paint floors to match the rest of a room's decor, and fill it with unique accent pieces such as teapot chandeliers, mirrors and custom shades. She custom-designs carpets, and her handpainted sinks and tiles are not only designed and painted on-site but also fired in kilns at the studio. Call for winter hours.

Margo's

876 Main St., Osterville • 428-5664

Opened in the spring of 1996, Margo's is an eclectic home decor store with a little bit of everything. You'll find home accessories, handpainted furniture and china with a colorful, country flair. The shop also offers a full home-decorating service and custom painting. In summer, it's open daily; off-season hours are usually Wednesday through Saturday or by appointment.

Oak & Ivory

1112 Main St., Osterville • 428-9425

This shop is owned and operated by a sixth-generation Nantucketer who makes classic Nantucket baskets on the premises. It also carries antique reproductions of tables, chairs, hutches, chests and side chairs. For a gift that represents the Cape's maritime history and traditions, you can't improve on the whimsical handmade Sailor's Valentine seashell boxes or the lightship baskets in precious metals and original scrimshaw. The shop is open daily.

The Shoe Salon

837 Main St., Osterville • 428-2410

No need to travel to New York or Paris for the finest in ladies' footwear — the Shoe Salon brings it to Cape Cod. You'll find shoes by Stuart Weitzman, Cole Haan, Van Eli and Peter Kaiser, along with accessories such as jewelry, handbags and even a select few sweaters. "We try to bring the unusual — we're not a me-too store," explains owner Pamela Boden. In addition to dressier shoes, the store carries men's and women's Mephisto walking shoes, which have been handmade in France for 30 years. Boden describes them as "the Mercedes-Benz of walking shoes." The shop is open daily in season, and Monday through Saturday in winter. A second Shoe Salon, in Chatham, 945-0292, is open April through the Christmas holidays.

Silva Jewelers

863 Main St., Osterville • 428-2872

Family-owned and -operated, Silva Jewelers not only sells but also designs and produces fine jewelry. Creator of the popular Mothers Basket line of birthstone jewelry, Silva Jewelers also has a line of nautical jewelry. The shop offers custom design, engraving, repairs, estate work and consignment. It's open daily.

Sign of the Owl Bookstore

13 Wianno Ave., Osterville • 428-9393

This longtime bookstore has a large children's section and is especially strong in literature, cookbooks, local-interest books and works by local authors. It also carries gift books, stationery and gift items, which change seasonally, and does gift-wrapping. One interesting bit of trivia: Although it has since changed hands, the shop was first started nearly 25 years ago by the wife of television personality Gene Reyburn. It's open daily.

Yankee Accent

23 Wianno Ave., Osterville • 428-2332

A cross between a gift shop and a gallery, this 24-year-old business with a nautical focus carries prints and originals by well-known local artists such as John Stobbart, Richard Sparre, Elizabeth Mumford and Nancy Braignton-Smith. It also carries gifts for the home and books by New England authors. The store is open daily from May to January and on Saturday only the rest of the year.

Cape Cod Natural Foods

Bell Tower Mall, 1600 Rt. 28, Centerville • 771-8394

A haven for the health-conscious, this

Clothing as shown by Bruno Duluc for KUSH

roomy store has what is probably the largest selection of organic produce on the Cape — more than 70 varieties including eight kinds of apples and six kinds of squash. It also features a huge selection of vitamins, minerals and homeopathic and herbal remedies, plus natural beauty aids and organic pet products.

Visit the store's six-table cafe and deli for hot vegetarian dishes, sandwiches and salads, along with organic milk, coffee, tea, fresh-squeezed orange juice and fruit and vegetable drinks. The store is open from 8 AM to 7 PM Monday through Saturday, and noon to 5:30 PM on Sundays.

1856 Country Store

555 Main St., Centerville • 775-1856

As the local children know, if you've only got a nickel in your pocket, you can still buy something sweet at this charming and historic country store in the heart of Centerville. Whether you're after penny candy, a daily paper or a souvenir of your vacation on Cape Cod, you'll find it here. And as you can tell from the benches out front marked "Democrat" and "Republican," the Country Store is a gathering place for adults (registered, opinionated and otherwise), teenagers and kids. On a hot day, this is where you'll find a cold soda, and on cold days, a cup of hot coffee.

The gift selection ranges from the popular Westerwald pottery (a line that features each village in Barnstable) to homemade jams, hand-dipped candles, and note and greeting cards. From gossip to Gummy Bears, the Country Store has it all! It is open daily.

Andi Carole

370 Main St., Hyannis • 771-7539

This classy boutique sells gorgeous designer clothing for women — clothes by small designer labels you won't find anywhere else. One of those designers is Andi Carole herself, a talented lady known locally for her crusade against litter and for her beautiful dresses with clean, flattering lines. She uses European fabrics with an emphasis on natural fibers, and the quality of the material shows in each piece. These dresses just fall so beautifully. "The thing about my dresses is you've got to see them on," says Carole, who opened this shop 11 years ago after a decade of designing in Europe. Everything she sells in the store is American made, including accessories and jewelry. And this is one of only a few shops that sells locally created Marsh Bears, adorable creatures that are much more than stuffed animals. Andi Carole is open daily.

Artifacts Fine Furniture and Interior Design

434 Main St., Hyannis • 790-3436

This store offers exciting interior-design expertise and a rich inventory of furniture with a contemporary, elegant and yet comfortable feeling. You can get everything here from entertainment centers, tables and chairs to Oriental rugs, mirrors, artwork and lamps. It also carries museum reproduction items in mahogany from the Caribbean, accessories from all over the world and traditional pieces in solid cherry, maple or pine. Run by designers, Artifacts does a lot of custom work. The store is open daily, with evening hours on Monday and Thursday.

FYI

Unless otherwise noted, the area code for all phone numbers in this guide is 508.

Black and White Books

100 W. Main St., Ste. 5, Hyannis • 862-0500

Mystery fans, here's your chance to tap the expertise of Rushton H. Potts, proprietor and respected mystery-book collector and dealer. His inventory of 7,000 hardcover books represents a decade of collecting. Whodunit fans will relish the novels of Raymond Chandler, Rex Stout and Dashiel Hammett as well as the works of first-time authors of mystery, science fiction, horror and fantasy. Patrons are invited to use the reference library, and Potts offers free advice too. The shop is open Tuesday to Saturday during the summer and by appointment at other times.

Boston Bed & Bath

Festival Plaza, Rt. 132, Hyannis • 778-2877

This store, the largest of Boston Bed & Bath's four Cape locations, has a seemingly endless inventory of sheets, comforters, pillows, blankets, towels, bath accessories and gifts — anything you could possibly need for

your home! See the writeup for the Falmouth location in the Upper Cape section of this chapter. There are also locations in Sagamore (Factory Outlet Mall, 833-0550) and Orleans (Skaket Corners, 240-1445).

Cape Cod Mall

Rt. 132 and Rt. 28, Hyannis • 771-0200

The largest mall on Cape Cod — really, the only "real" mall — has 90 shops including **Filene's**, **Macy's**, **Sears**, **Victoria's Secret**, **Lerner's**, **The Gap**, **The Disney Store**, **Waldenbooks** and several kiosks. The mall hosts special activities at various times throughout the year and offers monthly Kids Club activities. A nonsmoking facility, the mall has a large food court and is open daily.

Cape Town Plaza

Rt. 132, Hyannis • No central phone

Some of the larger stores you'll find here include **Filene's Basement**, **Kmart**, **Tweeters** and a very large and wonderfully stocked **Barnes and Noble Bookstore**, which sponsors author signings and social events. Our "Pick of the Plaza" is **Cape Cod Crafters**! The stores are open daily.

Colonial Candle of Cape Cod

232 Main St., Hyannis • 771-3916, (800) 437-1238

Founded more than 80 years ago by Mable Baker, who started out making bayberry candles for her friends and family, the Colonial Candle of Cape Cod today is a division of the largest candle company in the United States. In addition to outlet stores around the Cape, the Colonial Candle Company operates a Main Street gift store with candles and related accessories. You can also pick up your favorite tapers, jar or column candles at a considerably lower price next door at the seconds shop. The shop is open seven days a week. Other outlets are in Falmouth, Sagamore, West Dennis and Orleans.

The Crystal Pineapple

1582 Rt. 132, Hyannis • 362-1330

The Crystal Pineapple carries some 15,000 items made by crafters throughout the world.

A specialist in fine gifts and collectibles, the shop sells Austrian Swarovski crystal, cranberry glass and Italian Armani figurines, among other collectibles. You'll also find jewelry and unusual items such as (our favorite) a solar light-catcher that uses the sun, rather than wind, to make beautiful music. One room is devoted to angel-inspired items, and the lighthouse room showcases the local Highland Light, Nobska Light and Chatham Light in lighted and porcelain styles, along with lighthouse jigsaw puzzles. The store is open daily. West Barnstable has a second Crystal Pineapple, 362-3128.

Festival Plaza

Rt. 132, Hyannis • No central phone

The newest of the Hyannis plazas, this collection of stores includes **Boston Bed & Bath**, **Ben Franklin Crafts**, **Golf Market**, **Lenscrafters**, **Pier 1 Imports**, **Toys 'R' Us**, **Blockbuster Video**, **Purity** and **Paperama**. When you need a food break, fill up at the **Country Time Buffet**. The stores are open daily.

Nantucket Trading Company

354 Main St., Hyannis • 790-3933

If you like adding color and style to your kitchen, treat yourself to a shopping spree here. We love browsing in this spacious, two-level store, which carries glassware, dishes, cookware and a huge assortment of kitchen gadgets along with specialty foods such as Nantucket Coffee, tea, spices, garlic, vinegars and Cape's Kitchen pasta sauces and salsas. You'll also find terrific serving bowls, salad sets, cutting boards, placemats and napkins. This is a great place to shop for a gift, and the store's bridal registry is a neat alternative to the more traditional crystal and china registry. It offers UPS shipping and free gift wrapping. Nantucket Trading Company, which also has a location in Falmouth, is open daily, with expanded evening hours in the summer.

Nautical Books and Artifacts

1 Barnstable Rd., Hyannis • 778-2929

If it has anything to do with boats, you'll find it here. This shop, right near the corner of Main Street, offers nearly 600 new, used and rare books on whaling, shipwrecks, Coast Guard history, boat building, sailboat racing, navigation and just about anything related to boats and the sea. It also has ship models, marine art and artifacts. The shop is open Monday through Saturday and does mail order.

Plush 'n Plunder

605 Main St., Hyannis • 775-4467

When an off-Cape friend who is nuts about hats and vintage clothing came to visit, this is the first place we took her. She chose a black-veiled number from among the endless hats hanging on the walls and ceiling, and found some fancy gloves as well. If you want something different, this is the place to go. The shop is open year round.

Puritan Clothing Store

408 Main St., Hyannis • 775-2400

This 75-year-old family-owned retail clothing store represents three generations of commitment to Cape Cod and has a very traditional feel. We especially appreciate the attentive service we always get here. Puritan carries a complete line of men's and women's clothing, including sportswear and performance shoes (this store carries sports equipment). Puritan also rents and conditions skis.

The company introduced its own beautiful four-color Cape Cod tartan plaid several years ago and offers men's and women's clothing in this handsome material. Puritan has other locations in Chatham, Orleans, Falmouth, Cape Cod Mall and Mashpee. The stores are open daily.

Southwind Plaza

65 Independence Way (Rt. 132), Hyannis • 790-2844

The Southwind Plaza contains **Yield House**, **Bradlee's**, **Children's Orchard**, **Stride Rite**, **The Card Outlet** and **Stop and Shop**. The shops are open daily.

The Bird Cage

1064 Rt. 6A, West Barnstable • 362-5559

A delightful cross between a small museum, a yard sale, an art gallery and a nifty gift shop (which is closest to what it really is), The Bird Cage focuses on birds and anything else that has to do with the shore. The inventory covers everything from antique hunting and fishing gear to scrimshaw on mammoth tusks. It's worth going in just to satisfy your curiosity. Wooden decoys, which collectors know can be pricey (Lincolns and Crowells, for example, can sell for $10,000), represent a range of prices up to around $2,000. The shop is open daily from May through Christmas and at other times by appointment.

Black's Handweaving Shop

597 Rt. 6A, West Barnstable • 362-3955

Here's your chance to watch weavers at their looms as Bob, Jr. and Gabrielle Black create beautiful throws, shawls, scarves and placemats in their shop, which is attached to their home (.7 of a mile west of Route 149). Bob makes jacquard coverlets and throws and can personalize larger pieces by weaving names and dates into them. The Blacks do custom work so you can choose your own colors and designs. They weave about 90 percent of the shop's goods; the rest is the work of other handweavers. The Blacks have been weaving since the 1940s; they opened the shop in 1954 and over the years have woven pieces for customers worldwide. The shop is open daily.

Packet Landing Iron

1040 Rt. 6A, West Barnstable • 362-9321

Packet Landing's metalsmiths produce impressive ornamental ironwork that's displayed in a spacious, rustic gallery. Among the hand-wrought items are fireplace screens and tools, wall and table lamps, unusual curtain tiebacks and coat hooks and trees. One item unique to Packet Landing is a swing curtain rod that pivots, called a curtain crane. You'll also find plant stands, garden accessories, wrought-iron tables and outdoor furniture. Come here for hardware you can't find anywhere else, and for custom work that has enabled more than one customer to solve a technical problem. It's open daily.

Salt & Chestnut

651 Rt. 6A, West Barnstable • 362-6085

This is the only all-American weather vane shop anywhere, says owner Marilyn Strauss, who employs the talents of 33 crafters, mostly from New England, who work in copper, wood, glass and sheet iron. The shop offers custom designs, antique weather vanes, appraisals and lectures. One of the more unusual pieces produced here was a giant manicotti weather vane for the president of Prince Spaghetti, a pasta company. The store also carries chime towers for the garden and other unique items. The store is open daily year round but more by chance in January and February.

West Barnstable Tables

2454 Rt. 149, West Barnstable • 362-2676

In their 26th year of business in this large, year-round showroom, Stephen Whittlesey and Richard Kiusalas produce handmade custom furniture in a primitive style that retains and emphasizes the color and texture of the natural wood, much of which is about 100 years old. The shop also converts antique windows into frames for mirrors. Trestle, Shaker, farm table and pedestal legs are used on the distinctive tables; unique folk art cupboards are also created from antique wood and found pieces such as ship portholes. It's open daily.

The Whippletree

660 Rt. 6A, West Barnstable • 362-3320

Housed in a beautiful, 225-year-old barn, The Whippletree is filled with gifts and home accessories with a country flavor, including cotton coverlets, dried flowers and wreaths, greeting cards, candles and handcarved birds. Some popular collectible lines include Cats Meow, Snow Babies and Squashville. You can also select gifts for the holidays and items for children and babies. The Whippletree is open seven days a week from June to December and Thursday through Sunday the rest of the year.

Tern Studio

Rt. 149, West Barnstable • 362-6077

If you love wood — really fine wood, worked by a real craftsman — come visit Tern Studio, where Albert Barbour handcrafts fine wood furniture and one-of-a-kind wood turnings. Barbour uses all New England wood and often uses green wood for his turned pieces, then ages the finished pieces. The gallery is full of hand-turned bowls, candlesticks and vases — each a truly unique piece of art. You may also find a few pieces of furniture but since most of the furniture Barbour does is custom work, it doesn't stay in the studio for long. Photos of his pieces in their new homes line the walls of his studio. "My idea is, don't make the same thing twice," says Barbour, who has been plying his craft for more than two decades. "I don't want to become a factory." No chance of that; these far-from-factory creations must be seen to be appreciated. Tern Studio is open year round, "Six or seven days a week," the craftsman says.

The Picket Fence

4225 Rt. 6A, Cummaquid • 362-4865

Behind a picket fence is The Picket Fence, a great old barn filled with unique decorative items and collectibles. You'll find handpainted furniture, pottery, original dolls and a terrific assortment of holiday decorations. We always make a point of coming here at least once before Christmas. It's a fun place to browse, and it's friendly too. It's not uncommon, in November, to find an offering of hot cider and cookies greeting you. The shop closes after Christmas and opens again in spring.

The Barn & Co.

358 Rt. 6A, Yarmouthport • 362- 3841

Make a point of stopping by to admire the 155-year-old barn and the superb creativity of local and regional artists. You'll find Hearts Content handpainted clothing, Pat Gardiner dolls, Brewster native Marybeth Baxter's primitive cards and prints, Marstons Mills' Dust of the Earth pottery, lovely dried floral arrangements and everybody's favorite — angels, in cloth, ceramics and porcelain. Local basketmakers produce handsome items in the Shaker, traditional and Nantucket lightship designs. The shop is open year round with shorter winter hours.

Cape Cod Clockwork

586 Higgins Crowell Rd., West Yarmouth • 771-1082

Wendell Sharp, a certified master clockmaker, is the proprietor of the largest clock dealership on the Cape. He carries 20 or so grandfather clock designs plus a complete selection of Sligh and Howard Miller wall and mantel clocks, Chelsea ships clocks, Swiss music boxes and weather instruments. He is a dealer for the Wellfleet Clock Company, which makes tide clocks and shelf and wall clocks. Sharp's motto: "If you need a clock repaired/ Old or new/ Bring it in/ Wendell knows what to do." He is open Tuesday through Sunday in season, and Tuesday through Saturday off-season.

Cape Cod Crafters Outlet

851 Rt. 28, Victorian Village, South Yarmouth • 760-1677

This shop represents nearly 150 crafters who present a smorgasbord of artistic expression: handbags, baskets, quilts, birdhouses, doll clothes, paintings, tole art, bears, bunnies, flags, calendars, handpainted clothing, baby items, wood carvings, clocks, jewelry, rubber stamps, wood burnings, pressed flowers, shell craft, dried flowers, plant rooters and Victorian accessories. The shop is open daily, and there's another one in Hyannis.

Carver's Barn

64 Long Pond Dr., South Yarmouth • 760-5376

Would your neighbors in Kansas get a kick out of a "Circa 1992" sign for their house? Would a "Katie's Kitchen Is Always Open" sign make your best friend happy? Take your imagination to Carver's Barn and let resident carver Joe Gesullo, who co-owns and operates the shop with David Angelica, make you a personalized gift (it may take a few weeks). If you need something right away, choose from in-stock items: bird and fish carvings, decorated signs with scallop shells, pineapples (the traditional sign of hospitality) and folk art motifs. Prices vary; a simple personalized quarterboard costs around $70 to $80.

This colorful shop is also packed with antique and reproduction furniture — pine shelves and nightstands, Americana collectibles, stained glass and Christmas keepsakes — and conventional gifts such as cards and stationery, tapes and CDs. The shop is open weekends only from January to March and daily except Monday from April to December.

The Frame Shop

59 White's Path, South Yarmouth • 394-1729

Among the large selection of framed and unframed prints sold here are limited editions by Charles Wysocki (whose Americana scenes are very popular), camouflage art by Bev Doolittle and works by Paul Landry. Services include custom matting and framing, with approximately 600 moldings from which to choose. The shop, which has been at this location for 20 years and is owned by Bob and Lorraine Donnelly, is open Monday through Saturday year round.

The Mill Store
39 Rt. 28, West Yarmouth • 775-3818

This store has a large selection of unfinished furniture and craft items and is simply a fun place to explore if you are feeling creative or thinking it's time to make some changes in your personal space. Prices are excellent, and the store is open daily. The Mill Store has other locations in Dennisport, West Harwich and Plymouth.

Parnassus Book Service
Rt. 6A, Yarmouthport • 362-6420

With three floors of books in an 1840s-era general store, shelves clogged with books old and new, aisles often scattered with boxes and everywhere the exquisite aroma of old books, Parnassus is quickly assigned to the place in your memory reserved for completely satisfying experiences. The store carries extensive collections in such subjects as maritime history, fine arts, antiques, Cape Cod and Colonial American history. It is open Monday through Saturday year round.

19th Century Mercantile
2 N. Main St., South Yarmouth • 398-1888

Step through the door and into the past. Washboards, quilts and feather dusters from an earlier era share space with period clothing — spats, hoops and parasols — and old-time remedies such as slippery elm throat lozenges. The shop occupies a historic building dating to 1802. Originally a ropewalk, it was operated in the mid-1800s as a general store and would have been stocked with items you can find there today. Owner Barbara Amster, who dresses in period costume, has set aside a corner where children can play with old lesson books and clothes. Civil War and Revolutionary War re-enactors love this place. More fun: Groups and individuals can get gussied up in period costume and have a picture taken. The store is open year round, with a shortened schedule in the off-season.

The Silver Unicorn

941 Rt. 28, South Yarmouth • 394-8401

If you are looking for a keepsake of your visit to the Cape, stop in at the Silver Unicorn where you'll discover an extensive line of nautical jewelry — bracelets, charms, rings and earrings in gold and sterling silver — with a Cape Cod theme (maps, lobster traps and whale tails). The shop also has nautical glass sculpture. It's open daily.

Wild Birds Unlimited

1198 Main St., South Yarmouth • 760-1996

Bird lovers flock to this store for bird feeders (priced from $3 to $300) and plenty of seed and suet. But why stop there? The bird-themed paraphernalia goes on and on: handcarved birds, jewelry, music boxes, clothing, songbird tapes, videos, books and all kinds of educational materials. Do you want a birdbath? Wild Birds Unlimited has standing and hanging baths in wood, iron, concrete, ceramic and plastic that can be hung from trees, mounted on a deck or placed in your gardens. The store is open seven days a week.

Yankee Crafters Inc.

48 N. Main St., South Yarmouth • 394-0575

Thousands of pieces of handcrafted wampum jewelry — rings, pins, earrings and bolas — are offered at very reasonable prices. Also among the collections are Scandinavian jewelry, linens, calendars, crystal and Norwegian trolls. The building is listed on the National Register of Historic Places. Yankee Crafters is open daily.

The Basket Shoppe

28 Rt. 28, Dennisport • 398-6850

If you're a basket nut — one of those people who puts just about everything in baskets — you'll adore this shop. It sells all sorts of baskets at reasonable prices. We never leave here empty-handed. You'll also find high-quality wicker furniture, silk flowers and decorative accessories for the home. It's open daily.

Cape Cod Braided Rug Co.

259 Great Western Rd., South Dennis • 398-0089

These are the real things: braided rugs made right on the premises and in all sizes and colors. Bench and chair pads, rocker sets, stair treads and placemats are also available. The store also carries a varied selection of brand-name rugs. If you're lucky, you can watch the rugmakers in action. Since the hours of their operation vary greatly, we recommend you call in advance if you want to see a rug being made. The shop is closed on Sunday.

Armchair Bookstore

619 Rt. 6A, Dennis • 385-0900

The Armchair Bookstore in Yarmouthport and the Blue Heron Bookshop in Brewster combined in 1997 to offer a more expansive setting and a greater number of books. This family-run bookstore includes titles in literary fiction, history, nature, children's titles and toys, salty humor and more. Two golden retrievers, Chaps and Buzz, oversee the store and greet customers. Armchair is open 9:30 AM to 6 PM daily year round.

The Cape Cod Collection Ltd.

574 Rt. 6A, Dennis • 385-8366

This shop has lovely jewelry, including charm bracelets with gold or silver-plated Nantucket baskets, sand dollar and shell bracelets, even a nifty scallop-shell bracelet and earring set, cast from molds made from actual shells.

But the really unique aspect of this shop is its line of weather instruments made by Downeaster Mfg., also based here at the Cape Cod Collection. Their wind meters were mounted on the flagpoles at the 1996 Summer Olympics. We love the brass-encased Medallion series of tide clocks, wind meters, ship clocks and wind meters. Start your collection here! The store also features a selection of weathervanes, brass thermometers and classic ship models. It's open daily.

Ross Coppelman

1439 Rt. 6A, Dennis • 385-7900

To say Ross Coppelman's gold and silver creations are unique would be an understatement. This jewelry is lush, extravagant, bold and beautiful. Unusual and classic gemstones

are displayed in striking settings, many of them inspired by ancient Egyptian, Aztec and Roman designs but with a contemporary flair. Just west of the Route 134 junction, the shop has two showrooms of gold and silver jewelry and a workshop where it is created and produced. Coppelman, who opened his business in 1971, does a lot of custom jewelry, including wedding rings, and also resets stones. The shop is open daily in summer, and Monday through Saturday the rest of the year.

Fitzpatrick Irish Fashions and Jewelry

109 Rt. 28, West Dennis • 394-5831

Cape Cod has a large Irish population, and this store in the Windmill Crafters' Outlet is where they go to buy authentic Irish goods when they can't get to the homeland. The selection of imports is staggering: handknit fisherman sweaters, wool coats and jackets, kilts, Claddagh and Celtic jewelry, step-dancing shoes and a wonderful array of Beleek, Donegal and Royal Tara china. It's open daily year round.

Lady Bug Quilting & Knitting Shop

612 Rt. 6A, Dennis • 385-2662

In business since 1982, this shop started as a quilting supply shop then added the knitting component. Today it is equally strong in both areas. In the Kings Grant complex, the shop carries 100 percent cotton fabric, lots of yarn, needles and supplies, and books on both quilting and knitting. Owner Barbara Prue, who is proficient at both crafts, offers classes in knitting and quilting for all levels. The shop is open year round, daily in summer and Monday through Saturday the rest of the year.

Patriot Square

492 Rt. 134, South Dennis • 394-4129

Patriot Square is one of the mid-Cape's finer shopping plazas with a wide selection of shops and services. Nationally known stores include **CVS**, a **JC Penney** catalog store, **True Value Hardware**, **Royal Discount Books**, **Radio Shack**, **Marshall's** and **Stop & Shop**. There's even an **AAA** office in case you need help planning the rest of your trip! Fast-food eateries include Pizza Hut and Burger King.

Other stores specialize in video rentals, greeting cards and gifts, clothing, shoes, eyeglasses and more. Film fans will rejoice: The mall has a 12-screen movie theater! Need cash for a shopping safari? There's also a 24-hour ATM.

Tobey Farm Country Store

352 Rt. 6A, Dennis • 385-2930

Tucked inside this 300-year-old working farm — one of the best stops on the Cape for fresh fruits and vegetables — is a small shopping area featuring exquisite dried floral wreaths and centerpieces made from German statice, lavender, eucalyptus, rosebuds and yarrow at cut-rate prices. Freshly baked pies and a variety of locally bottled jams and jellies are irresistible. It's closed Christmas through mid-April.

FYI

Unless otherwise noted, the area code for all phone numbers in this guide is 508.

Lower Cape

Brewster Book Store

2648 Rt. 6A, Brewster • 896-6543

This delightful little shop is filled to the brim with hardcover and paperback books with a strong local author and local interest section and a terrific children's section. It's also got unusual cards and stationery. The shop holds regular book-signings, especially with local authors, and has some great sales! It's open daily.

Brewster General Store

1935 Rt. 6A, Brewster • 896-3744

Erected as a Unitarian church in 1852, The Brewster General Store is a landmark and a tradition. Revered by locals and visitors alike, it's a friendly, take-your-time kind of place where you grab a cup of coffee, a doughnut and a newspaper and sit out on the porch on one of the benches (actually old church pews) and watch the world go by. You can also buy linens, mugs, teapots, cookbooks, jams and T-shirts, among a great assortment of items. Children love coming in to pick out penny candy and put dimes in the turn-of-the-century player piano that gives the place a rollicking ragtime sound. On Sunday mornings the store fills up with folks getting their papers, and the coffee flows.

Upstairs you'll find antique linens, old milk bottles, sheet music, books and artwork, to name just a few of the items. In summer, the shed in the back of the store opens as **The Brewster Scoop**, serving up the finest in ice cream and low-fat yogurt. The shop is open daily.

The Cook Shop

1091 Rt. 6A, Brewster • 896-7698

Whether you are Julia Child or a child in the kitchen, you'll relish this gourmet gallery. The store is packed with all manner of cooking implements, along with spices, oils, vinegars, mustards, sauces and countless other palate pleasures. The second floor houses a wide selection of dinnerware, cutlery, containers and cookware. Bon appetit! The shop is open daily.

The Great Cape Cod Herb, Spice & Tea Company

2628 Rt. 6A, Brewster • 896-5900

Proprietor Stephan Brown runs the Cape's only all-natural herbal apothecary out of a rambling old horse stable. The more than 170 Western and Chinese herbs are stored in glass containers on rough-hewn shelves. Brown uses many of these herbs in his unique holistic teas, which, he promises, might cure such ailments as urinary tract problems, ulcers, sinusitis and sleep disorders. Mail orders are accepted; call (800) 427-7144. Brown also offers, on a some-

INSIDERS' TIP

A great time to check out shops you're unfamiliar with is during local festivals, such as Brewster in Bloom in April, Chatham's Spring Fling in May or Eastham's Windmill Weekend in September. As part of these celebrations, local businesses often hold open houses with refreshments, food samples or special discounts on certain items. See our Annual Events chapter.

what erratic basis, classes in natural healthcare, and plant and weed identification walks around his property. The shop is open daily.

Handcraft House

3966 Rt. 6A, Brewster • 240-1412

One of our favorites, Handcraft House (which really is in a former house) serves as a showcase for owner Eileen Smith's beautiful watercolors, many of them Cape landscapes. But it also carries a variety of fine, handcrafted items largely by New England craftspeople. You'll find colorful handwoven scarves, iron-forged candlesticks, wood marquetry boxes, glass suncatchers and jewelry, among many other items. The shop is open daily in season, on weekends in late fall and is closed from January to mid-April.

Lemon Tree Pottery

1069 Rt. 6A, Brewster • 896-3065

Opened in 1965, this shop has over the years blossomed into a showcase of pottery, ceramics, jewelry and other beautiful things. One specialty is very much in evidence outside the shop and throughout the Lemon Tree complex of shops: lawn ornaments — everything from fountains to rabbits and cats. The shop also sells terra cotta herb markers, dreamcatchers, handmade ceramic coat hooks in the shape of fish and colorful, hand-dipped tapers — a whopping 36 inches long and available in nine vivid colors. The shop is open daily.

Linda's Originals

220 Rt. 6A, Brewster • 385-2285, (800) 385-2284

The Yankee Craftsmen

220 Rt. 6A, Brewster • 385-4758, (800) 385-4758

Perched side by side on a hill, these two stores have been delighting collectors for a decade. Linda's Originals carries a wide range of handpainted clothing and handcrafted items and the largest selection of afghans on the Cape. The store is also home to the Cats Meow, a captivating collection of miniature handcrafted buildings. (This is the only place in the country where you can buy items from the Cats Meow Cape Cod Collection, such as the Cape Playhouse, Scargo Tower and the Chatham Lighthouse.)

The Yankee Craftsmen truly lives up to its name: The rooms are chock-full of collectible items made by crafters from the Cape and worldwide. It also has one of the largest collections of Byers Choice Carolers in the country as well as Harbour Lights lighthouses. If you can't find it here, friends like to say, it doesn't exist! In the summer, be sure to visit the lavish, award-winning flower gardens. The shops are open daily.

Punkhorn Books

627 Rt. 6A, Brewster • 896-2114

At first glance, you may think you've walked into a library. Owner David Luebke keeps his antiquarian books arranged in neat rows, according to the Dewey Decimal System. (Luebke's wife, Irene, also covers the books in see-through covers; she just happens to be a bookbinder.) The Luebkes run the bookstore out of the ground floor of their house, and they specialize in fine arts, biographies, natural history and the history of Cape Cod. They also have a fine selection of rare prints and maps. From June through October the book shop is open daily except Monday. In the off-season it's open by appointment only.

The Strawberry Patch

2550 Rt. 6A, Brewster • 896-5050

This red-shuttered old horse barn is the exclusive home of Hand-tiques, the name owner Mary Anne Boyd coined for her unique array of gifts. Many of the goods are displayed in antique display cases: a cast-iron stove holds cookie cutters and old post office boxes cradle candles.

In business more than 25 years, the shop carries lovely USA-made cotton throws, pillows and tablecloths, along with kitchenware, dolls, gifts, candy and Christmas decorations. Befitting a former equine home, the shop has several selling stalls, including the Teacher Stall (everything for a teacher or classroom) and the Fabric Stall (fabrics and other sewing necessities, including a wide array of threads stored in 1800s thread cases). A separate sale barn offers first-quality goodies at discounts of up to 50 percent. The Strawberry Patch is open daily.

Sydenstricker Galleries

490 Rt. 6A, Brewster • 385-3272

The colors are bold and bright. The designs, sharp and striking. The glass made here is so dazzling that several American embassies serve dessert to their guests on Sydenstricker plates, inspired by the art of ancient Egypt. Two sheets of glass are fitted into a terra cotta mold; the first sheet is decorated by shifting powered glass through a stencil. A five-hour fusing locks in the color. Choose from dishes in various sizes (some with a signature rippled edge), complete place settings, rectangular serving plates, candy dishes, even ashtrays. Two showcases are filled with glass paperweights. You can watch the glass being made Tuesday through Saturday from 10 AM to 2:30 PM. The shop is open daily.

Allen Harbor Nautical Gifts

335 Lower County Rd., Harwichport • 432-2467, (800) 832-2467

Even landlubbers will enjoy the incredible selection of items found here. There are jigsaw puzzles and calendars commemorating various Cape Cod landmarks, T-shirts and watches and jewelry (including a nifty charm bracelet that spells out "I love you" in colorful cloisonn, ship flags), doormats and decorative household treats. Allen Harbor also sells a great selection of tide clocks and wind and weather instruments. The shop is closed weekends during the off-season except at Christmastime.

Cape Cod Bonsai Studio

1012 Rt. 28, Harwich • 432-8400

Owner Michael Novik has planted his love and knowledge of gardening in Harwich, and the results are growing beyond belief. The studio has an abundance of bonsai trees — dwarf juniper, elm, boxwood and Japanese cherry — and tropical plants for sale, in individual ceramic planters or in groupings, meticulously arranged on spanking-clean shelves. You can also purchase accessories, including training wire, traditional ceramic planters and selected pieces of suiseki, stone forms resembling mountains that are also used as planters. The prices are quite reasonable, and Novik will help quench any fears non-green thumbers may have. He also offers courses and workshops in bonsai care and training. It's open by appointment in the off-season.

Cape Cod Cooperage

1150 Queen Anne Rd., Harwich • 432-0788

The Cooperage is a step back in time and a must-see for anyone who wants a glimpse of living Cape Cod history. This big old barn is the only place where cranberry barrels and rough-sawed fish boxes (both used today by people as storage containers) are made by hand, just as they were more than 100 years ago. The store also offers an incredible selection of handpainted furniture and staves, every conceivable arts and crafts notion, bevies of birdhouses and old-fashioned kids' toys, such as pull-along ducks and rabbits and hobby horses. Adjoining is a genuine blacksmith shop, where, every Saturday afternoon in July and August, you can watch blacksmith Robert Jordan making fences and kitchen tools. During season, you can also buy fresh-picked cranberries. It's open daily all year.

Cinnamon Stick

825 Main St., Harwichport • 432-3071

After eight years in its original location, Cinnamon Stick — also known as Andrea's Cinnamon Stick for proprietor Andrea Evangelista — moved to larger quarters down the road just after Christmas 1996. Now right next door to Cape Cod Divers on Route 28, the store still has the same homespun, cozy atmosphere but lots more of it! The shop has a huge selection of bears, both stuffed and resin, including Boyds Bears, North American Bear's Muffy Bear and the locally created Marsh Bears. You'll also find prints, cards, calendars, books, pottery, scrimshaw and Christmas ornaments, along with collectibles such as Nelson Stock villages. The shop is open year round, daily in summer and closed one or two days a week in winter (call for off-season hours). There's a sister store by the same name in Oracle Square, Orleans, 240-3635, that's open May through December.

Mid-Cape Coin

236 Main St., West Harwich • 430-2497

Owner Wayne Lizotte calls his store "the best little coin shop in New England." Who's to argue? He specializes in collector coins — true gems for the true numismatist. He also sells currency, buys and trades and offers professional appraisal services. Open daily in season, the shop's hours vary off-season.

Monahan and Company

540 Rt. 28, Harwichport • 432-3302

The oldest family-owned jewelry store in the country, Monahan still carries on the tradition started by founder Jerimiah Monahan in 1815: quality jewelry at fair prices. In 1995, the store closed its sister stores in Chatham and Vero Beach, Florida, to make its Harwich inventory even larger. It's open Friday and Saturday in the off-season.

The Potted Geranium

188 Rt. 28, West Harwich • 432-1114

Every room of this antique Cape Cod house is filled with wonderful home accessories, folk art, crafts and gifts. It's the kind of shop that puts you in a good mood the moment you walk in the door. You'll find such items as pewter bookmarks made in Chatham, locally produced Christmas ornaments shaped like weathervanes, handpainted mirrors and — the store's most unique item — handpainted napkin-ring sets made from cutaway miniature flower pots. If there's a new mom or baby on your gift list, visit the baby room for blankets, layettes, clothes and books. The former kitchen makes a fitting home for flavored teas and coffees, kitchen utensils and linens and a sampling of jellies and jams from the Chatham Jam and Jelly Shop. Hours vary in the off-season.

Sea Street Books

537 Rt. 28, Harwichport • 430-1816

This shop may be small, but it's got enough material for hours of browsing. We love the notes hung by strings inserted in selected books with comments and anecdotes that make deciding on a book much easier. It's also nice that the shop discounts books currently on the New York Times Bestseller List (25 percent off hardcovers, 10 percent for paperbacks). And it has a great children's section, complete with a small table and chairs, a basket of crayons and paper for little ones to draw on. That explains the many children's drawings hanging throughout the store. You'll also find tapes and compact discs of classical and jazz music. It's open daily.

Yankee Doodle Shop

181 Main St., Harwich • 432-0579

For more than 45 years, this has been one Yankee Doodle Dandy of a shop! Room after room of finished and unfinished quality country furniture, all made right on the premises, are offered at prices so low you'll question the price tag. The front porch, for instance, is home to at least 12 kinds of rockers, with prices averaging $75. There's also a wide selection of cast-iron doorstops and reproduction mechanical banks, hard-to-find wooden cupolas, folk art — even authentic spinning wheels! In the off-season, it's open Friday and Saturday only.

Amazing Lace

726 Main St., Chatham • 945-4023

In 1989 Donna Burns gave her store a proper name: It is amazing, and it is full of lace. And so much more. Vintage clothing fans will have a field day here choosing from such bargains as a 1950s coral silk brocade outfit (blazer and Capri pants) for $140 and a mint-condition 1957 wedding gown, complete with hoop skirt, at $250. We also loved the collection of turn-of-the-century folding fans — a steal at $75 each! The shop also has a nice selection of 1930s tablecloths and chenille bedspreads, just like Grandma had. In January and February it's open weekends only or by appointment.

Ben Franklin

631 Main St., Chatham • 945-0655

This is one of an increasingly rare breed of retail shop: an old-fashioned five-and-dime store. It's got a wide variety of merchandise, from art supplies and toys to greeting cards, mugs and T-shirts. We love to come here because it looks, feels and even smells like the stationery-variety store we remember from childhood. Kids gravitate to this shop because it sells baseball cards, model kits and basics such as Play-Doh and Silly Putty, and adults like it because it sells grown-up basics such as desk blotters, calendars and magazines. The shop is closed Sunday in the off-season.

Cabbages & Kings Books

628 Main St., Chatham • 945-1603

What a delightful shop! It has one of the largest children's sections we've come across in any bookstore and sells toys as well as books. We always have a tough time getting our little one out of this store. Adults will appreciate not only the nice selection of quality books but also unique greeting cards and stationery. The store will even gift wrap. It's open daily year round.

Chatham Candy Manor

484 Main St., Chatham • 945-0825, (800) 221-6497

People from all over the world have visited

Chatham Candy Manor for the caloric concoctions that are made in small batches, then hand-dipped every day in the same tradition started 50 years ago by the store's founder, Naomi Turner. The selection is endless: chocolate-dipped fruits (including apricots, strawberries and pineapples in dark or milk chocolate), hazelnut puree and chocolate treats shaped like scallops and our favorite, cranberry cordials (fresh fruit melded with bonbon creme and liqueur, then covered with pure chocolate). Even the barley lollipops are kettle-cooked and poured by hand. When holiday season comes around, watch for demonstrations of candy-cane making. Mail order is available; call for a brochure and price list. The shop is open daily.

Chatham Cookware

524 Main St., Chatham • 945-1550

Serious cooks will find everything they need — from wooden soup bowls to fancy pot holders — and everything they don't need but want — apple-shaped egg timers, anyone? The store also houses a small up-front bakery (all goods are made on the premises) and in the rear a small cafe in which you can feast on an ever-changing array of soups and sandwiches on delicious home-baked breads. Take-out treats include a wide array of goodies. You can bring home such homemade yummies as vegetable cheese chowder, Parmesan cheddar scones, blueberry/lemon strudel cake and almond yogurt loaf. The shop is closed on Tuesdays in January and February.

Chatham Glass Company

758 Main St., Chatham • 945-5547

Jim Holmes and Deborah Doane's glassworks are so beautiful they sell in such prestigious stores as Barney's and Neiman Marcus and are included in major museum and exhibitions worldwide. The colors are vivid (the color bars from which they choose, more than 70 in all, are imported from Germany), on a myriad of such witty and wonderful (and ever-so-functional) pieces as vases, dishes, trays and candlesticks. The husband-and-wife duo sign each original work, and you can watch the wonders being made in the workshop next door (open Monday through Friday in season). The gallery is open Monday through Saturday year round.

Chatham Jam and Jelly Shop

10 Vineyard Ave., Chatham • 945-3052

You can't leave Cape Cod without a jar of beach plum jam, and this is just the place to get it. The shop, on the corner of Route 28, sells more than 75 varieties of homemade preserves, and several concoctions (wild beach plum, cranberry and wild blackberry) are made from fruit handpicked on Cape Cod. The shop offers — even encourages — taste sampling, so you can't go wrong. Gift sets and mail order are available. It's open Monday through Friday.

Chatham Winery

The Cornfield, Rt. 28, Chatham • 945-0300

The Chatham Winery makes its own wines from flowers, honey and fruit, including apricots, pears, peaches, passion fruit, apples and, of course, grapes. The winery is famous for its Cranberry, a crisp, semisweet wine made from cranberries and packed in an award-winning lobster-shaped bottle. Cranberry and red raspberry vinegar are sold in the lobster bottles too. Gift boxes and baskets are also available, along with special souvenirs, such as novelty bottle bags and cork wreaths. Chatham Winery offers tastings daily and gives tours in the summer. It's open daily except on "really cold and/or snowy" Sundays.

The Dead Zone

647 Main St., Chatham • 945-5853

Since 1990 The Dead Zone has been paying homage to the legion of Deadheads — devout followers of the band The Grateful Dead. Inside you'll find reminders of the '60s and '70s: tie-dyed clothes in wild colors, irreverent bumper stickers, incense and love beads. Peace, baby. The shop is open daily.

The Pampered Palate

The Cornfield, Rt. 28, Chatham • 945-2663

This is one of those shops that smells so good you don't want to leave. The shelves of gourmet items, such as honey mustard, flavored vinegars and spices, will inspire you to go home and make your kitchen a creative work center. There's no need to do that, however, as you can get homemade, delectable goodies right here — everything from salads to pate. A great place pick up a gourmet picnic on your way to the beach, The Pampered Palate is open daily.

Pentimento

584 Main St., Chatham • 945-0178

This shop has wonderful ambiance — maybe it's the fact that it sells such indulgent items such as luxurious sweaters and blouses, pretty blank journals, fine stationery, scarves and jewelry. It also carries delightful children's books, whimsical picture frames and home accessories. It's closed January, February and March.

Scrimshaw by Marcy

333 Old Harbor Rd., Chatham • 945-0782

Animal activists need not worry: The scrimshaw sold here is antique and made long before any whale protection laws were put into effect. There's a nice selection, including whales' teeth with elaborate engravings and what are known as Sailor's Valentines — octagon-shape boxes with elaborately decorated shell lids that were made by natives on Barbados and given to sailors, who in turn gave them to loved ones upon their return home. The "scrimshaw" bookmarks, made from antique ivory piano keys, are a great bargain at just $14. It's closed in the off-season.

The Whale's Eye

6565 Orleans Rd. (Rt. 28), Chatham • 945-3084

Housed in an old barn, The Whale's Eye has an array of beautifully handpainted furniture and mirrors. All the work is done by Suzanne and John Rocanello, who opened the shop in the barn adjacent to their home in the late 1970s and soon after began doing craft shows all over the Cape (see our Annual Events chapter). At the shop, you'll see chests, boxes, tables and mirrors, many painted with nautical scenes. The Rocanellos do a lot of custom work, and if you bring in a fabric swatch or wallpaper strip, they'll be happy to use colors that will work with your decor. The shop is open daily in summer and a bit sporadically in spring and fall. "If the barn door is open, we're here," says Suzanne, but it's best to call first. It's open by appointment only in winter.

Yankee Ingenuity

525 Main St., Chatham • 945-1288

Half gallery, half gift shop, Yankee Ingenuity carries unusual items in a wide range of prices. On our most recent visit, we found delightful handcarved "Fishing Animals" for $15.95, an unusual driftwood mirror for $150 and a Tiffany-style lamp for $306. The shop is filled with interesting and beautiful things, from Impressionist-print umbrellas to jewelry, letter-openers and desk chimes. It's open daily.

Yellow Umbrella Books

501 Main St., Chatham • 945-0144

Yellow Umbrella has been offering locals

and tourists the latest in fiction and nonfiction bestsellers, used books and works by local authors since 1979. The store also has an extensive section on books about Cape Cod. It carries rare and out of print books, used hardcover and paperback books and will do special orders. Be sure to visit the outdoor bargain racks — any book is a buck. It's open daily year round.

The Baseball Shop

26 Main St., Orleans • 240-1063

Score a home run every time if you're looking for the latest in all things baseball. The store stocks more than 1,000 different baseball caps as well as trading cards, bumper stickers, autographed material and select clothing. It's open year round, daily in season and closed Tuesdays in winter.

Bird Watcher's General Store

36 Rt. 6A, Orleans • 255-6974, (800) 562-1512

This is a store for the birds. Literally. Since 1983 owner Mike O'Connor's entire focus is on the needs of both birds and bird watchers. This is the place to buy a bird feeder — the store carries more than 100, plus tons of bird feed to fill them! You can't be a bird watcher without binoculars, and Bird Watcher's carries some 40 types. It also stocks a comprehensive selection of bird books, T-shirts, socks, door knockers, welcome mats, sun catchers, magnets, gift wrap and note cards — all centered around birds. Even if you aren't into our feathered friends, you must stop here: Tell the super-friendly staff a joke, and they'll give you a gift. Now that's something to crow about! The shop is closed Thanksgiving and Christmas.

Booksmith/Musicsmith

Skaket Corners, Orleans • 255-4590

This is a great place to shop if you're into books and your other half is into music. You'll both be happy browsing here, as half the store is devoted to hardcover, softcover and paperback books, and the other half to compact discs and tapes. The store also sells calendars, magazines, cassettes and videos, and has a great children's corner in back complete with a small table and chairs where little ones can sit and read. It's open daily year round.

Boston Bed & Bath

Skaket Corners, Rt. 6A and West Rd., Orleans • 240-1445

Newly expanded in 1996, this store has a huge selection of items for the home. See our writeup for the Hyannis location in the Mid-Cape section of this chapter. The store is open daily year round.

Compass Rose Bookstore

Main St., Orleans • 255-1545

A nice roomy shop with a friendly, helpful staff, Compass Rose has a great collection of books, along with cards, stationery, date books and neat items such as rubber stamps and magnet poetry. It's nicely arranged and even has a small sitting area. Compass Rose holds frequent book-signings and events and is open daily.

Continuum

7 Rt. 28, Orleans • 255-8513

We've never seen so many different light fixtures in one place. Dan Johnson sells only quality restored lighting fixtures, or, as he calls them, "jewels for your home." At any given time, the shop will have in stock more than 400 lamps and 100 wall sconces ranging in price from several hundred to several thousands of dollars. Johnson also has a small but choice selection of old advertising signs and folk art, including wooden fish decoys. And being the die-hard Mickey Mouse lover he is, there's always a sale on something paying homage to the animated rodent. The shop is open daily during the season and Thursday through Saturday in the off-season.

INSIDERS' TIP

For unique, nature-inspired gifts, visit the Cape Cod Museum of Natural History in Brewster. In addition to exhibits, nature trails and educational programs, it's got a terrific gift shop!

The Goose Hummock Shop

Rt. 6A, Orleans • 255-0455

Outdoor enthusiasts find The Goose Hummock Shop ideal for one-stop shopping. From bait and fishing equipment to camping gear, firearms, clothing, canoes, kayaks and bicycles, it's all sold and serviced by a knowledgeable staff either here or in the store right behind the main one. Don't need any sand eels today? Then stop in for a tides chart and map — they're free! Check out the Hyannis location. The shops are open daily.

Hart's

78 Rt. 6A, Orleans • 255-1596

We would be lost without this shop, which carries fabulous women's clothing and unique gifts. This is the place to shop if you're looking for a special-occasion outfit that no one else will be wearing. And the prices are reasonable, especially during sales! The clothes have real panache, and the sales staff is helpful and friendly. We know one husband who relies on these good folks to help choose Christmas and birthday gifts. Hart's is open daily.

FYI

Unless otherwise noted, the area code for all phone numbers in this guide is 508.

Kemp Pottery

9 Rt. 6A, Orleans • 255-5853

Here's your chance to see a potter at work, as this is not only Steve Kemp's store but also his studio, and has been since 1978. His designs, often inspired by nature, include lamps, sinks, tiles, birdfeeders, fountains and sculpture, and many of them are made with Nauset Beach sand. Kemp also does unique bas-relief signs, several of which can be seen at the Cape Cod Museum of Natural History in Brewster. His functional pieces, including dinnerware, are lead-free and safe for the oven, dishwasher and microwave. The Kemps also have a shop in West Brewster. Hours vary in the off-season.

Kid & Kaboodle

115 Rt. 6A, Orleans • 240-0460

At last, a store that sells good children's clothing at reasonable prices! Whether you need a gift for a baby shower, playclothes for your toddler or a christening gown for your grandchild, this is the place to come. If you're shopping with little ones, they can play with the toys in the back room while you browse, but don't forget to visit that room yourself, as it's filled with great secondhand children's clothes at terrific prices! Kid & Kaboodle also carries maternity clothes and rents baby furniture. It's open daily.

S. Wilder and Co.

16 Rayber Rd., Orleans • 255-8330

Stepping into J. Robert Gellatty's showroom is like stepping back into time. The walls are lined with all sorts of indoor and outdoor lamps in all sizes, shaped from antique copper or brass and in designs such as nautical, Colonial and onion. Gellatty makes just about everything you see (except an occasional chandelier) at his work station. In fact, you can order a lamp and watch him make it before your eyes. He will custom-make your own design and does expert repairs. The store is open daily.

Oceana

1 Main Street Sq., Orleans • 240-1414

If you love beautiful things, you'll want to browse here. It's the kind of shop that inspires you to slow down and take your time, so tranquil is the ambiance. Oceana carries lovely jewelry, candlesticks, nature books and original art, wall hangings, rugs and handpainted tables, along with many other items. One unique creation that makes a great gift is an Oceana mussel shell wreath, either circular or heart-shaped and available in several sizes. The store even has a children's corner filled with nature-oriented toys, rubber stamps and wooden toys. Don't miss this shop; it's open daily.

Orleans Whole Foods Store

46 Main St., Orleans • 255-6540

This is a true health-food store, where you can buy grains and cereals in bulk, get fresh-ground peanut butter, vitamins and a wide variety of organic products, including produce. It's also a great place to grab a quick lunch, as the store makes healthy sandwiches, soups and sometimes pizza — sit on the bench out front and watch the world go by. But don't overlook its gift-shop potential: this good-for-you shop carries a nice selection of books, with an emphasis on spiritual, self-help and cookbooks, lovely, unusual greeting cards and Crabtree & Evelyn soaps and lotions, not to mention calendars and T-shirts. It's open daily.

The Card Shoppe

180 Brackett Rd., N. Eastham • 255-4478

It's so nice to know you don't have to drive to a big drug store to shop for cards. This little shop makes buying greeting cards a warm, friendly experience. There's always a good selection, and the sales are frequent and well-worth hitting to stock up! The store also carries gift items including Beatrix Potter music boxes and personalized gift baskets. It carries wedding invitations and offers UPS shipping. The Card Shoppe is open Monday through Saturday.

The Chocolate Sparrow

4205 Rt. 6, Seatoller Shops, North Eastham • 240-0606

Anyone who appreciates really good chocolate will love this shop — the aroma alone is heavenly. You'll find excellent fudge, hand-dipped chocolates and decadent truffles, all made here. If you come at the right time, you can watch them being made. The Chocolate Sparrow also has a Wellfleet location, 349-1333, open only in summer, and a coffee bar-chocolate shop in Orleans, The Hot Chocolate Sparrow (see our Restaurants chapter). The shop is open daily.

Collectors World

Rt. 6, Eastham • 255-3616, (800) 421-4270

This is one of those shops in which you'll find yourself wandering around and losing all track of time. The shop carries both antiques and new collectibles, including dolls, gnomes, model cars, lighthouses and cottage figurines. In the off-season hours are sporadic, but you can tell if the store is open if a red van is sitting in front.

Colonial Stoneware Trading Co.

2320 Rt. 6, Eastham • 240-7687

History comes alive in this unique shop, where you can not only buy authentic reproductions of blue and grey stoneware, but also watch it being made. Potters Tim Buchanan and Jim Phillips dress in period clothing and stage frequent demonstrations to explain how each piece is made and its historical significance. While you're there, be sure to visit Colonial Stoneware's Americana Museum, which has rotating displays. The shop is open daily from Memorial Day to Labor Day, and is also open in December through Christmas.

The Glass Eye

Rt. 6, Main St. Mercantile, Eastham • 255-5044

We love coming here on a sunny day, when light gleams off all the colored glass. But when it's cloudy, this shop will brighten your day. All the stained-glass work displayed in the gallery is done by owner John Knight, but the shop also carries blown glass by other artists. In addition to glass work, the gallery sells wonderful handmade paper creations by co-owner Donna Knight, who often puts on papermaking demonstrations. Be sure to visit the working stained-glass studio downstairs. Scrap glass is free for the asking, and you can even take lessons in the off-season. The shop is open daily, but closed on Sundays in winter.

Grandmother's Attic

4205 Rt. 6, Seatoller Shops, North Eastham • 255-7789

This children's book shop sells only the finest children's books and educational toys. Owner Shirley Weber, a former educator, also offers story hours and workshops for children

INSIDERS' TIP

Every Saturday from June to October you can buy the freshest Cape Cod-grown fruits and vegetables, cultivated mushrooms, local honey, herbs, flowers and plants, homemade jams and jellies — even freshly caught local fish — at the Orleans Farmers' Market, 19 West Road. It opens at 8 AM and closes at noon.

Plymouth gentian flowers decorate the rim of Mary Dunn Pond in Hyannis.

as well as occasional book signings. Adults can check out the shop's rental library, where you can borrow great hardcover bestsellers for $2 for three days. It's open Monday through Saturday.

Kristi Klein Originals

Rt. 6, Main Street Mercantile, Eastham • 255-9252

Although this shop also carries jewelry and accessories, the real attraction is Kristi Klein's Children of the World tapestry design, featured in vests, jackets, luggage, pillows and Christmas stockings. It's a beautiful design, charming yet classy, and a donation to children's charities is made on all sales. The shop is open daily.

Sunken Meadow Basketworks & Pottery

N. Sunken Meadow Rd., North Eastham • 255-8962

Hugh and Paulette Penney sell their handwoven baskets, textured with reeds and vines in a myriad of colors, and their handmade begging bowls, pinched pots and abstract wall pieces out of a barn studio nestled down a pine-needle path next to their house. The smell alone will keep you there for hours! The shop is open daily year round.

The Eclectic Company

93 Commercial St., Wellfleet • 349-1775

Here's a shop that lives up to its name, offering a diverse assortment of unique home accessories, clothing and jewelry. You'll find handpainted furniture, kitchenware and unique accents for your home, such as die-cut house numbers, made from house-shaped pieces of black steel. It's open daily.

Hatch's Fish and Produce

310 Main St., Wellfleet • 349-2810 for fish, 349-6734 for produce

In 1983 brother and sister Rob and Lauren McClellan took over ownership of this shingled fish shack (located in the parking lot behind town hall), and they kept alive the tradition of only selling the freshest locally caught fish and locally grown produce, in addition to such palate pleasures as homemade crab dips and pâtés. Rob will smoke any fish you'd like — the line for smoked salmon starts way over there. Hatch's is open daily from Memorial Day through end of September.

Herridge Books

E. Main St., Wellfleet • 349-1323

The books here are in such great shape that many customers cannot believe they are used. The store stocks the very best in dozens of genres from architecture to zoology. (A set of canary-yellow stairs, guided by a handrail made from an oar, lead to the basement and even more books. There's a good chance the store's official welcome cat, Checkers, will follow.) Bird lovers will relish the limited-edition Audubon prints that are based on originals and sanctioned by the Audubon Society. Don't forget to check out the small but delightful collection of hand-colored postcards sitting at the front register. Herridge Books is closed in the off-season.

Jules Besch Gallery

275 Main St., Wellfleet • 349-1231

Proprietor Michael Tuck's store bears testimony to his belief that letter writing need not be a lost art. Glorious blank and versed cards for everyday and special-occasion use line the walls of his gallery, named, he says with a wink, for his alter ego. Wooden racks hold luxurious wrapping paper sold by the sheet. The gallery also carries a staggering array of inkwells and ink, and fountain and quill pens. Take note, please, of one more item: handcrafted mirrors, framed with scraps of driftwood, shards of broken Blue Delft china, lobster claws, skate egg cases and other seashore treasures. It's closed in January, open weekends only from mid-February through mid-May and keeps regular hours the rest of the year.

The Kite Gallery

75 Commercial St., Wellfleet • 349-7387

The sky's the limit in this festival of everything fancy and high-flying. The pickings are far from slim: The shop has a huge selection of professional stunt kites, single-line kites and colorful (and, in some cases, elaborate) windsocks and flags. The Kite Gallery is closed in the off-season.

Salt Marsh Pottery

115 Main St., Wellfleet • 349-3342

Katherine Stillman's wheel-thrown pottery has a free and easy quality to it. Most of the plates and cups are designed with free-form pears (a homage to the pear tree in front of her studio, perhaps?) and abstract designs. All her wares are lead-free and can go from oven to dishwasher. We also give Katherine credit for her open-door policy: If you want to buy something and she's not there, simply leave cash or fill out a charge slip. Her trust is as beautiful as her pottery.

The Secret Garden

Main St., Wellfleet • 349-1444

It's not a secret any longer: This two-story garden is overrun with charming chattel, folk art, twig love seats, garden goodies, crushed-velvet hats, birdhouses, animal marionettes and an eclectic selection of jewelry. Kids go bonkers for the animal- and fish-shaped change purses from Tibet.

Wellfleet Flea Market

Rt. 6, within the Wellfleet Drive-in, South Wellfleet • 349-2520, (800) 696-3532

This outdoor extravaganza — more than 300 vendors selling everything from Gucci sweatshirts (seconds) and first-quality Woolrich vests to used books and African-American memorabilia at negotiable prices — has been a Cape Cod institution since 1957. Items we've found here include old license plates, new sweatshirts, designer men's shirts, used paperback books, great old prints and shampoo! Admission is $2 per car; walk-ins, $1 each. Two helpful hints: Eat before you go (the snack bar snacks are expensive and mediocre) and wear comfortable shoes. Many of the vendors accept credit cards. The market is open on Saturday and Sunday from mid-April to the end of November. In July and August, it's open Wednesday, Thursday, Saturday and Sunday, plus any official holiday Monday.

West Main Books

41 W. Main St., Wellfleet • 349-2095

This small bookstore, in business since 1972, packs a remarkable 14,000 volumes into two rooms. Because of the limited space, owner Joanna Fabris carefully selects each book so that she has the best of the best in each category. There is something for everyone from poetry to travel to children's books. During the summer West Main Books hosts book parties and readings. The shop is open year-round — daily in June, July and August, most everyday in the off-season and only on Friday and Saturday in the winter.

Atlantic Spice Company

2 Shore Rd., Truro • 487-6100, (800) 316-7965

Trust us when we say we're going to send you someplace spicy. This warehouse sells row after row of spices and herbs — from allspice to vanilla beans and everything in between. You can buy in bulk (1- or 5-pound packages), or if you're unsure of the potency of a particular spice, you can buy a smaller sampler bag — or ask for a taste. Atlantic also sells a wide range of teas (loose and in teabags), shelled nuts and seeds and baking items. The shop is open Monday through Saturday all year.

Susan Baker Memorial Museum

46 Rt. 6A, North Truro • 487-2557

Everyone has a right to his or her own idiosyncrasies, and Susan Baker is no exception. Not wanting to wait until she died to have her own memorial museum, she opened this pop palace in 1984. Once you spot Susan's work, you won't forget it. Startling and brightly colored pieces that are sometimes three-dimensional, sometimes satirical, sometimes taking the form of printed booklets (her oh-so-cute but crudely drawn cats and dogs are big sellers). Who says art can't be fun? The shop is open daily in season and erratically off-season (ring the bell at the side door if you'd like to see the collection in the off-season).

The Whitman House Quilt Shop

Rt. 6 at Great Hollow Rd., North Truro • 487-3204

It would be easy to call this store, sitting next to The Whitman House (see our Restaurants chapter), a class act: The building is a former schoolhouse and the oldest structure in Truro. The specialty here is Amish quilts, new and old, with prices that are more than reasonable. The two floors also showcase modern-day cranberry glass, teddy bears, a profusion of potpourri, brass beds and dolls. It's closed in the off-season.

Adams Pharmacy

254 Commercial St., Provincetown • 487-0069

Come to Provincetown's only drugstore to revel in the charm of a small-town apothecary. Adams was founded in 1870, and except for the products found on the shelves and the dates on the newspapers in the rack, we bet little has changed (except, perhaps, the prices of prescriptions and over-the-counter drugs). Adams even has one of those long steel lunch counters you never see anymore. A great way to learn about the town is to sit and order coffee early one morning, when the old-timers gather to exchange stories (both real and exaggerated) of days gone by. The store is open daily.

Cabot's Candy

276 Commercial St., Provincetown • 487-3550

Candy stores are a dime a dozen in Provincetown, but none comes close to Cabot's. The Cicero clan began making fudge and saltwater taffy on the premises in 1969, and they are the only ones making taffy this way on the Lower Cape. Stand inside or in front of the huge picture window and watch as a massive spool of taffy is tamed into individually wrapped bite-size pieces. (Ask for a free sample.) The flavors sometimes change, but you can be sure of finding cranberry, grape, chocolate, cherry, piña colada, peanut butter, licorice and orange-pineapple. Cabot's also sells sugar-free taffy. It's open only holidays and weekends in the off-season.

Galadriel's Mirror

246 Commercial St., Provincetown • 487-9437

This store is truly a gem — or more accurately, a lot of gems! You won't be able to

INSIDERS' TIP

For unique gift items — and treats for yourself! — watch for local crafts shows and fairs. See our Annual Events chapter for regularly scheduled crafts shows, and check the local newspapers for any impromptu events that may be held during the season.

resist running your fingers through the bowls of polished stones and touching the jagged edges of brilliant minerals. You'll find jade, rose quartz, topaz and other stones along with gold and silver jewelry. Take your time in here; there's a lot to see, and browsing among such beautiful things will put you in a tranquil mood. The shop, a fixture in Provincetown for 27 years, is open year round.

Good Scents

366 Commercial St., Provincetown
• 487-3393

In its 13th year, this small corner store is filled with all you need to pamper yourself — or someone else. There are lovely scented soaps, shampoos and lotions, along with bath brushes, luxurious robes and massage oils. Choose from a variety of skin-care products, and have lotions, shampoos and bath gels custom-scented with essential or perfume oils. Take them home and you'll know why they call this shop Good Scents. The shop happily makes up gift baskets and does mail order. It's open daily in season, closes for the month of January and has limited hours in the early spring.

Mad Hatter

360 Commercial St., Provincetown
• 487-4063

Hats off to this ingenious store, a meld of the whimsical and functional. Though Mad Hatter sells jackets, shirts and scarves, people head here for the crowning touch. Choose from zany headgear, such as a multicolor beanie with a propeller, or more traditional, classic designs. You can also get custom-made hats here. The shop is open daily in season and weekends from the beginning of January through mid-March.

Marine Specialties

235 Commercial St., Provincetown
• 487-1730

Marine Specialties is, hands down, the most unusual store in Provincetown. A cavernous former stable, the store is filled — and we mean filled, floor to ceiling — with the must-haves (candles, postcards and folding scissors) to the why-bothers? (porcelain urinals and Navy hymnals from the '40s). Marine Specialties carries an overwhelming supply of military surplus clothes from around the world. The back of the store has a more organized, quite complete, camping and fishing supplies area. The store is open daily in season and weekends only from Christmas through mid-March.

Norma Glamp's Rubber Stamps

212 Commercial St., Provincetown
• 487-1870

Owner Steve Katz gets our stamp of approval! Norma Glamp's is filled with row after row of rubber stamps, from goofy ones like Mickey and Goofy to every conceivable flower and animal and holiday motif you could think of. Celebrity buffs will want Lucy, Marilyn, Elvis, Bette (Davis, not Midler) and even the most famous Norma of all — Desmond. Norma's also carries a full line of embossing powders, ink pads, markers, stationery and other frivolous fare. The store also offers stamping classes. Think Steve looks familiar? You may have seen him sitting at the bar in "Cheers" — he was an extra on the sitcom for four years! The shop is closed mid-January through mid-March.

Northern Lights Hammocks

361 Commercial St., Provincetown
• 487-2385

Tootsies tired? Don't shop 'til you drop. Take a break by sampling one of the many hammocks here. The friendly staff will try its damnedest to get you to sample the swinging, swaying set, whether it be one made of rope, cotton, wood or canvas. (Your feet will thank you.) Some of the hammocks here are true works of art. One Mexican import features a polished wooden base that could work in the most chic of homes. The shop is open daily in season and weekends only off-season.

Now Voyager

357 Commercial St., Provincetown
• 487-0848

Diane Johnson and her partner, Nan Cinnater, named this bookstore after a line from a Walt Whitman poem and the Bette Davis classic. Both would have been proud. Besides specializing in mystery titles and the latest in

Photo: Cape Cod Chamber of Commerce

Glass collectors and admirers will love Cape Cod.

fiction and nonfiction, Now Voyager is also the Cape's largest supplier of gay and lesbian titles. There's a nice sampling of paperbacks as well as a small selection of CDs, cassettes and videos. Make sure you check out the shelves in the corner of the store (the front door hides them when it's open): Here, the owners sell used books at bargain-basement prices. The shop closes for a winter break in the month of January.

Provincetown Bookshop
246 Commercial St., Provincetown • 487-0964

Open since 1964, this year-round shop is filled floor to ceiling with hardcover, soft cover and paperback books, everything from poetry and plays to bestsellers with a good selection of Cape Cod books. Enter through the sliding wood door and you feel instantly at home. A great shop for browsing, it's open daily.

Recovering Hearts Bookstore and Gallery
2 and 4 Standish St., Provincetown • 487-4875

You don't have to be recovering to appreciate this specialty bookstore, which carries the best in self-help titles along with inspirational art and all sorts of things that help you feel better, such as candles, soaps and incense. It's closed in January.

Rilleau Sandal Shop
5 Allerton St., Provincetown • 487-3114

Loyal customers say these are the most comfortable sandals they've ever worn. First made by sculptor Roger Rilleau in 1940 after he mastered the art of traditional Grecian sandal making, they are often imitated. Today his son, Kim, carries on the family tradition. Besides footwear, the shop also sells buckleless belts, works of art in their own right. The store opens (and closes) frequently; call ahead for operating hours and for the times you'll be able to watch Rilleau at work.

There's No Place Like Home

150 Commercial St., Provincetown
• 487-6283

Kermit was wrong: It is easy being green. Just ask Home owner Woody Shimko. Woody founded this environment-friendly shop in 1992, and since then his loyal customers buy all kinds of recycled paper products, unbleached cotton clothing, natural soaps, even jewelry made out of recycled soda bottle caps and computer parts. The shop is closed in the off-season.

Small Pleasures

359 Commercial St., Provincetown
• 487-3712

If you love antique jewelry, this is a must-see shop. The lovely glass-topped display cases are packed with vintage treasures. You'll find rubies, emeralds, diamonds and moonstones in unique, original settings. The store also carries a selection of old silver spoons, tongs and other small items. The pleasure will be yours. It's open seasonally.

Tailwaggers

205 Commercial St., Provincetown
• 487-6404

A full-service pet palace, Tailwaggers offers all sorts of unusual dog and kitty treats, food by the can or bag, leashes and collars, beds and brushes, combs and other grooming aids. For pups who get chilly in winter, Tailwaggers offers an extensive line of winterwear. And it has such great toys for both felines and canines, the shop has been called a toy shop for pets. The wall behind the cash register is devoted to pictures of people with their satisfied pets. Tailwaggers is the only store in town to offer thirsty critters their own water dish. Open daily in season, Tailwaggers is closed Tuesday, Wednesday and Thursday off-season.

A number of antiques cooperatives and centers have sprung up on the Cape, providing one-stop shopping for those who like variety.

Antiques

There are those who come to the Cape not for its lovely beaches but for its proliferation of great antiques shops — and we don't blame them! Every town has more than a few places to browse among old things, with some dealers specializing in certain items such as pattern glass, early American furniture or old tools, and others carrying a smattering of diverse items. A number of antiques cooperatives and centers have sprung up on the Cape, providing one-stop shopping for those who like variety.

Listing every antiques shop could easily fill a whole book, so we've focused on our favorites here. You're sure to find others as you travel the Cape, particularly on the north side, where historic Route 6A is an antique-lover's paradise. At the end of the chapter, look for information on auction houses, where serious antiquers put their money where their mouths are.

If you want to get the most out of your antiquing adventure, three publications will be handy resources. Call for a copy of "Cape Cod Antiques & Arts," a monthly supplement of Cape Cod Community Newspapers, (800) 660-8999. Also, the *Cape Cod Times* publishes guides to Arts and Antiques during the peak season. For a complimentary copy write to: Cape Cod Times, Attention: Retail Department, 319 Main Street, Hyannis, Massachusetts 02601. The Cape Cod Antique Dealers Association Inc. issues a handy directory listing dozens of shops. For a free copy, send a business-size, self-addressed, stamped envelope to Liz Broadrick, 88 Corporation Road, Dennis, MA 02638.

Many antiques stores are open year round, though off-season hours vary greatly. Call ahead before you venture out.

Happy hunting!

Antiques Shops

Upper Cape

The Old House
294 Head of the Bay Rd., Buzzards Bay • 759-4942

The Old House, built around 1724, is a wonderful antique itself. The shop has been in business for more than 60 years and carries vintage collectibles such as Early American pressed glass, blown glass and china. The gift shop across the street specializes in new goods — linen calendars, Vermont country toys and character mice. The two shops are open from April to the end of December, every day except Sunday.

Pocasset Exchange
710 County Rd., Pocasset • 563-2224

A longtime Bourne antiques shop set off Route 28 at the corner of County Road and Barlows Landing Road, the Pocasset Exchange carries antiques, vintage jewelry and collectible linens, odd lots of glass and china, furniture and household objects. The Exchange is open Thursday, Friday and Saturday from April through November.

INSIDERS' TIP

If you are interested in a certain category of antiques, such as glass, silver or lusterware, take the time to read up on the subject before you buy, compare the offerings at different shops and consider membership in a club or organization connected with your specialty, such as the American Glass Club.

The Brown Jug

155 Main St., Sandwich • 833-1088

The inventory at The Brown Jug is mostly good quality Sandwich glass and Staffordshire china. You'll also find Tiffany lamps and vases, and French and English cameos. The shop, which has been in business for 60 years, is open seven days a week from April to Christmas, and by chance or appointment at other times of the year.

FYI

Unless otherwise noted, the area code for all phone numbers in this guide is 508.

Horsefeathers Antiques

454 Rt. 6A, East Sandwich • 888-5298

Owner Jeanne Gresham has created a distinctly Victorian and feminine feeling in this lovely shop, which carries table and bed linens, antique lace and trim, and a mix of everyday and special items such as china teacups and paper valentines. Antique christening gowns and other children's clothing are usually available. The shop is open year round, but it's best to call first in the off season, when hours vary.

Madden & Company

16 Jarves St., Sandwich • 888-3663

A tasteful shop that reflects both the old and new, Madden & Company displays fine antiques alongside country-flavored gifts and artwork. The inventory includes Americana, paintings, furniture, old wooden boxes, Nantucket lightship baskets, reproductions and specialty foods. The store is open Monday through Saturday from May through the Christmas holidays.

Sandwich Antiques Center

131 Rt. 6A, Sandwich • 833-3600

If this shop has the flavor of an auction preview, it may be because owner Russell Johnson has had a career as a highly successful auctioneer. In the antiques business for 18 years, Russell's very knowledgeable, and what he doesn't know he will gladly look up on a data base of all items sold at major auctions since 1988. The shop, located at the town's only traffic light, is home to 168 dealers displaying everything from Asian furniture and Russian silver to primitives. There are cases and cases of china, glass, silver and collectibles, and a reference room where you can either buy books or just look through them. Mr. Johnson will even photocopy a page or two for you. The center is open daily year round.

H. Richard Strand Antiques

2 Grove St., Sandwich • 888-3230

An antiques dealer in Sandwich for 26 years, Richard Strand is known for his Sandwich glass pieces. (The shop is across from the Sandwich Glass Museum.) He also carries other types of glass as well as Mandarin, Cantonese, German and English porcelain and other types of antiques ranging in price from $20 to $20,000. The shop is open daily year round.

The Weather Store

146 Main St., Sandwich • 888-1200

New Englanders have a long history of trying to understand, predict and maybe even outsmart the weather, which can be downright unpredictable in these parts. Testament to that history, this store is filled with antique weather instruments such as weather vanes, barometers, thermometers, books and compasses, along with marine antiques such as spyglasses and 19th-century maps. The store is open Monday through Saturday from April through the end of Christmas and by appointment at other times.

Aurora Borealis Antiques

104 Palmer Ave., Falmouth • 540-3385

Look for the quality line of Staffordshire, Orientalia, prints, furniture, nautical pieces,

INSIDERS' TIP

Teasel, a plant with a large thistle-like flowerhead, was used by early Cape settlers to card wool and to remove pilling from their woolen clothing. It is said that the idea for Velcro came from teasel, as well as the practice of "teasing" hair.

lamps, silver and glass. It is open daily except Sunday and Wednesday during the season and by appointment or chance in the off-season.

Uncle Bill's Country Store

Rt. 28, North Falmouth • 564-4355

Although this is primarily a gift shop, you will also find an upstairs room with a good selection of antique furniture, including tables, chairs, hutches and occasionally a period medicine chest. The store also has antique tools and railroad lanterns. The Country Store is open daily year round.

The Village Barn

606 W. Falmouth Hwy., West Falmouth • 540-3215

This lovely old barn, built around 1850, is home to eight dealers with an eclectic assortment of antiques on two floors, including some wonderful glass and china, furniture and linens. One dealer specializes in Cape Cod souvenirs and old advertising. The Village Barn is open year round, daily in season and generally weekends only from January to March, depending on the weather.

Mashpee Antiques

Mashpee Rotary, Mashpee • 539-0000

Lots of wood period furniture — sideboards, beds, even high chairs — from the late 1800s to the 1940s make up the large inventory in this family-run shop, launched in 1994. In addition to its extensive selection of china, pottery, prints, toys, jewelry and baseball memorabilia, the shop carries wood-care products and reproduction and antique hardware. Mashpee Antiques offers the only mirror re-silvering service in the area. The store is open daily year round.

Mid-Cape

Crocker Farm

1210 Race Ln., Marstons Mills • 428-3326

Primitives and folk art dominate this unusual collection of Early American accessories, decorative items and antiques for children. It's open year round, but hours are erratic, so it's best to call ahead.

The Farmhouse Antiques

1340 Main St., Osterville • 420-2400

Six rooms in this mid-18th-century building are chock-full of antiques: glass, silverware, fine paintings, furniture and usually several nice candelabra and lamps. The shop is open daily year round.

Stanley Wheelock

870 Main St., Osterville • 420-3170

In its ninth year, this established Osterville business is known for its general line of American, English and Continental furniture, decorative accessories, china, glass and fine prints. It is open regular hours from April through December and by chance or appointment from January through March.

Hyannis Antique Co-op

500 Main St., Hyannis • 778-0512

Some 50 dealers from throughout New England, including the Cape, have gathered an assortment of antiques into this year-round emporium, with additional inventory arriving regularly. Antique collectibles include china, glass, jewelry, golf equipment, postcards, military uniforms and weapons, Depression glass, Fiesta ware, toys (including dolls), art pottery and silver. Oak and pine furniture and Oriental and braided rugs are available as well. There's also a basement showroom, added last year, of used and reproduction furniture. The co-op, in business for eight years, is open daily, and there's plenty of free parking.

Maps of Antiquity

1022 Rt. 6A, West Barnstable • 362-7169

You could get lost among the thousands of original old maps in this interesting shop. The inventory consists mostly of 19th-century maps but it also includes 17th- and 18th-century ones, including those of Massachusetts townships and other New England states. European and world maps, railroad maps, coastal charts and early U.S. maps are part of the collection. The shop is open daily May through October, and does mail order the rest of the year; call or write for a catalog.

West Barnstable Antiques

625 Main St., West Barnstable • 362-5120

The ample inventory of furniture includes many desks, tables and occasional pieces, particularly in primitive and Shaker styles. The shop's Chinese exports, artwork, painted pieces and stoneware are also worth a look, and the shop has some sports memorabilia as well. The shop is open daily in season and Friday through Monday from January through March.

Salt & Chestnut

651 Rt. 6A, West Barnstable • 362-6085

In business more than 20 years, Salt & Chestnut carries antique weather vanes among its custom-designed new vanes in copper, wood, glass and sheet iron. The store is open daily year round but more by chance in January and February. (See our Shopping chapter for more about this shop.)

Owls Nest Antiques

4083 Main St., Cummaquid • 362-4054

Owls Nest Antiques, in its 24th year, specializes in children's items, doll furniture and dolls dating from 1850 to the present, including French and German dolls. You'll also find linens, quilts, glass, silver, fine china and even old wedding gowns. It's open daily except Sunday from April through October, and by appointment other times of the year.

The Picket Fence

4225 Main St., Cummaquid • 362-4865

Occupying an old carriage house and 1850 barn, The Picket Fence has a rich assortment of collectibles, antiques, glassware, furniture, lamps, baskets and even puppets. The Picket Fence also carries new merchandise (see our Shopping chapter) and is open daily April through December.

Yarmouthport Antiques

431 Rt. 6A, Yarmouthport • 362-3599

In its 12th year, this shop deals with Early American furniture, Chinese exports, patterned glass, china and pewter. The inventory also includes paintings, fireplace items, pottery and decoys. It is open daily May through October.

Constance Goff Antiques

161 Rt. 6A, Yarmouthport • 362-9540

A genteel air pervades this orderly shop,

INSIDERS' TIP

As you peruse the Cape's many antique shops, take time to chat with the dealers. They are by and large friendly people, and generally love to talk about their area of expertise. You can learn a lot, and meet some interesting people!

which features lovely items such as an antique English tea cart, estate jewelry, silver and just for fun, old sheet music. The shop, now in its 20th year, carries a large collection of English Flow Blue ironstone. It is open year-round.

Maritime Antiques

161 Rt. 6A, Yarmouthport • 362-1604

Located upstairs from Constance Goff Antiques, this well-regarded shop specializes in nautical pieces and is a regular stop for collectors of maritime paraphernalia. It's open daily in summer and by appointment in the off-season.

The Town Crier

153 Rt. 6A, Yarmouthport • 362-3138

An antiques shop since 1954, The Town Crier became a cooperative in 1980, making it one of the earliest antiques cooperatives on the Cape. It now has five dealer members, displaying a mix of items from old tools and postcards to dolls, glass and china. The shop, which is open May to mid-October, is housed in an 1840 building that has in years past been a store, post office and a meeting place for the ladies sewing circle.

Minden Lane Antiques

175 Main St., Yarmouthport • 362-0220

A year-round shop, Minden Lane Antiques carries period pieces for the home and garden, such as European and American furniture, including French and Italian tables and chairs. Other interesting items include antique signs, Oriental rugs, large outdoor urns and birdbaths. The shop is open Tuesday through Saturday.

Nickerson's Antiques

162 Main St. (Rt. 6A), Yarmouthport • 362-6426

In business since the late 1950s, Nickerson's is one of the oldest shops in the area. It specializes in 18th- and 19th- century furniture, from country pieces to formal tables, chairs and desks. Other collections include Oriental rugs, New England ship paintings and landscapes, and accessories in brass, china and wood. The shop is open daily May though September, and Friday through Monday the rest of the year.

Antiques Center of Cape Cod

243 Rt. 6A, Dennis • 385-6400

Entering its sixth year, this huge center has 140 dealers selling everything from wooden refrigerators to Shirley Temple dolls. In addition to the main building, with 18,000 square feet on two floors (be sure to go upstairs, where some real treasures are displayed), there is now a consignment warehouse in back. Certainly the largest antiques center on the Cape, this place can be a bit overwhelming to the uninitiated, but odds are you won't leave empty-handed. Put on your walking shoes and check it out! It's open daily all year except January through March, when it's closed on Wednesdays.

Red Lion Antiques

601 Rt. 6A, Dennis • 385-4783

With 17 dealers crammed into two floors, the Red Lion can only be described as eclectic. One dealer specializes in antique clocks and repairs them as well. You'll also find assorted china, silver and collectibles. It's open year round, daily in summer and Thursday through Monday the rest of the year.

Olde Towne Antiques, Harbeth Antiques

593 Rt. 6A, Dennis • 385-5202

Nine dealers occupy this 200-year-old livery barn, set back from the road next door to the Red Lion. You'll find a range of items in this clean, well-lit shop, including Harbeth's antique fishing gear and woodworking tools — specialities that draw buyers and browsers from all over. The shop also has books and linens. Old Towne is open daily all year.

Oxyoke

8 Searsville Rd., S. Dennis • 398-3067

Since 1948 owner George Marceline has been selling antique beds, hardware and hinges. He also refinishes and repairs old furniture. The shop is open daily year-round, but it's best to call first during the winter, as hours vary.

Lower Cape

B. Grant's Antiques and Books

1793 Route 6A, Brewster • 896-7198

Here is the kind of shop we love to poke around in. Located just west of Route 124, the shop has been in business 17 years and is chock full of primitives, kitchenware, glass, porcelain and nostalgia, in addition to a whole section of old and out-of-print books. An iron crib holds a collection of linens, quilts, pillows and an old Teddy bear, and there's even a sale box. It's open seven days a week May through October and by chance or appointment the rest of the year.

Kingsland Manor

440 Rt. 6A, Brewster • 385-9741

This place will take your breath away. Aptly named, Kingsland Manor is filled with an impressive and varied collection of antiques from Tiffany silver to Victorian furniture. We gazed for some time at a huge mirrored dark oak hall tree for $2,400 that was unlike anything we'd ever seen before. There's a collection of old canes with ivory and brass handles and a case full of military miniatures. A courtyard with a fountain leads to two outbuildings also filled with unusual and classic antiques. It's open year-round, seven days a week except, according to owner Norman Schepps, for Thanksgiving, Christmas Day and New Year's Day.

Monomoy Antiques

3425 Rt. 6A, Brewster • 896-6570

Housed in an 1860s carriage house on the corner of Crosby Lane, this neat-as-a-pin shop has lovely furniture, old light fixtures, sterling silver and books. There's also a great selection of old andirons and cooking utensils displayed in the building's original brick fireplace. In its fourth year, the shop is open daily from May through October and Friday through Monday the rest of the year.

Shirley Smith and Friends

2926 Rt. 6A, Brewster • 896-4632

Shirley Smith is picky about her friends, so the five other dealers who share space in this shop display only the finest antique furniture,

INSIDERS' TIP

When shopping for antiques look for lots of writing on the tag. The more information you have about the piece you are buying, the better. "Identification is key," said Shirley Smith, of the Cape Cod Antique Dealers Association Inc. A tag that reads: "1850s Connecticut cherry drop-leaf table, legs replaced," for instance, tells you a lot more than "drop-leaf table."

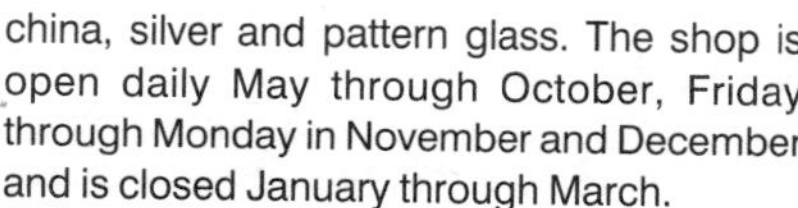

china, silver and pattern glass. The shop is open daily May through October, Friday through Monday in November and December and is closed January through March.

The Barn at Windsong
245 Bank St., North Harwich • 432-8281

A single-dealer antique shop for 25 years, this lovely old barn became a group shop about six years ago and now houses the wares of eight dealers, making it a browser's delight. Don't miss the linens, lace, old toys and children's books section, where we found an old wicker high chair in great condition for $300. Wander some more and you'll see collectibles, silver, Staffordshire and old European prints, along with a section filled with primitives, such as an 18th-century bottle box with a slant top and compartments. The shop is open daily April through November.

The Mews
517 Rt. 28, Harwich • 432-6397

Located at Ayer Lane, this shop is shared by four dealers who specialize in a range of antiques from early American pattern glass to primitives. You'll also find pottery, milk glass and oil lamps. The shop is open daily from May through October.

Patti Smith Antiques
51 Parallel St., Harwich • 432-3927

The "store" is run out of Patti's home and specializes in antique decorated stoneware. It's open by appointment only.

Bayberry Antiques
300 Orleans Rd., North Chatham • 945-9060

In its eighth year at this location (the shop was launched first in Brewster), Bayberry Antiques specializes in antique decoys, including Mason decoys and shorebird decoys. It's also strong in ephemera and paper items such as old postcards, Civil War memorabilia and books, Americana and maritime items. And Bayberry has a great collection of chocolate molds and ice cream molds. The shop is open Monday through Saturday from mid-May through October, and by chance or appointment through January.

Bob's Antiques
Shop Ahoy Plaza, 1579 Rt. 28, West Chatham • 945-4606

The clipper ship in the window shadowed by a crystal chandelier tells you that here is a shop with plenty of variety. This multi-dealer shop, which opened last year, has two floors filled with everything from primitives to art deco items. It's open daily in season, and Friday through Monday the rest of the year.

Chatham Antiques
1409 Rt. 28, South Chatham • 945-1660

Here's a wonderful selection of antiques

displayed in an antique setting! This Cape farmhouse (c. 1674) is filled with early American furniture, clocks, paintings, china, pewter, silver and glass. The shop, in business 18 years, is open May through October and by chance or appointment in the off-season months.

House on the Hill

17 Seaview St., Chatham • 945-2290

You'll find a delightful collection of baseball cards and sports memorabilia, political pins, toys, old advertisements, postcards and Cape Cod memorabilia here, along with glass, china and small furniture. The shop keeps extended hours in summer, usually until dusk, and is open by appointment the rest of the year.

The Spyglass

618 Main St., Chatham • 945-9686

This fascinating shop specializes in 18th- and 19th-century marine antiques. You'll find aneroid and mercurial barometers, globes, sextants, writing boxes, centuries-old maps and navigation charts, half models and other nautical memorabilia, along with early American portraits and what is probably the world's largest collection of antique floor-mounted telescopes. The shop, in business since 1981, is open year round, daily in summer but closed Sundays the rest of the year.

The Clock Shop at Pleasant Bay

403 Rt. 28, Orleans • 240-0175, (800) 325-6259

Clockmaker Gregory Scinto sells antique clocks along with new clocks in this small shop, which is filled with the peaceful sound of dozens of ticking clocks. See our Shopping chapter for more details. The shop is open year round — Monday through Saturday in season, Tuesday through Saturday in winter.

Lilli's Antique Emporium

255 Rt. 6A, Bayberry Square, Orleans • 255-8300

Windows lined with old, colored glass plates, cups and glasses fill this building with light and color. About 25 to 30 dealers display their wares here. You'll also find china, estate jewelry, linens and collectibles, and upstairs, old books, furniture and more. In its fourth year, the family-run Emporium (and yes, there really is a Lilli) is open year round, daily in season, closed Sundays the rest of the year.

Pleasant Bay Antiques

540 Rt. 28, South Orleans • 255-0930

This shop, housed in a 200-year-old barn and a portion of the attached house, is filled with some of the loveliest early American furniture you'll find anywhere, including tables, highboys, desks and four-poster beds. On our last visit, we counted no less than six grandfather clocks and fell in love with an 18th-century Connecticut cherry secretary priced at $9,500. Don't miss the decoy room, and be sure to go up to the loft, where a large tabby cat is likely to be napping on one of the many antique chairs. In its 27th year under owner Steve Tyng, the shop is open year round.

Collectors World

Rt. 6, Eastham • 255-3616

This spacious shop, in business 25 years, carries a mix of old and new, with antique collectibles and accessories as well as new collectibles. (See our Shopping chapter for more information). It's open year round except January, with limited hours in the off season.

INSIDERS' TIP

Legally, to be an antique an item must be at least 100 years old. But in today's market, you'll find younger items in many antiques shops — some of them in great demand. As one dealer pointed out, the antiques market goes through cycles in terms of what's hot and what's not; the best thing to do is go after what you really like, making sure, of course, that you buy from a reputable dealer.

Farmhouse Antiques

Rt. 6, South Wellfleet • 349-1708

Orientalia, vintage linen, decorative pieces and more ephemera — postcards, trading cards, advertising ads and magazines — than you'll know what to do with. You can also find restored antique lamps and lighting fixtures from The Continuum in Orleans (see our Shopping chapter) and original pieces by local artist Diane Vetromile, who has been known to cover an entire table with buttons to fabulous effect. The shop is open daily year round.

Wellfleet Flea Market

Rt. 6, South Wellfleet • 349-2520, (800) 696-FLEA

There's something for everyone here, and that includes antiques aficionados. Roughly 70 of the flea market's 200-plus dealers sell antiques, and if you're willing to walk a bit you're sure to come across some wonderful old treasures. This flea market, held on the grounds of the Wellfleet Drive-In Theater, is sprawling. See our Shopping chapter for more details. The flea market is held from April through Columbus Day on Saturday, Sunday and holiday Mondays, with additional days of Wednesday and Thursday in July and August. The rest of the year the flea market operates on random weekends, so call ahead to see if they're open.

Trifles & Treasures

11 Truro Center Rd., Truro • 349-9509

In business since 1983, this little shop offers antique boxes, chests, mirrors and tables, plus a bit of china and glass. It also has American country pine furniture and accessories and contemporary folk art. The shop is open daily June through mid-October and weekends in the spring and late fall.

West End Antiques

146 Commercial St., Provincetown • 487-6723

Launched in 1994, this well-regarded old shop offers a great collection of old Provincetown souvenirs, advertising and memorabilia, children's collectibles, clocks and lots of lovely glass, particularly Depression glass. It also has china and art pottery, especially Roseville. Open daily in summer, the shop is open weekends in spring and late fall and closed January to March.

The Emporium

220 Commercial St., Provincetown • 487-1948

Tucked inside this card and gift shop is a compact antiques shop with a nice selection of glass, silver and books, all at some of the best prices around.

Photo: Cape Cod Times

Fall foliage on Cape Cod is breathtakingly beautiful.

Clifford-Williams Antiques
225 Commercial St., Provincetown
• 487-4174

Perched above a cheese shop overlooking busy Commercial Street, Clifford-Williams is a place for serious antiques shoppers. Open year round, the shop carries a selection of decorative accessories and lighting.

Auction Houses

One of the best ways to pick up objects d'art and collectibles both new and old is at an auction. The Cape has nine auction houses, and items put on the block range from art deco vanity tables to 18th-century andirons. Keep in mind that a 10 percent buyer's premium is added onto all successful bids, and all items are bought as is, so check carefully for nicks, chips, tears, rips, discoloration and broken parts. And remember, bid with your head, not over it!

Upper Cape

The Bay Auction Company

111 Main St., Buzzards Bay • 759-2588

Year-round auctions are held on Friday starting at 6:30 PM. You can preview items starting at 2 PM on the day of sale.

Atlantic Auction Gallery

Factory Outlet Rd., Sagamore • 888-7220

Launched two years ago, this new kid on the block of Cape auction houses is establishing a reputation for high-caliber items. Auctions are held year round every other Thursday at 6:30 PM. Preview is held the day before the auction from 2 to 8 PM and the day of the auction from noon until right before the sale begins.

Sandwich Auction House

15 Tupper Rd., Sandwich • 888-1926

Auctions are held every Saturday night at 6:30 PM from Labor Day to Memorial Day and every Wednesday at 6:30 PM from the beginning of June through the end of August. Preview items beginning at 2 PM on the day of sale. Founded in 1974, this is the oldest weekly consignment auction house on the Cape.

Russell Johnson, Auctioneer

131 Rt. 6A, Sandwich • 833-3600

Mr. Johnson holds estate auctions from Boston to the Cape and Islands approximately four times a year; call for dates and preview times.

Mid-Cape

Mainsail Auction Company

70B Industry Rd., Marstons Mills • 420-6046

Mainsail holds auctions every other Monday at 6 PM year round, with a major Americana auction held every three months. Preview items from 1 until 6 PM on the day of the sale.

Cape Cod Antiques and Auction Service

2877 Falmouth Rd., Osterville • 420-0220

This company specializes in art glass and holds monthly auctions at 6:30 PM at the Holiday Inn, 707 Route 132, Hyannis, 775-6600. Previews are between 2 and 6 PM on the day of the sale.

Cape Cod Auction Gallery

451 Station Ave., South Yarmouth • 760-5444

Easy to find from Exit 8 off the Mid-Cape Highway, this year-round business holds general estate and specialty auctions every other Thursday at 6:30 PM, with preview hours from 2 to 6:30 PM the day before and the day of the sale.

Robert C. Eldred Company

1483 Rt. 6A, Dennis • 385-3116

More than 45 years old, Eldred is the oldest established auction house on the Cape. Last year Eldred again broke records in sales with $5.5 million, more than any other auction house on the Cape. The company holds at least 12 sales throughout the year; call for a free schedule. Items may be previewed the day before and the day of the sale.

Klinger & Company

153 Center St., South Dennis • 398-5285

The number of sales varies according to time of year; call for a schedule. This company holds at least six estate, specialty and general auctions a year, on Tuesdays at 6 PM at the Cape Codder Hotel, Route 132, Hyannis, 771-3000. You may preview items between noon and 5:45 PM the day before and the day of the sale.

Lower Cape

Merlyn Auctions

204 Main St., North Harwich • 432-5863

This company holds weekly auctions March through November on every Saturday beginning at 7 PM. You can look items over starting at 1:30 PM on the day of sale.

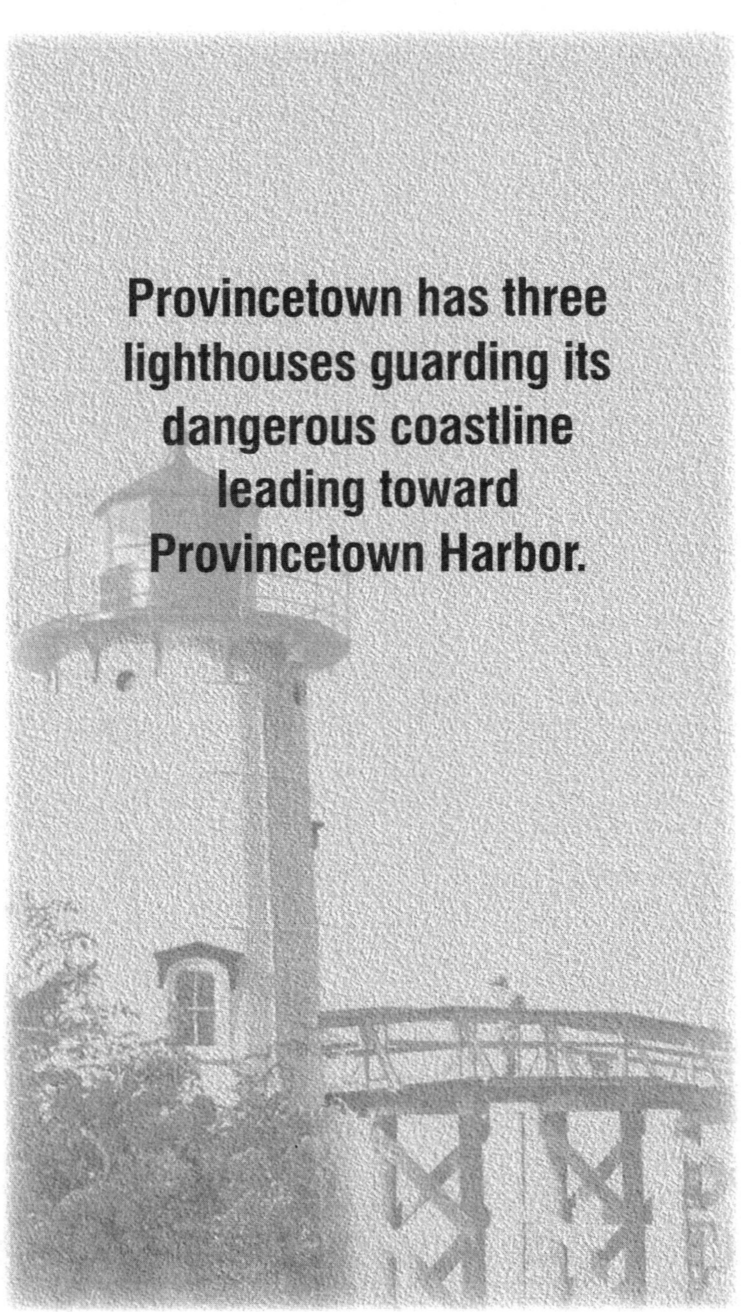
Provincetown has three lighthouses guarding its dangerous coastline leading toward Provincetown Harbor.

Attractions

There is so much to see and do on Cape Cod you may have to settle here as a permanent resident just to get to all the spots. From Aptucxet Trading Post along the Cape Cod Canal to Pilgrim's Monument in the heart of Provincetown there are interesting, fun, educational and exciting places to visit. Yet like New Yorkers who have never visited the Statue of Liberty or the Empire State Building, there are many Cape Codders who have not yet visited the Aptucxet Trading Post or climbed to the top of Pilgrim Monument. We hope that after reading this chapter, residents and visitors alike will feel the urge to visit our many Cape attractions.

Cape Cod is a peninsula of history. Before the white settlers arrived, some 5,000 Native Indians called this place home. The Pilgrims first landed here in 1620 and settled the Cape towns two decades later. Fishing ports sprung up, salt works harvested salt from the sea, bogs yielded cranberries, Cape whaling vessels combed the Pacific and Cape clipper ships sailed to the important ports of the world. Cape Codders fought in all the country's wars — even in the wars before there was a country to fight for. British ships bombarded Cape port towns during the American Revolution and War of 1812. A German U-boat fired on Orleans during the First World War. It was a Falmouth woman who penned "America the Beautiful." One of the first transatlantic wireless messages was sent from Wellfleet. President Cleveland had a summer place in Bourne. President Kennedy had his summer place in Hyannisport and even delivered his 1960 Presidential election victory speech from the National Armory building in Hyannis. All this history is remembered by the many historical societies and museums throughout the Cape's 15 towns. You'll read about a good many of these historic landmarks and museums in this chapter.

You could spend a lifetime studying Cape history; in fact, many of us have been doing just that. Yet there's more to the Cape than museums and historic sites. Cape Cod also hosts a number of fun spots for both the children and the child in all of us (you know what they say about all work and no play). The tail end of this chapter has a section entitled "Just for Fun." Don't forget to turn to other chapters such as Kidstuff and Summer Camps, Parks and Recreation, Beaches, Watersports and the chapters on Nantucket and Martha's Vineyard to complete the list of amusing and interesting stops along the way.

So let's begin here with a walk through the pages of Cape history as provided by the many museums and historic sites scattered about the old carriage routes of the Cape's 15 proud towns. As you travel these routes don't blink . . . you may miss something!

Museums and Historic Sites

Upper Cape

Aptucxet Trading Post
24 Aptucxet Rd., Bourne • 759-9487

In 1627 the Pilgrims of Plymouth constructed a trading post at this location to help them repay the debt they had incurred to make the *Mayflower* voyage. Here at this site they traded with the Dutch settlers of New Amsterdam and with the Native Indians of the area. Situated on the banks of the Cape Cod Canal, this replica trading post (built in 1930) has interesting displays that include Native American artifacts and a Rune stone supposedly chiseled by Vikings. Also on the grounds are President Grover Cleveland's personal railroad depot (President Cleveland had a summer place in Bourne) and the Dutch-style Jefferson Windmill shipped here from the Netherlands and once owned by 19th-century actor and Bourne resident Joseph Jefferson. The Aptucxet Trading Post (pronounced Ap-tuc-set) is open Tuesday through Saturday 10 AM to 5 PM and Sunday 2 to 5 PM from mid-April to mid-October. It is open seven days a week in July and August. Admission is $2.50 for adults ($2 for seniors, $1 per adult in a group tour) and $1 for children ages 1 to 12.

Briggs McDermott House

22 Sandwich Rd., Bourne • 759-6120

This 19th-century home with period furnishings has a famous ceiling made by Charles Raleigh. The house is open for tours from mid-June to mid-October on Tuesdays from 1 to 4 PM. Admission is free, but donations are gladly accepted. The house is run by the Bourne Society for Historical Preservation.

FYI

Unless otherwise noted, the area code for all phone numbers in this guide is 508.

Bourne Historical Center and Archives

30 Keene St., Bourne • 759-6928

Bourne is one of the few towns on the Cape with its own archival building. It contains assessors records dating to 1791, historic files, genealogical information, old photographs, artifacts and displays on the Cape Cod Canal and railroad. The archives, housed in the old Jonathan Bourne library building that later became the historical center, are accessible on Tuesdays from 9 AM to 3 PM throughout the year. There is no admission fee.

Dexter Grist Mill

Town Hall Square, Town Hall, Sandwich • 888-4910

For the first 15 years after the incorporation of Sandwich the residents of this first Cape Cod town had to travel to Plymouth to have their corn ground! Thomas Dexter of Sandwich remedied that situation. The original mill on this site was built by Dexter in 1654 to the joy of all residents. A stream running through the village was dammed to create its picturesque pond and herring run, which gives migrating herring a pathway from Cape Cod Bay to Shawme Pond. Dexter Mill, which is an authentic mid-17th century mill, offers a tour complete with fresh ground corn, and is open daily in the summer, with limited fall hours. Admission is $1.50 for adults, 75¢ for children ages 12 to 16 and free for children younger than 12.

Heritage Plantation

Grove and Pine sts., Sandwich • 888-3300

This immaculately maintained museum complex comprises about 76 acres of grounds with outdoor gardens, paths, sprawling lawns and the renowned Dexter collection of rhododendrons. An antique car collection, a military museum with antique guns and flags and a folk art museum with permanent and special collections delight visitors from around the world, as does a ride on the colorful restored 1912 carousel. The grounds also feature the Old East Windmill which was built at Orleans in 1800 and moved to Heritage Plantation in 1968.

The complex has a gift shop and cafe and hosts numerous special events and outdoor concerts. A shuttle bus with a wheelchair lift provides transportation around the grounds. The museum is open 10 AM to 5 PM daily from Mother's Day through October. Admission fees are $8 for adults, $7 for seniors, $4 for children ages 6 to 18 and free for children younger than 6.

Hoxie House

Rt. 130, Sandwich • 888-1173

This classic saltbox was presumably built around 1637 and is most likely the oldest house on Cape Cod. It was the home of the town's second minister, Rev. John Smith, his wife, Susanna, and their 13 children. It is named for Abraham Hoxie, a Sandwich whaling captain who bought it in the 1850s. Remarkably, its occupants lived without electricity, plumbing or central heat until the early 1950s. In the late 1950's the town purchased the Hoxie House and restored it to its current late-17th century condition. The museum is open daily from June through mid-October from 10 AM to 5 PM. Admission is $1.50 for adults, 75¢ for children ages 12 to 16 and free for children younger than 12.

Sandwich Glass Museum

129 Main St., at Tupper Rd., Sandwich • 888-0251

In 1825 Deming Jarvis arrived in Sandwich

to open the Boston and Sandwich Glass Company. Over the next 60 years this company provided many Sandwich people with jobs and brought much success to the town. Displays of exquisite antique glass at the Sandwich Glass Museum will delight both professional collectors and casual visitors. This museum contains one of the largest collections of blown, pressed, cut and engraved Sandwich glass in the United States. It provides a wonderful portrait of the glass-making industry and the town during its heyday through artifacts, equipment, old photographs and records. The museum has a gift shop and offers excellent lectures and exhibits throughout the year. It is open daily from 9:30 AM to 4:30 PM April 1 to October 1. In winter, the museum is open 9:30 AM to 4 PM Wednesday through Sunday. Admission is $3.50 for adults and $1 for children ages 6 to 16.

Thornton Burgess Museum

4 Water St. (Rt. 130), Sandwich • 888-4668

Born in Sandwich in 1874, Thornton W. Burgess was a prolific author of some 170 books who penned the popular children's series, *Old Mother West Wind* as well as *The Adventures of Peter Cottontail*. Although it is geared to children (see our Kidstuff and Summer Camps chapter), the museum's collection of Burgess books, photographs and memorabilia also is of interest to adults. The museum has a gift store and offers many special activities. The museum is open daily from April through December. It also operates the Green Briar Nature Center & Jam Kitchen, 888-6870, in East Sandwich, which is open Monday through Saturday 10 AM to 4 PM and Sunday 1 to 4 PM April through December. There is no fee, but donations are accepted. The Thornton W. Burgess Society is a nonprofit organization founded in 1976 "to inspire reverence for wildlife and concern for the natural environment."

Yesteryears Doll Museum

Main and River sts., Sandwich • 888-1711

This museum has extensive collections of toys from around the world, antique and contemporary dolls and doll houses, including some from Scandinavia, France, Indonesia and Spain. Fascinating miniature replicas of kitchens, a toy store, an apothecary and millinery shop contain tiny working stoves. The museum is open Monday through Saturday from 10 AM to 4 PM from mid-May to the end of October. Admission fees are $3.50 for adults, $2 for children.

Benjamin Nye Homestead

85 Old County Rd., East Sandwich • 888-4213

Another old and historic Sandwich house is this 17th-century home of Benjamin Nye, one of Sandwich's earliest settlers. A builder of grist and fulling mills, Nye built his house in 1685 much smaller than it is today. It was later expanded into a saltbox-style house and then enlarged into a Colonial. It was a private residence until l958 and has been operated as a museum since 1972. Furnishings and displays in the rooms reflect different periods of its history. Parts of the upstairs are left exposed to show the house's original construction. On occasion the museum offers special demonstrations of hearthside cooking, spinning and candle-making. The museum is open weekdays from noon to 4:30 PM from mid-June through mid-October. Admission fees are $3 for adults and $1 for children.

Bourne Farm

Thomas B. Landers Rd. and Rt. 28A, West Falmouth • 548-0711

This 1775 farm, now administered by the Salt Pond Area Bird Sanctuary Inc., has had only three owners over the course of two centuries. Many details of its construction are original. It is open Tuesday through Thursday from 2 to 4 PM in July and August. A $2 donation is asked from adults; children are admitted free. The Bourne Farm also hosts wedding receptions in the summer months.

Katharine Lee Bates Homestead

16 W. Main St., Falmouth • 548-4857

This is the childhood home of author and poet Katharine Lee Bates, who is known for her poem "America the Beautiful," later made into of one of the nation's favorite songs. Miss Bates was born in the house on August 12, 1859. The house, owned by the Falmouth Historical Society, is now a private residence and is not open to the public. Miss Bates wrote several poems about Falmouth, including "The Falmouth Bell," and taught English at Wellesley College. Her father, William Bates, was a Congregational minister in Falmouth who died when she was a small child. She visited the town many times as an adult and was buried at Falmouth's Oak Grove Cemetery after her death in 1929. Visitors can only view the house from the street since a family is currently living there!

Falmouth Historical Society

55 Palmer Ave., Falmouth • 548-4857

The Historical Society maintains and operates the Julia Wood House and the Conant House, the latter offering a display of Katharine Lee Bates memorabilia, antique glass, silver, china, Revolutionary War exhibits and whaling memorabilia. The Julia Wood House is a Georgian-style building that is furnished as a house museum. Because it was built by a doctor, one of its rooms is furnished like a doctor's office. The on-premises barn houses other exhibits. Both house museums are open Wednesday through Sunday 2 to 5 PM from mid-June to mid-September. The Historical Society also offers guided walking tours in the summer, Tuesdays at 4 PM, to view Falmouth buildings on the National Register of Historic Places. Admission to the museums is $2 for adults and 50¢ for children.

Bradley House Museum

573 Woods Hole Rd., Woods Hole • 548-7270

The third-oldest house in the village of Woods Hole, Bradley House was owned by 19th-century ship captain William Bradley, who was lost at sea. The structure now houses the Woods Hole Historical Collection of paintings, portraits, photographs and records. Two other houses were moved to the grounds in 1996: One is a boat barn that houses a number of small historic boats, and the other is an 1890s workshop that at one time belonged to a doctor who puttered with various hobbies including etching and tying fishing flies. During July and August the houses are open Tuesday through Saturday from 10 AM to 4 PM; in June and September you should call for hours. Admission is free (donations are accepted).

Nobska Light

Nobska Rd., Woods Hole • no phone

The original Nobska Light built in 1828 was not a freestanding lighthouse as it is today, but instead an octagonal tower perched atop the keeper's house overlooking the waters of Vineyard Sound. The current lighthouse was erected in 1876, and a fog bell was installed at the site the year before. In the 1980s Nobska was automated with a flashing beacon. It is named for the Nobsque Indians of the Woods Hole area.

Indian Meeting House and Burial Ground

Rt. 28 and Meeting House Rd., Mashpee • 477-1536

Dating back to 1684, this structure is the

oldest church building on Cape Cod. The wood for this meeting house was hauled by ox cart from Plymouth. It was built by a Native American congregation of "Praying Indians" in Santuit and was moved to the present location in 1717. The ancient cemetery surrounding it has a number of old stones. The church is opened in the summer for worship and memorial services, otherwise it is only open by appointment. Call the above number to make an appointment and to determine any fees.

Indian Museum

Rt. 130, Mashpee • 477-1536

This building was erected by descendants of Richard Bourne, the 17th-century minister and missionary who undertook the cause of the Native Mashpee Indians. The museum, which is owned by the town of Mashpee, contains local artifacts and a diorama depicting Wampanoag home life. Guides are all Wampanoag Indians, and the museum itself is run by Workers of the Wampanoag Tribe. Next to the museum is a herring run that helps migratory saltwater herring make their way up the Mashpee River to Mashpee Lake. Indian Museum is open Monday through Saturday, 10 AM to noon and admission is free (a fee is set for large groups) although donations are accepted.

Mashpee Town Archives

13 Great Neck Rd., Mashpee • 539-1438

Mashpee is one of the few Cape towns to have an archives building. The town's former library is ideally suited for storage of records, books and information, and it houses more than 300 volumes and public documents, some of which date back to 1692. The archives are open to the public Monday through Thursday, and on the first Saturday of the month, from 9 AM to 1 PM year round or by appointment. The museum is run by the volunteers of the Mashpee Historical Commission. There is no admission fee.

Mid-Cape

Centerville Historical Society

513 Main St., Centerville • 775-0331

Founded in 1952, this society maintains

the Mary Lincoln House with late Victorian displays, including a child's room, a doll and quilt room and a Colonial kitchen. Also on view are the personal collections of Charles Ayling, including Sandwich glass, military collections, Dodge MacKnight paintings, Elmer Crowell bird carvings and furniture. Other displays include marine artifacts, including tools, excerpts from ships logs and the wheel from the steamer *Portland*, which was lost in a gale on November 27, 1898. The Centerville museum is noted for its fine collection of period clothing, including shoes, jewelry and accessories.

The house is open from 1:30 to 4:30 PM Wednesday through Sunday from mid-June through mid-September. Admission is $2.50 for adults, $2 for seniors, $1 for children ages 6 to 17 and free for children younger than age 6.

Osterville Historical Society
Parker and West Bay rds., Osterville • 428-5861

The Osterville Historical Society operates a colorful museum within the Jonathan Parker House, which was built as a half-house in 1824. The exceptional displays include a large painting of George Washington at Valley Forge by Jean Baptiste Adolphe Gilbert, a Victorian Room and a children's room that contains dolls, toys and two beautiful dollhouses, one made in 1870. The Osterville Room contains maps and other archival material about the village. Displays of Sandwich glass, period furniture, Early American pottery, pewter and historical documents are also popular with visitors.

Out behind the Jonathan Parker house rests a boathouse containing historic Crosby catboats and Wianno Seniors and Juniors — all these styles of boats were designed in Osterville. Also on the grounds is the mid-18th century Cammett House, which is the second-oldest house in Osterville and provides a look at early architecture including a root cellar and beehive oven. From late June to mid-October the Historical Society museum is open from Thursday through Sunday, 1:30 to 4:30 PM. Admission is $2 for adults and free for children.

John F. Kennedy Hyannis Museum
397 Main St., Hyannis • 790-3077

Hyannisport summer resident John F. Kennedy brought energy and vision to our country's highest office. Opened in 1992, the JFK museum provides a multimedia exhibit that focuses on the late president's years on Cape Cod. Highlights include an 80-photo collection that spans his life and a video narrated by Walter Cronkite containing vintage footage and an oral history. The museum, which is open year round, is near St. Francis Xavier Church, where the Kennedy family has worshipped since the 1930s, the John F. Kennedy Memorial (see below) and the Kennedy Compound in Hyannisport. The museum is open from June through September seven days a week from 10 AM to 4 PM (opens at 1 PM Sunday). During the remainder of the year the hours are Wednesday through Saturday, 10 AM to 4 PM. It closes January 1 and reopens on Presidents Day in February. Admission is $3 for adults 17 and older; children younger than 17 are admitted free.

John F. Kennedy Memorial
Ocean St., Hyannis • 790-6320

This monument to our fallen president and fellow Cape Codder was opened in 1966. Situated along a quiet section of Ocean Street in Hyannis, it silently looks out over Lewis Bay. The moving memorial consists of a stone monument adorned with Kennedy's image and a fountain around which visitors can stand and reflect and remember the man who died so young and with so much still to achieve. It is open year round, and the fountain gladly accepts your pennies and your best wishes.

West Parish Meetinghouse
2049 Meetinghouse Way (Rt. 149), West Barnstable • 362-4445

The seeds of this historic church first sprouted in 1616, with the birth of the Congregationalists in England. One of the men leading the way was Rev. John Lothrop, who came across to land at Plymouth and then briefly settle in Scituate in 1634. Though the settlement of Barnstable began toward the east and the original meetinghouse was built in 1646 on Cobb Hill at Barnstable Village, this West Parish Meetinghouse, built in 1717, points to the growth in population that took place as the town found it necessary to split into east and west parishes. Though the original east parish meeting house in now long gone, the

West Parish building stands today as a proud reminder of those early years. The bell was made by Paul Revere, and the 1723 English gilded cock weathervane earned the church its nickname, "The Rooster Church."

Barnstable Court House

Rt. 6A, Barnstable • 362-2511

This granite building, constructed in 1832, has two cannons out on the front lawn that were hauled to Barnstable by oxen to defend the town's saltworks during the War of 1812. Also out on the front lawn is a life-size statue of James Otis Jr., who was known as the Patriot because of his speeches that rallied people to the Patriot cause prior to the American Revolution. Barnstable's Otis, who was a good friend of John Adams, the second president of the U.S., delivered a number of speeches in Boston and elsewhere that helped to move the colonies closer toward revolution. A fiery individual, Otis was once severely injured in a brawl and in 1783 his life was ended by a bolt of lightning. Six buildings comprise the governmental complex of Barnstable County, which has been the seat of the county court since 1685.

Donald Trayser Museum

Rt. 6A, Barnstable • 362-2092

This United States Customs House-turned-museum was built in 1856 and served as a customs house until 1913. Then it was a post office until 1959. The impressive red brick building now houses the collection of the Barnstable Historical Society, formed in 1939. Donald Trayser was a founding member of the historical society as well as a local historian. The displays include ship models, nautical equipment, farm and building implements, Native American artifacts, paintings and Oriental objects from days of the China trade. Also on the grounds is a recently renovated 17th-century wooden building that's reputed to be the oldest jail in the United States as well as a fish house with a display of fishing gear and a carriage house. The museum is open Tuesday through Sunday afternoons from mid-June through Columbus Day.

Sturgis Library

Rt. 6A, Barnstable • 362-6636

Along historic Route 6A in Barnstable Village rests what is believed to be the oldest house in the town of Barnstable. It also happens to be the oldest library building in the country. The oldest section of the Sturgis Library was built in 1644. Its first occupant was the town's first minister, Rev. John Lothrop who settled the town in 1639. On display at the library is Rev. Lothrop's bible. This building was also the birthplace and home of Capt. William Sturgis, who later presented the house to the town to be used as a library. The library has prestigious genealogical and maritime history collections, including many charts and maps.

The Olde Colonial Courthouse

Rendezvous Ln. at Rt. 6A, Barnstable • 362-8927

Built in 1772, this is a building where the very seeds of independence were planted. At this site on September 27, 1774, more than 1,500 people disrupted the court session in progress to protest a British ruling determining the manner in which jurors were to be selected. The protest ended peacefully. Today the building is the home of Tales of Cape Cod, an organization dedicated to the preservation of local history.

Sacrament Rock

Rt. 6A, Barnstable • No phone

This is the site of the first church service on the Cape, presented by Rev. John Lothrop in 1639 before there was a meeting house built. Unfortunately the rock was dynamited to make way for Route 6A. The pieces of the rock were collected and joined back together with cement along the side of the route, complete with a plaque telling of its historical significance.

Iyannough's Grave

off Rt. 6A, Cummaquid • No phone

Monuments to the great Indian Sachem Iyannough can be found all around Barnstable. The village of Hyannis and the section of the village of Osterville known as Wianno are both derivations of his name. In Hyannis, at the village green along Main Street, is a statue of the chief. Another monument to the Indian is his gravesite located just north of Route 6A in the Barnstable village of Cummaquid. The chief died of exposure in 1621 in his mid-twenties after being chased into a swamp by Pilgrim Myles Standish who, at the time, was butchering Indians of the area that he figured were of danger to the settlers. Iyannough displayed only good relations toward the white settlers, and it is difficult to imagine what was going through Standish's mind at the time. In the mid-19th century the sachem's grave was dis-

Photo: Jon Hamill, Cape Cod Times

Sailing is a popular way to spend a breezy day.

covered by a farmer plowing his field. A sign along Route 6A marks the spot.

Bangs Hallet House

Strawberry Ln. (off Rt. 6A), Yarmouthport • 362-3021

Owned and operated by the Historic Society of Old Yarmouth, this 11-room Greek Revival was built in 1840 for Thomas Thacher by adding on to the 100-year-old original house. The site is named for Capt. Bangs Hallet, who lived here after he retired from the China trades. You can tour the structure on Sundays 1 to 4 PM from June to October and on Thursdays 1 to 4 PM in July and August. Call ahead to arrange group tours. Admission is $3 for adults and 50¢ for children.

Col. John Thatcher House

Rt. 6A at Thatcher St., Yarmouthport • No phone

John Thatcher's father, Anthony Thatcher, was one of the founding fathers of Yarmouth, and this area of Yarmouthport is emblazoned with the Thatcher name. It's no wonder, John Thatcher himself fathered 21 children! Col. Thatcher's home, located directly across from the Yarmouthport post office, was originally built in the 1660s, although the year on the chimney reads 1680. The house was actually moved to its present location in 1680 and enlarged substantially to accommodate Col. Thatcher's growing brood. There are no tours given, but this significant Yarmouthport house is worth taking a look at.

Winslow Crocker House

250 Rt. 6A, Yarmouthport • 362-4385

A Georgian design, this house was built in 1780 at West Barnstable and moved to Yarmouthport. It has elaborate paneling, a large central chimney, a bowed roof and a fine collection of decorative arts from the 1600s to 1800s. Owned and operated by the Society for the Preservation of New England Antiquities, the Winslow Crocker House is open Saturday and Sunday from June through mid-October. Hourly tours begin at 11 AM, with the last tour beginning at 4 PM. Admission is $4 for adults, $3.50 for seniors, $2 for children ages 6 to 12, and free for children younger than 6 and residents of Yarmouthport.

Yarmouthport Village Pump

Rt. 6A at Summer St., Yarmouthport • no phone

Also known as the Simpkins Memorial Pump, this village pump was installed in 1886 to provide fresh water for the people and livestock of 19th-century Yarmouthport. The interesting feature of the pump is the wrought-iron memorial around it, donated by Mabel Simpkins in 1928 to remember her husband Nathaniel Stone Simpkins, who was a prominent member of the village and a lover of animals. Images of animals decorate the memorial.

Judah Baker Windmill

River St., South Yarmouth • No phone

Resting along the banks of Bass River is the Judah Baker Windmill, built in 1791. It was once a Dennis windmill named for the person who built it near Grand Cove. After changing hands a few times during the course of the 19th century, it eventually landed in the hands of Capt. Braddock Matthews, who moved the windmill to its current South Yarmouth location in 1863. It remained in operation until 1891.

Josiah Dennis Manse and Old West Schoolhouse

77 Nobscusset Rd. at Whig St., Dennis • 385-2232

This 1736 saltbox was the home of the town's founding father, Rev. Josiah Dennis, who lived here until his death in 1763. Look closely at the front of this house and you'll see that the windows on the left side are lower than the windows on the right, suggesting that this was once a half-house expanded at a later date. The manse is now a museum featuring period rooms and a library. A maritime room holds

INSIDERS' TIP

Pointing to the world of our ancestors are a number of grist mills and windmills in towns throughout the Upper, Mid and Lower Cape.

models, paintings and equipment from the Shiverick Shipyards, which produced eight large clipper ships during the mid-19th century. On the grounds of the manse is an 18th-century one-room schoolhouse. The museum, which is owned by the town, is open 2 to 4 PM Tuesday and Thursday during July and August and for groups by appointment. Admission is free.

Nobscusset Indian Burial Ground

Rt. 6A, Dennis • No phone

Although this is rather difficult to locate, it's well-worth the effort. Along the banks of Scargo Lake, known to the Indians of this area as Nobscusset Pond, lies the Nobscusset Indian burial ground. There are actually no stones here to see, only a plot of land encircled with a granite and iron fence, and a plague that identifies the spot as "The Burial Ground for the Nobscusset Tribe of Indians." The tribe's 17th-century sachem, Mashantampaine, is buried here. To locate the burial ground, look for a clearing in the bushes a few hundred feet west of the Scargo Lake town landing on Route 6A.

Scargo Tower

off Scargo Hill Rd., East Dennis • No phone

Scargo Tower is a 28-foot-high brick observatory sitting atop the 160-foot-high Scargo Hill, so you can imagine the sights you'll see on a clear day. Provincetown Monument across Cape Cod Bay can be seen, as can the white cliffs of Plymouth. In perfect atmospheric conditions you can just make out a suggestion of Nantucket off to the south. Built in 1902 and called Tobey Tower to honor early settler Thomas Tobey, it was given to the town of Dennis in 1929 and renamed Scargo Tower in favor of the Nobscusset Indian Princess of the same name. Below the tower and the hill rests Scargo Lake, which during the summer hosts swimmers, sailboats and canoes. Scargo Tower is open to the public and is a great place to stargaze.

Congregational Church of South Dennis

218 Main St., South Dennis • 394-5992

Known as the Sea Captain's Church because so many of its members were ship masters, this church was built in 1835. The south parish of the Dennis church was established here in 1794, later breaking away from the north in 1817. The current church replaced a small meeting house built in 1794. The church features a chandelier of Sandwich glass that was once lit with whale oil and the oldest operating pipe organ in the country. Built in 1765, the organ was installed here in the mid-19th century and attracts pipe organ enthusiasts from around the world. Behind the church is a cemetery with many stones bearing the names of ship captains as well as the words "Lost at Sea."

Jericho Historic Center

Old Main and Trotting Park rds., West Dennis • 398-6736

The town-owned 1801 Jericho House is a classic Cape-style house with a slightly bowed roof and is operated by the Dennis Historical Society. It was once owned by Cape writer Elizabeth Reynard (who wrote *The Narrow Land*) and her cousin, Virginia Gildersleeve, who presented the house to the town in 1962 to be used as a museum. It was dubbed Jericho by Reynard, who noted that when they originally bought the place the "walls were coming down." Behind the house is a barn museum with displays focusing on cranberry-growing implements, shipbuilding and saltworks — all 19th-century Dennis industries. The center is open from 2 to 4 PM on Wednesday and Friday in July and August. Admission is free, donations are accepted.

Old Bass River Light (West Dennis Light)

1 Lighthouse Inn Rd., West Dennis • 398-2244

Now the center section of the Lighthouse Inn at West Dennis Beach (see our Inns, Bed and Breakfasts and Guesthouses chapter), the Old Bass River Light was originally constructed in 1855 to become the Cape's 15th lighthouse. Though closed briefly from 1880 to 1881, it continued operation until 1914 when the opening of the Cape Cod Canal rendered it obsolete. In 1989 the lighthouse was reactivated as the West Dennis Light by the Stone family that owns and operates the Lighthouse Inn. They also operate the light itself, which blinks each evening from May 1 to October 31.

Lower Cape

Brewster Historical Society
3341 Main St. (Rt. 6A), Brewster • 896-9521

The Brewster Historical Society's museum has exhibits honoring the maritime history of Brewster and features memorabilia relating to the town, an early 20th century barber shop, a circa 1860 doll house and much more. Open on weekends only in June and September, Tuesday through Friday in July and August or by appointment, the focus of the exhibit is ever-changing. The Historical Society also operates the Old Higgins Farm Windmill (see below) and Harris-Black House, both at 785 Main Street (Route 6A) and both open June through September or by appointment.

Crosby Mansion
Crosby Ln. (off Rt. 6A), Brewster • 896-3491

Located within Nickerson State Park, this lovely home was built in 1888 by Albert Crosby for his wife, Matilda. An interesting note: The structure was built around the original four-room Cape house in which Crosby was born. Aside from being a residence, the building has been used as a music school and summer camp. As a result of being vacant for many years, the mansion fell into sad disrepair and was badly vandalized. In 1991, local volunteers organized and have put countless hours into preservation of the building. The house is maintained by the Friends of Crosby Mansion. There are no set hours, although the house is usually opened for the first weekend in May when the town celebrates Brewster in Bloom. Or you can call the number above to arrange a tour of the building. There is no fee to tour the house.

New England Fire & History Museum
1439 Rt. 6A, Brewster • 896-5711

See how fires were fought in the old days and witness firsthand the Chicago Fire of 1871 through the use of an award-winning diorama. This museum, generally considered to possess one of the most varied collections of fire memorabilia in the world, has more than 30 hand-drawn and horse-drawn fire-fighting apparatus on display as well as more than a thousand other items including the personal fire-helmet collection of famed Boston Pops conductor Arthur Fiedler. There is also a replica of an apothecary shop and an original Brewster blacksmith shop. The museum is open 10 AM to 4 PM on weekdays and noon to 4 PM on weekends from late May through mid-September. From mid-September through Columbus Day it's open from noon to 4 PM on weekends. Admission is $4.50 ($2.50 for ages 5 through 12).

Stony Brook Grist Mill

Off Stony Brook Rd., Brewster • No phone

This area was home to many mills over the centuries, beginning with the very first — a grist mill built by Thomas Prence in 1663. Nearby Prence's grist mill, a fulling mill was also built in the 1660s. The fulling mill burned in 1760 and the grist mill did the same in 1871. The country's first factory-produced woolen cloth was produced at a woolen mill built here in 1814. A new grist mill was constructed over the remains of the original in 1873, and it is this mill that we see today resting along Stony Brook. The mill is open to the public May through August. Adjacent to the mill is the Brewster herring run, where the annual migration of herring, also called alewives, occurs each spring.

FYI

Unless otherwise noted, the area code for all phone numbers in this guide is 508.

Cape Cod Museum of Natural History

869 Rt. 6A, Brewster • 896-3867, (800) 479-3867 (Mass. only)

With two floors of exhibits, this museum provides visitors with a good picture of life on Cape Cod. There are freshwater tanks to give you an idea of what's going on in the Cape kettle ponds and a saltwater tank to show you what lobsters and crabs do when they're not being dipped in butter. Other exhibits include a bird room, a dolphin and whale room, a woodland exhibit and rotating exhibits such as one on horseshoe crabs (do you know they've been on the planet for hundreds of millions of years?). Learn about coastal erosion, the archeology of Cape Cod or see what bees do in a working beehive. This museum is one of the best resources in the area for learning about the Cape's natural history. Many displays are geared to children, but all ages can learn here. Behind the museum is a vast salt marsh, which is an exhibit in itself. The museum has walking trails, lectures, special exhibits — including an impressive array of aerial photographs of the area — a library and gift shop. The museum is open year round — 9:30 AM to 4:30 PM Monday through Saturday and 12:30 to 4:30 PM on Sundays.

Old Higgins Farm Windmill

785 Main St. (Rt. 6A), Brewster • 896-9521

A smock-type windmill built back in 1795, this windmill was moved from Ellis Landing in Brewster to its current location in 1974. It ground its last bushel of grain back around 1900 and is today maintained by the Brewster Historical Society, which opens it to the public from June to September. Call the Historical Society number above for more information.

Brooks Academy Museum

80 Parallel St. (at rts. 124 and 39), Harwich • 432-8089

The Harwich Historical Society operates this museum, which is named for its builder, Sidney Brooks. It offers collections of Native American artifacts, Sandwich glass, a cranberry exhibit, early tools, implements and toys and historical documents, including genealogical information. Brooks Academy was known in the 1840s as the Pine Grove Seminary and was one of the first schools of navigation in the country. The building was sold to the town of Harwich in 1869 and used as a public school. The museum is open Thursday through Sunday, 1 to 4 PM, from June to Columbus Day. Admission is free.

Old Powder House

Rts. 124 and 39, Harwich • 432-8089

At the center of Harwich on the grounds of Brooks Academy is the old powder house that was enlisted during the Revolutionary War and the War of 1812 as an ammunition depot. It was in service from 1770 to 1864, storing shells and powder for town militia use. The militia trained nearby at Brooks Park, where a cannon used during the War of 1812 is on display.

Atwood House and Museum

347 Stage Harbor Rd., Chatham • 945-2493

Built in 1752, the Atwood House stands today as one of the oldest houses in Chatham. It was home to five generations of Atwoods and features a gambrel roof. Since 1926 the house has been the home of the Chatham Historical Society. The museum's eight rooms contain many historic collections and furnishings, including the Joseph C. Lincoln Room, which is a repository of the prolific Cape author's books and memorabilia. The museum also holds murals of 20th-century artist Alice Stallnecht-Wight, an antique Fresnel lens from Chatham Light, antiques, Sandwich glass, an international collection of seashells and artifacts. It is open mid-June to the end of September, Tuesday through Friday from 1 to 4 PM. Admission is $3 for adults, free for children younger than 12 and $1 for students who display a student card.

Chatham Light

Shore Rd., Chatham • No phone

In 1808 two wooden lighthouses were built on a cliff in Chatham east of the location of the current Chatham lighthouse . . . a cliff that no longer exists. These first two Chatham lights were range lights, meaning they were movable and could be aligned in such a way that mariners approaching Chatham by sea could find the channel to the harbor by lining up the two lights. By 1841, the cliff had eroded so much that both lighthouses tumbled to the beach below. Another pair of lighthouses were constructed on the cliff, this time made of brick and mortar. The cliff continued to erode at a rate of 20 feet per year until these new lighthouses were destroyed in 1879 and 1881. To replace them, two iron lighthouses were built. One is the current Chatham Light, the other was moved to Eastham in 1923 to become the current Nauset Light.

The Railroad Museum

153 Depot Rd., Chatham • No phone

On the appropriately named Depot Street is Chatham's Railroad Museum. It was built in 1887 and operated as a train depot until 1937, servicing more than 20,000 passengers per year. It was donated to the town in the 1950s and is today a museum offering many, many railroad-related items to the delight of railroad buffs. The building, listed on the National Register of Historic Places, offers displays of antique equipment and memorabilia as well as a caboose dating to 1910. It is open weekdays from May to September, and there is no admission fee though donations are accepted.

Old Godfrey Windmill

near Chase Park, off Shattuck Pl., Chatham • No phone

This wind-powered grist mill was built along Stage Harbor Road in 1797 by Col. Benjamin Godfrey. The mill ground corn until 1898. Over the 20th century it was twice damaged by storms and was closed until 1956 when it was given to the town. The mill was then moved to its current location at Chase Park. Managed by the Chatham Parks Commission, it is open every day except Tuesday throughout July and August.

Jonathan Young Windmill

Rt. 28, Orleans • 255-0767

This fine windmill was built in 1720 at South Orleans and moved in the mid-1800s to Orleans Center. It was then bought by private interests in 1897 and relocated again, this time to Hyannisport. In 1983 the mill was donated to the Orleans Historical Society and moved back to Orleans and placed at Town Cove Park where it was restored. The windmill is open to the public during the summer months.

French Cable Station Museum

Corner of Cove Rd. and Rt. 28, Orleans • 240-1735

Built in 1890, this is the U.S. terminal for the first transatlantic cable laid between the United States and France via Newfoundland. The cable was 3,000 miles long. Many of the original French cable operators emigrated to this country and settled around Orleans. This cable was used to transmit news of such important events

INSIDERS' TIP

Cape Cod is the site of more than 1,000 shipwrecks. In an attempt to prevent such disasters 18 lighthouses were erected around the Cape, and to save the crews of ships that did wreck, the United States Life Saving Service manned 13 stations along the lower Cape.

Daytrip to Plymouth

Plymouth is considered America's hometown. Rich in history and attractions, and within a 20 minute ride from the Bourne and Sagamore bridges, it makes for a perfect daytrip for those vacationing on Cape Cod.

The history of Plymouth is entwined with that of Cape Cod. The Pilgrims not only landed on Cape Cod first before settling at Plymouth five weeks later, but also were instrumental in the settlement of a number of Cape Cod towns. While anchored off Provincetown, the Pilgrims drew up the Mayflower Compact, a document that spelled out a democratic philosophy of majority rule and a government run by the people and not by a king.

The plight of the Pilgrims, a band of misfits escaping religious persecution to take their chances in the wilds and uncertainties of a New World, is truly one of the great stories of our country. Their ship, off course, arrived well north of its intended destination of Virginia. The Pilgrims arrived at Cape Cod in the late fall and settled at Plymouth toward the end of December without the supplies necessary to survive a long and cruel New England winter. Food was scarce, housing was inadequate, and all around them were Native Indian "savages." The Pilgrims managed as best they could despite their limited resources, yet by the end of that first winter half of the Mayflower Pilgrims were dead. As a testament to their will to survive, the Pilgrims secretly buried their dead so the natives would not know of their diminished numbers.

Their numbers would be reinforced with the ships to arrive in years to follow, particularly the *Anne* and the *Fortune*, whose passengers, along with the Mayflower Pilgrims, were referred to as "Old Comers" and were granted land privileges not available to the settlers who arrived later. Plymouth grew and became the hub of the Plymouth Bay Colony. The Indians, whom they feared, would turn out to be their saviors as they taught the Pilgrims how to plant in the rugged New England soil.

Today Plymouth is not only a wealth of early American history but also a beautiful coastal town where fishing and cranberry agriculture still thrive. We present here some of Plymouth's historical attractions. To gather more information about Plymouth, contact the **Plymouth Area Chamber of Commerce**, 225 Water Street, Plymouth, 830-1620 or the nearby **Massachusetts Visitor Information Center** at Exit 5 off Route 3, 746-1150 or 746-1152 (mailing address P.O. Box 1140, Plymouth 02362).

Plimoth Plantation

133 Warren Ave., Plymouth • 746-1622

To get a real feel for how the Pilgrims lived back in the early 17th century, plan to spend the good part of a day at Plimoth Plantation. Period houses are attended by skilled first-person interpreters who not only play the part but actually live the part and interact with visitors in a way which makes you feel like you're back in 1627. Also, at the Hobbamock's Wampanoag Indian Homesite are Native Americans who explain their people's way of life at the time of the Pilgrim settlement. Plimoth Plantation is open 9 AM to 5 PM from the end of March through the end November. Admission is $15 for adults and $9 for children 6 to 17. Children 5 and younger are admitted free of charge. You can purchase a combination ticket to Plimoth Plantation and the *Mayflower II* (see below) at a cost of $18.50 for adults and $11 for children. Adult group rates (for 15 or more people) are $12.75 for the Plantation and the *Mayflower II*.

— continued on next page

Mayflower II

State Pier, Plymouth • 746-1622

This is not the actual *Mayflower*, but it is a true replica that actually crossed the Atlantic in 1957 to arrive here as a gift from England. Docked at State Pier about 2.5 miles from Plimoth Plantation, it is a floating attraction that is a prerequisite visit for every Massachusetts schoolchild. An exhibit on the dock before you enter the boat tells a lot of its history and the history of those who sailed upon her. On board you receive a tour of the vessel courtesy of first-person interpreters who play the part of Pilgrims. As you look around the small 180-ton ship, imagine that more than 102 passengers and crew (along with their cargo and livestock) spent nearly three months crossing the Atlantic on board. In 1995 the *Mayflower II* made the trek across Cape Cod Bay to dock at Provincetown to commemorate the 375th anniversary of the drafting of the Mayflower Compact in Provincetown Harbor during 1620. Admission to the *Mayflower II* is $5.75 for adults and $3.75 for children ages 6 to 17. Children 5 and younger are admitted free. It is open to the public during the same hours as the Plantation (although July and August hours extend to 7 PM). See the Plimoth Plantation listing above for combined ticket prices for both attractions.

Plymouth Rock

Water St., Plymouth • No phone

This rock may or may not be the original rock upon which Pilgrims first stepped as they arrived here at Plymouth, but that is not really the importance behind this attraction. The rock, chiseled with the date 1620, rests within a stone memorial near the waterfront. It is symbolic of the Pilgrim's arrival here to build a new life based on religious and personal freedoms. Admission is free to this very popular attraction.

Plymouth National Wax Museum

Water St., Plymouth • 746-6468

Directly across from Plymouth Rock, atop the steep Coles Hill overlooking Plymouth Harbor, is the Plymouth National Wax Museum. The museum consists of some 180 wax figures displayed in 26 different scenes depicting Pilgrim life and history. The museum, and the gift shop on site, are open daily 9 AM to 5 PM from March through late November. The summer has extended hours. Admission is $5.50 for adults and $2.50 for children.

Massasoit Statue

Water St., Plymouth • No phone

Standing tall and strong and holding a pipe to symbolize the peace he waged with the Pilgrims, this larger-than-life statue of Massasoit looks out over Plymouth Harbor from his Coles Hill perch like some god from another age. Sachem of the Wampanoag Indians at the time of the Pilgrims' arrival, he

Photo: Cape Cod Times

Actors recreate the signing of the Mayflower Compact aboard the *Mayflower II*.

— continued on next page

chose the peaceful path and befriended the white visitors from across the ocean, helping them to survive in the 17th-century wilderness. Massasoit died in 1661, and with his passing went the peace. In 1675 and 1676 his son, Metacomet, known also as King Philip, led the Indians in a war to bear his name (the King Philip War). This uprising against the colonists was a last-ditch effort to win back all that the Native Indians of the area had lost over a half century's time. The uprising was put down and Metacomet, the son of the great chief Massasoit, was executed.

Pilgrim Hall Museum

75 Court St., Plymouth • 746-1620

Considered the oldest public museum in America, this museum has a fine collection of Pilgrim artifacts such as household objects, books, manuscripts and weaponry. Open from February through December, admission is $5 for adults, $4 for seniors and $2.50 for children age 5 to 12. There is a family rate of $12 for a family of four.

William Harlow House

119 Sandwich St., Plymouth • 746-0012

Built in 1677, this historical site offers fascinating glimpses at the 17th century through exhibits focusing on candlemaking and spinning. The museum provides a snapshot of daily life of the early colonists and also presents exhibits on textile arts. The museum is run by the Antiquarian Society, which has not yet determined its hours of operation for 1997 so call the above number for more information. Admission fees at this museum are $3 for adults and 75¢ for children.

Spooner House

27 North St., Plymouth • 746-0012

Also run by the Antiquarian Society, the Spooner House was constructed in 1747 and was home to generations of Plymouth Spooners for two centuries. The museum contains many original furnishings, Spooner family heirlooms, old letters and recipes and clothing from centuries ago. Admission is $3 for adults and 75¢ for children, Call the above number for hours of operation. The year 1997 marks its 250th anniversary.

Hedge House Museum

126 Water St., Plymouth • 746-0012

A third museum managed by the Antiquarian Society is the Hedge House, built in 1809. Once the home of a merchant shipowner, it was scheduled to be razed but was saved by a group of local women who founded the Antiquarian Society. Today it has collections of furniture, textiles and various changing exhibits. Admission is $3 for adults and 75¢ for children.

Court House Museum

Town Hall Square, Plymouth • 830-4075

This is the oldest wooden courthouse in the United States, built in 1749. The original courthouse was erected in 1686 and the current courthouse was constructed with some of the beams of the original. The museum includes numerous Colonial artifacts including exhibits relating to the Colonial court system.

Forefather's Monument

Allerton St., Plymouth • No phone

Also known as Pilgrim Monument, this 81-foot tall granite monument was erected in 1889 to honor the small band of Pilgrims who braved an ocean and the uncertainties of

— continued on next page

a wilderness world in order to provide a better life for themselves and the generations to follow.

Jenney Grist Mill

6 Spring Ln., Plymouth • 747-3715

This is a replica of the Pilgrims' grist mill that was originally constructed in 1636. It is located on a small pond, which makes for a beautiful setting. The mill, which is open year round, still operates.

Coles Hill (Sarcophagus)

Water St., Plymouth • No phone

During the first winter, the Pilgrims who died were buried on this hill in unmarked graves so the Indians of the area would not know of the high death toll amongst the new settlers. A granite sarcophagus was erected on the hill in 1921 to honor those dead.

Cranberry World Visitors' Center

225 Water St., Plymouth • 747-235

Though cranberry cultivation was first developed on Cape Cod, Plymouth's contribution to this thriving business is substantial. Cranberry World is part of Ocean Spray Cranberries Inc., which makes all those great cranberry-related beverages and products. The visitors center located along the Plymouth waterfront has exhibits that include cranberry harvesting tools (both antique and contemporary), outdoor demonstration bogs, a model of a cranberry farm and free refreshments. The center, which presents the history of cranberry cultivation, also includes a demonstration kitchen where you can taste cranberry-inspired foods. Cranberry World is open daily from May 1 to November 30, 9:30 AM to 5 PM. Admission is free.

Plymouth Bay Winery

170 Water St., Plymouth • 746-2100

This winery specializes in the production of fruit wines such as grape, raspberry and blueberry, but native cranberry wines such as Cranberry Blush and Cranberry Bay are the most popular. This farm winery gives wine tastings from March through December and produces about 3,500 cases each year. Visitors can, of course, purchase wines on site.

---

as Lindbergh's transatlantic flight in 1927 and the invasion of France by the Germans in 1940. The cable station was guarded by Marines during World War II because it provided an important link with U.S. operations in Europe. The station was closed in 1959, but all the original cables, instruments and other equipment are still in place. It is open Tuesday through Saturday from 2 to 4 PM in July and August and at special requests. No admission fee is charged though donations are accepted.

Orleans Historical Society Museum and Meeting House

3 River Rd., Orleans • 255-0767

Standing opposite Orleans Town Hall, the Greek Revival-style meeting house is a former Universalist church built in 1834. The Historical Society acquired it in 1971. Exhibits include collections of historic photographs, paintings, toys, costumes, china and farm implements. It also has displays of Native American artifacts and Coast Guard lifesaving equipment. Items salvaged from the November 1898 wreck of the *Portland*, one of the most famous New England shipwrecks resulting in the loss of all 176 lives, are on display here. One of the many interesting items here is a letter from Capt. Richard Raggot of the British Navy dated September 30, 1814, that contains the British demand for $1,000 to protect the town's saltworks from destruction (see

Photo: Steve Heaslip, Cape Cod Times

A quartet of pot-bellied pigs races the clock at the Barnstable County Fair.

our Historic Cape Cod chapter). The museum is open from 1 to 4 PM Monday through Friday in July and August and by appointment. Admission is free.

The Federated Church of Orleans
162 Main St., East Orleans • 255-3060

The original meeting house was built at this site in 1718. It was replaced in 1829 with the present church building that contains two red-oak portal beams hand-hewn from trees used to make the first congregation's church. The church was a focus of daily life for founders of Eastham, Orleans and Wellfleet. The church is open daily year round from 9 AM to 1 PM and 2 to 4 PM. Admission is free.

Eastham Grist Mill
Rt. 6, Eastham • No phone

Resting upon the town green in Eastham is the oldest and most widely known of all the Cape Cod windmills. The Eastham Grist Mill began life in Plymouth way back in the 1680s, which means that the corn it ground most likely found its way to the mouths of the sons and daughters of Pilgrims. It was later moved to Truro during the tail end of the 18th century, floated across Cape Cod Bay, and finally moved to Eastham in 1793. The mill remained in operation until the turn of the 20th century. It was first open to the public in the 1930s and saw restoration in the 1960s. Nowadays it is open during the summer months when visitors can see its original wooden machinery that still operates today — what craftsmanship! Admission is free, but donations are accepted.

Edward Penniman House
Fort Hill Rd., Eastham • 255-3421

Located within the boundaries of the Cape Cod National Seashore, the Penniman House in the Fort Hill area of Eastham points to the fortunes made by the Cape's whaling captains. Retiring from the sea in 1876, Captain Edward Penniman built this massive Victorian mansion on a knoll, with a cupola overlooking the Atlantic Ocean. Out in front of the house are the jawbones of a whale marking the entrance to the property, and telling of the former occupant's occupation. You can tour the house during the summer season; admission is free. The Penniman House is open weekends during the spring and fall and six days a week from June through Labor Day.

Eastham Schoolhouse Museum

Rt. 6 at Nauset and Schoolhouse rds., Eastham • 255-0788

This one-room schoolhouse was built in 1869 as an elementary school. Around the turn of the century the town had three such one-room schoolhouses that were later all brought together to one location and joined to form the Eastham Central School until 1936. Now the old schoolhouse has been restored to its late-19th century one-room status and serves as a museum of the Eastham Historical Society. It still has two doors marked as separate entrances for boys and girls. Exhibits include farming and household implements, Native American artifacts, shipwreck artifacts and displays pertaining to area history, including a 13-foot jawbone from a 65-foot finback whale. The museum is open weekdays in July and August. Admission is free.

First Encounter Beach

Samoset Rd., Eastham • No phone

At First Encounter Beach along the Cape Cod Bay side of Eastham's shore is a granite boulder with a plaque telling that this location was the site of the Pilgrim's first encounter with Native Indians. Unfortunately, this first encounter was not a friendly one. The Pilgrims, on their third day of exploring this new land, awoke to a volley of arrows that they answered with a volley of musket fire. Both parties departed, uninjured. Future relations between the two peoples would be much more cordial.

Nauset Light

Beach Rd., Eastham • No phone

Highland Light to the north had one tower. Chatham Light to the south had two towers. So to mark the cliffs of Eastham it was decided to give Nauset three lights. The first three lighthouses built on the cliff here were small brick towers constructed in 1837. These three lighthouses surrendered to cliff erosion in 1892 and their remains can be seen along Nauset Beach from time to time, especially in the early spring after a very stormy winter moves away the tons of beach sand. Three new towers, taller and constructed of wood, were constructed on the cliff to replace the original towers and were known as the Three Sisters. Two of these lighthouses were sold to private interests in 1918; otherwise they would have fallen over the rapidly eroding cliffs. The third light worked the cliff alone until 1923 when it too was sold. During that year the site saw the installation of the current Nauset Light, formerly one of the Chatham Twins. In 1996 Nauset Light was moved back from the cliff, as it was about to suffer the fate of the original brick lighthouses. As for the Three Sisters, they have been reunited and are now on display along Cable Road, just up the street from Nauset Light.

Swift-Daley House and Tool Museum

Rt. 6, Eastham • 240-1247

Built in 1741 by Joshua Knowles, this bow-roofed home has wide floorboards, a minister's cupboard, original wainscoting and an 8-foot-wide fireplace. The house once belonged to Nathaniel Swift, one of the principals of the Swift Meat Packing Company. Its eight rooms are filled with period furnishings, including artifacts and clothing from the Colonial through the Victorian eras. It is open weekdays from 1 to 4 PM in July and August.

The Tool Museum, behind the Swift-Daley House, has a display that includes numerous tools and implements collected in the area, including remnants of saltwork and cranberry-growing operations. The hours are the same as those of the Swift-Daley House. Both have free admission.

First Congregational Church

Main St., Wellfleet • 349-6877

This church holds the distinction as the only church in the world known to keep ship's time, thus revealing Wellfleet's proud history as a seafaring town. For those not familiar with ship's time, it takes the day and divides it into six four-hour segments representing watches. The first watch begins at 12:00 and concludes at 4:00 when the second watch begins. At each half hour during the watch, bells are chimed: one bell at 12:30, two bells at 1:00, three bells at 1:30 and so on until 8 bells are chimed and then the cycle begins again. Wellfleet's First Congregational Church was built in 1850 and contains an 1873 Hook and Hastings organ. To arrange a visit call the number above.

Marconi Wireless Site

Marconi Site Rd. (off Rt. 6), Wellfleet • 349-3785

Many believe this to be the site of the initial transatlantic wireless message when, in fact, the first such message was sent from England to Greenland in 1901, over a year before the South Wellfleet Wireless Transmitting Station sent its first message. Regardless, this site, now known locally as Marconi Wireless Site or Marconi Station, does hold its place as the site of the first wireless message sent across the Atlantic from the United States. On January 19, 1903, the airwaves crackled atop this windswept Wellfleet cliff — helping to change long-distance communication forever. Developed by the Italian physicist Guglielmo Marconi, the first Wellfleet telegraph transmitted a message from President Theodore Roosevelt to King Edward VII of England. On the evening of April 14/15, 1912, the station received a distress call from the *Titanic*. The station at South Wellfleet would only be in service until 1917 as cliff erosion was already threatening. Although erosion has destroyed much of the site, you can still view the footings of some of the towers (these towers stood over 200 feet high!) as well as a model of how the station looked back in 1903.

Wellfleet Historical Society Museum

Main St., Wellfleet • 349-9157

Occupying a former dry-goods store on Main Street and the Samuel Rider House on Gull Pond Road, the Wellfleet Historical Society displays include Cape Cod memorabilia such as ship models, whaling tools, antique housewares and tools, scrimshaw, Native American artifacts, Sandwich glass, a miniature doll collection and items from early Wellfleet town buildings.

The exhibits highlight prominent Wellfleet residents, such as Lorenzo Dow Baker, founder of the United Fruit Company empire, who was the first to import bananas into the United States in 1870; Luther Crowell, who invented a machine that made the square-bottom paper bag; Sarah Atwood, one of the country's first women lighthouse keepers; and Clarence John Bell, a horse-and-buggy era doctor who delivered 2,500 babies in Wellfleet. The museum is open Monday through Saturday with limited hours late June through early September. There is a nominal admission fee, and children younger than 12 get in free.

Highland Light (Cape Cod Light)

Highland Rd., Truro • No phone

Cape Cod's first lighthouse, appropriately named Cape Cod Light, was built on this cliff in 1797 and was lit by whale-oil lamps. By 1857 the tower was in danger of falling down so the current Highland lighthouse was constructed that year. Remarkably, the original whale-oil lamps were in use until the turn of the 20th century when they were replaced by a "modern" lamp system. The light system was updated with electricity as recently as 1932. Now with a range of some 20 to 30 miles, and sitting atop the cliffs of Truro, it is the first light transatlantic mariners see as they approach the northeast coast. The 80-foot tower was moved back from the cliff in 1996 and thus saved from the erosion threatening to take its life. It stands today not only as a monument to our Cape Cod heritage, but also to the Cape Codders of today who saved her from destruction. After all, is Cape Cod truly Cape Cod without the majestic sweep of Highland's beam? We think not.

Wreck of the Frances

Head of the Meadow Beach, Head of the Meadow Rd., Truro • No phone

This is a unique historic site in that it is a 19th-century shipwreck that can still be seen out in the water off Truro's Head of the Meadow Beach. A 120-foot German bark, the *Frances* wrecked here on the evening of December 26, 1872. Though all hands were saved by a crew of Truro volunteers headed up by Capt.

Boardwalks

To explore the Cape's beautiful extremities, such as marshes and cedar swamplands, there are a handful of boardwalks provided from Sandwich to Wellfleet.

The **Sandwich Boardwalk**, on the north side of the town beyond Jarves Street and the train depot, has a design that distinguishes it from any other as its middle section gracefully rises over a marsh creek. Completely rebuilt after a hurricane and a subsequent storm in 1991, the planks bear the names and messages of those townsfolk who donated them to the rebuilding project. The views are spectacular.

In Yarmouthport, follow Centre Street to its end and there you will find Grays Beach and its **Bass Hole Boardwalk**. Its 860 feet take you over a marshland sprinkled with wildlife and end at the mouth of a winding creek. You can watch fish and crabs performing the dance of life in the shallow waters below the wooden boardwalk.

Photo: Jack Sheedy

The boardwalk at Bass Hole in Yarmouthport offers a glimpse of life in the salt marshes.

Brewster has a boardwalk on Route 6A adjacent to the Cape Cod Museum of Natural History. Its wooden planks lead into a conservation area alive with all types of wildlife.

In **Eastham** is a boardwalk that leads off into the red-maple swamplands at the Fort Hill area off Route 6 and forms a circular trail (actually, a couple of trails). It's particularly beautiful during the autumn season when the canopy of yellow and orange leaves above seem to possess their own luminescence.

Uncle Tim's Bridge is popular amongst photographers and local artists who capture its image on film and on canvas. This boardwalk, which transverses **Wellfleet**'s picturesque Duck Creek, ends in a wooden viewing platform overlooking a conservation area. Another boardwalk in Wellfleet can be found at the **Marconi Wireless Site**. It leads you through the Atlantic White Cedar Swamp.

Edwin Worthen, the keeper of the newly built Highland Life Saving Station, Capt. Kortling of the *Frances* would die of illness three days later. Today the *Frances*' black iron hull pokes up here and there above the Atlantic waves and serves as a memorial to the more than 1,000 shipwrecks that have occurred along the outer Cape over the past three and a half centuries.

Jenny Lind Tower

off Lighthouse Rd., North Truro
• No phone

Back in the mid-1800s Jenny Lind was a legendary opera singer dubbed the Swedish Nightingale because of her sweet soprano. In 1850 showman P.T. Barnum had his private army of reporters churning out news stories about Lind a half-year before her arrival in

America, whipping the country in frenzy comparable to 1964's Beatlemania. The advance publicity worked. Her concert in Boston was so oversold that crowds rioted, forcing Lind to sing (for free) high atop a 55-foot stone tower at the Fitchburg Railroad Depot. In 1927, when it was announced that the tower was going to be destroyed, a wealthy Boston attorney shipped it piece by piece to a parcel of land he owned in North Truro. Today the tower and the land are part of the Cape Cod National Seashore. Though the tower is not officially open to the public, you can see it from the parking lot of the Highland Light as well as from the Highland Golf Links.

Truro Historical Society Museum at the Highland House

Highland Light Rd., North Truro • 487-3397

A turn-of-the-century hotel (built in 1907) houses the Truro Historical Society's collections. These include Native American artifacts, items dating to the 17th century, lifesaving equipment, 17th-century weaponry, antique fishing and whaling equipment, household items, shipwreck items, Sandwich glass and historic photographs. The museum is open from the beginning of June to late September, 7 days a week, 10 AM to 5 PM. A nominal admission fee of about $3 is charged. The museum is just a stone's throw from the Highland Lighthouse, and it is expected that the society will be holding daily tours of the historic lighthouse during the summer months.

Pilgrim Monument and Provincetown Museum

1 High Pole Hill Rd., Provincetown • 487-1310

The tallest granite structure in the United States, this 252.5-foot tower commemorates the Pilgrims' arrival in 1620. It was completed in 1910; Theodore Roosevelt had attended the laying of the cornerstone three years earlier. This is a beacon for the area, visible from the Cape Cod Canal on a clear day. For a spectacular view of Cape Cod Bay and the area, you can climb the 116 steps and 60 ramps to the top.

The museum has displays of Native American artifacts and antique china, pewter and silver. Other items of particular interest pertain to expeditions by Antarctic explorer Adm. Donald MacMillan and to the life of playwright Eugene O'Neill. The museum is open daily from 9 AM to 5 PM April through November (9 AM to 7 PM in July and August). The last admission is 45 minutes before closing. Parking is free. Admission is $5 for adults and $3 for children ages 4 to 12.

Provincetown Heritage Museum

356 Commercial St., Provincetown • 487-7098

Housed in a Civil War-era Methodist church built in 1860, the museum's collection includes one of the world's largest indoor schooner models, the *Rose Dorothea*, antique fire-fighting equipment and scenes from life in the past, including displays from each period of Provincetown's art colony. The museum is open daily from Memorial Day through Columbus Day, 10 AM to 6 PM. Admission is $3, and children younger than 12 get in free.

Old Harbor Life Saving Station

Race Point Rd., Provincetown • 487-1256

Race Point is now the home to the Old Harbor Life Saving Station that once protected the shores of Chatham. Built in 1898, it took its place as one of the 13 stations that lined the outer Cape beaches from Provincetown to Monomoy Point until the Life Saving Service was dissolved and became part of the Coast Guard in 1914. The Old Harbor Station was decommissioned in 1944 and sold off to private interests. It was acquired by the National Park Service in 1973 and moved up the coast by water during 1978, just ahead of the devastating Blizzard of '78. Now it rests at Race Point overlooking the Atlantic. Its boat room contains a surf boat and various lifesaving apparatus. The station is open to visitors during the summer months when boat drills are performed. Call the Province Lands Visitor Center at the above number for more details.

Race Point Lighthouse Long Point Lighthouse Wood End Lighthouse

Province Lands, Provincetown • No phone

Provincetown has three lighthouses guarding its dangerous coastline leading toward Provincetown Harbor. All three are located at the farthest reaches of Cape Cod where roads give way to ever-shifting dunes of sand. Race Point Light was built in 1876, replacing the original lighthouse built here in 1816. The current lighthouse is 41 feet tall. Long Point Light, at 36 feet, was originally installed along this lonely shore in 1827 and was replaced by the current Long Point Lighthouse in 1875. Today it is powered by solar energy. Between Race Point and Long Point rests the 45-foot-tall Wood End Light, which was built in 1873. Its light is also solar powered.

Just for Fun

Beyond interesting historical exhibits and museums preserving the antiquities of the area, the Cape also offers many attractions for those looking to participate in the present rather than admire the past. Cape Cod is brimming with fun attractions designed to keep you hopping. There's never a dull moment, as you'll soon find out for yourself. Below is a listing of some of the fun attractions you'll find on Cape (sans minigolf and amusement centers, which are covered in our Kidstuff and Summer Camps chapter). We do encourage you to look elsewhere in the book (i.e., Kidstuff and Summer Camps, Parks and Recreation, Beaches, Watersports) for a full account of things to do and places to visit. Enjoy!

Upper Cape

Cape Cod Glass Works
845 Sandwich Rd., Sagamore • 888-9262

Glass creations in all their glory are what you'll find at Cape Cod Glass Works near the Sagamore Bridge. You can watch artisans work their magic in the studio and then purchase their creations in the gallery. It's open 10 AM to 6 PM, daily in the summer and Monday through Saturday in the off-season.

Pairpoint Glass Works
Rt. 6A, Sagamore • 888-2344

At the Pairpoint Glass Works you can watch professional glassblowers working their craft. Pairpoint's history began with Boston's Mount Washington Glass Company, which relocated to New Bedford in 1867. This establishment is open Monday through Friday 8:30 AM to 4:30 PM throughout the year, and the on-site gift shop is open daily from 9 AM to 6 PM.

Sandwich Fish Hatchery
Rt. 6A, Sandwich • 888-0008

More than 80,000 trout are raised here to stock the state's various ponds. You can track the stages of fish development and even feed them. Admission is free. The hatchery is open year round from 9 AM to 3 PM. (See our Kidstuff and Summer Camps chapter.)

Cape Cod Children's Museum
Rt. 28, East Falmouth • 457-4667

Families can discover fun activities and learn something about the world around them in the process at the Cape Cod Children's Museum. Open year round, the hours are 10 AM to 5 PM Monday through Saturday and noon to 5 PM on Sundays. The museum is in the Falmouth Mall. Admission is $3 for adults, $2 for children age 1 to 4 and seniors. Children younger than 1 are admitted free. (See our Kidstuff and Summer Camps chapter.)

Marine Biological Laboratory
Water St., Woods Hole • 548-3705, ext. 423

A 1½-hour tour includes a slide show followed by a guided side trip to view undersea wonders. You can also visit the laboratory to watch scientists at work. Free tours are held

INSIDERS' TIP

Cape Cod's most famous shipwreck is the *Portland*, which sank in a gale north of Provincetown on the morning of November 27, 1898. The ship left India Wharf in Boston bound for Portland, Maine with a full load of Thanksgiving travelers and never made it. All 176 people on board were lost and the wreckage washed up on beaches from Chatham to Provincetown. Today, much of that wreckage can be seen in Cape museums.

at 1 PM Monday through Friday from mid-June through the end of August. Call to make reservations.

National Marine Fisheries Service Aquarium

Albatross and Water sts., Woods Hole • 548-7684

You'll find yourself face to face with marine life at this public aquarium. Three touch-tanks invite you to touch sea cucumbers, lobsters and starfish. Sixteen display tanks are teeming with fish and other undersea inhabitants. Admission is free at this aquarium, which is open daily from late June through mid-September and Monday through Friday the rest of the year.

Mid-Cape

Cape Cod Potato Chip Company

Breed's Hill Rd., Hyannis • 775-7253

Cape Cod Potato Chips is a success story that has made Cape Cod a household word among people around the country who appreciate a quality potato chip (we personally think they're the best in the universe). The company provides visitors with a chance to view the production of the almighty chip during a five-minute tour. From 9 AM to 5 PM, Monday through Friday throughout the year you can stop by for a free five-minute tour — and get a free crunchy sample in the process. And of course, you can purchase a supply to take home.

Cape Cod Scenic Railroad

Main St., Hyannis • 771-3788

The Cape Cod Scenic Railroad provides you with a whole different look at the beauty of Cape Cod. The train runs from May through December. Tickets cost $11.50 for adults and $7.50 for children ages 3 through 12 (seniors are $10.50). The two-hour ride takes you over the Cape Cod Canal via the magnificent railroad drawbridge. (See our Tours and Excursions chapter for more information).

ZooQuarium

674 Rt. 28, Yarmouth • 775-8883

Half zoo, half aquarium, all fun, the ZooQuarium has displays and exhibitions of all things native to the waters and lands of the Cape. Kids can pet a number of creatures, including llamas, sheep and pigs. Many of the animals living here were saved from certain death because of injury. The ZooQuarium is open daily from mid-February to late November. Admission is $7.50 for adults and $4.50 for ages 2 to 9. (See out Kidstuff and Summer Camps chapter.)

Cape Cod Discovery Museum

444 Main St., Dennisport • 398-1600

This is a great place to bring the kids on a rainy day or even on a sunny day. They can create bubbles deluxe or experiment with a number of musical instruments. There are blocks and puzzles and mind-expanding games on hand to keep your little rug rat entertained all afternoon. Admission is $2.50 for adults, $4.50 for children older than age 1. From mid-June through Labor Day the museum is open seven days a week from 9:30 AM until 7:30 PM. For the rest of the year (except Tuesdays from January through June) it is open Tuesday through Saturday 9:30 AM to 4:30 PM and Sundays noon to 4:30 PM.

Lower Cape

Bassett Wild Animal Farm

620 Tubman Rd., Brewster • 896-3224

The 20-acre Bassett Wild Animal Farm has tigers, lions, lemurs and monkeys, plus tamer creatures such as chickens, peacocks, ducks and friendly goats and lambs. The farm also offers hayrides and pony rides. It's open daily mid-May through mid-September. Admission is $5.75 for adults and $3.75 for ages 2 through 11.

The Brewster Store

1935 Main St. (Rt. 6A), Brewster • 896-3744

This 18th-century general store is definitely worth a stop. Norman Rockwell ambiance with a pinch of Aaron Copland thrown in for good measure, the classic building has attracted many local painters to capture its New England flavor with oil and watercolors. Inside you'll find a variety of items on sale, and the kids will have a blast filling bags with candy.

The store is open 365 days a year, 6 AM to 10 PM in the summer and 6:30 AM to 5:30 PM in the winter.

Salt Pond Visitor Center

Rt. 6A, Eastham • 255-3421

Here you can learn about the geological and natural elements that make up the outer shores of Cape Cod. Part of the Cape Cod National Seashore, the center has a fine exhibit room with displays on various Cape industries, lighthouses and the life-saving service. Also, there is an auditorium that shows short films on the National Seashore. The Salt Pond Visitor Center is generally open year round, 7 days a week from 9 AM to 4:30 PM except from early January to mid-February when it is only open on weekends. The summer has extended hours.

Province Lands Visitor Center

Race Point Rd., Provincetown • 487-1256

At the end of Cape Cod, this visitor center is managed by the Cape Cod National Seashore and has an observation deck that provides great views of Race Point, the Atlantic Ocean and Cape Cod Bay. Inside are maps, exhibits and rangers on hand to provide information and tours of the Province Lands area. The center is open April through November from 9 AM to 4:30 PM.

See villages and towns from the comfortable seat of a tall-windowed trolley or clip-clop down streets in a horse-drawn carriage.

Tours and Excursions

The Cape is beautiful from any perspective, whether it's riding in a car or walking on a beach. But to truly experience its many charms, try switching viewpoints. Get out on the water in a cruise ship or sailboat; take a train that chugs through country farms and hidden fields; or get a bird's-eye view from a plane or glider. See villages and towns from the comfortable seat of a tall-windowed trolley or clip-clop down streets in a horse-drawn carriage. Make the most of your visit by including a few of these tours, and you'll take home memories to treasure forever.

Here are some of our favorite tour and excursion companies, arranged by mode of transportation: boat, train, trolley and plane. Keep in mind that most of these tours are only offered in season, and reservations may be required.

Boat Cruises

Upper Cape

Hy-Line's Cape Cod Canal Cruises

Onset Harbor, Wareham • 295-3883

So many people pass over the Cape Cod Canal by car and wonder what it would be like to be on one of those boats down there. Find out! This is a great way to explore Buzzards Bay and the Cape Cod Canal. As you travel the length of the 7-mile-long canal, you may pass by tankers, sailing yachts, fishing boats or plush cruise ships. During the summer cruises depart daily from Onset Harbor in Wareham at 10 AM and 1:30 PM. A two-hour cruise costs $7 for adults and $3.50 for ages 6 to 12. A three-hour cruise costs $8 for adults and $4 for ages 4 to 12. Children younger than 4 ride free. Hy-Line offers a sunset cruise Monday through Saturday, for $8 for adults and $4 for children. If you want to enjoy some live music, take the Friday TGIF cruise, which has a cash bar and free popcorn, or the Saturday Moonlight and Music cruise. Both are for passengers 21 and older and cost $12 per person. Enjoy live Dixieland jazz on the Jazz Cruise on Thursday evenings from 7 to 9 PM or Sunday afternoon; the cost is $12 for adults and $6 for children.

Patriot Party Boats

Scranton Ave., Falmouth • 548-2626, (800) 734-0088

Docked at the entrance of Falmouth Harbor, Patriot Party Boats operates fishing and charter boats and the *Liberte*, a replica of a 1750 Pinky fishing schooner. *Liberte* makes four cruises a day. For fishing and sailing cruises, the fare for an adult is $20 ($14 for children 12 and younger). Charter rates are $60 per person. Call ahead to make reservations.

Through the Massachusetts Audubon Society and Ashumet Holly and Wildlife Sanctuary, Patriot Party Boats also offers nature cruises of the Elizabeth Islands. They depart on Sundays at 9 AM and return at 5 PM, with about 3½ hours allowed for a guided walk on Cuttyhunk Island, where the first European explorers landed in 1602. If you're planning on a long walk, wear appropriate footgear for tromping through water and marshy areas and bring binoculars. Short and medium-length walks take in the village and Lookout Hill. Everyone should bring a lunch. The cost is $45 for nonmembers and $40 for members, seniors and children. Call 563-6390 to make reservations.

Also on Patriot Party Boats, Ashumet Holly and Wildlife Sanctuary also offers a 2½-hour seal cruise in March and April and around New Year's Day. The boat departs from Falmouth Harbor and travels to the northern end of the Elizabeth Islands where harbor seals stay from October to mid-May before swimming northward to Nova Scotia. The cruise costs $25 for non-Audubon Society members and $20 for members, senior citizens and children.

Captain Kidd's Charter Service

180 Scranton Ave., Falmouth • 540-5955

This service operates the 32-foot *Antiqua* out of Falmouth Harbor and offers half-day and full-day trips and sunset and island cruises, as well as equipment and overnight accommodations on board.

FYI

Unless otherwise noted, the area code for all phone numbers in this guide is 508.

The Island Queen

Falmouth • 548-4800

For $10 round trip ($5 for children), you can take the 500-passenger *Island Queen* from Falmouth Harbor to Martha's Vineyard from Memorial Day weekend to Columbus Day. The trip is a leisurely 35 minutes each way, and food service is available on board, along with a full bar. The passenger-only vessel makes seven trips each day in summer, and reservations are not needed. The *Island Queen* is also available for charters.

OceanQuest Waterfront Park

Water St., Woods Hole • 385-7656, (800) 376-2326

Here's a great opportunity to learn and have fun, with an information-packed cruise that includes a hands-on science lesson for all ages. "It is geared to the general public — the nonscientist," says OceanQuest founder and director Kathy Mullin, a marine biologist who has worked on whale-watch boats for 10 years. "We take a sample of the ocean, and with that we look at temperature, depth, salinity, density, the pH, and we talk about the greenhouse effect and global warming." Passengers also get a chance to practice with a plankton tow, a trawl, microscope and lobster trap. Cruises are offered July 1 through Labor Day. The cost is $14 per adult ($10 for 12 and younger and free for children 3 and younger). Group rates are also available.

The Steamship Authority

Woods Hole • 477-8600

Although no commentary is provided, taking an island ferry (see our Getting Here and Getting Around chapter) is another excellent way to see the Cape from offshore. Steamship vessels depart from Woods Hole in Falmouth, offering scenic views of the Elizabeth Islands and the southeastern end of Buzzards Bay on the way to Martha's Vineyard. (In Hyannis, The Steamship Authority, 771-4000, provides service to Nantucket only.)

Mid-Cape

Eventide

Ocean St. Dock, Hyannis • 775-0222

This classic Cape Cod catboat makes about six trips daily out of Hyannis Harbor from mid-April through November. You have your choice of harbor cruises, a starlight cruise and a nature cruise to the Pine Cove Wildlife Sanctuary in Lewis Bay that departs at 10 AM. The 34-foot *Eventide*, which has a 38-foot-tall sloop-rigged mast, carries up to 22 people and is available for private parties. It can sail in only 30 inches of water, allowing it to get very close to the shore and attractions such as the Kennedy Compound and local lighthouses. Cruise prices are $16

INSIDERS' TIP

Small children like nothing better than a trolley ride. If you've got some time to kill, no need to plan anything elaborate or expensive — just buy a few tokens and take the family for a ride!

adults, $13 for senior citizens and $6 for children less than 90 pounds (Capt. Marcus Sherman explained that he goes by weight rather than age because Coast Guard regulations use 90 pounds as the cutoff for a child's lifejacket). Call ahead for reservations. When you arrive, look for the sign of the cat.

Hesperus

Ocean Street Dock, Hyannis • 790-0077

Built in Maine in 1937, this 50-foot John Alden sloop makes regular two-hour tours and full- or half-day cruises for parties of up to 22 people. It provides a great view of the Cape's southern coast as well as Hyannis Harbor and the Kennedy Compound. From June through October, the *Hesperus* makes regular sunset sails from 5:30 to 7:30 PM, and you can even arrange a moonlight sail.

Hy-Line

Ocean Street Dock, Hyannis • 778-2600

Hy-Line offers cruises of Hyannisport Harbor on board the *Patience*, a 1930s Maine coastal steamer and her replica, the *Prudence*. You'll see the Kennedy Compound in Hyannisport as well as Squaw Island, Great Island, the Hyannis Yacht Club and Point Gammon Lighthouse. Depending on the season, the schedule includes four to 17 trips a day between April and October. Family cruises in season allow children to sail for free, and two early evening cocktail cruises around Lewis Bay and Hyannis Harbor are very popular. The cost is $8 for an adult, $3.50 for ages 5 to 12 and free for children 4 and younger.

Hy-Line also has special excursions and regular ferry service from May to October to both islands. The company also offers an "Around the Sound" full-day cruise ($33 for an adult, $16.50 for ages 12 and younger) that includes stops on both Martha's Vineyard and Nantucket and offers a bus tour of each island. The ferry returns to Hyannis between 9 and 9:30 PM.

Windward Charters

Lewis Bay, Hyannis • 362-4925

With Windward Charters you can take a sightseeing cruise in Nantucket Sound. This one's a particularly nice outing that specializes in family trips. Windward Charters operates from early June to late September and also offers fishing trips.

Water Safari

Waterfront Park, Rt. 28, West Dennis • 362-5555

The only river cruise on Cape Cod, Water Safari takes you over the gentle waters of the Bass and Weir rivers on the *Starfish*, a custom-built, flat-bottomed vessel. You'll see Cape wildlife such as egrets, herons and terns, along with gorgeous riverfront estates, windmills and a lighthouse, with commentary by the knowledgeable Capt. Cliff Smith. Take your pick of four trips a day from late-May through Columbus Day. Refreshments are available on board, including a full bar. The cost for a 90-minute cruise is $10 for adults and $5 for children. Group rates are available.

Lower Cape

Cape Cod Museum of Natural History

Rt. 6A, Brewster • 896-3867, (800) 479-3867

During the summer months, the museum offers four-hour bird-watching trips to North Monomoy Island ($40, or $30 for museum members) and six-hour natural history cruises to South Monomoy ($65, $55 for members). Whenever there are enough people — usually every week or so — the museum arranges naturalist-escorted overnight cruises to Monomoy Island. Participants, who must bring their own food and water, get to sleep in the keeper's cottage attached to the 1820 lighthouse (on comfy mattresses provided by the museum). Since the island has no electricity, the lighting is provided by gas lanterns. What could be more rustic? The cost for this unforgettable experience is $120 for nonmembers, $100 for members. The Museum of Natural History also offers cruises of Nauset Marsh aboard the *Nauset Explorer*, a 17-seat motorized catamaran equipped with on-board aquariums and special optical equipment that allows up-close views of marsh life. The two-hour, naturalist-guided tour leaves from Orleans Town Cove, behind the Orleans Inn, and costs $24 or $20 for museum members; children 14 and younger are half price. Trips run twice daily in summer; call the museum for times.

If you'd like a tour where you do some of the work yourself, sign up for one of the Museum of Natural History's guided canoe trips. The trips are offered daily in season at one of 30 different sites, including rivers, ponds, inlets and bays, many of which are not accessible by any other means. All equipment (canoes, paddles, life jackets) and a snack is included. The cost is $22 for nonmember adults, $17 for members, $16 for nonmember children and $12 for member children. Children ages 7 and older are welcome but must be accompanied by an adult.

Catboat Charters

Saquatucket Harbor Marina, 715 Main St. (Rt. 28), Harwich • 432-3416

From May to October Capt. Jack Bradley sails his 22-foot traditional catboat *Jubilee* in Nantucket Sound on half-day (three hour), full day (six hour) and two to three-hour sunset cruises. He also does overnight cruises to Nantucket. The *Jubilee*, which Capt. Bradley says "was made for these waters", offers a smooth, comfortable ride to the six passengers it can accommodate, courtesy of her catboat design with a beam half as long as her length. The vessel is equipped with an auxiliary diesel engine. Troll fishing for blues and bass can be made part of the charter. Capt. Bradley has been sailing these waters for some 50 years; at age 11 he charged 50¢ per person for an hour's cruise in his first sailboat. For more current rates and reservations call the above number.

Chatham Harbor Tours

Chatham Fish Pier, Chatham • 255-0619

Get out on the water off the elbow of the Cape for a 90-minute narrated tour of North Beach, Pleasant Bay and the Chatham Break. Trips leave four times a day during the summer. The cost is $15 for adults, $10 for kids and free for children small enough to sit on their parents' laps. The popular sunset cruise, which features free steamers, is charter only: $100 for up to six people and $15 each for additional passenger.

Outermost Harbor Marine

Seagull Rd., Chatham • 945-2030

This is the place to go for seal cruises and shuttles to South Beach from late June through mid-September. The beach shuttle costs $9, and seal cruises are $15.

The Water Taxi

South Dock, Chatham Fish Pier • 430-2346

John McGrath carries on a tradition started by his grandfather, who launched the Water Taxi business back in 1944. He'll take you to Monomoy or North Beach or help you customize a seal-watching or sunset tour.

Seashore Park Boat Tours

Orleans Town Cove, Orleans • 240-3100

You can wander through the coves and creeks of Nauset Marsh in the *Blue Heron*, an open-air vessel that allows great views of shorebirds, wildlife, the site of a Colonial tidal grist mill, Champlain's 1605 landing site and burial grounds of many sailing ships of yore. You'll be treated to informative commentary and enjoy views you could never get from the shore. The *Blue Heron* cruises slowly on extremely calm waters, so sea sickness should not be a problem. The cruise is operated seasonally, and leaves from the dock behind the Orleans Inn. Tickets are $10.

Wellfleet Bay Wildlife Sanctuary

Rt. 6, Wellfleet • 349-2615

During the winter and spring months (December through April), the Sanctuary offers weekly seal cruises around Monomoy Island. In the spring and summer, the *Naviator* (see below) holds serious-only-need-apply weekly three-hour marine-biology cruises. During the summer, you can take daily seal and seabird cruises. The Sanctuary also offers a whale watch every June and September out of

INSIDERS' TIP

Remember, all water cruises and tours are dependent on the weather. If in doubt, call ahead to make sure your trip hasn't been canceled.

Photo: Cape Cod Chamber of Commerce

Provincetown from the water.

Provincetown (see our Whale Watching chapter). Tickets are $18 for Massachusetts Audubon members, $22 for nonmembers.

Naviator

Wellfleet Harbor, Wellfleet • 349-6003

In addition to fishing charters (see our Fishing chapter), Capt. Rick Merrill offers seasonal hour-long evening harbor cruises and a weekly marine-life cruise (in conjunction with the Wellfleet Bay Wildlife Sanctuary), on his 49-passenger vessel. The marine-life cruise is $20 for Massachusetts Audubon members and $25 for nonmembers, with a $5 discount form children younger than 15.

Erin-H

Wellfleet Harbor Marina, Wellfleet • 349-9663, 349-1999

Capt. Robert Hussey runs five- and eight-hour and all-day charters on his 36-foot *Erin-H* from mid-May through the end of September. Only six passengers are taken at a time.

Flyer's

131A Commercial St., Provincetown • 487-0898, (800) 750-0898

In business more than 50 years, this boatyard offers hourly shuttles between town and Long Point, the very tip of the Cape (see our Beaches chapter), on a 24-foot float boat. The cost is $10 round trip or $7 one way.

Hindu

MacMillan Wharf, Provincetown • 487-0659

A replica of the seaworthy schooners that sailed out of Provincetown during the 19th and early 20th centuries, the *Hindu* offers romantic moonlight cruises on Cape Cod Bay in July and August at $22 per person. It also offers daytime cruises with discounts for children.

Bay Lady II

MacMillan Wharf, Provincetown • 487-9308

This 73-foot vessel, which boasts 2,230

square feet of sail, offers two-hour sails across Provincetown Harbor and into Cape Cod Bay. Choose from morning, afternoon and sunset sails, priced at $10, $11 and $13 respectively. If you fall in love with the experience, ask about the frequent sailing discount and come back for more! Children younger than 12 sail for $5. The schooner sails from mid-May to late October.

Provincetown Harbor Cruises
MacMillan Wharf, Provincetown
• 487-4330

This company offers gentle 45-minute trips around the harbor. These are gentle, laid-back cruises, perfect for the very young and the elderly. Prices run about $6.

Train Tours

Mid-Cape

Cape Cod Scenic Railroad
252 Main St., Hyannis • 771-3788,
(800) 872-4508 (Mass. only)

There's something about a train that is pure magic. The rattle of the wheels, the mournful call of the whistle and the rocking motion cast a spell like no other. If you like trains, and want to see some out-of-the-way parts of the Cape, you'll love the two-hour excursion aboard the Cape Cod Scenic Railroad's vintage train. You'll get a glimpse of Cape Cod Bay, cranberry bogs, farmland and salt marshes and a narration of the Cape's history and folklore. The train leaves three times a day from the Hyannis station at Main and Center streets and can also be picked up in Sandwich twice daily at the Jarves Street station. All trips offer food service (sandwiches, cookies, snacks and beverages).

The Cape Cod Scenic Railroad operates on weekends in May and daily except Monday from June to late October. The fare is $11.50 for adults and $7.50 for ages 3 to 12. The Santa Express runs on weekends in December — a real must for families with young children! For a romantic evening without the kids, take the Dinner Train, a three-hour gourmet excursion. The Nature Train, a special ecology trip, is offered in partnership with the Cape Cod Museum of Natural History (896-3867). You'll enjoy commentary on natural history as the train chugs through salt marsh, field and forest, and in Sandwich you'll disembark for an hour-long exploration through tupelo groves and pine forests to the edge of the Great Marsh. The cost is $15 for adults, $12 for museum members, $10 for children, and $7 for museum member children.

Trolleys

Sightseeing Trolleys

Glasstown Trolley
Sandwich • 428-9973

Run by Aitchison Bus Co., the Glasstown Trolley has a regular route starting at the train station on Jarves Street and extending to the Heritage Plantation, Cape Cod Glassworks, through Market Square and past the harbor. The commentary offers details of the glass-factory era and the town's history. The trolley runs weekends only from Memorial Day through late June, then daily except Monday from late June through Columbus Day. The tours last about one hour, but if you want to get off along the route and do some sightseeing by foot, it is all part of the $5 price.

Provincetown Trolley
37 Court St., Provincetown • 487-9483

Take a ride on an old-fashioned open-air trolley for a 45-minute narrated tour through picturesque Provincetown. The trolley traipses along Commercial Street's waterfront and out to the Province Lands Visitor Center and National Seashore. The fare is $7 for adults, $6 for seniors and $5 for ages 12 and younger.

INSIDERS' TIP

For a spectacular view of the Cape's cranberry bogs, take an airplane sightseeing trip on a fall day.

Riders are allowed to get on and off at four stops. Trolleys depart from in front of the town hall every half-hour from 10 AM to 4 PM as well as hourly between 5 and 8 PM, from mid-May through late October. All aboard!

Public Trolleys

Many communities offer public trolley service that is used primarily for transportation (see our Getting Here and Getting Around chapter). But lots of people just hop on the public trolleys for a grand tour of the area. The trolleys listed below are operated by the Cape Cod Regional Transit Authority. For information on any of the routes call the CCRTA at 385-8326 or (800) 352-7155. Fares are 50¢ for adults and 25¢ for senior citizens and physically challenged people, unless otherwise noted.

Falmouth's Whoosh Trolley

This ride takes in Main Street to the Falmouth Mall on Route 28 and goes right into Woods Hole, including the Woods Hole Steamship Authority and the aquarium. The service runs from Memorial Day weekend to Columbus Day weekend, with two trolleys running seven days a week from June through Labor Day and limited service after that. The fare is 50¢ (children younger than 10 ride free). Call the Falmouth Chamber of Commerce, 548-8500, for information.

Mashpee Trolley

This summertime service covers Mashpee Commons, John's Pond, Route 151 and South Cape Beach. It runs daily from mid-June to Labor Day and connects with the SeaLine, which provides service to Hyannis and Falmouth, and connects with the Whoosh Trolley. Call the Mashpee Chamber of Commerce, 477-0792, for information.

Sea Line

A year-round service, the Sea Line runs between Hyannis and Falmouth, connecting with the Whoosh Trolley in summer and taking over the Woods Hole route when the Whoosh is not running. It runs six trips a day all year. The fare is $3.25 for the entire route, with a minimum fare of 75¢.

The Villager

Starting at the Plymouth & Brockton bus terminal in Hyannis, this year-round trolley travels to Barnstable Village and to the Barnstable County Complex. In the off-season, it makes stops at the mall and shopping areas on Route 132. In summer, when the Hyannis Area Trolley takes over the shopping route, The Villager is more of an express to Banstable Village, and also goes to Barnstable Harbor, where passengers can catch a whale-watch boat. The Villager makes eight round trips a day.

Hyannis Area Trolley

This summertime trolley has two routes, one down Route 132 to the mall and other shopping areas, and the other to Kalmus Beach, both docks and the marina.

YES Trolley

An acronym for Yarmouth Easy Shuttle, the YES Trolley runs down Route 28 and connects with southside beaches from June to Labor Day. It connects with SeaLine and the Coach of Dennis Trolley. Call the Yarmouth Chamber of Commerce, 778-1008, for more information.

Coach of Dennis Trolley

From mid-June to Labor Day, this trolley runs down Route 28, with a run down Lower County Road and also out Route 134 to Patriot Square.

INSIDERS' TIP

If you're vacationing in one particular town or village and plan on spending more than a couple of days at the beaches there, you may want to consider purchasing a weekly parking pass at town hall. The onetime fee will save you having to pay the daily parking fee, which over a few visits could end up costing more than a weekly pass.

H2O

New in 1996, this minibus runs down Route 28 from Hyannis to Orleans, taking in some of the beautiful parts of the road. It runs six trips a day all year, increasing to hourly trips in summer, and you can get on at regular stops or just flag the driver down! The entire ride takes an hour or so one way. The fare is $3.30 for the full ride, $1 minimum increasing by increments of 50¢ per town. Discount commuting passes are available.

Air Tours

Mid-Cape

Cape Cod Soaring Adventures

Marstons Mills Airport, Race Ln. and Rt. 149, Barnstable • 540-8081

On a clear day you can see Mt. Monadnock in New Hampshire from the cockpit of a glider floating 5,000 feet above the Cape. Fly with hawks and eagles during one of four different aerial tours of varying lengths up to 40 minutes. A 20-minute flight costs $60. Tours are available year round and can be tailored to your tastes. Instruction and rentals to qualified people are also available.

Cape Cod Flying Service Inc.

Marstons Mills Airport, Race Ln. and Rt. 149, Barnstable • 428-8732

This company offers sightseeing trips in a modern replica of a 1938 Waco biplane. The cost of a 20-minute tour for one passenger is $60; for two, $80. Half-hour sightseeing flights in an enclosed Cessna 172 are also available for $60, and the company offers aerial advertising and instruction.

Hyannis Air Service

Barnstable Municipal Airport, Rt. 132, Hyannis • 775-8171

This company gives year-round sightseeing flights in two Cessna 172s and a Piper Warrior. The pilots will tailor flights to the interest of passengers and fly-over places within a 50-mile radius of Hyannis, which includes Provincetown, Nantucket and Martha's Vineyard. Plane windows will open for aerial photographers. Fall cranberry bog tours are popular. The cost for one or two passengers is $49 for a half-hour tour, $89 for one hour and $169 for the two-hour "Grand Cape" tour. For three passengers, the fares are $69, $129 and $209 respectively.

Lower Cape

Cape Cod Flying Circus

Chatham Municipal Airport, 240 George Ryder Rd., Chatham • 945-2363, 945-9000

Cape Cod Flying Circus has three different tours and a choice of two planes (a two-seat biplane and a three-seat Cessna). The most exhilarating choice may be the 20-minute flight that includes upside-down acrobatics, loops and rolls. The other two choices are a sightseeing trip with aerial glimpses of Chatham, Monomoy and Pleasant Bay and a tame (by comparison) tour along the shores of the Cape. The business also offers personalized flight instruction. The cost is about $35 for three people to make a 20-minute trip to Orleans or over Monomoy, and the pilot will also fly over houses so you can wave at the kids or take a photo. The Circus operates daily year round except Christmas.

Willy Air Tours

Provincetown Airport, Race Point Rd., Provincetown • 487-0241

Daredevils will delight in taking a 15-minute flight over the tip of the Cape in a lemon-yellow 1930 Stinson SM-8A Detroiter dubbed "Willy." You'll love every chill and thrill. These unique tours are offered from the end of May through Columbus Day. The cost is $45 per ride, with a maximum of four passengers.

Unique Land Tours

Lower Cape

Art's Dune Tours

Corner of Commercial and Standish St., Provincetown • 487-1950, 487-1050

Since 1946, Art Costa has piled people of all ages into his four-wheel-drive vehicles for an hour-long journey to the outer reaches of the Cape Cod National Seashore, through fragrant pine woods, fields of beach grass and beach plum and, of course, sand dunes. You'll get to see the beach shacks of yesteryear, where many famous writers and artists lived, and have a chance to get out and stretch — a perfect excuse to snap some photos. The most popular tours are the sunset ones; get in line early! Tours are given from April through October and cost $9 per adult (the sunset tour costs $10).

Off the Beaten Track

190 Commercial St., Provincetown • 487-0854

What better way to learn about the history of Provincetown than by walking its tiny, narrow streets? Off the Beaten Track tours, which meet in front of Spiritus Pizza, allows you to step back in time while being entertained and educated on walking tours. You'll stop at numerous historical sites, including the oldest house in town, the site of an ancient Viking boatyard and the Pilgrims' first landing point. Tours last 90 minutes and cover nearly a mile. Tours are available from May through November by appointment only. The cost is $7 per person.

Rambling Rose Carriage Company

Commercial St. at Town Hall, Provincetown • 487-4246

There's nothing like a horse-and-buggy ride for truly relaxed sightseeing. You get an unhurried look at everything, and you can't help but feel special. Rambling Rose offers leisurely jaunts through town. Rates start at $17 for a 10-minute drive (and that includes a carrot, which you can offer your mane friend at the end of the trip).

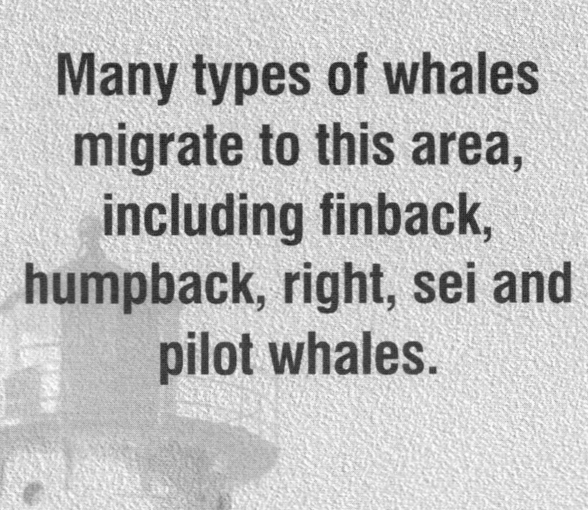

Many types of whales migrate to this area, including finback, humpback, right, sei and pilot whales.

Whale Watching

There's nothing like the thrill of seeing the largest creatures on earth up close in their native habitat. Cape Cod is one of the best places to do that because of its proximity to Stellwagen Bank, an annual feeding ground for whales. About 8 miles northeast of Provincetown, Stellwagen Bank stretches nearly 20 miles from the mouth of Cape Cod Bay into Massachusetts Bay, and has long been prime fishing ground because of the diversity of marine life it supports.

A protected National Marine Sanctuary since 1992 — the first area in the Northeast to receive that designation — Stellwagen attracts the whales who migrate here because of its abundant food supplies. Many types of whales migrate here every spring, including finback, humpback, right, sei and pilot whales. Each species has its own distinct diet, characteristics and habits, but generally, the whales begin arriving in this area in early spring and leave for warmer waters in early winter.

Humpback whales are the most popular species to watch because they are inquisitive enough to come close to the boats and they have an engaging tendency to perform. Humpbacks feed in the waters of Stellwagen Bank, rich with plankton, squid, herring, sand lance and other sea life. A mature humpback whale requires 800,000 calories a day, which translates to almost three-quarters of a metric ton of crustaceans and small fish. After feeding for six or seven months, they leave this area and fast until they return the next year. Humpbacks spend winters in the West Indies where they breed and give birth.

Different species of whales feed on different sea life. Right whales, for instance, feed mostly on plankton, miniscule organisms that float in the water. Whales follow the food sources, and whale watching boats follow the whales, so when you're out on one of these boats, you'll find yourself zipping around a bit until the boat operators get a handle on exactly where the whales happen to be. As you leave from either Barnstable or Provincetown, you'll generally see whale-watch boats from Plymouth and Boston approaching from the other direction as they all hunt for whale sightings. But fortunately for the whales, that's all they are hunting for. That wasn't always so, which is why many species are in danger of extinction.

Despite the fact that whaling was for centuries an important New England industry (see our Historic Cape Cod chapter), it is the 20th century that has brought some species to a point of near-extinction. Between 1910 and 1963, 140,000 humpback whales were killed; today only a few thousand survive. The right whale, so named because it is relatively slow-moving and floats when killed — therefore the "right" whale to take — is practically extinct; researchers estimate there are fewer than 300 northern right whales left in the sea today.

In 1975 a group of school children took the first whale-watching tour on the East Coast, conducted by Al Avellar of the Dolphin Fleet in Provincetown. More than 20 years later, tens

INSIDERS' TIP

Help save the whales — and maybe "adopt" one of your own, through the Whale Adoption Project, 548-8328, a Falmouth-based company devoted to raising funds for whale research, rescue and education. Sponsored by the International Wildlife Coalition, the Whale Adoption Project can be written at 70 E. Falmouth Highway, Falmouth 02536.

of thousands of people leave every summer from Plymouth, Barnstable and Provincetown to visit the summer homes of the whales.

During whale-watching trips, staff members, often naturalists or marine biologists, provide commentary about the natural history of the area, especially the whales and their habitat. When the scientists spot whales, the excitement in their voices is genuine; for many it's like encountering old friends. Those who have worked around whales for a long time can identify individual whales by markings on their tail flukes or body and often know specific details of their lives, from their offspring to their travel patterns.

The issues and restrictions that accompany whale-watching tours are far more complex than those for other types of tours. Disturbing or threatening the whales with the sounds of boat motors, the regular presence and proximity of people and pollution must be taken into account. State and federal agencies have developed guidelines for the whale-watching industry that are probably based as much or more on safety for the marine mammals as for the humans. For example, boats are prohibited from coming within more than 300 yards of most whales and 500 yards of the endangered right whale. Fines of $50,000 can be levied against anyone found guilty of harassing great whales.

FYI

Unless otherwise noted, the area code for all phone numbers in this guide is 508.

There is no question that whale watching has become an important part of the Cape's tourist economy. For one thing, it has extended off-season business in areas such as Provincetown. Since whale watching begins in April, many seasonal shops, restaurants and other businesses in Provincetown open then rather than waiting for Memorial Day.

Whale watching, a $100 million industry in New England, is extremely important to the economy of the Cape's outermost town, said Candace Collins-Boden, executive secretary of the Provincetown Chamber of Commerce. She noted that 1996 "was the best whale-watch season in about 10 years," in terms of the number of whales spotted. That fact was echoed by Lynn Hiller of the Center for Coastal Studies, a Provincetown-based nonprofit organization dedicated to the study of marine life. One day last October, she said, one whale-watch vessel saw 40 whales, whereas in previous years it was exciting to see one or two. Hiller attributed the increase in whales partly to plentiful food sources and explained that such things are cyclical in the natural world.

Although the whales feed underwater at Stellwagen Bank in Cape Cod Bay, they'll take time out to flirt with the whale-watching boats and will often swim alongside and underneath them for hours. You may also see other marine animals such as dolphins and porpoises.

The most exciting moment during a whale watch comes when one of the whales shoots straight up and out of the water, a move known as breaching. A collective "Ooh" rises from the boat, and all is quiet for an instant as viewers take in the awesome scene. After that, you'll be hooked, finding yourself telling your friends that they absolutely must experience a whale watch and offering to accompany them so you can experience it again!

In this chapter, we acquaint you with several of the organizations that conduct whale-watching excursions. Always call ahead to make sure the trips haven't been canceled because of weather or sea conditions. It is also a good idea to make reservations since seating is limited.

Cruise prices are competitive, and all companies offer a variety of discounts. Prices are generally a bit lower in the spring and fall — both great times to experience the Cape. Whale-watch tours run from mid-April through

INSIDERS' TIP

If you're going on a whale watch, don't forget to bring your camera, binoculars, sunscreen, motion sickness pills (available for free on board in case you forget them . . . or didn't think you'd need them) and a jacket. No matter how hot the weather, the temperatures at sea are always cooler.

Photo: Rob Schloerb, Cape Cod Times

Whale watching off Stellwagen Bank draws thousands of participants each year.

the end of October and usually last between three and four hours. Most companies offer three trips a day: The morning watch is ideal for families with small children; the afternoon trip is usually the most crowded; the sunset trip is the most romantic and beautiful, though it can be tough to see the whales at dusk.

All charters guarantee sightings; in the rare chance no whales are spotted, you'll be given a rain check to use at another time. It's always a good idea to make reservations, particularly in the busy summer season.

Mid-Cape

Hyannis Whale Watcher Cruises

Barnstable Harbor • 362-6088, (800) 287-0374

About 3 miles north of Hyannis in Barnstable Harbor, next door to Mattakeese Restaurant, this excursion goes across Cape Cod Bay to the Stellwagen Bank area. The company's new boat, a 110-foot cruiser that seats approximately 300 people, can move at 35 miles an hour. Travel time to reach the whales is often less than an hour and trips last three to four hours. Naturalists provide the commentary and also point out landmarks on the shore, including the 100-year-old cottage colony on Sandy Neck, a barrier beach at the entrance of Barnstable Harbor.

The cost is $22 for adults, $19 for adults 62 and older, $15 for children ages 4 to 12 and free for children 3 and younger.

Group rates for 20 or more are available. The boats are handicapped accessible. For educational groups, the Hyannis Whale Watcher Cruises also offers a floating classroom that makes morning nature trips into Cape Cod Bay.

Lower Cape

Dolphin Fleet

MacMillan Wharf, Provincetown • 349-1900, (800) 826-9300

Originator of the whale-watching industry on the Eastern Seaboard, the Dolphin Fleet always has a naturalist on board from the Center for Coastal Studies, which maintains an impressive database on whales. The naturalists provide informative and entertaining commentary about the whales, many of whom they know by name. We like the fact that whale

Photo: Steve Haeslip, Cape Cod Times

Windy days offer experiments in flight with just a kite and some string.

watches on this line are small; although the boats can hold more, the number of passengers is limited to 145. The central cabin is heated, and the galley serves a full breakfast. During peak season the Dolphin Fleet offers nine trips a day, The cost is $17 for adults, $15 for senior citizens, AAA members or discount coupon holders, and $14 for children ages 7 to 12. Children 6 and younger ride free.

Portugese Princess

MacMillan Wharf, Provincetown
• 487-2651, (800) 442-3188

With two 100-foot vessels, the Portugese Princess makes six trips a day in summer and two trips a day in spring and fall. Naturalists provide commentary and information and offer hands-on activities for children and adults. Full galley and bar service are available on board with the Happy Humpback Cafe offering Portugese specialties, hot dogs and snacks. The boats have heated cabins. Peak season rates are $16 to $18 for adults, $14.50 for children ages 7 to 16 and free for children 6 and younger.

Ranger V

MacMillan Wharf, Provincetown
• 487-3322, (800) 992-9333

This double-decker is the town's largest

INSIDERS' TIP

To help support the work of the Center for Coastal Studies, be sure to stop by their information and gift shop while you're in Provincetown. It's on Standish Street near the pier, right next to the Provincetown Chamber of Commerce.

whale-watching boat. It has a capacity of 541 passengers but limits whale-watching cruises to 380 people. The *Ranger V* also lays claim to being the fastest whale-watching boat on the East Coast and, because of its size, offers a fairly smooth ride. It has two galleys and bars and a state-of-the-art sound system for commentary by the marine biologist on board for every trip. This boat begins its season a bit later, in early May, but keeps going out longer than most other lines, until mid-November depending on the weather. Peak-season fees are $18 for adults, with discounts for senior citizens and AAA members, and free for children 9 and younger.

Cape Cod kids have
their own giant sandbox
to play in year round —
well, most of the year.

Kidstuff and Summer Camps

Cape Cod is a wonderful place to be a kid. We've met countless adults who say their idyllic childhood vacations here are part of what keeps them returning to the Cape — sometimes permanently.

What are the attractions for little people? Obviously, there are the beaches. Children of all ages love running in the sand, splashing in the surf, building sandcastles and hunting for seashells and beach rocks. Cape Cod kids have their own giant sandbox to play in year round — well, most of the year, although some tykes we know wouldn't mind a romp by the bay even in January! In summer, they love to share it with visitors, as children are famous for making new friends. But there's plenty to do on the Cape beyond beaches, from bumper cars and miniature golf to nature centers and museums. Kids can watch jam being made at the Green Briar Nature Center in Sandwich, feed the turtles and fish at the Cape Cod Museum of Natural History in Brewster, catch a dolphin and sea lion show at the ZooQuarium in Yarmouth or climb aboard a pirate ship at the Cape Cod Children's Museum in Falmouth.

There's so much for kids to do on the Cape that to detail everything would take a whole book. So we decided to simply offer a selection of what we consider to be the best and the brightest. We know you'll already be planning trips to museums (see our Attractions chapter) so we reserved this space for places especially geared toward children.

If you're looking for suggestions and ideas for kids who love the outdoors (as in biking and hiking, swimming and sunning), turn to our Parks and Recreation chapter or our Beaches chapter. During the summer, the Cape is alive with the sounds of music and puppet theaters and kiddie shows; take a look at our Arts and Entertainment chapter for more about these. Provincetown offers two exceptional kid-friendly tours: Rambling Rose Carriage Rides and the Provincetown Trolley Tour; see our Tours and Excursions chapter for more information.

Also included in this chapter are descriptions of summer camps, sports clinics and creative centers that have become dependable outlets for youthful curiosity and energy. You're sure to find some that inspire your children.

One last word. If you and your other half must get away for some time alone, babysitting services are available (see our Education chapter). Most hotels and accommodations keep a list of reliable sitters they've recommended in the past. The Children's Place, 240-3310, a regional family resource center in Eastham (serving the Lower Cape towns from Brewster to

INSIDERS' TIP

If you've got a long drive to face at the end of your Cape Cod vacation, put together a Car Kit of hands-on Cape memories for your kids to sift through in the car. Include things such as a bucket of sea shells and beach rocks, rinsed and dried; post cards of different places you visited; special books you bought during your trip and coloring books with Cape scenes.

Provincetown), keeps a list of recommended babysitters. And here's perhaps the Cape's best-kept secret: If you're staying on the Lower Cape (namely Provincetown), the Council on Aging, 487-7080, also offers a babysitting service. Senior citizens will watch your kid(s) either in their homes or at the places in which you're staying. Prices run between $5 and $8.50 per hour, depending on the number of children and the amount of notice given. It's not an all-day arrangement but perfect for parents who want to get away for a few hours of sightseeing or dinner.

FYI

Unless otherwise noted, the area code for all phone numbers in this guide is 508.

Aquariums and Animal Farms

Upper Cape

Sandwich Fish Hatchery

Rt. 6A, Sandwich • 888-0008

Fishing around to do something really different? Adults and kids alike will enjoy the Sandwich Fish Hatchery, where more than 80,000 trout are raised to stock state's various ponds. Kids will be able to track the stages of fish development and feed the critters (bring quarters!). Admission is free.

National Marine Fisheries Service Aquarium

Albatross and Water sts., Woods Hole • 548-7684

Please touch the specimens! That's the lesson stressed here at the public aquarium of the Northeast Fisheries Science Center. Children can feel around three touch-tanks and pick up such deep-sea wonders as sea cucumbers, lobsters and starfish. They can also look at creatures close up under a microscope and come eye-to-eye with marine life through the glass of 16 display tanks, including one with loggerhead turtles and another swarming with — eek! — eels. Don't forget to take a peek at the natural blue lobster; the odds of such coloring are 20 million-to-one! Student volunteers are on hand to answer kids' queries. The aquarium is open daily from late June through mid-September and Monday through Friday the rest of the year. Admission is free.

Marine Biological Laboratory

MBL and Water sts., Woods Hole • 548-3705, ext. 423

A visit here requires advance planning but is well-worth the effort. A 1½-hour tour includes a slide show followed by a guided side trip to say hello to squid, sponges, crabs and coral. As a bonus, there's a short visit to the actual lab, where kids can watch scientists at work. The facility gives tours at 1 PM Monday through Friday from mid-June through the end of August. Reservations are required, and the tour is free.

Mid-Cape

ZooQuarium

674 Rt. 28, Yarmouth • 775-8883

As its name implies, this place is half zoo and half aquarium — and all fun! One huge room houses tanks of fish, frogs and turtles, with a sandbox boat in the middle for tykes with a short attention span. When you walk out into the huge backyard, you'll think you're miles from the commercial bustle of Route 28. This is another world, where llamas, sheep, pigs and other animals wander in roomy pens and come over for a nuzzle or a nibble of corn. An antique miniature train is a nice diversion for kids who would rather touch wheels than fur, and the nearby classroom, with its touch-and-tell displays, is a fun place to learn. Don't miss the sea lion shows, which are held daily in summer. Willow and her friends love to perform, especially for children. The ZooQuarium is open daily from mid-February to late November. Admission is $7.50 ($4.50 for ages 2 through 9).

Lower Cape

Bassett Wild Animal Farm

620 Tubman Rd., Brewster • 896-3224

On this 20-acre farm, little ones can walk among tame chickens, peacocks and ducks

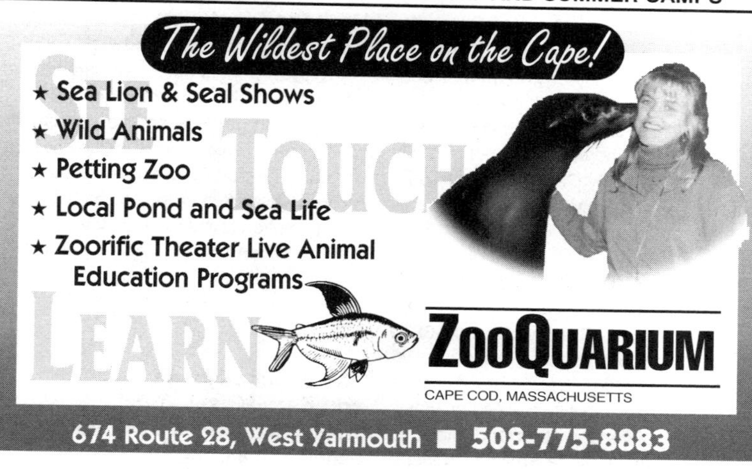

and pet the friendly goats and lambs. The tigers, lions, lemurs and monkeys hang out behind chain-link fences, staring back at visitors with equal curiosity. The farm also holds hayrides and pony rides. It's open daily mid-May through mid-September. Admission is $5.75 ($3.75 for ages 2 through 11).

Wellfleet Bay Wildlife Sanctuary
Rt. 6, Wellfleet • 349-2615

This Outer Cape treasure offers many fascinating programs, strolls and courses for children of all ages (these are detailed in our Parks and Recreation chapter). Nothing can be more rewarding than scavenging the seashore for shells and exotic animal life — scallop shells and skate cases, anyone? At low tide, you can walk about 2 miles out into the tidal flats of Cape Cod Bay, reachable from any beach in Brewster. Bring a pail, hike up your pants (or wear shorts) and start exploring!

Fun Museums and Nature Centers

Upper Cape

Cape Cod Children's Museum
Falmouth Mall, Rt. 28 • 457-4667

Learning is especially fun here. Attractions include a portable planetarium, a submarine, a dress-up castle (kids can use their imaginations to be anyone from Pocahontas to Frank Perdue) and an area where kids can be "morphed," that is, have their facial features superimposed on someone else's via a two-way mirror. But the biggest draw here is the 30-foot pirate ship on which you'll always find scores of Bluebeard wannabes scurrying up and down the three levels. A must! The museum also has two indoor sandboxes with a specially designed implement that allows kids to write with sand. The museum is open daily all year long, and monthly thematic programs with activities three times daily are held year round. Admission is $3 ($2 for ages 1 through 4 and for those older than 60).

Thorton W. Burgess Museum
4 Water St., Sandwich • 888-4668

The life and career of the Sandwich native and children's author who wrote thousands of stories and 170 books, including *Peter Cottontail* and the beloved *Old Mother West Wind* series, is chronicled here through memorabilia and exhibits. The cottage in which the museum is housed was the home of Burgess' eccentric aunt, a teacher who claimed she could talk with plants and wildlife. So it's only natural that there's a touch-and-smell herb garden here. In the see-and-touch room, kids are invited to guess what they're handling — is it a rubber snake? a feather? Story hours

(Burgess' tales, of course) are given on the front lawn three mornings a week in summer (in 1996 the schedule for story hours was Monday, Wednesday and Saturday at 10:30 AM, but at this writing a change was being considered, so call first). The museum is open daily mid-April through early December and Tuesday through Saturday the rest of the year. Donations are requested.

Green Briar Nature Center and Jam Kitchen

6 Discovery Hill Rd., Sandwich • 888-6870

You're still in Burgess country here: Remember the *Old Briar Patch*? That fictitious locale comes to life at this nature center, which abuts 57 acres of conservation land. Kids can visit frogs and turtles at the Smiling Pool and wander on the nature trails to look for signs of other critters. The Jam Center, established in 1903, is a kitchen nestled back in the woods where jams and jellies are still made the right way — by hand. Take a tour of the kitchen and see them being made, then buy some to take home. Donations are requested. You can also take one of the Center's regularly offered jam-making classes — they're available for both children and adults — and take home the fruits of your labor.

Yesteryears Doll Museum

Main and River sts., Sandwich • 888-1711

This 1833 Gothic Revival Church houses a collection of dolls from three centuries — everything from delicate, china-faced Victorian dolls to Barbie, who shares a case with G.I. Joe. Kids may not know what French bisque is, but there's no doubt when it comes to Shirley Temple. Don't miss the consignment shop and doll hospital in the museum's basement. The museum is open Monday through Saturday from 10 AM to 4 PM from mid-May through the end of October. Admission fees are $3.50 for adults and $2 for children.

Heritage Plantation

Grove and Pine sts., Sandwich • 888-3300

This is a perfect outing for parents and the kids-in-the-stroller set. You'll get to see everything — lush gardens and some magnificent collections — while giving the little ones a good workout. The old-fashioned, handcarved indoor carousel gives free rides with paid admission. The plantation is open early May to late October. Admission is $8 ($4 for ages 6 through 18).

Mid-Cape

The Jericho House and Barn Museum

Trotting Park Rd. and Old Main St., West Dennis • 398-6736

This museum boasts what we believe is the only "Driftwood Zoo" in the world. It's a collection of folk art animals made out of driftwood back in the '50s. Donations are requested.

Cape Cod Discovery Museum

444 Main St., Dennisport • 398-1600

Here, kids can pretend they are waiters, waitresses or chefs in a diner; play a see-through piano; have their silhouettes "frozen" in the shadow room; play with games, puzzles, brainteasers and building blocks; create masterpieces in the recycled art center; or blow bubbles the size of Montana at the Bubble Table. Kids can discover their musical talents in the music room and learn about electricity in the science area. There's something for all ages here. You may have a hard time, however, luring your little ones away from the gift shop. Launched in 1993 by special-needs teacher and mother Kate Clemens and her husband, Jim Nowack, Discovery Days is open Wednesday through Sunday year round. Admission to the museum is $2.50 for adults, $4.50 for children older than age 1. From mid-June through Labor Day the museum is open seven days a week from 9:30 AM to 7:30 PM.

INSIDERS' TIP

Put together a Cape Cod scrapbook with your children so they'll remember the things they did and the places they visited during their vacation — and can look forward to on their next visit!

The rest of the year (except Tuesdays from January through June) it is open Tuesday through Saturday from 9:30 AM to 4:30 PM and Sundays noon to 4:30 PM.

Lower Cape

Cape Cod Museum of Natural History

867 Route 6A, Brewster • 896-3867, (800) 479-3867

While this wonderful facility is great for people of all ages, it is family-oriented and very child-friendly. Take the little ones downstairs to a room full of hands-on exhibits, fish tanks and demonstrations that will entertain them for hours. They can observe the world of nature close up through whale displays, a working beehive and window bird feeder. The museum also has a nifty gift shop packed with educational yet entertaining souvenirs. The museum offers walking trails and numerous classes, programs and tours. Admission is $4 ($2 for ages 6 through 14) and free for members. (Tip: If you have children and live here or spend a significant portion of time here, a CCMNH membership is a great investment!)

New England Fire & History Museum

1429 Rt. 6A, Brewster • 896-5711

Children have always been fascinated by fire engines, and here they can view a whole history of them. Kids can climb on antique fire trucks and a fireboat, eye an animated diorama of the Great Chicago Fire and even gawk at the fire-helmet collection of the late composer Arthur Fiedler. The complex also has blacksmith and apothecary shops and a picnic area. It's open daily from late May through mid-October and the rest of the year by appointment for tours. Admission is $4.50 ($2.50 for ages 5 through 12).

Railroad Museum

153 Depot Rd., Chatham • no phone

Take the kids here for a look at old cars and cabooses, models, relics and photos. (The Museum is on the National Register of Historic Places.) The constantly playing soundtrack of wheels and whistles adds to the railway atmosphere and appeals to kids who love those noises! Donations are accepted.

Minigolf and Amusements

Upper Cape

Adventure Isle

343 MacArthur Blvd., Bourne • 759-2636, (800) 53-KARTS

You could spend days at this complex, located 2 miles south of the Bourne Bridge, and still not have enough time to do — and ride — everything. Where should you start? The complex has bumper boats, a .2-mile go-cart track, minibike run, batting cages, a video arcade and a 25-foot super slide. Oh, did we mention the minigolf course and NBA tournament basketball game? Adventure Isle is open daily mid-March through the end of November.

Sandwich Minigolf

159 Rt. 6A, Sandwich • 888-1579

This 27-hole course is built on a former cranberry bog, and the architectural trademarks of the Cape, such as covered bridges, windmills, whales and sea horses, are incorporated in its designs. Best of all: The course features the world's only floating green! It's open daily mid-May through mid-September.

Mid-Cape

Cape Cod Storyland Golf

70 Center St., Hyannis • 778-4339

This 2-acre, 18-hole course is one of the largest minigolf course in New England. It's designed as a mini-version of the Cape, with each hole representing a Cape Cod town. Reproductions of historic buildings, ponds and waterfalls abound. When you've had enough putting around, take a spin on the bumper boats. It's open daily from mid-April through the end of October. Admission is $5 ($4 for ages 12 and younger).

Rainy Day Doings

The gardeners among us welcome rainy days, knowing that without enough moisture the Cape would be bereft of many of the plants and flowers that make it beautiful. For those on vacation, however, a rainy day can be challenging, especially if there are children involved. While you might be content to curl up in your cottage with a good book listening to the rain drum musically on the roof, a few hours of that will drive even the calmest child stir-crazy. Coloring books and puzzles will work only just so long — after that you'll be forced to pile the family into the car in search of adventure. Here are a few of our favorite rainy-day activities; many of them are listed in this chapter.

Libraries: Every town has one, and on rainy days, the children's librarians expect crowds and often schedule extra activities accordingly. See the Yellow Pages in the phone book or look in the gray pages under individual towns for the address and phone number of the library nearest you.

Bookstores: We love to browse in bookstores on rainy days. A few of our favorites are Parnussus Books in Yarmouthport (great for old books), Armchair Bookstore in Yarmouthport; the Blue Heron in Brewster, Compass Rose in Orleans and the Yellow Umbrella in Chatham. For used paperbacks (a rainy day doesn't have to be expensive), visit Rodney's Bookstore on Main Street, Hyannis, or Annie's Book Stop in Orleans.

Cape Cod Museum of Natural History: This Brewster museum will keep children — and adults — amused for hours. It is busier than usual on rainy days, but the plus side is that you're sure to meet other families to chat with.

Cape Cod Discovery Museum: Right on Route 28 in Dennisport, this is a great place to take kids rain or shine — but especially rain!

Cape Cod Mall: Expect crowds at this Hyannis mall on rainy days, but at least it's a diversion. There are plenty of shops, plus three anchor stores (see our Shopping chapter) and a lively food court.

— continued on next page

Photo: Peter Barnes

Don't let a rainy day get you down — a Cape bookshop will keep you entertained for hours.

Arcades: If you can stand the noise, bring your kids to Ryan Family Amusements, located in Cape Cod Mall and in Falmouth, South Yarmouth and Buzzards Bay.

Bowling: This is more popular than you might think, and it's a great family activity, especially when skies are not sunny.

Beaches: As long as it's not stormy, there's nothing wrong with a walk at the beach in the rain. We especially like going to the beach when there's a light mist falling, and fog gives the shoreline a mystical, ethereal look. Best of all, there are no crowds!

Ryan Family Amusements

Cape Cod Mall, Rt. 132, Hyannis • 775-5566

With three other area locations, in Falmouth, South Yarmouth and Buzzards Bay, Ryan Family Amusements offers pinball, Skee-Ball and video games along with children's games such as ride-on horses, air hockey and basketball.

Pirate's Cove

723 Main St., South Yarmouth • 394-6200

Befitting the Cape's history, this course even has a pirate ship in a fake pond surrounded by waterfalls and cliffs. Forget squirting frogs — kiddie prizes include pirate eye patches, tattoos and flags. In 1997 they added an additional 18 holes of minigolf. Pirate's Cove is open daily from mid-April through Columbus Day weekend. Admission is $6 ($5 for ages 12 and younger).

Lower Cape

Bud's Go-Karts

362 Sisson Rd., Harwich • 432-4964

Unique to the Lower Cape, this long-established go-cart center, easy to find on the corner of Route 28 and Sisson Road, rings all summer with the delighted shrieks and shouts of children going FAST! and loving it. You can get on the course for $5.

Grand Slam Entertainment

322 Rt. 28, Harwich • 430-1155

Batting cages — including one with fastballs as fast as 90 miles per hour! — are ready and waiting for your little sluggers. There are also bumper boats and arcade games. A good time to come ride the boats is on a hot day, when the lines will be short because everyone else will be at the beach and the bumper rides will splash (and cool) you. It's open daily mid-April through mid-October.

Trampoline Center

Rt. 28, Harwich • 432-8717

Boiiiinnnng! Up they go! Kids will have a great time jumping to their hearts' content. A dozen large trampolines in a fenced-in outdoor area are set at ground level, so even the smallest of small fry can fly high. Remember to follow the two rules: no shoes and no flips. The center is open daily from mid-June through Labor Day. The cost is $3 for 10 minutes.

Cape Escape

14 Canal Rd., Orleans • 240-1791

Right near the Orleans Rotary, this fun little minigolf center features 18 holes set in nautical surroundings, complete with waterfalls, ponds, boats and a water wheel. It's also right next door to two very child-friendly restaurants. It's open seven days a week in season.

Gift Barn

Rt. 6, Eastham • 255-7000

Just 1 mile north of the National Seashore Visitor Center, this family-run complex offers an 18-hole minigolf course. It has an arcade with pinball, video games and redemption games — kids love them, because they get to pick out their own prizes. It's open daily June through September, but there's also a great gift shop with lots of stuff for kids that's open springtime until Christmas Eve. Mini-golf costs $3 per person, $1.50 for replays.

Playgrounds

Children love playgrounds, and there are plenty of them on the Cape. Just find an elementary school and you're sure to find a playground. Remember, these are open to the public only when school is not in session. Some towns have playgrounds that are not at schools, a great plus because they are more accessible. Here are a few of our favorites:

Barnstable: Behind Barnstable West Elementary School on Route 6A is a wonderful, castle-like wooden playground that will keep kids busy for hours.

Yarmouthport: On Route 6A at the end of Union Street is a wide-open, grassy park where kids can run, plus a playground they can climb, swing and slide on. It's also a great place to meet other parents.

Dennisport: Tucked away on a side street behind Main Street, not far from the Harwich line, is a lovely park with a gazebo, and next to it, a great little playground. It features a fun train, climbing tower with a twisty-tunnel slide, swings and tires for climbing.

Harwich: Behind the elementary school on South Street is the Castle in the Clouds, a wonderful, community-built structure with towers, bridges and slides. Just a short walk across the yard is a great preschool play area, with a wooden train, tires to climb on, swings and plenty of sand.

Chatham: Across the street from the Railroad Museum, behind the Chatham Elementary School, is the Play-A-Round Playground, a multilevel wooden structure of twisting turrets, chutes, slides and bridges. It includes a playing area for disabled children and a fenced-in area for wee ones.

Orleans: Our favorite for simplicity is the park-like play area on Eldredge Parkway, across from the police station and next to the tennis courts. It has swings, slides, a sandbox, lots of room to run and a couple of simple climbers, and it's perfect for preschoolers. If your kids are a bit older and seeking something more challenging, go down the street to Orleans Elementary School and walk behind the school to the big wooden structure with bridges and tunnels.

Wellfleet: At Baker's Field across from Mayo Beach (on Kendrick Avenue, just past the harbor) is a sandy, spacious playground with something for all ages, including a huge structure with ladders, bridges and slides. It's a perfect alternative if your kids are bored with the beach. They won't be bored here!

Tours

Cape Cod Scenic Railroad
Main St., Hyannis • 771-3788

Kids will love taking a ride on this line, especially during the holiday season when Santa's on board. (The trips sell out quickly; reserve early!) During the rest of the year, the vintage three-car choo-choo chugs along on a 42-mile, 1¾-hour trek between Hyannis and Sagamore, stopping at the Sandwich depot and the Cape Cod Canal. Views of cranberry bogs and salt marshes await you on the trip. There are four departures daily mid-June through late October and limited runs during May, late November and December. Check with the office about ecology discovery tours, which include an on-board naturalist and a stopover at a conservation preserve in Sandwich. These tours are, unfortunately, infrequently offered (see our Tours and Excursions chapter). Scenic tours cost $11.50 ($10.50 for seniors and $7.50 for ages 3 through 12).

Cape Cod Potato Chip Company
Breed's Hill Rd., Hyannis • 775-7253

Is there a kid anywhere who doesn't love potato chips? They'll love seeing them made even more. The company offers five-minute, self-guided tours daily year round — and, yes, you get free crunchy samples at the end. Bet you can't visit just once!

Read All About It

When searching for activities for your children on the Cape, don't overlook libraries, which offer a lot more than just books. Cape libraries tend to be social centers, busy, stimulating places that offer many programs and activities — especially for children! Almost all the libraries on the Cape offer summer reading programs in which youngsters keep track of the books they read. In addition, there are craft classes and story hours — a real boon for parents of preschoolers. Wherever you are on the Cape, you're not far from a library; be sure to check the Yellow Pages for the ones nearest you. Here are just a few of our favorites.

Upper Cape

Sandwich Public Library
142 Main St., Sandwich • 888-0625

The library holds story hours three days a week, for toddlers and preschoolers; call for times and registration. The library also offers a variety of children's activities throughout the year, including a summer reading club.

Mid-Cape

Sturgis Library
3039 Main St., Barnstable • 362-6636

This lovely old library offers a Tuesday evening story time all year, beginning at 7 PM — a great way to get the little ones calmed down and ready for bed! A preschool story hour is held Fridays at 10 AM from September to June. Preregister to make sure your child gets a sticker with his or her name on it. The library also offers story/craft programs, puppet shows and puppet-making workshops. Call or stop by for a copy of the Children's Room newsletter for dates and times.

Lower Cape

Eldredge Public Library
564 Main St., Chatham • 945-5170

Regular story hours are held all year on Wednesdays at 11:15 AM for children ages 2 to 4 and Saturdays at 11:15 AM for ages 5 and 6. A number of special programs are scheduled throughout the year, including storytellers, folk singers, craft classes and holiday parties; call for dates and times. The library has a great children's room with a preschool play

Photo: Michael Galvin

A participant in the watermelon eating contest on July 4th bites off more than he can chew.

area, board games for older children and a study area.

Eastham Public Library

190 Samoset Rd., Eastham • 240-5950

This library has a nice children's room, with a terrific play area for little ones and a helpful children's librarian. Story hours are held all year on Fridays at 10:30 AM, and in summer, an evening story hour (pajamas optional) is held on Tuesdays or Thursdays. The library offers a variety of children's activities during the summer, including writing, drama and crafts classes.

Provincetown Public Library

330 Commercial St., Provincetown • 487-7094

Toddler story time is held at 10:30 AM on Wednesdays all year, and a story time for all ages takes place Saturdays at 10:30 AM all year. The summer reading program includes all sorts of classes such as acting, puppet making, crafts and science. The library, which has a great (and very active!) children's room, always has a theme to give recognition to children. Last year, more than 2,000 stars were hung with the names of children who participated in the reading program. Look for balloons in 1997!

Summer Camps and Creative Centers

Many a Cape Cod resident has childhood recollections of learning to swim and sail at a Cape Cod summer camp. With its numerous beaches, ponds and woods, this area is ideal for providing youngsters with outdoor education and recreation. The Cape also has outlets for youthful energies at its sports clinics and art-fostering creative centers.

Upper Cape

Camp Lyndon Cape Cod YMCA

Lawrence Rd., South Sandwich • 362-6500

A day camp for boys and girls from ages 3 to 15, Lyndon offers archery, games, sports, sailing and boating, a ropes challenge course, arts and crafts, kickball and soccer. Swimming (including instruction) and horseback riding (ages 6 to 12) are part of the program. Special events and one overnight stay are included. Bus transportation is available.

Camp Burgess-Hayward

75 Stowe Rd., South Sandwich • 428-2571

Set on 400 acres of land in an area that encompasses three ponds, these two camps — Burgess for boys and Hayward for girls — are traditional overnight camps run by the South Shore YMCA for children ages 7 to 15. The waterfront facility allows for sailing, windsurfing, water-skiing, basketball, volleyball and tennis. Other aspects of the program include a 30-foot climbing tower, a low and high ropes courses, arts and crafts, photography, rocketry and horseback riding. Sessions run for two weeks.

Camp Farley 4-H Outdoor Education Center

615 Rt. 130, Mashpee • 477-0181

This 32-acre camp on beautiful freshwater Mashpee-Wakeby Pond has both day and overnight programs for children ages 7 to 14. Activities range from arts and crafts and recreation to boating, canoeing and horseback riding. Environmental and nature programs are also included. Kids will love the miniature farm yard with goats, sheep, pigs and chickens. The camp is open in July and August.

Animal Friends Summer Camp

97 Megansett Rd., Cataumet • 563-6116

Operated for 48 years by the Educational Department of the Animal Rescue League in Boston, this day camp gives children ages 6 to 13 the opportunity to be around all types of animals, from cows, pigs, sheep and goats to rabbits and gerbils. Campers learn about animal care, therapeutic pet visitation, farm life, ocean ecology, nature exploration and crafts such as candle-making and macrame. The camp sits on 24 acres on Squeteague Harbor in Buzzards Bay.

The camp offers two programs, one for children in grades 1 through 3 and another for children from 3rd grade to age 13. For more information, contact the Animal Rescue League in Boston, (617) 426-9170, extension 119.

Mid-Cape

Cape Cod Gymnastics

340 Hockum Rock Rd., Dennis • 385-8216

Open year round with a variety of classes, Cape Cod Gymnastics offers a seven-week summer program for children 8 and older that culminates with a week of intensive daily training. Other classes are available for children as young as preschool age, including one for preschoolers and parents to take together. The gym-dandy class is geared to 5 and 6-year-olds, and a variety of other classes are offered for different ages and abilities. "It can be competitive or noncompetitive," says owner Marcia Leonard. "It's healthy, and it develops coordination."

YMCA Camp 132

2245 Iyanough Rd., Barnstable • 362-6500

The Y offers a weeklong day program for children ages 5 to 12 at its well-equipped facility. Children participate in arts and crafts, archery, sports, swimming (including lessons) in the Y pool and Friday field trips (the Boston Aquarium and whale watching are two possibilities). Rates vary by age. YMCA membership is not required, but you save 5 percent by belonging to the association.

Families can also come here just for a day to participate in programs such as the Saturday mini-sports day in which children get to work out with a fitness trainer and learn a little about different sports they may want to try. The Y also has an active swim team, offers swimming lessons for ages 6 months and older and youth basketball. The school vacation Fun Club is a real boon for working parents.

Camp Wingate-Kirkland

White Rock Rd., Yarmouthport • 358-5816, 362-3798

Since the late 1950s, this coeducational overnight youth camp has been offering sports, water activities, arts and crafts, camp craft, music and drama. Children have their choice of a seven-week session or one of the two 3½-week sessions.

Fair Acres Country Day School

35 Fair Acres Dr., Marstons Mills • 420-3288

With pretty Shubael Pond at its doorstep, this day camp for children ages 3 to 9 offers certified Red Cross swimming instruction, arts and crafts, nature studies, sports, tennis and drama. The program runs during July and August.

Lower Cape

Cape Cod Museum of Natural History

Rt. 6A, Brewster • 896-3867

The emphasis here is on — what else? — the great outdoors. The museum offers one- and two-week day camps for children in grades 1 through 6 in which they learn about everything from birds to dinosaurs. They even get to set up their own freshwater and saltwater aquariums. Twice a week, the museum holds preschool classes for ages 3 to 6. Drop-in visits are encouraged. Once a week, special two-hour Camp Safari sessions permit children to explore the outdoor world of ponds, woodlands and marshlands. The museum also offers an archaeology camp for preteens, and a Marine Science Camp specifically geared toward junior high students, with trips to such Cape areas as Monomoy Island.

Wellfleet Bay Wildlife Sanctuary

P.O. Box 236, South Wellfleet • 349-2615

Kids who want to go nose-to-nose with nature will appreciate the one-week natural history day camps held in July and August. Kids and teens in kindergarten through 9th grades are eligible. Classes include such top-

INSIDERS' TIP

Do you remember the thrill of finding your first horseshoe crab on the beach? These big, strange but harmless creatures are actually not crabs at all — they're related to spiders and are one of the world's most ancient life forms.

ics as "Bugs, Bugs and More Bugs," "Investigating Marine Life" and "On the Forest Floor." Students in the 6th to 9th grade camps can head off on excursions, such as whale watching in Provincetown or canoeing through Nauset Marsh.

Brewster Whitecaps Baseball Clinic

Community Center Field, Brewster • 896-3913

Batter up! Every week in July and August, the Brewster Whitecaps team sponsors weeklong clinics on the art of baseball, from how to bunt to how to hit a home run. Open to boys and girls ages 7 to 14, the clinic meets at the Community Center Field in front of town hall.

Cape Cod Sea Camps

P.O. Box 1880, Rt. 6A, Brewster • 896-3451

Established in 1922, Cape Cod Sea Camps is the oldest residential camp on the Cape. With beautiful grounds that stretch to Cape Cod Bay, it offers a seven-week residential camp for ages 7 to 17 and a day camp for ages 4 to 17. Instruction covers all sorts of watersports, including sailing, swimming, windsurfing, water-skiing and canoeing.

Chatham A's Baseball Clinic

Veteran's Field, Chatham • 945-5199

The weekly training programs conducted by the Chatham A's team helps boys and girls ages 6 to 17 master the dos and don'ts of baseball. Classes are held at the field, between Main Street and Depot Road (the entrance is on Main Street) from late June to mid-August.

Creative Arts Center

154 Crowell Rd., Chatham • 945-3583

Budding DaVincis and Cassetts will love the year-round classes in drawing, painting, pottery, photography, sculpture and jewelry making. Classes are flexible and open to a wide range of ages and skill levels.

Family School Summer Camp

RFD 2, Brewster • 896-6555

The Family School Summer Camp gives children the opportunity to take part in a myriad of classes and activities, including field and racket sports, carpentry, canoeing, dance, drama, farming and horseback riding. Courses run a maximum of eight weeks. Children up to age 15 are eligible for the camp.

Photo: Vincent DeWitt, Cape Cod Times

A child holds onto a foam rubber Noodle toy at Kalmus Beach in Hyannis.

Woodsong Farm Equestrian Center

121 Lund Farm Way, Brewster • 896-5555

There's plenty of horsing around going on at Woodsong Farm Equestrian Center, and that's a good thing for youngsters wanting to learn more about horses. The Center welcomes ages 5 to 11 for weeklong day classes (each limited to six participants) who learn via video instruction, lectures, hands-on demonstrations and daily mounts. Morning-only and daylong classes are available year-round at the center, which also boards horses and has its own tack shop. Two separate summertime programs are offered for both novice and experienced riders.

Orleans Cardinals Baseball Clinic

P.O. Box 504, Orleans • 255-0793

The Cardinals offer what is perhaps the finest baseball clinic on the Cape — and very affordable. At seven weeks in duration, the camp assures that every boy and girl will emerge a winner. The clinic begins in mid-June and is open to ages 6 to 13.

Academy of Performing Arts

5 Giddiah Hill Rd., Orleans • 255-5510

There's no business like show business, and the Academy of Performing Arts is out to prove it. More than 20 instructors teach classes ranging from dance (ballet, jazz, line and tap) to drama and creative writing for children and adults. How about clown classes? Or sign up for classes in how to play a musical instrument, everything from piano, cello and flute to saxophone, viola and guitar. Courses run two weeks in July and August with a graduation ceremony — a public performance to show off newfound talent. (Don't worry, everyone applauds.)

Summer Day Programs

Cable Rd., Eastham • 255-8000

Visitors get to mingle with locals during various recreational day programs held at the playground of Nauset High School from late June through mid-August. Courses vary summer to summer, but expect such temptations as archery, soccer and arts and crafts. Programs are for children ages 6 to 13 and run from 9 AM to noon. Campers take swimming instruction on weekday mornings on Great Pond in Wiley Park (the entrance is on Herringbrook Road). Adults must register their child for any or all activities. Registration takes place at the high school or at Wiley Park beginning at 8:30 AM.

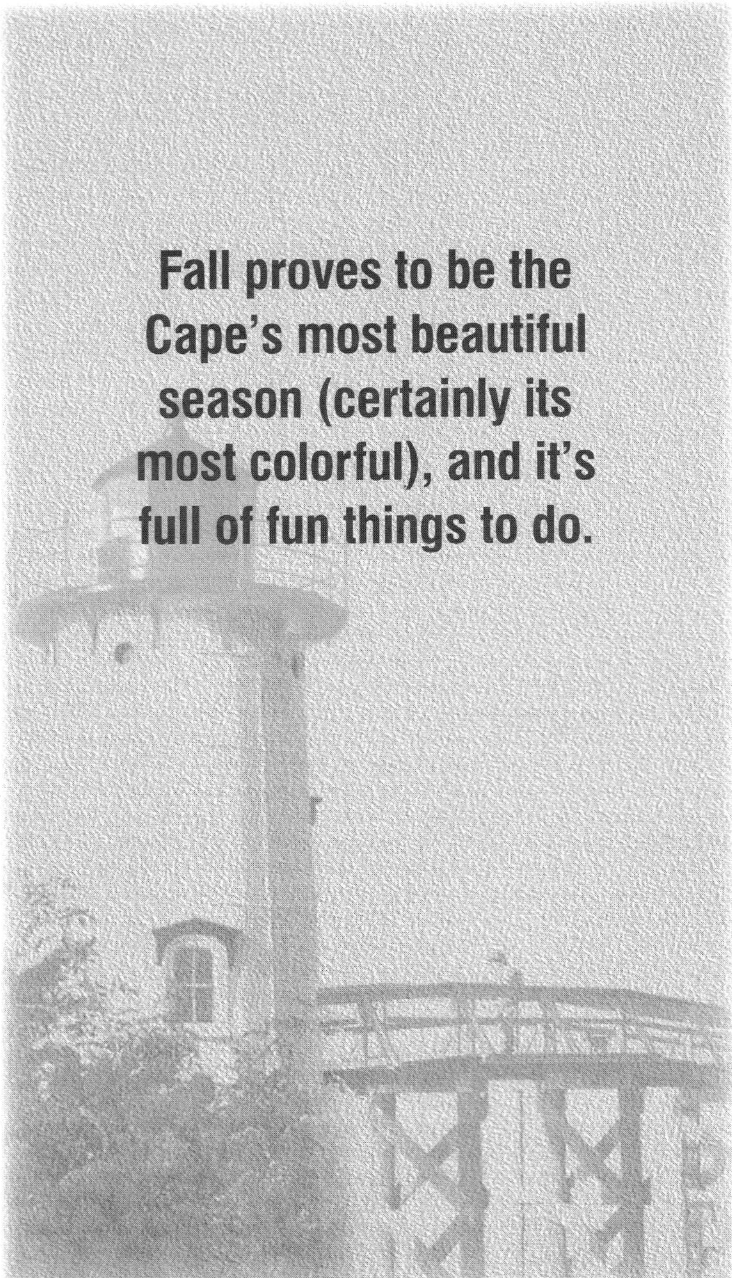

Fall proves to be the Cape's most beautiful season (certainly its most colorful), and it's full of fun things to do.

Annual Events

People on Cape Cod know how to have fun, and they prove it all year long with a full calendar of exciting annual events.

From Buzzards Bay Park to Provincetown's MacMillan Wharf, from Hyannis Village Green to Woods Hole's Nobska Light, from Eldredge Park in Orleans to the Barnstable Country Fairgrounds in East Falmouth, there are things happening throughout the 15 towns and the 12 months. And there's something on the docket for everyone.

The year begins with Chatham First Night, a town-wide celebration to usher in the new year. February keeps the fun coming with antiques shows and art auctions. Spring arrives in grand fashion with Falmouth's Annual Hat Parade, Easter egg hunts, home and garden shows and Osterville's Daff O'Ville Days.

The Brewster in Bloom Festival, walk-a-thons, biathlons, half marathons and a sailboat race from Hyannis to Nantucket and back wrap up the spring season.

June, heralding the beginning of the summer season, is a month full of strawberry festivals, chowder festivals and harbor festivals. The Blessing of the fleet at Provincetown is marked by a parade, events and religious observances. Across the Cape, the Cape Cod Baseball League begins action.

Fireworks, patriotic banners and flags mark the beginning of July, and arts and crafts fairs abound while village greens are alive with evening band concerts. The circus and fairs come to town, and in Mashpee the annual Wampanoag Powwow brings together Native Americans from across the nation for three days of tribal dances and events.

August begins with the Boston Pops Esplanade Orchestra at the Village Green in Hyannis. August is also the month when the Falmouth Road Race is run, the Cape Cod League holds its baseball playoffs and the annual Cape Cod Air show is held at Otis Air Base (unfortunately, in 1997 it is not being held but promises to return in 1998). Dennis holds its annual Festival Days and Orleans holds its annual Pops in the Park concert. Jimmy Connors, Bjorn Borg and other greats serve up the Mentadent Tennis Tournament of Champions in Mashpee.

Fall proves to be the Cape's most beautiful season (certainly its most colorful) and it's full of fun things to do. Pumpkins can be found at many autumnal roadside farm stands, but for a complete October experience you can obtain your grinning squash at the Bourne Farm Pumpkin Day or Harvest Day in Falmouth. The Cape Cod Marathon brings the physically fit to Falmouth at the end of October. Chatham by the Sea in November kicks off mid-month and continues through December. And what would December be without a Christmas Stroll?

Below, we present a rundown of some of the Cape's annual events. Since these events are worth traveling across the Cape for, we have arranged this chapter by month instead of region. You'll easily find what's going on when you're here by looking under the month categories. For a more complete listing of concerts and stage events, see our Arts and Entertainment chapter. For sporting events such as road races and triathlons, see our Spectator Sports chapter.

Unless we mention otherwise, the events listed here are free, with the exception of food costs.

January

Chatham First Night

Various sites in Chatham • 945-1122

As the old year becomes the new, the town of Chatham hosts a First Night celebration that includes a costumed road race, concerts and recitals, storytelling and hay rides. You can munch your way through the food concessions while awaiting a fireworks display at midnight over Oyster Pond. By purchasing a First Night button for around $5 you gain admission to all events; proceeds benefit the school's art and music departments. This New Year's Eve event is a great way to ring in another year on Cape Cod!

February

Early February

Cape Cod Kennel Club Show

Barnstable High School, 744 W. Main St., Hyannis • 394-1681

The Cape Cod Kennel Club holds two annual shows: The first is held on the first weekend of February at Barnstable High School and the other on the third weekend of September at the Barnstable County Fairgrounds, Route 151, East Falmouth. Any AKC-licensed dog that meets eligibility requirements is allowed to enter; applications must be submitted three weeks prior to the show. Spectator tickets cost $4 for adults and children older than 6; $2 for children younger than 6.

FYI

Unless otherwise noted, the area code for all phone numbers in this guide is 508.

Mid-February

President's Day Antique Show and Sale

Cape Codder Hotel, Rt. 132, Hyannis • 775-2280

Scheduled each year for the Saturday and Sunday of President's Day weekend, this show has more than 40 regional dealers who offer an array of antique furniture, glass and china. The doors open at 10 AM, and discount cards are available at the Hyannis Public Library, which sponsors the event. Admission is $3.

Second Annual Silent Art Auction

The Mews Restaurant, 429 Commercial St., Provincetown • 487-0600

The opening reception for this silent art auction, now in its second year, is held in the middle of February. Works of local artists remain on display until mid-March. This event is hosted by the Provincetown Repertory Theater.

Late February

Annual Close to Home Benefit

Provincetown Inn, 1 Commercial St., Provincetown • 487-9500

The Mayflower Room at Provincetown Inn is the setting for this annual evening of entertainment showcasing the talents of some 20 entertainers including singing, dancing, cabaret and comedy. It is held on the last Thursday of February. The Provincetown AIDS Support Group benefits from the proceeds. A $10 donation is requested.

March

Early March

Hyannis Half Marathon and 5-Mile Race

Barnstable High School, W. Main St., Hyannis • 888-4058

A 13.1 mile half-marathon and 5-mile race are run on the first Sunday in March. The races begin and end at Barnstable High School in Hyannis, and proceeds benefit the Barnstable High School scholarship for the cross-country team. Entry fees are $12 for the half-marathon and $10 for the 5-miler.

INSIDERS' TIP

September is the month when cranberries are harvested on Cape. A number of towns hold special festivals to honor the harvest of the native berry. Harwich holds a two-week celebration.

Mid-March

Annual Hat Parade & Tea Party

Main St., Falmouth • 540-2585

This annual event is a great way for all those Mad Hatters and March Hares out there to get into the spring spirit. In 1997 a tea party has been added to the usual hat parade format. Needless to say, Falmouth has a blast with this parade, which starts at 1 PM at the Village Green and ends at Peg Noonan Park where the Tea Party takes place. It's anybody's guess how many people will show up, but no matter how many participate, the hats are truly inspired, making it hard for judges to award prizes for creativity and originality. The Hat Parade is sponsored by the Falmouth Village Association.

Late March

Easter Egg Hunt

Falmouth Public Library, Main St., Falmouth • 540-2585

Hundreds of people hop over to the Falmouth Public Library to join in on this Easter fun. Children galore show up for this special event, usually held the day before Easter on the lawn of the library. (The eggs, by the way, are chocolate.) This is sponsored by the Falmouth Village Association.

April

Early April

Falmouth/Mashpee 31st Heart Fund Auction

Willowbend Country Club, 100 Willowbend Rd., Mashpee • 888-3300

Over the past 30 years this annual auction, which benefits the American Heart Association, has raised more than $1 million. Nearly 100 percent of this money stays on Cape for research and preventative medication. The event consists of a live and silent auction of such items as golf packages, tickets to major sporting events, tickets to the Cape Cod Symphony, gift certificates to area restaurants and even a chance to dive in the shark tank at the New England Aquarium! Tickets are $15.

39th Annual Rotary Home & Garden Show

Barnstable High School, W. Main Street, Hyannis • 362-5230

This annual two-day home show, now in its 39th year, is run by the Hyannis Rotary Club. About 125 display booths are set up in the Barnstable High School gymnasium and field house catering to all things that have to do with your home and garden — windows, landscape displays with water pools and gardens, underground water systems, security systems, pools, wooden playgrounds, etc. Tickets cost $2, and proceeds benefit local organizations.

Late April

Mashpee Daffodil Days

Mashpee Commons, Mashpee • 477-0792

With April come the daffodils, and Mashpee is one of a number of Cape towns to celebrate their return. Yellow is the color of the day as the Mashpee Beautification Council and the Mashpee Chamber of Commerce team up to sponsor town-wide events such as a pancake breakfast at Mashpee High School, plant sales and activities for the children.

Daff O'Ville Days

Various sites in Osterville • 428-6327

Sponsored by the Osterville Business and Professional Association, this village-wide celebration takes place during the last week in April. Events include an Arbor Day celebration, Mad Hatter Tea Party, bagpipe music, wine tastings and a book sale. The fun continues with outdoor grills, a fashion show and an antique car display. Special children's events keep the little ones busy, and daffodils beautify the village.

May

Early May

Cape Cod Marine Trades Boat Show

Marina Park, Scranton Ave., Falmouth • 548-2216

At Falmouth Harbor you'll be able to see every type of sailboat and powerboat from 40-footers to inflatables, some afloat and some on land. Marine dealers and boat manufacturers set up their wares, interspersed with information booths by such groups as boat insurance companies and the Coast Guard Auxiliary. Some of the proceeds from this three-day event go to the Cape Cod Regional Technical High School.

Brewster in Bloom

Various locations in Brewster • 896-8088

Spring has sprung, and Brewster is blooming! The Brewster in Bloom Festival includes four days of fun and games — a golf tournament, dance, flea market, road race, parade, band concert, crafts fair, food tasting and children's activities. And all the while there are more than 100,000 daffodils lining the streets! In 1997 the festival takes place in early May but some other years it falls in late April.

Old Timers Softball League

Fields throughout the Mid- and Lower Cape • 255-8206

The 55-plus players take the field across the Mid- and Lower Cape. Throughout the spring and summer these old timers provide exciting softball action, culminating in the Cape Classic Softball Tournament in September (see

INSIDERS' TIP

Interested in knowing more about annual events happening in a Cape town you'll be visiting? Call the town's chamber of commerce for a complete listing. Chamber phone numbers are listed in our Overview chapter.

below and our Spectator Sports chapter). Admission is free.

Mid-May

Cape Maritime Week

Cape-wide • 362-3828

History galore! Maritime Week is a major Cape-wide event that highlights the landmarks and sites comprising Cape Cod's wealth of maritime history. This mid-May celebration is coordinated by the Cape Cod Commission, which arranges lighthouse tours, Coast Guard open houses, special cruises, walks and lectures throughout the week. In Yarmouthport, a village that was once a major port, for example, you can take self-guided walking tours of sea captains' homes and attend open houses at museums, getting from place to place via the free trolley service.

Sixth Annual Cape Cod Canal Striped Bass Fishing Tourney

Bourne • 759-6000

For the sixth year, the Canal Region Chamber of Commerce is sponsoring this popular nine-day tournament to promote the natural resources of the Canal. It starts the third Saturday of the month. Sign up to win cash awards and prizes. Entrance fees are $20 for adults and $10 for children 15 and younger.

Herb Festival

Green Briar Nature Center, 6 Discovery Hill Rd., East Sandwich • 888-6870

Benefitting the Thornton Burgess Society, this event held over three days offers lectures on herbs, special demonstrations and exhibits and wildflower garden walks. You can get a taste of the herbs at a wonderful luncheon (reservations required) and buy plants just in time to start your own herb garden.

March of Dimes WalkAmerica

Falmouth • 790-1093

This is an annual fund-raising event that begins at Casino by the Sea in Falmouth Heights and is expected to follow the Falmouth Road Race route (see our Spectator Sports chapter). The course is 8 miles long.

Amateur Golf Tournament

Cranberry Valley Golf Course, 183 Oak St., Harwich • 430-7560

Find out if you have what it takes to hit 'em like the pros by entering the Amateur Golf Tournament at Cranberry Valley Golf Course in Harwich. It's held every Mother's Day weekend. The event is open to all amateurs with established USGA handicaps. Entrance fees are $95 per person or $190 for a team of two.

Spring Fling

Downtown Chatham • 945-5199

Chatham gets a little crazy with spring fever in May with its annual Spring Fling. There's a wild and crazy hat parade, clowns, jugglers, a pet show and face painting, Sponsored by the Chatham Merchants Association, this family-oriented event is held on the Saturday of Mother's Day weekend.

Late May

Rhododendron Festival

Heritage Plantation, Grove and Pine sts., Sandwich • 888-3300

One of the largest and best collections of rhododendrons is found in Sandwich, and many are in bloom for this event. Plantation tours, lectures and plant sales fill the schedule. Festival date varies depending on when the rhododendrons bloom so call ahead for the current year's schedule.

Johnny Kelley Half Marathon and Five Miler

Hyannis • 775-6800

This annual half marathon and 5-mile race is named for the man who ran in more Boston Marathons than any other runner. This race benefits the Cape Cod Hospital Foundation. (See our Spectator Sports chapter.)

Figawi Sailboat Race & Charity Ball

Hyannis • (800) 4HYNNIS

Generally considered the largest sailboat race on the East Coast, the Figawi usually draws more than 200 boats in a highly competitive race from Hyannis to Nantucket. A cocktail party greets contestants at Nantucket and the following day is filled with an awards ceremony, afternoon clambake and evening Memorial Day party. The reverse Figawi from Nantucket to Hyannis is followed by another party and another awards presentation! It's just party, party, party! It all takes place on Memorial Day weekend, launched by a black-tie Figawi Charity Ball (another party!) at the Tara Hyannis Hotel and Resort the weekend before the race. Proceeds aid local charities.

Artisan's Guild of Cape Cod Arts and Crafts Shows

Nauset Middle School, Rt. 28, Orleans • 385-4899

The 25-year-old Artisans' Guild of Cape Cod hosts five arts and crafts shows during the year; the first takes place on Memorial Day weekend. (The others are held in early July, early August, mid October and late November.) Summer shows are held on the front lawn of the Nauset Middle School, all others are held in the school's gymnasium.

Memorial Day Ceremonies

Various towns

Many towns on Cape hold Memorial Day ceremonies and parades, check the local papers for events. Memorial services are held at the National Cemetery in Bourne.

June

Early June

Annual Antique Show & Sale

Heritage Plantation, Sandwich • 833-2904

Now in its 19th year, this long-running show attracts more than 50 top-quality dealers from all over New England. Sponsored by the Cape Cod Antique Dealers Association, antiques lovers flock to this affair, where displays include baskets, antique jewelry, glass, decoys and tinware. Ticket prices are $8 for adults, $7 for seniors, $4 for children and free for children younger than 5.

Taste of Mashpee

Mashpee Commons, Mashpee • 477-0792

If you've got a hankering for some good food but you can't make up your mind what you want, stop by Mashpee Commons on a Sunday in early June. Under a tent is where you'll find a sampling from a number of area restaurants, all yours for one admission fee. Proceeds benefit the Mashpee Chamber of Commerce.

Hyannis Harbor Festival and Blessing of the Fleet

Bismore Park, Hyannis • (800) 4HYNNIS

This event has something special for everyone. The Harbor Festival features sailboat races, maritime exhibits, live music, food and crafts galore. You can also get your boat blessed. A Kids Fest at Aselton Park on Ocean Street features games, activities, rides, food and entertainment. And you can also get in on the annual WCOD Chowder Fest, a must for those seeking the best chowder on Cape; call the radio station at 775-6800 for information.

Mid-June

Cape Cod Baseball League

11 North Rd., Harwich • 432-3878

The 10 teams of the Cape Cod League play ball from mid-June to mid-August from Wareham to Orleans. Teams consist of college players from across the country. An all-star game is held at the end of July, and playoffs take place in mid-August (see our Spectator Sports chapter).

Heritage Week

Cape-wide • 888-1233

A "celebration of the cultural, historical and environmental heritage of Cape Cod," this observation has become an exciting annual event that involves museums, organizations and individuals in every town. During the week, you can take part in special walks and tours, open houses, lectures and theater productions throughout the Cape. Visitors and Cape residents alike will enjoy exploring cemeteries, windmills, waterfronts and main streets with a knowledgeable guide. Highlights for 1997 include costumed village tours, historical reenactments and a celebration of the history of Cape Cod theater. The weeklong schedule of events is sponsored by Heritage Cape Cod

Photo: Stephen Rose, Cape Cod Times

Fairgoers enjoy the Swinger at the Barnstable County Fair in Hatchville.

(phone number above). Obtain a calendar of events by calling 362-3225.

Late June

Strawberry Festival

St. Barnabas Church, Falmouth • 548-8500

About a century ago Falmouth was one of the largest producers of strawberries in the eastern United States. Today, locals mark this event on their calendars and it seems that everyone in town shows up to feast on fresh, luscious strawberries from Tony Andrews Farm in East Falmouth. You can also buy crafts and baked goods throughout the day.

NSRA Classic Car Parade

Main St., Falmouth • 548-8500

The Falmouth Village Association sponsors this annual antique car parade on Main Street. It is usually held on the fourth weekend of the month.

Willowbend Children's Charity Pro-Am

Willowbend Country Club, 100 Willowbend Rd., Mashpee • 539-5000

The greatest names in golf, including Greg Norman, John Daly and Nick Faldo, have competed in this annual Pro-Am with such pro sports stars as quarterback John Elway and Hall of Fame hockey defenseman Bobby Orr. The event benefits children's programs on the Cape (see our Spectator Sports chapter).

Sounds of Summer Pops Concert

Hyannis Village Green, Hyannis • (800) 4HYNNIS

Quickly becoming a tradition is this melodic summertime concert featuring Cape Cod's own symphony led by conductor Royston Nash. Woodwinds, brass and strings all come together at the Village Green in the center of the much happening Hyannis. Tickets are $10 for lawn seats, $20 for chair seats and $50 for table seats.

Lobster Roll Luncheon and Lawn Sale

First Federated Church, Main St., Hyannis • 775-0298

This year marks the 40th anniversary for this delicious luncheon series. Lobster rolls and other types of sandwiches are served. Proceeds from luncheon sales and the accompanying lawn sale benefit the church. The luncheon and sale are held every Friday afternoon from late June to early September. They even do take-out!

Brewster Home Tour

Various sites in Brewster • 896-3867, (800) 479-3867

If you've ever wanted to walk through some of the quaint and gorgeous homes in this Cape Cod village, here's your chance. The Friends of the Cape Cod Museum of Natural History sponsors this home tour in which various Brewster homes and gardens are open for visits on a Saturday in late June. Refreshments are included. Tickets can be purchased at the Cape Cod Museum of Natural History for $15.

Brewster Historical Society Antiques Fair

Drummer Boy Field, Rt. 6A, Brewster • 896-7389

You're bound to find something very old among the more than 75 dealers selling their wares at this very popular show and sale, now in its 24th year. It's held on the last Saturday of June on the Drummer Boy Museum grounds, and as a special bonus the on-site Old Higgins Farm windmill is open for the event.

The Blessing of the Fleet

Commercial St., Provincetown • 487-3424

This tradition of blessing the Provincetown fishing fleet dates back to 1947. It takes place in late June. Various religious and secular events mark the occasion, including a Friday night banquet and Sunday mass at St. Peter's Church followed by a jubilant, colorful parade to Fisherman's Wharf, where decorated vessels await the official blessing. This year's events (1997) will include a Portuguese festival and fireworks.

July

Early July

Independence Day Fireworks and Events

Various sites

Many towns across the Cape offer spectacular fireworks displays to celebrate Independence Day. Plan to arrive by dusk at one of the following locations: Falmouth Heights, Hyannis Harbor, Orleans and Provincetown Harbor. Hyannis also hosts a July 4th boat parade in the harbor, Falmouth has a blessing of the fleet, Harwich has a July 4th Family Fun Day with a craft fair and entertainment. Orleans has a parade as does Wellfleet, while Provincetown goes over the top with its festivities including a parade and street entertainment. The Community of Jesus in Orleans, 240-2400, hold a Star Spangled Spectacular Festival complete with a band concert and fireworks.

Mashpee Wampanoag Powwow

Douglas C. Pocknett Field, Rt. 130, Mashpee • 477-0208

Open to the public, this event is sponsored by the Mashpee Wampanoag Tribal Council and features tribal dances and other activities such as the native fireball game, princess contests, a road race, traditional clambake and Native American crafts. This popular three-day event attracts Native Americans from many other states and always takes place July Fourth weekend.

The Whale's Eye and All Cape Craft Shows

Various locations • 945-3084

All Cape Craft Shows consist of a series of 11 craft shows at various locations across the Cape. There are three shows in July at the Dennis-Yarmouth High School in South Yarmouth — a two day show early in the month, a one-day event mid-month and another two-day event late month. Also in mid-July, there is a two-day show at the Chatham Elementary School. In early August there are a two-day event at Chatham Elementary

School and a one-day show at Waquoit Congregational Church in East Falmouth. Mid-August sees shows again in Chatham and South Yarmouth; a late August two-day show at Ezra Baker Elementary School in West Dennis and another two-day event at Dennis-Yarmouth High. The Greek Orthodox Church is the site of a late-November two-day show.

Concerts in the Park

Buzzards Bay Park, Buzzards Bay • 759-6000

The music ranges from country and western to jazz and from show tunes to rock and roll at this music series held at Buzzards Bay Park gazebo. Join the fun every Thursday night during July and August. Admission is free.

19th Annual Arts & Crafts Street Fair

Main St., Falmouth • 548-8500

Hosted by the Falmouth Village Association, this event features more than 200 artisans and craftspeople displaying their wares. You'll also find plenty of food and fun entertainment throughout the day.

Clyde Beatty Cole Bros. Circus

Barnstable County Fairgrounds, Rt. 151, East Falmouth • 563-3200

Lions and tigers and bears, oh my! The circus returns to the Barnstable Fairgrounds in July to the joy of children across the Cape. For three days this three-ring circus entertains packed tents with acrobatics, animal acts and, of course, some clowning around.

PIXY Chili & Wings Challenge

Cape Cod Melody Tent, West End Rotary, Hyannis • 778-2888

Bring your appetite to this chili and wings fest sponsored by WPXC radio, a rock station on Cape. Twenty local restaurants that take chili and wings seriously cook up their very best recipes and let the public decide whose is the best. The afternoon also includes live music, known as the Rock and Rose Music Festival, which features a dozen local bands. Proceeds benefit a number of organizations including the Nam Vets.

Wellfleet Arts & Crafts Shows

Wellfleet Cinemas Complex, Rt. 6, Wellfleet • 349-9767

If you're in search of that perfect Cape Cod souvenir or piece of artwork to grace a wall back home, you're bound to find what you seek here. Shows are held throughout the summer: for two days during early July, two days during the first week of August, two days during the second week of August and another two days during the last week of August. You can call the above number for a schedule.

Mid-July

16th Annual Sandcastle Competition

South Cape Beach, Mashpee • 477-0792

South Cape Beach is the site of this annual sandcastle competition. Five categories: five to seven years of age, eight to 10, 11 to 13, 14 to 16 and family try their hand at sculpting sand. You are allowed three hours to produce your Camelot; judging is at noon. Preregistration is requested.

St. George's Greek Fair

St. George Greek Orthodox Church, Rt. 28, Centerville • (800) 4HYNNIS

This is a three-day fair like no other, featuring great food like you've never tasted before. Besides the wonderful Greek food (ah, the stuffed grape leaves and Retsina wine!) there's a great crafts fair and bake sale as well as

INSIDERS' TIP

Each August the annual Pops by the Sea concert is held on the Hyannis Village Green featuring the Boston Pops and an honorary guest conductor who leads the orchestra during the Washington Post March. Past guest conductors have been Walter Cronkite, Art Buckwald, Paula Zahn, Olympia Dukakis and Julia Child (who used, instead of a baton, a large wooden spoon!).

high-spirited dancing and a guided tour of the uniquely domed Greek Orthodox Church.

Cape Cod Book, Print and Paper Fair

Cape Cod Community College, Rt. 132, Hyannis • 888-6870

Sponsored by the Thornton Burgess Society in Sandwich, this event — known in the past as the Antiquarian Book Fair — is a good way to add to your collection of treasured books. Come and examine the antique or out-of-print inventory of more than 70 book dealers. Proceeds benefit the educational programs of the Thornton Burgess Society dedicated "to inspire reverence for wildlife and concern for the natural environment." (See our Attractions chapter.)

FYI

Unless otherwise noted, the area code for all phone numbers in this guide is 508.

Cape Cod Family Fair

Dennis-Yarmouth High School, Station Ave., South Yarmouth • 778-1008

The key word is fun, and the Cape Cod Family Fair features plenty of it with music, children's hands-on crafts and games, rides, shows, demonstrations, food and pony rides. This event is presented by the Yarmouth Chamber of Commerce. Parents, make sure this one is on your calendar. Admission is $2, and it's free for children younger than 12.

Sunday Evening Concerts

Drummer Boy Museum grounds, Rt. 6A, Brewster • 255-7045

Every Sunday evening throughout the summer musicians offer free outdoor concerts at the Gazebo at Drummer Boy grounds on Route 6A. It's a wonderful time complete with a view of Cape Cod Bay off in the distance.

22nd Annual Harwich Professional Arts and Crafts Festival

Brooks Park, Oak St., Harwich • 385-8689, (800) 441-3199

This mid-month event features more than 100 professional craftspeople and artisans offering their handcrafted works of art for sale. The arts and crafts festival is held over two days. A similar event is held in August (see below).

30th Annual Originals Arts & Craft Shows

Wellfleet Drive-In and Cinemas, Rt. 6A, Wellfleet • 349-9767

Some 125 artisans from Cape Cod and nationwide bring their handicrafts to sell mid-month on Tuesday and Wednesday. Some of the artwork you'll find here has shown in some of the finest galleries across the country. In the past this event has been held at the Nauset Regional High School, but in 1997 it will be held at the Wellfleet Cinemas complex.

Late July

Barnstable County Fair

Rt. 151, East Falmouth • 563-3200

A Cape Cod tradition for more than 130 years, the Barnstable County Fair regularly attracts well over 100,000 people during its annual weeklong run. Adults and children win prizes for baked goods, canned goods, homegrown fruits and vegetables, quilts and other handiwork as well as for the best sheep, pigs, cows and poultry. Top-name entertainment fills the bill in the evenings. A petting zoo and carnival rides and games make the Barnstable County Fair so exciting for kids. It's a Cape Cod classic.

Mashpee Night at the Pops

Mashpee Commons, Mashpee • 477-5400

Mashpee puts together an unbeatable combination: the Cape Cod Symphony Orchestra featuring conductor Royston Nash and a fireworks display. Just bring your own chair. It's sponsored by the Mashpee Community Concert Committee. It's generally held on the last Saturday in July.

August

Early August

Hospice of Cape Cod Auction

Ocean Edge, 2907 Rt. 6A, Brewster • 362-1103

The Hospice of Cape Cod holds its annual

auction in early August with the support of area merchants and artisans, who donate goods and services that fetch reasonable prices. This year marks the auction's 10th anniversary. Proceeds help support the Cape's only hospice. The auction is usually hosted by a celebrity chairperson; for the past few years it has been hosted by Orleans summer resident and actor Gavin MacLeod (of *Mary Tyler Moore* and *The Love Boat*) and his wife, Patti.

International Irish Festival

Massachusetts Military Reservation, Falmouth • 540-0111

Follow the sounds of the fiddle and bodhran to enjoy Irish singing and dancing, Celtic displays, an art gallery, horse show and poetry reading. It is typically held over three days in early August. Erin go bragh!

Pops by the Sea

Hyannis Village Green, Hyannis • 790-2787

This is it — the most popular concert on Cape! The Boston Pops Esplanade Orchestra comes to town with conductor Harry Ellis Dickson to perform some wonderful late-afternoon music, both classical and popular tunes as well as patriotic marches and sing-a-longs. Held at the Hyannis Village Green, the concert usually takes place on the first Sunday of the month and is sponsored by the Arts Foundation of Cape Cod. Lawn seats cost $15 ($20 the day of the concert) and premium seats cost $25.

22nd Annual Harwich Professional Arts and Crafts Festival

Brooks Park, Oak St., Harwich • 385-8689, (800) 441-3199

Held in the beginning of August, this event features more than 100 professional artists and craftsmen offering their handcrafted works of art for sale. This crafts festival is held over two days.

Fine Arts Work Center Annual Benefit Auction

24 Pearl St., Provincetown • 487-9960

You'll find a little bit of everything here — from works of fine art to jewelry to furniture to clothing. Merchandise and services are donated to this live auction by area merchants and residents; proceeds help support the Work Center's fellowship programs.

Mid-August

Peter Rabbit's Animal Fair

Henry T. Wing School, Rt. 130, Sandwich • 888-6870

The Thornton Burgess Society sponsors this event geared to younger folk, who will love the live animal exhibits, pet rabbit show, music, refreshments and games. Burgess items are available for purchase.

Falmouth Road Race

Falmouth • 540-7000

This year (1997) marks the 25th running of the Falmouth Road Race, an international event that attracts thousands of onlookers and some 8,000 runners from across the country and around the world to challenge its 7.1 mile course (see our Spectator Sports chapter for more information).

Mentadent Tennis Tournament of Champions

Willowbend Country Club, 100 Willowbend Rd., Mashpee • 539-5700

Some of the greatest names in tennis such as Jimmy Connors and Bjorn Borg have battled it out in this 35-and-older tourney held over five days (see our Spectator Sports chapter).

Centerville Old Home Week

Various sites in Centerville • 775-1787

Among the special moments of the Centerville Old Home Week are a reunion dinner, an ice-cream social with the legendary Four Seas ice cream, lectures, a tea party and country line-dancing outside in front of the recreation building. A good time is always had by all. Old Home Week takes place in mid-August, and proceeds benefit the Centerville Library.

West Barnstable Village Festival

Library and Community Center, West Barnstable • 362-3231

Look for free fun and community spirit with book sales, children's games and activities, a photography contest, raffles and plenty of food. This event is sponsored by the West Barnstable Fire Department and Whelden Memorial Library.

Craftsmen Fair

Drummer Boy Museum grounds, Rt. 6A, Brewster • 385-2970

The Society of Cape Cod Craftsmen has been sponsoring this popular crafts showcase for the past 45 years, making it the second-oldest crafts organization in New England! The three-day craft celebration featuring 50 craftspeople is held in mid-August.

Nauset Originals Art Show

Wellfleet Drive-In Theater & Cinemas, Rt. 6, Wellfleet • 349-9767

More than 200 Cape-based and national vendors gather outdoors on the third Monday and Tuesday of August to sell their wares at one of the largest summer art shows on Cape. Here you will find everything from pottery to paintings, clothes to china dolls. Refreshments are available.

Late August

Fourth Annual New England Jazz Festival

Mashpee Commons, Mashpee • 477-5400

This evening of music under the stars proves jazz is alive and well on the Cape. This popular summertime event features many local jazz musicians and is held at Mashpee Commons over Labor Day weekend and is sponsored by the Boch Center for the Performing Arts. Ticket prices range from $15 to $28 depending on who is performing.

Antique and Collectible Glass Show and Sale

Cape Codder Hotel, Rt. 132, Hyannis • 888-0251

The Sandwich Glass Museum has sponsored this late-August glass show for the past nine years. More than 60 glass dealers from throughout the United States display samples of antique and contemporary glass. Of course, rare and not-so-rare Sandwich glass are also on display. Proceeds from this event benefit the Sandwich Glass Museum. Admission is $5.

Dennis Festival Days

Various sites in Dennis • 398-3568, (800) 243-9920

Now in its 39th year, the Annual Dennis Festival Days is a weeklong end-of-summer celebration held at various locations in town. Activities include kite-flying and sandcastle-building contests, an antique auto parade, a jazz concert and cookout, river cruises, hay rides, farm tours, flower shows, an arts and crafts fair and fireworks at West Dennis Beach. One highlight that always brews excitement is the Annual Great Beer Race, in which waiters and waitresses from local restaurants weave through an obstacle course carrying pitchers of beer on trays.

Eighth Annual Pops in the Park

Eldredge Park, Orleans • 225-1386

Grab your lawn chair or blanket, pack a picnic dinner and enjoy the music. The Annual Pops in the Park, held in Eldredge Park in Orleans, is an outdoor concert by the Cape Cod Symphony Orchestra, conducted by Royston Nash. It's always an enchanted evening of music and fun. The concert is held the fourth Saturday of the month. Tickets cost $50 for table seats, $20 for chair seats, $15 for the lawn and $5 for children 16 and younger.

Carnival Week

Various locations in Provincetown • 487-2313

Just when you thought you had seen it all in P-town, along comes Carnival Week! Sponsored by the Provincetown Business Guild, this weeklong celebration features musical productions, guesthouse parties, balls, nightclub entertainment and an outrageous parade complete with floats and entertainers. A splendid time is guaranteed for all!

Provincetown AIDS Support Group Silent Auction

Universalist Unitarian Meeting House, 236 Commercial St., Provincetown • 487-9445

This Provincetown auction is held every Labor Day Weekend and is attended by tourists, residents and even some celebrities who bid on everything from works of art to furniture and jewelry. Proceeds benefit the town's AIDS support programs. Nearly every Provincetown artist contributes art work to this worthy cause.

September

Early September

Bourne Scallop Fest

Buzzards Bay Park, Buzzards Bay • 759-6000

For 28 years Bourne has hosted the largest scallop festival on the East Coast. Thousands converge on Buzzards Bay Park over three days to sample the seafood and attend the crafts fair. There are children's games, rides, plenty of entertainment and, of course, scallops!

Harwich Cranberry Harvest Festival

Various sites • 430-2811

Since it started as part of the National Bicentennial Celebration in 1976, the Harwich Cranberry Harvest Festival has grown into a weeklong town-wide extravaganza. The week is filled with many events, including a carnival, a parade, fireworks, a road race, an arts and crafts festival (the largest in New England), a classic car show, sailboat races, softball games, food tasting . . . the list goes on and on. This is the post-summer event you cannot miss!

Cape Classic Softball Tournament

Harwich High School, Oak St., Harwich • 255-8206

Held during the first weekend of the Harwich Cranberry Harvest Festival, this three-day tournament features seniors over the age of 55 from all over New England (see our Spectator Sports chapter).

Eastham Windmill Weekend

Various locations in Eastham • 255-6032

This is Eastham's big day! Windmill Weekend is a community celebration, featuring a parade, road race, games, sand castle competition, entertainment, kids' activities and an arts and crafts show. The whole event centers around the Eastham grist mill, which was built in Plymouth way back in the 17th century. The mill is opened to visitors during the festivities (see our Attractions chapter).

Mid-September

Coastweeks

Various locations • 289-2398, (617) 727-9530

This three-week, statewide coastal celebration includes a beach cleanup sponsored by Massachusetts Coastal Zone Management. It runs from mid-September to early October. For a calendar of events call 289-2398, or to volunteer for a beach cleanup call (617) 727-9530.

INSIDERS' TIP

The town of Orleans is celebrating its bicentennial in 1997 with a year-long celebration starting in March. A 200th anniversary Founder's Day observance was recognized on March 2 with a birthday celebration. A bicentennial Liberty Tree was planted on Arbor Day in April. The Fourth of July will feature a huge parade. At the end of August an Old Home Week is planned around the Cape Cod Symphony's "Pops in the Park" concert, an antique car parade, school reunions, dances, a beach party complete with bonfire and a half-marathon. A bicentennial dinner is scheduled for early September. For an up-to-date calendar of events write to: Bicentennial Commission, Orleans Town Offices, 19 School Road, Orleans, Mass. 02653. To learn a bit about the history of Orleans see our Historic Cape Cod and Attractions chapters.

Yarmouthport Historic Open House

Historic Society of Old Yarmouth, Strawberry Ln., Yarmouthport • 362-3021
Winslow Crocker House, 250 Rt. 6A, Yarmouthport • 362-4385

Two historic Yarmouthport homes are open to the public: the Winslow Crocker House, built in 1780, and the Bangs Hallet House, 1840. Both houses are filled with beautiful period antiques. The open house is sponsored by the Society for the Preservation of New England Antiquities, which owns the Winslow Crocker House, and the Historic Society of Old Yarmouth, which is headquartered in the Bangs Hallet House. (See our Attractions chapter for more information on both houses.)

Antiques Fair

Drummer Boy Museum, Rt. 6A, Brewster • 255-7045

This year (1997) is the premier for the Fall antiques fair to be held on the Drummer Boy Museum grounds in Brewster. See the listing for the Antiques Fair in June at the same location.

A Taste of Harwich

Cape Cod Regional Technical High School, Rt. 124, Harwich • 432-1600

Get a taste of Harwich, all under one roof. This evening event, sponsored by the Harwich Chamber of Commerce, allows you to sample fine cuisine from a number of Harwich restaurants. A Taste of Harwich takes place during the Harwich Cranberry Harvest Festival. First seating is $17 per person, second seating is $14.

Provincetown Art Association Annual Consignment Auction

460 Commercial St., Provincetown • 487-1750

Every year since 1979 this has been an auction (and art) lover's dream come true. The items put on the block here are consigned by collectors, assuring only first-rate works of art by area artists. Dealers and collectors from around the country attend. Proceeds help to fund the Provincetown Art Association's programs and exhibitions.

Late September

Sandwich Boardwalk Celebration

Sandwich Town Beach parking lot, Sandwich • 888-1233

In 1990 Hurricane Bob damaged the original Sandwich Boardwalk. The October 1990 "No Name Storm" sounded the death knell. Rebuilding the boardwalk was a community effort, and so is this celebration. Come enjoy professional kite-flying and live entertainment, special activities such as a bicycle safety clinic, a dunk tank, pony rides and a chance to make your own kite. A great way to close out the summer, it's usually planned for the fourth Sunday of September.

22nd Annual Bird Carvers' Festival

Cape Cod Museum of Natural History, 869 Rt. 6A, Brewster • 896-3867 ext. 15, (800) 479-3867

The Annual Bird Carvers' Festival is one of the oldest wildlife-carving exhibitions in the country. It is usually held on the third weekend of September. At the event, which is a fund-raiser for the Cape Cod Museum of Natural History, experience a world of decoys and miniatures as well as nature walks, carving demonstrations, birds of prey exhibits and bird-house-building tips.

Fall for Orleans Festival

Various sites in Orleans • 255-1386

We can't think of a better way to move from September into October than with the Annual Fall for Orleans Festival. This is a weekend-long showcase featuring an antique car parade, a fashion show, sidewalk sales, his-

INSIDERS' TIP

On Cape Cod there are three Barnstables: the village of Barnstable in the town of Barnstable in the county of Barnstable. One of the villages in the town of Barnstable is Hyannis (bet you thought Hyannis was a town!).

toric house tours, a Fall Ball and even a pet parade! The event is held the last part of September and the first part of October.

October

Early October

6th Annual Harvest Day

Falmouth • 548-5271

What better way to spend a crisp fall day than at Falmouth's Annual Harvest Day. The Cape Cod Farmers Market, face painting, pumpkin totem pole, pumpkin decorating, dried-flower arrangements — they add up to autumn fun. The Village Association sponsors this affair the first Saturday of the month.

Mid-October

Bourne Farm Pumpkin Festival

Rt. 28A, near Thomas Landers Rd., West Falmouth • 548-0711

At the Bourne Farm Pumpkin festival you can buy your Halloween pumpkin and receive a tour of the farm's 300-year-old house and grounds as well. This historic pumpkin fest usually takes place on the second Saturday in October.

Octoberfest

Mashpee Commons and Deer Crossing, Mashpee • 477-0792

Mashpee adds to the autumn fun with its very own two-day Octoberfest celebration complete with an arts and crafts show and rides for the children. The festivities are presented by Mashpee Leisure Services. This great family event is held over Columbus Day Weekend.

Yarmouth Seaside Festival

John Simpkins Elementary School, Rt. 28, South Yarmouth • 778-1008

The town of Yarmouth goes all out for this major event, so come enjoy a parade, arts and crafts, plenty of food, music, children's rides, demonstrations, races, competitions and a fireworks display. The festival is scheduled each year for Columbus Day Weekend.

Trash Fish Banquet

The Lobster Pot Restaurant, 321 Commercial St., Provincetown • 487-3622

The Center for Coastal Studies, which is based in Provincetown, presents this annual fund-raising event that features "trash" fish — fish you normally wouldn't eat either because its name or its physical appearance is not appealing. Chefs take these underutilized sea creatures and prepare them in a creative fashion . . . and they prove to be quite tasty indeed! Delicacies include monkfish, sand dabs, skate wings, smoked catfish chowder, marinated dogfish and pout parmesan. Yum! For more info, call the center at the number above.

Women's Week

Various sites in Provincetown • 487-4966

Women's Week, usually held mid-month near Columbus Day, is a weeklong festival of music, self-help and growth workshops, fashion shows and auctions. Many art galleries also hold events and exhibits honoring women. The bars and clubs are usually hopping with nationally known gay entertainers pleasing the crowds. Women's Week is sponsored by the Women's Innkeepers of Provincetown.

Fantasia Fair

Various sites in Provincetown • (207) 621-0858

Fantasia Fair is an annual event for transvestites, locals and visitors. For 10 days, the cross-dressers swing, socialize and attend workshops. The fair also includes a costume ball, talent show, and the Provincetown Art Association and Museum hosts a wine tasting.

Late October

Cape Cod Marathon

Falmouth • 540-6959

This 26.2 mile marathon, which begins and ends at Falmouth's Village Green, attracts more than 1,000 participants. Sponsored by the Falmouth Track Club, it is considered a Boston Marathon qualifying event (see our Spectator Sports chapter).

November

Early November

11th Annual Holiday Craft Fair

Cape Cod Regional Technical High School, Rt. 124, Harwich • 432-4500 ext. 225

This is a big one! Held annually at the Cape Cod Tech, this craft fair is now in its 11th year and features more than 125 artisans from up and down the East Coast. The fair, which features all handcrafted items, takes place over two days.

Mid-November

Chatham By the Sea

Various sites in Chatham • 945-1122

Chatham celebrates the holiday season early with Chatham By the Sea, which kicks off mid-November with candy-cane making demonstrations, arts and crafts fairs, a dinner dance at the Chatham Bars Inn and, of course, the arrival of Santa Claus. The event runs through New Year's Eve, culminating with the First Night celebration (see January listings).

Late November

Christmas in Orleans

Various sites in Orleans • 255-1386

Usually held during the last weekend of the month, this yuletide celebration features a candlelight stroll, tree decorating and lighting, caroling and a wonderful crèche display. Santa arrives by boat, then he and his elves take the little kiddies on hay rides to Snow Library where he poses for photos while Mrs. Claus reads stories. Refreshments can be found all around town.

December

Early December

Christmas Strolls

There's perhaps no more wonderful way to catch the holiday spirit than on a Christmastime stroll through one of the Cape's picturesque villages. The museums, historic homes, bed and breakfasts and stores all open their doors to the public, all in good holiday cheer. Expect to see Santa commanding the attention of wide-eyed children and to hear carolers' songs filling the air with traditional holiday song. Besides getting you in the spirit, the strolls are also a great way to get your holiday shopping done.

Many towns and villages have Christmas strolls, they are generally planned for early December. Here are some of them:

- Sandwich Stroll (during Christmas in Sandwich)
- Falmouth Christmas Stroll (during Christmas by the Sea)
- Hyannis Christmas Stroll
- Barnstable Village Christmas Stroll
- Centerville Village Christmas Stroll
- Yarmouthport Christmas Stroll
- Osterville Village Christmas Open House
- Harwich Stroll (during Christmas Weekend in the Harwiches)
- Orleans candlelight stroll (during Christmas in Orleans)

Christmas in Sandwich

Various sites in Sandwich • 759-6000

Here is small-town New England at its loveliest. The celebration runs for over two weeks, starting with carols and a stroll throughout the village to view the Christmas lights that twinkle in and around the village's historic homes. The celebration continues with church fairs, music, plays and open houses at museums, bed and breakfasts and shops in the village, exhibits and demonstrations. Christmas in Sandwich is sponsored by the Canal Region Chamber of Commerce.

Christmas by the Sea Weekend

Various sites in Falmouth • 548-8500

Falmouth's Christmas by the Sea is a gala five-day celebration beginning midweek and running throughout the weekend. It features a fashion show, Christmas caroling at Nobska Lighthouse, Proper English Teas, concerts and other performances, bazaars, Santa's arrival by boat and the lighting of Falmouth Village Green complete with caroling. The festivities include the annual Christmas Parade down Main Street to the Village Green on Sunday.

Hyannis Christmas Harbor Lighting and Stroll

Bismore Park, Ocean St., Hyannis • (800) 4HYNNIS

Hyannis is ablaze with Christmas cheer from the gaily lighted harbor homes and buildings to the holiday boat parade in Hyannis Harbor. Highlights of the three-day festivities include free harbor tours, free chowder, hot chocolate and other goodies. The boat parade is usually held during the first week of December, followed in the next few days by the Hyannis Christmas Stroll on Main Street. Come enjoy the holiday decorations, hay rides, special activities and free refreshments. Santa Claus makes an appearance, and don't miss the lighting of the Village Green!

Annual Lighting of the Monument

1 High Pole Rd., Provincetown • 487-3424

Every winter, volunteers drape Provincetown's Pilgrim Monument with some 5,000 lights, turning the world's tallest granite structure into the world's tallest granite Christmas tree (over 250 feet tall — see our Attractions chapter). The monument remains lit nightly through New Year's Day. Carols and refreshments at the town hall complete the scene.

Mid-December

Christmas Weekend in the Harwiches

Various sites in Harwich • 432-1600, (800) 441-3199

During the second week of December the town of Harwich gets into the Christmas spirit with three days of strolls, entertainment, open houses and fun activities for the whole family. At Brooks Park there is a Christmas tree lighting and carols are sung. The events are sponsored by the Harwich Chamber of Commerce, which can be reached at the two numbers above.

Arts and Entertainment

Cape Cod is living proof that you don't have to go to a big city to get a taste of culture. What's great about this vacation paradise is that here you can lie on a beach and visit art galleries and museums all on the same day! On any given night you can see a play, attend an art opening, go to a concert or see a foreign film. The Cape has some 125 different arts organizations, according to Jane Thompson-Renzi, president of the board of directors of the Arts Foundation of Cape Cod, which sponsors many events, including Pops By the Sea, and supports many arts efforts from museum exhibits to music festivals and dance performances. "There's so much to do down here," said Ms. Thompson-Renzi, explaining that one of the missions of the Arts Foundation, established in 1987, is to make sure visitors know that. The Cape is known for its great summer theater, but there's some great theater to be enjoyed in the winter months as well. (We must have something to keep us sane through those long, quiet months.)

For music lovers, there's the New England Jazz Festival, Jazz By the Sea, the Cape Cod Symphony Orchestra, even a bit of opera. For big names in entertainment, check out the Cape Cod Melody Tent in Hyannis, where there's not a bad seat in the house.

Visual arts thrive on the Cape, which attracts painters like moths to a flame. It's the light, many say, but it's more than that. There is something indefinable about Cape Cod that attracts creative souls. Countless artists have made this place their home, and galleries abound, many of them located in the artists' homes.

First, let's look at theater, which has a long and distinguished history on the Cape. Then we'll move on to music, art galleries and art museums and cinemas that go beyond box-office hits. There's plenty here to get off the beach for — take a break from the sun and bathe in creativity instead.

Theater

The diversity of theater offerings on the Cape is amazing, considering the size of this peninsula. In any given season you can see musicals, comedy, original works and reworked classics. And ticket prices are a fraction of what you might pay in Boston or New York to see a production of equal caliber; most companies listed here charge about $15 a seat.

The Cape's theater legacy dates to 1915, when a group of washashores (including writers John Reed and Susan Glaspell) gathered in Provincetown to write, produce and stage plays. The following year, they were joined by an aspiring playwright named Eugene O'Neill. On July 28, 1916, his first play, *Bound East for Cardiff*, was staged in a waterfront fish house to tremendous success. Two years later the group named themselves the Provincetown Players and, alas, moved to New York City to continue their work. The Provincetown Players never returned to town, but other theatrical troupes popped up, most short-lived. In 1940, the Provincetown Playhouse-on-the-Wharf opened, producing more O'Neill plays than any other theater. It was destroyed by arson in 1977; all that remains is the former box office on Gosnold Street, now the Julie Heller Gallery. There is now, unbelievably, no permanent theater in this otherwise theatrical town.

On a brighter note, however, a group founded in 1995 intends to build a theater on the grounds of the Provincetown Monument and Museum. Provincetown Repertory Theatre is staging its 1997 productions in gallery space at the museum and hopes to break ground in 1998 for a permanent venue right next door, according to founder and director Ken Hoyt. "Of all the towns I've ever been in, I've never seen a place where theater belongs more than Provincetown," Hoyt observed. The company, he said, will do at least one O'Neill play a year, along with newer works. The Provincetown Theatre Company has been doing plays at the Provincetown Inn and will probably continue to do so this summer.

FYI

Unless otherwise noted, the area code for all phone numbers in this guide is 508.

A handful of theater companies on the Cape have demonstrated real staying power. The deepest bow goes to the Cape Playhouse in Dennis, the oldest summer professional theater in the country. It celebrated its 70th season in 1996 and continues to draw major talent and big-name stars. The Barnstable Comedy Club dates back to 1922 and is the third-oldest continuously operating theater in the country. The Harwich Junior Theatre was founded in 1952, the Chatham Drama Guild is in its 65th season and the Academy of Performing Arts in Orleans has been delighting audiences since 1975.

Here's a Cape-wide look at theater.

Upper Cape

Theater on the Bay

Trading Post Corners, Monument Beach • 759-0977

Founded in 1985, Theater on the Bay has earned a reputation for producing adventurous and quality theater. In 1994 it won the George McConville Award for the best theater on the Cape. Open year round, it stages an average of eight shows a year, including musicals, dramas, comedies and original works. The 1997 lineup included *Spiked Heels* in April and the musical comedy *Archy and Mehitibel* in early summer. January's sold-out operetta *Hansel and Gretel* will return in December 1997 as a holiday show. In between plays, the theater holds coffeehouses showcasing hot local bands; in June it also does a show with storytelling and music for Juneteenth, a world-wide black celebration.

Woods Hole Theater Company

68 Water St., Woods Hole • 540-6525

Established in 1974, this company presents six or seven shows a year at the Woods Hole Community Hall and sponsors occasional productions by other theatrical troupes. The group's goal, explains President Lydia Sargent, is to provide a wide variety of theater for the community, from comedy and satire to drama and classics. Examples of the company's productions include 1997's Ayn Rand courtroom drama *Night of January 16th*, an evening of "scenes, solos and sundries" by WHTC board members, and *No Tea For A Rebel*, a new play about Benjamin Franklin.

Falmouth Theater Guild

Highfield Theater, off Depot Ave., Falmouth • 548-0400

This group, established in 1957, puts on three shows a year including at least one musical. Its season runs from September to June, when the theater space is taken over by the College Light Opera Co. The Guild sometimes performs a holiday show in December.

Oversoul Theater Collective

Mashpee High School, Mashpee • 477-3210

The Cape's only multicultural/multi-ethnic theatrical troupe, Oversoul began as a "guerrilla improv comedy troupe," explained co-founder Morgan James Peters. It now leads a double life with regular performances and an ongoing educational program called the Living Theater Institute. "We ain't just theater," quipped Peters, but he is very serious about the educational component of Oversoul's work, which he describes as "an institution for scholarly research and multicultural and performing arts education." Oversoul, he said, hopes

to someday have its own theater where it can offer both performances and classes. For now, shows and classes are held at Mashpee High School, and the group also does regular coffeehouse presentations at the Unitarian-Universalist Fellowship Hall in Falmouth.

Mid-Cape

Barnstable Comedy Club
3171 Rt. 6A, Barnstable • 362-6333

The nation's third-oldest continuously operated theater, the Barnstable Comedy Club has been offering audiences the best in comedy, drama and music since 1922. The group stages four major productions every year, with 10 performances of each show, beginning in September and running through Memorial Day. The club's motto is "Let's produce good plays and remain amateurs," and that's a formula that works well here. "I think we're one of the healthiest theater companies on the Cape," said club president Linda Stevens. And though the performers are all volunteers and nonprofessional, remember their names: Past "nobodies" have included Geena Davis and Kurt Vonnegut!

Cotuit Center for the Arts
737 Main St., Cotuit • 428-0669

This four-year-old arts center began with a focus on visual arts but has branched into theater as well. Drama classes are included in its offering of courses for children, teens and adults. Productions include works such as *Hamlet* and *Tragic Secrets* and *Wandering Christmas,* both Edward Gorey productions.

The Janus Players of Cape Cod Community College
Rt. 132, West Barnstable • 375-4044

The group is composed of drama students and area residents. It stages one show every spring. Performances are held at either of the college's two performing spaces.

Cape Playhouse
Rt. 6A, Dennis • 385-3838, 385-3911

America's oldest professional summer theater, the Cape Playhouse has drawn top entertainers since it first opened on July 4, 1927. The list of actors who have performed here reads like a who's who in theater; among them are Bette Davis, Tallulah Bankhead, Humphrey Bogart, Henry Fonda (with his then 20-year-old daughter, Jane), Lana Turner, Helen Hayes, Jessica Tandy, Anne Baxter, Paulette Goddard, Gertrude Lawrence, Gregory Peck, Olivia de Havilland and John Raitt. Cape resident and performer Pat Carroll, who not only stars in shows but also directs them here, serves on the board of directors, as do Gavin MacLeod and Julie Harris.

The theater itself is a former Unitarian meetinghouse dating to 1838. The original pews are cushioned for comfort, and the theater is air-conditioned. You can take a free behind-the-scenes tour during the season; call for exact dates and times. Children's theater is performed twice on Fridays in the summer. Tickets are sold via subscription, though good-location single seats are usually available. The season begins in late June and runs to mid-September, with two-week runs of six plays, ranging from musicals and comedies to mysteries.

The 26-acre grounds of the playhouse, overseen by a foundation named for Playhouse founder Raymond Moore, are also home to the unique Cape Cinema (see the section on cinemas later in this chapter) and the Cape Museum of Fine Arts (see the gallery section, below).

Lower Cape

Cape Cod Repertory Theater Company
3379 Rt. 6A, Brewster • 896-1888

Cape Rep, which celebrated its 10th anniversary in 1997, operates the Cape's only outdoor theater, a lovely venue set among the pines off Route 6A across the road from the state park in East Brewster. As of last year, the group has an indoor theater at the same site. Cape Rep offers such productions as *Light Up the Sky* and *Alice In Wonderland*. In October Cape Rep brings back its popular *Dressing Them Up*, with many of the same actors who have delighted audiences in past years. Cape Rep also offers a Broadway musical dinner revue at the Old Sea Pines Inn, 2553 Route

6A, Brewster, 896-6114, on Sunday evenings from June through September. The company stages children's theater every Tuesday and Friday morning at 10 AM in July and August.

Harwich Junior Theatre

Corner of Division and Willow sts., West Harwich • 432-2002

The Jester greets you at every performance at the Harwich Junior Theatre, giving you a glimpse of the fun to come. Founded in 1952, this year-round company stages delightful family shows including drama, musicals, comedies — even Shakespeare. Besides producing four shows a season, HJT offers year-round classes and workshops for children.

Chatham Drama Guild

134 Crowell Rd., Chatham • 945-0510

In its 65th season in 1997, the Guild does four major shows a year, ranging from musicals to comedy and mystery. One year the Guild staged *Fiddler On the Roof* in conjunction with Chatham High School, making it an educational experience for the students who participated as well as a grand experience for the audience. The organization also does children's plays as matinees.

Monomoy Theatre

776 Main St., Chatham • 945-1589

Nineteen ninety-seven marks the 40th anniversary of the Ohio Players at this theater, which was once owned by the wife of the president of Ohio University. The theater is still owned by the same family and is run by Ohio University's School of Theatre Arts. Held during the summer season are a half-dozen other productions ranging from comedy to drama and thrillers. Monomoy has a tradition of closing its season with a Shakespearean play.

Academy of Performing Arts

120 Main St., Orleans • 255-1963

Founded in 1975, the Academy stages between 10 and 12 productions throughout the year — musicals, dramas, comedies and everything in between — many of them works by local and regional playwrights. The quality of performances is high. One yearly highlight is the program of new works produced in March. The building itself dates to 1873 and once served as Orleans Town Hall; the Academy is in the midst of a fund-raising campaign to renovate and upgrade the building. The Academy also offers a plethora of courses in dance, musical instrument instruction and acting at its new teaching facility on Giddiah Hill Road (see our Education chapter).

The Stages Theater Company

Community of Jesus, Rock Harbor, Orleans • 240-2400

The Stages Theater Company, known until 1995 as the CJ Players, produces between four and six shows year round, three of them beneath a huge tent outdoors. With a troupe of 30 actors ranging in age from 8 to 65, the company stages dinner theater performances in the off-season and occasional dessert theater evenings in summer.

The Highlanders

Nauset Regional Middle School, Rt. 28, Orleans • 255-6343

For its 40th anniversary in 1997, The Highlanders staged *Brigadoon*, which was "the show that kicked it off way back when," noted director Peter Earle. The group does a big-time Broadway musical every April with large casts and lots of flash. Past hits include *Oliver* and *South Pacific* — "Tried and true musicals," as Earle puts it.

Wellfleet Harbor Actors Theater (W.H.A.T.)

Town Pier, Wellfleet • 349-6935

W.H.A.T. co-founders and directors Gip Hoppe and Jeff Zinn bring something different to the theater experience on Cape Cod, providing, as Hoppe puts it, "an alternative to the tradition summer-stock straw-hat stuff." The group stages six shows a year from May through October, tempting audiences with everything from David Mamet to John Patrick Shanely.

Provincetown Repertory Theatre

Pilgrim Monument and Museum, Provincetown • 487-0600

This group stages performances in July, August and September and holds a lecture series in June. Still in temporary quarters, the company, founded in 1996, is raising money

to build a new theater to be its permanent home right here on the grounds of the monument and museum. Founder Ken Hoyt says each season will feature at least one O'Neill play, along with new works.

Music

There is music in the salt air on the Cape, especially during the summer, when crowds of people make for a celebratory atmosphere that just cries out for accompaniment. There are free outdoor concerts in many towns (see our Sounds of Summer close-up in this chapter), some regular events so popular many visitors plan their vacations around them (such as Pops in the Park and Jazz By the Sea) and a number of venues that offer great live music. The Cape Cod Melody Tent is the place to go for big-name entertainment in summer; it really is a tent — a huge one — and it's a terrific place to see a concert. The Cape will soon have another large entertainment venue when The Boch Center for the Performing Arts opens in 1998 with two performing spaces, indoor and outdoor, in Mashpee. Here's a listing of some of the best musical venues on the Cape. Look in the *Cape Cod Times*' Friday entertainment section for exact dates and concert schedules.

Upper Cape

College Light Opera Company

Highfield Theater, off Depot Ave., Falmouth • 548-0668, Winter number (216) 774-8485

Formerly affiliated with Oberlin College, the College Light Opera Company stages nine musicals a summer, each running a week, from the last week of June through the last week of August. Shows include Gilbert and Sullivan and heaps of Broadway classics.

Woods Hole Folk Music Society

Woods Hole Community Hall, Water St., Woods Hole • 540-0320

Here's something to liven up those quiet winter months. From October to May, the Woods Hole Folk Music Society stages concerts on the first and third Sundays of the month. The programs often attract nationally known performers; for example, the 1996-97 season included Northern Lights, Peggy Seeger, Roy Bookbinder, Oscar Brand, David Mallett and Kim and Reggie Harris. It also marked the Society's 25th season. Admission runs about $7, with discounts for members, seniors and children.

Boch Center for the Performing Arts

Various venues • 477-2580

With ambitious plans for an 850-seat indoor theater and an outdoor theater that will accommodate 2,000, the center, which will be located on Great Neck Road in Mashpee when completed in 1998, has been holding concerts to benefit its building fund. Locations include Sandwich High School, Mashpee High School and, in season, the tent at Mashpee Commons.

New England Jazz Festival

Mashpee Commons, rts. 28 and 151, Mashpee • 477-5400

The festival is a three-day celebration headlined by such icons as Thelonious Monk Jr., Gary Burton, Dorothy Donegan, Marian McPartland and Dave McKenna. The event was staged for the first time in 1994 as a benefit for both The Boch Center for the Performing Arts and the Cape Cod Jazz Society.

INSIDERS' TIP

You don't always have to go to a gallery to see an artist at work. We often see artists set up easels and work outdoors at scenic spots throughout the Cape, including Nauset Light in Eastham and the windmill on Route 6A in Brewster. There's something very inspiring about watching an artist capture the light and beauty of a place that suddenly seems even more lovely for our appreciation of its artistic value.

Heritage Plantation

Pine and Grove sts., Sandwich • 888-3300

When summer heats up, so does the rockin' and rollin' with at the Plantation's annual Rock & Roll Ramble, usually held in June. The Plantation also hosts dozens of other concerts, from Scottish pipe bands to the New Black Eagle's Jazz Band and Big Band dance music, through Labor Day. Museum admission ($8 for adults, $7 for those older than 60 and $4 for ages 6 through 18) is charged for all concerts.

Opera New England of Cape Cod

Sandwich • 775-3974

Opera New England of Cape Cod hosts Opera Northeast of New York City, a touring company whose members stage operas at the Sandwich High School, Quaker Meetinghouse Road, East Sandwich, every spring and fall. The company celebrated its 20th anniversary in 1997. Opera New England of Cape Cod also sponsors bus trips to catch the latest operatic fare in Boston and Manhattan.

Mid-Cape

Benefit Coffeehouse

Liberty Hall, Main St., Marstons Mills • 775-5165, 428-1053

Since 1990, New Age acoustic and folk-rock music have filled Liberty Hall. The concerts given here are held as benefits for a number of causes, including area families in need, children suffering from cancer and conservatory groups. Tickets range between $8 and $12.

Cape Cod Melody Tent

W. Main St. and West End Rotary, Hyannis • 775-9100

The Cape Cod Melody Tent is the Cape's premier summer showcase, an outdoor tent (one of only 10 left in the country) in which many big names in show business appear — Steve and Eydie, Liza, Willie, Aretha, Reba and Tony Bennett, to name a few. The big white tent is pitched at the end of May and is taken down mid-September. Shows sell out fast; check the box office for last-minute seat cancellations. Ticket prices vary from $25 to $50.

The Melody Tent also features children's theater and musical productions every Wednesday morning during the season; ticket prices are $5.25.

Cape Cod Symphony Orchestra

Village Green, Main St., Hyannis • 790-ARTS

The orchestra's Sounds of Summer concert every July on the Village Green is a widely attended event. The 90-member orchestra, conducted by Royston Nash, features guest artists and the best in Americana. Patron tickets run about $50; lawn seats, $4.

Jazz By the Sea

Village Green, Main St., Hyannis • 790-ARTS

Presented by the Arts Foundation of Cape Cod, Jazz By the Sea is an annual explosion of the best sounds this side of New Orleans. Locals Marie Marcus, John Salerno and Carol Sloane often drop by. The event takes place in early August. VIP table seating runs about $25; lawn seats are $5.

Pops By the Sea

Village Green, Main St., Hyannis • 790-ARTS

The Boston Pops Esplanade Orchestra is another crowd-pleaser. Tickets run as high as $100 (VIP tables) to as low as $4 (lawn seats.) Funds benefit the Arts Foundation of Cape Cod. Pops By the Sea features a famous guest conductor every year (Olympia Dukakis in 1996!)

Summer Concerts

Guyer Barn Gallery, 230 South St., Hyannis • 790-6370

The 1865 barn housing the Guyer Barn Gallery turns into a hip, modern-day coffeehouse, swinging with everything from country-western to folk and rockabilly every Saturday evening in July through September. A nominal admission fee is charged.

P.M. By the Sea

Sandy Neck Beach, Rt. 6A, West Barnstable • 771-8298

Here's a truly Cape Cod experience: Sit on the beach before a bonfire on a moonlit evening and listen to folk music, poetry and other low-key entertainment. P.M. by the Sea stages these delightful events on the Friday night closest to the full moon in summer. The fun begins at dusk, and it's a great family venue. A donation of $5 is requested. Ages 12 and younger are admitted free.

The Sounds of Summer

Just about every town on the Cape offers free outdoor summer concerts. Here's a list of our favorites.

Falmouth

Join the crowds at the Town Band Shell, on the west side of Inner Harbor, every Thursday evening during July and August for concerts performed by the Falmouth Town Band.

The Falmouth Village Association presents a Friday night concert series in Margaret E. Noonan Park on Main Street. Call 548-8500 for a schedule of both series of concerts.

Sandwich

The Sandwich Town Band, under the direction of Wil Harrigan, performs free concerts on Thursday evenings at the Henry T. Wing School Bandstand, Route 130, 888-7892.

Mashpee

Mashpee Commons, which is just off the rotary at routes 28 and 151, offers an extensive free concert series. The sessions, held under the festival tent, feature everything from R&B favorites to ragtime, Bourbon Street blues and Big Band. Call 477-5400 for a complete schedule.

Mashpee Community Concerts, 477-6992, holds one concert (with a breathtaking fireworks finale) on the last Saturday in July at the Mashpee Commons.

Barnstable

The Barnstable Band, under the direction of John P. Hagon, marked its 47th season of free concerts in 1997. The concerts, with selections ranging from Sinatra to Sousa, begin in early July and run through the end of August at various locations throughout the Cape.

Yarmouth

The Cape Cod Symphony Orchestra, 362-1111, performs regularly at the Mattacheese Middle School, Higgins Crowell Road, from May through October.

Also, you can attend free band concerts every Monday evening in July and August at the Mattacheese Middle School's band shell.

Dennis

Both town greens (on Route 6A in Dennis and Route 28 in Dennisport) are the sites for free concerts in July and August.

Photo: Peter Simon

Outdoor concerts are a great, and often free, way to spend a summer evening.

Brewster

The Brewster Town Band, founded in 1994 under the direction of Bruce Abbott,

— continued on next page

presents free concerts in Drummer Boy Park, Route 6A, West Brewster, every Sunday in July and August.

Harwich

Brooks Park, Oak Street, is the setting for concerts on Tuesday evenings in July and August.

Chatham

Up to 6,000 music lovers pack Kate Gould Park every Friday night from July through Labor Day to hear the town's brassy band perform. Why not join the fun? It's been a summer tradition for the past 60-plus years! The park is next door to the Chatham Wayside Inn, 512 Main Street.

Music for a Summer's Night is a series of Sunday evening concerts held at the First United Methodist Church, 16 Cross Street, 945-0474, from Independence Day Weekend through Labor Day. Though admission is free, a freewill offering is taken before each performance.

Lower Cape

Monomoy Chamber Ensemble
Various venues • 945-1589

Based in Chatham, the Monomoy Chamber Ensemble has been presenting the finest in chamber and classical music for 27 years. Concerts, performed by an ensemble of eight musicians, feature works by Bartok, Mozart, Brahms, Dvorak and Martinu and are held at various locations. MCE also features a free children's concert once a summer.

Cape Cod Symphony Orchestra
Eldredge Park, Rt. 28, Orleans • 255-1386

In August, the CCSO offers its annual concert to benefit the Orleans Chamber of Commerce Scholarship Fund. Lawn tickets cost about $11; patron tickets are more.

Community of Jesus Orchestra
Rock Harbor, Orleans • 240-2400

The Community's concert band and orchestra perform several events during the year, including an annual Fourth of July star-spangled concert celebration with a fireworks display launched over the water as its grand finale. Tickets cost about $25 ($15 for ages 10 and younger) and include a fried-chicken dinner. The Community of Jesus also is home to Gloriae Dei Cantores, a 40-member choral group that was founded in 1976. The group travels and performs internationally.

Cape and Islands Chamber Music Festival
Various venues • 255-9509

For three weeks in August, the Cape and Islands Chamber Music Festival holds concerts in various venues. One highlight: a screening of a musically themed film (such as *Immortal Beloved* and *Amadeus*), in which a quartet "demonstrates" the music used in the film. Concert tickets average $20.

First Encounter Coffee House
Samoset Rd., Eastham • 255-5438

The coffeehouse, also home to an 1899 Unitarian Universalist church, boasts some of the biggest names in acoustic and folk music, including Wellfleet's own Patty Larkin and James Taylor's brother, Livingston. Admission runs about $10 (see our Nightlife chapter).

The Beachcomber
Cahoon Hollow Rd., Wellfleet • 349-6055

Once an 1897 lifesaving station, The Beachcomber is the place to go on the Lower Cape for the best in reggae and rock. Admission fees are nominal (see our Nightlife chapter).

The Provincetown Muse Series
Provincetown Town Hall, 260 Commercial St. • 487-0955

Held each summer since 1982, this concert series features some of the most-respected names in jazz, classical, world and folk music. Some recent artists who have wowed crowds include Holly Near, Maxine Sullivan, Cris Williamson, Shawn Colvin and Odetta; 1996 marked the 10th consecutive visit by the Klezmer Conservatory Band. Admission runs about $17.

Dance

Cape Dance Theater of Cape Cod Community College

Rt. 132, West Barnstable • 375-4044

Comprised of faculty, students and area residents, this 16-member dance troupe mainly focuses on modern dance, though it has broadened its scope in recent years to include such traditional fare as ballroom dancing. Noted Boston choreographer Nicola Hawkins teaches master classes and choreographs compositions at CDT. Her results can be witnessed during the troupe's three annual shows staged at the college's Tilden Arts Center.

North Atlantic Dance Art

Nauset Regional Middle School, Orleans • 896-9939

Known as DanceArts, this company was founded in 1981 by Skip Warren and Thomas Vacanti, and was originally based in Boston before moving to the Cape in 1995. The company does about three modern dance and ballet productions a year. DanceArts is also planning an outdoor dance series. The company also has a Young Artists program that provides year-round training to serious students of ballet at three locations in Eastham, Brewster and Chatham.

Art Galleries

The Cape's unique light and natural beauty was drawing artists here even before Charles Hawthorne founded the Cape Cod School of Art in Provincetown in 1899. And it continues to attract painters, sculptors and other artists. That explains the profusion of galleries here, particularly in the Lower Cape towns of Wellfleet and Provincetown. Many galleries are run by working artists, and you can often catch a glimpse of the artist at work while you're browsing in galleries with attached studios.

Here are some of our favorite galleries. Remember that hours vary greatly during the off-season so it's best to call in advance.

Upper Cape

The Giving Tree

550 Rt. 6A, East Sandwich • 888-5446

This very unusual gallery embodies its theme, "Where Art Meets Nature." Artwork is set outdoors amidst perennial gardens, wild bamboo, a salt marsh and a 52-foot suspension bridge over a creek. Statuary, mobiles and wind chimes in metal, wood, ceramics and con-

Historic Dennis Village

crete range in size from small (a mobile) to 7-feet tall (sculpture). The gallery also has one-of-a-kind jewelry and unique home accessories such as sun catchers made from Cape Cod shells. More than half of the 120 artists working here are locals. Relax in the coffeehouse (you can sit outside too) with espresso, latte, teas or iced drinks. The Giving Tree is open daily from mid-April through Christmas and by appointment the rest of the year.

Sandwich Art Gallery

153 Main St., Sandwich • 888-8835, (800) 833-2098

Housed in an antique building in the heart of Sandwich village, this gallery displays original oils, pastels and watercolors as well as signed, limited-edition lithographs. The gallery represents a wide variety of artists, and works include an in-depth representation of American Impressionism and folk art. The gallery offers a variety of sizes and prices. It's open daily March through December, and by appointment in January and February.

Falmouth Artists' Guild

744 Main St., Falmouth • 540-3304

What began as an informal gathering of people painting and studying together has grown into the premier art space on the Upper Cape. The Falmouth Artists' Guild offers 10 shows a year (all but the members' show are open to everyone); four shows are juried. During the winter holidays, the Guild also has a holiday craft/art show. The Guild offers classes for children and adults.

The Market Barn Gallery

15 Depot Ave., Falmouth • 540-0480

The Market Barn Gallery is housed in a barn behind the Market Bookshop and holds seasonal exhibitions of local artists. Open daily mid-June through mid-September, the Market Barn Gallery also hosts poetry readings in summer and opening receptions every two weeks when exhibits change.

Gallery 333

333 Old Main St., North Falmouth • 564-4467

This gallery is also housed in a barn, this one almost 200 years old. The work of almost 40 artists is on display. 333's openings are quite popular.

Woodruff Gallery

Mashpee Commons, rts. 28 and 151, Mashpee • 477-5767

John Richardson Woodruff considers his gallery more than just an exhibition space. Here you can watch John, his wife, Amy, and selected guest artists as they create their works of art, which cover every available inch of wall space. Woodruff also offers art instruction and custom framing and sells a wide range of art supplies.

Woods Hole Gallery

14 School St., Woods Hole • 548-7594

Since 1963 Edith Bruce, owner of the Woods Hole Gallery, has been cultivating the newest and freshest talent in the world of art. The collections here are superb, representing only New England artists in a range of media including pastels, watercolors, oils and acrylics. Ms. Bruce, an artist herself, also restores paintings and teaches art. The gallery is open June through September and is closed Wednesdays.

Mid-Cape

Cotuit Center for the Arts

737 Main St., Cotuit • 428-0669

This center behind Cotuit Grocery has rotating exhibits of artwork by students, teachers and others all year long; it offers classes in visual arts, drama and music.

Birdsey Gallery

12 Wianno Ave., Osterville • 428-4969

This friendly gallery, housed in an old build-

INSIDERS' TIP

The dune shacks in Provincetown have housed such notables as Tennessee Williams, Eugene O'Neill, Jackson Pollock and Jack Kerouac.

West Barnstable Tables

Primitive furniture & folk art emphasizing the natural texture & colors found in Antique Wood.

Handmade Furniture by:
Richard Kiusalas
Stephen Whittlesey

Route 149, (Exit 5, North)
W. Barnstable, MA 02668
Open seven days 9-4 (508) 362-2676

MAPS OF ANTIQUITY

Authentic Antique Maps
Framing

Shop open May - October
mail order year round
catalogs issued

508-362-7169
1022 Rte. 6A • West Barnstable, MA 02668

TERN STUDIO

fine furniture, gift items, bowls, vases, restorations & refinishing

Albert O. Barbour
Furnituremaker
Rt. 149, W. Barnstable
(508) 362-6077

Accessories and accents for home & garden
Production & custom ironwork
Blacksmith on premises

Decorative & Functional Forged Ironworks

1040 Route 6A • West Barnstable, MA
508-362-9321

500 YEARS OF HISTORY AND FOLKLORE!

This beautiful hand-crafted map is lithographed on parchment and suitable for framing.

Size is 22" x 28". Pricing is as follows: unframed $14.99 + $3 shipping & handling. MasterCard & Visa accepted.

Send check or money order to Michael L. Welch, Vinland Adventure Co., 991 Oak St., West Barnstable, MA 02668 or call Toll Free 1-800-959-0410 or (508) 362-4908.

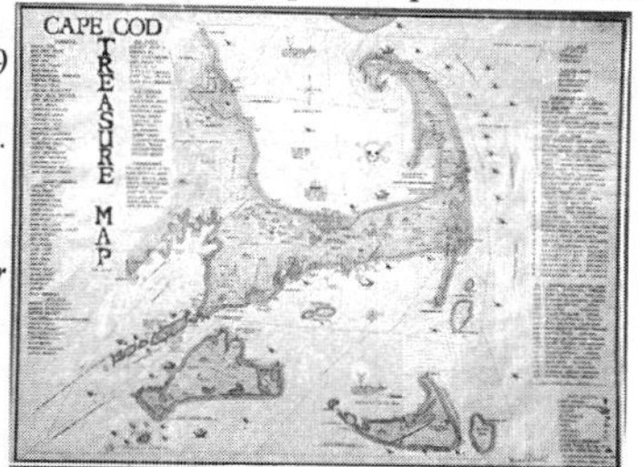

Includes:
Famous Explorers
Shipwrecks of Value
Pirates & Witches
Famous Ghosts
Lost Islands
Lighthouses
The Vikings
Old Fort Sights
Old Tavern Sights
The Pilgrims
& Much, Much More!

VINLAND ADVENTURE CO.

Also available at the Crystal Pineapple Shops–Hyannis

ing with lots of character, represents more than 40 different artists. "What we look for is diversity, so there's something for everyone," says owner Suzanne Cartstensen. That goes for price, too. You can pick up a lovely framed print here for a mere $35, or you could spend as much as $3,500 for an original painting. Some of the popular artists whose work graces Birdsey's three rooms include Martha Cahoon, Jane Shelley Pierce, Vern Broe, Susie McLean and Neil McAulliffe. There are plenty of local artists in the mix if you're craving a Cape Cod or New England scene. In its 17th year, this gallery actually welcomes children, and treats them to helium balloons. While you browse, your little ones can pet Olivia, the Carstensens' very friendly English cocker spaniel. The gallery is open daily May through December, and Saturdays or by appointment in winter.

FYI

Unless otherwise noted, the area code for all phone numbers in this guide is 508.

Cape Cod Art Association
3480 Rt. 6A, Barnstable • 362-2909

The nonprofit Cape Cod Art Association was established in 1948 and offers year-round art exhibitions, five for members only and four open to area residents. Exhibitions change every three weeks. Some shows are juried, and artists are always present at openings. The CCAA also hosts two levels of art classes, for kids ages 6 to 10 and 11 to 14.

Cummaquid Fine Arts
4275 Rt. 6A, Cummaquid • 362-2593

Cummaquid Fine Arts is itself a work of art: an 18th-century home set on more than 4 acres of lush green. Inside are works by Cape and New England artists such as Orleans artist Rosalie Stambler Nadeau and Susan Carey, along with a sprinkling of antique decorative pieces.

Higgins Art Gallery
Cape Cod Community College
Rt. 132, West Barnstable • 362-2131

The exhibition space at the Higgins Art Gallery is not large, but the works are always refreshing. They mount several shows each year.

The Gallery at C3TV
307 Whites Path, South Yarmouth • 394-2388

The Gallery at C3TV is a small but appealing space located within the offices of the Cape's community-access TV station. The gallery hosts a different show every three weeks or so.

William R. Davis Fine Arts
633 Main St. (Rt. 6A), Dennis • 385-4170

Marine artist William R. Davis works in oils to create luminous scenes; his paintings have a unique quality of light. You'll find seascapes, yachting scenes and still life original paintings, along with limed-edition prints. The gallery is open year round.

Worden Hall
1841 Rt. 6A, East Dennis • 385-9289

Behind the majestic door of Worden Hall lies artwork that since 1965 has awed its audiences. The works of owner Donn DeVita and his late wife, Nancy — landscapes and seascapes, mostly in oils — compete for attention. Donn also creates what he calls "unusual art," for example, drawing with a knife instead of a pencil, then filling the broken surface with color.

Lower Cape

Ruddeforth Gallery
3753 Main St. (Rt. 6A), Brewster • 255-1056

Debra Ruddeforth's oils and watercolors are soft, lush and inviting; they include many Cape landscapes as well as florals and still lifes. The year-round gallery also displays photographs by Tom Ruddeforth.

Struna Galleries
3873 Rt. 6A, Brewster • 255-6618

Timothy Struna's pen-and-ink renderings are so distinctive you'll know them anywhere. He also works in watercolors and acrylics, and we highly recommend a visit to his cozy gallery.

Cape Cod Celebrities

You may not bump into them on the street or find them right next to your blanket on a public beach, but a number of celebrities make their home on Cape Cod and the islands.

Some, like Gavin MacLeod, Spike Lee and Walter Cronkite, just spend summers here. But others, such as Carly Simon, Pat Carroll and Norman Mailer, make the Cape and islands their year-round home.

Close-up

Other stars love to visit — we've heard of sightings of Barbra Streisand, Joan Rivers and Dustin Hoffman. Phil Donahue and Marlo Thomas have been known to drop in by way of the water at the Chatham Bars Inn.

The celebrities who live here have strong feelings about the Cape. Here, a half-dozen celebs tell why they love it so.

Photo: Janet Donnelly, Cape Cod Times

Pat Carroll

—

Pat Carroll
Harwichport

"I lived in Los Angeles for 33 years, but after the big earthquake of 1994, I made a list of possible places to which I could relocate. On the list was Cape Cod, and I thought, 'I love the ocean, I have friends on the Cape, and I started my professional career there. Why not the Cape?'

"I love my house. It faces a cranberry bog and is surrounded by trees, so it's like living in a tree house. I feel so peaceful, so content there . . . the house is a perfect nesting place for me. The Cape is simply marvelous! And I've noticed that the older people on the Cape are so active, so alive, so healthy. The people here are real, so friendly. I stop and talk to everybody. I am so at home here I don't believe it!"

Mary Higgins Clark
Dennis

"I began fantasizing about the Cape when I was writing radio shows about the environment. I read so many books for research, and the Cape sounded like the most idyllic spot in the world. I kept thinking, 'Don't worry. I'm gonna get there one day. Hang in there.'

"My first visit was in 1968. It cost me $16 to fly round-trip! I got off the plane and thought, 'Wow! The Cape really does live up to its reputation.' I felt like I had been here before . . . that's how restful and at peace I felt. There is truly no other place like the Cape. The beaches, the dunes, the way the light plays games in the sky, the countless stars at night, the friendliness of the people. Take it from an Insider: Once you visit, you won't want to leave."

Photo: Vince DeWitt, Cape Cod Times

Mary Higgins Clark

—

— continued on next page

Photo: John Hamill, Cape Cod Times

Edward Gorey

Edward Gorey
Yarmouthport

"I love Jack's Outback. I've been eating breakfast and lunch there every day for the past eight years. I love going to Hallet's for ice cream. I love browsing at Parnassus Books. I love going to the movies at the Cape Cinema. And I love being able to do it alone, without people staring. Now go away."

Julie Harris
Chatham

"In 1978, my then-husband and I were renting a home in Arlington, Virginia, but we wanted to live by the sea. My aunt lives in South Chatham, and after visiting her one summer, we simply fell in love with the area. The Cape really keeps me humming. I love visiting Provincetown; it's so friendly and bouncy. I love going to local theater; the Harwich Junior Theater, the Academy in Orleans and the Wellfleet Harbor Actors Theater put on some great shows. But best of all, I love taking my canoe out in the salt marsh behind my house. That really keeps me going."

Photo: Sherwood Landers, Cape Cod Times

Julie Harris

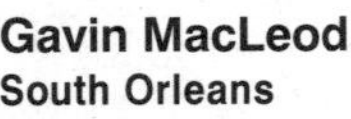

Gavin MacLeod
South Orleans

"The first time my wife, Patti, and I came to the Cape was about 10 years ago. We were driving from Boston to the Cape Playhouse, and just as we rounded a bend on Route 6A, Patti said, 'You know, this place is so beautiful I could live here.' I, of course, agreed. So we looked around and bought a gorgeous saltbox. My work keeps me away from it more than we like, but we always make it back for at least several weeks in the summer.

"I love the Cape because I can wind down, and people treat me like a regular Joe. I love going to the auctions at Eldred's in Dennis, I love the Cape Museum of Fine Arts, I love watching the Orleans Cardinals play. I also love going to my local post office, where these four guys are always sitting around talking about politics and the world. I walk in, and I become one of them! I'm no celebrity, just someone who, like them, gets a little fatter, a little older, a little grayer as the years progress. And that's perfectly all right."

Photo: John Hamill, Cape Cod Times

Gavin and Patti McLeod

— continued on next page

Photo: Steve Haeslip, Cape Cod Times

Norman Mailer

Norman Mailer
Provincetown

"My wife and I are very fond of Provincetown. We love spending the long stretches of winter there. Whenever I'm on the road for business, the town always draws me back; it nourishes my soul and my writing. Provincetown is perhaps the most generous small town in America, full of wonderfully goofy aspects and sweet freedom."

Underground Gallery

673 Satucket Rd., Brewster • 896-6850

The Underground Gallery is an architectural wonder supported by tree trunks and nestled under tons of earth. But the real attractions are the vivid, distinctive watercolors by Karen North Wells. The works of her husband, architect and artist Malcolm Wells — who designed the gallery — are also on display, as are a sampling of books, puzzles and furniture.

Winstanley-Roark Fine Arts

2759 Rt. 6A, Brewster • 896-1948

The oils and pastels found at Winstanley-Roark Fine Arts — nudes, landscapes and still lifes — are the work of husband-and-wife team Robert K. Roark and Anita Winstanley Roark. They also sell antique etchings and offer framing services.

Private Collection Gallery

515 Main St. (Rt. 28), Harwichport • 430-0303

Located next door to Wild Oats Natural Foods, this gallery represents about 15 local and New England fine artists with both traditional and contemporary works in all mediums. Open year round (daily in season, closed Wednesdays in winter) the gallery's roster of artists includes Georgia Dearborn, Mary Napoletano Johnson and Zoltan Szabo.

Just Africa Gallery

586 Rt. 28, Harwichport • 432-8098

This unique, exciting gallery boasts a fine collection of contemporary stone sculpture from Zimbabwe alongside batiks, textiles, pottery, wood carvings and masks. There's a second Just Africa gallery in Hyannis at 433 Main Street, 775-0448.

The Artful Hand Gallery

459 Main St., Chatham • 945-4933

The Artful Hand displays an innovative collection of contemporary American arts and crafts created by award-winning and emerging new artists. The Artful Hand has another Cape gallery at 47 Main Street, Orleans, 255-2969, and at Copley Place, Boston.

Creative Arts Center

154 Crowell Rd., Chatham • 945-3583

The Creative Arts Center has two galleries hosting at least 10 members-only shows a year. The center also offers a wide range of classes.

The Gallery at Chatham

595 Main St., Chatham • 945-5449

Filled with natural light, this gallery curls around a balcony in the second floor of a small shopping mall (elevator access is available). A variety of fine artists are represented here, including James Maddocks, Marilyn Schofield and Peter Quidley. In addition to paintings,

Photo: Vincent DeWitt, Cape Cod Times

A resident of Yarmouth sweeps sawdust in front of his lobster bouy-bedecked shed.

you'll find pottery, stained glass and photographs. It's open year round.

Munson Gallery

880 Rt. 28, Chatham • 945-2888

Founded in 1955, the Munson Gallery is one of the oldest galleries on the Cape. It's also one of the best, offering a perfect meld of new and well- established artists.

Addison Holmes Gallery

43 Rt. 28, Orleans • 255-6200

One of the newer galleries on the Cape, Addison Holmes represents a number of acclaimed fine artists, including Lois Griffel, Charles Kolnik and Gerry Gilmartin. The two-level gallery, in a former home on Town Cove, is bright and inviting. It's open year round.

Hogan Art Gallery

39 Main St., Orleans • 240-3655

Highlights at the Hogan Art Gallery are the highly colorful whiteline prints of Ruth Hogan and the tromp l'oeil painted furniture of Suzanne Thibault.

Tree's Place

Rt. 6A, Orleans • 255-1330

The collection of paintings in the newly expanded gallery space at Tree's Place couldn't have been better coordinated. The works are all different yet blend perfectly, leading the visitor in a natural line from wall to wall and room to room. Featured artists include Sam Barber, Thomas Higham and Michael Whelan. You'll also find the delightful, rich folk art of Elizabeth Mumford; the soft, graceful realism of Betsy Bennett; the vibrant, powerful compositions of Pamela Pindell; and Joseph McGurl's American luminism. Don't forget to go upstairs, where a beautiful assortment of gifts awaits, and stop in the Tilery, which has a wonderful array of tile works from around the world. Tree's Place is open year round.

Blue Heron Gallery

Bank St., Wellfleet • 349-6724

The Blue Heron Gallery has one of the finest collections around of representational contemporary art, including works by Donald Voorhees, Olaf Palm and Steve Allrich. It's

open daily May through mid-October with shorter fall hours.

Cove Gallery
Commercial St., Wellfleet • 349-2530

Cove Gallery displays works by such internationally recognized artists as watercolorist Wolf Kahn and children's book illustrator Tomie DePaolo. Step outside and see the peaceful garden overlooking Duck Creek. The Cove also does custom framing.

Jacob Fanning Gallery
25 Bank St., Wellfleet • 349-9546

The Jacob Fanning Gallery is overrun with cockroaches, crickets and opossums. But don't call an exterminator: The creatures, made from pieces of recycled metal and brightly painted, are the whimsical one-of-a-kind sculptures by local artist Stephen Thomas. It's open daily in summer, and by appointment only in winter.

Kendall Art Gallery
40 E. Main St., Wellfleet • 349-2482

This gallery represents 30 contemporary artists including Harry Marinsky, whose massive bronze sculpture, *Made for Each Other*, greets visitors outside the gallery. Artist in residence Walter Dorrell does his Wellfleet watercolors in his "floating" studio, a canoe he takes into the town's kettle ponds.

Left Bank Gallery
25 Commercial St., Wellfleet • 349-9451

In its 27th year in 1997, Left Bank represents more than 25 local and nationally known artists such as Rosalie Nadeau, Margaret Babbitt, Timothy Struna and Vincent Amicosante. It also hosts changing exhibitions. Check out the Potter's Room, filled with American crafts, and the outdoor sculpture garden. The gallery is open daily May through mid-October, and closed Tuesday and Wednesday in the off season.

Swansborough Gallery
Main St., Wellfleet • 349-1883

The five levels of this gallery, located at the corner of School Street, are filled with a mix of paintings, sculpture, prints and photographs by more than 30 acclaimed artists. It's open daily in season.

Karol B. Wyckoff Gallery
1 Bank St., Wellfleet • 349-1443

Karol Wyckoff's incredible watercolor landscapes must be seen to be appreciated. As beautiful as the Cape scenes they depict, the paintings draw you in, casting a delicate spell. If you can't swing an original, look for limited-edition prints. The gallery also offers bird carvings, ceramics and cards. It's open Monday through Saturday in season.

DNA Gallery
288 Bradford St., Provincetown • 487-7700

Ever since the DNA Gallery opened in 1994, it has been a welcome artistic refuge for those seeking the latest in environmental art. DNA also ties in its openings with various readings, films and musical events.

Julie Heller Gallery
2 Gosnold St., Provincetown • 487-6499

This gallery is almost exclusively devoted to the works of those artists who helped establish Provincetown as an art colony. Look for important (and costly) works by Milton Avery, Ross Moffett, Blanche Lazzell and Henry Hensche. Heller also represents a small number of artists who she feels are carrying on the Provincetown tradition.

INSIDERS' TIP

Several free brochures can help make your gallery-going easier. Write away for: *Cape Cod Art Galleries*, Publications of New England, P.O. Box 660, Yarmouthport 02675; *The Galleries and Potteries of Brewster*, The Studio/Gallery Association of Brewster, P.O. Box 1149, Brewster 02631; *Galleries of Wellfleet Guide*, P.O. Box 916, Wellfleet 02667; and *Provincetown Gallery Guide*, Provincetown Gallery Guild, P.O. Box 242, Provincetown 02657.

Cortland Jessup Gallery
432 Commercial St., Provincetown
• 487-4479

The Cortland Jessup Gallery is noteworthy because it refuses to remain stagnant. Cortland curates exhibitions ranging from haunting color-reversal X-rated prints to the silk-screen prints of feminist Kate Millett and the collages of performance artist Pat Delzell.

Long Point Gallery
492 Commercial St., Provincetown
• 487-1795

Since 1977 the Long Point Gallery has been one of the town's most important cooperative galleries. Many of the works shown here are by such Provincetown masters as Robert Motherwell, Paul Bowen, Paul Resika, Tony Vevers and Robert Beauchamp — sometimes for sale, sometimes not.

Rice/Polak Gallery
430 Commercial St., Provincetown
• 487-1052

Also in the East End, right next door to Cortland Jessup, is the Rice/Polak Gallery, where you'll find works in various mediums by local artists. The highlight, however, is the annual photography show in which the works of female photographers come into focus every October in celebration of Women's Week (see our Annual Events chapter).

Rising Tide Gallery
494 Commercial St., Provincetown
• 487-4037

The cooperative Rising Tide Gallery is housed in a late-1800s schoolhouse and features the works of members who have roots on the Lower Cape. Group shows are held at the beginning and end of every season. Look for the somber landscapes and nudes of local abstract expressionist Michael Rogovsky.

Wohlfarth Galleries
234 Commercial St., Provincetown
• 487-6569

Wohlfarth Galleries is the only venue exclusively devoted to traditional photography. An adjacent gallery exhibits other mediums.

Art Museums

The Cape's three art museums are treasures not only for their wonderful collections but also for their very existence, as they preserve much of what is important to Cape Codders. In addition to making art accessible to people, these institutions hold keys to both the past and the future, showing the legacy left by early artists and encouraging a new generation. The cultural events they sponsor sustain and nurture the community's passion for the arts.

Cahoon Museum of American Art

4676 Falmouth Rd. (Rt. 28), Cotuit • 428-7581

Housed in a 1775 Georgian Colonial farmhouse, the Cahoon Museum features a permanent collection of primitive-style paintings by the late Ralph Cahoon and his wife, Martha Cahoon, who still lives on the Cape and is still creating art. The museum has five special exhibitions each year. The building was actually the Cahoons' home and studio for 37 years. It is just east of Route 130.

In addition to the Cahoon paintings, the museum has a gallery of marine paintings and examples of American Impressionism and the Hudson River School. Founded in 1984, the museum also has a gift shop where you can purchase Cahoon prints and other items, and it offers memberships to help support its work. Talks, classes and demonstrations are held throughout the year. Admission is by donation. The museum is open Tuesday through Saturday and is closed in February.

Cape Museum of Fine Arts

Rt. 6A, on the grounds of the Cape Playhouse, Dennis • 385-4477

Founded in 1985, this museum houses a collection that dates from the late 1800s to the modern era, with more than 800 works by such icons as Charles Hawthorne, Paul Resika, Martha Cahoon and Chaim Gross. New acquisitions unveiled in early 1997 include several oils by Provincetown painter Gay Dickerson, a pastel by Rosalie Nadeau, watercolors by John Hare and prints by Edward Wilson and George Elmer Brown.

The museum sponsors frequent classes, trips, a winter lecture series and a film series (see the listing for ReelArt! in the Cinemas section later in this chapter). One special exhibit set for the spring of 1997 is a retrospective of the work of Betty Lane, who lived in Brewster most of the later years of her life. Admission is $2 for adults, free for those 16 and younger. The museum is closed Mondays in the off-season.

Provincetown Art Association and Museum

460 Commercial St., Provincetown • 487-1750

Regarded as one of the most important art institutions in the world, PAAM was established in 1914 to "promote education of the public in the arts and social intercourse between artists and laymen." Since then, its collection has grown to more than 1,700 works, all by artists associated in some way with Provincetown. The four exhibition spaces are wonderfully lighted, perfect for the numerous shows and various juried shows that happen here. One highlight: the shows curated by students of the town's grammar and high schools, the brainstorm of Executive Director Robyn Watson, who initiated the project in 1991 with a class of 2nd graders. Since then, grades 4, 6 and 8 have also participated. The project will end in 2002, the year the original 2nd-grade "curators" will be in the 10th grade.

PAAM also has an Adopt a Painting program in which patrons can underwrite the restoration of a favorite work. The museum has a nifty gift shop chock-full of artwork, books, posters, clothing, note cards and other items. It also sponsors lectures, courses, craft fairs and readings, such as Stephen Murphy's annual summer "O'Neill-By-the-Sea" festival. Admission is $3. The museum is open daily in summer, and off-season hours fluctuate so call ahead.

Cinemas

Moviegoers have some unique options on the Cape. Although there are multiplex movie theaters throughout the Cape (in Mashpee, Hyannis, Dennis and Harwich), there are a few theaters that offer something different than the current box-office hits. If you prefer art and

INSIDERS' TIP

For environmentally minded art, check out the Cape Cod Museum of Natural History's rotating "Personal Response to the Earth" exhibits, which feature Cape photographers and artists. The museum is on Route 6A in Brewster.

foreign films to the latest thriller, or you like the idea of watching a movie in a different setting, check out these unique venues.

Cape Cinema

Cape Playhouse grounds, Rt. 6A, Dennis • 385-2503

Insiders know that the Cape Cinema, built in 1930, is the place for serious movie-watching. The theater shows the finest in foreign, independent and art films from April through November, and its small size assures a sellout every time.

Getting there early will not only guarantee you a seat but also will give you time to bask in the cinema's beauty. The exterior was designed in the style of the Congregational Church in Centerville, and the interior ceiling is covered with a 6,400-square-foot mural of heavenly skies designed by Rockwell Kent and executed by Jo Mielziner. (Kent also designed the stage's golden sunburst curtain.)

ReelArt!

Cinema at the Cape Museum of Fine Arts, Cape Playhouse grounds, Rt. 6A, Dennis • 385-4477

ReelArt! offers first-run, independent and foreign films in the museum's 92-seat downstairs auditorium. Screenings run Thursday through Sunday year round. Admission is $5 ($4 for seniors and matinees).

Wellfleet Drive-in

Rt. 6, Wellfleet • 349-2520, (800) 696-3532

It's the only one of its kind left on the Cape — and one of a few left in the country. Ever since it opened in 1957, the Wellfleet Drive-in has been one of the most popular after-dark spots. Admission is $6 for adults, $3.50 for children ages 5 through 11 and senior citizens age 60 and older, and free for children four and younger. The huge parking lot is also home to the Cape's largest flea market (see our Shopping chapter).

Holiday Inn

Rt. 6A, Provincetown • 487-1771

Every night all year, the Holiday Inn shows free recently run movies — actual reel-to-reel 35mm prints, not large-screen VCR projection — in their Whaler Lounge. The popcorn is also free.

Appreciation of the
natural world is one of
the best uses of your
time on Cape Cod.

Parks and Recreation

The Creator was truly on top of the game when creating Cape Cod. This peninsula is a wonder of nature, a pile of glacial debris, which has over the thousands and thousands of years been sculpted by the winds and tides into a work of art. These outposts are a delicate blending of land and sky and sea, the three elements working together to create a place like no other.

Beaches, hiking and biking trails, bridle paths, picnic areas and nature sites are plentiful on the Cape, and we give you an overview of our favorite places in this chapter. If you came here to get a close look at coastal flora and fauna, you're in luck: Our parks and conservation areas are home to rare and not-so-rare (but still lovely) natural habitats. Cape Cod's beauty can be observed on foot, on horseback or on bicycle, and we've provided information on all of the above. For those who aren't so much into nature but instead favor health clubs, tennis courts and the tamer waters of heated indoor swimming pools, we've included descriptions of places you can go for those leisure and fitness activities.

Despite the fact that development on Cape Cod has been the most contentious issue of the last two decades, nearly one-third of the Cape's total acreage is use-restricted or designated conservation land. The largest such parcel is the 27,700-acre Cape Cod National Seashore (see our close-up in this chapter).

Centuries ago, municipalities had little need to worry about open space on the Cape, aside from woodlots and common grazing lands. Today, however, parks and conservation areas are a guarantee that public lands will be available for the benefit and enjoyment of generations to come. Open space also provides a recharge area for the sole-source aquifer beneath the Cape. This huge underground freshwater supply is critical to all life here. Conservation land, therefore, supports a habitat for both people and wildlife such as white-tailed deer, coyotes, possums, woodchucks, skunks, birds and fish.

A number of organizations contribute to the preservation of Cape lands. Among them is the Association for the Preservation of Cape Cod, 255-4142, which is an excellent source of information about conservation lands, including areas of critical concern throughout the region. The Massachusetts Audubon Society, (617) 259-9500, owns and manages extensive properties in Osterville and Wellfleet, and The Trustees of Reservations, 921-1944, is a private nonprofit conservation organization that has acquired more than 20,000 acres of land in Massachusetts, including the Mashpee River Reservation in Mashpee.

Appreciation of the natural world is one of the best uses of your time on Cape Cod. A number of organizations have long been involved in teaching people to understand, enjoy and protect the Cape's unique environment, which has dense woodlands, pine barrens, saltwater estuaries and 365 freshwater lakes and ponds. Among them is the Cape Cod Museum of Natural History, 869 Route 6A, Brewster, 896-3867, (800) 479-3867, with its extensive nature trails, museum, staff scientists, library and gift shop (see our Attractions chapter).

Just a note of caution: Before heading off to explore, make sure you can readily identify the distinctive three-leaf pattern and shape of poison ivy. And don't get ticked off if we remind you about those nasty Lyme Disease-carrying ticks. They are most prevalent in tall grass and bush, especially from April through October. Your best protection is to tuck your long pants into socks, stay out of shrubbery and spray your clothes with a DEET-based insecticide. It's a good idea to wear light colors so the ticks are easier to see and remove. Check your pets too.

Cape Cod has about 150 beaches, each with its own character; see our Beaches chapter to narrow your search. If you're into watersports, fishing, boating or golf, we have chapters devoted to those pursuits too. Come to think of it, you may need to set aside another week or two to do it all!

FYI

Unless otherwise noted, the area code for all phone numbers in this guide is 508.

Natural Areas and Walking Trails

Cape Cod is a garden paradise erupting with beauty. Visitors tend to gravitate more toward the extremities — the beaches — and for good reason. But the Cape is also graced with inland beauty from Bourne to Provincetown. We encourage you to wander inland and discover parts of the Cape we Codders consider some of her most beautiful hideaways.

Upper Cape

Bourne Scenic Park
Scenic Hwy., Bourne • 759-7873

Bourne Scenic Park, situated along the Scenic Highway, is operated by the Bourne Recreation Department primarily as a campground (see our Campgrounds chapter), but the roadways and a huge swimming pool are open to the public.

Four Ponds Park and Town Forest
Barlows Landing Rd., Bourne • 759-0623

Four Ponds Park and the abutting Town Forest off Barlows Landing Road comprise roughly 300 acres laced with marked hiking trails and points for fishing for pickerel and trout. Although no prominent structure remains, the area used to be part of the Pocasset Iron Works. You can park in the lot on the right of Barlow's Landing Road about a mile from MacArthur Boulevard. This is a nice area for bird-watching, and you might see deer too.

Nivling Alexander Reserve
Shore Rd. and Thaxter Rd., Bourne • 563-2800

The Nivling Alexander Reserve is a half-mile circular wooded trail passing through 40 acres of land along Red Brook Pond and cranberry bogs. The entrance is at Shore Road and Thaxter Road. For more information, contact the Bourne Natural Resources Department at the above number.

Boyden Farm
Cotuit Rd., Sandwich • 888-4200

Boyden Farm is a 48-acre conservation area that fronts Peters Pond. It has walking trails, fishing areas and a small parking area along the road. Bring your binoculars to the wildlife field where you may spot deer, eagles and wild turkeys, which have been successfully released on the Cape in recent years.

Maple Swamp
Service Rd., Sandwich • 888-4200

Maple Swamp is a large 500-acre conservation area spreading out along a service road parallel to Route 6 between exits 3 and 4. It is closed to vehicles and has numerous trails and roads for walking (no biking). Parking is limited along the road. Here you can find all types of wildlife, including white-tailed deer. The kettle-hole ponds and irregular terrain are typical of the topography that glaciers created thousands of years ago. The elevation at Maple Swamp ranges from 40 feet above sea level to 250 feet at one of the highest points of land on the Cape.

Ryder Conservation Area
Cotuit and S. Sandwich rds., Sandwich • 888-4200

The lovely 243-acre Ryder Conservation Area is accessible from Cotuit and S. Sandwich roads. It offers about 5 miles of walking trails. Wakely Lake has fishing areas and a boat ramp and is an excellent area for canoeing and swimming. Nature lovers will appreciate the large holly and beech trees and old overgrown bogs. Lifeguards are on-site during the summer months (Ryder Conservation Area is open May to October). A local beach sticker is required, contact the above number for more information.

Spring Hill Conservation Area

Salt Marsh Rd., Sandwich • 888-4200

You'll discover the Spring Hill Conservation Area at the end of Salt Marsh Road off Foster Road. An open barrier beach community with piping plover and lease terns, this area is accessible for saltwater fishing in Cape Cod Bay.

Talbot's Point Conservation Lands

Old County Rd., Sandwich • 888-4200

Talbot's Point Conservation Lands on Old County Road has a relatively level trail system through a red pine forest planted for soil control by the Conservation Corps during the Great Depression. Its 112 acres abut a saltwater and freshwater marsh, and walkers may see shore and upland game birds as well as osprey. The park features a freshwater bubbling spring. Call conservation agent Mark Galkowski at the above number for more information.

Scusset Beach Reservation

Scusset Beach Rd., Sandwich • 888-0859

Scusset Beach Reservation on the north side of the canal (see our Campgrounds chapter) is a large state-run park that is mostly used for camping, but hiking and fishing are permitted. A 1-mile trail through Scusset visits Sagamore Hill, which offers a panoramic overlook of Cape Cod Bay. You can also learn about World War II coastal fortifications and Native American meeting grounds. The U.S. Army Corps of Engineers gives free guided tours of the area in the summer.

Shawme-Crowell State Forest

Rt. 130, Sandwich • 888-0351

This large 742-acre state-run park is used mostly for camping and offers an abundance of wildlife, flora and fauna. There are 285 campsites. Toilets and hot water are available at a cost of only $6 per night. There are several hiking trails and hunting is allowed within this huge state forest. A hike to Mt. Perry is well-worth the trip for from the summit you can view all of Cape Cod Bay. A camping permit allows campers to use Scusset Beach.

The Briar Patch

Rt. 6A, East Sandwich • 888-6870

The Briar Patch is a 57-acre conservation area off Route 6A in East Sandwich. This pleasant area of white pine , black locust trees and meandering trails was a source of inspiration to Thornton W. Burgess, who wrote *Old Mother West Wind* and hundreds of other children's books in the early 20th century.

Murkwood Conservation Area

Rt. 6A, East Sandwich • 888-4200

To explore the 79-acre Murkwood Conservation Area, park at the East Sandwich Fire Station on Route 6A and walk across the street. Basically a peninsula surrounded by water, this former farmland abuts Scorton Creek, and you might be fortunate enough to see eagles, osprey, shorebirds and white-tailed deer. The area's several miles of trails pass through swampy areas and pine woods, and the marsh views are nice.

Ashumet Holly Wildlife Sanctuary

Currier Rd., Hatchville (Falmouth) • 563-6390

Owned by the Massachusetts Audubon Society, the Ashumet Holly Reservation and Wildlife Sanctuary, off Route 151 on Currier Road, is a popular 45-acre preserve that is open from sunrise to sunset all year. Along the trails you can see flowering magnolias, dogwood, rhododendron and rare wildflowers such as the Plymouth Gentian. The grounds include 65 varieties of holly trees as well as Franklinia trees, named in honor of Benjamin Franklin, which are actually a type of tea plant. In the spring, swallows nest in the Ashumet barn. The sanctuary offers workshops, bird walks and field trips during the year and trips to the Elizabeth Islands near Falmouth (see our Tours and Excursions chapter). Activities usually cost $3 for nonmember adults and $2 for children, seniors and members. Admission is $3 for adults, $2 for seniors and children and free for members.

Beebe Woods

off Depot Ave., Falmouth • 457-2536

Beebe Woods was a generous gift to the town from benefactor Josiah K. Lilly. Located past Highfield Theater at the end of Depot Avenue, the wooded grounds of the 334-acre estate have extensive trails and are open to the public for walking, cross-country skiing, horseback riding and bird-watching.

Bourne Farm

W. Falmouth Hwy. (Rt. 28A) or Palmer Ave., Falmouth • 548-0711

The 33.9-acre Bourne Farm is owned and operated by Salt Pond Area Bird Sanctuary Inc. You can take an afternoon tour of a 1775 farmhouse and barn with an old cattle tunnel every Tuesday through Thursday in the summer. This former working farm has hiking paths and a parking area. Call about special activities and classes offered throughout the year.

Frances A. Crane Wildlife Management Area

Ashumet Rd., Falmouth • 759-3406

Frances A. Crane Wildlife Management Area is a 1,700-acre reserve regulated by the Massachusetts Division of Fisheries and Game. The land is an extensive sand plain with mostly pitch pine and little deciduous growth. It is stocked with game during the fall hunting season and should not be considered safe for recreational activities then. At other times of the year, it is a popular place for walking and horseback riding. Hobbyists take note: The area has a model airplane flying strip.

Goodwill Park

Palmer Ave., Falmouth • 457-2543

The 85-acre Goodwill Park is a spacious wooded area with a lovely pond. The park is open daily from 8 AM to 4 PM for hiking, swimming, Frisbee-playing and canoeing. With a pretty freshwater beach, restrooms, barbecue grills and play equipment, this is a good place for families and picnickers. To bring a large group, call the parks department at the above number to reserve the pavilion area.

Washburn Island

Waquoit Bay, Falmouth • 457-0495 ext. 100

Washburn Island is a 334-acre wooded island in Waquoit Bay that is managed by the state Division of Forests and Parks within the Department of Environmental Management (see our Campgrounds chapter). It is only accessible by boat and has no fresh water. If you wish to camp on the island you must purchase a permit. Call the Waquoit Bay National Estuarine Research Reserve at the above number for more information.

John's Pond Park

Hoophole Rd., Mashpee • 539-1414

John's Pond Park is a 258-acre area with a trail system and a 1,200-foot sandy beach. Nature lovers can watch herring swim up the Quashnet River in the spring and fall and explore an extensive area of cranberry bogs. As you head toward North Falmouth, you'll find the park off Route 151 past the Barnstable County fairgrounds; turn right onto Currier Road, then right on Hoophole Road and right again onto Back Road. John's Pond Park is just beyond the trailer park.

Lowell Holly Reservation

S. Sandwich Rd., Mashpee • 740-7233

At the Lowell Holly Reservation, marked by a small sign on Sandwich Road (the entrance is opposite a sign that says "Carpe Diem"), you'll find a delightful 1.5-mile trail among American beech, huge holly and white pine trees and rhododendron. There's a perfect little swimming beach with a picnic table on the Cape's largest (and perhaps most beautiful) lake. Birders have spotted eagles, osprey and hawks here. Once owned by James Lowell, former president of Harvard University, this 135-acre property is maintained by The Trustees of Reservations. The parking fee on summer weekends is $6; on weekdays admission is free.

Mashpee River Woodlands

Quinaquisset Rd., Mashpee • 539-1414

The 400-acre Mashpee River Woodlands has 8 miles of hiking trails along the Mashpee River, a protected waterway that is perfect for canoeing, bird-watching and walking. "You can

Photo: Vincent DeWitt, Cape Cod Times

There are plenty of places to enjoy nature throughout the Cape — just you and your best friend.

get up there and think you are in the middle of Maine," commented conservation agent Bob Sherman, noting that this area is a good place to see the natural transition between freshwater and saltwater habitats. Coming from the Mashpee Rotary, follow Route 28 toward Hyannis to the first right, Quinaquisset Road.

South Cape Beach

Great Neck Rd., Mashpee • 457-0495

At the end of Great Neck Road is South Cape Beach, where the state maintains a public beach, parking lot and conservation land with 3 miles of sandy roadways suitable for hiking. Here you can explore both freshwater and saltwater wetlands. There is a fee for parking. For more information about South Cape, contact the Waquoit Bay National Estuarine Research Reserve at the above number.

Pine Barrens

Great Neck Rd. S., Mashpee • 539-1414

The Pine Barrens is a 300-acre reserve that has about 4 miles of marked walking trails. For more information about other smaller conservation areas and guided walking tours, contact conservation agent Bob Sherman at the number above.

Mid-Cape

Crocker Neck Conservation Area

Santuit Rd., Cotuit • 790-6245

The 52-acre Crocker Neck Conservation Area in Cotuit is a peninsula created by Shoestring Bay, Popponesset Bay and Pinquiskset Cove. It is wooded and has an interpretative trail with permanent numbered markers and an observation deck overlooking tidal pools. The area also has saltwater marshes. You can park in a lot off Santuit Road.

Long Pond Conservation Area

Santuit-Newtown Rd., Cotuit • 790-6245

A community garden with two observation decks overlooking the 37-acre Long Pond are features of Long Pond Conservation Area. An interpretative network of trails totaling 2 miles passes through fields and woodlands. A parking entrance on Newtown Road is about 2.5 miles from Route 28.

Burgess Park

Rt. 149, Marstons Mills • 790-6345

Burgess Park is a 17-acre park with a Frisbee golf course, walking trails, a playground, volleyball court, croquet area, horseshoe pits and barbeque grills. The park over-

From Sea to Shining Sea: The Cape Cod National Seashore

As someone who spent a lot of time on the Cape, John F. Kennedy not only saw the lighthouses, but he also saw the light. Perhaps his greatest accomplishment as President of the United States (especially to Cape Codders and environmentalists) was achieved on August 7, 1961 — the day he signed a bill making the Cape Cod National Seashore a reality.

It was, and remains, a Cape Cod Camelot. The CCNS, the first of its kind in the nation, consists of approximately 27,700 acres of federally protected undeveloped uplands, bogs, pitch pine forests and ponds in six towns (Chatham, Orleans, Eastham, Wellfleet, Truro and Provincetown); almost half of Wellfleet and about 70 percent of Truro fall within the National Seashore. Although there was actually some local opposition to the Seashore at the time of its formation, today nearly everyone agrees it was the best thing that ever happened to the Lower Cape.

Your first priority should be to stop at the CCNS **Salt Pond Visitor Center**, off Route 6, Eastham, 255-3421. Besides getting free hiking and bike maps and a host of other informational necessities, you can view free videos and tour a first-rate museum featuring early Cape Cod artifacts, including mementos belonging to sea captain Edward Penniman and his wife. (Take a peek into the seafaring diary she kept while accompanying the captain on several trips.) The Penniman's French Second Empire-style house is owned by the CCNS and is open to the public (see our History chapter).

Beaches

The CCNS boasts six protected beaches, comprising nearly 40 miles of the finest seashore on the Atlantic coast: **Coast Guard Beach** and the adjacent **Nauset Light Beach** in Eastham; **Marconi Beach** in South Wellfleet; **Head of the Meadow** in North Truro; and **Herring Cove** and **Race Point** in Provincetown. (You could, if you choose, make your way from Eastham to Provincetown by walking along the sand at low tide, though many opt to bike their way on the paved Cape Cod Rail Trail.) All CCNS beaches have lifeguards, restrooms and showers except for Head of the Meadow. A food stand is available only at Herring Cove. Parking costs $5 per day; a $15 season pass is good at any time at any CCNS beach and is a better buy if you're planning on spending lots of time at various (or even the same) beaches.

Hiking Trails

Bummed out on beaches? Then take a hike. The National Seashore boasts nine hiking trails that meander through various kinds of terrain. One of our favorite walking spots is **Fort Hill** in Eastham, where trails meander through fields with stunning water and marsh views, through woods and through a cedar swamp. Watch out for monster poison ivy plants on the edge of the trail! Stop and see the Captain Penniman House while you're there. We're also partial to the Seashore's longest and most difficult trail: **Great Island** in Wellfleet. Accessible by driving out past the harbor to the parking area, the trail is an uphill, downhill 8-mile (round-trip) saunter through soft sand, pitch pines

— continued on next page

Photo: Cape Cod Chamber of Commerce

Cape Cod National Seashore.

and marshes that offers breathtaking views of Wellfleet Bay. Look for fiddler crabs, fast-moving, harmless and ugly little black creatures so named because the males have one oversized claw that's reminiscent of someone playing a fiddle. Be sure to check the tides, since much of the trail is flooded at high tide. We speak from bitter experience when we say it's slow going slogging back over the soft-sand high ground if you've timed your hike poorly.

In Truro, there's the **Pilgrim Spring Trail**, an easy .75-mile walk through bayberry and blueberry woodlands and the half-mile **Cranberry Bog Trail** (the name says it all). In Wellfleet there's the moderately difficult **Atlantic White Cedar Swamp Trail**, a 1.5-mile venture through natural wonders. In Provincetown, check out the 1-mile **Beech Forest Trail**, where you'll circle a freshwater pond as you walk among American beech trees, sheep laurel, yellow and gray birch and swamp azalea. The **Seashore** is also a front-runner when it comes to having handicapped-accessible facilities. Several of its hiking trails and nature paths are wheelchair-accessible. The **Buttonbush Trail**, an easy quarter-mile path next to the Salt Pond Visitor Center in Eastham, has Braille map interpretations along the way.

Tours

The CCNS also offers an abundance of guided tours, interpretative nature walks, lectures, classes, demonstrations, family-oriented beach walks and evening campfire talks throughout the year. The Salt Pond Visitor Center is also home to an outdoor amphitheater, which is the setting for musical and educational programs on summer nights. Some events cost a nominal fee; many are free. Call for a full schedule.

A second visitors center, the **Province Lands Visitor Center**, Race Point Road, Provincetown, 487-1256, provides many of the same offerings; it is closed from Thanksgiving to mid-April. The Salt Pond Visitor Center is open daily, but only on weekends during January and February. When the visitors centers are closed, you can still obtain help at the CCNS administrative offices, Marconi Station, off Route 6, 349-3785.

looks Hamblin Pond, and it's an easy walk to the pond's beach.

Centerville Recreation Building

Main St., Centerville • 790-6345

The children's playground at the Centerville Recreation Building on Main Street is popular with families. The facilities, which include a portable toilet, are handicapped-accessible.

Bridge Creek Watershed

Rt. 149, West Barnstable • 790-6245

To reach Bridge Creek Watershed you can park at either the fire station on Route 149 or at Church Street (which can be found off Parker Road off Route 6A). This conservation area is marked by mapped, well-cleared trails for you to explore.

Sandy Neck Recreation Area

off Route 6A, West Barnstable • 790-6245

The Sandy Neck Recreation Area has about 4.8 miles of sandy trails bordered by wildflowers and cranberries. It's a nice place to canoe and fish. You can plan your hike from a trail map at the beach guard station. Parking is available.

West Barnstable Conservation Area

Rt. 149, West Barnstable • 790-6245

West Barnstable Conservation Area is an extensive 1,114-acre area with 15 miles of trails, one of which is called the Trail of Tears. A good number of the trails are geared toward mountain biking. You'll find limited parking at the intersection of Popple Bottom Road and Route 149, or off the service road.

Hathaway Pond Recreation Area

Old Phinney Ln., Barnstable • 790-6245

The Hathaway Pond Recreation Area in Barnstable has oak and pine forests, two ponds, an interpretative trail and a picnic area within its 94 acres. The entrance is on Phinney's Lane near Route 132.

Horse Pond Conservation Area

Higgins Crowell Rd., West Yarmouth • 398-2231

Located near the Mattacheese School, this 5,073-foot hilly trail is marked by pitch pines, white oaks, sassafras and blueberry bushes as well as huckleberry. Though the trail is joined by side trails that lead off toward longer journeys, the main trail keeps Horse Pond within sight.

Meadowbrook Road Conservation Area

Meadowbrook Rd., West Yarmouth • 398-2231

Meadowbrook Road Conservation Area is a pretty walking area. It has a 310-foot-long boardwalk over a freshwater marsh that leads to a scenic overlook of Swan Pond. Benches provide a good place for a reflective moment or to examine the beautiful salt marsh vegetation that grows so abundantly here.

Raymond J. Syrjala Conservation Area

Winslow Gray Rd., West Yarmouth • 398-2231

The Raymond J. Syrjala Conservation Area is about a half-mile from Route 28. The 3,540-foot trail encircles a kettle-hole pond that serves as a great frog pond. The trail itself is spongy due to the decaying leaves and pine needles that comprise it. Many species of vegetation, such as red maple, pitch pine and blueberries, are marked.

Dennis Pond Conservation Area

Willow St., Yarmouth Port • 398-2231

As its name suggests, this conservation area is adjacent to Dennis Pond and features a 3,285-foot trail that leads through woodlands of red maple, white pine and sweet pepperbush. Your walk will take you through the many faces of Cape Cod woodlands, including an old bog, pine forests and a small swamp. Moss is plentiful in some spots, fallen pine needles in others. There's a small parking area out on Willow Street where you begin your journey.

Crab Creek Conservation Area

North Dennis Rd., Yarmouth Port • 398-2231

Five-inch-long blue crabs (Callinectes sapidus) are abundant in this area, and their presence here has lent this conservation area its name. A 500-foot trail follows a creek that joins Follins Pond with Mill Creek. It is a prime fishing spot and features a dock just for that purpose. Besides the creek and the crabs, there is also an old bog and plenty of red maple, cranberry, pitch pine, blueberry and poison ivy.

Callery-Darling Conservation Area

Center St., Yarmouth Port • 398-2231

The Callery-Darling Conservation Area is a great place to spot woodland and water birds, such as the gangly great blue heron, which fishes in both fresh and salt water and is the largest heron in North America. There is a trail system here comprising some 2.4 miles wandering through lands where foxes, rabbits and even deer make their home.

Botanical Trails

Rt. 6A, Yarmouth Port • 398-2231

In Yarmouth, the Botanical Trails behind the Yarmouth Port post office on Route 6A are owned by the town. The area has a little herb garden and a 150-year-old weeping beech tree. There is a gate house at the beginning of the trail where trail guides can be obtained and where a donation is requested (50¢ for adults, 25¢ for children). The main trail is approximately 1 mile in length, while the pond trail around Millers Pond adds another half-mile to the trek.

Bass Hole (Gray's Beach)

Centre St., Yarmouth Port • 398-2231

Bass Hole, also called Gray's Beach, at the end of Centre Street, is the place to stroll along the boardwalk, put your toes in the water and enjoy the beach, playground and barbecue facilities. Many consider this the best place to watch a sunset on Cape Cod.

Simpkins Neck Romig-Jacquinet Conservation Area

New Boston Rd., Dennis • 760-6123

Simpkins Neck and the Romig-Jacquinet Conservation Area are two connected parcels of land that are largely surrounded by marshlands. Once you find the entrance (off New Boston Road, two houses past Berrien Studios on your left) you can follow the trail to the edge of the marsh. You'll have to work your way through some underbrush, but once you do, you can actually walk out to the marsh. Bird watchers will be in heaven, as will wildlife lovers, since Simpkins Neck is also refuge to raccoons and deer.

Crowe's Pasture

South St., East Dennis • 760-6123

Nature lovers will relish Crowe's Pasture, a bayfront 50-acre-plus site off South Street at the end of Quivet Cemetery. Follow the dirt road (about 2.5 miles round-trip) and revel in an oasis of seals, marsh hawks and wild apple and cherry groves. It's also a great place for four-wheel-drive vehicles.

Fresh Pond Conservation Area

Rt. 134, South Dennis • 760-6123

Fresh Pond Conservation Area, right on Route 134, is 90 unspoiled acres of blueberries and wild cranberries, with the occasional fowl thrown in for good measure. You have your choice of four informal trails of various lengths.

Indian Lands Conservation Area

Main St., South Dennis • 760-6123

Some of the Cape's most awesome flora and fauna abound at Indian Lands Conservation Area, a 2-mile walk that hugs the banks of Bass River. Birders can easily spot kingfishers and blue herons in the winter. You know summer's around the corner when the lady's slippers start sprouting in May. We know of a hiking aficionado who found, on three separate occasions, Indian artifacts of the Native Americans who lived here centuries past.

INSIDERS' TIP

Birdwatching is a big hobby on the Cape. You may want to pick up Peter Trull's book *The Common Birds of Cape Cod*. The Cape also has a number of stores that cater to this growing hobby, including the Birdwatcher's General Store in Orleans and Wild Birds Unlimited in South Yarmouth.

Lower Cape

The Lower Cape is dominated by the expansive Cape Cod National Seashore, one of America's most beautiful recreational shorelines. See our "From Sea to Shining Sea" close-up for details on the Seashore's beautiful natural areas in the towns of Eastham, Wellfleet, Truro and Provincetown. Adding to this bounty of natural areas are other excellent parks and wildlife refuges, including the magnificent Monomoy National Wildlife Refuge.

Nickerson State Park

Rt. 6A, Brewster • 896-3491

This 1,779-acre wonderland has 8 miles of bike trails that link with the Cape Cod Rail Trail. Then there are the hiking trails — miles of paths that meander through the woods. Some of them wind past the park's two main attractions, Flax and Cliff ponds. The trails are also great for cross-country skiing in winter, if the Cape is blessed with a real snowfall (yes, it does happen!). Hike out to Higgins Pond, a major migration stop for endangered birds such as osprey and the peregrine falcon. You'll also see cormorants, wrens, osprey, hawks, owls, warblers, thrushes, great blue herons, Canada geese and the common loon — it's bird-watcher's heaven. Nickerson also has bayfront land on the north side of Route 6A (an easy walk from the park's entrance on the south side of the road) and regularly offers ranger-guided interpretive programs and walks that cover plant and wildlife in a variety of habitats.

The Cape Cod Museum of Natural History

869 Rt. 6A, Brewster • 896-3867

This renowned facility maintains three important trails. The 1.3-mile John Wing Trail, just west of the museum's parking lot and named in honor of Brewster's first European settler, cuts its way through 140 acres of beach plum, golden aster, salt reed grass and bush clover, around a sassafras grove and salt marshes, ending on a tidal island with an unsurpassed view of Cape Cod Bay. One word of caution: During high tides the causeway is covered, making entry to the island (and exit off it) nearly impossible. If the water rises while you're there it can get as high as your knees, so be sure to check the tides in the museum before you go. The other two trails, also part of the museum, are the North Trail, a quarter-mile-long path that serves as a primer for plant identification, and the South Trail, four times the length of its sister, cutting through cattail marsh and poison ivy — lots of it.

Spruce Hill Conservation Area

3341 Rt. 6A, Brewster • 896-3701

This 25-acre parcel, hidden behind the Brewster Historical Society Museum on the eastern end of town, features a half-mile-long former carriage road leading to Cape Cod Bay and an expansive beach. Rumor has it that the trail was once used by bootleggers during Prohibition. Fragile plant life is abundant here, so please, as always, stay on the official path.

Punkhorn Parklands

Run Hill Rd., Brewster • 896-3701

Here you'll find a maze of 45 scenic trails tossed throughout more than 800 acres of quarries, pine, oaks, marshes and meadows, a tranquil paradise interrupted only by warbling birds, howling coyote and the occasional mountain bike. Along the paths you'll spot old pumps once used by cranberry growers to flood these former bogs.

Bell's Neck Road Conservation Area

off Bell's Neck Rd., Harwich • 430-7506

One of the finest bird-watching spots on the Lower Cape, this magnificent 245-acre utopia of marshlands, herring runs, reservoirs and tidal creeks is a favorite stop for the Cape Cod Bird Club, 432-2528, which leads frequent walks here.

INSIDERS' TIP

To get the most out of a nature walk, go with an expert. Guided walks for small groups are offered in different areas of the Cape by naturalist Lee Baldwin of Cape Cod Naturally, 432-0805, and in Falmouth by Alison Robb of Nature's Circle, 540-2408.

Thompson's Field
Rt. 39, Harwich • 430-7506

This field is a wildflower wonder: 93-acres of the best blooms on the Cape. Look, but please don't pick! It's also a great place for stargazing.

Monomoy National Wildlife Refuge
Chatham • 945-0594

Accessible from Chatham only by boat in good weather conditions, Monomoy is a 2,750-acre, two-island wilderness area, one of only four remaining between Maine and New Jersey. Acquired by the federal government in 1944 and now under the administration of the U.S. Fish and Wildlife Service, Monomoy has no electricity, no human residents, no vehicles, no paved roads — just more than 285 species of birds, saltwater and tidal flats, bayberry and beach plum thickets, freshwater ponds, a non-working lighthouse (built in 1823, restored in 1988) and a 9-mile-long barrier beach. Beach areas are closed from April to mid-August so that the nesting areas of piping plovers and terns won't be disturbed.

Quiet is the best word to describe Monomoy. In the winter, thousands of seals take harbor here. Monomoy is an important stop along the North Atlantic Flyway, and in May and late July migrating waterfowl and shorebirds stop here for a rest. Monomoy was once attached to the mainland; a 1958 storm severed the relationship. Twenty years later, another storm divided the island into two. The Cape Cod Museum of Natural History, 896-3867, and the Wellfleet Bay Wildlife Sanctuary, 349-2615, offer regular guided tours. Morris Island, a 40-acre island accessible by car and foot, is home to migrating warblers, and tidal flats provide food for oyster-shucking birds. Check your tide chart before visiting: The ¾-mile-long interpretive walking trail closes during high tide.

Wellfleet Bay Wildlife Sanctuary
Rt. 6, Wellfleet • 349-2615

The Massachusetts Audubon Society operates this 1,000-acre-plus tract of saltmarsh, forest, beach, tidal flats and moors. What was once a turnip and asparagus farm is now a haven of self-guided nature trails and superb bird-watching, along with a natural history day camp for children and week-long field trips for older folk. Guided walks, canoe cruises through Nauset Marsh, Monomoy cruises and seal and whale-watching trips are regularly sponsored. The excursions are extremely popular and book up faster than you can say "humpback" (see our Whale Watching chapter). The 1.5-mile Goose Pond Trail, part of the 5 miles of trails, offers a look at a diversity of habitats and leads to the shore. It's an excellent place for viewing shore birds, hawks and herons. If you're still getting to know Mother Nature, borrow or purchase a copy of the 32-page plant identification booklet at the trailhead. In keeping with the theme of preservation, the $1.6 million visitors center, built five years ago, uses passive solar heating and composting toilets. It's open year round.

Recreation

Biking Trails

Cape Cod is serious about its bike paths. Most towns have areas where you can ride, but there are three major bike trails set aside for those who prefer two wheels: the paths that run along both sides of the Cape Cod Canal; the Shining Sea Bikepath in Falmouth; and the Cape Cod Rail Trail that runs from Dennis to Wellfleet. Remember to always wear a helmet and please obey the rules of the road.

Upper Cape

Cape Cod Canal
Buzzards Bay • 759-4431

One of the most popular outdoor recreational facilities is the Cape Cod Canal area in Bourne and Sandwich. Owned and operated by the U.S. Army Corps of Engineers, the 8-mile-long paved service roads that run along both sides of the canal are relatively level and are used morning, noon and night in every season by bikers, in-line skaters, walkers and dog-walkers. The views are appealing — cormorants dive for fish while towering tankers and elegant sailboats pass by within a few hundred yards. Or watch as the railroad bridge lowers to allow the Cape Cod train to pass over the Canal.

The path, considered the longest trail in

Massachusetts without interruption, can be accessed at many points along its length. Those access points along the north side of the Canal are at the northeast of Bourne Bridge, Herring Brook Fishway in Bournedale, Scusset State Park and at the east side of the Sagamore Bridge. South side accesses are along Pleasant Street in Sagamore, the southeast side of the Bourne Bridge and the Boat Basin off Freezer Road in Sandwich. The access roads are marked so you should be able to find your way.

Shining Sea Bikepath

Woods Hole • 548-7611

A favorite with bikers, hikers and in-line skaters, the Shining Sea Bikepath runs a little more than 3.1 miles from the Woods Hole Road near Locust Street to Railroad Avenue in Woods Hole near the Steamship Authority docks (there is talk of extending it). You can park at Locust Street, or there is also some parking available at the Steamship Authority Parking Lot. The route follows the shore and provides a classic view of Martha's Vineyard and Nobska Light. Along the way you'll come upon a public beach where you can stop for a swim and a picnic. Other smaller routes connect with the Shining Sea Trail.

FYI

Unless otherwise noted, the area code for all phone numbers in this guide is 508.

Lower Cape

Cape Cod Rail Trail

Dennis to Wellfleet • 896-3491

This 25-mile paved trail runs from Dennis to Wellfleet, following the old rail bed and offering cyclists, walkers and others who use the trail a glimpse of a part of Cape Cod many visitors never see. Along the wooded trail you'll pass ponds, cranberry bogs, fields and woods. It's especially peaceful in the off-season. Be aware that it can get busy in summer, making it especially important to obey the common-sense rules you'll find posted along the route. Helmets are required by state law for cyclists younger than 12 (they're also recommended for older children and adults), ride to the right, call out a warning before passing and pull off the trail when stopping. The trail, which was expanded two years ago (the Eastham to Wellfleet leg in the new portion), features three tunnels, two in Brewster and a new one in Eastham, and is patrolled in summer by police officers — on bikes, of course! The officers are there to help, so feel free to ask questions about regulations or the distance from one point to another. Sadly, there are not many restrooms along the route, but there are facilities at Nickerson State Park in Brewster, and a new composting toilet in Eastham.

Parking areas for trail access are in Dennis on Route 134; Harwich on Headwaters Road near Route 124 and at the Pleasant Lake General Store on Route 124; in Brewster on Route 137 and at Nickerson State Park off Route 6A; in Orleans at the court house on Rock Harbor Road; in Eastham at the Cape Cod National Seashore Visitor Center; and in South Wellfleet at the South Wellfleet General Store just off Route 6.

Nickerson State Park

Rt. 6A, Brewster • 896-3491

The park has several loops of often hilly paved trails that connect with the Cape Cod Rail Trail.

Cape Cod National Seashore

Rt. 6, Eastham • 255-3421

At the Visitor Center, right near the Cape Cod Rail Trail (exit the trail at Locust Road and cross Route 6 at the traffic light) is a lovely trail that goes out to Coast Guard Beach with a few scenic view benches to stop at along the way. You'll love crossing the wooden bridge over the

INSIDERS' TIP

Canada geese, often mistakenly called Canadian geese, were named after John Canada, the Bostonian who "discovered" them. These large birds are frequent visitors to the Cape as they migrate south for the winter.

Photo: Vincent DeWitt, Cape Cod Times

Greenbrier Nature Center in Sandwich is part of Thornton Burgess Society.

salt marsh just before you reach Coast Guard Beach. In Provincetown, the Seashore has miles of trails — you could ride around all day!

Bike Rentals

The Cape has plenty of shops that rent and sell bicycles and cycling equipment. Below we list a few that happen to be close to the major bike routes.

Upper Cape

P&M Cycles
29 Main St., Buzzards Bay • 759-2830

This bike rental outfit is right on the Cape Cod Canal bike trail. It rents bicycles by the hour, day, week or month and has the largest selection of used bicycles to choose from on the Cape.

Holiday Cycles
465 Grand Ave., Falmouth Heights • 540-1701

If you're vacationing in Falmouth you'll want to spend some time on the Shining Sea Bikepath. It would help a lot if you had a bicycle, so you'll definitely want to stop by Holiday Cycles for bike rentals and any equipment you might need.

Mid-Cape

Barbara's Bike and Sport Equipment
430 Rt. 134, South Dennis • 760-4723

Barbara's is right at the parking lot at the beginning of the Cape Cod Rail Trail. It rents bicycles by the hour, day or week for all members of the family, from toddlers to teenagers to grandparents.

Rick's Rollers
240 Lower County Rd., Dennisport • 760-6747

Rick's specializes in sales and rentals of all types of things with wheels attached. With a rental it also provides all protective gear for free.

Lower Cape

Idle Times Bike Shop
Town Center Plaza, Rt. 6, North Eastham • 255-8281

With three other shops, one at the entrance to the Cape Cod Rail Trail on Route 134 in Dennis, one in Brewster and one in Wellfleet, Idle Times boasts the largest fleet of rental bikes on the Cape. It also sells bikes and accessories. The North Eastham and Dennis shops are open year-round, and the other two are seasonal.

Little Capistrano Bike Shop
Salt Pond Rd., Eastham • 255-6515

This friendly shop is just across Route 6 from the Cape Cod National Seashore Visitor Center, right near the Cape Cod Rail Trail and the Seashore bike trails. It offers rentals, sales, accessories and repairs. It's open April through December, and by appointment only January through March.

Bowling

Sometimes you just get the urge to bowl a few strings. The Cape can accommodate this urge with a number of fine alleys.

Upper Cape

Ryan Family Amusements Center Bowling & Miniature Golf
200 Main St., Buzzards Bay • 759-9892

This popular Upper Cape facility has candlepin bowling, a pro shop and a game room while next door is an 18-hole miniature golf course (Bourne Bridge Adventure Golf). Ryan hosts leagues as well as good old recreational bowling and offers birthday party packages.

Ryan's Family Amusements Center
23 Town Hall Sq., Falmouth • 540-4877

Falmouth has plenty of fun spots to explore, and the Ryan Family Amusements Center is one of them. It offers candlepin bowling alleys for leagues as well as for nonleague recreational bowlers. There is a pro shop on site and the facility hosts birthday parties.

Trade Center Bowl & Amusements
89 Spring Bars Rd., Falmouth • 548-7000

This bowling facility features ten pin with computer scoring. There are leagues for children and high schoolers as well as moonlight bowling. Also on premises are pool tables, video games, a pro shop and a snack bar.

Mid-Cape

Cape Bowl
441 Main St., Hyannis • 775-3411

Cape Bowl in the heart of downtown Hyannis features ten pin and hosts leagues for all ages. Some lanes have built in bumpers for kids and other lanes even glow in the dark. There's a pro shop, video games and souvenir and gift shops on site.

Ryan Family Amusements Center
Rt. 28, South Yarmouth • 394-5644

A very busy recreational hot-spot, this Ryan Family Amusements Center has both ten pin and candlepin lanes, a pro shop and a game room. Like the other Ryans Family centers on the Cape, the Yarmouth facility hosts leagues and birthday parties.

Lower Cape

Orleans Bowling Center
Rt. 6A, Orleans • 255-0636

With 14 lanes, this is an all-candlepin bowling center. Even during league events, there are lanes available for the public. Weekend nights are popular for families. The center is open year-round from 9 AM to 10 PM Monday through Saturday, and on Sundays opens at noon.

Fitness Clubs and Indoor Swimming

With hundreds of miles of coastline, it seems redundant for the Cape to offer so many swimming pools. (It's just that we Cape Codders love the water so much!). Most hotels and motels have a pool or two. The resorts around the Cape normally have a couple. And a number of health and fitness clubs also offer indoor swimming facilities. In fact, indoor pools are an excellent resource for those who want instruction, physical therapy and aerobic exercise as well as an opportunity to continue their favorite form of exercise all year.

The Cape has a number of health and fitness clubs where you can continue your exercise routine while you're on vacation. Fees and access to facilities vary, but generally the fitness centers are open all year.

Upper Cape

Massachusetts Maritime Academy

Taylor's Point, Buzzards Bay • 564-5690

Massachusetts Maritime Academy has beginner swimming lessons, lap swimming, competitive swimming, a masters group and water polo for all ages. And a big plus: The pool has a giant water slide.

RMA Nautilus Racquetball & Fitness Center

MacArthur Blvd., Bourne • 759-7111

RMA Nautilus Racquetball & Fitness Center has a full complement of Nautilus equipment and free weights plus cardiovascular equipment. Racquetball court fees average $10 per hour. Soothe those aching muscles in the sauna, spa and steam rooms.

Sportsite

315 Cotuit Rd., Sandwich • 888-7900

Sportsite offers classes in aerobics, step and body-shaping and has Nautilus and cardiovascular equipment. Children's programs and child care are other features here.

Woman's Body Shopp

Canterbury Plz., 331 Contuit, Sandwich • 888-4700

The Woman's Body Shopp has two locations: Canterbury Plaza, Sandwich, and 155 Attucks Lane, Hyannis, 771-1600. They offer more than 100 aerobic classes per week, a full cardiovascular room, swimming lessons, full dance programs and a Nautilus and free-weight room. The center also offers babysitting, tanning, a hot tub, steam room and a beauty shop.

Sandwich High School - Sandwich Community School

365 Quaker Meeting House Rd., East Sandwich • 888-5300

The Sandwich Community School coordinates public use of the constantly busy Sandwich High School swimming pool. The pool offers lessons, family and lap swims, water aerobics and a masters program.

Falmouth Health and Fitness Inc.

133 E. Falmouth Hwy., Falmouth • 540-6180

Falmouth Health and Fitness Inc. has a Stairmaster, treadmill and NordicTrack equipment and offers boxing and slide, step and water aerobics.

Falmouth Sports Center Health Club

33 Highfield Dr., Falmouth • 548-7384

The Falmouth Sports Center Health Club offers Nautilus, free weights and cardiovascular equipment. The club also has a physical therapy department.

World Gym of Cape Cod

Dear Crossing, Rt. 28, Mashpee • 477-3332

World Gym is a state-of-the-art fitness club featuring the best in equipment and instruction. More than 35 aerobic classes are held each week. There is no initiation fee and monthly fees start at $30.

Mid-Cape

The Fitness Club of Cape Cod

55 Attucks Ln., Hyannis • 771-7734

The Fitness Club of Cape Cod offers a whirlpool and sauna, fitness equipment, racquetball, a tanning salon and basketball and wallyball courts. This club is open daily year round.

R&R Fitness Center

12 Thornton Dr., Hyannis • 778-6446

This fitness center has many bikes and treadmills available and offers more hammer-strength equipment than any other club on the Cape. There are men's and women's locker rooms as well as personal trainers.

YMCA

2245 Iyanough Rd., West Barnstable • 362-6500

The Cape's only YMCA has water exercise, water jogging, lap swimming and lessons as well as special arthritis exercise classes. The club also has fitness equipment, saunas and aerobic classes. You do not have to be a member to use the facility; the guest fee is $6 per day.

Bass River Athletics Club

1067 Rt. 28, South Yarmouth • 398-0131

Bass River has lots of cardiovascular equipment as well as Nautilus, free weights, aerobics, step aerobics and racquetball courts. After your workout you can relax in the whirlpool, steam room or sauna. The club has trainers available and offers a babysitting service.

Mid-Cape Racquet & Health Club

193 White's Path, South Yarmouth • 394-3511

Mid-Cape is a complete fitness center with Nautilus and free weights and a personal training program. After your workout, enjoy the sauna, steam and whirlpool. Facilities include a juice and wine bar. The club is a popular choice for private soccer or basketball parties for kids. Mid-Cape Racquet Club is open daily year round.

David's Gym

50 Rt. 134, South Dennis • 394-7199

David's Gym claims no one does fitness better. Indeed! How's this for starters: step and cardio aerobic classes, hi-tech Cybex equipment, one-on-one training, whirlpool and sauna, professional and amateur boxing and karate training, all offered in a super-clean, super-friendly environment.

Lower Cape

Ocean Edge Resort

2660 Rt. 6A, Brewster • 896-8671

This resort has two indoor pools (one Olympic-size lap pool is by the golf course on the south side of Route 6A and the other is behind the conference center on the north side) and two fitness centers (again, one on each side of Route 6A). You can purchase winter pool memberships at incredible off-season prices (only $450 per family or $325 per individual) from the beginning of October until May 1. Prices are prorated if you join after October. The resort also offers day and weekend passes. Morning water aerobic classes are open to the public for $5, $3 for seniors and $2 for members.

Chatham Health & Swim Club

251 Crowell Rd., Chatham • 945-3555

This members-only facility has an oversize swimming pool, hot tub, steam room, lockers, aerobics studio with daily classes and a tanning salon.

Cape Cod Divers

815 Main St., Harwich • 432-9035

Swim and dive lessons are given by certified professionals year-round in an indoor heated pool. If you just want to take a dip, you can use the pool for a $4 fee.

INSIDERS' TIP

Norse explorers who are believed to have discovered Cape Cod around A.D. 1000 called the land Vinland because of the abundance of vines they found here.

Norseman Athletic Club

Rt. 6, North Eastham • 255-6370

This club features a large swimming pool. It also has a whirlpool, steam and sauna rooms, Nautilus and free weights, racquetball and squash courts, tanning booths, six indoor tennis courts and a friendly, knowledgeable staff . There's even an indoor basketball court. Hungry after all that exercise? Pay a visit to the healthy snack bar. Nonmembers pay a rate of about $12, which allows unlimited use of all facilities. Budget-stretching weekend rates for families are available.

Willy's Gym Orleans Market Place

Rt. 6A, Orleans • 255-6826

This popular facility is sort of a clearinghouse of fitness for the mind and body. Here, you can take part in everything from t'ai chi to traditional yoga, from Indonesian martial arts to massage. Each week, Willy's offers more than 60 classes in step, aerobics and dance. They even have specially tailored kids' fitness classes.

Provincetown Inn

1 Commercial St., Provincetown • 487-9500

For just $4 a day ($2 for kids), you can bask in the warm waters of the inn's large, heated indoor pool, which, believe it or not, is the shape of a Pilgrim hat! A perfect escape for rainy days. Alas, the pool closes for the winter.

Mussel Beach Health Club

35 Bradford St., Provincetown • 487-0001

This is the premier fitness club in town — it's so popular that they've moved several times within the last few years to bigger and bigger headquarters. Most of the clientele is male, with finely chiseled bodies and oh-so-perfect physiques. Make use of the top-of-the-line equipment, the treadmills and the cardio room, and you, too, could be mistaken for Adonis.

Provincetown Gym

170 Commercial St., Provincetown • 487-2776

This club caters to men and women and features complete free weights and cardiovascular equipment. Many fitness buffs like the intimacy afforded them here as well as some of the best (and toughest) trainers around. The club offers classes in t'ai chi and yoga.

Horseback Riding

The Cape has a number of good stables for boarding, riding lessons and trail rides. You can even get in beach riding if you want.

Upper Cape

Fieldcrest Farm

774 Palmer Ave., Falmouth • 540-0626

Fieldcrest Farm offers riding instruction, boarding and training and has a large indoor ring and a complete tack shop with saddles, bridles, clothing and supplies. Group rates are $18 for a half-hour, $25 for 45 minutes and $30 for an hour. Private rates are $30 for a half-hour and $35 for 45 minutes.

Haland Stables

Rt. 28A, West Falmouth • 540-2552

In West Falmouth, Haland Stables provides a guided trail ride through pine woods and cranberry bogs. Only walking and trotting are allowed on the trails, and all riding is English-style. Appointments are required, and both private and group lessons are offered. Rates are $15 for a half-hour and $24 for an hour.

Maushop Stables

Sampson's Mill Rd., Mashpee • 477-1303

Mashpee's Maushop Stables focuses on riding lessons but will conduct trail rides by appointment. It also offers boarding services, a summer camp and an indoor arena. The group rate is $15 per hour, while private rates are $25 for a half-hour and $40 for an hour.

Mid-Cape

Holly Hill Farm

Flint St., Marstons Mills • 428-2621

Holly Hill offers lessons running from $25 to $50 per hour. This Marstons Mills establishment is a show stable of hunters and jumpers and provides such services as boarding and training. There are no trails on site.

Sandy Neck Beach

Barnstable • 362-8306

Sandy Neck Beach, Barnstable, is an excellent place to ride if you have your own horse. Trails wind 7 or 8 miles through dunes and past bogs. During the summer, horses are permitted on the beach anytime Monday through Thursday, until noon on Friday and not at all on weekends. The rest of the year, they are allowed on the beach on weekends as well. You will need to obtain a horse pass, good for one year, at a cost of $10 for each horse. Passes are available at the Sandy Neck gatehouse; also stop here if you have more than two trailers.

Common Sense Farm at Salt Meadows

226 Great Western Rd., South Dennis • 398-3644

This Dennis establishment offers trail rides, English and Western instruction and a summer day camp. All services are provided by appointment.

Lower Cape

Moby Dick Farm

Great Fields Rd., Brewster • 896-3544

This friendly, year-round equestrian center offers instruction and, since it's only a clip-clop away from the wooded Punkhorn Parklands, miles of trails! The staff is specially trained to handle beginners. For seasonal fun, ask about hayrides, sleigh rides and carriage rides. Trail rides cost $35 and last 1½ to two hours. We highly recommend them. You'll learn a lot about the natural history of the area, and come back to the stable as refreshed and invigorated as only a good trail ride can leave you!

Woodsong Farm

Lund Farm Way, Brewster • 896-5555

Right next to Nickerson State Park, this facility offers riding lessons and boarding and boasts a lovely network of trails. Unfortunately, the trails are only for use by those who board horses here. Lund Farm also hosts horse shows — terrific ones, we might add, that are great fun on a summer day — and offers summer programs for kids.

Nickerson State Park

Rt. 6A, Brewster • 896-3491

The park has one marked bridle trail and a network of other trails. There is no fee to ride here.

Deer Meadow Riding Stables

Rt. 137, Harwich • 432-6580

This stable offers year-round guided trail rides and riding at $20 for one hour, $14 for a half-hour. They also give lessons (English and Western style) and offer pony rides. If you already own a horse, Deer Meadow will board it for you.

Bayberry Hollow Farm

W. Vine Street Ext., Provincetown • 487-6584

Know a child celebrating a birthday on the Cape? We've got the perfect present — pony rides! Bayberry Hollow offers kid-friendly rides on kid-friendly ponies, either on their land or yours, for all occasions. The farm is open all year long; appointments are a must.

Nelson's Riding Stables

43 Race Point Rd., Provincetown • 487-1112

This facility is famous for its guided Western-style one-hour trail rides through the woods, dunes and Province Lands of the Cape Cod National Seashore. It's worth the $25 just for that breathtaking first sight of the Atlantic as you break out of the dunes. Nelson's also offers two-hour sunset rides on the beach. These trips are for experienced riders only (ages 13 and older). The stables are open

INSIDERS' TIP

Thrust some 40 miles out into the ocean, Cape Cod is a natural wonderland. Many species of animals and birds stop along our shore as they migrate north and south. For instance, it is not uncommon to see seals along the beach or perched upon a boulder off shore.

from mid-April through the end of October; call for off-season hours.

If you own your own horse, you can also ride specially designated trails in the Province Lands as well as on park fire roads at Cape Cod National Seashore. A complete listing of these trails, along with rules and regulations, can be found in a free booklet available at the visitors center, 349-3785.

Ice-skating and Hockey

Most people don't associate Cape Cod with ice-skating, yet the Cape is a hot spot on ice. Last year, the Falmouth High School hockey team won the state championship at the Fleet Center in Boston (where the Bruins play). Todd Eldredge, a world champion men's figure skater, hails from Chatham and Olympic medalists Nancy Kerrigan and Paul Wylie have both trained at the Tony Kent Arena in South Dennis. Rentals are available at most rinks (though Falmouth does not offer rentals). Since times for public skating change frequently, your best bet is to call ahead for hours. Below are some of the Cape's rinks.

Upper Cape

Gallo Ice Arena

231 Sandwich Rd., Bourne • 759-8904

Located along the Cape Cod Canal, the Gallo Ice Arena plays host to hockey schools, camps and clinics as well as figure-skating camps and public skating. There is a pro shop on site. The arena is open from June to April (it's closed in May).

Falmouth Ice Arena

Palmer Ave., Falmouth • 548-9083, 548-0275

Ice-skating is offered on a 85-by-185-foot rink including youth and adult ice-hockey programs, figure-skating programs and public skating. There are a pro shop and a snack bar on site.

Mid-Cape

Joseph P. Kennedy Skating Rink

141 Bassett Ln., Hyannis • 790-6345, 790-6346

Named for Joseph P. Kennedy, the brother of John F. Kennedy who was lost during World War II, this rink in the center of Hyannis is used for local hockey games and figure-skating as well as public skating.

Tony Kent Arena

8 S. Gages Way, South Dennis • 760-2400, 760-2415

Olympians Nancy Kerrigan and Paul Wylie have both practiced and performed here. The rink is home to Dennis-Yarmouth youth hockey as well as figure-skating and learn-to-skate programs. The rink also offers public skating.

Lower Cape

Charles Moore Arena

O'Connor Way, Orleans • 255-2971

This arena offers in-line skating and roller-skating during the summer and ice-skating the rest of the year. It also hosts a kids-only Rock Night on Friday (see our Nightlife chapter).

Tennis

Nothing like a little tennis to burn off some calories and work up a hankering for a dip at the local beach or nearby swimming pool. Serves and volleys can be found around the Cape, at indoor clubs and at outdoor public courts at the many schools and parks sprinkled about the peninsula.

Annual local tournaments are held at the Cape Cod Community College in Barnstable, Mid-Cape Racquet Club in South Yarmouth, Eldredge Park in Orleans as well as at many other spots (see our Spectator Sports chapter). Town recreation departments usually offer instruction on public courts during the summer. Here are some of the tennis clubs and public courts located around the Cape.

Upper Cape

Falmouth Sport Center

33 Highfield Dr., Falmouth • 548-7433

If you're staying in Falmouth and want to play some tennis, you're in luck. The Falmouth Sports Center has six indoor courts, three outdoor courts and three racquetball courts. The center also has a physical therapy department and a health club. Membership is not required. One hour of court time costs $16 per person for nonmembers, $8 for members. There are leagues, round robins, ladders, matches and lessons available. The Sports Center is open year round.

Southcape Resort

950 Falmouth Rd., Mashpee • 477-4700

Southcape Resort and Tennis Club in Mashpee is a year-round timesharing facility with two indoor and three outdoor courts that are available to the public. The courts are open day and night. The cost is $24 per hour. (See our Hotels and Motels chapter).

Public Tennis Courts

The following list shows courts available in the various towns. It's best to call ahead to determine when the courts are available.

Bourne Memorial Community Building, Buzzards Bay, 759-0650

Bourne Town Hall, 24 Perry Avenue, Buzzards Bay, 759-0680

Bourne High School, 75 Waterhouse Road, Bourne, 759-0670

Chester Park, Monument and Arthur avenues, Monument Beach, 759-0600

Clarke Field, Clark Road, North Sagamore, 759-0600

Oak Ridge School, Quaker Meeting House Road, Sandwich, 833-0111

Sandwich High School, Quaker Meeting House Road, Sandwich, 888-4900

Forestdale Elementary School/Henry T. Wing School, Route 130, Sandwich, 888-4361

East Falmouth Elementary School, 33 Davisville Road, East Falmouth, 548-1052

Lawrence School, 113 Lakeview Avenue, Falmouth, 548-0606

Falmouth High School, Gifford Street Ext., Falmouth, 540-2200

West Falmouth Park, Blacksmith Shop Road, West Falmouth, 457-2567

Nye Park, County Road, North Falmouth, 457-2567

Bell Tower Field, Bell Tower Lane, Woods Hole, 457-2567

Mashpee Middle School/Coombs Elementary School, 150-152 Old Barnstable Road, Mashpee, 539-1446

Mid-Cape

Mid-Cape Racquet Club & Health Club

193 White's Path, South Yarmouth • 394-3511

Mid-Cape Racquet Club has nine indoor tennis courts, but that's only the beginning. There are also courts for basketball, squash and racquetball, and a complete fitness center (see Fitness Clubs below). You do not have to be a member to play here. The club has programs and instruction for children and adults. Court fees for nonmembers are $14 per person for singles and $11.50 for 1½ hours for doubles. The Racquet Club has day-care facilities and a juice and wine bar. Mid-Cape Racquet Club is open daily year round.

Sesuit Tennis Centre

1389 Rt. 6A, East Dennis • 385-2200

The year-round Sesuit Tennis Centre will satisfy the needs of both novice and pro, with three outdoor Plexi-pave courts, ball machines and lessons. The center handles certified racket stringing, and the pro shop has a variety of tennis equipment and apparel. As their motto says: "If it says tennis, we have it."

Public Tennis Courts

Grade 5 School, Hyannis, 790-6458

Hyannis Middle School, 895 Falmouth Road (Route 28), Hyannis, 790-6460

Osterville Bay School, West Bay Road, Osterville, 428-8538

Cotuit Elementary School, 140 Old Oyster Road, Cotuit, 428-0268

Centerville Elementary School, Bay Lane, Centerville, 790-9890

Barnstable-West Barnstable School, Route 6A, Barnstable, 790-6345

Dennis-Yarmouth High School, Station Avenue, South Yarmouth, 398-7630

Wixon Middle School, Route 134, South Dennis, 398-7697

Lower Cape

Ocean Edge Resort

2660 Rt. 6A, Brewster • 896-9000

The outdoor courts here are meticulously

maintained. Fees are about $12 an hour per person, but that doesn't stop the five clay and six Plexi-pave courts from filling up fast. Reservations are suggested at least two weeks in advance. In the off-season, only resort guests can use the courts.

Wychmere Harbor Tennis Club

792 Main St., Harwich • 430-7012

Regular patrons swear by the facility's courteous, knowledgeable staff, well-stocked pro shop and the daily round robins. The six Har-Tru and three Omni courts aren't bad either. Wychmere also offers private and group instruction as well as adult and junior clinics.

Chatham Bars Inn

297 Shore Rd., Chatham • 945-0096

This resort is the epitome of luxury, and playing on one of the four all-weather, waterfront courts is no exception. Court fees are $15 an hour for non-guests (guests play free) and lessons are $60 an hour. The pro shop, open seasonally, is first-rate, and the resort also offers a variety of tennis clinics.

Norseman Athletic Club

Rt. 6, North Eastham • 255-637020

This club has six superb courts that can be used by nonmembers at a walk-in fee of $12 per person, per day, on an availability basis.

Oliver's Clay Tennis Courts

Rt. 6, Wellfleet • 349-3330

Oliver's boasts seven clay and one Truflex court. Oliver's also offers lessons, arranges matches and strings rackets. Greenery camouflages the courts, but even if you miss the sign, you won't miss the big-bucks cars out front. It's open seven days a week, mid-May through mid-October.

Chequessett Yacht & Country Club

Chequessett Neck Rd., Wellfleet • 349-3704

This club has five all-weather asphalt bayfront courts (with wind screens) open to the public. Lessons are also available seasonally. The club is open seven days a week from March 1 through December 1.

Provincetown Tennis Club

286 Bradford St., Provincetown • 487-9574

The private club offers five clay and two hard-surface courts for nonmembers. Daily, weekly and monthly membership fees are available for nonmembers (in addition to court fees). Games can be arranged, and the club also restrings rackets. In July and August, the club holds professional-caliber open tournaments.

Bissell's Tennis Courts

21 Bradford St. Ext., Provincetown • 487-9512

Its location, tucked away behind The Moors restaurant, makes Bissell's hard to find. You have your choice of five clay courts. Bissell's offers lessons at reasonable prices.

Public Courts

Four courts are behind the Brewster Police Department, near the Old Town Hall on Route 6A, Brewster

Brooks Park, Route 39 and Oak Street, Harwich

Cape Cod Technical High School, Route 124, Harwich.

Depot Road near the Railroad Museum, Chatham

Chatham High School, Crowell Road, Chatham

Kitty Lane, South Chatham.

Eldredge Park, Route 28 and Eldredge Parkway, Orleans

Nauset Regional High School, Cable Road, Eastham, (available only during school summer vacation. There's a nominal fee, payable at the courts.)

Mayo Beach, Kendrick Street, Wellfleet

Motta Field, near the Pilgrim Monument, Provincetown

Prince Street, near the high school, Provincetown

Skateboarding

Skateboarders have gained a few alternatives to parking lots and sidewalks. A number of towns have begun developing skateboard parks. Kids pay a nominal fee to use parks, and must adhere to a roster of common-sense rules. Helmets are a must! Two new skateboard parks are in Harwich at Brooks Park on Route 39 and Oak Street, and in Chatham behind the elementary school on Main Street.

Parking is a big consideration when you're planning a day at the beach. Most beaches either charge admission or require a parking sticker, generally available at town halls or, in some cases, at certain beaches.

Beaches

Cape Cod has some of the most beautiful beaches in the world. Nothing defines the Cape better than its beaches, which are the primary draw for many visitors. Even if you're not a sunworshipper or a surfer, it's wonderful being near the shore and breathing in the salt breezes. There is nothing more healing, more rejuvenating, than a walk on the beach. Lose yourself in the hypnotic rhythm of the tide, sense the vastness of the ocean whose waters stretch far beyond the horizon, hear the heartbeat of the earth in the waves that pound the shore. Or just come and play: Run along the tideline; try your luck at surfcasting; build sandcastles. Watch the surfers at the ocean beaches, or if surfing's your thing, join them. Look for delicate shells and pretty rocks, smooth as robin's eggs from untold years of rolling with the tides. Lie in the sun. This, after all, is what you came here for.

With some 150 saltwater and freshwater beaches, the Cape offers something for everyone in the way of beaches. Some Cape beaches have rough-and-tumble waves great for surfing, such as Newcomb Hollow in Wellfleet; others are gentle and quiet, like Brewster's Breakwater Beach or Coporation Beach in Dennis. Some are broad, like Nauset in Orleans, and others are narrow, such as Nobska in Falmouth. Some are rocky, like Town Beach in Sandwich, and some are all sand as is Craigville Beach. But every one is a wonderful place to spend time.

Water temperatures vary depending upon where you choose to plunge in or wiggle your toes. The bays and sounds, for instance, are relatively shallow bodies of water and warm up faster than the Atlantic, which reflects rather than absorbs light and heat. In the height of the summer, average temperatures in Cape Cod Bay on the north side are in the 60s and 70s, while ocean temps on the east side linger in the mid 50s, rarely getting higher than the low 60s.

And then there are the freshwater lakes and ponds, which have calm waters and nice beaches, many with picnic facilities. The 700-acre Mashpee-Wakeby Pond is the Cape's largest freshwater body.

A few words of caution are in order to make your days at the beach safe and serene. Lifeguards are posted at many beaches to oversee hundreds of swimmers, but their watchfulness should not be a replacement for adult supervision of children. Also, children should not take water toys such as flotation rings or rafts, into the ocean because they can be quickly carried out to a depth that's over their heads. And while many of us remember digging in the sand to "bury" each other as children, that activity can be dangerous as well, which is why notices at the Cape Cod National Seashore warn against it.

The National Seashore, while we're on the subject, contains some of the loveliest beaches on the Cape. Stretching from Chatham to Provincetown, it has ocean beaches in Eastham, Wellfleet, Truro and Provincetown; see our Parks and Recreation chapter for details about the park.

Parking is a big consideration when you're planning a day at the beach. Many beach lots fill quickly on nice summer days (Nauset Light Beach in Eastham, for instance, is generally full by about 10 AM in July and August). Most all beaches either charge admission or require a parking sticker, generally available at town halls or, in some cases, at certain beaches. We've detailed the procedure in each town in the write-ups below. A note of caution: If you park illegally, you will be ticketed and fined. Often public transportation is an option — the trolleys that operate in some towns, such as Hyannis and Harwich, are great for beach transportation. Or, ride a bike — admission to most beaches is free for those who walk or bike in.

Keep in mind that all public beaches have

regulations regarding issues such as dogs (prohibited on many beaches during the season, or on others, allowed only during certain times), open fires (allowed by permit only) and alcoholic beverages (in general, not permitted). Heed the rules that are posted; they are in place for the safety and comfort of everyone.

The beaches we include here have lifeguards during the summer unless otherwise noted. Many have restrooms and changing facilities, while some only have portable toilets. Some have snack bars, and virtually all are included in the routes of local ice cream trucks, whose bells call children in from the water faster than you can say Creamsicle. You may bring your own picnic to the beach, but please don't litter (and this includes cigarette filters) — leave the beach as lovely as you found it.

Ready for a day at the beach? Grab your sunscreen, shades, a blanket or beach chair and follow us!

Upper Cape

The Upper Cape towns have coastlines that touch the waters of Cape Cod Bay, Buzzards Bay, Vineyard Sound, Nantucket Sound and the Cape Cod Canal. Bourne, Falmouth and Mashpee all have beaches on the south side of the Cape with its warm waters. On the north side, Sandwich's bay beaches are influenced by a different tidal system and are colder. Another influence on Sandwich beaches is the man-made Cape Cod Canal, which interrupts the natural sweep of wind-carried sands along the shore. As a result, Sandwich beaches tend to be rockier than others, but they are distinctly charming. On a clear day you can see the Pilgrim Monument in Provincetown 26 miles across the bay.

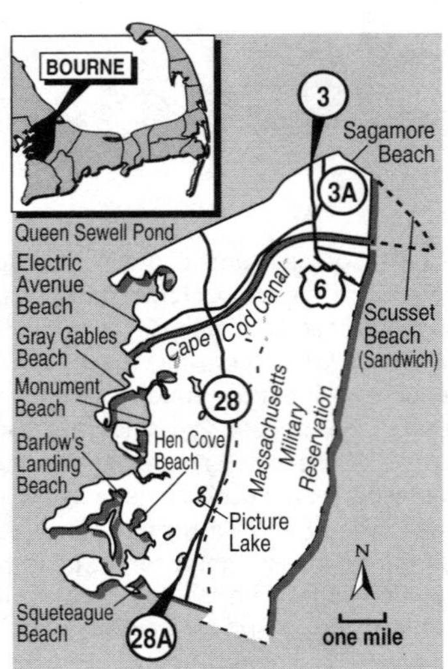

Bourne

Bourne is home to a number of fine saltwater beaches stretching across its more than 50 miles of coastline along Buzzards Bay. The town also has about 2 miles of frontage on Cape Cod Bay to the north as well as a couple of ponds available for freshwater swimming. In Bourne, resident and nonresident beach parking stickers from the Natural Resources Office, Bourne Town Hall, 24 Perry Avenue, Buzzards Bay, 759-0623, are required if you want to park at a town beach. These public beach parking stickers cost $15 per season for residents and $20 for nonresidents.

Electric Avenue Beach on Buzzards Bay rests at the entrance to Buttermilk Bay near the Buzzards Bay rotary at the west end of the Cape Cod Canal. Lifeguards are on duty at this beach.

INSIDERS' TIP

Parking lots at Provincetown beaches fill up fast, usually by 10:30 AM, earlier on a scorcher. If possible, use the Beach Shuttle, a yellow school bus that makes frequent pickups and drop-offs between just about every motel and guesthouse in town and the Beach Point area of North Truro and Herring Cove and Race Point beaches. Cost is $1.25 one way.

Monument Beach along Shore and Emmons roads has public parking and looks out upon the Bourne entrance to the Cape Cod Canal and the Monument Beach Marina. Situated at a small harbor, it is a pleasant place to spend the day in the sun and water. Lifeguards are on duty. There is a concession stand and bathhouse on site.

At the southwest end of the entrance to the Cape Cod Canal is where you can find **Gray Gables Beach** in the village of Gray Gables. It is here where President Grover Cleveland used to spend his summer vacations when he was President during the 1880s and 90s. Gray Gables has lifeguards and portable toilets. There are no concessions.

A popular northside option is **Scusset Beach** on Cape Cod Bay. This large, clean state-run beach is largely in the town of Sandwich yet you approach it by taking Meetinghouse Road off the Sagamore Rotary just before the Sagamore Bridge. From Meetinghouse, take Scusset Beach Road into Sandwich to the beach parking area where you'll pay a fee of $2 (or $15 for a season pass). This beach has a snack bar and bathhouse available.

Sagamore Beach at the Sagamore Highlands is really three interconnected beaches on the mainland side of the Cape Cod Canal. These northside beaches can be found off Samoset Road. Though there are no concession stands at these beaches, there are lifeguards on duty and portable toilets available.

Off Barlow's Landing Road in Pocasset is the appropriately named **Barlow's Landing Beach**. Overlooking beautiful Pocasset Harbor, this beach has lifeguards and portable toilets but no concession stands.

Hen Cove Beach, also known as Pocasset Town Beach, is on Hen Cove in Pocasset, which empties into Red Brook Harbor. The beach is well-protected by both the cove and harbor making it a nice place for the kids. There are lifeguards on duty and portable toilets but no concession stands.

Another well-protected beach is **Squeteague Beach** at Cataument's Squeteague Harbor. There are no lifeguards or concessions at this beach though there is one portable toilet.

Freshwater swimming can be found at **Queen Sewell Pond** in Buzzards Bay, just south of Little Buttermilk Bay. There are lifeguards and portable toilets at this beach.

Another freshwater pond open to swimmers is **Picture Lake** located off Williams Avenue between County Road and Route 28 in Pocasset. This beach has lifeguards but no bathroom facilities.

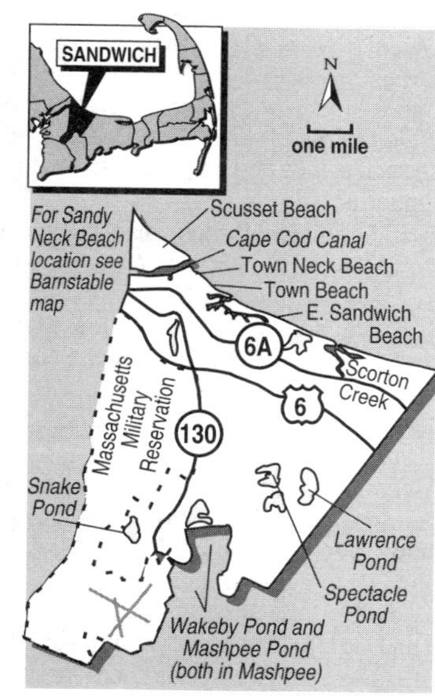

Sandwich

Sandwich has saltwater access along the north shore of the town that borders Cape Cod Bay. A portion of this north shore lies on the other side of the Canal (the mainland side). Although deprived of the large harbors, coves and bays present in many of the other Cape towns, Sandwich has a number of fine freshwater ponds in the southern portion of the town including Peters Pond and Snake Pond, the latter offering a public beach. Sandwich also has frontage on a portion of Mashpee's Wakeby Pond, just enough to sneak in a beach.

For parking purposes, resident stickers are sold at the Sandwich Town Hall, 888-4910, in Sandwich Village. The cost is $15 for residents, $20 for nonresidents. Nonresident stickers are valid at all beaches except Snake Pond and

Sandy Neck (see below). One-day parking stickers cost $4.

Town Neck Beach, at the end of Town Neck Road, offers the perfect place to watch boat traffic pass on the Cape Cod Canal. Though there are no lifeguards on duty, there are restrooms and a concession stand.

Town Beach rests at the entrance to Sandwich Harbor. This Sandwich beach can be reached by taking Town Neck Road to Freeman Avenue. Nearby is the famous Sandwich boardwalk crossing Mill Creek which winds through the picturesque marshes along the north side of Sandwich. Town Beach offers concession stands and bathroom facilities but no lifeguards.

East Sandwich Beach, also known as Springhill Beach, is off Route 6A at the end of Ploughed Neck Road where it empties into North Shore Boulevard. Just to the east is Scorton Harbor and the beautiful Scorton Creek. The parking area accepts permits only. The beach has no lifeguards, concession stands or toilet facilities.

A beautiful beach with high sand dunes that stretches for miles along Cape Cod Bay is **Sandy Neck Beach**. Off Route 6A at the extreme eastern boundaries of the town, this beach is within both Sandwich and Barnstable. Daily parking is $4. The beach offers lifeguards, concessions stands and bathroom facilities. Many people enjoy taking a four-wheel-drive vehicle onto Sandy Neck Beach for a day of fishing and swimming; this requires buying a permit through the Town of Barnstable. Your four-wheel-drive vehicle must undergo an inspection at the gatehouse for proper emergency equipment such as a tow rope, shovel and spare tire. Call the Sandy Neck gatehouse, 362-8306, Sandy Neck administration, 790-6350, or the Town of Barnstable at 362-8300 for more information. The beach is open year round.

For freshwater swimming, check out **Snake Pond** on Snake Pond Road in Forestdale. This beach is ideal for inexperienced swimmers, kids and those who just want a quick dip. This pretty little pond is often crowded in the summer and is available to residents only. A lifeguard is on duty. There are concessions and toilet facilities.

Sandwich has a beach on the Wakeby portion of the beautiful **Mashpee-Wakeby Pond**. The beach, which can be found off Sandwich-Cotuit Road, has a large parking area, restrooms and a big gazebo for grilling and picnics. Lifeguards are on duty.

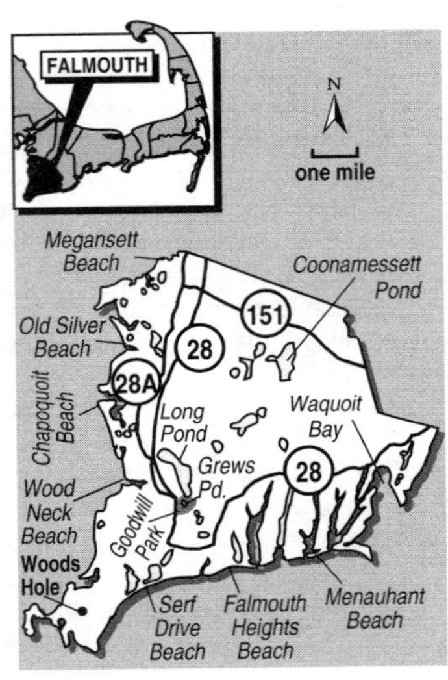

Falmouth

Falmouth offers more miles of coastline than any other Cape town. This coastline is blessed with many fine harbors as well as a number of wonderful beaches. The southern shoreline borders Vineyard Sound while the western side overlooks Buzzards Bay.

Beach stickers are available at the Surf Drive bathhouse. Guest stickers, for visitors to Falmouth, cost $125 for the summer, $40 for one week, $50 for two weeks, $65 for three weeks and $75 for four weeks. Residents can pay $20 for a two-year sticker or $10 for one year. Some of the beaches in town have daily parking fees; see the individual beach listings below for the details. Or you can call the Falmouth Beach Committee, 548-8623, for more information. Some accommodations in town offer guests a temporary pass that's treated the same as a resident sticker.

Along Vineyard Sound, **Surf Drive Beach** is the closest beach to Falmouth village center. This beach offers lifeguards, a bathhouse with showers and a concession stand. The waters here are warm and calm. The views include Martha's Vineyard across the Sound and Nobska Light nearby. A small inlet to the north of the beach is popular with families who have little kids. Daily parking runs $8.

Old Silver Beach in North Falmouth is as popular as it is beautiful. The Buzzards Bay waters here are warm and ideal for youngsters. A creek splits the beach in two, one side is for residents and the other side for visitors to the town. Lifeguards watch over the swimmers. A concession stand keeps hunger at bay. Portable toilets and showers are available. The daily parking fee is $10 for guests (nonresidents).

Another North Falmouth beach is **Megansett Beach** on Buzzards Bay. As with Old Silver Beach, the waters here are rather warm. The beach has lifeguards yet no concession stands or bathhouses. Parking is by resident sticker only.

Chapoquoit Beach rests along Buzzards Bay just south of West Falmouth Harbor. This residents-only beach has lifeguards, concessions and toilet facilities in the form of portable toilets. The beach is off Chapoquoit Road.

Wood Neck Beach can be found at the mouth of the saltwater Little Sippewissett Lake in West Falmouth. It's waters are warmed by Buzzards Bay. Wood Neck has concessions and portable toilets on site as well as lifeguards. Parking is by sticker only.

Overlooking Vineyard Sound and Martha's Vineyard beyond is **Falmouth Heights Beach**. The waters here are warm and inviting. Falmouth Heights has lifeguards on duty and portable toilets are available. Though there are no concession stands there are a number of places nearby to get something to eat.

Two other wonderful Vineyard Sound beaches are **Menauhant** and **Bristol**. Both southside beaches have lifeguards, concession stands and portable toilets. Menauhant also has showers. Bristol Beach is accessible by sticker only. The parking fee at Menauhant is $8 per day.

Grews Pond is a wonderful little freshwater pond in Goodwill Park off Gifford Street just north of Falmouth center. The pond has lifeguards on duty and toilet facilities are available. There is no charge for public parking.

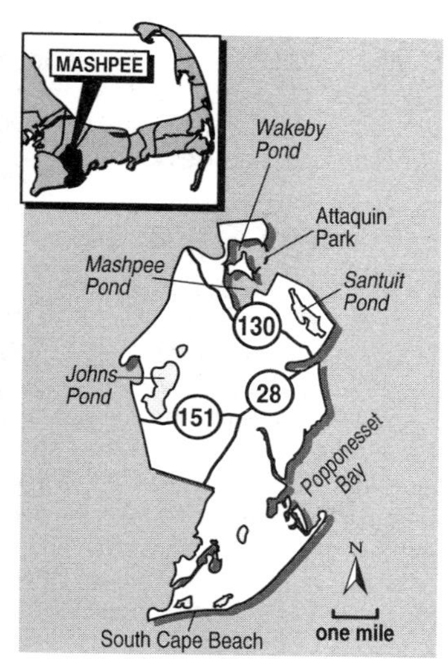

Mashpee

The southernmost portion of Mashpee touches Nantucket Sound, Waquoit Bay and Poponesset Bay. Within the town are a number of large ponds: Ashumet and Johns Ponds in the west, Santuit Pond in the east, and the connected Mashpee and Wakeby Ponds along the northern border with Sandwich. Residents can obtain town beach stickers for $15 at the clerk's office at town hall on Great Neck Road; call the Mashpee Town Offices at 539-1446 for additional information.

South Cape Beach on Nantucket Sound is a great, unspoiled place to enjoy sand, sea and sun. Only about 3.5 miles from the Mashpee Rotary at the end of Great Neck Road South, the beach is operated by both the town, which has a parking lot and requires a resident sticker, and by the state Department of Environmental Management, which has a large public parking lot and charges nonresidents of Mashpee $2 per day. Lifeguards are on duty and toilet facilities are available.

For freshwater swimming, go to **Attaquin Park** on the 700-plus acre Mashpee-Wakeby Pond, the Cape's largest freshwater body. The park, off Route 130 at the southern end of the pond, has a swimming area, lifeguards, toilet facilities and a state boat ramp with parking available.

Another popular freshwater spot is **Johns Pond** off Route 151 and Currier Road. It has a public beach complete with lifeguards, a volleyball net and toilet facilities.

Mid-Cape

The beaches of the Mid-Cape can be found on two separate bodies of saltwater — Nantucket Sound to the south and Cape Cod Bay to the north. The southside waters are always warmer while tidal flats on the bay side of the Mid-Cape heat the northside waters as they ebb and flow over the sand. On the whole, beaches in this long middle area of the peninsula are not as affected by currents and rips as on the Lower Cape. There are also a number of beautiful lakes and ponds offering freshwater options.

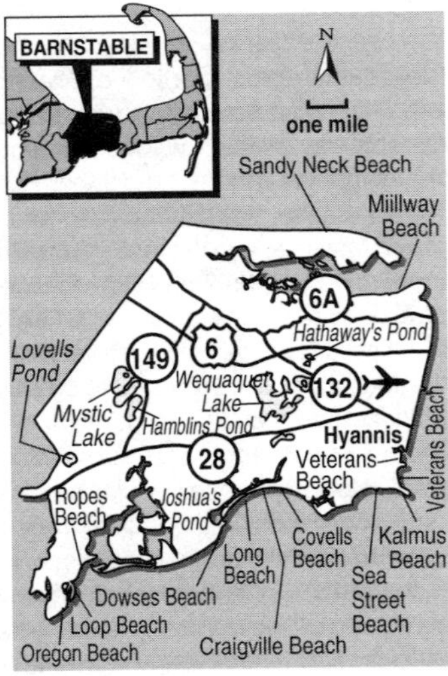

Barnstable

Barnstable has saltwater beaches on the north side and south side of the town. Most of the beaches rest along the warmer Vineyard Sound, although the town's largest beach, Sandy Neck, lies along Cape Cod Bay. The town also has a number of ponds and lakes available for freshwater swimming. The largest is Lake Wequaquet in Centerville at 650 acres. Residents of Barnstable can purchase beach parking stickers for $15; a second sticker for the same residential address costs $10. Weekly nonresident stickers run $25 while a day beach parking pass costs $8. (Sandy Neck day passes on weekend and holidays is $10.)

Cotuit has three fine beaches, all for residents only. **Oregon Beach** off Main Street has no lifeguards or restroom facilities, nor does **Ropes Beach**, located in the protected Cotuit Bay. Cotuit's **Loop Beach**, also off Main Street, does have lifeguards and bathroom facilities. Neighboring Osterville has a fine saltwater residents-only beach at the end of Wianno Avenue called **Dowses Beach**. Lifeguards oversee Dowses' Vineyard Sound waters. Toilet facilities are available as are concessions.

The often-crowded **Craigville Beach** off Craigville Beach Road in Centerville (Craigville) is a favorite with sunbathers and swimmers. On Vineyard Sound, this beach has a large parking lot and a bathhouse with outdoor showers. There are lifeguards on duty.

Two nearby residents-only beaches in Centerville are **Covells Beach** along Craigville Beach Road to the east of Craigville Beach and **Long Beach** on Long Beach Road to the west. Covells has lifeguards and restrooms; Long Beach has neither.

Hyannis has three beaches open to the public and one residents-only beach, **East Beach**. East Beach, just west of Hyannis Harbor, has no food or bathroom facilities and no lifeguards on duty.

As a windsurfing beach, **Kalmus Beach** at the end of Ocean Street in Hyannis is considered by some to be the best on the Cape. One of two beaches in Hyannis Harbor, Kalmus has a windsurfing area, snack bar, bathroom facilities and a picnic area. The beach is protected by lifeguards.

Sea Street Beach at the end of Sea Street is the second public beach in Hyannis Harbor and is within walking distance of many accommodations in Hyannis. This beach has a bathhouse, snack bar and picnic area. Lifeguards are on hand.

With a delightful view of Lewis Bay, **Veterans Beach** on Ocean Street in Hyannis is a popular place where families enjoy picnics and cookouts shaded by a pine grove. The facilities include a bathhouse, snack bar, picnic area and playground. Lifeguards are on duty. The Kennedy Memorial (see our Attractions chapter) is adjacent to Veterans Beach.

At 6 miles in length, **Sandy Neck Beach**, north of Route 6A in West Barnstable, is the town's longest beach. The road that leads to the beach, Sandy Neck Road, actually connects with Route 6A just over the town line in East Sandwich. Sandy Neck Road then works its way north into West Barnstable before reaching the beach parking lot. This beach offers swimming, fishing, camping and hiking. Facilities include indoor restrooms, showers and a snack bar. Lifeguards work this beach (see the Sandwich section).

Next to Barnstable Harbor at the end of Millway along the north shore of the town is **Millway Beach**. This residents-only beach offers a great view of the boat traffic entering and leaving the harbor, including the whale-watching vessels going out to Cape Cod Bay. Across the waters is Sandy Neck with its decommissioned lighthouse at the point. Millway has lifeguards and restroom facilities.

For freshwater swimming, check out the residents-only **Hamblins Pond** off Route 149 in Marstons Mills. Lifeguards, restrooms and a picnic area are here. Another Marstons Mills pond is **Lovells Pond** off Newtown Road. Lovells has lifeguards and restrooms. **Joshua's Pond** on Tower Hill Road in neighboring Osterville has bathroom facilities and a playground for the kids. Joshua's Pond also has lifeguards.

Lake Wequaquet on Shootflying Hill Road in Centerville is a freshwater playground. The lake is almost 2 miles long and roughly a mile wide. Bathroom facilities are on site, as are lifeguards. Wequaquet is a residents-only beach.

Hathaway's Pond off Phinney's Lane in Barnstable is open to the public. The pond's facilities include restrooms and a picnic and playground area. Lifeguards are on duty.

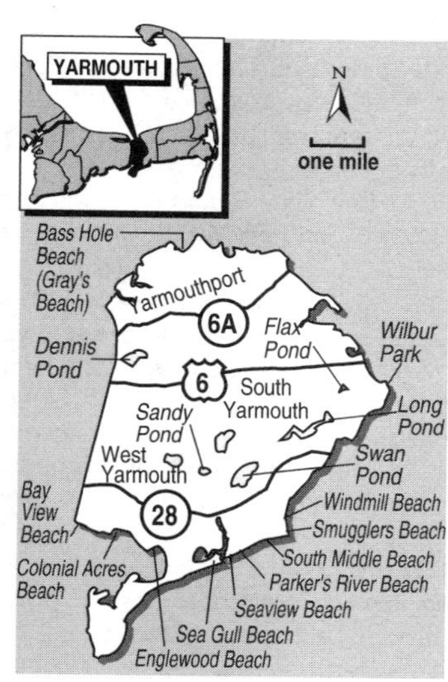

Yarmouth

Yarmouth has coastlines to the north on Cape Cod Bay and to the south on Nantucket Sound and Lewis Bay. The west side of the town borders Bass River to the south and Garden Creek to the north. The north side of the town on Cape Cod Bay is only about 1.5 miles long and is largely marshland, save for a small beach at Bass Hole on the east end. The south side has many fine beaches. There are also a number of freshwater ponds. Beach parking stickers cost $15 for residents of Yarmouth; $8 for a second sticker. Nonresident stickers run $75 for the season and $30 for a week. Four beaches in town have daily rates (see below). Stickers are available at the town hall on Route 28. Call the Recreation Department, 775-7910, from 7 AM to 3:30 PM for more information. The Yarmouth Chamber of Commerce, 657 Route 28, West Yarmouth, 778-1008, also sells beach stickers.

Off Sea Gull Lane, which is off South Sea Street in West Yarmouth, is where you'll find **Sea Gull Beach**. Offering plenty of parking

INSIDERS' TIP

Nude sunbathing is not allowed on any beach. National Park Service rangers, as well as local police, strictly enforce this law.

spaces, this is Yarmouth's largest and most popular beach, especially with high school and college students. Sitting just west of Parkers River, it has lifeguards, toilet facilities, a few picnic tables and concessions. The daily parking rate at Sea Gull Beach is $8.

From **Bay View Beach**, which is at the end of Bay View Street in West Yarmouth near the town line with Barnstable, you have a good view of Lewis Bay and the thousands of boats that enter Hyannis Inner Harbor every year. Bay View Beach has lifeguards on duty and bathroom facilities.

Colonial Acres Beach at the end of Standish Way in West Yarmouth has portable toilets and a new bridge out to the beach. Lifeguards keep an eye on things. The beach is at Lewis Bay.

Englewood Beach, also in West Yarmouth and also on Lewis Bay, is at the end of Berry Avenue. Englewood has a small parking lot, restroom facilities and lifeguards.

On the east side of the mouth of Parkers River is **Sea View Beach** off South Shore Road in South Yarmouth. This southside beach is protected by lifeguards, has a picnic area and portable toilets. Parking costs $7 for the day.

To the east of Sea View Beach along the Cape's southern shore is **Parkers River Beach**, which has restroom facilities, a concession stand, outdoor showers, swings and good parking as well as lifeguards. The beach rests along the warm waters of Nantucket Sound. It costs $7 a day to park.

South Middle Beach on South Shore Drive in South Yarmouth is a residents-only beach offering a large parking lot and restroom facilities. Lifeguards keep an eye on the activities out on Nantucket Sound.

Smugglers Beach (also known as Bass River Beach) is a good family beach with a fishing pier, a large parking area and a snack bar. This beach, located at the mouth of Bass River in South Yarmouth, also has lifeguards and bathroom facilities. The daily parking rate is $8.

About a half-mile up Bass River is where you'll find **Windmill Beach** off River Street. It is a small beach with no lifeguards or toilet facilities, but the views of the river are spectacular. Nearby is the Judah Baker windmill built in 1791.

Wilbur Park and its beach area are about 4 miles up Bass River where Highbank Road bridge connects South Yarmouth with the village of South Dennis. Though there are no lifeguards or bathroom facilities, Wilbur Park has a picnic area and a boat ramp.

The only beach on the north side is **Bass Hole**, also known as Gray's Beach. It is at the end of Centre Street off Route 6A in Yarmouthport and is considered by many to be one of the great sunset spots on the Cape. Bass Hole is at the mouth of Garden Creek and has a long boardwalk that extends over the salt marsh and offers an excellent view of coastal plant and marine life as well as nature's beauty. Across the river is Dennis' Chapin Beach. Bass Hole Beach is rather small and at low tide has very little water, which makes it perfect for small children (just pay attention to the tidal current in the creek). Bass Hole Beach has a large picnic area complete with a pavilion and bathroom facilities. There are lifeguards on duty.

In addition to its wealth of saltwater beaches, Yarmouth also has four public beaches at freshwater ponds. **Sandy Pond** off Buck Island Road in West Yarmouth offers not only a beach for swimming but also playing fields for softball, basketball and soccer, tennis courts and a playground. The beach has lifeguards on duty and a comfort station.

Long Pond is off Indian Memorial Drive in South Yarmouth. Lifeguards are on duty and portable toilets are available. The beach also has a playground on site. An Indian burial ground is nearby.

Also in South Yarmouth, **Flax Pond Recreation Area** has picnic areas, tennis and volleyball courts and softball fields. Toilet facilities are provided and lifeguards are on duty.

INSIDERS' TIP

Never leave your pet in the car in hot weather — even with the windows cracked.

Dennis Pond off Summer Street in Yarmouthport requires a town beach parking sticker. You'll find lifeguards and toilet facilities at this pretty pond located just a stroll from Yarmouthport village.

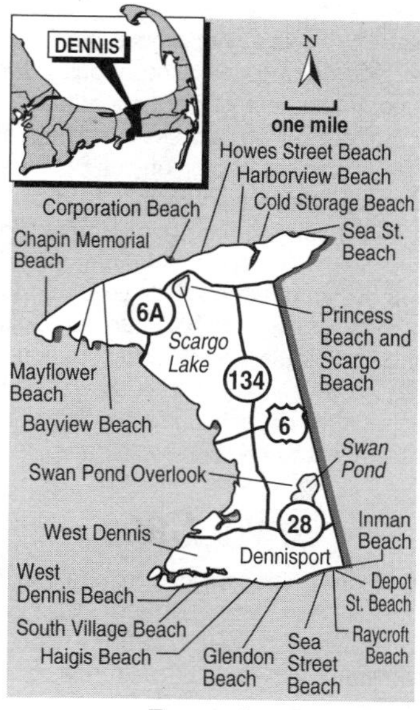

Dennis

With fine beaches on both the north and south sides of town, its no wonder that so many tourists make Dennis their vacation destination. There are eight beaches on Cape Cod Bay and another eight on Nantucket Sound. If you prefer freshwater swimming, Scargo Lake offers two beaches. Residents pay $15 for a beach parking permit while nonresidents pay $125 for the season. A seasonal pass can be gained for $100 if you can produce a lease for four or more weeks. Weekly stickers run $25 while daily parking costs $8. Stickers can be obtained at the Dennis Town Offices on Main Street in South Dennis, 394-8300.

Chapin Memorial Beach on Chapin Beach Road at the northwest corner of Dennis is a favorite among owners of four-wheel-drive vehicles. At low tide, shellfishers will delight in being able to walk more than a mile out into the tidal flats of Cape Cod Bay. The beach has no lifeguards though restrooms are available. Across the water is Yarmouth's Bass Hole and Gray's Beach.

Also on Cape Cod Bay is **Mayflower Beach** at the end of Beach Street. In addition to restrooms and concessions, this beach features a boardwalk that stretches from the large parking lot over the dunes to the beach below. Mayflower Beach is protected by lifeguards.

Bayview Beach at the end of Bayview Road is a residents-only beach. Though there is a boardwalk leading to the beach, there are no restrooms or concession stands. Lifeguards are on duty.

The crescent-shaped **Corporation Beach**, off Corporation Road and hugging Cape Cod Bay, is a popular spot on hot summer days. The curve of the beach forms a tidal pool that's perfect for children. A concession stand, restrooms and showers are available. Lifeguards are present. On a bluff overlooking the Bay is a swing set to keep the kids happy.

Howes Beach is a small public beach off Howes Street, just east of Corporation Beach. Howes has a boardwalk and lifeguards but no restrooms or concessions.

Two East Dennis residents-only beaches are on each side of Sesuit Harbor. On the west side is **Harborview Beach**, which has no facilities although a lifeguard is present. **Cold Storage Beach** on the east side of the harbor has restrooms and lifeguards but no concession stands.

The last public beach on the north side is **Sea Street Beach** at the end of Sea Street in Quivet (East Dennis). Sea Street has lifeguards, restrooms and a boardwalk leading to the beach. There are no concession stands.

There is perhaps no more popular Mid-Cape beach than **West Dennis Beach**, off Davis Beach Road in West Dennis. Situated on a narrow patch of sand on Nantucket Sound just east of the mouth of Bass River, the beach stretches for more than a mile. Beachgoers begin to arrive here by 10 AM, but since the parking lot has room for more than 1,000 cars, you'll rarely have to worry about finding a space. The eastern end of the beach is reserved for Dennis residents; the western end, however, is less crowded and open to everyone. A well-equipped snack bar concession, restrooms and showers provide all the comforts while 10 lifeguard stations make this a safe, secure haven. At the beach is the Old

Bass River lighthouse (see our Attractions chapter).

About three-quarters of a mile east of West Dennis Beach is **South Village Beach** by the mouth of Swan River. South Village has parking for both residents and nonresidents. Toilet facilities and lifeguards are on site. There are no concession stands.

A number of Dennisport beaches are provided for the multitude of tourists who rent cottages in this south side village. **Haigis Beach** lies where Ocean Drive meets Old Wharf Road. Lifeguards are on duty and toilet facilities are available. There are no concession stands but there is a small store right across the street from the beach.

Further down Old Wharf Road is **Glendon Beach** opposite Glendon Road. Like Haigis, Glendon has lifeguards and toilet facilities. Again, there are no concession stands although a small store is just a short walk away.

Sea Street Beach at the end of Sea Street in Dennisport is perhaps a half mile east of Glendon Beach. Like Glendon and Haigis, the Nantucket Sound waters here are warm and the beaches are marked with rock jetties. Sea Street Beach has restroom facilities, concessions and lifeguards on duty.

The next two beaches do not have lifeguards, restrooms or concessions. **Raycroft Beach** is at the end of the short Raycroft Parkway off Old Wharf Road. To the east about a couple of hundred yards is **Depot Street Beach** at the end of (you guessed it) Depot Street.

At the end of Inman Street off Chase Avenue is the final saltwater beach in Dennisport. Flanked by motels with private beaches on either side up and down the popular Chase Avenue, Inman is a public beach that offers toilet facilities but no concessions. Lifeguards keep tabs on what's going on out in the water.

Scargo Lake is a nearly 50-foot-deep, 50-plus acre freshwater sandy-bottomed kettle hole nestled at the bottom of Scargo Hill. The lake is home to two popular beaches: **Princess Beach**, off Scargo Hill Road, and **Scargo Beach**, off Route 6A. Princess Beach has restrooms and a picnic area as well as lifeguards. Scargo Beach, narrow and tree-lined, also has toilet facilities and a lifeguard.

Lower Cape

Beaches in this area are on Cape Cod Bay, Nantucket Sound and the Atlantic plus numerous freshwater ponds. The **Cape Cod National Seashore**, 349-3785, has great beaches in Eastham, Wellfleet, Truro and Provincetown. Admission to any CCNS beach from June to Labor Day is $5 per car; $15 buys you a season pass good at all CCNS beaches — a wise

Photo: Steve Heaslip, Cape Cod Times

Beachgoers get a taste of heavy surf as they wade at Nauset Beach in East Orleans.

investment if you'll be staying a while or visiting often over the course of the summer. Those older than age 62 can get a Golden Age Passport for $10, good at all national parks. Admission is $3 for walkers or bikers. Lower Cape beaches, as a rule, are relatively undeveloped; most have no real restroom facilities but do have and portable toilets. Most Lower Cape beaches do not have concession stands; we've noted the exceptions.

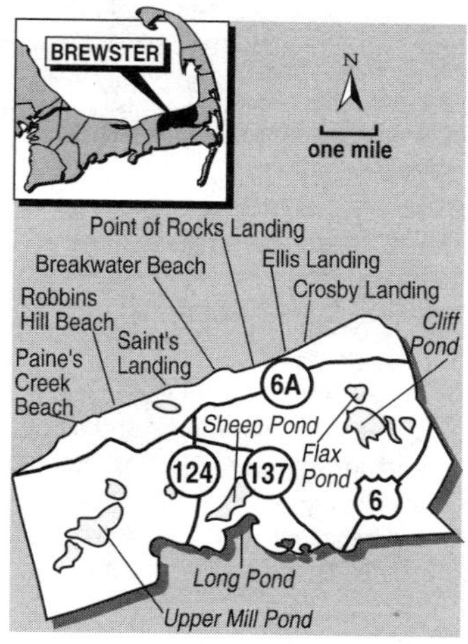

Brewster

Brewster has eight public beaches on Cape Cod Bay, plus a couple of beaches on freshwater ponds, the largest being **Long Pond**, which lies half in Brewster and half in Harwich. Parking permits for town beaches are available in the lower level of town hall at the rear entrance on Route 6A, 896-4511, from 9 AM to 3 PM daily. The cost is $5 for residents, and for nonresidents it's $8 a day, $25 a week, $45 for two weeks or $75 for the season. Facilities are limited at Brewster beaches. There are no snack bars (personally, we like it that way), though the ice cream truck cruises the beach parking lots on summer days. Portable toilets are the best you'll do for bathrooms. The only lifeguarded beach is at Long Pond, where the town holds its swimming instruction program.

Going from west to east, **Paine's Creek** is the first town beach on the bay. As its name implies, it is fed by a creek and is perfect for children. Parking, however, is limited. Off Lower Road, **Robbins Hill Beach** and **Saint's Landing Beach** are both pretty and quiet, and, like all Brewster beaches, are incredible at low tide when the flats seem to go on forever. **Breakwater Beach** is a popular spot for families. At the end of pretty Breakwater Road off Route 6A by the Unitarian church, the beach is bordered by grassy dunes, and there is plenty of parking. **Point of Rocks Landing** is nice and quiet, but has virtually no parking. **Ellis Landing** and **Crosby Landing** are both great beaches; Crosby is larger and has more parking and is walkable from Nickerson State Park across 6A. Within Nickerson State Park, **Flax Pond** and **Cliff Pond** are great for swimming and picnicking.

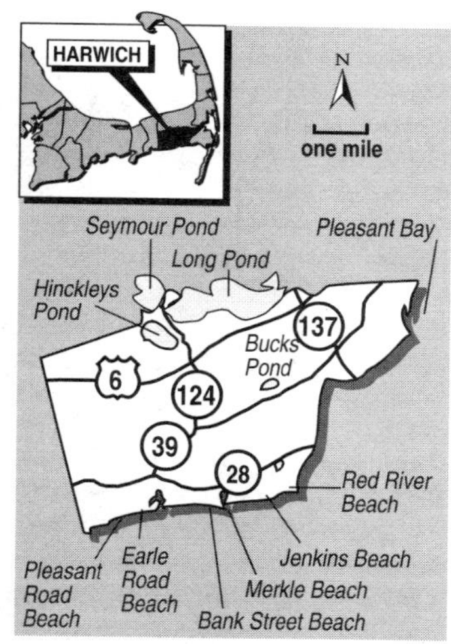

Harwich

Harwich has 16 beautiful beaches on Nantucket Sound, plus four on freshwater ponds. Stickers are required for parking, and are available at town hall on Route 39, 432-7638. The cost for nonresidents, who must show proof of renting in Harwich, is $25 for a week, $40 for two weeks and $50 a season for temporary residents. The exception is Red River Beach, off Depot Road in South Harwich, where you can park daily, for $5 on weekdays, $10 weekends. To avoid the beach-sticker issue entirely, take advantage of the town's free beach trolley, which operates daily from late June to early September and runs along Route 28 with stops at most public beaches. The town's larger beaches — **Red River**, **Bank Street** and **Pleasant Road** — have lifeguards and restrooms; a few of the smaller ones like **Earle Road** and **Cahoon's Landing** are equipped with portable toilets. Other small beaches on Nantucket Sound in Harwich are **Jenkins Beach**, right next to Saquatucket Harbor, and **Merkle Beach**, tucked next to Wychmere Harbor.

Harwich also has four freshwater beaches: **Bucks Pond**, off Route 39; **Pleasant Bay**, off Route 29; **Hinckleys Pond** and **Seymour Pond**, both off Route 124; and **Long Pond**, off Long Pond Drive. (Town beach stickers, available at town hall, are required to park at Long Pond; none of these ponds have lifeguards or restroom facilities.)

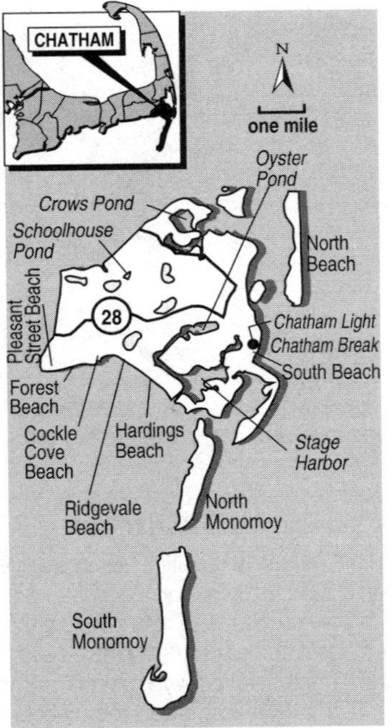

Chatham

Parking permits are required at most of Chatham's nine beaches; the exceptions are Forest Beach Road and Pleasant Street beaches, both in South Chatham, which have limited but free parking. Stickers good at the other beaches can be obtained at the booths at Hardings, Cockle Cove and Ridgevale beaches, where daily parking is allowed for a $7 fee. A one-week sticker is $35, and a season sticker is $60. Residents and property owners can get season stickers for $15 at the permit department on George Ryder Road, 945-5180. Only four beaches have lifeguards: Hardings, Cockle Cove, Ridgevale and Oyster Pond. Those beaches also have restrooms; other town beaches have portable toilets. Lifeguarded **Cockle Cove Beach**, off Cockle Cove Road, is the best choice for families with little ones. It also has restrooms, and parents will appreciate the calm waves and long stretches of soft sand. **Hardings Beach**, off Hardings Beach Road, has a concession stand for snacks, restrooms and quietly pounding surf. **Ridgevale Beach**, between Hardings and Cockle Cove (at the end of Ridgevale Road) also has lifeguards, restrooms and a concession stand in summer. Also on Nantucket Sound are **Pleasant Street Beach** (where you don't need a sticker to park) and **Forest Beach Road Beach**. Those seeking solitude should head over to Atlantic Ocean-fronted **North Beach**. Located at the southern end of Orleans' Nauset Beach, it's accessible only by boat. Area water taxis will take you there (and bring you back) for about $10 round-trip per adult.

The remote **South Beach**, off Morris Island Road just beyond the Chatham Light and also on the Atlantic, provides solitude without requiring a boat. It has no parking lot, so you'll have to walk or bike there. The most desolate stretches take quite a hike, but the quiet and grandeur cannot be beat.

Oyster Pond, an inland saltwater pond off Stage Harbor Road that's connected to Nantucket Sound via Stage Harbor and Oyster Creek, is calm and relatively warm and has a lifeguard in season; it also has restrooms. **Schoolhouse Pond**, situated on Schoolhouse Road in West Chatham, is also worth a visit for its tranquility, but note that parking is limited to Chatham residents.

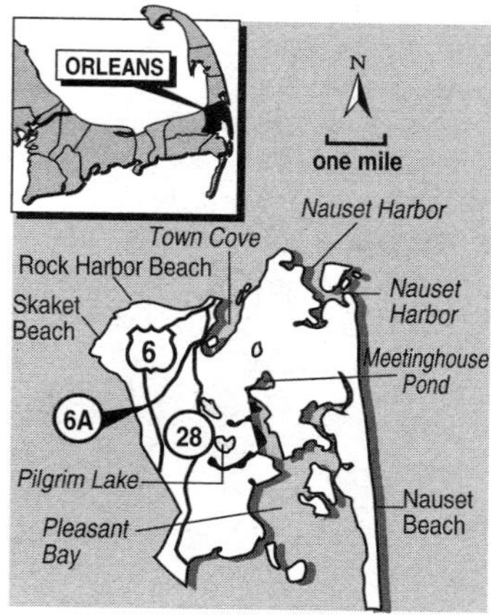

Orleans

Orleans has only a few public beaches, but when one of them is beautiful **Nauset Beach**, famous for its wide expanse, big Atlantic Ocean waves and lovely dunes, and the other is **Skaket Beach** on Cape Cod Bay, one of the best places to watch a sunset, who could ask for more? Residents get beach stickers for free; renters (who must show proof of renting in Orleans, such as a lease or rent receipt) can get stickers for $25 a week, $45 for two weeks or $65 for the season. People who are renting in nearby towns can get a one-week sticker for $30 or a season sticker for $100. All nonresident stickers are issued at Nauset Beach, 240-3780, where daily parking is available for $8. The same price applies to Skaket Beach, and the one-day permit entitles you to go to either beach — or both — during that day.

Nauset Beach, at the end of Beach Road in East Orleans (just follow Main Street east), has lifeguards, a snack bar and restrooms. You can rent beach chairs and umbrellas too. Four-wheel-drive vehicles are permitted on one section of the beach, except when plovers and other birds are nesting, but you must have a permit from the Orleans Parks and Beaches Department, 18 Bay Ridge Lane, 240-3775; the cost is $110 for a year; $55 off-season.

Bayside Skaket Beach, 255-0572, off Skaket Beach Road, is just as popular as Nauset and also has restrooms. Parking is limited, and the lot fills up fast. At low tide, people flock here for the chance to walk a mile or so through the beach grass and onto the flats. At high tide, it's great for frolicking in the water.

If you don't want to swim, but just want to get your feet wet, stop at the little beach at **Rock Harbor**, another great place for sunsets. One secret gem is the tiny beach that is reachable by walking down the trail at **Paw Wah Point Conservation Area**, off Namequoit Road. You'll even find a few picnic tables scattered here and there.

Orleans has a freshwater pond worth visiting: **Pilgrim Lake**, off Kescauogansett Road, features a lifeguard in season as well as changing rooms, picnic areas, a small beach and even a dock should you decide to moor your boat while taking a dip.

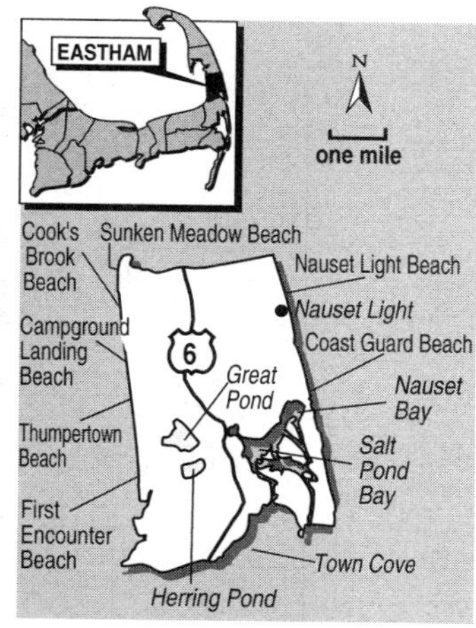

Eastham

Parking at Eastham's town beaches requires a sticker, available at the Natural Resources building on Old Orchard Road, 240-5972. Stickers are free for residents; for nonresident renters the cost is $20 for one week, $30 for two weeks and $50 for the season. Visitors can park for $5 a day. One caveat: Although Eastham resident stickers are good for both town and National Seashore beaches, visitor stickers are good only at town beaches and not Seashore beaches.

While the National Seashore beaches have lifeguards in season, Eastham town beaches do not, with the exception of **Great Pond Beach**, on Great Pond Road, and **Wiley Park**, on the other side of Great Pond Road off Herringbrook Road. Wiley Park also has a small playground and restrooms, and is great for families. Town beaches that dot the bay side include **First Encounter**, which is lovely but can get crowded. To get away from it all, drive beyond the main parking lot and find a spot down by the river, where the beach is lovely and the water is calm. First Encounter is one of the few beaches with real restrooms, the other two being Wiley Park and **Cook's Brook**; the others have portable toilets.

Moving up the bay coast, you'll find **Thumpertown Beach**, which is lovely but has limited parking and a stairway to the beach. Just north of Thumpertown is **Campground Beach**, which has lots of parking and easier access to the beach but can get cramped at high tide. Cook's Brook is quiet and pretty, as is **Sunken Meadow**; both have limited parking and are frequented largely by the occupants of nearby cottages. On the ocean side are two popular Cape Cod National Seashore beaches — they're easy to find, just turn east at the Visitors Center off Route 6 and keep driving. **Coast Guard Beach** has virtually no parking at the beach, but there is a large lot just a half-mile away that is serviced by a frequent shuttle bus. Or, park at the Doane Rock picnic area and hike through the woods and over the boardwalk — a pretty walk but long if you're carrying much gear. Just to the north is **Nauset Light Beach**, whose namesake lighthouse was moved back from an eroding cliff in 1996. The lot here fills up fast. If you're really desperate, you can park at the high school on Cable Road, but it's a healthy walk from there.

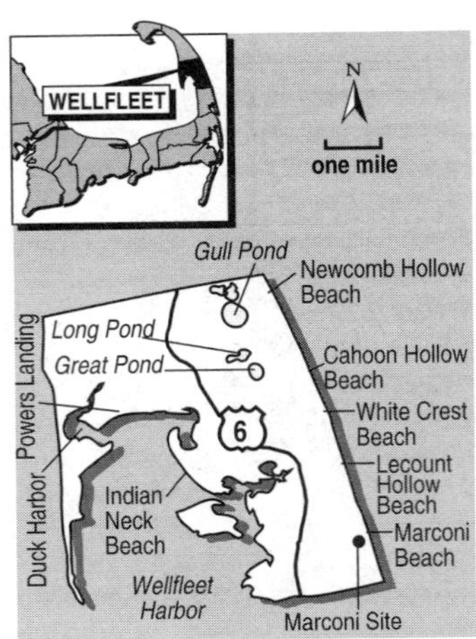

Wellfleet

Many of the beaches in Wellfleet require a town sticker; renters can buy one at a specially marked booth on the town pier in July and August, for $25 a week or $75 for the season. These include the bayside **Duck Harbor**, at the very end of Chequessett Neck Road; **Indian Neck Beach**, off Pilgrim Spring Road; nearby **Burton Baker Beach**; **Powers Landing**, off Cequessett Neck Road; and the Atlantic-sided **Newcomb Hollow Beach** and **LeCount Hollow Beach** (also called Maguire Landing).

With the exception of Duck Harbor, all the bayside beaches are really on the harbor, with views of Great Island, which juts into the bay, cradling the harbor. **Great Island** is National Seashore territory and more for hiking than beaching (see our Parks and Recreation chapter), but if you really want to get away from it all, put on your backpacks and hiking shoes and trek out to Great Island's remote shores. Indian Neck Beach is perhaps the nicest of all,

INSIDERS' TIP

Cape Codders have a long history of moving houses and other buildings. Ask about the history of any given building and you're likely to be told it once stood somewhere else — on the other side of town, or in many cases, closer to the shore.

with its soft, sandy stretch looking out over the harbor and the bay beyond. Adjacent Burton Baker Beach is the only town beach that allows windsurfing but only at certain times of the day. Windsurfers should pick up a copy of the regulations at the beach sticker booth at Wellfleet Harbor.

Beach stickers are also needed to park at **Great Pond** (off Cahoon Hollow Road), **Gull Pond** (off Gull Pond Road) and **Long Pond** (off Long Pond Road). Just past the harbor on Kendrick Avenue is **Mayo Beach**, perfect for families with children. Here you can see boats heading in and out of the harbor, and you can actually park for free here if you can get a space. Right across the street is a terrific playground, so if the kids get restless and bored with the beach (and they do) you can take them over to Baker's Field for some swinging, climbing and sliding. You'll also find full restrooms at Baker's Field, an easy stroll across the street from Mayo Beach. Other town beaches have portable toilets. There are no food concessions.

On the Atlantic, **Cahoon Hollow Beach** attracts a big college crowd, who later in the day flock to the beach-side Beachcomer (see our Nightlife chapter). The lot fills up quickly, and you can opt to use a beach sticker or pay a daily parking fee of $10. The same goes for **White Crest Beach**, just to the south. The waters at White Crest Beach (also called Four Mile Beach and Surfer's Beach) are rougher, making it ideal for the surfers who flock here. Please note that White Crest is not the place to bring young kids, seniors or the handicapped: A steep dune with no staircase leads down to the beach.

The National Seashore's **Marconi Beach** will take your breath away with its beauty. Parents will appreciate the easy access from the parking lot to the beach itself. In-season facilities here include full restrooms and outdoor showers.

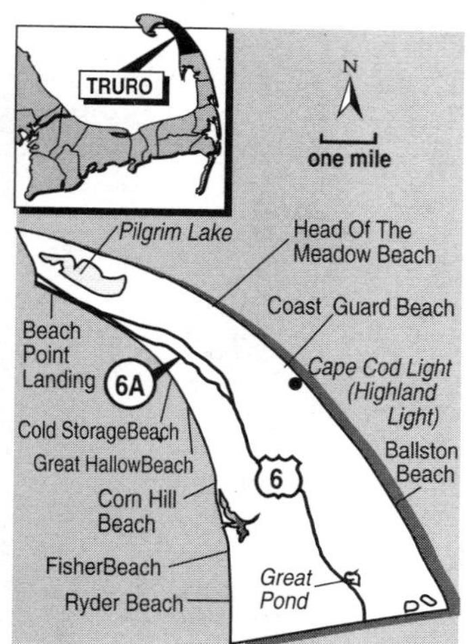

Truro

You'll need a sticker, available to renters in the Beach Commission office behind the Truro Center Post Office, to gain access to just about all of the beaches in Truro. The cost is $10 a year for residents; for nonresidents, it's $20 for one week, $30 for two weeks, $60 for four weeks and $100 for the season. All the town beaches are equipped with portable toilets. If you want the real facilities, go to the National Seashore's portion of Head of the Meadow on the ocean side. **Head of the Meadow Beach** is half-owned by the town and half by the Seashore. Both sides have lifeguards in season, so this is a good choice for families with children. Another plus is that the ice cream truck cruises this lot. If you don't have a beach sticker, you can park at the town portion of Head of the Meadow for $5 a day. The same goes for **Corn Hill Beach**, on the bayside; all other Truro beaches require stickers to park.

INSIDERS' TIP

Don't hit the beach without the essentials: sunscreen and a bottle of water or juice. It's easy to burn and easy to become dehydrated sitting in the sun.

Photo: Cape Cod Times

Children can spend hours playing in the sand.

Also on the ocean side, **Ballston Beach** and **Long Nook Beach** are very popular, so you must get there early to get a parking space. Long Nook is quiet and banked by dune cliffs; Ballston requires some walking to get out to the beach so if you have lots of gear to carry it can be awkward. Another Truro beach on the ocean side is **Coast Guard Beach** (not to be confused with the National Seashore beach by the same name in Eastham). On the bay side, **Corn Hill** (also on the ice cream truck's route) has plenty of parking and is popular with families. This picturesque beach is right at the mouth of the Pamet River, and you'll see boats heading in and out of the harbor.

In the southern end of town, also on the bay side, is **Ryder Beach**, which has been something of a well-kept secret. It's a lovely beach but not heavily frequented, so it's a nice choice for those who want to get away from crowds. Just north of that is **Fisher Beach**, which is nice but has only a tiny parking lot. North of Corn Hill is **Great Hollow Beach**, which is lovely and quiet; and then **Cold Storage Beach**, also called Pond Village, which is very popular so get there early in the day.

On Route 6A near the Provincetown line is **Beach Point Landing**, often called Topmast because parking is right next to the Topmast Motel.

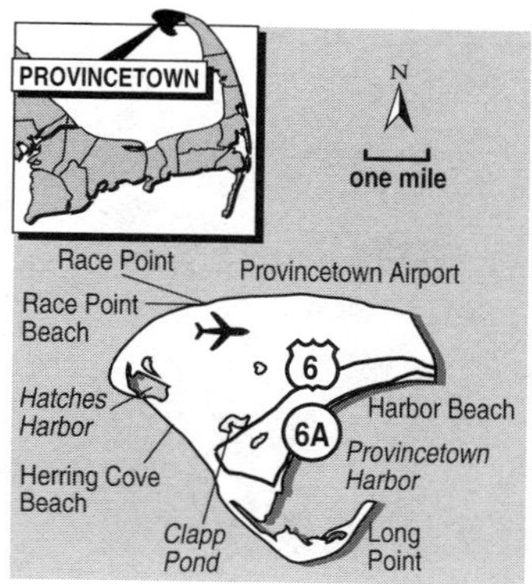

Provincetown

Provincetown is unique in that it has no real town beaches — and thus, there is no such thing as a Provincetown beach sticker. The two main beaches here are both part of the National Seashore: **Herring Cove** and **Race Point**. The waters are warmer and calmer at Herring Cove, but sun worshippers often prefer Race Point since it faces north and gets sun all day long. Still, everyone agrees that the sunsets at Herring Cove are unparalleled and the finest on the entire Cape. Expect hundreds, perhaps thousands, of people on the beach during the summer. National Seashore beaches have lifeguards, full restrooms and outdoor showers.

Harbor Beach, running parallel to Commercial Street alongside the bay, is ideal for those more interested in a walk at water's edge than a swim. There's no beach lot per se, but the closest parking is the town lot at MacMillan Wharf, which has hourly rates.

If you really want to get away from it all, head for the very tip of Cape Cod: **Long Point**, where Long Point Lighthouse still stands. You can get there by two routes, one by land, the other by sea. Take a two-hour walk, leaving from the Breakwater, on a jetty/footpath at the western end of Commercial Street adjacent to the Provincetown Inn. It's a long, romantic walk — and a longer walk back. Or, hop aboard a water shuttle from **Flyer's**, 131 A Commercial Street, 487-0898. The shuttle leaves every hour and costs $5 one way, $8 round trip.

Hatches Harbor, off Herring Cove, is a natural harbor reachable only two ways: either by a long walk along Herring Cove Beach or by a short drive with a four-wheel-drive vehicle over the sand. Its remoteness makes Hatches a perfect spot for those seeking solitude. On any given (hot) day, there's usually just a handful of visitors, most of them townies. The area surrounding Hatches was once home to early fishing settlements, saltworks, shipwrecks and the Race Point Lighthouse.

If you plan on arriving at the Cape by boat, you'll want to contact a marina early enough to assure that there'll be a slip waiting for you.

Boating and Watersports

A good part of the reason why people come to the Cape is to leave the land and step into the rising and falling waves of the sea. Twentieth-century sailors in pleasure boats and fishing boats follow in the watery footsteps of our 18th and 19th century ancestors who went to the sea to earn their living. In this sense, the sea — the bays, the sounds, even the ocean east of the lower Cape — is familiar to us. We feel at ease upon its waves. We understand its ways, its rhythms, its tides. We feel at home in this realm where our ancestors sailed. The waters off Cape Cod are in essence an extension of Cape Cod. Nantucket Sound and Cape Cod Bay are as much a part of the peninsula as the villages of Cotuit and Cataumet are on dry land.

In this chapter we explore the different ways people can get on the water. Each town has numerous boat ramps, marinas and boatyards, as one would expect in a spot surrounded by water. And, if you didn't bring one along with you, boats are available for rent — from high performance motor boats to sailboats, canoes to kayaks, paddleboats to Hobie Cats.

Watersports have become the rage for those who like to push the watery envelope. Jet Skis, sailboards and Parasailing have all turned the Cape into a saltwater playground. Surfing is superb on the outer Cape's unprotected oceanside beaches, where the waves are untamed and crash with a resounding boom.

During the summer months the harbors and marinas around the Cape are very busy spots. If you plan on arriving to the Cape on your own boat you'll want to contact the marina early enough to assure that there'll be a slip waiting for you. Any other questions can be directed to the harbormasters — we've provided their phone numbers in this chapter for your convenience.

Please remember to keep safety close at hand. Make sure life jackets and emergency supplies as well as first aid supplies are accounted for and in working order. If you're cruising the coast make sure you have an accurate navigation chart. Keep an eye on the weather and don't take any chances if you see fog rolling in. The waters around the Cape, especially along the outer Cape and the Buzzards Bay and canal areas, can be a little tricky.

But most of all, have fun! That's what it's all about, folks. Enjoy!

Boating

Boat Ramps and Town Landings

Bourne and Sandwich offer boating access to the Cape Cod Canal, the world's widest sea-level canal, and to two beautiful bays. Adjacent to Waquoit Bay, Mashpee is perfectly situated for touring the southern shore of the Cape, Nantucket and Martha's Vineyard.

Falmouth has 14 harbors and extensive boating facilities. An outstanding port halfway between Boston and Newport, Falmouth Harbor is protected, has deep water, full-service marinas, charters, rentals and plenty of mooring and slip space.

The Mid-Cape area offers everything a boater could possibly want. On the north side, you have access to Cape Cod Bay, Sandy Neck Beach and wonderful fishing for bass, bluefish and bluefin tuna. On the south side, Nantucket Sound, the islands of Nantucket and Martha's Vineyard and fishing for bass and blues draw anglers and pleasure boaters alike.

In the Lower Cape, Wychmere Harbor is considered one of the prettiest harbors on the Cape. Slips and moorings here are available, albeit infrequently, through the town. Call the harbormaster for availability. Pleasant Bay and Chatham Harbor provide access to Nantucket Sound, the Atlantic Ocean and Monomoy Island. On the Bay side, Orleans, Eastham, Wellfleet and Truro offer many town landings that allow you to spend a day on Cape Cod Bay, while Provincetown Harbor allows you to set sail from a harbor where whaling and fishing boats of the past made history.

Cape Cod boat ramps come in a variety of forms: sand, gravel and asphalt. Some town landings provide free use, others require a sticker so you'll want to inquire at the local town hall (phone numbers are listed in our Overview chapter). You'll find public boat ramps at the following locations.

FYI

Unless otherwise noted, the area code for all phone numbers in this guide is 508.

Upper Cape

Buzzards Bay: Buttermilk Bay

Bourne: Electric Avenue, Monument Beach, Barlow's Landing, Cape Cod Canal on Jefferson Road

Pocasset: Shore Road, Red Brook Harbor

Sandwich: Sandwich Basin

Woods Hole: Eel Pond

Falmouth: Great Pond, Green Pond, Falmouth Inner Harbor, Quinsett Harbor

West Falmouth: West Falmouth Harbor, Megansett Harbor

Waquoit: Waquoit Bay

Mashpee: Mashpee Neck Road

Mid-Cape

Osterville: Bay Street, Dowses Beach, East Bay Road, Oyster Road

Cotuit: Old Shore Road

Marstons Mills: Prince Avenue

Centerville: Coddington Road

Hyannis: Lewis Bay on Arlington Road

Barnstable: Scudder Lane, Mill Way Beach/ Barnstable Harbor

Cummaquid: Bone Hill Road

West Yarmouth: Bayview Road

South Yarmouth: Bass River

Yarmouthport: Bass Hole on Center Street

East Dennis: Cold Storage Road

South Dennis: Mayfair Marina, Follins Pond, Kelley's Bay

West Dennis Road: Uncle Freeman's Landing, Uncle Barney's Road, Horsefoot Road, Grand Cove

East Dennis: Sesuit Harbor, Sesuit Neck Road

Lower Cape

Brewster: Paines Creek, Point of Rocks

West Harwich: Herring River

Harwichport: Allens Harbor, Wychmere Harbor, Saquatucket Harbor

East Harwich: Round Cove/Pleasant Bay

North Chatham: Crows Pond, Ryder Cove, Strong Island Road

Chatham: Oyster Pond/Oyster Creek, Shore Road, Stage Harbor

West Chatham: Hardings Beach

Orleans: Town Cove at Asa's Landing, Rock Harbor, Town Cove on Cove Road

East Orleans: Meetinghouse Pond, Pochet Neck, Mill Pond Road, Nauset Harbor on Tonset Road

South Orleans: Arey's Pond, Quanset Pond

INSIDERS' TIP

President John F. Kennedy owned a Wianno Senior, which he sailed in the waters off Hyannisport during his summer vacations.

Eastham: First Encounter Beach on Samoset Road, Cole Road, Rock Harbor, Seaview Avenue, Hemenway Road, Salt Pond

North Eastham: Campground Beach, Silver Spring Beach,Steele Road, So Sunken Meadow Road

Wellfleet: Town Pier

Truro: Ryder Beach Road, Corn Hill Beach, Great Hollow Beach, Long Nook Beach

North Truro: Shore Road

Provincetown: Provincetown Harbor

Harbormasters

Harbormasters are on hand at most Cape harbors, taking care of all the business that goes on at these busy places. They make sure the docks and facilities are in working order and can assign you with a slip or mooring. Besides overseeing such functions as pump-out service, they're also the enforcers of harbor rules and regulations. Phone numbers for harbormasters are:

Bourne	759-0623
Falmouth	457-2550
Mashpee	539-1450
Sandwich	883-0808
Barnstable	790-6273
Yarmouth	790-3116
Dennis	385-5555
Harwich	430-7532
Chatham	945-5185
Orleans	240-3755
Eastham	240-5972
Wellfleet	349-0320
Truro	349-2555
Provincetown	487-7030

Marinas and Boatyards

Upper Cape

Bourne Marina

1 Academy Dr., Buzzards Bay • 759-2512

In town, within easy walking distance of shops, restaurants and family recreational facilities, Bourne Marina has 156 slips and can accommodate 60-foot boats with a 6-foot draft. It has fuel, water and 30- and 50-amp electrical service, pumpout facilities as well as restrooms, showers, lockers and a laundry area. You'll have use of a community lounge, a pressure washer and pumpout, and a marine and grocery store. The marina is open from May to October 31.

Monument Beach Marina

Emmons Rd., Phinney's Harbor, Monument Beach (Bourne) • 759-3105

Monument Beach Marina has 62 leased slips and 40 moorings as well as fuel and pumpout services, restrooms and showers. The marina can accommodate boats up to 44 feet long. The marina is open from mid-April to October 31.

Kingman Marine

1 Shipyard Ln., Cataumet (Bourne) • 563-7136

The 235 dock slips here can accommodate vessels up to 100-feet long. The marina offers water, 110- and 220- volt outlets and fuel. There are also restrooms, a laundry and showers on site as well as a restaurant, shops and a marina store. The marina is open year round.

Parker Boatyard

68 Red Brook Rd., Red Brook Harbor, Cataumet (Bourne) • 563-9366

Parker Boatyard carries both gas and diesel fuel and has 130 moorings with launch service and limited overnight dock space. The facilities include bathrooms, showers and a picnic area with grills. A complete yacht yard that specializes in sailboats, Parker's does repairs, repowering, awlgrip work, rigging and spar work, hauling, launching and winter storage. Though the boatyard is open year round, the marina is closed for the winter months.

The Sandwich Marina

Ed Moffitt Dr., Sandwich • 833-0808

This marina on the Cape Cod Canal has 180 commercial and recreational slips and offers water, electricity and diesel fuel as well as showers, parking, a playground area, a boat ramp and winter storage. Stores are within walking distance. Open year round, the marina can accommodate boats as long as 70 feet.

Woods Hole Marine

91A Water St., Woods Hole • 540-2402

Woods Hole Marine has a full-time mechanic available and can handle boats up to 65 feet long with about 37 moorings and 28 slips. Facilities include dinghy docks, showers, toilets and a pumpout boat that services five harbors in the area. The facility has water and 15-amp electrical service and is within walking distance of a convenience store, shops and restaurants. It's open from early spring to the end of October.

Fiddler's Cove Marina

42 Fiddler's Cove Rd., North Falmouth • 564-6327

Well-located for access to the Cape Cod Canal, Fiddler's Cove is a marina and boatyard with complete marine service. The facility has no moorings, but it has 135 slips and offers power, fuel, water and cable. It can accommodate boats up to 80 feet in length with a 7½-foot draft. The marina has a 34-ton travel lift for launching or hauling. The marina is open year round.

East Marine

Falmouth Heights Rd., Falmouth • 548-2704

An active boatyard since 1914, East Marine has 19 slips but no moorings and carries both No. 89 and No. 93 gas and marine diesel fuel. It offers 30- and 50-amp power, showers, cable TV and telephone. A pumpout facility is nearby. It is open year round, does repairs and has a 35-ton travel lift and boat storage. It can handle boats up to 50 feet. The marina is within walking distance of Main Street facilities.

Falmouth Harbor Marine

53 Falmouth Heights Rd., Falmouth • 457-7000

Falmouth Harbor Marine offers gas and diesel fuel and repair service for inboard and outboard motors, including Yamaha and Mercruisers as well as hauling, launching and storage. The boatyard, which is open year round, has 4 slips yet no moorings.

Falmouth Town Marina

Scranton Ave., Falmouth • 457-2550

This marina has seasonal and transient slips, which can be reserved, but there is a waiting list for seasonal slots. The marina accepts boats up to 100 feet. It offers water, electricity and shower facilities, and you can get fuel nearby. The marina is open from the beginning of April to the end of October.

Falmouth Marine Service

278 Scranton Ave., Falmouth Inner Harbor, Falmouth • 548-4600

Falmouth Marine has 30 slips and 16 moorings. It can accommodate boats up to 90 feet with an 11-foot draft and haul boats weighing up to 70 tons. A full-service yacht yard with stock room, gas and diesel fuel, electrical hookups and pumpout service, Falmouth Marine also offers a passenger ferry service to Edgartown. The year-round facility is within walking distance of restaurants and shops.

MacDougalls

Cape Cod Marine Service, 145 Falmouth Heights Rd., Falmouth • 548-3146

MacDougalls is a full-service boatyard with a sail loft and an engine shop. It rents 70 slips and 20 moorings, has electrical service, gas, ice and a marine store as well as a railway and a 50-ton travel lift. The facility is open year round and offers storage. A sailboat dealership on the premises, CWS Yacht Sales, 548-7700, sells new and used sailboats from 16 to 72 feet.

Edwards Boatyard

Rt. 28, East Falmouth • 548-2216

Edwards Boatyard has seven moorings and 48 slips. It has showers and restrooms, gas and diesel fuel, ice, pumpout facilities and a marine store as well as four railways, a boat-launching ramp and storage. This is a full-service yard that does safety and environmental inspections, has a factory-trained staff for repairs and is a Boston Whaler dealer. A family business for 44 years, Edwards is open year round (daily in season and five days a week in winter).

Quissett Harbor Boatyard

36 Quissett Harbor Rd., Quissett Harbor, Falmouth • 548-0506

Located in a small harbor in a wooded area, this boatyard is a lovely place to tie up for the night. It has 86 moorings and offers repairs, water, electric hookups and ice, but no fuel. Quissett Harbor Boatyard is open year round with limited hours during the winter months.

The Half Tide Marina

Frog Pond Close Rd., Mashpee • 477-2681

This full-service marina has 60 slips and 15 moorings. There are restrooms and some supplies available, along with boat sales, storage and all types of repairs.

Little River Boatyard

15 Riverside Rd., Waquoit (Mashpee) • 548-3511

Little River Boatyard is a rack and storage facility that does repairs, sells gas and ice and rents ice eaters (things that keep ice from forming around docks). It is open daily from 7 AM to 7 PM year round.

New Seabury Marina

Rock Landing Rd., New Seabury, Mashpee • 477-9197

New Seabury has five transient slips and gas, water and electric service as well as a marina store. It can accommodate boats up to 39 feet in length. The marina is accessible to numerous recreational facilities, golf and restaurants. New Seabury Marina is open from May to October.

Mid-Cape

Crosby Yacht Yard

72 Crosby Circle, Osterville • 428-6958

A popular rendezvous for yacht clubs and boating groups, Crosby Yacht Yard can accommodate power and sailboats up to 105 feet. It has both slips and moorings, shower and laundry facilities, fuel, water, ice, electricity and a marine store. Repair service is available seven days a week. The facility has travel lifts, marine railways, inside and outside storage and launch service. The home of the Cape Cod cat boat, Crosby's is a boat builder and an authorized dealer for J-Boat and Phoenix power boats and offers full brokerage services. There is a restaurant on the premises. Crosby Yacht Yard is open year round.

Nauticus Marina

West Bay Rd., Osterville • 428-4537

This marina is open from May to November and can accommodate boats up to 120 feet with a 6-foot draft. It has 100 feet of transient dockage and 15 slips for seasonal use. Electrical, water and cable service are available, but the marina has no gas nor does it offer repair service. The marina is within walking distance of village shops and restaurants.

Oyster Harbor Marina

122 Bridge St., Osterville • 428-2017

Oyster Harbor Marina has 110 slips and 30 moorings; it can accommodate boats from 8 to 100 feet long and has gas and diesel fuel, pumpout facilities, a 55-ton travel lift and storage. The full-service boatyard offers a marine store, restrooms, showers and carpentry, mechanical and electronic repairs as well as sales in yachts and outboard motors. Open year round, the marina is within walking distance of Osterville.

Hyannis Marina

21 Arlington St., Hyannis • 775-5662

Offering a calm, sheltered refuge, Hyannis Marina has more than 160 slips, diesel fuel and gasoline, water and electrical hookups and a complete parts and service department. The marina can accommodate everything from motor boats to mega-yachts up to 160 feet. It has a full restaurant and bar, swimming pool, cabana bar, courtesy and rental cars, showers, complimentary telephone and TV service, a coin-operated laundry and game room. The facility also includes an electronics and canvas shop, valet rack service, a marine store and emergency service. It is open year round.

Barnstable Marine Service

Barnstable Harbor, Off Mill Way, Barnstable • 362-3811

Barnstable Marine has 35 slips for boats up to 52 feet. They sell diesel fuel and gasoline, have showers and restrooms, bait and tackle, ice and snacks, haul-out facilities with a 20-ton travel lift and full mechanical, carpentry, finishing and repair services and yacht brokerage services. It is open year round and is a short walk from village shops and stores.

Ship Shops

Pleasant St., South Yarmouth • 398-2256

Ship Shops is a full-service boatyard in South Yarmouth with a limited number of transient slips and moorings. It sells gas and diesel fuel and has a marine shop. Ship Shops is open year round.

Bass River Marina

Rt. 28, West Dennis • 394-8341

Bass River Marina is open year round and offers 185 slips. This mid-Cape marina on the beautiful Bass River has gas and pumpout facilities.

Mayfair Boat Yard & Marina

181 Old Mayfair Rd., South Dennis • 398-3722

There are 85 slips at the year-round Mayfair Boat Yard. It also has gas and a dump facility for porta potties.

Northside Marina

Sesuit Harbor, 357 Sesuit Neck Rd., East Dennis • 385-3936

This northside marina on Sesuit Harbor offers 120 slips, storage, gas, diesel and pumpout facilities. The marina is open year round.

Lower Cape

Harwichport Boat Works Inc.

4 Harbor Rd., Harwichport • 432-1322

A year-round facility, Harwichport Boat Works offers a handful of guest mooring spots both here and in the inner harbor. This is a full-service marina, offering storage, gas and diesel, boat and engine sales and repairs. The yard is also renowned for its restoration work; wood and glass are its specialties. Tie-ups are short-term only.

Allen Harbor Marine Service Inc.

335 Lower County Rd., Harwichport • 432-0353

The year-round facility on picturesque, protected Allen Harbor was founded in 1927 and is another full-service yard, offering 52 slips and 35 moorings, a gas dock, repairs, sales and storage (they literally shrink-wrap your boat for the winter). Beside Allen Harbor Marine is a town-owned docking ramp.

Saquatucket Harbor

Municipal Marina , 715 Main St. (Rt. 28), Harwichport • 430-7532

This marina was voted the No. 1 Marina in Lower Cape by *Cape Cod Life* magazine. The marina, just a quarter-mile from the village and the largest municipal marina on the Cape, has 192 slips and a dozen visitor slips. Services and amenities include washers, dryers, restrooms, showers, pumpout service and 20/30-amp/110 volt electrical service. The marina is open from early May to mid-November.

Outermost Harbor Marine

83 Sea Gull Rd., Chatham • 945-2030

Outermost Harbor Marine offers 65 slips and only three moorings. It has a gas facility, hauling and launch service, storage and a marine hardware and supplies shop. It also specializes in fiberglass repairs. The facility is closed January and February.

Stage Harbor Marine

Bridge St., Chatham • 945-1860

Stage Harbor Marine has 33 slips and 33 moorings, gas and pumpout facilities and a first-rate repair shop. Stage Harbor is open year round.

Chatham Yacht Basin

Barn Hill Ln., Chatham • 945-0728

Open year round, Chatham Yacht Basin has 30 moorings and 70 slips on pretty Oyster River. Chatham Yacht Basin is a full-service marina.

Oyster River Boatyard

Barn Hill Ln., Chatham • 945-0736

Instead of moorings, Oyster River Boatyard offers 20 floating docks. It also has 22 slips, but don't count on getting one anytime soon as there is a long waiting list. The year-round boatyard also has a gas facility and repair service.

Ryder's Cove Boatyard

Town Landing, 46 Ryder's Cove Rd., Chatham • 945-1064

Ryder's Cove has 36 slips and 73 moorings. The marina offers gas and seasonal rack storage. It is also a certified Johnson motors specialist. Ryder's Cove is open throughout the year.

Arey's Pond Boat Yard

Arey's Ln., Orleans • 255-0994

This year-round boatyard has 60 protected moorings off Pleasant Bay that can accommodate boats up to 30 feet. It also offers custom wooden boat building and repairing and sells new and used boats and skiffs. Arey's Pond Boat Yard offers a sailing school in the summer.

Nauset Marina

off Barley Neck Rd., Orleans • 255-3045

Open year-round, this marina has 55 slips, 45 moorings and 40 dry land rack seasonal storage spaces as well as gas (no diesel) and pumpout facilities.

Rock Harbor

Rock Harbor Rd., Eastham • 240-5972

There are 39 municipal town slips at Rock

Harbor. The waiting list, though, is 12 years! Rock Harbor offers perhaps the lowest prices on the Eastern seaboard — $20 a foot, versus the usual $40 found everywhere else. Rock Harbor (half of it is owned by the town of Orleans) is the only place on the Cape at which you can moor at the front of Cape Cod Bay. You must supply and anchor your own mooring; the fee is $10.

Wellfleet Marine

Town Pier, Wellfleet • 349-2233

This year-round marina offers seasonal moorings by the night, week and month on a first-come, first-served basis. It also has a gas facility as well as diesel; pumpout is done via the harbormaster's boat. Several slips are available through the harbormaster.

Provincetown Marina

Fisherman's Wharf, Provincetown • 487-0571

Located smack in the middle of town, Provincetown Marina has more than 200 berths and 100 moorings, with launch service from 7 AM until midnight (later on weekends). Three launches operate from Memorial Day through Columbus Day weekend. The marina also has a pumpout station, trash dumpster and gas dock as well as showers, telephones, soda machines and a coin-operated laundry. Coverage is provided 24 hours a day on Channel 9. The marina is open from Memorial Day through Columbus Day weekend.

Provincetown Yacht and Marine Marina

MacMillan Pier, Provincetown • 487-9256

This newer marina has 22 slips, available by the night, week or month. The marina also offers water and electrical hookups, showers and a pumpout station. Though this is one of the smallest marinas in New England, it can hold very large boats because it has 10 feet of water at low tide.

Boat Rentals

If you're in the mood to do a little sailing or motoring upon the waves, you may want to consider renting a boat. There are many rental outfits across the Cape to help you out, and some of them are listed below. Those looking for charters and cruises, where you can sit back and enjoy the sights while someone else does the sailing, should refer to our Tours and Excursions chapter. Or, if you wish to mix a little fishing in, see our Fishing chapter for charters.

Upper Cape

Cape Water Sports

145 Falmouth Heights Rd., Falmouth • 548-7700

This company at MacDougalls Marine in Falmouth's Inner Harbor rents sailboats by the day or week. Selections include Hunter and Beneteau brands ranging in size from 27 to 45 feet.

Cape Yacht Charters

490 Sippiwissett, Falmouth • 540-5395

Cape Yacht Charters is a personalized service that matches sailors and sailboats. It is a bare boat charter service, as opposed to a crewed charter. The boats, all based in Falmouth, range in size from 28 to 45 feet and are often booked a year in advance.

INSIDERS' TIP

The hurricane season just happens to coincide with prime boating time. Contact the National Hurricane Center at (900) 933-2628 for advisories. To prepare your boat for bad weather, seal hatches, portholes, windows, doors and vents with duct tape. At a slip or tie-up, make the lines as long as possible, set extra anchors and add extra fenders and chafe protection. Take valuables and electrical equipment off the boat and do not remain on board during a hurricane.

Mid-Cape

Cape Cruzin Boat Rentals

Hyannis Marina, Arlington St., Hyannis • 760-3818

Cape Cruzin rents Sea-Doo and Wave Runner vehicles that seat up to three people and offshore performance boats at the Hyannis Marina during the summer. It also offers Para-Sailing.

Cape Cod Boats

Bass River Bridge, Rt. 28, West Dennis • 394-9268

Spend the day on Bass River by renting a motorboat, Sunfish sailboat, canoe, runabout or windsurfer. Want to spend the time fishing? You'll also find bait, tackle, even licenses — year round.

Cape Cod Waterway Boat Rentals

Rt. 28, Dennisport • 398-0080

You can rent manually powered and electric paddleboats, canoes and kayaks for use on Swan River, Swan Pond and Nantucket Sound. The shop is open from early May through mid-September.

Lower Cape

Jack's Boat Rentals

Rt. 6A, Nickerson State Park, Brewster • 896-8556

Almost nothing beats sailing Flax Pond on a warm summer day, and Jack's Boat Rentals is the place for one-stop shopping. It's all here: Sunfish, sailboards, seacycles, pedal boats, canoes and kayaks. Jack's also offers windsurfing and sailing lessons. Jack's has other locations at Gull Pond in Wellfleet, 349-7553, and a retail shop on Route 6 in Wellfleet, 349-9808.

Cape Water Sports

Rt. 28, Harwich • 432-7079

This year-round facility is the largest rental company on Cape Cod. Here, you can find all kinds of boats, including canoes, Daysailers, Hobie Cats, windsurfers, paddleboats and sailboats up to 42 feet long — perfect for a jaunt on the gentle Herring River.

Wellfleet Marine

Town Pier, Wellfleet • 349-2233

From mid-June to mid-October Wellfleet Marine rents (by the hour or day) Stur-Dee Cat 14-foot sailboats, 14-foot skiffs (with 6 horsepower motors), 19-foot Rhodes sloops and 21-foot MacGregor Sloops for use in Wellfleet Harbor.

Flyer's

131A Commercial St., Provincetown • 487-0898, (800) 750-0898

Ever since it opened its doors in 1965, Flyer's has satisfied the needs of boaters. No wonder it boasts the largest rental fleet on the Cape! Find powerboats, sloops, catamarans, Sunfish and rowboats here. Flyer's also rents fishing equipment, including an Early Bird's Special for early risers: outboards, drop lines and bait at great prices. Flyer's is open from mid-May to mid-October.

Boating Equipment

Harborside Marine & Sports

56 Scranton Ave., Falmouth • 548-0143

Harborside Marine sell canoes, kayaks, marine supplies, dinghies, inflatable boats and Evinrude outboard motors. It also has fishing

INSIDERS' TIP

The catboat was first built in Osterville as a small, easy-to-handle fishing boat which, because of its design, was nearly impossible to capsize. It was designed for the single fisherman. Today's catboats are purely recreational. Visit the Osterville Historical Society to see an old boathouse complete with a Wianno Senior and Junior as well as all the tools of the catboat building trade (see our Attractions chapter).

supplies, foul weather gear, camping equipment and services outboard motors and boats.

Edwards Boatyard Inc.
1209 East Falmouth Hwy., East Falmouth • 548-2216

Edwards Boatyard provides service on all types of boats and offers a mobile repair service. The marine store has a complete supply of parts and accessories. It has an outboard, diesel and inboard engine shop and provides towing and salvage service.

Anchor Outboard Co. Inc.
365 West Main St., Hyannis • 775-3454

Besides selling small boats and engines, this Hyannis outfit services what its sells. Anchor Outboard also sells marine supplies and services Evinrude, Johnson and outboards.

E & B Discount Marine
1166 Rt. 132, Hyannis • 790-1425

E & B Discount Marine provides "anything for the boat . . . except the boat." Here you'll find an assortment of marine supplies. It provides electronic repairs on products it sells as well as propeller repairs. E & B also offers in-store seminars, free of charge.

Catboat Curtains
49 Harborview Rd., Barnstable • 362-7059

Do you wish you had a little more privacy when you're tied up at a marina, or have you wondered where you could find sheets for the V-berth? This company makes custom sheets and curtains to fit any boat, no matter what shape or size. They'll visit you anywhere on the Cape, Nantucket and Martha's Vineyard to get measurements from your power or sailboat. What a great idea! Catboat Curtains is open year round.

Sailing Lessons

More than 40 yacht clubs and sailing associations around the Cape and islands offer opportunities for sailing to members and nonmembers. A number of towns offer instruction including: Barnstable, 790-6345; Falmouth, 457-2567; Harwich (to residents), 430-7553; Sandwich, 888-4361; and Yarmouth, 398-2231. Here are a few other possibilities to get you out on the water.

Cape Cod Sailing
Eventide, Hyannis • 771-7918

If you've always wanted to learn how to sail, Cape Cod Sailing offers extensive lessons in two- to five-day sails in the area. Instruction includes basic maneuvering, the anatomy of a boat, engine maintenance, sail and sheet handling, anchoring and mooring and other pertinent subjects. Small groups, families and couples are welcome. Cape Cod Sailing offers cruising and sailing lessons on a 36-foot sailing yacht. Classes, some specially geared to women, are held Monday through Friday from June to October.

FYI

Unless otherwise noted, the area code for all phone numbers in this guide is 508.

Arey's Pond Boat Yard
Arey's Ln., So. Orleans • 255-0994

This marina offers private lessons and extensive hands-on group lessons from Memorial Day to Labor Day. Instruction takes place on gorgeous Pleasant Bay.

Chequessett Yacht & Country Club
Chequessett Neck Rd., Wellfleet • 349-0198

In season, from early July through the end of August, Chequessett Yacht & Country Club offers eight-week junior and adult sailing instruction programs.

Capt. Bob Rice
Brewster • 896-2730

Rice shares his more than 20 years of sailing experience in an extensive, totally hands-on six-hour course. His "classrooms" are either a small boat (in Brewster's Punkhorn Parklands) or large boat (Saquatucket Harbor in Harwichport). He promises to have the patience of a saint with novices; intermediate sailors will love his overnight learning excursions on Nantucket Sound. Lessons are held from Memorial Day to early October.

Flyer's
131A Commercial St., Provincetown
• 487-0898, (800) 750-0898

From mid-May to mid-October Flyer's offers personalized lessons on beginner and intermediate levels, including hands-on, video instruction.

Watersports

Surfing and Windsurfing

Waves crash along the outer Cape's shores every second of every hour of every day, waves that strike with a thunderous boom strong enough to pound the shoreline smooth and shake the dunes beyond. Upon this Atlantic shoreline surfers can be found challenging these monstrous waves.

The beaches from Wellfleet to Orleans provide the best surfing on the peninsula. Here the wave is an untamed beast. It travels for miles and miles across unbroken stretches of ocean stumbling only slightly over the shoals protecting this coastline. Yet the shoals only seem to heighten the oncoming wave's power and resolve. The wave builds, sprouts a whitecap atop its peak, curls, builds some more and then races toward shore like some serpent awakened from a watery sleep. There are a number of shops around the Cape which cater to the surfing crowd who attempt to tame these "serpents."

Windsurfing, sometimes called boardsailing, depends on maneuvering a sail that pivots 360 degrees on top of a rudderless board. It is more related to sailing than surfing and was accepted as an official Olympic sport in 1992. Five years ago, the largest boardsailing regatta in the country was hosted by the Hyannis Yacht Club in coordination with the U.S. Windsurfing Organization and the International Mistral Class Organization.

In 1994 the three top windsurfers in the world, Robby Nash, Bjorn Dunkerbeck and Anders Bringdal, participated in the New England Windsurfing Show held at Kalmus Beach in Hyannis.

Considered to be one of the best places for boardsailing in the United States, Kalmus Beach is protected and has steady winds that usually blow 10 to 20 knots. Chapoquoit Beach on Buzzards Bay in Falmouth has also been the site of national competitions and is popular with advanced-intermediate to advanced windsurfers. Old Silver Beach on Buzzards Bay in North Falmouth and most of the Vineyard Sound shore are well-suited to basic boardsailing skills. Other popular beaches where you can ply the waters include Chapin and Corporation beaches in Dennis on Cape Cod Bay and West Dennis Beach on Nantucket Sound.

Photo: Steve Heaslip, Cape Cod Times

Jet-skiers splash around Lake Wequaquet in Centerville.

The following establishments sell and rent equipment or make repairs.

Cape Sailboards

661-D Main St., Falmouth • 540-8800

This is a full-service store with active wear, sailboards, accessories, wet suits, Boogie Boards, snowboards and skateboards. Board and sail repairs are available; the shop is open March to December.

Boarding House Surf Shop

302 Main St., Hyannis • 778-4080

This year-round Hyannis shop sells everything to do with the three sports of surfing, skateboarding and snowboarding. They offer all the clothing and accessories you'll need as well as videos to help you learn the techniques and a repair service.

Sound Sailboards

223 Barnstable Rd., Hyannis • 771-3388

In business since 1988, Sound Sailboards sells boards and sails, masks, wet suits and hoods and offers lessons and rentals. It is open from April through December seven days a week.

Monomoy Sail and Cycle

275 Orleans Rd., Chatham • 945-0811

Monomoy Sail and Cycle rents sailboards for use on Nantucket Sound and Pleasant Bay. Remember that while Pleasant Bay offers calm, delightful waters, Southern Pleasant Bay is much rougher — and potentially dangerous.

The Pump House Surf Company

9 Cranberry Hwy., Orleans • 240-2226

Offering a complete line of surf boards as well as clothing, swimwear and eyewear, The Pump House is an ideally located Lower Cape surf shop convenient to the Atlantic side beaches. It provides a repair service, a surf report, rentals and offers lessons. The Pump House is open weekends from early April to the end of May, seven days a week until October, and then weekends from October to December.

Nauset Sports

Rt. 6A, Orleans • 255-4742

This year-round shop rents and sells the latest in wetsuits, boards (sail, surf, skim and body) and essential windsurfing and surfing equipment.

Jasper's Surf Shop

Rt. 6, Eastham • 255-2662

Jasper's has a large selection of surf boards and equipment and sells some sailboards, swimsuits, wet suits and lifeguard equipment. Repairs are done in the summer only. In the off-season, the shop takes mail orders via telephone.

Jack's Boat Rentals

Gull Pond, Wellfleet • 349-7553

In addition to everything needed for on-the-water adventures, Jack's also rents Boogie Boards. It has two other shops in Brewster and on Route 6 in Wellfleet offering Sunfish, seacycles, canoes and sailboards.

Diving

Whether you use a mask and snorkel or scuba equipment, you can find as much adventure below the waves as on top of them, for the New England waters contain unique topography and marine life as well as hundreds of shipwrecks. Many wrecks lie around North and South Monomoy Islands off Chatham. Among these are the *Pendleton*, a 540-foot oil tanker that sank in 1952, and the *Alva*, a 285-foot steamer that was the private yacht of William K. Vanderbilt and sank in 1891 after colliding with the steamer *Dimmock* in

INSIDERS' TIP

Have you ever been sitting in a boat 5 miles offshore watching clouds build on the horizon and wishing like heck you knew more about interpreting weather signs? A video produced by meteorologist John Ghiorse is available to help boaters read weather indicators. For more information, write to John Ghiorse, Dept. C, 165 Fairway Drive, Seekonk, Massachusetts 02771.

heavy fog. Treasure salvors such as Barry Clifford, who located the pirate ship *Whydah* off Wellfleet, use sophisticated side-scan sonar to locate wrecks, but a diver with basic equipment and some coordinates can enjoy wreck diving too.

Beach diving is also popular on the Cape, especially at Corporation Beach in Dennis and Sandwich's Town Beach, which is considered safe and easy for beginners because the current is light and the rocky bottom is interesting. Divers see plenty of striped bass, bluefish, tautog, flounder, sea robins, sea urchins and starfish.

Several books about underwater exploration in the area are available, including three by Donald L. Ferris and Bill Dubiel: *Beneath the Waters of Cape Cod*, *Beneath the Waters of Massachusetts Bay* and *Exploring the Waters of Cape Cod: Shipwrecks and Dive Sites*, which has information on 94 dive sites, maps, photos and loran numbers.

The ocean side of the Cape has more currents and shoals; the bay side is colder and calmer. The visibility tends to be better in Cape Cod Bay and on the southern sounds than in Buzzards Bay. Just as winds alter the landscape, currents cause underwater changes, so you should consult the staff at local dive shops for suitable areas and current conditions for diving.

Check with one of the following dive shops for instruction, information or gear.

Aquarius Diving Center

3239 Cranberry Hwy., Buzzards Bay • 759-3483

This full-service scuba shop provides instruction, sales and service, charter diving anywhere on the Cape and dive travel arrangements. The Diving Center is a Scuba Pro dealer that specializes in low-stress fun dives. "What we mean by that is easy, relatively shallow dives," says Steve Carey. "We keep the dives at 50 feet or less, and average around 20 to 30 feet." Aquarius is open year round.

Aqua Center

2 Freezer Rd., Sandwich • 888-3444

Aqua Center is open year round and has diving equipment, masks, snorkels and fins. It offers instruction and equipment rental.

East Coast Divers

237 Falmouth Rd., Hyannis • 775-1185

Open year round, East Coast Divers offers scuba lessons, equipment and service and sells lights, compasses, pressure gauges, wet suits, boots and hoods. Courses cover ice diving, beginner and dive master instruction, search and rescue, CPR and equipment repair.

Sea Sports

195 D Ridgewood Ave., Hyannis • 790-1217

A full-service scuba diving shop, Sea Sports caters to snorkelers and has "everything you need to go diving." Sea Sports organizes an informal dive club and weekly night dives and also has a full-service surf shop. The shop is open year round.

Cape Cod Divers Inc.

815 Main St., Harwichport • 432-9035, (800) 348-4641

Considered by many to be the premier scuba shop on the Cape, Cape Cod Divers, established in 1980, is a full-service, year-round rental and sales center and the perfect spot for beginners to learn. Beginners are taken on dives in Provincetown Harbor, where they can scuba among shipwrecks. More experienced divers are taken to wrecks off Monomoy Island. During the winter, Cape Cod Divers offers certification in its indoor heated pool. Certification is offered year round.

Canoeing and Kayaking

One of the most exciting ways to explore the Cape is by canoe or kayak. Gliding through shallow water along coastal inlets, marshes and rivers permits you to see the land from the perspective of the earliest inhabitants. Nature lovers, especially bird-watchers who get close glimpses of great blue herons, osprey and snowy egrets, rave about the experience. Seeing the land from offshore also helps you appreciate physical characteristics that are often unnoticeable from foot or car. Some people consider a kayak easier to maneuver than a canoe because you are lower in the water, but operating a two-ended paddle can require some coordination.

Water conditions range from easy to challenging. A lot of people enjoy kayaking in Waquoit Bay, which allows them to explore Washburn Island. Other good spots include Barnstable Harbor and Pleasant Bay in Chatham and Orleans. As far as equipment goes, sea kayakers should have a whistle, horn, strobe light, bilge pump and a spray skirt to keep water out.

The Cape Cod National Seashore, 255-3421, (see our sidebar in Parks and Recreation) offers two guided canoe trips a day, depending on tides, from July 4 through Labor Day (and sporadically from Memorial Day to July 3 and from the Labor Day to Columbus Day). The trips begin at Salt Pond Visitors Center and wind their way through Nauset Marsh, where you can spot a spectacular display of wildlife, including migrating birds such as egrets and cranes. Reservations are accepted in person only for the first trip of the day. Two-hour trips cost $10 and tickets for the first trip can be reserved up to seven days in advance; the second trip is first-come, first-served.

The following establishments offer sales, rentals, repairs or tours.

Cape Cod Coastal Canoe & Kayak

36 Spectacle Pond Dr., Hatchville (Falmouth) • 564-4051

Now in its fourth season, Coastal Canoeing offers nature trips guided by a naturalist. Some excursions are regularly scheduled while others are arranged through the Cape Cod Museum of Natural History and the Thornton Burgess Society. Equipment, instruction and snacks are provided. You can visit about 14 areas around the Cape, including Barnstable's Great Marsh, Barnstable Harbor, Phinney's Harbor in Bourne, Great Island in Osterville, Nauset Marsh in Eastham, the Mashpee River, Scorton Creek in Sandwich and Waquoit Bay in Falmouth. Other popular outings off Cape are to the North River, a beautiful marsh area that crosses under Route 3, and to the Taunton River. Organized by Shirley and Fred Bull, Coastal Canoeing operates April through October. The trips last three hours, and you can bring a picnic.

Harborside Marine and Sports

56 Scranton Ave., Falmouth • 548-0143

This store carries the classic Old Town brand canoes and kayaks as well as other models of kayaks, both flatwater and seagoing, in one- and two-seaters, some with a rudder. The shop also sells fiberglass dinghies, aluminum dinghies from 10 to 12 feet long, paddles, oars and other boating equipment. Harborside Marine is open year round.

Eastern Mountain Sports

233 Stevens St., Hyannis • 775-1072

Open year round, this store has access to sit-on-top kayaks, which have no cockpit and are often used by scuba divers. It carries flatwater kayaks, which are shorter, and sea kayaks, which range from 15 to 22 feet and are used for touring since they have a lot of storage capacity. Eastern Mountain Sports carries a full range of paddles, flotation vests, safety equipment, maps and charts, camping and backpacking equipment and clothing.

Cape Cod Waterway Boat Rentals

Rt. 28, Dennisport • 398-0080

This company rents canoes and kayaks for use on Swan River, Swan Pond and Nantucket Sound. The shop is open from the beginning of May through mid-September.

Goose Hummock Shop

Town Cove, Orleans • 255-2620

Goose Hummock offers a large selection of canoes and kayaks for rent — from a half-day up to a week. A Saturday morning 2½-hour Introduction to Kayaking course is offered that covers basic paddle strokes and other topics. Goose Hummock also hosts half-day guided kayak trips during the season on the Orleans Cove.

Jack's Boat Rentals

Rt. 6, Wellfleet • 349-9808

Explore the Cape's hidden ponds, inlets and marshes on guide-led interpreted kayak eco-tours. Tours are given from Memorial Day through Columbus Day weekend. Since no experience is needed, beginners and children are especially welcome. Times vary because of the fluctuating tides. Jack's, which also has locations at Nickerson State Forest in Brewster, 896-8556, and Gull Pond in Wellfleet, 349-7553, also rents single and double kayaks and canoes.

Wellfleet Bay Wildlife Sanctuary
Rt. 6, Wellfleet • 349-2615

Wellfleet Bay Wildlife Sanctuary offers guided canoe trips with an environmental slant all over the Cape from the beginning of April through the end of October. Trips through marshes and ponds, from Chatham to Provincetown, are the specialty here, and you won't find more knowledgeable guides anywhere else on the Cape. The fee is nominal, and it's best to make reservations.

Jet Skiing

If surfing the Lower Cape is just too tame for you, check out the action on the motorized miniboats — they go by such brand names as Jet Ski, Waverunner, Sea-Doo and others — available at rental places around the Cape. Here are two places to get you started:

Cape Cod Windsurfing Academy & Watersports Rentals
134 Menauhant Rd., Falmouth Heights • 495-0008

Located on beautiful Vineyard Sound, this outfit at the Surfside Holiday Hotel rents all types of watercraft including Jet Skis. It also rents kayaks and sailboards for windsurfing.

Cape Cruizin Boat Rental
Hyannis Marine, Arlington St., Hyannis • 862-2520, (800) 760-3818

Cape Cruizin specializes in performance craft rentals. Here you can rent fast-moving Jet Skis as well as 28-foot performance boats by the half day, day and week. You can even soar above the water Parasailing. Afterwards, you can rest at a poolside grill and bar.

Cape Cod is blessed
with 360 ponds and
lakes, many of which
are teeming with bass,
trout, white perch and
pickerel.

Fishing

Fishing has a rich history on the Cape that goes back to its very beginnings, and continues today to be an important part of the local economic base. Before the white settlers, the Native Indians of the area understood well the importance of the sea. They were the Cape's great fishermen. Unearthed shell heaps along the coves and along the banks of rivers tell of their love for the shellfish of the area. The first white settlers to these parts were farmers. The crops yielded by the Cape's soil were not as bountiful as these settlers had hoped; therefore other avenues had to be explored to supplement the early Cape Codder's diet as well as pocketbook. It didn't take long for Cape Codders to realize that the real money was to be made off shore, harvesting fish from the sea. Bay whaling was also practiced to great success.

Centuries later the Portuguese arrived here to add yet another layer to the Cape's fishing heritage. Their contribution is substantial as evidenced by the growth of Provincetown as a major fishing port during the 19th and early 20th centuries.

Though commercial fishing still exists around the Cape, today fishing has largely become a recreational pastime that rivals its commercial cousin. In this chapter, we give you an overview of the sport, along with places to go and people to see to help make your fishing experiences memorable.

If you love to fish, you'll be in good company on the Cape. Anglers of every stripe come here for the great saltwater and freshwater fishing. Saltwater anglers go after striped bass, blues, bonito, false albacore, Spanish mackerel and cod and fluke, while freshwater anglers find trout, small and largemouth bass and yellow perch. The fishing season typically begins in the warmer Vineyard Sound waters, and as the season progresses Cape Cod Bay becomes a busy place. You start catching fish in early May in the saltwater and catch striped bass through November. Ice fishing is also popular in many of the larger lakes and frozen harbors.

No license is required for saltwater fishing. However, in order to fish in the freshwater ponds and lakes, you'll need to purchase a license, which you can obtain from the town clerk (see our Overview chapter for town hall addresses and phone numbers) and at many of the tackle shops around the Cape.

The **Massachusetts Division of Marine Fisheries**, 563-1779, can be reached Monday through Friday from 7 AM to 4:30 PM. They can provide you with current information about species availability and regulatory restrictions, which often change.

Shellfishing for mussels, clams and quahogs is also quite popular around the Cape. Get a license and a clam rake or just a trowel and dig for your chowder. Types of shellfish available, regulations and licensing fees vary considerably town by town. Contact the individual towns.

If you want to know more about fishing, attend a meeting of the Cape Cod Chapter of **Trout Unlimited**, which meets at Liberty Hall, just off Route 149 in Marstons Mills, on the second Wednesday of the month from 7 to 9 PM from September through May. The meetings are open to the public. Members and guest speakers discuss local fishing with an emphasis on conservation of the area's natural waterways. The group has a strong interest in freshwater and saltwater fly-fishing.

The best advice we can offer is to stop by a local bait and tackle shop for tips on where, when and what to fish. See our tackle shop recommendations later in this chapter.

Harbormasters are another good source of general information, but they can be hard to track down since their work frequently takes them away from their offices. Their phone numbers are listed in our Boating and Watersports chapter.

And if you want to see where most of the Cape's trout start out, visit the **Sandwich Fish Hatchery** on Route 6A, 888-0008. More than 80,000 trout are raised here to stock the state's ponds. Admission is free (see our Attractions chapter).

Freshwater Fishing

Since Cape Cod is surrounded by ocean, bay, sound and canal, it's sometimes easy to forget that it's also home to many freshwater fishing opportunities. The area is blessed with 360 ponds and lakes, many of which are teeming with bass, trout, white perch and pickerel as well as many of the other species such as sunfish, catfish and crappie. If you're fishing any of the Cape's freshwater ponds or lakes, it's helpful to know the feeding habits of the two main freshwater gamefish of the area — bass and trout. Bass are best caught on an overcast day with a temperature of about 70 degrees. Bass like to hide among the weedy sections of the pond and do not travel in schools so its best to move around a bit. Trout are also caught on cloudy days and go after live bait although they will respond to lures and flies. Trout prefer clear, moving water in the 60 degree range. While bass are by nature curious fish, trout are rather cautious. Both fish are good eating!

> **FYI**
>
> Unless otherwise noted, the area code for all phone numbers in this guide is 508.

A license is required to fish the Cape's freshwater ponds, lakes, streams and rivers. Licenses can be obtained at town halls or at certain bait and tackle shops. Typically, licenses are not required for children younger than 15.

Below we've listed some of our favorite fishing holes around the Cape.

Upper Cape

Flax Pond in Bourne is a good place to catch both bass and pickerel. This shallow pond with a maximum depth of six feet can be accessed from the northwest off Old County Road.

Lawrence Pond is Sandwich's largest pond at nearly 140 acres. It has a maximum depth of 27 feet and a boat ramp at the southeastern corner off Great Hill Road. Here you'll fish for white perch, pickerel and bass.

Peters Pond, Sandwich's second largest body of water, is stocked with trout. Pickerel and white perch are also here. A boat ramp is at the extreme eastern shore off John Ewer Road. The depths of this pond exceed 50 feet.

Snake Pond in Sandwich is more than 30 feet deep. Bass and pickerel can be caught here. Access is from the south off Snake Pond Road.

Spectacle Pond of Sandwich is stocked with trout and is also home to numerous white perch, bass and pickerel. Access can be made from the southwest shore off Pinkham Road.

Deep Pond in Falmouth is a bit misleading as there are several deeper ponds in town. At a maximum depth of nearly 30 feet, the pond is stocked with trout. You can access the pond from the southwest off Sam Turner Road.

Grews Pond is another trout-stocked Falmouth pond. A boat ramp south of the pond provides access. Maximum depth is 35 feet.

Jenkins Pond, between Goodwill Park Road and Pumping Station Road in Falmouth, has a maximum depth of more than 50 feet and is home to bass, white perch and pickerel. Much of this nearly 90-acre pond is more than 20 feet deep.

Ashumet Pond in Mashpee is trout stocked and is also full of bass and pickerel. Access can be found along the western shore off Currier Road in Falmouth.

Johns Pond of Mashpee achieves a maximum depth of 60 feet where stocked trout, pickerel, white perch and bass swim. There is a boat ramp to the east off Hooppole Road providing access to this greater than 300-acre body of water.

Mashpee Pond and **Wakeby Pond** in Mashpee are connected, combining for more than 700 acres of water. Mashpee Pond is the deeper of the two at nearly 90 feet. Both ponds are stocked with trout and also harbor bass, pickerel and perch. Access Mashpee Pond at a boat ramp on its southern shoreline just north of Route 130.

Mid-Cape

Hamblin Pond in Marstons Mills is stocked with trout and also provides good bass and pickerel fishing. There is easy access from Route 149 by taking the road adjacent to the small cemetery.

Hathaway Pond in Barnstable is stocked with trout and has a maximum depth of nearly 60 feet. A boat ramp can be found on the southern shore off Phinneys Lane near the intersection of Route 132.

Lovells Pond in Marstons Mills is larger than 50 acres and is stocked with trout to join the bass and pickerel. Access can be found along the southern shoreline off Newtown Road.

Shallow Pond in Barnstable lives up to its name — maximum depth is less than 8 feet over its nearly 70 acres. This is mainly a pickerel pond. It sits between Route 132 and Huckins Neck Road.

Wequaquet Lake, between Centerville and West Barnstable, is a huge lake by Cape Cod standards —650 acres — though its depth rarely exceeds 25 feet. This lake is stocked with northern pike and is also home to many bass, white perch and plenty of pickerel. Access can be found along the northern shore off Shootflying Hill Road.

Dennis Pond in Yarmouthport is a great place to fish for pickerel and bass. Access points are along the west side of the pond off Willow Street and along the east side off Summer Street.

Long Pond in South Yarmouth is stocked with trout. You can also catch bass, white perch and pickerel in this largely shallow pond with a maximum depth of 30 feet. There is a boat ramp on the south side of the pond north of the point where Route 28 and Wood Road intersect.

Fresh Pond in South Dennis is a shallow pond — about five feet deep — with access on its east side off Route 134. Pickerel can be caught here.

Scargo Lake in East Dennis achieves a maximum depth of about 50 feet over its 50-plus acres. The lake, which is stocked with trout, also has white perch and bass. Two access points can be found, one along the north side off Route 6A and another at the northeast corner off Scargo Lake Road.

Lower Cape

Cliff Pond in East Brewster is stocked with trout to swim in its nearly 200 acres. Access can be gained from the east off Nook Road and the west off Pond Road, both within Nickerson State Park. Nearby Little Cliff Pond is also trout stocked.

Flax Pond in East Brewster is trout stocked. It is more than 70 feet at its deepest point, and its waters are home to bass and pickerel. Access is from the northwest off Deer Park Road within Nickerson State Park.

Long Pond on the Brewster and Harwich town line is very large, spanning nearly 750 acres. In some spots the waters exceed 50 feet, with just more than 60 feet being its greatest depth. Here you'll find plenty of bass biting along with white perch and pickerel. Access is from the east off Route 137 and south off Long Pond Drive as well as from the north off Crowells Bog Road (east of Route 124).

Sheep Pond is a 150-acre Brewster pond stocked with trout. Bass and pickerel also swim in its depths, which exceed 60 feet. Access is from the southwest off Route 124. (Take Fisherman's Landing Road.)

Seymour Pond on the Brewster/Harwich line has pickerel, bass and white perch. It is about 180 acres in area and about 40 feet at its deepest point. It can be accessed from the east off Route 124.

Goose Pond in Chatham is trout stocked. Access is gained from the north off Old Queen Anne Road to Carriage Drive to this 50-plus-foot pond.

Schoolhouse Pond in Chatham is a small 20-acre pond stocked with trout. Maximum depth is about 50 feet. Access can be gained from the northwest off Old Queen Anne Road.

Baker's Pond in Orleans is trout stocked. A small pond at 28 acres, its maximum depth approaches 50 feet. Access is from the east off Bakers Pond Road.

Crystal Lake in Orleans has bass and pickerel along with stocked trout. Access points can be found along the northwest off Route 28 and southeast off Monument Road.

Great Pond is Eastham's largest pond at 110 acres. Bass and pickerel can be caught here. Access can be made off Great Pond Road.

Herring Pond of Eastham reaches a maximum depth of about 35 feet. Its 40-plus acres are trout stocked, and bass, white perch and pickerel can also be found here. Access to the pond is from the southwest off Crosby Village Road.

Gull Pond in Wellfleet is stocked with trout, though you'll also catch bass, pickerel and perch here. There is a boat ramp along the west side of the 100-plus acre pond off Schoolhouse Hill Road. Maximum depths here exceed 60 feet.

Long Pond in Wellfleet is like two ponds, the east side dropping to more than 30 feet and the west side going a bit deeper — over 50 feet. Access to this bass and pickerel pond can be found along the northwest side off Long Pond Road.

Great Pond in Truro is a small trout-stocked pond that drops to greater than 35 feet in its center. There is access at the southwest tip just off Route 6.

Pilgrim Lake in Truro, just before entering Provincetown, is a bit deceiving for its size. At 350 acres in total area, its deepest waters are scarcely six or seven feet. White perch and pickerel can be found here. Access is from the south off High Head Road.

Saltwater Fishing

The entire Cape coastline is potential fishing grounds. At any given hour on any given day during spring, summer and fall you are bound to find somebody casting from a jetty or dropping a line off a bridge. When the blues are running the beaches are lined with surf casters hoping to snag a big one.

A license is not required in the state of Massachusetts for saltwater angling for recreational purposes — this includes all tidal waters of Cape Cod Bay, Nantucket Sound and the Atlantic Ocean. There are limitations and restrictions for certain saltwater fish, including minimum size of catch, number of fish you can take in a day and, in some cases, what months of the year you can take them. There are also rules on how you can catch a particular species.

Other examples include a 28-inch minimum size on striped bass — and you can only take one a day. If you are after cod and haddock, you can only take a combination of 10 fish. On the other hand, bluefish have no minimum size requirement, and the possession limit is 10. (By the way, bluefish have very sharp teeth and literally attack when out of the water, so watch your fingers.) Regulations are known to change from time to time so it is best to contact the Massachusetts Division of Marine Fisheries at (617) 727-3193 for the latest rules and regs. Or visit any bait and tackle shop — they should be able to help you out.

Below is a quick listing of some of the more popular coastal fishing locations from Bourne to Provincetown.

Upper Cape

If you're in Bourne, try the **pier at Shore Road** in Pocasset or anywhere along the **Cape Cod Canal**.

In Sandwich, the jetty at the **Sandwich basin** is a good spot, or else the jetty or pier at **Scusset Beach**, the jetty at **Sandwich Beach** or along **Scorton Creek** off Route 6A.

Falmouth, with its long coastline and finger inlets, has many locations including the bridge at **Green Pond** as well as the jetties at **Falmouth Harbor**, **Woods Hole** and **Great Pond**.

Mashpee Neck Road and **South Cape Beach** in Mashpee are great spots, as is the jetty at **Dead Neck**.

Mid-Cape

In Barnstable give **Barnstable Harbor**, **Craigville Beach** and **Sandy Neck Beach** a try.

Bass Hole (Gray's Beach) in Yarmouthport is a wonderful spot to kill a couple of hours (even if the fish aren't biting). Other spots in the town of Yarmouth are **Seagull Beach** and the jetty at **Bass River Beach** and the **Bass River Bridge** linking Yarmouth with neighboring Dennis.

Dennis has a number of hot spots, including jetties at **Corporation Beach**, **Davis Beach**, **Cold Storage Beach** and **Sesuit Neck Beach**. **Chapin Beach** is also a good spot.

Lower Cape

Cast your line at **Paine Creek** and **Point of Rocks** in Brewster, or at **Bridge Street**, **Harding Beach** or **Nauset Beach** in Chatham.

Rock Harbor in Orleans is a nice spot, as is the Orleans' portion of **Nauset Beach**.

When in Eastham, take your rod over to **Sunken Meadow Beach**, **First Encounter Beach**, **Coast Guard Beach** or even **Nauset Light Beach**.

Wellfleet's **town pier** is a popular fishing spot. Also in Wellfleet is **Cahoon Hollow**, **Duck Harbor Road** and the jetty at Indian Neck.

Head of the Meadow Beach, **Highland Light Beach** and the jetty at **Corn Hill Beach** in Truro are all spectacular spots.

In the fishing port of Provincetown you can cast your line off historic **MacMillan Wharf** or at various spots along Provincetown's equally historic harbor.

Shellfishing

There's perhaps nothing more relaxing than an early morning's jaunt to the local shellfish beds to dig for tasty critters hiding in the mud flats. Oysters, quahogs, clams, the very thought of them makes our lips smack with images of a steaming bowl of chowder or a nice stuffed quahog. Yum!

Regarding all shellfish, you need to consult the local town hall for restrictions and permits. Regulations and minimum size requirements can be a little confusing at first. The minimum size of a good oyster is one with a certain shell diameter (currently 3 inches), while a minimum quahog size is measured in shell thickness (1 inch). Conch is measured in shell width (2¾ inches), and sea scallops must meet a certain shell height (3½ inches).

Each town has its own restrictions in terms of possession limits. You'll also want to find out which beds are open and which are closed and what types of shellfish are available for the taking. Contact the town hall for local regulations and limits. (See the Town Halls listings in our Overview chapter.) We find that when the rules are followed the chowder tastes a whole lot better!

Fishing Charters

Lower Cape

Cool Running Charters

Falmouth Inner Harbor, Scranton Ave., Falmouth • 457-9445, 426-3786 beeper

Capt. Dan Junker of the *Relentless* is fully insured and U.S. Coast Guard-licensed. From mid-May to mid-October, the 27-foot, six-passenger J.C. Sport Fisherman takes daytrips to the waters off Nantucket, Martha's Vineyard and the Elizabeth Islands. The catch usually ranges from stripers, blues, yellowfin and bluefin tuna, bonita, albacore and mako and blue sharks. The crew instructs new anglers in the fundamentals, and the charter price includes use of fishing gear. Passengers bring their own lunch. By the way, in Jamaica, "cool running" means "peace be the journey."

Cygnet

Falmouth Inner Harbor, Falmouth • 548-6274

Cygnet is a 31-foot sportfishing boat available for charter in Vineyard Sound and Nantucket Sound from May to October. Parties up to six go after blues, bass and tuna.

High Hopes Fishing

Falmouth Harbor, Falmouth • 457-9014

Operating out of Falmouth Harbor, Captain Jim Stevens' 31-foot Bertram *High Hopes* has been going after stripers, blues and yellowfin tuna for the past five seasons. A half-day charter is about six hours, while a full day can run from eight to 10 hours. Jim, who is United States Coast Guard licensed, and his mate will even fillet and package your catch. *High Hopes* can take up to six people at a time and operates from early May to the end of October.

Patriot Boats

Falmouth Inner Harbor, Falmouth • 548-2626, (800) 734-0088

The family-owned and operated boats depart from the entrance of the harbor for half- or full-day deep-sea fishing trips with bait and tackle included. Services include a water taxi service and excursions on board the *Liberte*, a replica of a 1750s pinky schooner (see our Tours and Excursions chapter).

Mid-Cape

Barnstable Harbor Charter Fleet

Millway Rd., Barnstable • 362-3908

In Barnstable, the Barnstable Harbor Charter Fleet offers four-, five-, six- and eight-hour fishing trips on approximately 10 charter boats.

Helen H Deep Sea Fishing

Pleasant St., Hyannis • 790-0660

The *Helen H* is a large offshore fishing boat

INSIDERS' TIP

The Sport Fishing Information Line, (800) ASK-FISH, is an excellent source of current information about freshwater and saltwater fishing. You can learn the best places to fish, location of boat launches, license requirements, general regulations and stocking and award programs.

with a sun deck and restrooms. In the summer it makes trips daily at 8 AM and 1 and 6 PM and goes to Georges Bank on Sundays. The fishing is year round on the *Helen H,* which carries about 100 passengers during the spring, summer and fall and about 40 people during the winter.

Navigator

Hyannis Harbor, Hyannis • 771-9500

The *Navigator* is a modern deep-sea fishing boat suited to families. It makes three fishing trips daily, the last one at 6 PM. This vessel has a full galley serving food and drinks. Besides going for blues, *Navigator* also offers tuna fishing.

Windward Charters

Lewis Bay, Hyannis • 362-4925

You can take a four-, six- or eight-hour fishing and sightseeing cruise in Nantucket Sound. This one's a particularly nice outing for families and children. Windward Charters operates from early June to late September.

Lower Cape

Golden Eagle

Harbor Rd., Harwich • 432-5611

Families will enjoy a trip aboard the 42-foot *Golden Eagle* out of Wychmere Harbor. From mid-June through mid-September, she offers two daily four-hour fishing trips as well as the popular evening charters for bluefish three nights a week during July and August. Fish-cleaning service is also available, and the Golden Hook Award is given for the largest fish caught each trip. During May and October the Golden Eagle makes one six-hour trip a day and two four-hour trips on weekends.

Mooncusser

Wychmere Harbor, Harwichport • 240-2021

The Cape's South Shore is packed with blues, bass and cod, and Capt. Steve Dion's 30-foot bass boat, *Mooncusser*, knows just where to find them. *Mooncusser* operates from Memorial Day until mid-October.

The Banshee

Stage Harbor Marina, Chatham • 945-0403

The Banshee is owned and operated by Captain Ron McVickar, who loves sharing his 36 years of fishing expertise with new friends. The vessel specializes in light tackle (no line in excess of 30-pound test is used), assuring the best deep-sea adventure possible. From early May to early November *The Banshee* goes after striped bass and blue fish.

Rock Harbor Charter Fleet

Rock Harbor, Rock Harbor Rd., Orleans • 255-9757, (800) 287-1771

With its 18 boats, Rock Harbor is the Cape's largest charter fleet. From mid-May through mid-October, U.S. Coast Guard-licensed captains offers four- and eight-hour tuna, mackerel, bluefish and striped bass fishing expeditions.

Nekton

Rock Harbor, Orleans • 255-1289

The 36-foot award-winning sportfishing vessel *Nekton* is captained by Steve Peters. Offshore trips include those for cod and flounder, which feed near the location of the wreck of the target ship, *S.S. James Longstreet*. In the summer fish for stripped bass and bluefish; during the spring go after flounder. The *Nekton* sails from early May to late October.

Columbia

1 Bayview Drive, Orleans • 240-1613

The 43-foot Columbia offers four-hour half days and eight-hour full days of bass and blue fishing from mid-June through the beginning of October.

The Naviator

Town Pier, Wellfleet • 349-6003

Some say the star of *The Naviator* is its captain, Rick Merrill, a 30-year veteran of Cape Cod waters. Others say it's the 60-foot boat herself. Fishing trips are held from mid-May to Columbus Day. In conjunction with the Massachusetts Audubon Society, *The Naviator* hosts cruises to view seals and sea birds from Columbus Day until December. Marine life cruises are held in the early evenings during July and August.

Cap'n Bill and Cee Jay

MacMillan Wharf, Provincetown • 487-4330, (800) 675-6723

The party fishing boats of *Cap'n Bill* and *Cee Jay* leave MacMillan Wharf twice a day for bountiful bluefish and fluke expeditions. They also offer night fishing trips for the serious angler. Rod, reel and bait are included on all trips.

Shady Lady

Bradford St. Ext., Provincetown • 487-0182

There's nothing shady about a charter on the *Shady Lady*. From mid-June through the beginning of October, you can enjoy a half-day or full day of sportfishing. Expect everything from blues to bass, cod to tuna.

Fishing Guides

The fish are out there . . . but how do you go about catching them? For a truly Cape Cod fishing experience, enlist an expert to show you the way it's done. The following guides provide the expertise and the equipment needed for fly- or spin-fishing for striped bass and bluefish as well as other species such as tautog, fluke, mackerel, scup, cod, shark and tuna. Call ahead to schedule your outing. Prices depend upon the length of the session and number of people in your party. It's great fun. A guide will certainly increase your odds of catching a fish — and a few good fish tales — to take back home. And if you don't catch anything, at least you can tell all your friends about the big one that got away!

INSIDERS' TIP

If you don't intend to eat the fish you catch but are only fishing for recreation, you are encouraged to release your fish as quickly as possible to limit any pain and trauma the fish may experience from the ordeal.

Upper Cape

Gene Burke
Falmouth • 548-5519, 548-6900

For guided shore fishing in the Upper Cape (Cape Cod Canal and Vineyard Sound), the approximate cost is $200 for five hours for up to three people.

Mid-Cape

Bob Alexander
Hyannis • 790-8600

Alexander specializes in sight-fishing from a boat with fly or light spinning tackle. He operates mainly in the northern Mid-Cape area, from Barnstable Harbor to Brewster flats. The cost is approximately $150 (minimum) for two hours and $75 for each additional hour.

Lower Cape

Chris Benson
Harwich • 432-1200

Benson is a specialist in saltwater fishing in the crystal-clear Monomoy flats of the Lower Cape. The cost ranges from $195 to $350 for a full day of fishing.

Capt. Danny Marini
Harwich • 432-1200

Fish from a skiff in Pleasant Bay on the

Photo: Michael Gavin

Surfcasters reel in bluefish.

Lower Cape. A full day of fishing costs $195 to $350.

Peter Alves

Harwich • 432-1200

Alves offers wade fishing outings in local estuaries and Monomoy on the Lower Cape. The cost is around $195 to $350 for a full day.

Tony Stetzko

Orleans • 255-2357

A day of fishing in the surf in the Nauset area of the Lower Cape will cost about $150 to $225.

Bait and Tackle Shops

If you're ready to go after the big ones you'll want to first stop in at one of the following bait and tackle shops to stock up on the tools of the trade. From rods and crawlers to lures and reels, you're certain to find what you need. Besides, there's nothing like a basket of slippery eels to get your fishing day off to a good start! You'll also want to get your hands on a current tide chart, and these are generally available free or for a nominal price at bait and tackle shops.

Upper Cape

Red Top Sporting Goods

265 Main St., Buzzards Bay • 759-3371

With the Cape Cod Canal at its doorstep, this shop is just a few steps from one of the richest sources of saltwater fish — striped bass, bluefish, flounder, tautog and mackerel — in the region. The year-round shop (hours are limited in winter) sells fishing tackle and other outdoor gear. It also handles fishing licenses and has tide charts. And the staff's advice on what's biting is as current as you're going to get.

Sandwich Ship Supply

68 Tupper Rd., Sandwich • 888-0200

This shop carries an extensive line of equipment, bait and tackle, safety gear, flags, clothing, maps, anchors, chains, ropes and other nautical necessities.

Eastman's Sport & Tackle

150 Main St., Falmouth • 548-6900

Open year round, this large upper-Cape shop carries all types of fresh- and saltwater fishing tackle including extensive fly-fishing gear. At Eastman's you can obtain Massachusetts, New Hampshire and Maine fishing licenses as well as clamming equipment and tide charts.

Mid-Cape

The Fly Shop

1022 Rt. 6A, West Barnstable • 362-1500

The Fly Shop is open year round for the sale of fly-fishing equipment and related accessories, including rods, reels, lines, fly-tying material, fishing books and some clothing. It is a Cortland Pro shop and a local outlet for Sage and Scott rods. Tide charts are available, but licenses are not.

Goose Hummock Shop

Rt. 28, Hyannis • 778-0877

Goose Hummock carries a full line of fishing equipment, outdoor clothing and hunting and hiking gear as well as canoes and kayaks. Check out the monthly calendar of fishing-related events and the company's extensive outdoor adventure program. Goose Hummock is open year round, offers fishing licenses and has an extensive inventory in both sales and rentals. Tide charts and advice are free. Fly-fishing guide Andy Little conducts trips of three hours and longer.

INSIDERS' TIP

One of the best sources for up-to-date fishing news and tips can be found in Molly Benjamin's fishing columns in the *Cape Cod Times.* Look for it in the sports section on Sunday and on the "Outside" page on Friday.

Sports Port

149 W. Main St., Hyannis • 775-3096

One of the Cape's oldest tackle shops still run by its original owners, Sports Port sells all salt- and freshwater tackle as well as shellfishing gear and fly-tying equipment. Along with live bait for both fresh and salt water, the Sport Port will also offer you fishing information so you'll know what's biting where. This shop is open year round.

Truman's

608 Main St., West Yarmouth • 771-3470

Open year round, Truman's supplies fishing tackle, fly-fishing equipment, shell-fishing gear and provides rod and reel repair. Also available are live bait, tide charts and fishing licences.

Riverview Bait & Tackle

1273 Rt. 28, South Yarmouth • 394-1036

This store, just a half-mile west of Bass River, sells offshore tackle, bait, custom rods and reels, nautical charts and fly-fishing supplies. It also rents equipment and offers rod and reel repair. It's open year round.

Bass River Bait & Tackle

42 Rt. 28, West Dennis • 394-8666

Bass River sells rods and reels, bait, fishing licenses and a full line of supplies for freshwater and saltwater fishing. It also rents rods and reels. The shop is open year round.

Lower Cape

Fishing The Cape

Rt. 137, East Harwich • 432-1200

An Orvis fly-fishing shop that is open year round, Fishing The Cape has all the accessories for both saltwater and freshwater fly-fishing and is a complete outfitter, providing local fishing guides and arranging fishing trips for both fresh water and salt water. Tide charts are also available.

The big feature here is the Orvis Fly Fishing School, which offers 2½-day sessions every weekend between mid-May and September 1. Class size averages about 16 students for each session. Call owner Bob Benson for more information.

Goose Hummock Shop

Rt. 6A, Orleans • 255-0455

For more than 50 years (1996 was its 50th anniversary) Goose Hummock has been catering to the needs of Lower Cape fishermen. This shop carries a full line of fishing equipment, including a newly expanded line of major brands of fly-fishing equipment, outdoor clothing, hunting and hiking gear, canoes and kayaks. Goose Hummock is open year round, offers fishing licenses and has an extensive inventory in both sales and rentals. The tide charts and advice are free. Fishing guide Sean Fields conducts trips of three hours and longer.

MacSquids

85 Rt. 6A, Orleans • 240-0778

Make MacSquids your one-stop tackle shop: It sells bait, rods, reels, freshwater and saltwater tackle and lures — even clamming gear. Rod and reel rentals are available, and the store offers free tide charts. It's open year round.

Blackbeard's Bait & Tackle

50 Brackett Rd., Eastham • 240-3369

You can buy or rent rods and reels and purchase bait and clamming gear here. Blackbeard's also does rod and reel repairs. The shop is open seasonally.

The Cape's 432 public
holes offer a variety of
challenges for the
seasoned golfer or the
occasional duffer.

Golf

There are a lot of reasons to visit the Cape, just as there are a lot of reasons why people decide to make the Cape their permanent home. Twenty-seven of those reasons comprise this chapter.

We refer here to the 27 public golf courses from Falmouth to Provincetown. Falmouth alone has five courses, Barnstable and Yarmouth each have four. These courses range in size from the 1275 yard Woodbriar in Falmouth to the 6525 yard Dennis Pines (the New Seabury Blue course is 17 yards shorter at 6508). The oldest public course is Highland Golf Links, which was established in 1892 atop the cliffs of Truro; the newest is Olde Barnstable Fairgrounds, opened for business exactly 100 years later in 1992.

The Cape's 432 public holes offer a variety of challenges for the seasoned golfer or the occasional duffer. You could find yourself driving over rivers, ponds, sand traps, marshlands, cranberry bogs, even swamps. Some courses feature immaculate landscaping (Ocean Edge comes to mind), while other courses, such as Highland, utilize the natural Cape terrain to form the best Scottish links experiences this side of Glasgow. Water hazards may include Vineyard Sound, Bass River or even the Quashnet River of Mashpee. A hook may land you in a conservation area, a slice may send you into a pine forest. You may even find yourself chipping out of a smallpox cemetery (see Kings Way Golf Club).

Because of the Cape's generally mild temperatures, you can play golf just about 12 months of the year (although we suggest thermal underwear and ear muffs during January and February). Eighteen of the courses are open year round, and two courses have honor play during the winter months, which means that you can slip a five or 10 dollar bill in a slot at the clubhouse door and head out to shoot nine or 18 or whatever you're in the mood for (or should we say fore!).

Some golfers say this area has the best courses in the country, and we, of course, agree with them. It is not surprising that golfers feel that way considering that a number of Cape Cod courses have been designed by such renowned golf course architects as Donald Ross, Herbert Fowler, Brian Silva and Geoffrey Cornish (if they're not household names to you, then you'll have to trust us that they're impressive course designers).

Drawn by the quality of the courses and the weather, state amateur and professional championships as well as regional events are regularly held on Cape Cod. Willowbend, a private course with stadium holes designed to accommodate large crowds, sponsors the annual Children's Charity Pro-Am attracting such pros as Greg Norman, John Daly, Brad Faxon, Andrew Magee and Nick Faldo as well as Vicki Goetze of the LPGA (see our Spectator Sports chapter).

In an area where municipal courses are often better than the best private courses in other parts of the country, players are in good company with native Cape Codders Carri Wood, Sally Quinlan and Jim Hallet, who have all played in the PGA or LPGA, as well as newcomer John Curley who was a former U.S. Amateur semifinalist. Young people, and those not so young, can learn the skills of the sport through local school programs and course pros. Catering to the golf crowd, there are a number of golf specialty shops in many of the towns. Driving ranges can be found at about half of the Cape's courses as well as at other locations such as the Longest Drive in Dennis, where you can work on that slice before hitting the links.

And if you yearn for a view of the first tee from your own backyard, the Cape is home to several golfing communities where luxury homes and condominiums line the fairways and greens of some of the best courses in the region (see our Real Estate chapter).

In the sections that follow, we describe some of Cape Cod's best golf courses that are open to the public. As we mentioned above, most of the courses are available for year-round play, and each offers a unique personality of its own. Whether you're a scratch golfer or a hacker, the Cape offers many a challenging hole. And it's a funny thing, down here on the Cape even a slice looks pretty when its tailing off into a colorful autumn cranberry bog or marshland. Yet nothing is as rewarding as snagging that first Cape birdie. You can almost hear the crowds cheering from the grandstand!

FYI

Unless otherwise noted, the area code for all phone numbers in this guide is 508.

Courses

Upper Cape

There are 11 public courses in the Upper Cape towns of Sandwich, Falmouth, and Mashpee. All except one consists of 18 holes. Two reside at the beautiful New Seabury resort in Mashpee.

Holly Ridge Golf Club

121 Country Club Rd., South Sandwich • 428-5577

Set within a residential community on some 90 acres, Holly Ridge is an 18-hole, 2952 yard par 3 public course designed by golf course architect Geoffrey Cornish. The signature hole here is the 7th, which has a pond to avoid on your tee shot. The course has a driving range, practice green, pro shop, and a restaurant and lounge (Holly Ridge Grill). Reservations are accepted up to seven days in advance for tee times. Greens fees are $20 for 18 holes, $13 for nine holes and just $10 for 18 holes from December 1 to February 28. Holly Ridge is open year round and offers an extensive lessons program and free clinics every Saturday from April to September. Carts are $17 for 18 holes and $3 for pull carts.

Round Hill Country Club

1 Round Hill Rd., East Sandwich • 888-3384

Round Hill offers a 5920 yard public 18-hole, par 71 course for individual play or golf outings and tournaments. Facilities also include a driving range, two practice greens, a clubhouse and pro shop. The 100-acre setting features views of Cape Cod Bay. The 420-yard par 4 9th hole forces you to shoot into the wind at an elevated green. You can reserve a tee time by calling up to seven days in advance, and you may want to use a cart to scale the hills (they don't call it Round Hill for nothing!). Rates during the peak season are $36 on weekends and $27 on weekdays for greens fees and $12 for cart rental. Off-season rates drop to $20 on weekends and $14 on weekdays. You may want to ask about their spring and fall specials. The course is open year round.

Woodbriar Country Club

339 Gifford St., Falmouth • 540-1600

Woodbriar is an attractive 1275 yard 9 hole par 3 public course that is open year round and features lots of water. Actually the course is 56 par going out and coming back in again — eight par 3s and one par 4 just to keep things interesting. The longest hole here is the 215-yard 5th hole, which has a stream to cross (in fact, this hole was recently upgraded to a par 4). Greens fees are very reasonable: $18 for 18 holes on weekends, just $16 during the week and $10 from November 1 until April 1. Woodbriar has a practice green and offers food and drink inside the clubhouse. The scenic course is situated right next to the Coonamesset Inn (see our Restaurants chapter). The course is open seasonally. Tee times are on a first come, first served basis.

Falmouth Country Club

630 Carriage Shop Rd., East Falmouth • 548-3211

Falmouth Country Club is a 6227-yard, par 72, 18-hole course. It is open year round and features a beautiful par 4 fourth hole with a pond guarding the front of the green. The course itself is wide open without many trees and is relatively flat, making it perfect for walkers, for beginners and for people who slice or hook. It also has a nice practice range, putting green and pro shop and offers rental equipment and carts. Greens fees are $25 on weekdays and $35 on weekends. Off-season fees drop to $20 for weekdays and $30 for weekends. Golf carts rent for $11 per person or $22 per cart. Tee-time reservations can be made up to seven days in advance.

Ballymeade

125 Falmouth Woods Rd., North Falmouth • 540-4005

Ballymeade, which is about 8 miles from the Bourne Bridge, is a relatively new semiprivate 6100-yard, 18-hole, par 72 course. Known for its high-quality play, Ballymeade has hilly, rocky terrain and narrow tree-lined fairways. The panoramic views are stunning, especially from the par 3 11th hole, which is one of the highest points on Cape Cod offering fantastic views of Buzzards Bay. Ballymeade also has a fully stocked pro shop and PGA teaching pros.

Reservations for tee times should be made seven days in advance. The greens fees in the summer are $75 on weekends and $58 during the week, and $50 and $40, respectively, during the off-season. Fees include the use of a cart, which is mandatory. The course is open year round and has a driving range and a putting green complete with a bunker so you can practice those pesky sand shots.

Cape Cod Country Club

Theatre Dr., North Falmouth • 563-9842

Cape Cod Country Club's course is considered one of the best, a classic New England course with small greens. This well-kept 6000-yard, par 71 public course has 18 holes among rolling fairways and elevated greens. The 9th hole is a par 3 that requires your tee shot to clear a pond before the green and avoid two ponds on either side of the green — good luck. Cape Cod Country Club offers rental carts and equipment, a pro shop and lunch counter. There is a practice green so you can work on your putting, and lessons are available. Fees are $35 on weekends and $28 on weekdays, and a cart is an additional $11 per person. Reserve your tee time a week ahead. The course is open year round.

Paul Harney Golf Club

74 Club Valley Dr. (off Rt. 151), East Falmouth • 563-3454

Owned and operated by the former PGA golf pro Paul Harney, this 18 hole executive course offers outstanding play with five par 4 holes and 13 par 3s, totaling some 3600 yards (par 59 if you're counting). The 16th hole is a par 3 with an elevated tee and a pond protecting the green some 230 yards from the tee. Those who frequently play this course note that if you stray you'll end up in the trees. There are plenty of ways to get into trouble here, so you'll want to hit your shots long and straight. Greens fees are $25. Carts are $10 for a nine-hole game and $20 for 18 holes. Play is based on a first come, first served basis. Weekends are busy and the course does not take reservations; still, it's a good idea to call ahead to see how long the wait might be. This course is open year round and has a practice green to putt on while you wait for your tee time.

Quashnet Valley Country Club
309 Old Barnstable Rd., Mashpee • 477-4412

Water hazards in the way of rivers, cranberry bogs and even swamp lands come into play on 15 of Quashnet Valley's 18 holes, so you'll definitely want to bring along plenty of extra golf balls if hooking and slicing is part of your game plan! Set among the pretty bogs is this semiprivate par 72 course that features the Quashnet River running through its 6093 yards. The course is a nature lover's bounty and borders conservation areas. All the holes require concentration, but the 6th is a particularly demanding 430-yard par 4 that will take your best drive and approach shot to a two-tiered elevated green with water on the right and woods on the left. The facilities include a pro shop, driving range and a practice green. Memberships are available. Cart rentals are $12.50 per person for 18 holes. Greens fees are $30 Monday through Thursday and $35 on Fridays, while weekend fees are $60 including a cart. The course is open year round and offers rates in the area of $25 weekdays and $30 weekends during the winter months.

New Seabury Country Club
off Great Neck Road S., New Seabury (Mashpee) • 477-9110

Distinguished by two renowned championship courses overlooking Vineyard Sound, the New Seabury Country Club has long been considered one of the top-100 golf courses in the United States. Since the Blue Course and the Green Course were built in the early 1960s, New Seabury has hosted tournaments and championships by the LPGA, NCAA, New England Intercollegiate Golf Association, the Massachusetts Open, the American Junior Golf Championship and others.

Many of the front nine holes of the 6508-yard, par 72 Blue Course run along the coast offering spectacular ocean views and some potential high winds. The signature hole is the 2nd hole, a par 4 with outstanding ocean views. The back nine is wooded and hilly, as is the 5900-yard, par 70 Green Course.

Greens fees run about $75 on the Blue Course and $50 on the Green Course. Cart rentals add another $15. Off-season rates run $60 for the Blue and $50 for the Green before Thanksgiving and $40 and $30 between Turkey Day and May 1. Call for tee times. Reservations are accepted one day in advance. Both courses are open year round.

Mid-Cape

Ten (yes, 10!) public courses can be found in the three Mid-Cape towns of Barnstable, Yarmouth and Dennis. Among them is one 9-hole course, three par 3 courses, one 4100-yard executive course and five with distances exceeding 6000 yards. On average, there are 13,300 yards of golf per town!

Cotuit High Ground Golf Course
31 Crockers Neck Rd., Cotuit • 428-9863

If you're looking for an inexpensive round of golf, then throw your clubs in the car and head for the Cotuit High Grounds. Greens fees are $10 and just $7 after 4 PM. Seniors and juniors pay only $7. This is a semiprivate nine-hole, par 3 course (actually there is one par 4 hole so the total par is 56 for a round of 18 holes). The yardage of 2580 is known for its small greens and narrow fairways. On the par 3 5th hole you will need to make sure your

INSIDERS' TIP

For the most current golf information, including prices and tee times as well as golf packages, call The Cape Golf Report's information hotline at (800) TEE-BALL. Or you can tune into Tom Martin's 60-second Tee Ball Tips on WKPE-FM (104.7), airing Monday through Saturday at 6:20 AM and 4:50 PM during the spring, summer and fall.

drive clears the swamp, otherwise you'll be in knee-deep trouble. Open year round, reservations are not required during the week; for a weekend tee time plan on calling ahead during the week. There is a putting green and small pro shop available as well as pull carts and three or four riding carts. Individual memberships can be had for $350.

Hyannis Golf Club

Rt 132, Hyannis • 362-2606

Hyannis Golf Club offers a 6000-yard, 18-hole, par 71 course that's open year round. A favorite hole is No. 2, a 420-yard par 4 that features a marsh before the elevated tee. (The marsh is particularly beautiful in autumn). This fine course is home of the Cape Cod Open and the Canal Classic, two of the major golfing events on the Cape. Mickey Herron, the director of golf at the course, operates a golf school here. The club has 1 and 3 PM specials as well as senior citizen specials on Tuesdays and Thursdays. Facilities include a full pro shop, driving range, two putting greens and rental carts and equipment. Greens fees range from $35 on weekdays to $45 on weekends, and carts are $26 a day for two people or $13 per person. Reservations, which are accepted anytime, are recommended in the summer. On site is the Iyannough Hills Food and Spirits restaurant.

Tara Hyannis Golf Course

West End Rotary, Hyannis • 775-7775 ext. 473

Golf Digest rated this course as the toughest par 3 on the Cape. The resort offers a picturesque 2621 yard, 18-hole par 3 course with five water holes. Play is excellent year round. The resort also has two putting greens and a fully equipped pro shop with equipment and cart rentals. Greens fees range from $20 on weekdays to $25 on the weekend. Rates after December 1 drop to as low as $12 until March 1. Tee-time reservations are definitely advisable and can be accepted one month in advance. Memberships are available. Inquire about senior citizen specials and special golf programs (some include dinner). As for the holes, the 3rd hole is considered the toughest on the course — it is very challenging and the only way you'll ever make par is to hit it straight as an arrow.

Olde Barnstable Fairgrounds Golf Course

1460 Prospect St. (Rt. 149), Marstons Mills • 420-1141

This relatively new 6113-yard course, built in 1992, has difficult par 5s and tricky contoured greens. The 18th hole is a par 5 with a big holly tree in the middle of the course that comes into play as you consider your second shot. Facilities at the par 71 course include a fully stocked pro shop, a huge practice range and putting green. Pull and motorized carts and rental clubs are available. Another nice feature is a full-service restaurant (Fairways Restaurant) where you can sit on the deck and watch biplanes and gliders take off and land at the small Cape Cod Airport across the street. The fees are $44 during the summer, $35 during the fall and $24 from December 1 until May. Carts are $11 per person ($22 for two). Olde Barnstable Fairgrounds is open year round and reservations can be made anytime after January 1 if you plan on paying in advance, otherwise you can call two days in advance.

Bass River Golf Course

62 Highbank Rd., South Yarmouth • 398-9079

The signature hole on this appropriately named golf course is No. 6, a par 3 right on the tidal Bass River. In fact, if you are going west over the Bass River Bridge look to your right and you can see the hole across the water. Views of scenic Bass River are just one of the nice things about this course, one of the busiest in Massachusetts. The 5734-yard 18-hole, par 72 public course hosts more than 65,000 rounds of golf a year. A fully stocked

INSIDERS' TIP

Cape Cod has more than 120,000 yards of public golf courses, about 68 miles. That's like golfing from the Cape Cod Canal to the tip of Provincetown.

pro shop, snack bar and practice green are additional amenities. This is a "ride, carry or pull" year-round course with summer rates in the area of $37 a round. Winter rates drop to about $30 from November 1 through May ($17 after noontime . . . of course the sun sets around 4:30 PM so you may be able to squeeze in a dozen and a half if you move it along). Carts are $22. Reservations are best made four days in advance or anytime after January 1 if you plan on prepaying.

Bayberry Hills

W. Yarmouth Rd., South Yarmouth • 394-5597

Known as an excellent public course, this challenging, wide-open 6067-yard, par 72 course has 18 holes, plus two practice greens and a large driving range. If we had to pick a hole to tell you about, it would be the par 4 4th hole with a hidden green down below a hill — and a hidden water hazard to boot! This course hosts about 45,000 rounds a year, and yet it's closed December through March. Peak-season fees are $37, and carts cost $22. Off-season fees are the same as the Bass River course: $30 before noon and $17 after noon throughout November (both courses are run by the town of Yarmouth). We recommend you call four days in advance to reserve your tee time or anytime after January 1 if you are prepaying your greens fees.

Blue Rock

off High Bank Rd., South Yarmouth • 398-9295

A favorite of longtime Cape golfers, Blue Rock is rated as one of the best par 3 golf courses in the Northeast. Well-designed and beautifully maintained, this public 18-hole, 2890-yard course is open year round and has holes that range from 103 yards to 248 yards. We know of someone who, in her very first time golfing, parred the 1st hole! There are a number of beautiful holes, many crossing a river that runs through the course. Both the 9th and the 18th are long par 3s that require you to drive over the river to an elevated green. Facilities include two practice greens and a golf school run by award-winning PGA pro Bob Miller. The course is open year round. The on-site Best Western Blue Rock Motor Inn, which is open from April to November, offers a number of golf and stay packages. Summer greens fees are $22 on weekdays and $26 on weekends. Only pull carts are available. By the way, those rates drop to $16 after 4 PM. Reservations can be made one week in advance.

Kings Way Golf Club

64 King's Circuit (off Rt. 6A), Yarmouthport • 362-8870

A 4100-yard, well-trapped, 18-hole, par 59 executive course, Kings Way features an unlucky 13th hole. The hole is unlucky in the respect that on the right side of the green is a smallpox cemetery bearing the stones of two 19th-century Yarmouth men who died of the disease. The 10-year-old semiprivate course is similar to a Scottish links course with flat, beautifully maintained fairways and rolling greens. The club offers a practice green, pro shop, lessons, carts, equipment rentals and a restaurant. Very popular is its "9 & Dine" special, which includes nine holes of golf and dinner at the on-site Fearrington's Restaurant for one low price. Greens fees are $45 for 18 holes and a cart, $33 in the fall. Kings Way, which offers 13 par 3 holes and five par 4s, is closed December 1 through March 15.

Dennis Pines

Rt. 134, East Dennis • 385-8347

The tournament-caliber Dennis Pines sits on 170 acres of pine forest and boasts 18 holes, 6525 yards and a par of 72. This year-round course has narrow fairways, and ex-

INSIDERS' TIP

When calling for rates and tee times, keep in mind that most golf courses consider "weekdays" to mean Monday through Thursday and "weekends" Friday through Sunday. Holiday greens fees are typically charged at the weekend rate, but you are advised to call ahead to confirm.

Photo: Cape Cod Times

A heron spreads its wings on a grassy shore.

pect to contend with some ponds and pine woodlands (many of which are quite playable). Hole 12 is a devilish par 5 dogleg left that requires a trio of real good, accurate shots if you are going to get on the green in three. Four of the 18 are water holes. Reservations are suggested four days in advance during the season, though you can reserve a tee time six months in advance with prepayment. In the summer season greens fees are $35. These drop to $25 during the off-season. Carts are $21 and club rentals are available.

Dennis Highlands

825 Old Bass River Rd., Dennis • 385-8347

Opened in the mid-1980s, Dennis Highlands has become a favorite among locals and tourists. Besides a superb 6076 yard, 18-hole, par 71 course, it also offers a large two-tier practice range, a putting green and a full pro shop. The 175 rolling acres are dotted with stands of pine and oak. The 6th hole, a tricky par 4, has a very difficult two-tiered green. Reservations are suggested during the summer/fall season; they are accepted up to four days in advance or up to six months in advance if you are prepaying. Summer fees are $35, and off-season the greens fees drop to $25. Carts are $21. You may have noticed that the greens fees and the telephone numbers for Dennis Pines and Dennis Highlands are the same. That's because they are both owned and run by the town of Dennis. Although the Pines is open year round, the Highlands is closed from December through March.

Lower Cape

Of the eight Lower Cape towns, five have golf courses. Brewster and Harwich each have two while Chatham, Wellfleet and Truro have one each. Four of the seven are 9 hole golf courses averaging 2580 yards; the three remaining 18-hole, par 72 courses (two in Brewster and one in Harwich) average 6200 yards.

Captains Golf Course

1000 Freeman's Way, Brewster • 896-5100

Captains Golf Course was ranked the best new public course by *Golf Digest* magazine in 1986. Open year round, its 18 holes feature 6176 yards and a par of 72. The course is well-bunkered, and all the holes are named for Brewster sea captains. The 14th hole is a very difficult par 5 and is the only hole in the course with water, which must make its namesake Captain Myrick very happy. In season, greens fees are $40. Off-season fees drop to between $20 and 35. Carts are $24 for 18 holes and $13 for nine holes. Seasonal specials are available. Reservations are required during holidays and weekends, and you can set up a tee time two days in advance or more than two weeks in advance with prepayment. You can make tee-time reservations and get course conditions by calling the automated message board at the above number. The course has a driving range, putting green and pro shop. Captains is closed January and February.

Ocean Edge Golf Club

832 Villages Dr., Brewster • 896-5911

Avid golfers will relish the Ocean Edge Golf Club, which features a championship-style, 18-hole course sporting five ponds and Scottish potbunkers. Open all year long, the course boasts 6127 yards of lush green fairways and a par of 72. Hole 8 is an incredibly long 601-yard par 5 (get out your Big Bertha!). In-season greens fees are $54, and cart fee is around $14 per player. Off-season fees are $40 for greens and, again, $14 for a cart. Unless you're a guest of Ocean Edge Resort, reservations are mandatory two days in advance. The spectacular Ocean Edge Resort, which spans both north and south of Route 6A in Brewster, features a driving range, two putting greens and a fully stocked pro shop. Although open to the public, resort guests receive preferred tee times.

Cranberry Valley

183 Oak St., Harwich • 430-7560

After 17 holes of golf you are faced with an interesting 18th at Cranberry Valley — a par 5 double dogleg right that is essentially a horseshoe! This course is home to an 18-hole championship layout, spread over rolling fairways fringed with pines and cranberry bogs. The first three holes on the back side have water. Cranberry Valley features 6296 yards totaling a par 72. On site are a driving range, putting green and pro shop. Reservations are required in season and can be made up to 10 days in advance. Those who prepay can reserve a tee time after March 1 for any date throughout the rest of the year. Clubs and cart rentals are available. Greens fees are $40 in season and $30 off-season (after mid-October). The course is open year round, but temporary greens are in effect from December through the beginning of March.

The Harwich Chamber of Commerce holds the Amateur Golf Tournament at Cranberry Valley Golf Course over Mother's Day weekend (see our Spectator Sports chapter).

Harwichport Golf Club

51 South St., Harwichport • 432-0250

This pocket-size course is a real charmer. It reminds us of the kind of courses our dads used to play. Its 9 holes total 2538 yards and 34 par (68 if you play it twice). It may be small but it's not easy, and there's plenty here to challenge you. For instance, the 8th hole is a par 4 dogleg left to a small green. (Unfortunately we read the scorecard wrong and thought it was a dogleg right . . . needless to say we lost our drives!) The Harwichport Golf Club offers relatively flat terrain, and a flat greens fee structure as well. Fees are $21 for 18 holes and $13 for nine, both during the summer and the fall. The course closes December 1 and reopens "sometime in the spring." Reservations are not needed, it's first come, first served. There are no riding carts here (they're not necessary), but there are plenty of pull carts available. There's a putting green and the most quaint clubhouse you'll ever lace up your golf shoes in. (The coffee alone is worth the greens fees.) By the way, a membership costs $295.

Chatham Seaside Links

209 Seaview St., Chatham • 945-4774

Nestled amongst Chatham's beautiful ocean community of incredible houses and summer homes, the 9-hole Chatham Seaside Links offers an intimate golfing experience. The 9th hole, a par 4, offers views of the ocean. At 2400 yards, this is a par 34 course with a clubhouse that is open from April 1 to December 1, although the course itself remains open to the public throughout the winter on the honor system. Just slip $5 into the box and tee off for as many holes as you like!. The course sits right next door to the magnificent Chatham Bars Inn and is often packed with tourists. Greens fees are an amazingly low $13 for nine holes, $22 for 18. Tee times are determined on a first come, first served basis. There is a practice green and pro shop at the course.

Chequessett Yacht and Country Club

Chequessett Neck Rd., Wellfleet • 349-3704

This nine-hole Wellfleet course provides breathtaking views of Wellfleet Harbor and Cape Cod Bay beyond. The nine holes come to a par 35, or 70 if you play 18, and total 2584 yards (5168 yards for 18). On site is a pro shop and a putting green. The course is open to the public from the second week of March through the end of November, and then from November to March the course is available via the honor system ($10). Greens fees during the summer season are $25 for 9 holes and $38 for 18. Off-season rates go as low as $12 for 9 holes and $18 for 18. Nonmembers must reserve tee times at least five days in advance. In spring 1996 the club added man-made water hazards just to make it a bit more challenging. A par 4, hole No. 3 features an elevated tee and an elevated green with a valley in between — and a fabulous view of Cape Cod Bay all the way.

Highland Golf Links

Highland Light Rd., North Truro • 487-9201

This is the granddaddy of all Cape Cod courses, a rugged links course where the winds offer as big a challenge as the natural roughs that accent the fairways. Founded in 1892, Highland is the oldest public course on the Cape and one of the 10 oldest in America. Its nine holes and 2789 yards are perched high along windswept bluffs overlooking the Atlantic. The Highland pays homage to Scottish tradition with open and unirrigated fairways, punctuated by deep natural rough and moorlands and festooned with sand, wild cranberry, beach plum, thicket, Scotch broom and heath. At this truly special course it is not uncommon to spot whales spouting in the Atlantic or fishing vessels fighting the waves as they trudge up and down the coast. From the course you can also view Highland Lighthouse and Provincetown's Pilgrim Monument.

Reservations are mandatory and require 48 hours notice. The course is most crowded on weekends, especially Sundays. Greens fees are $16 for nine holes and $30 for 18. Carts are $21 for 18 holes and $13 for nine. Highland is open from April 1 to November 1, and cart and club rentals are available.

Instruction

Many of the courses on the Cape offer lessons from golf professionals who can help you work on all facets of your game. These pros can tell you why you're slicing and hooking or why you just can't seem to get the ball in the hole. You're best bet is to call any of the golf courses featured above and inquire about

INSIDERS' TIP

The Cape Cod Chamber of Commerce's "Golf Map of Cape Cod" lists dozens of courses on the Cape and islands. And best of all, it's free! Write to the Chamber for your copy: Route 6, Hyannis 02601.

lessons. Or you can take a look at our short list below.

Upper Cape

Holly Ridge Golf Club

121 Country Club Rd., South Sandwich • 428-5577

The year-round Holly Ridge Golf Club offers two LPGA professionals who provide lessons. You can learn from Jane Frost through her golf school or else via a private 45 minute lesson costing $100. The course's other pro, Jean Enright, can also provide private lessons at a rate of $35 for a half-hour and $70 for an hour.

Mid-Cape

Hyannis Golf Club

Rt. 132, Hyannis • 362-2606

PGA pros Mickey Herron and Sue Kaffenburgh, along with instructors Mike Boden and David Porkka, offer individual and group lessons. Their instruction focuses on all skill levels. The club has a great practice facility as well as state-of-the-art video equipment to allow golfers to analyze their own swing and problem areas. Individual lessons cost $35 for a half-hour.

Olde Barnstable Fairgrounds Golf Course

1460 Prospect St. (Rt. 149), Marstons Mills • 420-1141

PGA professionals Gary Philbrick and Mike Haberl provide lessons year round to improve all areas of your game from driving to putting and all those tricky shots in between. Their individual half-hour rate is $30.

Blue Rock Golf Course

off High Bank Rd., South Yarmouth • 398-9295

Head professional Bob Miller, along with assistant professionals Pat Fannon and Nick Stefos, can help you correct that hook, slice or show you how to make that perfect approach shot. Besides offering a golf school from late spring to early fall, they also provide individual lessons: $40 for a half-hour lesson with Bob Miller, $32 for Pat Fannon and Nick Stefos. Available year round, there are even indoor facilities available if the weather outside is frightful.

Driving Ranges

There are some 20 driving ranges on the Cape where you can practice your wood and iron shots. Many of these ranges are at the public courses, though some can be found at other facilities from Bourne to Eastham.

Upper Cape

Bourne Sports World, Route 28, Bourne, 759-5500

Adventure Isle, Route 28, Bourne, (800) 53-KARTS

Holly Ridge Golf Club, 121 Country Club Road, South Sandwich, 428-5577

Round Hill Country Club, 1 Round Hill Road, East Sandwich, 888-3384

Falmouth Country Club, 630 Carriage Shop Road, East Falmouth, 548-3211

Ballymeade Country Club, 125 Falmouth Woods Road, North Falmouth, 540-4005

Quashnet Valley Country Club, 309 Old Barnstable Road, Mashpee, 477-4412

New Seabury Country Club, off Great Neck Road S., New Seabury (Mashpee), 477-9110

Mid-Cape

Olde Barnstable Fairgrounds Course, 1460 Prospect Street (Route 149), Marstons Mills, 420-1141

Hyannis Golf Club, Route 132, Hyannis, 362-2606

Bayberry Hills Golf Course, West Yarmouth Road, South Yarmouth, 394-5597

In-Putt Indoor Entertainment & Golf Practice Center, 41 Long Pond Drive, South Yarmouth, 394-5300

Bass River Sports World, Route 28, South Yarmouth, 398-6070

Dennis Pines, Route 134, East Dennis, 385-8347

Dennis Highlands, 825 Old Bass River Road, Dennis, 385-8347

The Longest Drive, 131 Great Western Road, South Dennis, 398-5555

Lower Cape

Captains Golf Course, 1000 Freeman's Way, Brewster, 896-5100

Ocean Edge Golf Course, 832 Village's Drive, Brewster, 896-5911

Cranberry Valley, 183 Oak Street, Harwich, 430-7560

T-Time Family Sports Center, Route 6, Eastham, 255-5697

Services

With so many golf courses around, you won't be too surprised to learn that there are a number of golf stores that cater to the hackers and swingers amongst the population. Whether you're in the market for new equipment (perhaps a new set of clubs, a golf bag or a new pair of shoes), a repair of your existing equipment or just need a dozen balls, you will more than likely find what you need at any of the following golf establishments.

Upper Cape

The Swing Shop

413 Rt. 6A, Sandwich • 888-2820

At The Swing Shop you'll find a complete supply of golf equipment, providing everything you'll need to fill your bag and lower your score. The shop also provides club repair and regripping services. It's open year round.

Nevada Bob's

Route 28, Falmouth • 540-9200

One of the largest golf retailers on Cape, this Falmouth shop specializes in club repair, regripping and custom fitting while offering a complete supply of golf equipment. Open year round, there is a second office in Hyannis.

Mid-Cape

Fit to a Tee

11 Enterprise Rd., Hyannis • 771-8333

Fit to a Tee specializes in manufacturing custom clubs. It also does club repair and has a teacher who provides lessons. Fit to a Tee is open year round.

Golf Day

411 Barnstable Rd., Hyannis • 790-7888

This year-round shop has a large supply of golf equipment and offers regripping and club repair. Golf Day also has golf videos and books available to help you improve your game.

Nevada Bob's

Rte. 132, Hyannis • 775-9300

Providing a complete supply of golf equipment, Nevada Bob's is a year-round shop that also offers club repair, custom fitting and regripping.

The Golf Market

1070 Rt. 132, Hyannis • 771-4653

The Golf Market can provide you with all the golf equipment, sportswear and accessories you'll need to hit the links. It also provides regripping service. The Golf Market is open year round.

Lower Cape

Club House Golf Shop

119 Rt. 137, Harwich • 432-3524

Club House Golf Shop offers a full line of golf equipment, clothing and accessories. Open year round, it also provides club repairs, regripping and club rentals.

Old-time baseball is alive and well on Cape Cod in the form of the Cape Cod Baseball League.

Spectator Sports

Cape Cod is known for a host of things: spectacular beaches, magnificent lighthouses, rich history and devotion to the arts to name a few. Yet Cape Cod is also known for sporting events, primarily baseball, road races, golf, tennis and even soccer. If baseball is your game, then you'll have plenty to watch with the Cape Cod Baseball League running from mid-June to mid-August. Golf enthusiasts will enjoy the Willowbend Children's Charity Pro-Am while tennis buffs will want to secure court side seats for the Mentadent Champions Tennis Tournament. Cape Cod is also home to the Falmouth Road Race in August, attracting world class runners from around the world. Not to be outdone, the Cape Cod Crusaders bring professional soccer to the peninsula throughout the summer. In this chapter we have listed some of the major spectator sports events in the area. For exact schedules and dates, check the sports section of the *Cape Cod Times*.

Baseball

Cape Cod Baseball League

11 North Rd., Harwich • 432-3878

Old-time baseball is alive and well on Cape Cod in the form of the Cape Cod Baseball League.

Imagine the late-afternoon summer sunlight filtering across the ball field, casting players' shadows upon the grass of the outfield. Listen for the reverberating pop of a ball into a mitt or the resounding crack of a bat connecting with a pitch — perhaps two of the greatest sounds this country has ever produced.

Imagine the taste of a hot dog with plenty of mustard, the anticipation of the batter awaiting the pitch, the call of the umpire, the coaches' subtle maneuvering, which novices to the game don't even notice and devotees to the game are always second-guessing. Imagine the swing, the crack, the roar of the crowd. For just a dollar donation at the gate you can gain admission to all of these sensations and watch future big-leaguers play the game as it was meant to be played.

This year marks the league's 112th season of play, making it the oldest continuing amateur summer baseball league in the nation. The first game was played on July 4, 1885, with Sandwich hosting Barnstable on a field that no longer exists. The historical significance of that game is documented at Cooperstown's National Baseball Hall of Fame.

What was begun over a century ago as local recreation is now considered one of the choice amateur baseball organizations in the nation. Some 300 ballplayers from colleges and universities across the country are recruited each year to play on the 10 teams of the Cape league. Major league scouts attend many of the games, especially the league's all-star game, looking for the next Ted Williams or Sandy Koufax. The ballplayers, many of whom come from as far away as California and Florida, are hosted by local families who provide lodging and meals.

Some 150 major league baseball players had their beginnings in the Cape Cod Baseball League. Among them are 1995 American League Most Valuable Player Mo Vaughn, first baseman for the Boston Red Sox. He played for the Wareham Gatemen. Jeff Bagwell of the Houston Astros, who won the MVP honor for the National League in 1994, once played for the Chatham A's. Chicago White Sox first baseman and 1993 and 1994 American league MVP Frank Thomas was once an Orleans Cardinal. The list of major leaguers who have played in the league goes on and on.

The Cape League season runs from mid-June to mid-August. Each team plays a 44-game schedule — that's 220 games across the Cape each summer! An all-star game is held in mid- to late July, and playoffs are held around the second week of August.

Home parks help keep this great American pastime alive. Fields are located at Spillane Field in Wareham, Massachusetts Maritime Academy in Buzzards Bay, Guv Fuller Field in Falmouth, Lowell Park in Cotuit, McKeon Field in Hyannis, Red Wilson Field at the Dennis-Yarmouth Regional High School in South Yarmouth, Cape Cod Regional Technical High School in Harwich, Whitehouse Field at Harwich High School, Veterans Field in Chatham and Eldredge Park in Orleans. Games are typically held at 1, 5 and 7 PM. Printed schedules are available in many local stores and newspapers.

FYI

Unless otherwise noted, the area code for all phone numbers in this guide is 508.

The Bourne Braves and Brewster Whitecaps joined the league in 1988. At that time it was decided to split the 10 teams into two divisions, East and West, thus setting the stage for playoffs at the end of the season. The top two teams in each division face off, with the winners going on to the dramatic best of three championship series.

Many of the fields, if not all, offer concession stands, but no one will complain if you pack a meal and make a picnic out of it. Since the league's 10 fields are located within a 50-mile radius of each other, it is possible to visit all the fields throughout a summer. Last summer we watched games at half of the parks.

Senior Babe Ruth League

Falmouth • 563-9442

Other baseball events, such as the Senior Babe Ruth league featuring 16 through 18 year olds, are also on tap Cape-wide. Games are played during June and July at many fields across the Cape with playoffs held in mid-July. In 1996 Cape Cod hosted the New England Senior Babe Ruth Championships which consisted of all-star teams from all over the six-state region, including, of course, Cape Cod. In fact, in recent years five Cape teams have made it all the way to the Senior Babe Ruth world series. In 1991, the Cape was the site of the national playoffs, drawing scouts from colleges across the country.

American Legion Baseball

Buzzards Bay • 830-5055

During the summer months, American Legion baseball games can be seen at fields in Sandwich and Falmouth. The Cape has two American Legion teams: Post 188, which plays their home games at the Sandwich High School field, and Falmouth, which plays its games at the Guv Fuller field in Falmouth. Both teams are in zone 10 that includes a dozen American Legion teams from Southeastern Massachusetts. They play 26 regular season games from the first week of June to the last week of July. Playoffs begin during the first part of August, with the winners going on to championships in Massachusetts, then New England and, eventually, the national world series. Players range in age from 16 to 18. The Cape teams recruit from the Bourne to Dennis-Yarmouth areas.

Softball

Any spring or summer evening, or weekend morning for that matter, you can find a men's or coed softball game at a field nearby.

Cape Senior Softball Classic

Eastham • 255-8206

For a special treat, check out the Cape Cod Old Timers League in the Mid- and Lower Cape towns. The season runs from early May to the Sunday before Labor Day. We attended the annual Cape Senior Softball Classic, a three-day tournament in early September. This event features surprisingly entertaining softball from these spry players 60 years of age and older. Teams come from as far away as

INSIDERS' TIP

In the 19th century fish used to be dried on fish flakes that lined the wharves of such fishing villages as Dennisport and Harwichport.

Connecticut and New Hampshire, and there are divisions for 65 and 70-plus.

Road Races

With its fabulous scenic routes, it's no wonder Cape Cod hosts so many road races. The warmth of the sun, the scent of the pines, the sparkle of the ocean — this is truly a runner's paradise.

Topping the bill is the Falmouth Road Race, which combines a challenging 7.1 mile course with spectacular ocean views. Besides Falmouth, though, there are a number of other races held across the Cape in Hyannis, Centerville, Dennis and Harwich to name a few towns. Most are serious road races, some are purely for the fun of it and a good number are for charity. Some even coincide with an annual town celebration such as the Harwich Cranberry Harvest Festival and some are held once a week such as the SportsEast Friday Night 5-miler in Hyannis.

Let's begin with the Falmouth Road Race and then take a look at some of the other races across the Cape.

Falmouth Road Race

Falmouth • 540-7000

For those who run, or who like to watch other people run, Falmouth is a mecca of sorts. The streets here are painted with the race's proud history, and we don't only mean the Start and Finish lines painted upon the asphalt or the mile markers that follow the flow of footfalls. Even in the chill of winter you cannot escape the drama of the race as you walk or drive the fabled route. With the heat of August come the runners and the crowds to cheer them on.

Considered one of the country's best nonmarathons, the Falmouth Road Race had its beginnings back in 1973. Today the world-class annual event, which is held on the second Sunday in August, attracts more than 8,000 runners from around the world to challenge its demanding 7.1-mile course. Some great names in marathon running who have competed here include Alberto Salazar (he won this race in 1981 and 1982), U.S. gold medalist Frank Shorter, four-time winner of the Boston and New York marathons Bill Rodgers as well as U.S. gold medalist Joan Benoit Samuelson, Grete Waitz, Lorraine Moller and Lynn Jennings.

Last year's race saw three records crumble. Kenyan Joseph Kimani had the winning time of 31:36 minutes for the men, while fellow countrywoman Catherine Ndereba came in at 35:37 minutes. Wheelchair winner Craig Blanchette of Washington was among the record breakers, crossing the finish line at 24:01 minutes.

Of course, the thing that sets Falmouth apart from other road races is the incredible Cape Cod scenery, from the course's Woods Hole start to its Falmouth Heights finish. Between those two points runners pass the refreshing waters of Vineyard Sound and the stoic white column of Nobska Light. The race attracts some 70,000 spectators who line the streets.

For that one day a year, Falmouth's population becomes that of a small city. So if you wish to attend the event, we strongly advise that you make your accommodations reservations well in advance. If you are interested in participating in the Falmouth Road Race, call the number above; entries close May 15.

Upper Cape

Coast Guard 10K Road Race

Mass. Military Reservation • 968-6448

Though the Falmouth Road Race is the biggest act on the Cape in terms of footracing, the Cape hosts dozens of other competitions,

INSIDERS' TIP

Cape Cod (or more specifically, South Chatham), is the home of men's figure skating champion Todd Eldredge, who won the world title in March 1996. Also, Tony Kent Arena in Dennis has been the practice rink for Olympic medalists Nancy Kerrigan and Paul Wylie.

such as this race to benefit the Coast Guard's Morale, Well-being and Recreation Program. This 10K road race at the Massachusetts Military Reservation is usually held in April, about a week or two prior to the Boston Marathon. In fact, many runners use it as a warmup for the marathon. An entry fee of $10 to $15 gets each of the 100-200 participants a T-shirt.

Jane and Joe Donovan Road Race

Monument Beach • 759-2707

This 7.1 mile race in Monument Beach takes place on the first Sunday in June. Named for the late husband-and-wife team who started this race years ago, proceeds benefit the Shrine Hospital in Boston.

Sportsite Health and Racquet Club 5K

Sandwich • 888-7900

Held in mid-November, this 5K road race takes place in Sandwich. It benefits the Sandwich Junior Golf Association.

Falmouth Main Street Mile

Falmouth • 457-2567

Sponsored by the Falmouth Track Club, this 1-mile race always takes place on the Sunday after Labor Day. If you want to take part call Helen Kennedy at the number above.

Heart Beat Hill Race

Falmouth • 457-4620

This 2-mile run (and walk) is more of a health event than a competitive race. Taking place in September, it is sponsored by Falmouth Hospital and benefits the high school scholarship program.

Chase the Turkey Trot

Falmouth • 563-2968, 563-5208

This 4-mile run, held at the end of November, takes place at Falmouth Academy and Beebe Woods. Proceeds benefit the International Myeloma Foundation.

Cape Cod Marathon

Falmouth • 540-6959

In late October the 26.2-mile Cape Cod Marathon is held. This race, which attracts about 1,000 participants, is a Boston Marathon qualifying event and also includes a team relay event. It begins and ends at the Falmouth Village Green and is sponsored by the Falmouth Track Club. Part of the race traces the Falmouth Road Race course. The men's and women's winners each receive $1,300. The team relay portion of the race benefits the Leukemia Society of America.

Mashpee 5K Woodland Run

Mashpee • 539-1446

Held on the last Saturday in July, this Mashpee 5K race starts at Heritage Park and concludes at K.C. Coombs Elementary School. The course takes runners through a wooded section of Mashpee, and all ages are invited to participate. There are eight divisions, and the winner in each division receives a plaque. The overall male and female winners also receive a trophy.

Mid-Cape

Osterville Run for the Library

Osterville • 428-5757, 428-9115

Held in mid-July, this 4.1-mile race takes place in Osterville to benefit that village's public library. Some 400 runners participate.

Centerville Old Home Week 5K Road Race

Centerville • 775-1856

Starting at Covell's Beach and finishing at the Centerville Elementary School, this race benefits the Centerville Library. It usually takes place the third week of August. More than 150 contestants participate in age groups ranging from 13 and younger to 69. There's even a special race for the kiddies afterwards at the Centerville Elementary School.

INSIDERS' TIP

During the latter quarter of the 19th century, horse racing was big on Cape Cod. Thousands would attend the races at trotting parks in Falmouth, Marstons Mills, Barnstable Village, Hyannis, West Dennis and Harwich.

Johnny Kelley Half Marathon and Five-Miler

Hyannis • 775-6800

Named for the octogenarian who ran in more Boston Marathons than anyone, this half-marathon and 5-mile race are held on the Sunday of Memorial Day weekend. Proceeds benefit the Cape Cod Hospital Foundation, a favorite charity of Kelley.

SportsEast Friday Night 5-Miler

Hyannis • 771-6226

Every Friday night throughout the year the streets of Hyannis host this 5-mile road race. During the spring and summer the race begins at 6 PM; 5:30 PM during the fall and winter months. Up to 30 runners take part each week, and there is not an entrance fee.

Photo: Ron Schloerb, Cape Cod Times

A determined player completes a double play during an American Legion Baseball game.

Hyannis Half Marathon and Five-Miler

Hyannis • 888-4058

This run is held on the first Sunday in March. The format has been changed for 1997 to a 13.1-mile half-marathon and 5-mile race (instead of a full marathon as in years past). The race begins and ends at the Barnstable High School and attracts some 1,500 participants. Those interested in running should send an SASE to P.O. Box 1992, Hyannis, 02601. The proceeds of this race go toward a Barnstable High School scholarship for the cross country team.

Hyannis Main Street Mile

Hyannis • 775-8877

Benefitting the Hyannis Public Library new book fund, this race, as its name suggests, takes place on Main Street in Hyannis. It starts on the east end and finishes on the west end of town. The 1-mile race usually takes place on the third Sunday in October, although we're told that in 1997 it may be held in September.

Pete's Preservation Parade

West Barnstable • 888-1789

This 4-mile run in early September begins at the West Barnstable Community Center at routes 149 and 6A. Walkers are also invited to participate.

Cross Country Conservation Caper

South Dennis • 385-1349, 428-4925

This series of 2.5 mile races takes place over an eight-week period from mid-June to early August. There is one race each week beginning at the Dennis Town Hall. The course winds through conservation lands, hence its name. It benefits the Cape Cod Flyers, a youth track program.

20th Annual Dennis Road Race

Dennis • 394-8300

Three hundred runners compete in this 5-mile road race. Held in late August, it begins at Wixon School on Route 134.

Lower Cape

19th Annual Brew Run

Brewster • 896-6574

The Brew Run is a 5.2-mile race sponsored by the Brewster Rescue Squad and the Wood Shed to benefit Brewster Rescue and Safety. To register, send a SASE to the Wood Shed, Box 967, Brewster 02631. It is held in mid-August.

5K Run for MS

Brewster • 896-3491

This 5K race is held in early October to benefit multiple sclerosis research. The race takes place at Nickerson State Park in Brewster.

Irish Pub Road Race

West Harwich • 432-8808

Sponsored by the Irish Pub in West Harwich, this 5.25-mile road race takes place in August to raise money for the Harwich Ambulance Fund. It begins and ends at the Irish Pub on Route 28, West Harwich, where afterwards a party is held with an awards ceremony and live entertainment.

Cranberry Harvest Festival Road Race

Harwich • 432-0100

Harwich Center is the site for this 5.75-mile race, held in September as part of the Harwich Cranberry Harvest Festival, an annual town-wide 10-day celebration to mark the harvest of the native berry. The race benefits the "We Love Our Kids" program.

INSIDERS' TIP

The old Cape Cod Coliseum, now a warehouse building on White's Path in South Yarmouth, was at one time home to professional hockey on Cape Cod. Four different minor league teams came and left between 1972 and 1981. Also, a number of Boston Bruins pre-season exhibition games were played at the Coliseum.

John Gray Half-Marathon and Five-Miler
Orleans • 888-4058

This half-marathon and 5-mile road race attracts about 500 runners. It is held at the Nauset Regional Middle School in Orleans on Labor Day Weekend to benefit the Nauset area schools athletics.

Triathlons, Biathlons and Walkathons

Upper Cape

Coast Guard Air Station Biathlon
Otis Air Base • 968-6448

Held at Otis Air Base over Memorial Day weekend, this biathlon event combines running, biking and some more running for a change. It benefits the Coast Guard Morale Well-being and Recreation program.

March of Dimes WalkAmerica
Falmouth, Hyannis • 790-1093

The March of Dimes holds two walkathons, one in Hyannis in late April and another in Falmouth in mid-May. The Hyannis walkathon is a 5-mile scenic walk that begins at the National Guard Armory. The Falmouth event begins at Casino by the Sea and is usually follows part of the Falmouth Road Race route. WalkAmerica was the first walking event in the nation and is now in its 27th year.

New England Triathlon Tour/ Falmouth Sprint
Falmouth • 477-6311

A .25-mile swim, 9-mile bike and 3.1-mile run comprise this triathlon event. The fun begins at Surf Drive Beach in Falmouth Heights and normally takes place in late July.

Mid-Cape

New England Triathlon Tour/ Hyannis Sprint I and II
Hyannis • 477-6311

Craigville Beach is the starting point for this triathlon, consisting of a .25 mile swim, 10-mile bike and 3.1-mile run. Sprint I is held in mid-June while Sprint II takes place in early September.

Lower Cape

Harwich Cranberry Festival Bridge to Bridge Swim and Run
West Harwich • 432-0100

This biathlon begins with a .8-mile swim from Wixon dock on the Herring River to the town dock at Route 28. It is then followed by a 3.1-mile run from the town dock to Pleasant Road Beach. This event is usually held on a weekend in mid-August, but it depends largely on the tides. Proceeds go to the "We Love Our Kids" program.

Golf

Cape Cod is synonymous with golf. Upon this sand trap of a peninsula are more than two dozen public golf courses, so no matter where you are, somebody is teeing one up not too far away. (See our Golf chapter for a list of courses.) A number of tournaments are held on Cape Cod for amateurs and pros alike. Space does not permit listing all the Cape's tournaments, so we encourage you to check with local golf courses and watch the *Cape Cod Times* sports pages for upcoming matches. Among some of the most notable tourneys are the following.

INSIDERS' TIP

Perhaps the best place to watch the Falmouth Road Race is anywhere along Grand Avenue in Falmouth Heights. The finish line is at the ballfield along this route. While you're waiting for the runners you'll have the views of Vineyard Sound to keep you occupied.

Upper Cape

Willowbend Children's Charity Pro-Am

Willowbend Country Club, 100 Willowbend Rd., Mashpee • 539-5000

This is the premier golf tournament on Cape Cod, attracting some of the biggest names in golf, professional sports and some 15,000 fans. It takes place at the beginning of July at Willowbend in Mashpee. Since the first tournament in 1992 it has raised about $450,000 to benefit children's programs on Cape Cod.

Greg Norman won 1996's Pro-Am with a record score of 67 for the round. Other popular pro golfers in the event included Nick Faldo (fresh from his 1996 Masters win), Andrew Magee, Bruce Lietzke and, of course, John Daly, who dazzled the crowds with his mammoth 300-plus yard drives. On the amateur side were such great sports names as Hall of Fame Boston Bruins defenseman Bobby Orr, Dallas Cowboys running back Emitt Smith and Denver Broncos quarterback John Elway. This is a tournament not to be missed.

All the holes here are beautiful and offer you unrestricted views of the competition, but plan to set aside some time to watch the drives along the par 5 10th hole, especially when Daly steps up to the tee. We've seen him hit a wedge to the green on his second shot!

Tickets are a very reasonable $20 for the one-day event, and it benefits a great cause.

Junior Team Championship

Quashnet Valley Golf Club, Old Barnstable Rd., Mashpee • 477-4412

Held in late August, this championship tourney features members of the Junior Golf Association of Cape Cod, ages 7 to 18.

Mid-Cape

Canal Classic

Tara Woods Golf Course, West End Rotary, Hyannis • 775-7775
Hyannis Golf Club, Rt. 132, Hyannis • 362-2606

In late August the Canal Classic is held at the Tara Woods Golf Course and the Hyannis Golf Course. This unique invitational tourney is a combination of scramble and best ball at two different courses on the same day. Two-man teams play nine holes at one course and then nine holes at the other.

Dennis Highland Fourball

Dennis Highland Golf Course, 825 Old Bass River Rd., Dennis • 385-8347

Held in late September at the Highland course in Dennis is this best ball tournament featuring teams of two players each.

Lower Cape

Amateur Golf Tournament at Cranberry Valley Golf Course

Cranberry Valley Golf Course, 183 Oak St., Harwich • 430-7560

This Harwich tournament is held over Mother's Day weekend. Players need only a USGA handicap to participate.

Cape Cod Junior Open and Captains Junior Golf Day

Captains Golf Course, 1000 Freeman's Way, Brewster • 896-5100

Held each August at Captain's Golf Course in Brewster, both of these events are held on the same day and feature juniors age 7 to 18 years old.

Tennis

As with golf, it is impossible to list all the Cape's tennis tournaments. It is estimated that the Cape's 30 private and public tennis courts hold in excess of 100 tournaments, 30 of which are played at Mid-Cape Racquet Club in South Yarmouth. Imagine the number of serves we're talking about! Below is a sampling of the events, starting off with the granddaddy of all tennis events on Cape.

Upper Cape

Mentadent Champions Tennis Tournament

Willowbend Country Club, 100 Willowbend Rd., Mashpee, • 539-5700.

It just so happens that the premier tennis

tournament on Cape Cod takes place at the same place where the premier Cape golf event is held — Willowbend in Mashpee. This tourney, for ages 35 and older, is held in mid-August and features some of the greatest names in tennis. Jimmy Connors, Bjorn Borg, Roscoe Tanner, Guillermo Vilas, Eddie Dibbs, John Lloyd and last year's winner, Andres Gomez, have all competed here for some $150,000 in prize money.

Imagine seeing Connors and Bjorg face off as they did in the 1970s. The Champions of Tennis circuit allows us to relive these classic matchups from decades ago.

The tournament is held over five days, typically from Wednesday through Sunday. Singles and doubles semi-finals are held on Saturday and finals on Sunday. Ticket prices range from $15 to $50 depending on seat location and day (for instance, least expensive tickets are available on the first day of the tournament while the tickets for the finals are the most expensive). A couple of thousand spectators attended last year's finals between Connors and Gomez, so you'll want to purchase your tickets early.

Mid-Cape

Cape Cod Community College Open

Cape Cod Community College, Rt. 132, West Barnstable • 375-4015

Held over a two-week period during the second and third weeks of July, this tennis tournament at the college features men's and women's singles and doubles matches. Junior and adult divisions are based on age, not experience. There is also a wheelchair division. Matches typically take place between Wednesday and Sunday over the two-week period.

Mid Cape Open

Mid-Cape Racquet Club, 193 Whites Path, South Yarmouth • 394-3511

These matches take place over a two-week period in August at various locations around the Cape and feature singles, doubles and mixed doubles. Semi-finals and finals are held at the Mid-Cape Racquet Club. There are divisions for all ages and skills levels.

Woody Tournament

Sesuit Tennis Club, 1389 Rt. 6A, East Dennis • 385-2200

Only wooden rackets are allowed at the Woody Tournament, held at the Sesuit Tennis Club in late July. Featuring singles, doubles and co-ed matches, the tourney usually takes place over three days.

Lower Cape

Lower Cape Open

Eldredge Park, Orleans • 255-4349

In this August tournament, players in age groups from younger than 11 to 70 and older battle it out at Eldredge Park in Orleans. There are singles and doubles competitions.

Provincetown Tennis Club Year-Rounders Tournament

Provincetown Tennis Club, Bradford St., Provincetown • 487-9574

Originally started more than 20 years ago as a tournament for local year-rounders, the tournament has expanded to include seasonal residents as well as players from outside of Provincetown. The fun begins in mid-June with men's and women's singles, doubles and mixed doubles, culminating in the finals held on the July 4 weekend.

INSIDERS' TIP

The Shining Sea Bikepath gets its name from Katharine Lee Bate's famous poem "America the Beautiful": ". . . from sea to shining sea." She was born in Falmouth in 1859.

Soccer

Cape Cod Crusaders

Barnstable High School, Hyannis
• 790-4782, (800) 9-CRUSADE

Professional soccer has come to Cape Cod in the way of the Cape Cod Crusaders. Out of some 90 professional teams of the United System of Independent Soccer Leagues throughout the country, the Crusaders are one of only six New England teams. The team plays two dozen games each summer season, half of them on their home field at Barnstable High School. There's usually at least one game held each weekend from April to mid-August. Game time is 7:30 PM. For the other half of the games they travel to New Jersey, New York and as far south as North Carolina for matches. The season concludes with national championships on Labor Day Weekend. The Crusaders, of the Pro League, have participated in post-season play two of the past three years.

Players come from as far away as Ireland and England, while others hail from more nearby New England colleges. Games can draw up to 2,000 spectators. Ticket prices in 1996 were $6 for adults and $4 for children younger than 12. Call for ticket and schedule information.

Cape Cod Soccer League

Various locations • 896-3271

During the months of June and July the amateur Cape Cod Soccer League is in action with eight teams playing around the Cape. Teams include such good ol' Cape Cod names as Chatham Fog and Harwich Hurricanes.

Massachusetts Maritime Academy

Taylor's Pt., Buzzards Bay • 830-5000

During September and October you can catch college soccer games at the Massachusetts Maritime Academy in Buzzards Bay. The Mass Maritime Buccaneers compete against some 20 local colleges and are members of the Massachusetts State College Athletic Conference. To watch the Bucs in action, contact Mass Maritime for info on upcoming matches.

College Sports

In addition to soccer, Massachusetts Maritime Academy hosts other sporting events, such as football, volleyball and cross-country. Home games are held at Mass Maritime, Taylor's Point in Buzzards Bay. For schedules, call Mass Maritime at 830-5000 or check the *Cape Cod Times* sports section.

Lacrosse, Field Hockey, Volleyball

Cape Cod Summer Lacrosse League

Falmouth, Sandwich, Barnstable and Hyannis • 420-3061

Developed by the Native Americans, lacrosse is considered North America's oldest sport and is Canada's national sport. (We bet you thought it was ice hockey!) This amateur summer lacrosse league is comprised of four teams: Falmouth, Sandwich, Barnstable and Hyannis. Playoffs are held in mid-August. Players are recruited from some 400 schools and colleges. The season runs from late June to mid-August.

Third Annual Cape Cod Classic

Dennis-Yarmouth High School, South Yarmouth • 398-7630

This field hockey event is held at the Dennis-Yarmouth High School in mid-August and features some of the best high school field hockey players from across the New England region. The tournament consists of eight all-star squads. There is also a skills competition.

INSIDERS' TIP

Alistair Cook once described Highland Golf Links in Truro as "the most perfect example of the typical British or Scottish links in the United States."

Jose Cuervo Series Tournament

Craigville Beach • 790-6888

For a number of years now, amateur volleyball has attempted to gain a foothold on the beaches of Cape Cod. This tournament is usually held over Labor Day weekend at Craigville Beach and features plenty of spikes. It is a two-day tournament featuring men's, women's and coed divisions, and it's free for spectators.

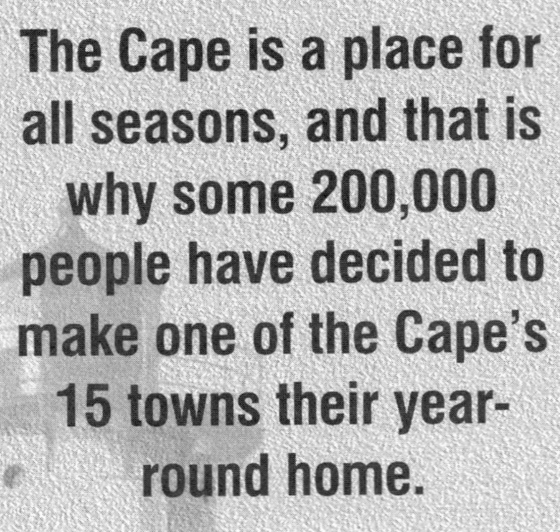

The Cape is a place for all seasons, and that is why some 200,000 people have decided to make one of the Cape's 15 towns their year-round home.

Real Estate

People have been interested in acquiring property on Cape Cod since the early 17th century when settlers first began to migrate to these parts. The Plymouth Court spent so much of its time resolving land ownership issues that a local court was established in Barnstable to relieve the overtaxed Plymouth system.

Of course, the first to call Cape Cod home were the Native Indians. No doubt, they chose Cape Cod for many of the same reasons why people today are still choosing to make Cape Cod their home or home away from home. It is one of those magical places where land and sea meet to form a place rapidly approaching nirvana. The climate is pleasant — the summers cooled by a refreshing ocean breeze, the winters warmed by this same ocean air thus making a Cape winter less harsh than those throughout the rest of New England (although the winter of 1996 made liars out of everyone who has ever said "it doesn't snow on Cape Cod" . . . oh well, upon us all a little snow must fall!).

Though known as a summer vacation spot, the Cape's most beautiful season is arguably autumn. It is truly a place for all seasons, and that is precisely why some 200,000 people have decided to make one of the Cape's 15 towns their year-round home.

There is such a range of housing available on this picturesque peninsula that to hear people describe the Cape's architecture you would think they were talking about a dozen different places. We're surrounded by water, and there are hundreds and hundreds of waterfront properties looking out over the bays and the sounds, the canal and the foaming Atlantic. Inland, you'll find neighborhood communities just like you might find in any town across the country. Old sea captain's homes and other antiquities are available if you'd rather live in a piece of history than in something more contemporary. There are full-Cape homes, three-quarter Capes, half-Capes and even some quarter-Capes. There are saltboxes, Colonials, Greek Revival houses and Federal dwellings. There are condominiums, second homes, investment homes and cottages and cottages and cottages. We have such a variety that the best advice we can give is to see it all firsthand. Get your hands on a map of the Cape at any of the local newsstands or bookstores and drive the nearly 75 villages and sub-villages that comprise the 15 towns.

Perhaps you'd like a house off in the rurals of Wellfleet or Truro, where the Cape is less densely populated, or perhaps an antique gem along Route 6A in Barnstable, Yarmouthport, Dennis or Brewster. Maybe you'd like to look out over the waters of a lake or perhaps even one of the hundreds of kettle ponds that are sprinkled across the glacially created terrain. How about a farmhouse? Or a more contemporary dwelling? What about something along a golf course or near a river? Perhaps even something with a widow's walk!

At the time of this writing (January 1997), there are some 6,000 properties available for sale across the Cape as listed by the Multiple Listing Service (MLS). The last few years have seen a steady increase in number of sales, and 1996 proved to be an excellent year for many of the Cape's Realtors. In fact, the 1996 fall season was particularly good and even December, typically a slow month, was still busy at many offices. Despite increased sales, home prices have remained relatively fixed. Cape Cod is as good a buy today as it has ever been!

Betsy Warren, the current President of the Cape and Islands Board of Realtors and last year's President of the Cape Cod and Islands Multiple Listing Service feels "very, very positive about the real estate market" and expects 1997 to be an even more exciting year than last year. Besides those looking for second homes, rental properties and investment opportunities, today's buyers also include the large market of people relocating to the Cape for retirement, those who are moving up to a larger house to accommodate lifestyle changes (such as a growing family), and those younger Cape Codders representing first-time homebuyers. With increasing job opportunities, there has been a healthy trend of younger people staying and buying on Cape.

Many real estate companies offer a number of programs designed to cater to the needs of their clientele. For instance, if you're in the market for your first home you may want to ask your Realtor if he or she has any first-time homebuyer programs or deals with any financial institutions or mortgage companies that offer first-time homebuyer mortgages. These typically include lower down payments and/or fewer points. If you are a first-time homebuyer, or even someone in the market for a second home, you may want to inquire at a bank or mortgage company about prequalification. Once you are prequalified you'll know exactly how much house you can afford, and your Realtor will know what price ranges to avoid.

FYI

Unless otherwise noted, the area code for all phone numbers in this guide is 508.

Besides primary homes and second homes, the Cape is also known for its rental properties. Many a future year-rounder started out on the Cape with a cottage rented during the summer. A summer rental property close to the beach can fetch between $600 and $800 a week during the summer. Over the course of a 10-week season this can add up to $6,000 to $8,000, which can nearly carry your mortgage! (For rental information, see our Vacation Rentals chapter.)

The Cape is also a wonderful spot to retire. Besides a more temperate climate, the Cape offers lower tax rates than those throughout the rest of Massachusetts and also many activities for the older than 60 crowd (see our Retirement chapter).

During the 1970s and '80s the Cape experienced a building boom. Though there are some 6,000 existing properties on the market, new homes are still being built. Land is available in many of the Cape's towns, but you may want to check on restrictions. For instance, some towns require that you purchase an acre, so you may want to call the town offices for all the specifics before you decide to build in a particular town.

The **Cape Cod & Islands Board of Realtors**, 350 Station Avenue in South Yarmouth, 394-2277, is a good year-round source of information. For those who are interested in building or remodeling, real estate agencies generally have ample information about local builders.

Another source of information is the **Home Builders Association of Cape Cod**, 189 Harbor Point Road in Barnstable, 362-4755. This association represents approximately 80 builders and suppliers throughout the Cape who work on new homes and remodeling projects.

The sections that follow provide you with a good range of real estate professionals available on the Cape. At the end of the chapter, look for a listing of the Cape's exclusive golfing communities. No matter what you choose to live in, or where, you really can't go wrong on Cape Cod. People have been settling here for more than 350 years, and the vast majority have been happy with their choice!

Real Estate Agencies

Upper Cape

Cape Coast Realty

18-B MacArthur Blvd., Bourne • 759-9517

This year-round real estate office handles properties in Bourne, Sandwich and parts of Falmouth and deals primarily with residential properties, many of which are waterfront. Cape Coast is a member of the Multiple Listing Service.

ERA Bayside Professionals

2 Williams Ave., Pocasset • 564-6365, (800) 878-3722

This 17-year-old office has 8 full-time agents serving the Bourne, Falmouth, Mashpee, Sandwich and Wareham areas. The company deals almost exclusively with residential property sales and vacation and year-round rentals. ERA offers home warranty, referrals throughout the country, a nationwide Multiple Listing Service and will actually buy your home if they cannot sell it. ERA also sends a monthly mailing of new listings to potential buyers.

Jack Conway and Company Inc., Realtor

128 Rt. 6A, Sandwich • 888-2300

The 40-year-old Conway and Company has 35 offices and approximately 650 brokers and sales staff from Boston and the South Shore to the Cape. It deals with residential, commercial and investment properties and has a financial service division that works with out-of-town buyers. The office also has specialists in development, sales and project making and remodeling. Conway operates a school of real estate licensed by the Commonwealth of Massachusetts. The relocation service provides information and introductions to the community at no extra cost. The company has an in-house insurance company and other offices located in Falmouth, Pocasset and Dennis.

Eagle Associates Real Estate

116 Rt. 6A, Sandwich • 888-4366

This office has much to be proud of. Principals Frank Murphy and Betsy Warren have combined 56 years of experience in Cape Cod real estate. Betsy was named Cape and Islands Realtor of the year in 1995, president of the Cape Cod & Islands Multiple Listing Service for 1996 and is now president of the Cape Cod & Islands Board of Realtors for 1997. Established in 1974, the office now has four brokers and deals primarily with the sale of land and residential and commercial property. The company covers real estate in the Upper and Mid Cape areas from Sandwich to Barnstable and stresses the importance of personalized service.

Ermine Lovell

881 Palmer Ave., Falmouth • 548-0711

Ermine Lovell was selling real estate in Falmouth in 1929, long before many of us were even born, much less thinking of buying property. She is also an ardent conservationist who has set up the Salt Pond Areas Bird Sanctuary in West Falmouth and bought the 18th-century Bourne Farm to preserve as a museum (see our History and Attractions chapters). The company, which has four full-time brokers, deals primarily with properties in Falmouth, Woods Hole and Pocasset and Cataumet in

INSIDERS' TIP

In Wellfleet, the zoning laws demand that condominiums can only be single cottages, not multiple-unit dwellings.

Bourne. Options include land, waterfront and residential properties and a very busy summer-rental business.

Harriet Dugan Realtors

598 Main St., Falmouth • 548-4093

Harriet Dugan knows Falmouth real estate like the back of her hand. After all, she was born and brought up in Falmouth and has been in the real estate business for 40 years. The company handles a full range of properties and services, including commercial land sales and leases and waterfront property. The office, which also handles summer rentals, specializes in properties in Mashpee and Falmouth.

Vincent Associates

159 Main St., (Town Hall Sq.), Falmouth • 548-6500

This real estate agency has been in business in Falmouth for close to 30 years. It offers primarily residential land and dwellings but also deals with commercial transactions and conducts home appraisals. Most of the agency's property listings are in Falmouth, but the office does not restrict itself to sales and rentals only in this area. Vincent has winter, summer and year-round rentals.

Great Bay Associates

77 Cypress St., East Falmouth • 540-3775

The Realtors at Great Bay Associates have been handling the sale of property in Falmouth for over 18 years. Although they can sell property all over the Cape through the MLS system, they specialize in waterview or near-the-water properties in the East Falmouth area, more specifically on the Maravista, Acapesket and Davisville finger peninsulas on Little, Great, Green and Bourne pond inlets, which spill into Vineyard Sound. Great Bay deals primarily with residential properties — primary homes, second homes and investment properties as well as land. The friendly staff also handles the summer rentals on the properties they sell (see our Vacation Rentals chapter).

Century 21 Regan Realtors

9 Steeple St. (at Mashpee Commons), Mashpee • 477-5200, Massachusetts only (800) 780-5299

Started in 1982, Regan Realty is a large office (12 brokers and associates) that specializes in affordable waterfront properties from Falmouth to Hyannis, including Sandwich. The office has a rental division and also deals with new construction, land sales and condominiums as well as commercial properties. Computerized resources, primarily MLS and the Internet, and appraisals and competitive market evaluations are available. Through Century 21, the Mashpee office is linked with listings, referrals and relocation services and general information from 6,000 other offices worldwide.

Mid-Cape

The Buyer Brokerage of Osterville

874 Main St., Osterville • 420-1804, (800) 290-1804

This three-year-old company acts exclusively as a buyer's broker, counseling the buyer of a property throughout the home-purchase process. Partners Jane Tardanico and Stephen Perry serve as advocates for the buyer; Perry participated in establishing the National Association of Exclusive Buyer Agents in 1993. The six-broker Osterville office specializes in properties in the Mid-Cape area and relies heavily on their team approach. The first real estate office in the Osterville area to offer exclusive buyer representation, this firm charges no additional fee for their service (beyond the sales commission).

RE/MAX Liberty

3860 Falmouth Rd., Marstons Mills • 428-2300

A national franchise, RE/MAX has a service approach to real estate and handles many of the details that usually fall to the client, such as inspection of septic systems and smoke detectors. This office focuses on residential and commercial sales and rentals. It has more than a dozen full-time brokers, including owners/brokers Don MacEachern and Deborah Schilling, who maintain a high level of activity within their primary market area from Dennis to the Cape Cod Canal. RE/MAX brokers donate a portion of their commissions to the Children's Miracle Network, a nonprofit program that benefits hospitalized children.

Wianno Realty

68 Wianno Ave., Osterville • 428-8800

This real estate office is run by Jim and Gail Crocker, who have been in business together for the past 11 years. Jim, a lifelong Cape Codder, has been a Realtor for the past 13 years. Their listings cover Osterville, Cotuit, Centerville and Marstons Mills. Jim is a licensed Title V inspector. The company's primary focuses include residential properties, second homes, land and development. Jim, who last year (1996) served as a trustee and vice-chairman of the Osterville Free Library, is now on the steering committee of the Osterville Business and Professional Association.

Prudential Prime Properties

619 Main St., Centerville • 775-1976, (800) 924-1144

This office has been associated with Prudential for four years, which links it with a 25-office consortium called New England Prime Property that has offices in Maine, Massachusetts, Rhode Island and Connecticut. The company has 14 full-time brokers (including a relocation broker) located in two offices — the other office is at 3 Barnstable Road in Hyannis, 790-1986 and (800) 773-1986. Prudential Prime Properties can provide building, mortgage and insurance services through its corporate network. The office deals extensively in waterfront village and golf course properties as well as new construction and commercial properties.

Today Real Estate

1533 Falmouth Rd. (Rt. 28), Centerville • 790-2300, (800) 966-2448

Established in 1985, this large and active real estate company has three offices (one on Route 130 in Sandwich, 888-8008, (800) 792-6456, and another on Route 28 in South Yarmouth, 398-0600, (800) 966-0369). It has more than 40 brokers and claims it has sold the most units of any company Capewide since 1990. Today specializes in residential property, both owner-occupied and investment properties. Today Real Estate also publishes and distributes its own listings catalog. The office deals with properties from the Cape Cod Canal to Orleans.

Strawberry Hill Real Estate

880 W. Main St., Hyannis • 775-8000

Principal Adrienne Siegel has been selling

INSIDERS' TIP

The main roads of many Cape villages feature 18th- and 19th-century homes, and in some places you can find homes that date back to the 17th century.

real estate on Cape Cod for 15 years and has been owner/operator of this office for five years. The agency deals primarily with Centerville and Hyannis property and with the Mid-Cape area in general. She and five other brokers sell mostly residential real estate — single family homes, land, condos, estate sales and waterfront — with prices ranging from $50,000 to $500,000.

Realty Executives

1582 Rt. 132, Hyannis • 362-1300

A national firm, Realty Executives is generally credited with starting the concept of 100 percent commission, a motivating factor that allows a broker to earn nearly the entire sales commission rather than splitting it with the agency. About 95 percent of calls to the office are generated by agent advertising. The Hyannis office, along with offices on Cranberry Highway in Buzzards Bay, 743-4600, and at the junction of routes 137 and 39 in East Harwich, 432-5100, have between 300 and 400 listings. For regional referrals, Realty Executives has six or seven other offices scattered throughout Massachusetts.

Walsh Realty

610 W. Main St., Hyannis • 775-7330

A well-respected Hyannis company, Walsh Realty has been in business since 1973 in the Centerville-Craigville-Hyannisport area. The primary business is residential home and land sales as well as condominiums, and summer and year-round rentals.

Bay Harbor Realty Inc.

3224 Main St. (Rt. 6A), Barnstable • 362-5505

Ruth Cutler and Marge Gibson are the principals of this office, which covers the Mid-Cape area from Sandwich to Orleans. Cutler has been active in real estate for 17 years, while her partner has 27 years experience. This office has four full-time and four part-time Realtors, and deals with properties from the upper end to starter homes.

R.J. Norton & Co. Realtors

3221 Rt. 6A, Barnstable • 362-2120, (800) 321-2120

As an affiliate of the prestigious Sotheby's International Real Estate system, R.J. Norton

Photo: Ron Schloerb, Cape Cod Times

A family settles in for a day at the beach.

is a leading Realtor in the area with an average sale of $200,000 on the Cape's northside from Sandwich to Barnstable. Owner Bob Norton is a longtime Cape resident. His company is Sotheby's agent from Sandwich to Dennis. If a property is listed on the Cape, Sotheby's has the capacity to advertise it worldwide. The company has about 12 full-time real estate brokers and two other offices at 137 Route 6A in Sandwich, 833-3333, and 598 Route 6A in East Sandwich, 888-1555.

Bill Harrison, Realtor

299 Rt. 28, Cape Realty Building, West Yarmouth • 771-7974

A Realtor since 1957, Harrison and the six other brokers in his office deal primarily in residential property in the Mid-Cape area in Barnstable, Yarmouth and Dennis. The staff is experienced and lives in the area. The full-service real estate office deals with listing and selling property. Harrison is a member and past president of the Cape Cod & Islands Board of Realtors. A professional Realtor for the past 40 years, he has been named Realtor of the Year, is a certified residential specialist and a graduate of the Realtor Institute in Washington, D.C.

Peter McDowell Associates

585 Main St. (Rt. 6A), Dennis • 385-9114, (888) 385-9114

11 Rt. 28, Dennisport • 394-5400

Serving the Dennis, Yarmouth, Barnstable, Brewster and Harwich areas for the past 30 years, Peter McDowell Associates has two offices in the town of Dennis — one on the northside and the other on the southside. A well-respected real estate company, it offers many fine residential properties for sale in the five-town area as well as hundreds of rental properties in the town of Dennis.

Steele Associates

1372 Rt. 134, East Dennis • 385-7311

Independently owned and operated by Joseph D. Steele, this 12-year-old full-service real estate agency has developed a specialty of handling beachfront property, particularly along the northside section of Dennis. The agency also handles the sale of residential homes, condominiums, land and commercial properties in the towns of Yarmouth, Brewster and Harwich. Steele Associates has a staff of eight agents offering the highest degree of personal service.

James E. Mischler Real Estate

Intersection of rts. 28 and 134, West Dennis • 394-3330 (800) 863-3330

Established in 1979 by Jim and Rita Mischler, James E. Mischler Real Estate specializes in the sale of property on or near salt water. The company handles sales throughout the Cape from their central West Dennis location as well as some 400 vacation rental properties near the water in the towns of Dennis, Harwich and Brewster.

Reef Realty Ltd.

24 School St., West Dennis • 394-3090, (800) 346-4059

Since it was established in 1985, this firm has won numerous local and regional sales awards including Most Listings Sold in Dennis and Most Listings Sold Cape-wide. The staff of nine Realtors handles an extensive number of sales properties, both residential and commercial. Reef Realty Ltd. is also the Cape's largest residential custom building company and developer with more than 100 years of combined experience. They are members of the Cape Cod Home Builders Association as well as the National Home Builders Association. Reef Realty's slogan is "Cottage to castle, Sandwich to Eastham," which tells at a glance what they handle and where.

Lower Cape

Bay Village Realty-Better Homes and Gardens

1990 Main St. (Rt. 6A), Brewster • 896-6200

Established in 1978 with a primary market area covering all the mid- and lower-Cape towns, Bay Village has all types of properties for sale, from large commercial spaces to tiny seaside cottages. More than 60 agents work in the six Bay Village offices (other offices, which also handle real estate sales and rentals, are located in Harwichport, Chatham, Orleans and Wellfleet; there is also a rental office in East Orleans). The Brewster office serves as the exclusive agency for Cobb's Pond, a condominium complex on Cape Cod Bay. The commercial division, Business Locators of Cape Cod, can be reached at 255-8200.

Great Locations Real Estate

2660 Rt. 6A, Brewster • 896-2093, (800) 626-9984

This unique real estate office specializes in vacation, second homes and retirement properties in the Brewster, Dennis and Orleans areas (although it does cover the whole Cape). It offers expert property management and rental management on the properties it sells, which include condominiums as well as private homes. A full-service real estate agency, the properties it lists range from $49,000 condominium units to $369,000 waterfront homes.

Stonybrook Realty and Building
84 Mate's Way, Brewster • 896-9717

This office opened two years ago as an outgrowth of a home-building business. Stonybrook's market area ranges from Yarmouth to Wellfleet, with a primary listing area consisting of the towns from Yarmouth to Brewster. The office has a unique 24-hour real estate hotline, 896-9045, which potential buyers can call to receive a 90-second message describing a property of interest. The messages can be accessed using codes shown in Stonybrook's newspaper ads.

Coldwell Banker/ Murray Real Estate
1011 Rt. 28, South Harwich • 432-6600

Murray Real Estate has been serving the towns from Falmouth to Chatham since 1974, both as an independent agent and Coldwell Banker affiliate. The company's listings encompass a wide range of residential and commercial properties. There are also offices in Hyannis at 1481 Route 132, 362-6700, and in Dennisport at 63 Lower County Road, 394-2114.

Connolly Real Estate
894 Main St. (Rt. 28), Chatham • 945-4663

A full-service brokerage for both sellers and buyers, this office is run by Marie Connolly, who has served as state director for the Massachusetts Association of Realtors. In business for six years, the office handles commercial and residential properties primarily in Chatham, everything from "quaint cottages to waterfront homes."

Pine Acres Realty
938 Main St. (Rt. 28), Chatham • 945-1186

One of the earliest real estate offices in Chatham (Pine Acres opened in 1948) this company has many exclusive properties along Chatham's waterfronts as well as in the towns of Harwich and Orleans. It is an affiliate of

Photo: Cape Cod Times

The Sandwich Boardwalk offers a place to fish, swim or just stroll down to the beach.

Christie's Great Estate, which is a high-end referral network. Pine Acres Realty has 10 brokers and offers one-stop service in terms of being able to rent the properties it sells.

Sylvan Realty

33 Cross St. (Town Hall Sq.), Chatham • 945-7777, (800) 473-3432

2469 Rt.. 28, South Chatham • 432-2344

Sylvan is a full-service real estate company that specializes in Lower Cape properties, particularly in Chatham, Brewster and Orleans. Exclusive listings include homes, cottages, condominiums, land and commercial properties. A member of the Multiple Listing Service, Sylvan offers a fax back service which allows potential buyers to call a special phone number, 945-1435, to obtain a fax message with information on a property of interest.

Compass Real Estate

2 Academy Pl., Orleans • 240-0022, (800) 834-0061

If you buy a property from Compass, owner Aleta G. Pruesse throws in a celebratory bonus: free dinner at the Wheel Haus Cafe, the restaurant that she and her husband, Uli, also own. The firm handles the sale of residential properties as well as summer rentals throughout the Lower Cape (from Brewster and Harwich to Provincetown) in all price ranges. Compass, housed in the offices aside the cafe, has a staff of eight Realtors. There's also a Compass office at 282 Main Street in Wellfleet, 349-1717, (800) 834-0703, that handles sales and summer rentals.

The Real Estate Company

5 South Orleans Rd. (Rt. 28), Orleans • 255-3456

207 Main St., Orleans • 255-5100

Situated across the street from the Christmas Tree Shop in Orleans, this office, along with its sister office on Main Street, primarily handles sales in the greater Orleans area as well as Eastham and Brewster. This full-service agency also offers waterfront/waterview rentals from Rock Harbor to Nauset Beach. Between the two offices there are a dozen sales agents and five rental agents.

INSIDERS' TIP

Zoning is a hot topic on the Cape, so before you buy any property here, go to a zoning board meeting in your area of interest and talk with a member about your concerns.

Anchor Real Estate
Rt. 6, Eastham • 255-4949

Susanne Goodrich, who was named Massachusetts Realtor of the Year in 1993, opened this office in 1980. In 1996, Anchor was recognized by MLS as the leader in listings sold for the town of Eastham as well as total sales in the town. Anchor's staff includes seven brokers who all live and work in Eastham. Their primary focus is sale of residential homes and vacant land throughout the lower Cape, particularly in Eastham, Wellfleet and Truro. The staff also offers more than 200 summer rental properties (see our Vacation Rentals chapter).

Outer Cape Realty
5150 Rt. 6, North Eastham • 255 0505

The oldest real estate company in Eastham, Outer Cape was established in 1956. This office features a friendly staff of four Realtors who offer single-family homes, cottages and beautiful waterfront homes in the Eastham and South Wellfleet area.

Chequessett Village Real Estate
1 W. Main St., Wellfleet • 349-3411, (800) 334-0909

Known as one of the first real estate offices in Wellfleet (and the oldest surviving one in town), Chequessett Village has been privately owned and operated for more than 40 years. It handles Wellfleet properties, commercial and residential, in all prices ranges.

Duarte/Downey Real Estate Agency
12 Truro Center Rd., Truro • 349-7588

This Truro real estate agency first opened its doors for business in 1937. A full-service brokerage with four Realtors, Duarte/Downey offers residential properties including single-family homes, cottages and condominiums in its primary market area of Truro and Wellfleet. The agency also features waterfront homes and land as well as rentals in the Truro area.

Truro Real Estate
Rt. 6 at Fisherman's Rd., Truro • 487-4225

Chuck Leigh founded this company eight

years ago and offers residential homes, condominiums and cottages as well as land and commercial sale properties in its primary market area of Wellfleet, Truro and Provincetown. Many of the properties are in and around the Cape Cod National Seashore. Truro Real Estate has three Realtors covering the lower Cape.

Harborside Realty

162 Commercial St., Provincetown • 487-4005, (800) 838-4005

This five-year-old agency handles properties in Provincetown — from residential homes and condominiums to guest houses and commercial properties. Realtor Len Bowen has been in the business for 25 years.

Golf Communities

If your idea of living well is rolling out of bed and right onto the first tee, you may be interested in one of the Cape's superlative golfing communities. These developments feature luxury homesites, some of which are built right alongside the property owners' private course. Most of the communities have clubhouses and other recreational facilities — swimming pools and tennis courts, for example — to appease the nongolfing members of the family.

Ballymeade

Rt. 151, North Falmouth • 457-4455

Situated on 934 acres of land, Ballymeade has permits for 257 housing units. The feeling of the property is New England country colonial with a contemporary Cape flair. The property's rolling hills permit distant waterviews and gorgeous sunsets. Ballymeade offers a challenging 18-hole golf course (see our Golf chapter), a large clubhouse, 10 tennis courts, a swimming pool and a restaurant.

The property includes duplex townhouses with wonderful views of Buzzards Bay and the golf course. Ballymeade is 6 miles from Falmouth and 7 miles from the Bourne Bridge. A lot of residents here commute to work in Boston. Among the favorable features are spacious grounds, a limited number of residences and the conservation area. Ballymeade has a building division and works with buyers on designs.

New Seabury Resort & Conference Center

155 Rock Landing Rd., New Seabury (Mashpee) • 477-9400, (800) 999-9033

New Seabury is a premier golfing and resort community with two championship courses (see our Golf chapter), including the Blue Course on Vineyard Sound and the challenging Green Course. The complex also boasts 16 outdoor tennis courts, walking and riding trails, 3 miles of beachfront and outstanding dining facilities in the area. The resort is about 3 miles from Mashpee Commons and abuts South Cape Beach and conservation land.

Condominiums here are referred to as villas, and three different communities are available. Beautifully situated on the water, Maushop, for example, is styled after a Nantucket village — crushed seashell paths and white picket fences — and consists of mostly two-bedroom villas. The Mews units have a contemporary New England style and are scattered among the golf courses. These villas on one or two floors are built on small lots that utilize the outdoor areas and maintain privacy. Tidewatch condominiums, in the original area New Seabury developed on the water, are like a hotel with a common area. The units have two and sometimes three bedrooms, and some are on three levels. Most are an easy

INSIDERS' TIP

The Cape Cod house was built by early settlers as an economical dwelling in terms of heating with its central chimney feeding many hearths throughout the house. Full Capes are distinguished by two windows on either side of the front door; three-quarter Capes have two windows to one side of the door and one to the other. A half Cape has only two windows to either the right or left of the door.

walk to the country club. Beautiful oceanfront house lots are available in a new 25-lot village called the Seaside, which is situated on the golf course. Some properties here have a pool and two-car garage.

Kings Way

Sales Office, Rt. 6A, Yarmouthport • 362-8800

Situated off Route 6A in Yarmouthport near the Yarmouth-Dennis line, Kingsway is a condominium community with an 18-hole executive-style golf course (see our Golf chapter), a clubhouse, tennis court, swimming pool, country store and meeting house. The townhomes range in size from 1,300 square feet to 1,800 square feet. All units have a minimum of two bedrooms, two bathrooms, a two-car garage and a full basement. Carriage homes range from 900 to 1,200 square feet and include two bedrooms, two baths, an attached one-car garage, a private courtyard entrance and a deck or patio overlooking the golf course. Out of the planned total of 450 units, more than half are presently occupied. Residents are predominantly retired. The community's builder is The Green Company, which started Kings Way in 1987.

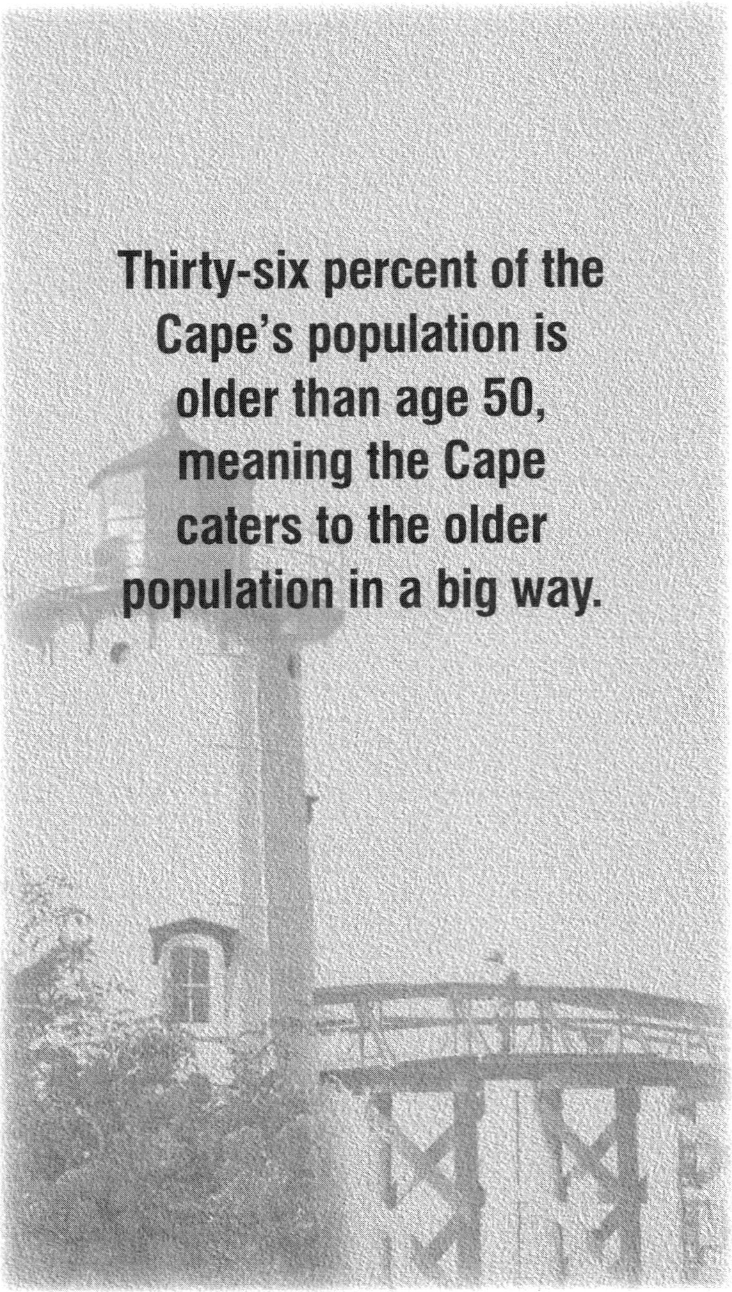

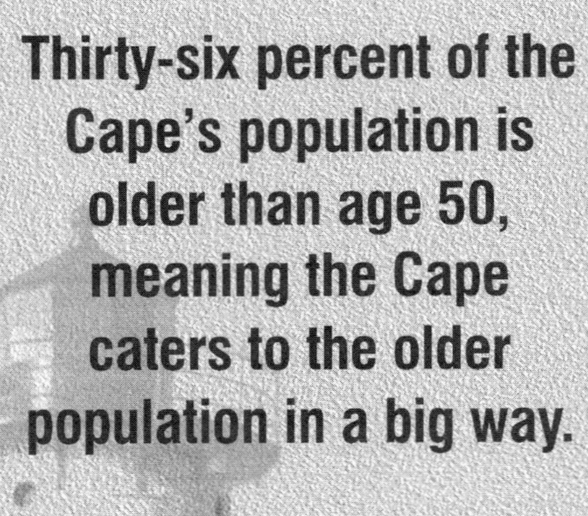

Thirty-six percent of the Cape's population is older than age 50, meaning the Cape caters to the older population in a big way.

Retirement

Many people dream of retiring to Cape Cod. The peninsula offers a serene quality of life, magnificently beautiful scenery, clean beaches with warm, comfortable waters, affordable living with lower real estate taxes, a temperate climate, dozens of golf courses that remain open all year long (weather permitting) and so many other one-of-a-kind attributes.

Those who appreciate history will enjoy the fact that Pilgrims helped to settle much of the Cape, and three towns (Sandwich, Barnstable and Yarmouth) date back to 1639. Those who admire natural beauty will enjoy the Cape Cod National Seashore that features mile after gorgeous mile of protected beaches. Those who enjoy the arts will enjoy the many galleries, museums and theaters sprinkled throughout the Cape's towns, not to mention the Cape Cod Symphony. Cape Cod truly has something to offer everyone.

Thirty-six percent of the Cape's population of 200,000 is older than age 50. As you can well imagine, that means the Cape caters to the older population in a big way. For instance, every town on the Cape has a council on aging designed to identify the needs of the older Cape population and then enact programs to satisfy those needs. Also, there are a number of assisted-living communities that provide the very best of both worlds — independent-living options coupled with healthcare and supportive services.

In this chapter, we offer information about resources and services for retirees as well as descriptions of retirement villages and nursing homes.

Agencies and Centers

You certainly won't ever be bored with all that the various Cape Cod councils on aging have to offer. Each council has put together a full docket of activities designed to keep older adults on the move. With councils operating in each town from Bourne to Provincetown, the Cape Cod Council on Aging provides programs specific to the particular needs of the local populations while offering basic cultural, social, health and well-being activities and information to improve the quality of a retiree's life.

You can learn a hobby, perhaps how to knit, quilt, sew, paint or even carve wood. You can learn good health management and have regular medical screenings for high blood pressure, diabetes, hearing and visual impairment and other physical and mental health concerns. You can take yoga classes. You can participate in good nutrition programs through home-delivered or on-site meals. Or you can participate in any of the councils' fun-packed activities such as dining clubs, cribbage matches, choral groups, bingo games, birthday parties, film festivals and daytrips.

The councils are open year round. Below is a brief summary of each agency, but we urge you to telephone the centers themselves to see if they provide the services you require. We have found that the majority of the centers have their own newsletters, so you may want to ask that they send you one so you can see for yourself what the center is all about.

Upper Cape

Bourne Council on Aging
239 Main St., Buzzards Bay • 759-0654

The Bourne council operates a food pantry and a nutrition center and provides counseling, social support, exercise clubs, art classes, and health and fitness clinics. The council runs bingo, cribbage, Scrabble and whist games while also offering a number of services from knife-sharpening to outreach programs. Transportation via minibus for shopping and medical appointments is also provided.

Sandwich Council on Aging

270 Quaker Meetinghouse Rd., East Sandwich • 888-4737

The Sandwich council provides a screening service through Benefit Access Screening, which helps to determine if senior citizens are eligible for the more than 70 benefits available. Some of these benefits include legal, financial, medical and recreational assistance as well as outreach counseling, elder services lunches, hearing tests, transportation to local stores, flu clinics and even foot care programs. Each New Year's Day the center hosts a community breakfast.

FYI

Unless otherwise noted, the area code for all phone numbers in this guide is 508.

Falmouth Council on Aging

300 Dillingham Ave., Falmouth • 540-0196

At the active Senior Citizen Center activities include dancercize, oil painting, quilting, bridge, chess and much more. Health clinics and health information and education are also provided. Eligible seniors receive home-delivered meals via the Meals on Wheels program, and elder transportation is available within the town of Falmouth.

Mashpee Council on Aging

500 Great Neck Rd., North Mashpee • 539-1440

This council, located at the Carol H. Jacobson Senior Center, offers a busy schedule of arts and crafts as well as physical activities. Seniors benefit from blood pressure clinics, flu shots, smoking cessation classes, chiropractic wellness workshops, outreach programs and sessions by support groups such as AA and Al-Anon. The center also offers insurance counseling and has a program that provides transportation to medical appointments and shopping.

Mid-Cape

Barnstable Council on Aging

198 South St., Hyannis • 790-6365

Seniors in the town of Barnstable can benefit from the wide array of services available to them at the Barnstable Council on Aging. Legal and financial consultation as well as tax assistance are provided. Seniors may receive Meals on Wheels, borrow medical equipment, receive flu shots or get blood pressure consultation, foot care advice and overall medical counseling. There are recreational and cultural programs and even a pot luck luncheon each month.

Yarmouth Council on Aging

528 Forest Rd., South Yarmouth • 394-7606

The Yarmouth Council offers health-related programs, including breast cancer screening and diabetic screening, pedicares and even the services of a psychotherapist. Their educational programs range from bank-statement balancing to computer classes. Recreational activities include duplicate bridge, Scrabble, beano and pool. Other services include legal assistance, the telephone lifeline and insurance advice.

Dennis Council on Aging

1045 Rt. 134, South Dennis • 385-5067

The Dennis Senior Citizens Center offers a host of benefits, including programs on financial management and income tax preparation, Meals on Wheels and even lunch on weekdays (reservations are necessary). The council sponsors programs and workshops on various topics such as medical issues. It also provides transportation for shopping and makes telephone calls to seniors who live alone. This center is networked with several illness-related support groups.

Lower Cape

Brewster Council on Aging

1673 Main St., Brewster • 896-2737

The council in Brewster offers an array of programs and services including home support, legal and financial aid, an outreach program, a sight-loss program, a senior dining program and support groups for those with arthritis and those mourning the death of a loved one. Seniors can have their blood pressure checked and receive flu shots. Recreation includes bridge, Scrabble, chess, swimming, art and a men's coffee club.

Harwich Council on Aging

728 Main St., Harwich • 430-7550

The list of services offered by the Harwich council seems endless. Blood pressure clinics, hearing clinics, outreach programs, health insurance counseling, legal advice as well as support groups for alcohol abuse and sight loss are all provided. Equipment (walkers, wheelchairs, etc.) is loaned free of charge. Volunteers provide seniors with rides to medical appointments. A noonday meal is provided at the Brewster council, and Harwich seniors are invited to join Brewster seniors for lunch.

Chatham Council on Aging

193 Stony Hill Rd., Chatham • 945-5190

The Chatham council's outreach program provides a mobile book service, health insurance counseling, tax preparation services, medical transportation, shut-in telephone reassurance services, flu and pneumonia clinics and free medical equipment. Special events include cooking classes and beginner's bridge while weekly activities include exercise classes and a walking club. Meal service is provided weekdays through Elder Services; reservations are required.

Orleans Council on Aging

150 Rock Harbor Rd., Orleans • 255-6333

This center offers classes in line dancing, bridge, bowling, watercolor painting, tennis and fitness, and a special program called Cameo in which participants have their life stories videotaped for themselves and future generations to enjoy. Movies are shown on Mondays while lunch is served at the center on Tuesday and Thursday; reservations for lunch must be made by calling the Nutrition Center at 255-9871 at least 24 hours in advance.

Eastham Council on Aging

1405 Nauset Rd., Eastham • 255-6164

Ongoing services at the Eastham center include computer classes, painting and craft classes, beano and open bridge. The travel club's day and overnight trips keep the seniors on the move (they're even working on putting together a trip to Eastham, England!). Through the AARP a "55 Alive" safe driving class is offered. A noon meal is provided every Monday and Wednesday; reservations are required. The center also is home to the Lower Cape Adult Day Care Center, which includes a full day's worth of programs.

Wellfleet Council on Aging

95 Lawrence Rd., Wellfleet • 349-2800

At the Wellfleet Council you can play cribbage, bridge and beano, take an art class or receive answers to your legal, insurance and tax questions. The council also provides personal and fire safety programs as well as support groups for people with cancer, heart problems, stroke and sight loss. Senior meals are served on Tuesdays; reservations must be made by calling 349-6325.

Truro Council on Aging

19 Town Hall Rd., Truro • 349-9525

This center offers many workshops and services, including blood pressure, foot care and flu shot clinics, insurance and tax counseling, fitness classes, financial assistance referrals and even a course designed to teach safe driving habits to seniors. Outreach touches on such topics as fuel assistance, emergency food distribution, health proxy services, transportation to medical appointments and services for the homebound. Meals on Wheels and emergency food distribution is also provided.

Provincetown Council on Aging

26 Alden St., Provincetown • 487-7080

The Provincetown Council keeps the seniors busy with yoga, oil painting, swimming, chair caning, bingo, Scrabble, aerobics and strength training. Hearing tests, massages and smoking cessation programs are also provided. Van transportation takes seniors to Hyannis on Monday, Orleans on Tuesday, to

INSIDERS' TIP

The Cape Cod Old Timers is a softball league for men older than the age of 55. There's also a 65 and older league as well as a league for seniors 75 plus.

the local A&P on Wednesday and to Wellfleet on Thursday. Senior dining is provided on Wednesdays at noon; reservations are required.

Retirement Communities

Retirement communities include three basic types — independent living, assisted living and independent living with some assistance.

Independent living is just what it sounds like. Seniors enjoy all the independence of living on their own but with the added advantages of being part of a community. Assisted living is a senior housing alternative that combines independent living with personalized support services. Healthcare needs are also included and programs are designed to cater to the senior's individual situation. Meanwhile, independent living with some assistance is somewhere between the two. It is for the senior who is largely self-sufficient, but requires some assistance from time to time. Below we've listed the retirement community options on Cape Cod.

Upper Cape

Heritage at Falmouth

140 Ter Heun Dr., Falmouth • 457-6400

Located on the grounds of Falmouth Hospital, Heritage is an assisted-living community offering 56 apartments including studios and one- and two-bedroom units complete with a private bath and kitchenette. All utilities and maintenance are provided, as are three daily meals, housekeeping, personal care, transportation and activities including social events, wellness classes and lectures. Opened in the fall of 1995, Heritage is owned by the Falmouth Hospital Foundation.

Woodbriar

339 Gifford St., Falmouth • 540-1600

Woodbriar, opened in 1976, has the distinction of being Cape Cod's first retirement community. It can accommodate approximately 120 residents and provides three levels of care: independent living, special care and assisted living. Residents can choose between a single room or a suite, both with private bath. Meals, which are included in the monthly charge, can be served in the senior's room or in the dining room. Also included in the monthly charge are all utilities and maid and linen services. The facility is adjacent to a golf course, has a swimming pool and offers daily planned activities such as movies, exercise groups and shopping trips.

Mid-Cape

Heatherwood at Kings Way

100 Heatherwood Dr., Yarmouthport • 362-9889, (800) 352-0365

Located at the beautiful condominium community King's Way, Heatherwood is certainly one of the Cape's premier retirement communities. It offers 115 one- and two-bedroom independent-living units as well as 14 assisted-living units. Amenities include a meal plan, housekeeping, maintenance, transportation, social activities and arts and crafts. The facilities include a greenhouse and resident storage areas. A doctor visits once a week.

Heatherwood also shares numerous amenities with Kings Way, including walking trails, tennis courts, swimming pools and of course, the challenging Kings Way golf course. (See our Golf chapter.) Surface and underground parking is plentiful, and each resident has a security and emergency response system.

Mayflower Place

579 Buck Island Rd., Yarmouth • 790-0200

This 10-year-old retirement community has 102 units as well as an on-site 72-bed skilled-nursing facility (see the Nursing Home section later in this chapter). The smallest unit (called the Chilton) has a kitchen, living room and bedroom and one and a half baths while

INSIDERS' TIP

For free information for the 50-plus crowd, check out *Prime Time*, a monthly publication of the *Cape Cod Times*.

Photo: Vince DeWitt, Cape Cod Times

Salty dogs share a view.

the largest (the Allerton) also has a dining room and two full baths totaling 884 square feet. The facility offers support services and a medical clinic staffed 24 hours a day by RNs and certified nurses aides.

Mayflower Place has an on-site library, post office, chapel, theater, dining room, two craft rooms, pub, greenhouse, beauty parlor, bank, game room, exercise room and an indoor swimming pool.

Thirwood Place

237 N. Main St., South Yarmouth • 398-8006, (800)248-5023

With a total of 186 units, this facility situated on 45 acres overlooking Flax Pond offers both assisted and independent living. The amenities at this impressive retirement community include an auditorium, swimming pool, dining room, arts and crafts room, post office, greenhouse and billiard room. Many services are provided including activities programs, transportation, a nurse who is available daily and emergency-trained personnel who are on hand around the clock. All meals, utilities, housekeeping and laundering is included in the monthly fee. Pets are welcome.

Lower Cape

Brewster Place

855 Harwich Rd., Brewster • 896-3252

This newly established assisted-living community provides 68 apartments, each with a kitchenette and private bath. Opened in November 1996, Brewster Place offers independence supported by 24-hour assistance and plenty of personal touches including a staff nurse. The monthly charge includes three meals a day, housekeeping, personal care needs, utilities and wellness programs including both physical and social activities. Transportation is also provided for local errands. Laundry facilities are on each floor. Brewster Place is next to Brewster Manor, in fact, the two buildings are connected (see the Nursing Home section of this chapter).

Harwich House

26 Pleasant Lake Ave., Harwich •432-5291, (800) 529-5291

Harwich House is near the junction of routes 124 and 39. This retirement community offers 18 one- or two-bedroom condominium units. Staff is available 24 hours a day. The facility provides a dining room where dinner is served for a nominal fee. The development's laundry facilities are shared. This independent-living facility as well as The Melrose and Chatham House are managed by Wise Properties.

The Melrose

601 Main St., Harwichport • 430-7496, (800) 529-5291

Opened in August l996, The Melrose is built on the same site as the popular Melrose Supper Club. In fact, part of the original building's exterior has been incorporated into the new 29-unit housing complex. All two-bedroom apartments feature full kitchens and private laundry rooms. Meals are also provided at a nominal charge in the common dining room. The monthly service fee includes 24-hour assistance. The independent-living facility, which is managed by Wise Properties, is handicapped-accessible and provides an elevator.

Chatham House

33 Cross St., Chatham •945-2239, (800) 529-5291

This 10-unit cooperative apartment complex is set in the bustling yet beautiful downtown Chatham. Within walking distance are many shops, restaurants, churches, and the impressive Eldredge Library. The one-bedroom apartments share laundry facilities. Meals are served in a common dining room. Chatham House is fully handicapped accessible and is managed by Wise Properties.

Winstead Retirement Center

328 Bank St., Harwich • 432-4586

Winstead offers its senior residents a choice of accommodations: a private room and bath, a studio apartment with bath and kitchenette or a full one-bedroom apartment. Residents are offered independent and assisted living as well as independent living with some assistance. The monthly fee includes three meals per day and local transportation. This facility also provides an elder day care center five days a week. The daily rate for day care (which in 1996 was $40) includes three meals, coffee hour, a snack as well as a full list of activities.

Orleans Convalescent and Retirement Center

60 Daley Terrace, Orleans • 255-2328

This Orleans retirement center, built in 1969, was one of the early pioneers providing supportive living concepts for older adults. It has 19 apartments (with garages and security systems) ranging in size from studios to two-bedroom units. The evening meal, which can be served either in the common dining room or in the privacy of the individual apartments, is included in the monthly fees, as are housekeeping and laundry services. This facility also offers a 33-bed private skilled-nursing facility with 24-hour medical coverage (see the Nursing Home section of this chapter).

Nursing Homes

Nursing homes are long-term care facilities that can be utilized for short-term care as well. Twenty-four hour a day skilled-nursing care is provided as well as various services including rehabilitation and activities.

Many people may think of nursing homes as facilities where seniors go to live out the rest of their years under the care and supervision of nurses and nurses aides. For some seniors this is true. Yet, nursing homes also provide valuable short-term care for seniors recovering from an illness or surgery. In these cases, the nursing home offers recuperative services for those that don't require the level of care or the cost of a hospital. Below is a list of many of the nursing homes found on the Cape.

Upper Cape

Cape Cod Nursing & Retirement Center

Lewis Point Rd., Buzzards Bay • 759-5753

This nursing home is housed in three buildings, one of which was built in 1890. In the 1950s it became a home for elderly women, and today it is a full-service nursing home with 99 beds. Services include recreational, physical, occupational and speech therapy. All insurances are accepted (i.e., Medicare, Medicaid and private insurance).

Bourne Manor

146 MacArthur Blvd., Bourne • 759-8880

Now in its ninth year, the Bourne Manor has 142 beds and accepts all types of insurance. This facility offers short- and long-term rehabilitation, including physical, occupational and speech therapy.

Cape Heritage Nursing & Rehabilitation Center

37 Rt. 6A, Sandwich • 888-8222

This 123-bed facility, opened in 1987, provides clinical services, including skilled nursing, long-term care and comprehensive physical, occupational, speech, recreational and respiratory therapy. Wound care and IV therapy are also provided. Facilities include a lovely dining room and common rooms. The activities department plans many outings and in-house activities. It accepts all types of insurance.

Center for Optimum Care of Falmouth

359 Jones Rd., Falmouth • 457-9000

Known as the Freedom Crest of Falmouth Nursing Care Center for 8 years, this center changed its name when it changed hands in 1995. This 120-bed nursing home facility offers full rehabilitation services as well as an Alzheimer's disease unit. All insurances are accepted.

Falmouth Nursing Home

545 Main St., North Falmouth • 548-3800

Just over a quarter-century old, the 121-bed Falmouth Nursing Home offers full in-house rehabilitation services, including physical, occupational and speech therapy. This facility also has an Alzheimer's disease and dementia unit. All insurances are welcome.

JML Care Center

184 Ter Heun Dr., Falmouth • 457-4621

This facility is affiliated with Cape Cod Healthcare Inc., a major healthcare provider on the Cape. JML's services include pain and diabetes management, oncology and IV therapy. Rehabilitation services include a range of physical and occupational therapy and a speech-language program. Adult day care is provided on site. The center has an attractive dining room and a spacious outdoor patio. JML Care accepts all types of insurance.

The Royal Megansett

209 County Rd., North Falmouth • 563-5913

This 78-bed facility offers water views as well as skilled nursing and rehabilitation services. Included in these services are physical, occupational and speech therapy as well as hearing and nutritional services and respite care for short-term needs. Skilled and intermediary nursing care is also provided. There are daily activities and outings for residents. Established as a nursing home in 1954, this facility has sweeping views of Buzzards Bay (in fact the dining room itself has beautiful water views). There are common rooms and an activity room on each floor.

INSIDERS' TIP

During the late 18th century "Sleepy" John Sears was an East Dennis sea captain who, after a long career, retired from the sea to experiment with the distillation of salt. Although his East Dennis neighbors ridiculed his backyard hobby early on, calling it "Sears' Folly," he eventually succeeded in harvesting salt from sea water. As a result, an entire industry was born. Salt works were erected all across the Cape bringing fortunes to their owners.

Mid-Cape

Cape Regency Nursing & Rehabilitation Center

120 S. Main St., Centerville • 778-1835

This attractive 120-bed facility, now in its 15th year, offers comprehensive nursing services and rehabilitation services, including physical, occupational, recreational and speech therapy as well as respiratory therapy and subacute care. Cape Regency accepts all insurances.

Mayflower Place

579 Buck Island Rd., Yarmouth • 790-0200

A 70-bed nursing home, this facility is on the grounds of the Mayflower Place retirement community (see Retirement Communities earlier in this chapter). The nursing home provides 24-hour skilled nursing care and offers physical, occupational and recreational therapy. All insurances are accepted.

Windsor Nursing Home

265 North Main St., South Yarmouth • 394-3514

This 120-bed nursing home facility is right next to Thirwood Place retirement community, although the two are not related in any way other than being friendly neighbors. Windsor provides its residents with physical, occupational, recreational and speech therapy as well as dental and podiatry services. All insurances are welcome.

Eagle Pond Nursing Home

One Love Ln., South Dennis • 385-6034

In a tranquil, wooded section of South Dennis far removed from the well-traveled routes is the Eagle Pond Nursing Home, a 142-bed long- and short-term nursing facility. Besides offering physical, occupational and speech therapy, Eagle Pond's staff also offers respiratory therapy and is skilled in dealing with those seniors with Alzheimer's disease. All insurance types are taken at Eagle Pond.

Lower Cape

Brewster Manor

873 Harwich Rd., Brewster • 896-7046

This multilevel skilled-nursing facility maintains 173 beds, providing short-term rehabilitation services and extended care including physical, occupational, recreational and speech therapy. Brewster Manor is attached to Brewster Place, a new retirement complex that opened in 1996 offering assisted living apartments (see the Retirement Communities section of this chapter). All types of insurances are accepted at Brewster Manor.

Cranberry Pointe at Harwich

111 Headwaters Dr., Harwich • 430-1717

This 126-bed skilled-nursing facility is situated among the cranberry bogs of Harwich, hence its name. It is a two-story complex offering such amenities as a beauty salon, a gift shop and an ice cream parlor. Cranberry Pointe offers complete rehabilitative services. It accepts all types of insurance plans.

Liberty Commons Nursing Home

390 Orleans Rd., North Chatham • 945-4611, (800) 770-7100

Liberty Commons is a 132-bed facility that has various types of care available, from short-term rehabilitation to a long-term Alzheimer's secure unit. This complex's dining room is in a beautiful atrium, complete with safe terraces upon which residents can dine while savoring the sights of Pleasant Bay. Liberty Commons accepts all types of insurances.

Orleans Convalescent Home

Rt. 28 and Daley Ter., Orleans • 255-2328

This two-year-old Orleans nursing home has 50 beds and is also the site of the Orleans Retirement Center (see Retirement Centers section). It provides physical, speech and occupational therapy and accepts private insurance.

INSIDERS' TIP

In the town of Dennis, South Dennis is actually north of both West Dennis and Dennisport. In the town of Chatham, West Chatham is really east of South Chatham.

Cape End Manor

100 Alden St., Provincetown • 487-7090

This 60-bed, skilled-nursing facility is the only municipality-owned and -operated facility on the Cape. It offers complete rehabilitation services to its residents, many of whom have included local writers, chefs, painters, historians, and, of course, fishermen. Cape End Manor accepts all types of insurances.

Rest Homes

Designed for those seniors who do not require nursing services on a regular basis, rest homes are an alternative to nursing homes and retirement communities, providing a less expensive long-term care option. Periodic medical services are provided as well as 24-hour supervision and three meals a day.

Upper Cape

Fraser Rest Home

125 Main St., Sandwich • 888-0880

A 10-room rest home along historic Main Street in Sandwich, Fraser offers round-the-clock nurse's aide service. There is a registered nurse on staff as well as an activities director. Also provided are mental health and community support programs. This Sandwich home is associated with the Fraser Rest Homes in Hyannis and Falmouth. All types of insurance are accepted.

Fraser Rest Home

Pine St., Falmouth • 563-3522

This 23-bed facility has been a rest home for a half-century. It offers all the services that the Sandwich Fraser Rest Homes provides.

Mid-Cape

Fraser Rest Home

349 Sea St., Hyannis • 775-4881

This 35-year-old, 35-bed rest home, located on quiet Sea Street in Hyannis, provides all the same services as the Fraser Rest Homes in Falmouth and Sandwich.

Lower Cape

Rosewood Manor

671 Main St., Harwich • 432-0135

The Cape Cod cottage-style Rosewood Manor is termed a "bridge facility," bridging the gap between assisted living and long-term care. This facility, complete with a fireplace in the living room and beautiful gardens out of doors, has accommodations for 33 residents and offers an around-the-clock nursing staff. It provides residents with respite, hospice and long-term care.

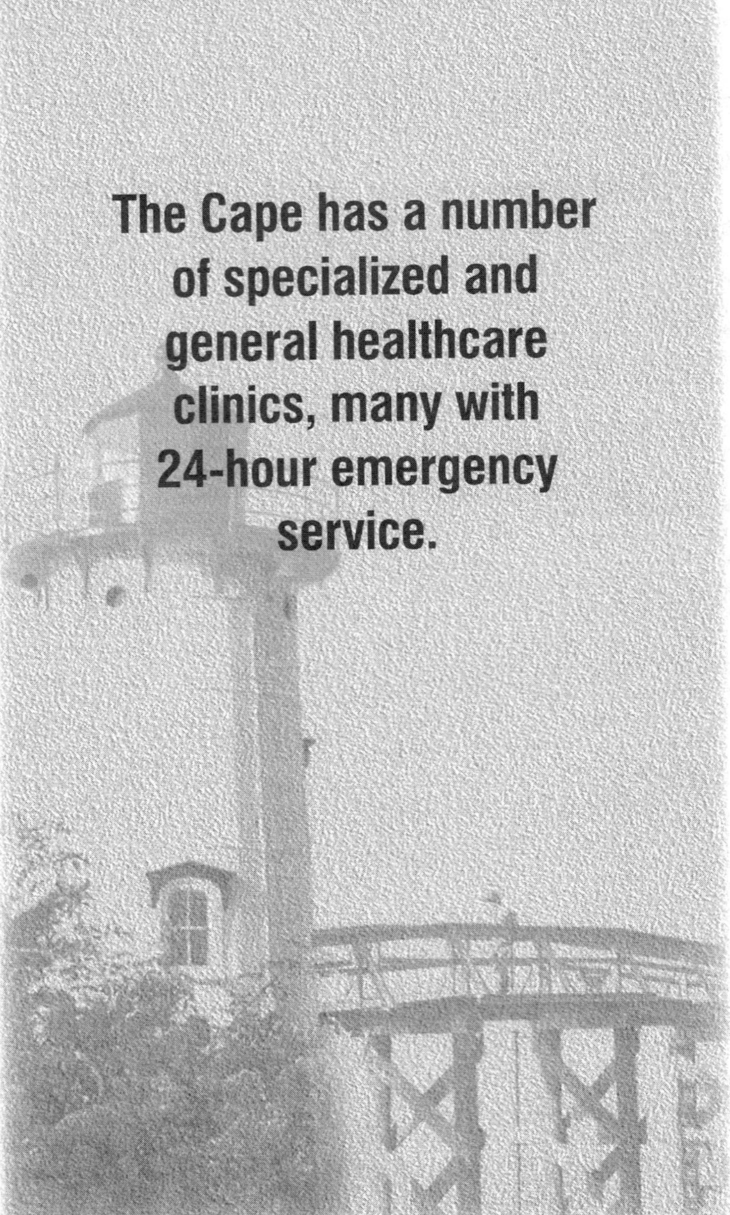
The Cape has a number
of specialized and
general healthcare
clinics, many with
24-hour emergency
service.

Healthcare

Healthcare is of primary importance to Cape Codders. Many of us have chosen to live here because of life-quality issues, and good health is one of them. We are blessed with a number of facilities that help us stay healthy; more and more of those facilities have been able to offer us sophisticated healthcare services that once required a trip to Boston. Those who live and work here are also concerned with being able to meet the healthcare needs of visitors. For that reason, rescue units in every town are well-equipped and well-prepared, with extra staff on hand or on call in the busy summer months. Medical clinics as well as many family practices accept walk-in patients.

The Cape's two hospitals joined forces in June of 1996 in order to offer better coordination of care and more services. Cape Cod Hospital and Falmouth Hospital, along with 22 healthcare providers already included in the two hospital systems, are now affiliated under the ownership of a parent corporation known as Cape Cod Healthcare Inc. In addition, there are a number of specialized and general healthcare clinics, many with 24-hour emergency service. Many of them are listed in this chapter.

If you have a major medical emergency, dial **911** to reach a rescue unit. Another valuable resource is Ask-A-Nurse, (800) 544-2424, which is available 24 hours a day and provides accurate answers to healthcare questions.

Hospitals

Upper Cape

Falmouth Hospital
100 Ter Heun Dr., Falmouth • 548-5300

Falmouth Hospital is an 84-bed facility that offers an excellent full-time emergency room and an intensive care unit, maternity and pediatric units, occupational and physical therapy, older adult healthcare services and a full range of diagnostic testing, including MRI, CAT scan, ultrasound, mammography and nuclear medicine. The hospital is situated at the center of a large medical complex that includes the JML Care Center, a 56-bed assisted-living facility known as Heritage at Falmouth and private medical offices. The hospital's new wing, completed in May 1996, houses a maternity department and a large surgical center that specializes in outpatient services. Also included in the new wing is the Women's Health Resource Center, which offers educational services, a library and a computerized data base.

Falmouth Hospital has 100 affiliated physicians in all major specialities, and operates four medical offices in the area: the John Lewis Medical Center on Route 130 in Sandwich, 888-2882; Mashpee Medical Associates, 19 Steeple Road, Mashpee, 477-4400; Bourne Medical Associates, 120 Clay Pond Road, Bourne, 759-7117; and Women's Health Group of Upper Cape Cod, 200 Jones Road, Falmouth, 548-4865.

Affiliated with the hospital, The Visiting Nurse Association of Upper Cape Cod offers Care on Call, 548-5577, a private-duty nursing service; two adult day healthcare centers in Sandwich; child care and maternal and child home healthcare. For information on any of the VNA's services call 548-0411. For a free courtesy bus ride to the hospital call (800) 352-7155. Also affiliated with the Hospital, and operated by Cape Cod Healthcare Inc., is the JML Care Center, which offers nursing-home care, short-term rehabilitation service and an adult day health program.

Mid-Cape

Cape Cod Hospital

27 Park St., Hyannis • 771-1800

This is a large medical complex of more than 12 buildings offering 24-hour medical care with on-call specialty consultation. With 258 beds and nearly 250 affiliated physicians, it is the largest surgical center on the Cape and Islands and the only one with an inpatient/outpatient psychiatric center. It is a regional center for cancer and radiation treatment and features a new emergency wing completed two years ago, a new maternity unit done in 1996 and a new cardiac catherization lab — a service that patients used to have to travel to Boston for.

The family-care assisted-living program allows senior citizens and HIV patients to stay at home during treatment. The hospital also has short-and long-term rehabilitative care, and has two off-site nursing homes, The Manor and The Pavillion, for extended care.

The Spaulding Cape Cod Hospital Rehabilitation Center and Sports Medicine Complex here is an outpatient facility for physical and occupational rehabilitation. An extensive new radiation department provides MRI testing. The hospital has a large surgical day-care center and numerous support groups for bereavement, cancer, maternity bereavement, Weight Watchers, smoking cessation and domestic violence. Its Young At Heart senior fitness program has been very successful.

FYI

Unless otherwise noted, the area code for all phone numbers in this guide is 508.

Clinics

Upper Cape

Bourne Health Care

304 Main St., Buzzards Bay • 759-5731

Three hospitals (Falmouth and two off-Cape in Wareham and Plymouth) are within 20 minutes' drive of this year-round walk-in clinic, and a physician is on call at all times. Medical services include minor surgical procedures, lab and x-ray, immunizations and allergy injections. Major insurance and Medicare are accepted. The office is open Monday through Friday from 8:30 AM to 5 PM and on Saturday from 9 AM to 4 PM. It is closed on Sunday.

The Rehabilitation Hospital for the Cape and Islands

off Rt. 6, Exit 3, East Sandwich • 833-4000

A new independently owned hospital, The Rehabilitation Hospital offers comprehensive rehab treatment for adult inpatients and adult and child outpatients. It has 60 beds and a staff of more than 150. Resources include a therapeutic pool, a home-activities apartment, specialized evaluations (including hearing) and orthotics and prosthetics clinics. The hospital provides treatment for a variety of conditions from amputation to work-related and sports injuries as well as for complex medical conditions such as joint replacement surgery, neurological and chronic pain, spinal cord and brain injuries and stroke.

Mashpee Family Medicine

Summerfield Park, 800 Falmouth Rd. (Rt. 28), Mashpee • 477-4282

This family practice sees patients of all ages, from infants to centenarians. Open from 8 AM to 5 PM Monday through Friday, and 9 AM to 1 PM on Saturdays, the practice offers walk-in care between 9 and 11 AM and 1 to 3 PM. Offering both family and urgent care, Mashpee Family Medicine accepts most insurance plans, including Pilgrim, Prucare, HMO Blue, HCVM and PHCS. The office prides itself on offering same-day care.

Mid-Cape

Cape Cod Breast Evaluation Center

off Lewis Bay Rd., Hyannis • 771-4708

Patients can obtain a mammogram or ultrasound in the office, have a physical exam and receive results the same day. Although appointments are generally scheduled well in advance, there are generally a few open slots at this year-round facility. The office is open from Monday through Friday from 9 AM to 5 PM.

Health Stop of Hyannis

Capetown Plaza, Rt. 132, Hyannis • 771-7520

You can see a physician by appointment or on a walk-in basis here any day of the year. The hours are 8 AM to 8 PM Monday through Friday, 9 AM to 5 PM on Saturday and 11 AM to 5 PM Sunday.

Mid-Cape Medical Center

355 Rt. 28, Hyannis • 771-4092

Open since 1981 for daily year-round healthcare, this walk-in center has on-duty physicians and provides medical, lab and x-ray service. It does immunizations for patients 12 and older, PAP smears and gynecological exams, and routine physicals. The center also treats minor injuries, such as cuts, abrasions, lacerations and simple fractures. The center, which is about a mile from Cape Cod Hospital, accepts most types of insurance. It opens at 8 AM every day and stays open until 7:45 PM Monday through Thursday, 4:30 PM Friday and Saturday and 1 PM Sunday. In most cases, you do not need an appointment.

Cape Cod Artificial Kidney Center

241 Willow St., Yarmouthport • 362-4535

This is a year-round, out-patient hemodialysis unit. It does not usually have a waiting list. Hours are Monday through Saturday 8 AM to 4:30 PM.

Cape Cod Medical Center

434 Rt. I34, Dennis • 394-7113

This full-service facility with two attending physicians welcomes walk-in patients. The center accepts most insurances and credit cards. In the winter, the center is open Monday through Friday, 8:30 AM to 5:30 PM; Saturday, 9 AM to 3 PM. In summer, the center is also open on Sundays from 8:30 AM to 2 PM.

Lower Cape

Medicenter Five

525 Long Pond Dr., Harwich • 432-4100

Local residents and visitors depend on this not-for-profit medical center that provides comprehensive care for everything from fractures to hives. In the winter, Medicenter Five is open Monday through Friday 8 AM to 5 PM and Sat-

INSIDERS' TIP

While you're packing for your vacation, include copies of your health insurance plan and prescriptions. You'll have the information on hand should you need it.

Who To Call In An Emergency

Emergency	**911**
Battering/Physical Abuse of Women (Independence House)	**428-4720**
Child Abuse (Department of Social Service)	**(800) 792-5200**
Disabled Persons Abuse	**(800) 426-9009**
Drug Abuse and Crisis Intervention	**(800) 234-0246**
Drug and Alcohol Abuse Hotline	**(800) 252-6465**
Elder Abuse Hotline	**(800) 992-2275**
Emergency Mental Health Services	**778-4627, 778-4628**
Helping Our Women (HOW)	**487-HELP**
Missing Children Hotline	**(800) 843-5678**
Parental Stress Line	**(800) 632-8188**
Poison Hotline	**(800) 682-9211**
Rape Crisis Line	**428-4720**
Runaway Hotline	**(800) 231-6946**
Samaritans Suicide Prevention:	
Cape-wide	**(800) 893-9900**
Falmouth	**548-8900**
Buzzards Bay	**759-2828**
Barnstable	**375-0020**

urday 8 AM to 1 PM. In the summer, weekend hours change to Saturday from 8 AM to 6 PM and Sunday noon to 5 PM. The center accepts most insurances and major credit cards.

Orleans Medical Center
225 Rt. 6A at Bayberry Sq., Orleans • 255-9577

Established in 1984, this center offers walk-in attention for urgent medical needs. It is open all year Monday through Friday from 8 AM to 4 PM. In July and August, the center is also open Saturday from 8 AM to noon. It accepts some insurance plans and MasterCard and Visa.

Outer Cape Health Services
Rt. 6 at Briar Ln., Wellfleet • 349-3131

Outer Cape Health Services offers a full range of services for acute and chronic medical conditions. It has its own lab and x-ray facility, and a team of physicians, nurse practitioners, physician assistants and nurses. Walk-in care is available on a first-come, first-served basis. The center accepts most insurances and credit cards and sliding-scale payments. Winter hours are 8 AM to 5 PM Monday through Friday, plus extended evening hours until 8 PM on Wednesday and Friday. In summer, it is also open Saturday and Sunday from 9 AM to 5 PM.

Outer Cape Health Services
49 Harry Kemp Way, Provincetown • 487-9395

The coverage here is the same as at the Wellfleet center. Winter hours are 8 AM to 5 PM Monday through Friday, with evening hours until 8 PM on Tuesday and Thursday, and 9 AM to noon on Saturday. Summer hours are the same except Saturdays, when the facility stays open until 1 PM.

Alternative Healthcare Practitioners

The Cape is home to a large number of chiropractors as well as other alternative healthcare practitioners, including acupuncturists, massage therapists and nutritionists. What draws many people to these practitioners is that their focus is on health and prevention, rather than the treatment of illness (though they do that too). We've listed just a few; check your local phone book for more.

Upper Cape

Holistic Health Associates
68 Tupper Rd., Sandwich • 833-0433

This center offers chiropractic treatment, massage, reiki, nutritional counseling, hypnotherapy, acupuncture, acupressure and vibrational sound therapy (music designed for certain energy centers of the body). The backbone of the center is Back In Motion Chiropractic, where Dr. Larry Shell uses a variety of chiropractic techniques and therapeutic exercise. He also has an office at Sportside Health Club, 888-7900, in Sandwich. Holistic Health Associates is open 9 AM to 5 PM Monday through Friday, and 9 AM to noon on Saturday. Appointments are needed.

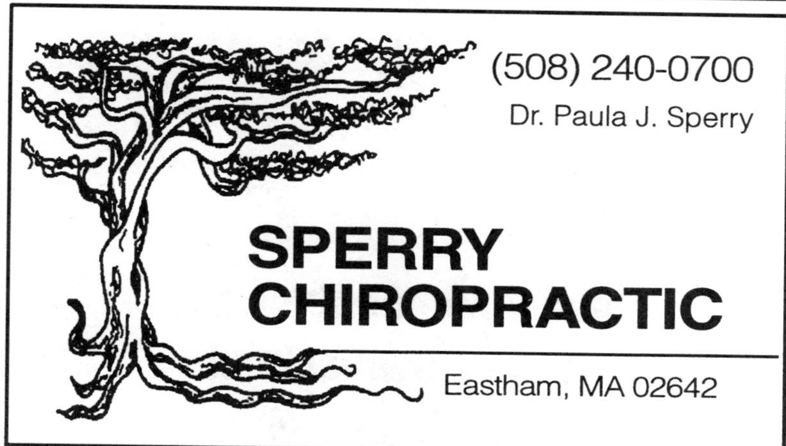

Mid-Cape

Great Marsh Chiropractic
1049 Main St. (Rt. 6A), West Barnstable • 362-4533

Great Marsh has two staff chiropractors, Dr. Christian Smith and Dr. John Dorris, along with a massage therapist who is on hand during office hours. The center is open Monday to Friday, with evening hours on Thursday.

Lower Cape

Sperry Chiropractic
Rt. 6, Eastham • 240-0700

"Don't let a bad back spoil your vacation," says Dr. Paula Sperry, who has been treating residents and visitors on the Lower Cape for more than a decade. And she treats more than bad backs: bring your neck aches and headaches to her office, just north of the Orleans-Eastham rotary. The office is open Monday through Friday, with evening hours on Monday, Wednesday and Friday, and is also open Saturdays in summer.

Off-Cape Area Hospitals

Jordan Hospital
275 Sandwich St., Plymouth • 746-2000

A growing hospital in Plymouth, Jordan Hospital offers radiation therapy, 12 LDR (labor/delivery/recovery) rooms, a newly renovated emergency room, a new rehabilitation services department and a new transitional-care unit. Imaging processes here include x-ray, mammography, MRI and CAT scan; the hospital also has an extensive cancer center for radiation and chemotherapy and a cardiac care unit.

A community health-education department offers classes to the public on CPR, First Aid, women's health and smoking cessation (some classes require a fee, others are free). The hospital supports a large number of help groups, from infant loss to parenting and cancer support.

Tobey Hospital
43 High St., Wareham • 295-0880

This is an 89-bed acute-care hospital that offers a full range of inpatient and outpatient care and services, including a 24-hour emergency room, extensive medical and surgical care, maternity care, rehabilitation and diagnostic and cardiac testing. The hospital has a staff oncologist, and all staff physicians are emergency-care specialists. The hospital is about 10 minutes from the Bourne Bridge.

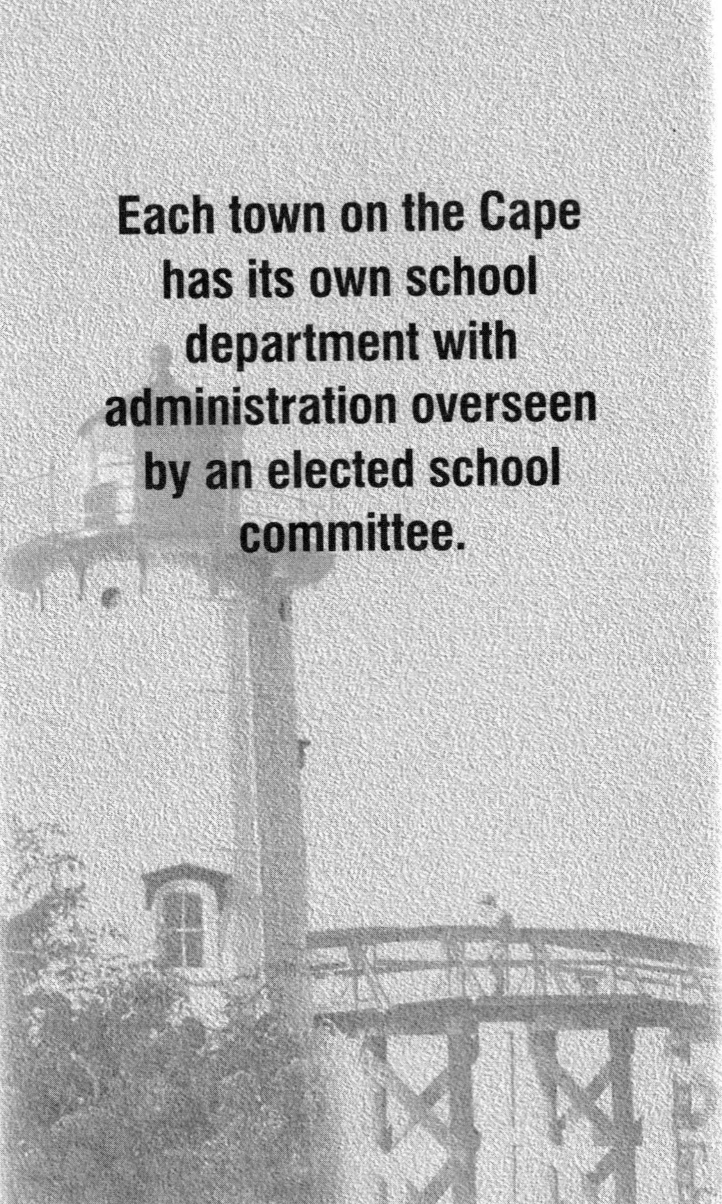

Each town on the Cape has its own school department with administration overseen by an elected school committee.

Education and Child Care

Cape Codders of all ages find plenty of educational opportunities here, from career training to enrichment courses. To start with, the Cape has excellent public schools that prepare students to move on to colleges anywhere in the United States, including Ivy League schools and top-ranked state and private schools. There are two private schools at the high-school level and two technical schools. Several colleges offer extension courses on the Cape, and Cape Cod Community College in Barnstable has ties to the University of Massachusetts at Dartmouth.

Just about every town on the Cape offers enrichment classes for adults, and exciting nondegree programs are available for senior citizens, including the Academy for Lifelong Learning, 362-2131; Wisdom Institute, 775-1384; Lifetime Learning Program, 225-2792; and Elderhostel, (617) 426-8056. Community schools programs in most towns provide all ages with academic and recreational opportunities. The arts are strong and valued on the Cape, and schools emphasize visual arts, theater and writing. And, befitting the region's maritime tradition, the Cape has two educational programs dedicated to the sea: the Massachusetts Maritime Academy in Buzzards Bay and the SEA Semester offered at Woods Hole.

For the littlest learners, there are a number of preschool and child care centers. We'll begin with a rundown on the Cape's public schools, then move on to private schools, preschools and child care centers.

Public Schools

Each town on the Cape has its own school department with administration overseen by an elected school committee. The Cape's two regional school systems (Dennis-Yarmouth and Nauset) have both regional and local school committees and all schools now have school advisory councils. Many schools now offer after-school programs so that children whose parents are still working in the afternoon don't have to go home to an empty house. Some public schools, such as Barnstable, also offer preschool programs, but most preschools are operated privately; see the end of this chapter for information on preschools and child care.

Bourne has six schools, including one high school, two middle schools and three elementary schools, serving a student population of 2,500. Three of the schools are on the Massachusetts Military Reservation, one is in Sagamore and the rest are in Bourne.

Falmouth's school system serves 5,218 students in seven schools — five elementary, one middle and one high school.

Mashpee's tremendous residential growth in recent years increased school population to 1,621 students in early 1997 and required a new building. The town is phasing in full-grade use of the new high school that opened in the fall of 1996 to allow students who began their high school education in neighboring Falmouth (about 300 Mashpee students had attended Falmouth High School before construction of the new high school in Mashpee) to graduate from the same high school. The Coombs School is for preschool through grade 6, and the relatively new Quashnet school serves kindergarten through grade 6 in a school-within-a-school format.

Sandwich has a public high school built in 1975 and three schools for kindergarten through grade 8 in the village, East Sandwich and Forestdale. One of the two fastest-growing towns in the state in recent years (Mashpee heads the list), Sandwich schools are still considered crowded despite building two new schools in recent years. With 3,702 students enrolled as of early 1997, the town has been considering whether to build another school. The high school is a focus for many activities in the community, including night classes and swimming programs operated by the Sandwich Community School; call 888-5300 for information.

The Upper Cape is also home to a technical school that serves 500 students in grades 9 through 12 and at the postsecondary level. Upper Cape Cod Regional Technical School, located on Sandwich Road in Bourne, also accepts students from outside the Upper Cape area on a tuition basis. The LPN (licensed practical nurse) program graduates about 30 students a year. The high school offers instruction subjects as diverse as carpentry, cosmetology and culinary arts, among many others.

In the Mid-Cape area is the largest school system on the Cape — naturally located in the largest, most populated town. The Barnstable School System has more than 7,000 students in 13 schools, including a large high school.

Serving both Yarmouth and Dennis is the Dennis-Yarmouth Regional School District with a total enrollment of 4,509 students in eight schools. The regional high school on Station Avenue in Yarmouth has 1,148 students from both towns, each of which have their own middle and elementary schools. The high school, which has 1,152 students, is the site of most classes in the adult education program.

In the Lower Cape, Chatham operates three schools, Depot Road School (kindergarten and grade 1), Main Street School (grades 2 through 6) and the Chatham Junior and Senior High School. As of early 1997, the town's enrollment stood at 354 students in prekindergarten through grade 6, and 303 students in grades 7 through 12. The school system offers adult education courses three times a year (contact Beth Eldredge, 945-0133, Monday through Friday, after 3:30 PM). Harwich schools serve 627 children in preschool through grade 4 at Harwich Elementary School, 460 students in grades 5 through 8 at Harwich Middle School and 400 students in grades 9 through 12 at Harwich High School. Adult education courses are offered in the fall and winter (contact Millie Winston at 432-2166 for more information). Harwich is also home to Cape Cod Regional Technical School, which has an enrollment of more than 500 students from Mashpee to Provincetown. The students alternate between attending technical and academic classes, and earn both high school diplomas and certification in such fields as electrical engineering, plumbing, auto maintenance, computer technology, horticulture, cosmetology and graphic arts. One of only two technical schools on the Cape, Cape Cod Tech has become so sought after that it has had to turn students away in recent years.

FYI

Unless otherwise noted, the area code for all phone numbers in this guide is 508.

Nauset Regional School District includes the towns of Brewster, Orleans, Eastham and Wellfleet. Each has its own local elementary school. Brewster, which has seen tremendous growth in the last decade, now has two schools, Brewster Elementary School and the new Eddy Elementary School, which opened in the spring of 1997. Together they serve an enrollment of 737 students in kindergarten through grade 5. Orleans Elementary School has 338 students in kindergarten through grade 5, Eastham has 358 and Wellfleet Elementary is the district's smallest school with 181 students. Students from all four towns attend Nauset Regional Middle School in Orleans, which has an enrollment of 693 students in grades 6, 7 and 8, and Nauset Regional High School in Eastham, which in 1996 was renovated and expanded to serve a student population of about 950 in grades 9 through 12. Adult continuing education courses are held at the middle school three times a year; for information call Kelly Bigos at 255 -4300.

The Lighthouse Charter School in Orleans is an independent public school with open enrollment for grades 6 through 8. The only one of its kind on the Cape, it was formed under the state's Education Reform Act and opened in September 1995 as one of a handful of experimental public schools across the Commonwealth. With a philosophy based on the developmental progress of individual students, the school has an enrollment of 162. Tuition is free; however, students must meet admission requirements, and preference is given to students living in Orleans and the Nauset District.

Truro has no middle or high school of its own, but has an excellent elementary school. Truro Central School has 168 students in preschool through grade 6. Older students attend either Nauset Regional Middle School and then Nauset Regional High School or Provincetown Junior and Senior High School.

Provincetown's school system is comprised of two schools. Veteran's Memorial Elementary School serves 179 students from preschool through grade 6, and Provincetown Junior and Senior High School has 178 students in grades 7 through 12—some of whom, as explained above, come from neighboring Truro. The high school has its own student-produced radio program that airs on WOMR (92.1 FM).

Public School Phone Numbers:

Bourne School Department	**759-0660**
Falmouth School Department	**548-0151**
Mashpee School Department	**539-1500**
Sandwich School Department	**888-1054**
Upper Cape Cod Regional Technical School	**563-5515**
Barnstable School Department	**790-6440**
Dennis-Yarmouth Regional School District	**398-7600**
Chatham Public Schools	**945-5130**
Harwich School Department	**430-7200**
Cape Cod Regional Technical High School	**432-4500**
Nauset Regional School District	**255-8800**
Lighthouse Charter School	**240-2800**
Truro Central School	**487-1558**
Provincetown Schools	**487-5000**

Private Schools

Upper Cape

Falmouth Academy
7 Highfield Dr., Falmouth • 457-9696

A college preparatory school with 190 students, the Academy provides a core curriculum (science, math, English, history and a foreign language) for grades 7 through 12, plus an inclusive athletic program and numerous elective courses, including chamber orchestra, volunteer work and boating. Situated on the beautiful Beebe Woods property donated to the town by the late Josiah Lilly of Lilly Drug Company, the school has an aggressive financial aid program; nearly 40 percent of the students receive some type of financial aid.

Mid-Cape

Cape Cod Academy
50 Osterville-W. Barnstable Rd., Osterville • 428-5400

In its 21st year in 1997, this private school has an enrollment of 250 students from kindergarten through 12th grade. Students come from as far away as Wellfleet and Duxbury. The student/teacher ratio is 7-to-1, and the average class size is 13 to 14 students. According to John Potter, director of admissions, 100 percent of the students go on to college. Sports, arts, computer science for all grades, advanced placement courses and foreign languages are areas of emphasis. The school, which recently added a new student activity center with a gymnasium, also has a strong financial aid program.

Trinity School of Cape Cod
10 Carter Rd., Yarmouth • 394-4118

Opened in 1967, this interdenominational Christian education school has about 110 students in preschool through grade 9. The curriculum is traditional and Bible-based, according to new headmaster Tom Hoffrage. French is taught in grades 3 through 9, and writing skills are emphasized in every grade. The school holds weekly chapel and has several bell choirs.

Lower Cape

Family School-Saltbox School

3570 Rt. 6A, Brewster • 896-6555

Housed in two buildings in a pleasant wooded setting with outdoor play areas and a pool, The Family School offers programs for infants, toddlers, preschoolers and elementary school students through grade 5 as well as an after-school program and a summer camp. Accredited by the National Academy of Schools, The Family School places an emphasis on nurturing and the developmental stages of each child, and accepts state-funded voucher programs for tuition.

The Laurel Schools

1436 Rt. 137, Brewster • 896-4934

This private, state-certified school offers programs for preschool through grade 8, with a focus on individualized instruction that encourages children to develop into self-starters and perpetual learners. With an enrollment of about 130 students, Laurel stresses environmental studies, language arts (including French) and creative and artistic expressions. The school also offers a series of after-school arts classes.

Higher Education

Upper Cape

Massachusetts Maritime Academy

101 Academy Dr., Buzzards Bay • 830-5000, (800) 544-3411

The Massachusetts Maritime Academy is the oldest continuously operating maritime academy in the country. Graduates obtain a bachelor's degree in engineering. Programs include marine safety and environmental protection with a focus on work in maritime or industrial fields. The four-year co-ed course of study includes practical experience on the training ship *Patriot State*, which gives students an opportunity to visit numerous countries during their education. The academy also has a state-of-the-art oil-spill simulator and a ship's bridge simulator.

SEA Semester

171 Woods Hole Rd., Woods Hole • 540-3954

This unusual college program offers the academic equivalent of a full college semester on board the *Westward*, a 125-foot staysail schooner or the *Corwith Cramer*, a 134-foot brigantine. The *Cramer* is named for the founder of SEA who designed a program for college students that enabled them to spend six weeks on shore studying oceanography, nautical science and maritime studies, followed by six weeks at sea practicing oceanography. Each student is also expected to complete an academic project. The staff, which conducts six programs a year, is comprised of experienced oceanographers and scientists, and the ships' captains are master mariners. During the summer the vessels go to the North Atlantic, and in the winter they visit the Caribbean and the Gulf of Mexico. High school and teacher training programs are also available.

Mid-Cape

Cape Cod Community College

Rt. 132, West Barnstable • 362-2131

Set on 120 acres a few miles from Hyannis, Cape Cod Community College has 3,900 students enrolled in credit courses and an average of 4,100 per semester in both day and evening courses. The college offers associate of arts and associate of science degrees. Roughly 63 percent of the students are women. The average age is 26, but students range in age from 16 to 75. A joint admission program with the University of Massachusetts guarantees that if a CCCC student graduates with at least a 2.5 average, he or she will be accepted into the UMASS school system, which involves four universities and 15 community colleges. The two-year college provides a strong background in the arts, humanities and sciences, has a popular nursing program and offers hotel and restaurant management, dental hygiene and criminal justice courses. In Hyannis, the Adult Education Center is part of the Community College that concentrates on adult literacy, English as a second language and computer training.

Fisher Junior College

142 Corporation Rd., Hyannis • 771-6610

Located behind Cape Cod Mall, Fisher is a two-year business school granting certificates and degrees in such areas as computer support specialist, accounting, paralegal, criminal justice, medical assistant, health information technician, medical coding and office administration. The Red Cross-certified nursing assistant program is one of the most popular. The school has approximately 900 students and has a nearly 100 percent employment placement record.

Arts Education

Mid-Cape

Cape Cod Conservatory

Rt. 132, West Barnstable and Beebe Woods • 362-2772, 540-0611

The Conservatory's main facility is in its 40th season of teaching music, art, dance and drama and also offers classes at the Beebe Woods Center. The Conservatory has about 1,200 students, mostly from the Cape. Dance classes for adults and children include ballet, tap and jazz; drama, art and cartooning classes are offered for children. Adults may take courses in oil painting, monotype and music

Photo: David Lane

A family sits in Orleans Town Cove Park.

instruction in all instruments. High school students comprise about 60 percent of the music classes, but classes are open to all ages.

Cotuit Center for the Arts

737 Main St., Cotuit • 428-0669

This four-year-old arts center began with a focus on visual arts, but has branched into theater as well. Open year round, it offers classes for adults, teens and children. Classes include painting, drawing, creative writing, drama, mixed media, guitar and foreign language through the arts. It also presents art exhibits, plays and seminars throughout the year. It's located behind Cotuit Grocery.

Lower Cape

Academy of Performing Arts

5 Giddiah Hill Rd., Orleans • 255-5510

Associated with the Academy Playhouse, this school offers a variety of performance classes, including dance, acting, voice and music lessons. Classes are for the young to the young-at-heart and are given in two 18-week sessions. The academy also offers a summer camp.

Truro Center for the Arts at Castle Hill

Castle and Meetinghouse rds., Truro • 349-7511

One of the Lower Cape's most respected nonprofit educational institutions, Castle Hill has for 25 years offered classes with instructors who are both talented and distinguished. Housed in an 1880s barn with an adjacent windmill that contains the school's administrative offices, this unusual school offers a full range of courses in painting, sculpture, printmaking, pottery, poetry, playwriting and fiction. Course offerings vary from year to year; the 1997 listing includes interpretive watercolor with Elizabeth Pratt, landscape in oils with Robert Douglas Hunter, figure sculpture with Penelope Jencks, handmade books with Susan Lightcap and poetry with Marge Piercy, to name just a few. There are classes for children, a lecture series and artists receptions. Classes are held in July and August.

The Cape Cod School of Art

48 Pearl St., Provincetown • 487-0101

Founded in 1899 by Charles Hawthorne, the painter who is credited with transforming Provincetown into an important art colony, the Cape Cod School of Art is now run by noted impressionist Lois Griffel. The studio itself is a large rustic barn, but most of the teaching is done outdoors — something Hawthorne encouraged his students to do. Griffel herself teaches workshops in "Painting the Impressionist Landscape," one of the school's most popular classes. Other well-known local and nationally known artists teach weeklong workshops in pastels, figure painting and watercolor.

Hawthorne School of Art

29 Miller Hill Rd., Provincetown • 487-1236

Charles Hawthorne built this studio in 1899 (not to be confused with the Cape Cod School of Art he also founded; see above) high upon a sand dune. In 1989, Olga Opsahl-Gee and her husband, Peter Gee, reopened the studio with the hopes of "creating new artists on Cape Cod." They offer weeklong classes and workshops in such areas as raku pottery, experimental painting, fiber craft and photographic imaging, taught by local and world-renowned instructors. The school also has special drop-in children's workshops, a perfect (and creative) way for parents to have a little time to themselves!

Fine Arts Work Center

24 Pearl St., Provincetown • 487-9960

Founded in 1968 by a group of artists and writers (including poet Stanley Kunitz and art-

INSIDERS' TIP

How's this for obscure Cape Cod trivia? Poet Sylvia Plath's mother once taught at Cape Cod Community College! (Sylvia herself worked as a waitress at a Cape resort during her sophomore and junior years in college.)

ist Robert Motherwell) as a place where new talent — both writers and visual artists — can be nurtured, this former lumberyard has since become one of the leading artistic training grounds in the world. More than 1,000 people apply for the competitive Winter Program each year; only 20 (10 in each category) are accepted. Residencies, which run from October through April, include room and board plus monthly stipends of $375 for writers and $450 for visual artists (the additional monies are to purchase materials). The application deadline is February 1. Classes are taught by some of the biggest names in the arts world, including Grace Paley, James Lechay and Tama Janowitz.

The open-enrollment Summer Programs are series of weeklong and weekend workshops in creative writing and visual arts. These workshops run from June 22 to August 29 and cost $425 for the week or $225 for a weekend, not including accommodations. (Most people stay at nearby inns and guesthouses.) Numerous distinguised faculty, including Michael Mazur, Grace Paley and Bernard Chate, conduct the workshops. The center hosts scores of readings and benefits throughout the year; one exceptional highlight is the annual auction (see our Annual Events chapter). Free catalogs are available; write to the address above.

Other Schools

Sylvan Learning Center
11 Enterprise Rd., Hyannis • 778-6284

Whether exceptional, average or learning disabled, students benefit from this program, which stresses supplemental education rather than tutoring. The Sylvan program is often used by people in preparation for taking standardized tests or starting back to school. Students at Sylvan range in age from 5 to 47, but the most typical age group is 11 to 16.

The Inquiring Mind
475 Rt. 6, Eastham • 240-5028

Probably the most unconventional school around, The Inquiring Mind is in the home of retired professor John Clark, who offers classes on Chaucer, Shakespeare, Beowulf, the short story, poetry, history of the English language and writing, among others. We've met a number of people who have taken classes with Dr. Clark, and all rave about the experience. With small classes in a homey setting — actually a living room in the Clarks' 1830 home — this enterprise gives students of all ages a chance to explore topics in depth in a relaxed atmosphere.

Child Care

Although the Cape has a large retirement population, it is also filled with young families who live here year round. As in other areas of the country, many families need more than one income to get by so child care is especially important. A number of family day-care providers have sprung up in response to that need along with a growing number of preschools. In some cases, preschools also offer infant care and toddler programs.

Preschools and child-care centers must be licensed by the state or show that they are exempt from licensing. You can check the compliance record of any Cape child-care center by calling the **Massachusetts Office for Children** at its Lakeville office, 947-1133.

One important resource for referrals is the **Childcare Network of Cape Cod**, 115 Enterprise Road, Hyannis, 778-9470, (800) 845-1999, a nonprofit agency that maintains a list of all preschools and day-care facilities in the area. They know where vacancies are and which centers are licensed to take drop-in students and can also refer families to other services children may need. On the Lower Cape, check with **The Cape Cod Children's Place**, 995 Nauset Road, Eastham, 240-3310, a re-

INSIDERS' TIP

Katharine Lee Bates, the Wellesley College professor who wrote "America the Beautiful" in 1893, was born in Falmouth and spent her childhood there. A statue of Bates stands in front of the Falmouth Library.

gional family resource center that not only offers child care but also has information on local child-care providers and preschools and other services that families may need.

Despite the number of preschool and daycare centers that have opened on the Cape, there are still gaps; many Cape residents work at night and must rely on family members or local babysitters. The Children's Place in Eastham (see above) maintains a list of referrals for babysitters on the Lower Cape. You might also check the bulletin boards at libraries for local babysitters, who often advertise their services there. There no "tot-drop" places and no 24-hour childcare services. There are no babysitting services on the Cape, but on Nantucket, there's **Nantucket Babysitters Service**, 228-4970.

Some families opt for au pairs. One resource for au pairs is **E.F. Au Pair** in Cambridge, Massachusetts, (800) 333-6056, which operates a cultural exchange/childcare program in which young European men and women come to the United States for one year and in exchange for room and board and a stipend will provide up to 45 hours a week of child care for a host family. Nannies are another option; agencies that serve the Cape include **The Original Nanny Service** in Worcester, 755-9284, and **Abetter Nanny** in Waquoit, 548-3739.

Libraries

Upper Cape

Sandwich Public Library, 142 Main Street, Sandwich, 888-0625

Jonathan Bourne Library, 19 Sandwich Road, Bourne, 759-0644

Falmouth Library, 123 Katherine Lee Bates Road, 457-2555

East Falmouth Library, 310 E. Falmouth Highway, 548-6340

North Falmouth Library, Chester Street, 563-2922

West Falmouth Library, 575 W. Falmouth Highway, 548-4709

Mashpee Public Library, Route 151, Mashpee, 477-0323

Mid-Cape

Centerville Library, 585 Main Street, 775-1787

Cotuit Library, 871 Main Street, 428-8141

Hyannis Public Library, 401 Main Street, 775-2280

Marstons Mills Public Library, 2160 Main Street, 428-5175

Sturgis Library, 3090 Main Street, Barnstable, 362-6636

Whelden Memorial Library, 2401 Meetinghouse Way (Route 149), West Barnstable, 362-2262

Cape Cod Community College, Route 132, Barnstable, 362-2131

South Yarmouth Library, 312 Main Street, South Yarmouth, 760-4820

West Yarmouth Library, Main Street, West Yarmouth, 775-5206

Yarmouthport Library, 297 Hallet Street, Yarmouthport, 362-3717

Dennis Memorial Library, 1020 Old Bass River Road, 385-2255

Jacob Sears Memorial Library, 23 Center Street, East Dennis, 385-8151

South Dennis Free Public Library, Main Street, South Dennis, 398-8954

West Dennis Free Public Library, 272 Main Street, West Dennis, 398-2050

Lower Cape

Brewster Ladies' Library, 1822 Main Street, Brewster, 896-3913

Brooks Free Library, 739 Main Street, Harwich, 430-7562

INSIDERS' TIP

Early Cape settlers mistook native osprey for buzzards, thus the name Buzzards Bay — or so goes one theory on the area's curious name.

Chase Library, 5 Main Street, West Harwich, 432-2610

Harwichport Library Association, 47 Bank Street, Harwichport, 432-3320

Eldredge Public Library, 564 Main Street, Chatham, 945-5170

South Chatham Public Library, Main Street, South Chatham, 945-1815

Snow Library, 67 Main Street, Orleans, 240-3760

Wellfleet Public Library, 55 W. Main Street, Wellfleet, 349-0310

Eastham Public Library, 190 Samoset Road, Eastham, 240-5950

Cobb Memorial Library, 13 Truro Center Road, Truro, 349-6895

Pilgrim Memorial Library, 36 Shore Road, North Truro, 487-1125

Provincetown Public Library, 330 Commercial Street, Provincetown, 487-7094

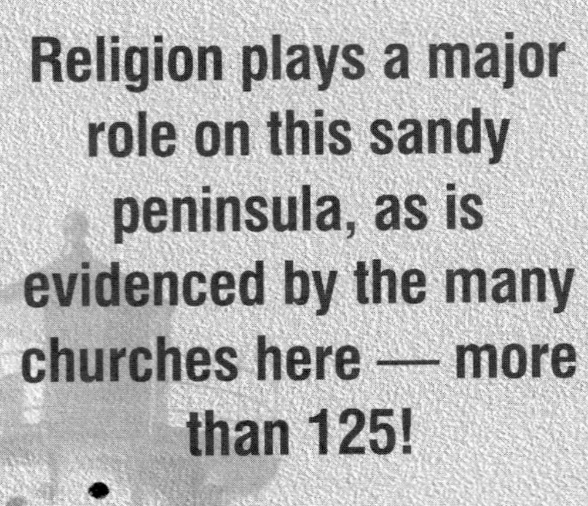

Religion plays a major role on this sandy peninsula, as is evidenced by the many churches here — more than 125!

Worship

Religion has long played a role in the makeup of Cape Cod, beginning with the Native Indians thanking their Great Spirit for all the life-giving gifts they received each day. The religion of the Wampanoag Indians was the only religion of the area for 10,000 years, until white settlers came at the beginning of the 17th century.

Our Religious Roots

This migration commenced with the landing of the Pilgrims in 1620. These 102 hearty souls braved the vast Atlantic and hardships in the New World so that they may be free to live and worship as they pleased. Half of them did not survive the first winter and would never realize that dream. What faith it must have taken for the others to go on — faith in oneself, faith in one's mission and faith in one's God. It is upon this Pilgrim faith that the settlements of the area were built.

England's established church of the time was the Church of England. In opposition to this establishment were the Pilgrims, separatists seeking to forge their own church. Their pilgrimage to Plymouth brought more settlers in the years that followed, settlers bringing a Congregational church with more conservative ideas with them. They established settlements all along the northeast coast, including the Cape, as early as 1637.

As soon as enough Congregationalists gathered and built a meeting house (and encouraged a minister to relocate to their corner of the wilderness to preach to them) they were in line for incorporation. Incorporation brought more settlers to add to the flock. As the flock grew and people began to settle in the outlying areas, east and west parishes and north and south parishes were established. Many of these local parishes would lead to the incorporation of completely separate townships in years to follow. (See our Historic Cape Cod chapter.)

In those days, religion and community meant the same thing. The meeting house served as both the religious and political center of the community. Church and state were one and the same (and would be until 1692 when a charter provided religious freedom). All members were expected to contribute to the church that had earned their township incorporation.

Congregationalists were not the only ones settling during the 17th century. By the mid-1600s Quakers began to find their way on the Cape to settle in Sandwich, Falmouth, Barnstable and later Harwich. These Quakers, whose religion taught them to tremble or quake at the fear of God's wrath, attempted to gain converts from the Congregationalist flock, and in some cases succeeded. Despite their efforts the Quakers were singled out as heretics. Many were forced through repeated persecutions to flee town for other parts. Some, such as John Wing of Falmouth, relocated to a remote wilderness lying between Yarmouth and Eastham to begin the settlement of what would become the town of Harwich. Quakers tended to settle in parts where people were few, such as in the South Yarmouth, which became a Quaker village. The Quakers were followed by Baptists, who settled at Harwich during the mid-18th century and later spread outward across the Cape.

By the late-18th century a new religious tour de force arrived on Cape Cod. In England Methodism grew from the spiritual awakening of John Wesley in 1738. Great Britain and Ireland saw the spread of this new religion, and by the latter quarter of the 18th century, Methodism made its way across the Atlantic. The first Methodist meeting house on the Cape was erected in Harwich in 1792, followed by another in Bourne in 1794. By the early to mid-19th century, Methodism had rattled the Congregational spires and the latter began to see many divisions and splinter groups emerge.

The middle of the century was a religious revolution on Cape Cod, as small religious sects began to form from factions of the more established churches of the day. During this period, the town of Dennis saw its church separate into a half-dozen groups, while in neighboring Harwich no less than 15 divisions formed from the church in that town. Each group had its own issues, its own agenda, and its own particular belief system that set it apart from the others. It was during this time that the Unitarian Universalists came into being. By the end of the century, though, many of these groups were able to resolve their differences and they came back together.

Meanwhile, Catholicism began to emerge with the flow of Irish immigrants during the 1830s and throughout the 19th century. The first Catholic parish was established in Sandwich in 1830 as Irish were settling there to work in the factories. A second parish was erected in 1869 at Harwich. Portuguese fishermen in Provincetown had already brought their Catholic church along with them. Cape Verde Islanders, who settled in Falmouth as farmers, did the same. As the 20th century arrived and people began to migrate southward from around Boston, the Catholic population of the Cape began to grow. Today this once predominantly Protestant peninsula, settled initially by Congregationalist, is largely Roman Catholic.

Worship Today

Despite more than three centuries of changes and growth, religion continues to play a major role on this sandy peninsula, as is evidenced by the many churches here — more than 125! The Cape remains largely Christian, although there are a pair of Jewish synagogues and other groups such as Baha'i spiritual assemblies. For a listing of all church locations across the Cape, consult the Yellow Pages of the local phone book. Most Cape Cod newspapers have information on services. The *Cape Cod Times* prints its listing on Saturday. Also, the **Cape Cod Council of Churches** located on Main Street in Hyannis, 775-5073, is an excellent source on what's available here in terms of worship. The Council, which celebrated its 40th year in 1996, operates a food and clothing service center in Dennisport and encourages the various religious societies to work together in an effort to provide for the Cape community.

United Church of Christ churches, which grew from the old Congregational parishes, comprise the largest Protestant contingency on the Cape. Three UCC churches can be found on the upper Cape, seven in the mid-Cape area and six along the lower Cape. Among them are a number that lie along Main Street in the following towns: Sandwich, Falmouth, Centerville, South Dennis, Harwich, Harwichport, East Orleans, Chatham and Wellfleet. Other UCC churches are located in North Falmouth, Waquoit, Cotuit, West Barnstable, West Yarmouth, Dennis, and Truro. The **First Congregational Church** of Yarmouthport is not a member of the United Church of Christ, retaining its original congregational charter as a member of the National Association of Congregational Christian Churches.

There are some 15 **Baptist** churches on the Cape — American Baptist, National and independent. Five of these churches are in the upper Cape, six are in the mid-Cape and four are along the lower Cape. Baptist churches can be found in the towns of Bourne, Sandwich, Falmouth, Mashpee, Barnstable, Yarmouth, Brewster, Chatham and Eastham.

United Methodists have 14 churches; five in the upper-Cape towns of Bourne and Falmouth, two in the mid-Cape towns of Barnstable and Yarmouth, and seven in the lower-Cape towns of Harwich, Orleans, Chatham, Eastham, Wellfleet and Provincetown.

INSIDERS' TIP

Some of the greatest food on Cape Cod can be had at the St. George Greek Fair held at the Greek Orthodox Church in Centerville during the month of July. See our Annual Events chapter.

Roman Catholic churches account for 21 of the Cape's more than 125 places of worship. Adding seasonal parishes brings the total number of Catholic churches closer to 30. There is at least one Roman Catholic church in each of the Cape's 15 towns. The town of Falmouth has four Catholic churches, as does Barnstable. Although the Protestants on Cape have more church buildings, the average membership of a Catholic parish is much larger than that of a Protestant congregation. As a result, the Cape is predominately Catholic by a ratio of nearly 2 to 1. President John F. Kennedy was a member of the St. Francis Xavier Church in Hyannis, where he and his brothers, Joe, Bobby and Ted, served as altar boys.

Episcopalians arrived at Woods Hole in 1852 and at Sandwich in 1854. Today they are well-represented on the Cape. There are 11 **Episcopal** churches located in Buzzards Bay, Sandwich, Woods Hole, Falmouth, Osterville, Barnstable, South Yarmouth, Harwichport, Orleans, Chatham and Provincetown. Three **Assembly of God** churches can be found in Hyannis, Dennisport and Wellfleet. **Lutheran** churches are in Falmouth, West Barnstable, East Harwich and Brewster. **Pentecostal** churches are in Mashpee and Dennisport. Two **Church of Jesus Christ of Latter Day Saints** congregations are on Cape Cod, one in Cataumet and the other in Brewster.

Community Churches can be found in Mashpee, East and West Dennis as well as in South Chatham. For **Unitarian Universalist** parishes you'll want to look in the towns of Falmouth, Barnstable, Brewster and Provincetown. **Society of Friends** are in West Falmouth and South Yarmouth (once known as Quaker Town and Friends Village). In East Falmouth and South Dennis you can find a **Church of the Nazarene,** while Buzzards Bay, Sandwich, Falmouth, Hyannis, Brewster, Harwichport and Orleans all have **Christian Science** churches. **Jehovah's Witnesses** can be found in four locations across the Cape: Hatchville, Hyannis, Harwich and Eastham. West Barnstable has a **Presbyterian** church and Centerville is home to a **Greek Orthodox** church with its Byzantine building erected in 1949.

Rounding out the Christian places of worship are two **Christian Missionary** churches in Buzzards Bay and Brewster and two **Federated Churches** in Cotuit and Hyannis. **Seventh Day Adventists** are located in Osterville. **Full Gospel** churches are in Sandwich, Mashpee, West Barnstable and Dennisport and the **Church of New Jerusalem** (a.k.a. Swedenborgian) was established in 1870 in Yarmouthport. Orleans is home to the **Chapel of the Community of Jesus**, Hyannis is home to the **Salvation Army,** which holds services, and South Dennis is home to an **American Apostolic Catholic Church**.

Hyannis has a **Zion Union Church** that caters to the black members of the community. **Interdenominational** parishes are in Centerville and Hyannis, **nondenominational** parishes are in Sandwich, Mashpee and Marstons Mills, a **Christadelphian Ecclesia** parish is in Cataumet and an **Evangelical Covenant** church is in Brewster. **Unity** churches are located in Centerville and Yarmouth.

Cape Cod also hosts the **Falmouth Jewish Congregation** in Hatchville (East Falmouth). It is housed in what was once the East End Meetinghouse of the United Church of Christ, founded in 1797. The **Cape Cod Synagogue** in Hyannis was erected in 1949. There is also a **Lubavitch Chabad Jewish Center** in Hyannis.

Baha'i World Faith spiritual assemblies can be found on Cape Cod. Groups meet every 19 days for feasts and services. The Baha'i belief is one of world peace, social justice and the reunification of all humanity.

Last, but by no means least, the **Wampanoag Indians** of Mashpee hold services at the Old Indian Meeting House on Route 28 in Mashpee. Built in 1684, this meeting house is the oldest church on Cape Cod.

Cape Codders, as a rule,
like to stay informed,
especially when it
comes to local news.

Media

Cape Codders, as a rule, like to stay informed, especially when it comes to local news. And that's not hard to do here. The Cape has a daily newspaper, several weekly newspapers, special-interest magazines, a public-access television station and a range of radio listening choices to keep residents and visitors informed and entertained. In this chapter is a composite of our media choices — newspapers, magazines, cable TV services and radio and television stations.

Newspapers

Cape Cod Times

319 Main St., Hyannis • 775-1200, (800) 451-7887 (Mass. only)

The Cape's only daily paper, the *Cape Cod Times* covers news throughout the area, including Martha's Vineyard and Nantucket, as well as state, national and world news. It is delivered to subscribers in the morning. It has a daily circulation of approximately 52,000 and Sunday circulation of 64,000. The newsroom and business offices are in Hyannis, and there are bureau offices in Falmouth, Sandwich, Orleans and Provincetown.

Started in 1936 as part of the *New Bedford Standard Times* (some old-timers still refer to the paper as the Standard Times) the *Cape Cod Times*' offices in downtown Hyannis date to 1938. In 1966 the paper was acquired by Ottaway Newspapers Inc. (a Dow Jones subsidiary), which has 20 daily newspapers and 550,000 circulation coast-to-coast.

In addition to the daily newspaper, the *Cape Cod Times* also publishes *PrimeTime*, a free monthly magazine with an age 50-plus target audience; *CapeWeek*, a weekly events magazine; and special seasonal and topical editions, including the popular *Summer Times* series published three times during the summer.

In 1996, the *Cape Cod Times*' 60th anniversary, the newspaper published the first edition of the *Insiders' Guide® to Cape Cod, Nantucket and Martha's Vineyard*, the first of this nationally distributed series in New England. This 1997 book is the second edition and has been completely updated and expanded.

Barnstable Patriot

326 Main St., Hyannis • 771-1427

The oldest newspaper on Cape Cod, the *Barnstable Patriot* was launched in 1830. It publishes every Thursday and covers the town of Barnstable and its seven villages, with a focus on county government. Weekly sections deal with such topics as senior citizens, sports and libraries. Barnstable High School and Cape Cod Academy students regularly put together a page of the paper.

Bound volumes of the *Barnstable Patriot* going back to 1926 are available at the newspaper office; bound and microfilm copies in Sturgis Library in Barnstable go back to the first issue.

The Falmouth Enterprise

Depot Ave., Falmouth • 548-4700

This biweekly paper celebrated its 100-year anniversary in 1995. Owned by the Hough family of Falmouth, who also publish *The Bourne Enterprise*, *The Mashpee Enterprise* and the *Upper Cape Local*, *The Falmouth Enterprise* and its sister publications cover local news throughout the Upper Cape. The Falmouth and Mashpee papers are distributed on Tuesday and Friday; the *Upper Cape Local* is mailed once a week. *The Bourne Enterprise* comes out on Fridays. These papers include calendars of events, arts and entertainment, and weddings and births. The papers have a total circulation of about 43,000 and are sold at newsstands and by subscription. Home delivery is available.

Cape Cod Community Newspapers

923-G Rt. 6A, Yarmouthport • 362-2111
5 Namskaket Rd., Orleans • 255-2121

Owned by Fidelity, this large newspaper group publishes six local weekly newspapers, including *The Sandwich Broadsider*, *The Bourne Courier*, The *Mashpee Messenger*, *The Register*, *The Harwich Oracle* and *The Cape Codder*. The combined weekly circulation on the Cape is about 40,200.

All the papers are sold on newsstands and by subscription. *The Cape Codder* covers the eight Lower Cape towns from Brewster to Provincetown and comes out on Tuesdays and Fridays; the Friday edition has two sections. *The Register*, which comes out on Thursdays, covers Dennis, Yarmouth and Barnstable. The newspapers are community-oriented, general interest papers that report on news and events.

Cape Cod Chronicle

60 Munson Meeting Way, Chatham
• 945-2220

Established in 1965, the *Chronicle* is the Lower Cape's only independent weekly newspaper. Published on Thursday, it focuses on Chatham and Harwich and is chock-full of news, features, sports, community service listings, entertainment news and even a crossword puzzle.

The Advocate

100 Bradford St., Provincetown • 487-1170

The Advocate calls itself Provincetown's "hometown newspaper," and rightfully so: It's been published for nearly 130 years! The weekly paper, published on Thursday and covering Provincetown, Truro and Wellfleet, reports on town meetings, social events and political shenanigans with the usual small-town charm. It also features a weekly column detailing fun news bits such as in-town celebrity sightings.

Provincetown Banner

167 Commercial St., Provincetown
• 487-7400

The *Banner* debuted in May 1995, and although some residents wondered if there was room for a second local paper, it has thrived. Published on Thursdays, it's a particularly well-designed paper with bold graphics.

FYI

Unless otherwise noted, the area code for all phone numbers in this guide is 508.

Out of Town Newspapers

You can get local and Boston newspapers just about anywhere on the Cape, and many stores sell out-of-town newspapers such as the *New York Times* as well. Some stores offer a larger selection and offer newspapers from Providence, Worcester and more far-flung places. A few news dealers with good selections are **Way's Center News**, 424 Main Street, Hyannis, 775-0422; **The Brewster Store**, 1935 Route 6A, Brewster, 896-3744; and **Dick's Coffee Bar**, Post Office Square, Main Street, Orleans (no phone).

Magazines

Cape Cod Life

4 Barlow's Landing Rd., Unit 14, Pocasset
• 564-4466

Launched in 1979 by local publisher Brian Shortsleeve, this glossy, attractive magazine comes out six times a year and is sold by subscription and on newsstands. *Cape Cod Life* also puts out an annual home and garden issue in June that covers gardening, interior decorating, house styles and architecture.

The full-color magazine concentrates on local people, historic and current topics, events and activities. Topics include art, cooking, nature, shopping, dining and lodging on Cape Cod, Nantucket and Martha's Vineyard. Noted for its beautiful photography, *Cape Cod Life* runs an annual photo contest. Back issues

INSIDERS' TIP

Vacation over? Buy a copy of the Patti Page hit song, "Old Cape Cod." As you listen, the memories will come flooding back!

Photo: Cape Cod Times

Any place is a good place to be with friends on the Cape.

and a number of good books about the Cape can be ordered through the magazine.

Provincetown Arts

650 Commercial St., Provincetown • 487-3167

It's slick, glossy and ultra-thick, and, according to publisher Chris Busa, focuses on "the artists and writers that make up Provincetown's artistic colony." The magazine sells for $6.50 an issue, is sold in bookstores nationwide and is published every July.

Television

Although the Cape has only one station of its own, C3TV, we get lots of others. Most are from Boston, a few are from Providence. Station numbers may vary according to which cable company serves your area of the Cape.

WBZ (CBS), Boston, channel 4

WCVB (ABC), Boston, channel 5

WLNE (ABC), Providence, channel 6 (46 in Mashpee, 49 for Harron cable customers)

WHDH (NBC), Boston, channel 7

WJAR (NBC), Providence, channel 10 (50 in Mashpee and for Harron customers)

WPRI (CBS), Providence, channel 12 (52 in Mashpee).

In addition, there's a plethora of cable stations available, depending upon the cable package you (or the place where you are staying) pay for. On the Lower Cape, channel 8 is community programming, with offerings from taped selectmen's meetings to theatrical performances.

C3TV

307 Whites Path, Yarmouth • 394-2388

C3TV, Cape Cod's public access community television center, is a versatile community resource that airs social, political and cultural programs from 9:30 AM until midnight. C3TV is also a community media center with conference and workshop space and a gallery that hosts 10 community art exhibits a year. The station is funded by the towns of Barnstable, Yarmouth, Dennis, Harwich and Chatham.

C3TV has two studios used to produce such programs as "Books and the World," "Dr. Wheels," "Going to the Dogs," "The Cooking Connection" and others. Programming covers local sports, selectmen's meetings and committee meetings.

Cable Television

Adelphia Cable Communications

91 Industrial Park, Plymouth • 747-3300, in Falmouth 548-7784

This company serves Falmouth and Martha's Vineyard and carries all major broadcast and satellite stations. It also has an FM station.

Continental Cablevision

Deer Crossing, Rt. 28, Mashpee • 477-7733

Serving Mashpee in the Upper Cape and Brewster to Provincetown in the Lower Cape, Continental offers about 70 channels, including premium stations such as HBO, Cinemax, Showtime and three pay-per-view channels, a home and garden channel and fX.

Harron Cable

49 Bournedale Rd., Bournedale • 888-5444

Harron Cable serves Sandwich and Bourne and has approximately 52 channels, including CNN, Discovery, SEGA Channel, Family Channel, Science Fiction, TNT and premium channels such as HBO, Showtime, Disney and The Movie Channel. It also offers community access and pay-per-view programming.

Photo: Peter Simon

Splashing through the surf is a perfect way to spend the day.

TCI Cablevision of Cape Cod
10 Old Townhouse Rd. E., South Yarmouth • 771-3700

TCI serves Barnstable, Yarmouth, Dennis, Harwich and Chatham with 52 channels, nine premium channels and three pay-per-view channels. It also offers Prime Star, a satellite-dish viewer service, and the popular C3TV public-access programming.

Continental Cablevision
15 Locust Rd., Orleans • 255-5735

This community access station serves the towns of Brewster, Orleans, Eastham, Wellfleet, Truro and Provincetown and is free to any resident or employee of these towns. Continental has two studios (in Orleans and Provincetown), and programming on channel 8 runs the gamut from the serious to the downright silly. Hey, this is community access!

Radio Stations

Classical
WFCC 107.5 FM

Community
WOMR 92.1 FM (Provincetown)
WCCT 90.3 FM (Cape Cod Tech)

Contemporary/adult/easy listening
WCOD 106 FM (adult contemporary)
WQRC 99.9 FM (easy listening, jazz)
WRZE 96.3 FM (Top 40)
WJCO 93.5 FM (adult standards)
WOCN 103.9 FM ("memory music" from 1930s to '80s)

Rock
WPXC 103 FM (classic rock)
WMVY 92.7 FM (adult rock)
WCIB 102 FM (classic rock)
WKPE 104.7 FM
WKPE 1170 AM

Talk
WUOK 1240 AM (talk/sports)
WXTK 94.9 FM (news/talk)

Nantucket

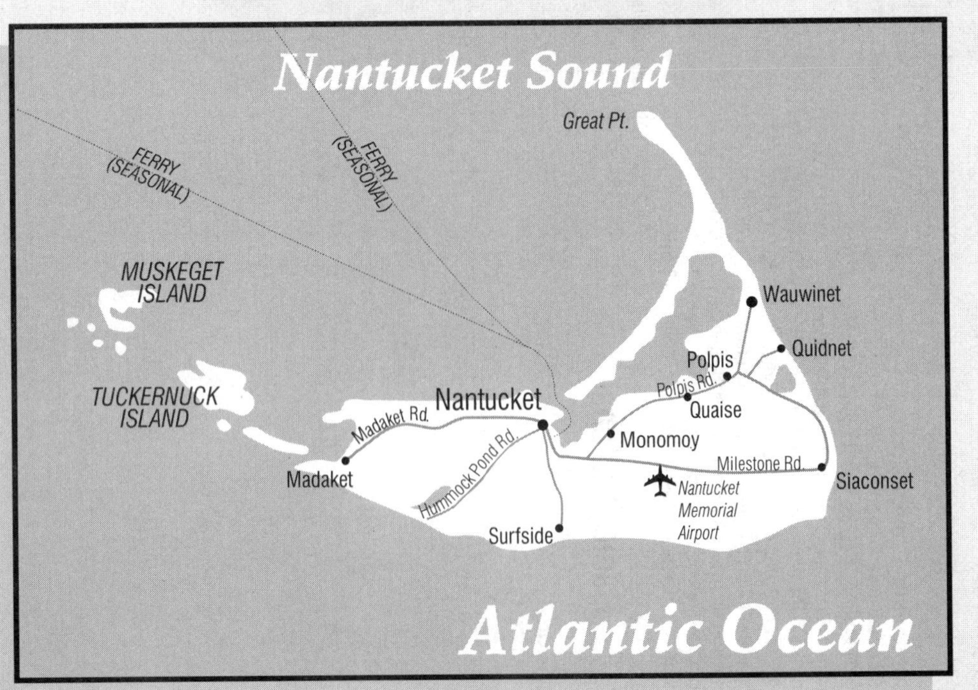
Nantucket Sound
Great Pt.
FERRY (SEASONAL)
FERRY (SEASONAL)
MUSKEGET ISLAND
TUCKERNUCK ISLAND
Wauwinet
Quidnet
Polpis
Polpis Rd.
Quaise
Nantucket
Madaket Rd.
Hummock Pond Rd.
Monomoy
Milestone Rd.
Siaconset
Madaket
Nantucket Memorial Airport
Surfside
Atlantic Ocean

Nantucket

Colorful blossoms spill out of window boxes and wave in the warm breeze. Tall hedges front grey-shingled homes that once sheltered the families of ship captains. Landscapers sweep leaves from immaculate lawns bordered by colorful gardens. Fragrant pink roses climb tall white picket fences. This is Nantucket, 30 miles at sea and in many ways a world unto itself. The name means "faraway island," and that is true in many respects.

Unlike Martha's Vineyard, which sprawls in full view of Cape Cod, Nantucket is out of sight of the mainland. Perhaps that's why Nantucketers have always been a particularly independent breed, and why the community here is so close-knit. In the cobblestone streets and brick sidewalks of Nantucket Town, friends call out greetings and stop to chat, and everyone seems to know each other. No one seems hurried, and the word "stress" begins to seem like a foreign term you have no use for.

It doesn't take long to feel at home here. Far away though it may be, Nantucket is still accessible, and while it's nice to stay a few days or even a week or two (we'd love an even longer stay), it is possible to take a daytrip here from Cape Cod. The trip from Hyannis is a little more than two hours by boat and only 15 minutes by air. However long or short your stay, you'll know as soon as you arrive that Nantucket is unlike any place you've ever been. We especially enjoy arriving by boat and seeing the whole town come into view like a postcard as the vessel rounds Brant Point. You'll notice the buildings here are almost exclusively grey weathered shingle with white trim, one of the indications that construction and alterations are strictly monitored here. In 1970 the entire island was established as a Historic District, which means that all construction must be accepted by the Historic District Commission, the Nantucket Building Department and the Planning Board. While residents may grumble or joke about the stringent regulations, there's no arguing with the results: Nantucket has an incredibly quaint and unspoiled appearance.

Islanders have also taken care to preserve the land here. More than 11,800 acres — 36 percent of the island — are protected from development, much of that through the Nantucket Conservation Foundation, which owns and manages more than 8,348 acres. History, of course, has also been carefully and lovingly preserved. This community, which has a year-round population of roughly 6,500, maintains more than a dozen museums. Make sure you fit in at least one or two of them, to get a real taste of the island's history, which is really its essence.

Nantucketers are generally friendly and good-humored, but if you sense that your car is distinctly unwelcome on Nantucket, you are right. When you prudently decide it is too expensive to bring a vehicle to the island, you might go through a slight withdrawal before you realize how freeing it is to walk from Point A to Point B without worrying about parking, tickets, gas and unfamiliar street signs. Nantucket forces you to forsake some aspects of modern life, and you find that you grow more and more comfortable with that fact.

Despite their sterling silver door knockers and look of high-end prosperity, Nantucket's people have ridden out rough economic times throughout history. These are people who know how to make tough choices, and for much of this century they have had to fight that fatal human urge to kill the goose that lays golden eggs by exploiting what makes money. More than 100 years ago, folks discovered that what made money on Nantucket was not whaling, sheep herding or farming but tourism. Realizing that services and property were at a premium, residents wisely made provisions for the future by preserving open space and historic structures.

Nantucket is a complex place. Despite an

emphasis on structural conformity, it has always been characterized by individuality and the wild, natural beauty of its moors, stretches of beach and bogs. And yet it also has enough sophisticated shops and great restaurants to please the most demanding urbanite.

Don't mistake being physically remote for being culturally isolated or provincial, however. Travelers from around the world come here. (The Nantucket Chamber's book has a greeting in six languages.) In 1993 the Nantucket Elementary School was selected from 177 schools nationwide to receive an award for overall excellence. With graduating classes that average 50 to 60 students, the school has teams in football, swimming and soccer. Its football team was singled out last fall by *Sports Illustrated*, which sent a writer and photographer to spend time with the team.

FYI

Unless otherwise noted, the area code for all phone numbers in this guide is 508.

Area Overview

Nantucket Town, the most concentrated part of the island, is situated around the harbor. Most businesses and accommodations are located here, so if there is no town named in an address for any of the following listings, assume it is in Nantucket Town. We'll tell you if a business or accommodation is located in any of the outlying villages, which are less populated and more seasonal. The village of **Madaket**, to the west, consists of residences and a few businesses. The residential village of **Cisco** is on the island's southern shore. The village of **Siasconset**, more commonly referred to as Sconset, is a bustling summertime resort on the eastern end of the island known for its excellent restaurants and rose-covered cottages with sweet names such as Little House and Auld Ange Syne, the oldest cottage on the island. Look for the images of spouting whales cut into the privet hedges. The old schoolhouse, now a fire station, was used until 1957.

If you're an artist, bring your sketch pad. Nantucket's air is full of moisture, and it is warmer in winter and cooler in summer than the rest of the area, which results in achingly beautiful flowers and gardens. You'll want to take lots of photographs or at least pick up one of several good pictoral books on Nantucket.

Wildlife on Nantucket consists of deer, pheasant, rabbits and squirrels. Forty years ago, squirrels were nonexistent on the island because they, like the deer, had been hunted out. Their recent reappearance has been attributed to stowaways on logging trucks. Today the island is host to several grassland-nesting birds species, including short-eared owls and northern harriers, that are scarce on the mainland but thrive here because there are fewer natural predators. Nantucket is a popular spot for birders, and it's easy to see why: Some 354 bird species have been recorded here. The island abounds with wild blueberries, blackberries, beach plum and elderberries. The 260-acre Milestone Cranberry Bog is one of the largest in the United States. The highest point of land is Folger Hill, which at 109 feet, is a foot higher than Altar Rock.

It's true that much of Nantucket shuts down in the off-season, but even in the quiet months, it's a beautiful place. Nantucketers, however, may be less than eager to share that. "Don't tell anyone how great it is in the off season," said one resident. "We like it quiet then."

Someone once wrote: "Nantucket constantly pulls at my heart, and everyone I know who lives here or visits here is touched by this miniature world of open space and devoted people. Her boundaries simultaneously challenge our lives and add comfort to our souls."

Amen.

History

Indian legend has it that the giant Maushop created Nantucket and Martha's Vineyard from the sand in his moccasins. The scientific version, though less romantic, is consistent with what we know about the formation of Cape Cod. Prehistoric glaciers deposited sand, rock and rubble in the area. As the glaciers melted, the water level rose. About 6,000 years ago, Nantucket Sound was flooded, separating the Cape from the islands. By roughly 2,000 years ago, Nantucket and Martha's Vineyard had taken the general form they have today.

Native inhabitants lived on the island for hundreds of years; about 1,500 of them were here when the first English people arrived. In 1602 Nantucket was sighted by Bartholomew Gosnold on the bark *Concord*. He noted the island in his log but did not land. In 1641 Lord Sterling, a representative of Charles II, deeded the island to Thomas Mayhew and his son, whose family had first settled on Martha's Vineyard and grazed sheep out on Nantucket.

After about 15 years, the Mayhews sold shares to nine settlers from mainland New England who wanted to escape the religious tensions there. By 1700, the island population consisted of approximately 800 Native Americans and 300 European settlers, who lived together in relative harmony. Tristram Coffin is considered the patriarch of the island. Benjamin Franklin's grandfather, Peter Foulger, lived on Nantucket, and like his grandson was a versatile person, respected as a preacher, poet, artisan, Indian interpreter and Clerk of the Works. Three ships involved in the Boston Tea Party were out of Nantucket.

Many Nantucketers supported themselves by raising sheep and producing wool — at one time, there were 10,000 sheep on the island. In time, however, the islanders turned to whaling, first from offshore and then from whaling boats. Adding tryworks (huge pots used to melt down whale blubber) to the whaling vessels revolutionized Nantucket's whaling industry. No longer did the ships have to return to port to process and store the blubber, so they could remain at sea longer. According to the New Bedford Whaling Museum, the longest whaling voyage lasted 11 years.

Alternately tedious and strenuous, boring and dangerous, whaling was the heart of Nantucket's economy for more than 100 years. Historical books such as *Nantucket Then and Now* by John McCalley and *Away Off Shore* by Nathaniel Philbrick describe with gritty detail the island conditions, often sad and brutal, during Nantucket's era of whaling. It was common knowledge that you could "smell a whaler before you could see it."

The Great Fire of 1846 (preceded by another big fire eight years earlier) destroyed hundreds of waterfront businesses connected to whaling; the loss gutted the town economically as well as physically. This catastrophe, compounded by the effects of silt building up in the harbor, the discovery of oil and the California Gold Rush in 1849, doomed the whaling industry. In 1869 Nantucket's last whaling ship, the *Oak*, sailed out of the harbor.

As the 19th century drew to a close, islanders turned to tourism for their livelihood. At first, a mere trickle of wealthy summer people came to Nantucket to enjoy boating and saltwater bathing. But with the introduction of steamboat service from New Bedford, vacation travel to Nantucket boomed. Today, 40,000 to 50,000 people visit Nantucket on a busy weekend.

Getting Here

Nantucket may be an offshore island, but it's not hard to get here. Excellent year-round ferry and air service provide access to residents and visitors from all parts of the United States and the world.

By Air

In season, frequent flights leave from Barnstable Municipal Airport in Hyannis and land at Nantucket Memorial Airport, which accommodates anything from twin-engine Cessnas to 19-seat Beechwoods and jets. The aerial views are utterly spectacular and the speedy 15-minute flight gives you added time to enjoy the island. (Bear in mind that the cost is roughly two-thirds more to fly to Nantucket rather than take the ferry.)

Nantucket Memorial Airport
30 Macy Ln., Nantucket • 325-5300

Located off Old South Road, Nantucket Memorial is the second-most active commercial airport in Massachusetts. Air service is available from Boston, Hyannis, New Bedford, Martha's Vineyard, New York and Newark as well as through private charter. The flight to Nantucket takes about 30 minutes from Boston, 15 minutes from Hyannis and a little more than an hour from New York City. Car rental agencies and taxi service are available on site. For private planes, the airport offers servicing and repair facilities; fuel is available 24 hours a day.

The following charter and commercial airlines are based at Nantucket Memorial Airport.

Ocean Wings Air Charter
Memorial Airport • (800) 253-5039

The only Nantucket-based air-charter service, Ocean Wings Air Charter offers 24-hour year-round service to any New England, United States or Canadian destination. This company has a private hangar and offers flight instruction. Ocean Wings also has winter service based in Puerto Rico and the Caribbean.

Colgan Air
(800) 272-5488

This carrier offers regular, year-round service between the island and Hyannis, Boston and New York, and seasonally from Newark.

Continental Express
(800) 525-0280

In season, this airline offers three to four daily flights between Newark and Nantucket.

Island Airlines
228-7575, (800) 248-7779

This airline provides 11 round trips daily between Hyannis and Nantucket, year round, with additional flights on weekends.

Nantucket Airlines
228-6234, (800) 635-8787

Cape Air
771-6944, (800) 352-0714

A merger of these two airlines made it possible to offer more than 20 daily flights, with year-round shuttle service between Nantucket and Hyannis on Nantucket Air and regular service to New Bedford, Boston, Martha's Vineyard on Cape Air. In the peak season the company offers more than seven flights daily to Boston. Charter service is also available.

USAir Express
(800) 428-4322

This carrier provides five daily flights in season to Boston, with connecting flights to LaGuardia and also to Martha's Vineyard.

By Sea

If you'd prefer to spend a few hours enjoying a ride on Nantucket Sound — sunshine, sea breezes and perhaps a glass of wine on the upper deck of a passenger ferry — you

Photo: Rob Benchley, Nantucket Beacon

Boats in Nantucket Harbor sit idle during a morning fog.

can take advantage of regular ferry service throughout the year from Hyannis and Woods Hole. The standard ferry ride is about two hours. The *Grey Lady*, Hy-Line's speedy new catamaran (named after the island's longtime nickname, a reference to the fog that surrounds Nantucket at times), makes the trip from Hyannis in an hour.

Ferry boats departing from Hyannis provide daily transportation to Nantucket year round. (Note: Falmouth's ferry service only goes to Martha's Vineyard, not Nantucket.)

Freedom Cruise Lines

Saquatucket Harbor, Rt. 28, Harwichport • 432-8999

This relatively new line, a real boon to Lower Cape-based residents and visitors, provides seasonal passenger-only service to Nantucket and offers private charters. Travel time is 1½ hours. There are a bar and snack bar on board the 66-foot boat. The round-trip cost is $32 for adults and $25 for children 12 and younger.

Hy-Line Cruises

Ocean Street Dock, Hyannis • 778-2600
Straight Wharf, Nantucket • 228-3949

Hy-Line offers seasonal passenger-only ferry service between Nantucket and Hyannis from May to October. Reservations are not required, and the trip takes about two hours. The one-way cost is $11 for adults and $5.50 for children ages 4 to 12. First-class tickets cost $21 one-way. The number of daily departures ranges from six in season to one in late spring and fall. Hy-Line also offers seasonal ferry service between Martha's Vineyard and Nantucket.

Hy-Line's luxurious high-speed catamaran, the *Grey Lady*, launched in December 1995, provides year-round all first-class transportation. The *Grey Lady* seats 40 and makes five round trips daily to Nantucket. Travel time is only one hour. One-way for adults is $29 ($52 round trip), and tickets for children are $23 one-way ($39 round trip). Children younger than 1 ride for free. Reservations are strongly advised for the *Grey Lady* because of its limited seating capacity; call 778-0404. You can bring your bicycle on any of Hy-Line's boats for an additional charge of $4.50 one way or $9 round trip.

The Steamship Authority

S. Dock St. • 477-8600 (reservations)
Hyannis • 540-1394 (TDD)

The Steamship Authority provides year-round transportation to Nantucket from Hyannis for passengers, vehicles, bicycles and pets. Reservations are required for vehicles but not for passengers. With indoor and outdoor seating, the ferries can accommodate about 1,000 passengers. Each vessel has a full concession stand and a bar that serves beer and wine. If you decide to leave your car behind, parking costs $7.50 per day.

The trip takes about 2 hours and 15 minutes. The one-way cost is $11 for adults and $2.50 for children ages 5 to 12. Children younger than 5 ride free. Bring your bicycle along for an additional $5 each way. In season the ferries make six daily departures from Hyannis (three off-season), with additional ferries scheduled at major holidays, when the island draws larger than normal crowds for such events as the Christmas Stroll and Daffodil Festival. (See our Annual Events section in this chapter.)

Reservations for an automobile cost $101 one way from May 15 to October 14. The fare drops to $77 from mid-October through December and is also $77 March 15 through May 14. From January 1 through March 14, the one-way fare for cars is a low $55. Make your reservations several months in advance. The Steamship Authority recommends that you 1) have several alternatives for departure dates, and 2) arrive at least 30 minutes before departure to avoid your space being released to standbys. Be aware that the penalty for canceling an auto reservation can be as high as the full ticket price. Refunds will be given only if the reservation is cancelled at least 14 days in advance; after that it is possible to reschedule without a refund.

INSIDERS' TIP

A plaque and a stone boulder in a field off Madaket Road mark the site of Benjamin Franklin's mother's house.

By Private Boat

The boating crowd will find superb facilities within Nantucket harbor, which has moorings, tie-ups, fuel and food service. Most of the island's restaurants, accommodations and attractions are within easy walking distance. For more information, call the **Town Pier** at 228-7260, the **Nantucket Boat Basin** at 228-1333 or (800) NAN-BOAT, or **Nantucket Moorings** at 228-4472.

Marine supplies are available at **Island Marine Service**, 228-9095; **Madaket Marine**, 228-9086; and **Nantucket Ship Chandlery**, 228-2300, at the harbor.

Getting Around

Nantucket Town is the main part of the 50-square-mile island, which has only a few paved roads. Madaket Road leads to the community of Madaket, about 5.5 miles from town. Hummock Road leads to Cisco Beach, about 4.5 miles away; Surfside Road leads to Surfside Beach, about 2.5 miles from town; and Siasconset is about 9 miles from town along Milestone Road. Take Polpis and then Wauwinet Road to get to Wauwinet, an area roughly 5.5 miles from town. Past Wauwinet is conservation land on Great Point. The Nantucket Memorial Airport is about 2.5 miles from town.

By Shuttle Bus

A highly successful means of coping with traffic and transportation has been the use of shuttle buses, which in 1996 provided more than 196,000 rides between June and September. It may even bring romance: last fall, a couple who met on the shuttle were married on Nantucket!

Nantucket Regional Transit Authority
228-7025, TDD 325-0788

Nantucket Regional Transit Authority has expanded the shuttle service to serve the entire island, with routes to Sconset and Madaket and loops out to Surfside Road (there is no service to Surfside Beach) and Miacomet. Downtown shuttle stops are on Washington Street and Salem Street; other stops are located on the routes. The South Loop bus runs every 10 minutes and costs 50¢, as does the Miacomet Loop bus, which runs every 15 minutes. Two different routes run regularly to Sconset and cost $1; there is no service to the airport. Service to Madaket runs every 30 minutes and costs $1. Three-day, weekly, monthly and season passes are available. Senior citizens older than 65 and children younger 6 ride free. Buses are handicapped accessible and have bicycle racks. Service runs from June 1 to September 30, seven days a week from 7 AM to 11:30 PM.

By Car

One important piece of advice concerning cars is politely but firmly spelled out in the Nantucket Chamber of Commerce guidebook: "Unless it is absolutely necessary, please do not bring your car to Nantucket. By leaving it behind, you are helping us to preserve our historic downtown district." As the guidebook states, Nantucket Town was designed during the 18th century; the narrow lanes can become congested with traffic, especially during the summer months, and parking can be difficult. You really don't need a car here, particularly for daytrips; you can walk to just about anyplace in town and get out of town by bike, bus or taxi. We actually welcome the freedom of not having a car during our stays; it seems to immerse us more completely in the far-away-from-the-world feeling that being on Nantucket brings.

If you won't part with your car, be prepared to part with your money because it is expensive to bring a car to the island (see the Ferry Service section). You'll need a beach vehicle permit to drive on beaches; contact the Nantucket Police Department, 228-1212. A special permit is also required for driving on property managed by the Nantucket Conservation Foundation (reach them at 228-0006 from late-May through mid-October and at 228-2884 the rest of the year). Permits cost $75 per year (no daily rate).

There are no in-town parking lots, only street parking; it's free, but the one-hour limit is enforced. A final note: Nantucket has many one-way streets, so watch for signs.

Car Rentals and Taxis

Once on the island, transportation is not difficult to arrange. Taxis meet incoming flights at the airport and incoming ferries downtown. Car rental agencies are located at the airport and in town.

If your auto needs run to the four-wheel-drive variety, you'll want to call **Nantucket Windmill Auto**, 228-1227, (800) 228-1227, at the airport. This year-round full-service agency has a fleet of Jeeps, Wranglers and Explorers along with the more traditional sedans, vans and station wagons. They also provide free pickup service at your hotel or guesthouse or at The Steamship Authority.

Some of the other rental services on the island include: **Affordable Rentals**, 6 S. Beach Street, Nantucket, 228-3501; **Budget Rent-A-Car**, 228-5666, (800) 486-5666; and **Hertz Car Rental**, 228-9421, (800) 654-3131. The latter two are at the airport.

By Bicycle and Moped

Bicycles are an excellent way to get around because the island is relatively flat and bike paths stretch from town to Siasconset, Surfside and Madaket (but the wind can sometimes make biking a challenge!). Mopeds are faster, but inexperienced drivers can get in trouble with sand on the roads. To avoid getting ticketed (or hurt), please familiarize yourself with local regulations and observe them. Rental agencies can inform you of the regulations.

Do not ride bikes on sidewalks or mopeds on bike paths, and heed one-way street signs and other street signs. Front and rear reflectors are required.

The following shops have bike and moped rentals (Young's also repairs bikes). All are within walking distance of the ferry dock.

Cook's Cycle Shop Inc., 6 S. Beach Street, 228-0800

Holiday Cycle, 4 Chester Street, 228-3644

Nantucket Bike Shops, Steamboat Wharf and Straight Wharf, 228-1999

Young's Bicycle Shop, Steamboat Wharf, 228-1151

Accommodations

According to Nantucket Chamber of Commerce figures, the island has nearly 1,400 rooms available per night, a figure that does not include home rentals. Nantucket has outstanding accommodations of all types — single cottages, small guest houses, many bed and breakfasts, hotels and even a hostel — and we've chosen a list of what we consider some of the very best.

Rates tend to be pricey during the summer. It's safe to say you're not likely to find anything during the busy season for much less than $110 a night, with the exception of the youth hostel. In some cases, you can get a good deal by settling for a shared-bathroom arrangement. At the high end, $700 a night and $20,000 a week are possible. Most places have lower rates in the off-season. Many of the smaller inns do not allow children, while some allow children older than a certain age. One innkeeper hedged, "It depends on the child." Families with children might be better off renting a cottage or staying at one of the larger resorts that accommodates children.

It is always wise to inquire about the specific policies of any facility concerning, children, pets, cancellations and refunds. Most places accept major credit cards; we tell you of those that do not.

Nantucket has no private campgrounds, and public camping is also prohibited. The closest you'll get to camping is the hostel, which offers dormitory-style accommodations.

Price Code

The following key is based on the average cost of a night's stay in a double-occupancy room during the busy season, minus tax and special charges. Massachusetts charges a state tax, which adds about 5.7 percent to a bill.

$	**Less than $75**
$$	**$76 to $110**
$$$	**$111 to $175**
$$$$	**$176 or more**

Reservation and Information Services

If you're planning a vacation on Nantucket, reserve your accommodations well in advance — many places are booked months ahead of time. One innkeeper we talked to said summer guests often reserve rooms before they leave for the October Cranberry Festival and the Christmas Stroll (see our Annual Events section of this chapter), and then reserve their summer vacation slot while here for the holidays.

However, people's plans do change, and cancellations can easily create the opportunity for you to get a room in a first-rate inn without reserving far in advance. That's where reservation services come in especially handy. Here are a few resources to try.

Nantucket Chamber of Commerce

48 Main St., Nantucket • 228-1700

Call or write for an extensive brochure that covers everything you could want in the way of accommodations. The office is open year round. A $5 charge covers mailing expenses.

Nantucket Visitors Services and Information Bureau

25 Federal St. • 228-0925

This town-run bureau, along with the Chamber of Commerce and the Nantucket Lodging Association, has compiled a detailed list of accommodations. The staff can tell you on a day-by-day basis where vacancies exist, but they do not make bookings. The office is open daily year round.

Nantucket Accommodations

4 Dennis Dr. • 228-9559

This well-established year-round reservation service will book rooms for you (their fee is $12). They also have house rental listings.

Nantucket Vacation Rentals

6 Ash Lane • 228-3131, (800) 228-4070

If you have questions about rental houses, cottages and apartments, give Nantucket Vacation Rentals a call. The office, at Nantucket Real Estate Co., is open all year.

Accommodations Et Al

11 India St. • 228-0600, (800) 673-4559

This year-round reservation service represents a group of historic inns, bed and breakfasts and cottages distinguished by fireplaces, harbor views and antique furnishings.

The Nantucket Concierge

P.O. Box 1257, Nantucket 02554 • 228-8400

You name it, Carolyn Hills will arrange it. She books accommodations, makes reservations for airline tickets, dinner and entertainment, arranges the delivery of everything from flowers to birthday cakes and can get tickets for anything on island. She can fix you up with swimming or sailing lessons and tennis court time, as well as golf lessons and tee times. Need a babysitter while you're out on the town? She can arrange that too.

Inns, Bed and Breakfasts and Guesthouses

Anchor Inn

$$$ • 66 Centre St. • 228-0072

Located next door to the historic Old North Church just outside of town, this old sea captain's home retains its original antique paneling and random-width floorboards. The comfortable common room has a fireplace, and guests enjoy home-baked muffins, coffee and other goodies each morning on the bright enclosed breakfast porch. Each of the 11 guest rooms is named for a Nantucket whaleship and has a private bath; most have queen canopy beds.

Centerboard Guest House

$$$-$$$$ • 8 Chester St. • 228-9696

This immaculate Victorian-style guesthouse has six rooms, beautifully decorated with fresh flowers and lace; some have lovely painted murals in pale pastels. One suite has a private Jacuzzi and fireplace, and there is also a cottage available with a whirlpool bath and private garden. Rooms offer a private bath, telephone, refrigerator and television, and your hosts serve a continental breakfast. The facility is nonsmoking.

The Century House

$$$ • 10 Cliff Rd. • 228-0530

Nestled partway up the hill between Cliff Road and Centre Street, this is the oldest operating guesthouse on the island. Built in 1833 by Capt. Robert Calder, it became a rooming house in 1870. It was purchased in 1984 by its present owners, Gerry Connick and JeanEllen Heron, a husband-and-wife team who lovingly restored the old building. Guests are treated to a veritable feast each morning, including "Gerry's famous granola," homemade coffee cake, bagels and breads. Guests can relax anytime in the comfortable common room. An interesting touch: All 14 rooms are hung with lovely and varied paintings done by artists who have stayed here. The Century House is open from mid-May through mid-October.

Centre Street Inn

$$$ • 78 Centre St. • 228-0199, (800) 298-0199

Built in 1742, this was originally the residence of Peter Folger, a whale-oil trader. It became a boarding house in 1875. A close walk from both town and beaches, it offers 13 guest rooms with antique brass or canopy beds, private or shared baths. Innkeepers Sheila and Fred Heap purchased the inn four years ago, and have since redecorated each room with floral fabrics and custom painting, including some whimsical touches such as ivy surrounding a mirror. The large common room, where a continental breakfast is served each morning, is especially inviting, and guests can enjoy a cup of coffee or tea there any time of day. The inn, which is a nonsmoking facility and welcomes children older than eight, is open April to mid-December.

Eighteen Gardner Street

$$$$ • 18 Gardner St. • 228-1155, (800) 435-1450

The smell of fresh-baked cookies often pervades this charming old inn, where a plate of cookies is left by the staircase for guests to grab as they come in from a day of shopping, biking or sunbathing. This air-conditioned inn has 18 guest rooms, including singles, doubles and a two-bedroom suite, furnished with antiques and period reproductions. Many rooms have queen-size four-poster beds, and some have fireplaces that are great in the off-season. Owner Tim Madden bought the inn last year and has since redone the elegant dining room, where guests help themselves to a sumptuous continental breakfast. Downtown is a pleasant five-minute walk from the inn, or you can pedal there on one of the bicycles set aside for guests' use. The inn is open year round.

Fair Gardens

$$$$ • 27 Fair St. • 228-4258, (800) 377-6609

The inn is charming, but you'll especially

love the outdoor gardens in the backyard. The setting is in a very quiet neighborhood within a few minutes' walk of town. Some rooms have a fireplace and a canopy bed, and you can order room service for breakfast if you wish, but that means you'd have to turn down having breakfast outdoors in the Shakespearean herb garden.

Hawthorn House

$$$ • 2 Chestnut St. • 228-1468

Right in town, this homey, historic house offers nine guest rooms decorated with antique furnishings, original artwork by local artists, and in many cases, handmade quilts. A separate cottage is also available. Coffee is offered in the cozy upstairs common room, and guests receive a coupon good for a full breakfast at one of several restaurants in town. Deisel, a grey tabby cat, can often be found sitting sentinel on the front steps of Hawthorn House, which is open year round.

House of the Seven Gables

$$$ • 32 Cliff Rd. • 228-4706

This has long been a favorite of ours. Located a short walk from town up on quiet Cliff Road, this place exudes Victorian charm — maybe it's all those gables. Built in the 1880s, it was originally the annex for the Sea Cliff Inn, an old, established Nantucket hotel that was destroyed in 1972. Each of the 10 rooms is different, but all are nicely done, with floral wallpaper, quilts and antiques. Most have private baths, and some have water views. Guests are served a continental breakfast in their rooms, and can sit in the common room in the evening. No smoking is allowed at the inn.

Jared Coffin House

$$$-$$$$ • 29 Broad St. • 228-2400, (800) 248-2405

Jared Coffin, a successful Nantucket merchant, built a handsome brick house for his wife, but she complained that it was too far from town (eight blocks). So he built this fine three-story brick house, which also apparently failed to please her. Eventually, the Coffins moved to Boston, and the house has been an inn ever since.

The inn is now one of the best-loved accommodations on the island. The elegant Jared Coffin House is one of four buildings comprising the year-round inn. Sixty guest rooms and suites have single, double or queen-size beds and private baths and telephones. Furnishings are Colonial and Victorian, highlighted by lace curtains, parquet floors, canopy beds and Oriental rugs.

Breakfast at Jared's is such a treat that people who are not staying at the inn often go there for their first meal of the day. One local resident confided she breakfasts there once or twice a week just to experience a truly civilized morning repast. Guests of the inn get a full breakfast included in the room rate. Jared's also serves dinner, and the rustic Tap Room downstairs is great for a more casual lunch, dinner or snack.

Martin House Inn

$$$ • 61 Centre St. • 228-0678

Polished mahogany, classic paintings and Oriental rugs characterize this elegant 1803 mariner's home, which became an inn in the 1920s. A piano graces the common room, where window seats beckon, and a continental breakfast is served at a large, beautifully appointed table. Many of the 13 guest rooms

FYI

Unless otherwise noted, the area code for all phone numbers in this guide is 508.

INSIDERS' TIP

Take home a piece of Nantucket by seeking out locally made products. Two of our favorites are Nantucket Tea Traders teas, available in a number of local shops, and the Nantucket Beach Chair, which is so nice you may just want to park it in your living room instead of taking it to the beach. Handcrafted by Nantucket resident Robert Sarisian, these folding chairs are made of smooth hardwood with a canvas seat and back in classic Nantucket red denim. Look in Island Breezes and other shops.

have four-poster beds, fireplaces and private baths. Guests can sit on the veranda in summer, or curl up in front of the fire in the cooler months. The inn, open year round, is located just a short walk from town.

The Nesbitt Inn

$$ • 21 Broad St. • 228-0156

If you don't mind sharing a bathroom, this historic inn is a great value. Innkeepers Dolly and Nobby Noblit are two of the friendliest hosts you'll ever meet, which is no doubt part of the reason guests come back year after year. It must be genetic: Dolly is a third-generation innkeeper, part of the same family that has had the Nesbitt Inn since 1914. Built in 1872, this is the oldest inn built for that purpose on the island. The regal staircase, wide hallways and comfortable rooms seem to take you back in time — as does the claw-foot tub in one of the bathrooms. Guests can lounge in the common room or on the wide front porch. Children are welcome — there's even a play yard they can use — but not pets. A continental breakfast is included in season; the inn is open year round.

Ships Inn

$$$ • 13 Fair St. • 228-0040

Open seasonally, this inn began as the home of Capt. Obed Starbuck, who built it in 1812; many of its rooms are named for the ships he commanded. The antiques-filled home is also distinguished as the birthplace of Lucretia Coffin Mott, the first female abolitionist and advocate of women's suffrage. The inn has a romantic downstairs restaurant and bar that is open to the public for dinner; continental breakfast is available for guests.

The Woodbox

$$$, no credit cards • 29 Fair St. • 228-0587

Built in 1709, this is known as the oldest inn on the island, and the original, unpainted wood paneling, hand-hewn beams, low ceilings and huge old fireplaces bear witness to its history. Period antiques and reproductions are used throughout, and, as you might expect for a very old structure, the rooms are quite small. It is open from June through December. The inn's restaurant serves breakfast and dinner.

Hotels and Resorts

Harbor House

$$$$ • S. Beach St. • 228-1500, (800) ISLANDS

This outstanding resort hotel complex has 111 fine rooms, many of them in townhouses, one cottage, a lovely dining room, tennis courts, nightly entertainment in season, a outdoor heated pool, concierge and, well, just about anything a person could want in a hotel. The decor is traditional Nantucket, the brick sidewalks and street lighting are all part of the historic ambiance here. Business conferences and tour groups are notably well-handled at the Harbor House. This facility, which does not allow pets, is open April through December. Note: Whether you stay here or not, make a point of enjoying the buffet Sunday brunch at the Harbor House's restaurant, The Hearth.

The White Elephant

$$$$ • Easton St. • 228-2500, (800) ISLANDS

One of the island's premier facilities, The White Elephant is an expansive harborfront complex that offers everything from regular hotel rooms and deluxe suites to cottages. If you want truly luxurious accommodations, book into the Breakers, a separate and more contemporary section with water-view rooms and suites with private patios.

The White Elephant has 68 guest rooms and 32 one-, two- and three-bedroom cottages, some with full kitchens. Outdoor facilities include a swimming pool and a private dock for smaller boats. You can eat breakfast, lunch and dinner in the dining room, The Regatta, which has an outstanding view of the harbor and is open to the public. A full-time concierge can assist you with your plans. The White Elephant is air-conditioned and does not allow pets. It is open from mid-May until the end of October.

Wauwinet Inn

$$$$ • 120 Wauwinet Rd. • 228-0145, (800) 426-8718

If you want an ocean view, privacy, natural beauty, country tranquility, premier service and accommodation, you'll find it here. This ultra-romantic deluxe country inn is 8 miles from town between the bay and the ocean. It offers a 25-bedroom inn for adults only as well as five family cottages. Toppers, the elite restaurant, is open to guests for three meals and to the public for lunch and dinner. The picnic basket menu is fantastic.

The Wauwinet is open from May through October. Rates include a full breakfast, recreational activities such as tennis, bicycling (bikes provided by the inn), sailing, kayaking and cruising the bay. A daily wine-and-cheese tasting, nature excursions and four-wheel-drive trips along the 20 miles of nearby beach are also complimentary. The Wauwinet is a nonsmoking inn and does not allow pets.

Cottages

Bartlett's Beach Cottages

$$$$ • Hummock Pond Rd., Cisco • 228-3906

If you've always dreamed of waking up in a rustic cabin on Nantucket Island, throwing on your bathing suit and heading down to the ocean for an early morning swim, call and reserve one of these quaint year-round cottages. Located 4 miles from town, the cottages can accommodate one to 12 people. Pond boats are provided.

The Summer House

$$$$ • South Bluff, Siasconset • 257-4577

Eight rose-covered cottages are beautifully situated on a bluff overlooking the ocean. Five of the cottages have one bedroom, two have two bedrooms and one is a suite. All have bathrooms, two have kitchenettes. Guests have beach access, and there is also a topnotch restaurant. The Summer House is open from late April through October.

Wade Cottages

$$$$ • Siasconset • 257-6308

The grounds of this former estate are delightful, and you'll enjoy the solitude of a private beach. The accommodations include guest rooms with private or shared bathrooms, apartments with one to four bedrooms and cottages with three, four or five bedrooms. The facility is open from late May to October.

Wharf Cottages

$$$$• Swain's Wharf and Old South Wharf, Nantucket • 228-4620

Wharf Cottages are ideal for boaters who want to come ashore to dry out, stock up on supplies and buy a newspaper. They're also great for families with older children. All 22 cottages have full kitchens and water views. These cottages are open from late May to late September.

Hostel

Star of the Sea Youth Hostel

$ • 31 Western Ave. • 228-0433

Those who enjoy roughing it can make this their base for biking or backpacking getaways. This hostel, once a historic lifesaving station, has 49 beds, cooking facilities and beautiful sunset views from its location just across from Surfside Beach. Reservations are required in season (you can call for reservations beginning Dec. 1), and the cost is $12 a night for members and $15 for nonmembers, plus a linen rental charge if you don't bring your own. It's open from April 25 until right after the Cranberry Festival in late October (see our Annual Events section).

Vacation Rentals and Real Estate

Despite the fact that Nantucket has strict building regulations, it has an active and extremely pricey real-estate and new construction market. In 1995, the average inventory was about 300 homes, which was considered low, but, then, builders weren't constructing as many speculation houses. You won't find many California-style homes here; in fact, the handful of stucco dwellings stand out among the clapboard, shingle and brick everywhere. New homes and mansions with every amenity blend in and are hard to spot among the old historic homes.

The low end of the market is high here. A basic home or handyman's special can go for $175,000 or more, and new three-bedroom homes can start at $250,000. That's understandable when you realize the cost of land — which is limited on an island — is very high here. The price of most available lots is as much as most people would expect to pay for a house and lot elsewhere. If you can afford it, there are some great listings in the higher end of the market. You can get a classic antique in the heart of the historic district for anywhere from $700,000 to a few million, and a waterfront mansion may go for $5 million and up.

Nantucket's land bank tax plays an integral role in the real-estate scene, with 2 percent of the profit from the sale of land or a building going into the fund, which is used to buy and retain land for preservation.

Most of Nantucket's larger real estate offices have a rental department, in case the price of buying is out of the question or you're here strictly for R&R.

The Nantucket Listing Service, which is comparable to MLS, is another resource for prospective buyers.

The following agencies represent the best sources on the island for real-estate purchases and rentals.

Century 21 - Nonie Slavitz Real Estate

16 Macy Ln. • 228-1118, (800) 423-1167

This office has about 12 Realtors and handles vacation and seasonal rentals, year-round and vacation housing, and commercial rental and sales. It is open year round.

Coffin Real Estate

51 Main St. • 228-1138, (800) 662-8260

Open year round, this long-standing and experienced real-estate office offers seasonal and vacation rentals, and residential and commercial land sales.

Congdon & Coleman Real Estate Inc.

57 Main St. • 325-5000

Established in 1931, Congdon & Coleman is one of Nantucket's oldest firms. The full-service company offers sales, appraisals, year-round rentals and summer rentals by month or season. The office is open year round and has about 12 brokers.

Denby Real Estate Inc.

5 N. Water St. • 228-2522

Associated with Sotheby's, this 26-year-old business offers fine homes for sale and rent. Rentals range from weekly rates of $1,000 per week to $125,000 for seasonal waterfront property. The office also does appraisals and subscribes to the Nantucket Listing Service, which is comparable to MLS.

Island Properties

5 S. Beach St. • 228-6999

Island Properties offers both sales and rentals (long- and short-term). Home sale prices range from $175,000 to several million dollars. The 10-year-old firm is open year round.

The Maury People Inc.

35 Main St. • 228-1881
Sconset Rotary • 257-4050

One of the largest and most active offices on Nantucket, The Maury People has extensive sales listings throughout the island and approximately 1,500 rental listings. Open daily year round (the Sconset office is open May through October), the Main Street office has 15 Realtors on staff and has been doing business on Nantucket for 25 years. The specialities here are historic and beach homes.

Rental properties represent a range of rates; a beach cottage may rent for $1,500 per week, a mansion for $20,000 a week. The price of houses may range from a $200,000 home to a $5 million mansion.

Restaurants

The caliber of dining facilities on Nantucket makes this one island you wouldn't mind being stranded on. It could take all summer, or possibly longer, to sample all the great restaurants here, and there is plenty of variety. It is not, however, what you would call cheap.

Dinner for two at some restaurants can easily cost $120. (At one place the inexpensive wine by the glass is $12.) Not all Nantucketers ride around in Mercedes Benzes, so obviously there are ways to eat out without applying for a second mortgage. One idea: Go out for lunch instead of dinner at your favorite elegant restaurant. And look into more casual places for dinner, or restaurants that offer bistro or tavern menus in addition to full dinners.

For a quick bite, duck into one of the two Main Street drugstores, Congdon's Pharmacy or Nantucket Pharmacy, which both have sit-down counters and friendly atmospheres. They're located side by side, so if one counter is crowded (as is often the case) try the other. And you thought soda fountains had gone out of style!

While we have given you a great head start on finding your own special place among Nantucket's long list of restaurants, consider yourself morally and gastronomically obliged to do your own research. Most of the places we have included are open year round, but they may take a much-needed break sometime after New Year's; it's best to inquire about winter hours at any facility.

As a general rule, you don't have to dress up for dinner here, but there are exceptions. Chanticleer, for instance, requires jackets for men. It's a good idea to ask about a restaurant's dress code when you call for reservations.

Price Code

We've included the following pricing codes as guidelines in helping you decide where to dine. The key is based on the average price of dinner for two, excluding appetizers, alcoholic beverages, dessert, tax and tip. Most restaurants accept major credit cards; we'll tell you the ones that do not.

$	**Less than $20**
$$	**$21 to $49**
$$$	**$50 to $80**
$$$$	**$81 and more**

Arno's Restaurant

$$ • 41 Main St. • 228-7001

A popular, reasonably priced meeting place for working folk, families and hungry tourists, Arno's serves a big breakfast (until 2 PM), lunch and dinner. Get a window table and people-watch while you enjoy your food. We suggest you try the surf 'n' turf. Children have their own menu. Arno's is open year round.

The Atlantic Cafe

$$ • 15 S. Water St. • 228-0570

We find ourselves coming back to this casual, congenial place time and again whenever we're on Nantucket because we know we'll always get a great meal at a reasonable price. The waiters and waitresses are super-friendly, and children are welcome here with high chairs and a children's menu. Popular menu items include seafood dishes such as scallops, swordfish and fried clams and hearty appetizers such as nachos and fried zucchini sticks. In operation since 1978, the cafe serves lunch and dinner daily year round; the full menu is available from mid-morning to late night.

Black-Eyed Susan's

$$ • 10 India St. • No phone

This casual little place has great food at great prices and until recently was something of a local secret. Its breakfast menu offers traditional favorites along with some jazzier dishes, and in the evening the place is transformed into a bring-your-own-bottle bistro. (They do not serve liquor.) Dinner menus change every other week; some recent offerings include ancho chili penne with smoked crimini mushrooms and watercress pesto, North African spiced chicken served on tabbouleh fennel salad and steak Diane served with grilled oysters. The restaurant is nonsmoking, and is open April through October or longer.

The Boarding House

$$$ • 12 Federal St. • 228-9622

In Nancy Thayer's novel *Belonging*, which is set on Nantucket, the sophisticated, affluent heroine Joanna Jones dines twice at The Boarding House. The lady, however fictional, knows her restaurants. Chef-proprietor Seth Carter Raynor's innovative cuisine has both Mediterranean and Asian influences; yellowfin tuna with wasabi aioli and soy ginger glaze and grilled quail with citrus vinaigrette are two examples of dishes that appear on the ever-changing menu. Choose from a lighter bistro menu or more formal fare, and sit in the romantic, smoke-free lower dining room with low-beamed ceilings and fresco walls, in the comfortable bar area or, in summer, outside on the patio. The Boarding House serves lunch and dinner and is open year round.

The Brotherhood of Thieves

$, no credit cards • 23 Broad St. • No phone

Low, oak-beamed ceilings, wood paneling and lots of candlelight create a wonder-

fully warm and cozy atmosphere. The food is terrific, and there's lots of it. The corkscrew fries served with burgers and sandwiches are terrific, and the chowder is hard to beat. It is casual, offers pub fare and is open daily year round for lunch and dinner, with evening entertainment. The Brotherhood does not take reservations, so you may have to wait for a table outside in a line. But it's worth it!

Caffe Bella Vita

$$ • 2 Bayberry Ct., Nantucket Commons • 228-8766

If the urge for authentic Italian food hits when you are surrounded quite literally by seafood, stop in here for some linguine alla carbonara or ziti con salsa. Or try the tonna griglia (grilled tuna) if you feel obligated to have fresh fish while on Nantucket. The chef makes delicious sauces! You'll love the outdoor patio, perfect for a candlelit dinner or a relaxing lunch. The year-round cafe is just outside of town — the perfect opportunity to work off dinner by walking.

Cap'n Tobey's Chowder House

$ • Straight Wharf • 228-0836

This moderately priced tavern-style restaurant offers a menu and prices that families can appreciate. The clam chowder is widely and highly recommended. It is open daily for lunch and dinner in season, and closes in October.

The Chanticleer

$$$$ • Nine New St., Siasconset • 257-6231

The Chanticleer has perhaps the best wine list on the island, as *Wine Spectator* has duly and consistently noted, and the classical French cuisine is legendary. Chef-proprietor Jean-Charles Berruet has been at The Chanticleer for 27 years.

The restaurant's annual opening on Mother's Day is an anxiously anticipated event; it closes in October. In June, when the roses are out and hanging baskets of pink fuchsias are everywhere, go for lunch in the rose garden — and don't plan anything for the rest of the afternoon. Quintessential Nantucket!

Cioppino's

$$ • 20 Broad St. • 228-4622

An intimate atmosphere adds to the dining experience here, where you'll find a friendly maître d' and sophisticated fare, including the restaurant's signature dish, made with fresh local shellfish, lobster and shrimp over linguini. The menu, which changes seasonally, may include hazelnut-crusted salmon, tournedos of beef and vegetarian pasta, to name just a few compelling entrees. There's also a refreshing array of salads and tempting desserts. Cioppino's is open for lunch and dinner from May to December, and has a small bar as well.

The Club Car

$$$ • 1 Main St. • 228-1101

Located near the waterfront with a ringside seat on Main Street, this well-regarded restaurant skillfully combines casual dining and elegant eating. The menu is rich and varied — you may find anything from rabbit to octopus — and the food is consistently excellent. If your budget is tight, have lunch at the bar in season and look for dinner specials off-season. If, however, rack of lamb is a favorite of yours, just remember that you only live once.

The lounge is the last-known existing railroad car from the Nantucket Railroad Company. The Club Car is open seasonally, from May to October, serving lunch and dinner.

DeMarco

$$$$ • 9 India St. • 228-1836

This restaurant has outstanding Northern Italian food, an absolutely superb wine list (more than 100 Italian selections!) and a wonderful atmosphere. We once dined at a windowside table where the moon peeked in from above, adding to the romance. If the menu offers swordfish, don't pass it up. Owner Don DeMarco has operated the restaurant for many years. The menu changes regularly, and

INSIDERS' TIP

Thirty-six percent of Nantucket — 11,800 acres — is protected from development.

breads and desserts are made on the premises. DeMarco is open from April to December. Reservations are advised.

Espresso Cafe

$ • 40 Main St. • 228-6930

This is a favorite caffeine-refueling stop for us when we've been cruising the shops for hours and can't walk another step. Choose from cappuccinos, cafe lattes or just plain old fresh-brewed coffee, served in large white mugs. Try one of their desserts or croissants, or for a more substantial meal, soups, chili, sandwiches or pizza. It's a good place for a quick breakfast or lunch, and you can eat inside, beneath a lovely old tin ceiling or outside in the tree-shaded courtyard. Espresso Cafe is open from morning to late night during the summer; hours are shorter in the off-season.

Le Languedoc

$$$ • 24 Broad St. • 228-2552

This family-owned restaurant is known and loved by an appreciative following for its warm, intimate and comfortable atmosphere, excellent service and wonderful wine; it's one of the few places you can get superior wines by the glass. You can choose between a more elaborate and pricey menu upstairs and a more casual and affordable but equally fine cafe menu downstairs or on the outdoor terrace in summer. The restaurant is open for dinner daily in season. Lunch and dinner are available in the fall from September through Christmas Stroll (the first weekend in December; see Annual Events), and then it closes until April.

Moona Grille

$$ • 122 Pleasant St. • 325-4301

Opened in October 1995 by Everett and Linda Reid, Moona Grille offers original dishes such as lobster black bean hash, risotto of fresh asparagus, eggplant and spring peas, and fried squid salad at very reasonable prices. The menu changes monthly at this year-round restaurant, where breads and desserts are made fresh daily. Although it is in a relatively new building, the Reids have created an 1800s atmosphere with lots of interesting architectural details.

Provisions

$ • Straight Wharf • 228-3258

This year-round gourmet deli is a popular place among both locals and visitors, who come for hearty soups, salads and terrific sandwiches. Or you can opt for pâtés or cheeses with French bread, and treat yourself to a cappuccino. In fine weather the benches outside are filled with people enjoying their lunches. Provisions is open for breakfast, too, and they'll pack picnic lunches for you to take along.

RopeWalk

$$ • 1 Straight Wharf • 228-8886

Nantucket is surrounded by water, yet this is one of the few eating places with a water view. Situated near the wharves, RopeWalk is a convenient place to eat before or after you catch the ferry for lunch and dinner. You'll find ample indoor seating or you can eat outdoors at the raw bar. It's very casual, the food is good (especially the crab cakes) and some say the calamari is the best on the island. RopeWalk, which is open seasonally, is run by the same people who run The Club Car.

The SeaGrille Restaurant

$$ • 45 Sparks Ave. • 325-5700

The creative and well-prepared seafood, especially the lobster bisque, makes The SeaGrille popular with locals. One hard-working islander says she eats there two or three times a week and has never had a bad meal. The handpainted murals set a nautical tone, and the specials, bouillabaisse and quesedilla salad (which challenges even big eaters) are just samplings on a menu known for its upscale seafood at reasonable prices. The SeaGrille serves dinner nightly and lunch Monday through Saturday year round.

The Second Story

$$ • 1 S. Beach Rd. • 228-3471

Yes, it is on the second story, but the candlelit decor and handpainted walls, to say nothing of the exciting menu make it worth every step. The menu includes imaginative selections of such classics as duck, salmon and chicken with terrific sauces. It is open year round for lunch and dinner.

Something Natural

$ • 50 Cliff Rd. • 228-0504

This is a great place to stop on your way out to Madaket. Pack one of their incredible, healthy sandwiches in your bike pack and you'll have something to look forward to when you stop — if you can wait that long. You might just want to stay and eat at one of the shaded picnic tables, where you're likely to see a number of locals filling up on their lunch break. The homemade breads alone are wonderful, and if you really want to indulge, try one of their fresh-baked chocolate chip cookies. It's open from April to October.

FYI

Unless otherwise noted, the area code for all phone numbers in this guide is 508.

The Summer House Restaurant

$$$$ • 17 Ocean Ave. • 257-9976

Set on an ocean bluff with a dark green interior and white wicker furniture, The Summer House conjures up the very image of, well, summer. One of the loveliest restaurants on the island (and one of the few that is actually on the water), this is a place people come to for special occasions as well as for the excellent food. It's open for lunch by the pool, just below the restaurant, and dinner in season.

21 Federal

$$$ • 21 Federal St. • 228-2121

With polished wood, linen and candlelight, this place is quietly sophisticated — and the food has the same quality. Entrees such as braised lamb shank and sauteed breast of duck are simply and elegantly prepared, and first courses include some unusual appetizers such as tuna tartare. Do not skip dessert, which might be hazelnut and raspberry Dacquoise with coffee butter cream, or warm berry compote. 21 Federal is open for lunch and dinner April to December.

Vincent's

$$ • 21 S. Water St. • 228-0189

This bright, friendly little restaurant serves up generous helpings of Italian dishes, including seafood specialties and all sorts of pastas, at great prices. Open from May to late fall, Vincent's is housed in the only surviving Humane Society building on Nantucket, one of the houses of refuge that preceded the U.S. Lifesaving Service. Now it's a lifesaver for hungry visitors and residents.

Shopping

If you love small shops with fine merchandise, you'll find paradise in Nantucket Town. Just as the island's old-time sea captains traveled the world and brought home exotic wares of distant ports, today's shopkeepers import the best from all over, without neglecting the quality items produced right here on the island. You'll find everything from gold jewelry and pearls to beautiful handwoven shawls and the lightship baskets Nantucket is famous for.

Most of the shops listed below are open all year; we'll let you know when hours are seasonal.

Claire Murray

11 S. Water St. • 228-1913

Claire Murray's handmade rugs, both finished pieces and kits, fall into a unique class of artwork. Beautiful, colorful and cheerful, some patterns are simple enough for beginners, others are a challenge to accomplished rug makers, but all are visually exquisite. You can buy a finished rug for $70 to $3,000, and kits average about $130 each. Needlepoint and counted cross-stitch kits, gift items and cotton throws are also available. Classes are offered with a purchase. Also check out Claire Murray's new beautifully illustrated book; it's a wonderful gift.

Cold Noses

1 Courtyard, Straight Wharf • 228-5477

How many shops get letters from dogs? Owners Barbara and Ralph Maffei readily comply with orders from pooches all over the country requesting mail-order doggy snacks. This shop has everything for the canines in your life and gifts for felines too! Those much-in-demand homemade dog biscuits come in an assortment of flavors, shapes and sizes and contain no salt, sugar or soy. The shop stocks other healthy pet foods as well. The Maffeis,

Photo: Cape Cod Times

Sandcastle building is fun for the young and young at heart.

who also have a shop in Boston, cram a lot into this small shop, including dog clothing, greeting cards, pillows and collars with matching human belts. Cold Noses will definitely warm your heart.

Cross Rip Outfitters

24 Easy St. • 228-4900

If there's an angler on your gift list, be sure to stop here. In addition to rods and reels, this shop has a great collection of fishing-related gifts, including beautiful painted mugs, ties, jewelry, hats, shirts, sunglasses and even stationery. Cross Rip also offers fly fishing instruction, equipment rentals and a guide service.

Erica Wilson Needle Works

25 Main St. • 228-9881

This store has lovely original gifts, including darling animal hangers, handpainted quilts and handknit sweaters from England and Ireland, bears and other stuffed animals and children's clothing. Unique needlepoint kits work into patterns adapted from famous tapestries and original designs, which range in price from $20 to $1,200 for a rug.

Diana Kim England, Goldsmiths

56 Main St. • 228-3766

Seven goldsmiths contribute to the elegant handmade jewelry sold here, much of which is produced in the studio upstairs, including earrings, pendants and bracelets in 14- to 18-karat gold and ivory. Among the most popular pieces are the gold lightship basket charms, some of which have moving parts. Prices here range from about $70 to $2,400. The shop is closed from January to April.

Flowers at the Boarding House

12 Federal St. • 228-6007

The sweet fragrance of flowers envelopes you as soon as you step into this florist/gift shop. Every nook and cranny is filled with lovely things, including potpourri, fancy pillows and soaps. This is a great place to shop for that perfect wedding or shower gift — or treat yourself! The small ceramic Nantucket tote bag is a perfect memento, but don't limit yourself to the gift shop. We once received a beautiful bouquet of fresh flowers from the adjoining florist shop that made our little bed and breakfast room both fragrant and homey. The florist shop offers a vast selection of topiary and fresh flowers and offers worldwide flower delivery.

Handblock

42 Main St. • 228-2358

This visually-enticing boutique carries unique clothing for women and children, plus some wonderful gift items including gorgeous pottery, jewelry and lifelike stuffed cats and dogs. In the rear of the shop are shelves and shelves of colorful linens, woven pillows and blankets and beautiful hatboxes.

The Hub

31 Main St. • 228-3868

This is the place to go to buy a newspaper — just about any newspaper. The Hub also sells magazines, books, lottery tickets, post cards and sundries, and offers photocopy and fax service. As its name implies, it's generally a lively place, great for chatting with perfect strangers.

The Kiteman

7 Cambridge St. • 228-7089

While you're in the childlike, carefree mood that Nantucket inevitably inspires, why not pick up a great kite and head for a sandy beach? The Kiteman (a.k.a. Al Hartig) sells a huge selection of Valkyrie and Ace kites to a high-flying clientele.

The Lion's Paw

0 Main St. • 228-3837

Baskets, pillows, hooked rugs, linens and boldly colorful ceramics make up the bulk of inventory in this delightful, spacious store. This shop has a terrific selection of tablecloths and also displays beautiful handpainted furniture and accessories and unique gift items.

Mitchell's Book Corner

54 Main St. • 228-1080

If you love books, you won't be able to resist this corner shop. The Nantucket Room is especially engrossing, with titles such as Nathaniel Philbrick's *Away Off Shore*, deservedly touted as one of the most readable Nantucket histories, Francine Mathews' *Death in Rough Water*, Martha Lawrence's *Lightship Baskets* and John McCalley's *Nantucket Then and Now*. Mitchell's also has a great general inventory and a large selection of quality children's books.

Murray's Toggery

62 Main St. • 228-0437

Family-owned and operated, Murray's celebrated its 50th birthday in 1995. There is a reason for its longevity: It's got everything. You'll find shoes, sweaters, hats and Estee Lauder products, and it is the largest men's clothing store on Main Street. Started by Philip Murray, the popular Nantucket Red menswear line originated here from a type of slacks made in France. It has now expanded to coats, jackets and caps.

Nantucket Country

38 Centre St. • 228-8868

"I only buy things I would put in my own home," says Cam Dutton, who opened this two-story antiques shop in April 1996. Chock full of one-of-a-kind pieces, from a Passier hunt saddle to a lovely 18th-century tilt-top tavern table, the shop specializes in old quilts and folk antiques. It has a few new items as well, such as hooked rugs and country accent pieces. It's open year round, but weekends only in the quiet off-season.

Bill and Judy Sayle's Nantucket Lightship Baskets

112 Washington St. Ext. • 228-9876

Beautiful, practical, versatile — and undeniably expensive — the traditional Nantucket lightship baskets that are exquisitely handmade by Bill and Judy Sayle range in size from miniatures as small as a thimble to ones as big as a baby's cradle. Woven with a fine caning material, the baskets are made with a cherry wood bottom, oak stays, oak handles and leather hinges, and the lids are decorated with carved ivory or scrimshaw scenes. Both Bill and Judy create the baskets, and Bill handcarves the decorative whales, shells or birds in ivory. (It was Bill's mother, Mickey, who first suggested putting a lid on the traditional lightship basket and his father, Charlie, who carved the first decoration on a basket made in 1948 by Jose Reyes.)

The prices vary according to size, the type of wood used for the tops and the type of decoration. Miniature baskets can range in price from $195 to $525, and medium-covered baskets with a carved sperm whale on the lid can start around $775. The Sayles' shop is open weekdays from 10 AM to 3 PM and weekends by appointment year round (unless they take a winter break after the holidays).

Nantucket Bookworks

25 Broad St. • 228-4000

This year-round store not only has a wonderful collection of books and plenty of room to browse, but a fun assortment of greeting cards, stationery, blank books and other gifts for writers. It has a great children's section, and gifts for all ages are scattered throughout the store. Even the cash register receipts are fun, each with an interesting quote from notable literary figures. In business 25 years, Nantucket Bookworks keeps long hours, so you can browse after dinner!

Nantucket Looms

16 Main St. • 228-1908

Nantucket Looms displays beautiful handwoven throws, mufflers and shirts and small elegant toiletries, jewelry and oversize mugs. Local and international craftsmen have contributed to this rich assortment of clothing and gift items, including decorative birdhouses and dog doorstops, handmade sweaters and handpainted furniture. Their cotton fishermen's sweaters are classics.

The Nantucket Sleighride

3 India St. • 325-4980

With ivy growing across the front of the building, this shop is as pretty outside as in. It carries Christopher Radko Christmas ornaments, which collectors consider the ultimate in glass, as well as other Christmas collectibles by Miriam Mandell and Ginny Moore and copies of 19th-century candle molds. Although the Nutcracker is usually a male figure (had you ever thought about that?), here you can get a female Christmas Nutcracker.

Nantucket Gourmet

4 India St. • 228-4353

This store has everything for the true or aspiring gourmet, from every imaginable kitchen gadget to Nantucket-made jams and jellies, mustards, cranberry marmalade, mustards, vinegars and teas. The peppergun, an unusual one-handed grinder invented by Tom David of Nantucket, is particularly popular. The shop also has a full deli with more than 40 types of cheeses and other edibles for party platters and picnic lunches.

Nina Hellman

48 Centre St. • 228-4677

Here is a wonderful collection of marine antiques — everything from old anchors, tools and ship lanterns to intricate ship models and ships in bottles. The shop also has a great collection of old scrimshaw, prints, Nantucket memorabilia and a great collection of old books on whaling, sailing and other nautical topics. It's open from Daffodil Weekend to Christmas.

The Fragrance Bar

5 Centre St. • 325-4834

Step into this old-time apothecary-like shop for an unforgettable olfactory experience. Perfumer John Harding will custom-mix essential oils to arrive at the fragrance you're looking for or match you with one of hundreds of his existing blends identical to popular fragrances. Since they contain no alcohol or other additives, the scents have amazing staying power. The shelves here are also filled with lotions, bath gels, shampoos and soaps that can be custom-scented.

INSIDERS' TIP

Fall is a wonderful time to visit Nantucket. The swamp maples and cranberry bogs make for beautiful fall color, and the island is quieter too.

Sweet Inspirations

26 Centre St. • 228-5814

Chocolate, chocolate, chocolate. Those who love the stuff will find a haven in Sweet Inspirations, where the glass-front display cases are filled with plates of all sorts of positively inspired creations. Try one of their heavenly truffles, chocolate buttercrunch, chocolate-covered cranberries or, our personal favorite, a simple square of dark chocolate wrapped in foil embossed with a tiny Nantucket Island. Sweet Inspirations has lovely collectible tins to fill with the chocolates of your choice and does mail order too.

Weeds

14 Centre St. • 228-5200

A new and beautiful take on the Nantucket Lightship basket is a line of porcelain and fine bone china designed by Weeds founder and owner George Davis for Wedgewood and available exclusively at the shop he launched more than a decade ago. There's a lot more to see in this year-round shop, which sells antique and reproduction furniture, hat boxes, tins, garden items and gifts to fit every price range.

Entertainment and Nightlife

The streets of Nantucket are wonderfully quiet when the stars come out, but if you're a night owl there are some lively spots. Also consider taking in some of the cultural arts offerings of Nantucket. During the summer season, theater is performed on the island.

The Theatre Workshop of Nantucket

Bennett Hall, 62 Centre St. • 228-4305

If you're a fan of community theater, attend a production by this organization, which showcases local talent year round for enthusiastic audiences.

Actors Theater

1 Centre St. • 228-6325

This company, which stages productions in the basement of the Methodist Church, combines professional and amateur talent in new productions in the summer. The small stage lends an intimate flavor to the plays performed by this talented ensemble.

Movies

Check out the **Dreamland Theater** on S. Water Street, 228-5356, and the **Siasconset Casino** in Siasconset, 257-6585. Both are open seasonally. The **Gaslight Theatre**, on N. Union Street, 228-4435, is open year round.

Rose & Crown

S. Water St. • 228-2595

In town, the Rose & Crown is a lively night spot that often has live entertainment; it is closed in winter.

Chicken Box

14 Dave St. • 228-9717

Heading toward Surfside Beach, you can find this super-casual, year-round bar, better known as The Box. The Box has live bands seven nights a week from Memorial Day to Labor Day and every weekend the rest of the year.

The Muse

44 Surfside Dr. • 228-6873

The Muse is another popular watering hole that has live entertainment on weekends, usually bands but occasionally DJs. It also offers Keno and video trivia games.

Harbor House

S. Beach St. • 228-1500

For more low-key entertainment, try the Harbor House where The Hearth hosts a folk duo on Friday and Saturday nights springtime though December.

The Brotherhood of Thieves

23 Broad St. • No phone

This is a cozy eatery that often has a solo guitarist or folk duo perform on weekends.

The Tap Room at the Jared Coffin House

29 Broad St. • 228-2400

You won't find hard rock here, but often this downstairs respite will feature folk music with a guitarist adding to the homey, old-fashioned atmosphere. Have a bite to eat and then linger over conversation and drinks to hear the music.

Photo: Rob Benchley, Nantucket Beacon

A lone scalloper heads out into Nantucket Harbor at sunrise during opening week of Nantucket's Bay Scallop season.

Cross Rip Coffee House

Methodist Church, 2 Centre St. • 228-4352

Here's a great alternative to bars: entertainment in an alcohol-free environment. The coffee house offers varied entertainment year round, from comedy acts to folk music.

Arts

Visual Arts

Nantucket Island School of Design and the Arts

23 Wauwinet Rd. • 228-9248

If the visual arts are your love, contact the school and take some classes. The school offers courses for academic credit and enrichment to both children and adults in such subjects as drawing, painting, photography, clay, textiles and crafts. The school has accommodations on Washington Street on the harbor.

Shredder's Studio

Salros Rd. off Appleton Rd. • 228-4487

Shredder's offers oil painting, watercolor, jewelry making and basketry classes to adults and young adults and watercolor, ceramics and other classes for children. It even has a preschool creative workshop for little budding artists.

Galleries

Robert Wilson Galleries

34 Main St. • 228-2096

While in Nantucket, be sure to visit this gallery, which has exquisite landscape and still-life renderings in oils and watercolors.

The Little Gallery
Straight Wharf • 228-0294

The Little Gallery is operated by the Artists Association of Nantucket. You can buy a remembrance of Nantucket and support local artists at the same time.

The Nantucket Gallery & Frame Shop
23 Federal St. • 228-1943

This gallery is owned by artist Marshall DuBock, who sells Nantucket scenes. (See our close-up in this chapter for more about DuBock).

The Gallery at Four India Street
4 India St. • 228-8509

This gallery is open year round. It has 19th- and 20th-century oils, pastels, watercolors, sculpture and bronze work, 80 percent of which is the work of local and regional artists.

Attractions

Nantucket's place in history is richly illustrated in the island's museums and historic buildings. You can visit them for an Insiders' view of the past, including the whaling period that shaped Nantucket's salty character. Be sure to allow plenty of time to see everything, including the three picturesque lighthouses that dot the shoreline.

Historical Sites and Museums

The Whaling Museum
Broad St. • 228-1736

Originally a candle factory, this superb museum offers displays of whaling equipment, scrimshaw, early records and the skeleton of a 43-foot finback whale. Don't miss the lively lecture on the history of whaling, presented 3 times a day. The museum is open on weekends starting in April and daily in May; it closes just after Columbus Day. Admission is $5 for adults and $3 for children.

Nantucket Historical Association Sites
2 Whalers Ln. • 228-1894

The association maintains and operates 11 historic sites and buildings, including the **Friends Quaker Meeting House and Fair Street Museum**, 7 Fair Street; the **Old Mill**, Mill and Prospect streets, which has original mechanisms and stones; the **Old Gaol**, Vestal Street, which is nearly 200 years old and is one of the oldest jails in the United States; and the **Hadwen House**, 96 Main Street, which contains the architectural detail and furnishings characteristic of the 19th century.

These facilities are open to the public daily from mid-June to Labor Day (some stay open longer). A general pass is $10 for adults and $5 for children. The association's gift shop, 228-5785, is next to the Whaling Museum.

Maria Mitchell Birthplace
1 Vestal St. • 228-2896

America's first woman astronomer, who taught at Vassar College in 1865, is memorialized in her preserved home. The Maria Mitchell Society, 228-9198, works to preserve her contributions. You can tour the home from June through August. The admission fee for nonmembers is $3 for adults and $1 for children.

The society also operates the **Maria Mitchell Observatory**, next door at 3 Vestal Street, 228-9273, and the **Marine Aquarium** at 28 Washington Street, 228-5387.

The Hinchman House
7 Milk St. • 228-0898

Wildlife enthusiasts will appreciate the natural history collection of living and preserved varieties of wildlife here. The staff conducts children's nature classes, and bird and nature walks. The Hinchman House is open for self-guided tours June through August. Admission is $3 for adults, $1 for children.

Macy-Christian House
Liberty St. and Walnut Ln. • 228-1894

Built in 1723 and restored in the late-19th century, this house has furnishings and architecture representative of the Colonial and Colonial Revival periods. Daily tours are available, and admission is $2 for adults and $1 for children.

The Oldest House

Sunset Hill • 228-1894

This Colonial saltbox was built in 1686, nearly 100 years before the American Revolution, for Jethro and Mary Gardner Coffin as a wedding present from their parents, ending the notorious feud between the two families. Admission is $3 for adults and $2 for children. It is open seasonally.

Nantucket Atheneum

Lower India St. • 228-1110

The recently renovated handsome Greek Revival library is one of the oldest continuously operating libraries in the country; Maria Mitchell was the first librarian. It contains some 40,000 volumes as well as paintings, ship models, scrimshaw and sculpture, and also has a wonderful new children's room. Be sure to visit the Upper Hall, where such figures as Daniel Webster, Ralph Waldo Emerson, Henry David Thoreau and Frederick Douglass once spoke.

The Life Saving Museum

Polpis Rd. • 228-1885

This is an authentic re-creation of the original 1874 station built in Surfside to assist mariners. It is open daily from mid-June to mid-September.

Peter Foulger Museum and Research Center

Broad St. • 228-1655

This facility includes the Historical Association's archives and is open year round. The museum has permanent and rotating exhibits pertaining to Nantucket history.

The African Meeting House

Five Corners • 228-4058

This small post-and-beam building was built around 1827 by African-American island residents, who used it as a school, church and meeting house. The building, which is the only remaining public African-American landmark, is owned by Boston's Museum of Afro-American History, which is working to restore it. Tours are available by appointment.

The Coffin School

4 Winter St. • 228-2505

Completed in 1854, this Greek Revival building succeeded the island's first school on Fair Street after the Great Fire of 1846. Around the turn of the century, the school became a center for nautical training and home economics for the Nantucket Public Schools. It now houses the Egan Institute of Maritime Studies, and is open to the public from June to October, offering lectures, exhibits and history videotapes.

Lighthouses

Brant Point Light

Harbor entrance

Built in 1746, Brant Point Light is the second-oldest lighthouse in the United States. Photographs of its Christmas wreath have graced numerous magazine pages. This is the lighthouse you see when entering the harbor on the ferry.

Great Point Light

Great Point

Destroyed by a storm in 1984 and rebuilt, Great Point Light sits at northern tip of the island in an area frequented by bird-watchers and picnickers. (See our Natural Areas section.)

Sankaty Head Lighthouse

Sankaty Bluff

Picturesque red-and-white Sankaty Head Lighthouse is perched on Sankaty Bluff at the eastern end of the island. It overlooks the sea and a golf course.

Tours and Excursions

Nantucket's experienced tour guides show off their island with the love and pride of a gardener showing off a bed of roses. You'll get a history lesson, personal insights and priceless anecdotes, and witness the easy camaraderie of islanders, who are likely to roll down the car window and give the traffic cop — probably a friend — a hard time.

Most tours will meet you at a central location or pick you up. The cost is generally about $10 per person.

Ara's Tours

P.O. Box 734, Nantucket 02554 • 228-1951

In its 11th season, Ara's offers two basic tours: a 1½-hour tour that covers 30 miles with guided commentary in an air-conditioned van for $10 per person at 10 AM, noon and 2 PM; and a 3-hour, four-wheel-drive beach tour that begins at 4 PM and takes you to the island's northernmost point for $40 per person. Naturalist and photographer Ara Charder provides the commentary and always stops for photos. The van tour can accommodate 14 people, and the four-wheel drive tour 8 people per vehicle. Private tours are also available.

Barrett's Tours

20 Federal St. • 228-0174
In Eastern Mass. • (800) 773-0174

Barrett's provides narrated bus tours of Nantucket daily April through November and also offers shuttle-bus service to Jetties, Surfside and Madaket beaches and to Siasconset. A family-owned and -operated business for 75 years, Barrett's also offers tours and transportation for special groups, such as wedding parties, with group rates for 20 or more people.

Betty's Tour and Taxi Service

61 Polpis Rd. • 228-5786

For a tour of the island's homes, beaches, bogs, lighthouses and historic sites, ride with Betty — she seems to know every back road on the island — or Ed. Scheduled tours are at 9:30 and 11:30 AM and 2 and 4 PM and by appointment in the off-season.

Grimes Tours

22 Pleasant St. • 228-9382

A descendant of one of the original settlers of Nantucket, Robert Pitman Grimes provides a personal tour in his Suburban with commentary gleaned from research and personal experiences. Tours start at 10 AM, 1 and 3 PM and usually take about 1¾ hours. You can schedule a private tour for as many as eight people by appointment.

Walking Tours of Nantucket Town

228-1062

Former Nantucket selectman and local official Roger A. Young provides a fascinating 2-hour guided walking tour from June 1 to September 30. It's best to call for reservations. His daily tour starts at 9:30 AM and focuses on island history and historic sites. "I tell stories," Young says. "Some are true and some aren't true. People tell me I should write a book." Tours cost $10 a person.

Gail's Tours Inc.

257-6557

A sixth-generation native, Gail Nickerson Johnson has a wealth of knowledge and a great sense of humor, which she shares generously on her tours. Her two vehicles can accommodate a total of 13 people. She offers sightseeing and private tours, including sunset, picnic or beach excursions. Regular tours depart at 10 AM and 1 and 3 PM.

Whale Watching and Cruises

Whaling as an industry played a key role in the history of Nantucket. Visit The Whaling Museum to trace its impact (see our Attractions section in this chapter). But today's emphasis is on watching rather than killing these magnificent creatures. For a real adventure, try an all-day whale watch. If you just want to get out on the water, there are a number of boats available for tours. We've listed a few of them.

Nantucket Whalewatch

Straight Wharf • (800) 322-0013, outside Mass. (800) 942-5464

In July and August the whale-watch vessel *Yankee Spirit* departs on Tuesdays only from Straight Wharf for an all-day trip to whale feeding grounds at the Great South Channel. Naturalists with the Center for Oceanic Research and Education of Gloucester provide the narration. The cost is $65 for adults and $45 for children younger than 12. The traveling time is about two hours each way, and full galley services are available.

Anna W II

Straight Wharf • 228-1444

This boat offers several trips daily in season, starting with a morning 1½-hour lobster trip ($22.50 for adults, $17.50 for children 4 to 12). Captain Bruce Cowan is a naturalist and very knowledgeable about marine life as well as boats. The afternoon ice cream cruise, on which children are invited to help steer the boat between bites of ice cream, is very popular with families, and the evening sunset cruise is both romantic and relaxing. Bring your own beverages. The Anna W II also offers afternoon shoreline cruises in summer and seal cruises from November to late April.

The Endeavor

Straight Wharf • 228-5585

This Friendship sloop, owned and operated by Jim and Sue Genthner, offers four daily sails around Nantucket Sound plus a sunset cruise. You can also arrange private charters and parties. Ask about the Songs and Stories of the Sea trip, which is fun for children ages 4 to 8, and the Fiddlin' on the Sea trip, which provides whaling-era instrumental music for families with older children. Rates range from $15 per person for a one-hour sail and $22.50 for a 1½-hour sail to $30 for a 1½-hour sunset sail.

The Genthners also offer you the unique opportunity of exploring the inner harbor in the *Wanderer*, an authentic 30-foot reproduction whaleboat, which can be rowed or sailed. Aside from learning about Nantucket whaling life, passengers can explore beaches, bird watch or have a picnic lunch. Trips can be arranged from June through September, and rates depend on length of trip.

Beaches

When you're on a relatively small island, it's hard to get away from the beach. Aw, what a pity.

Whether you go to an ocean beach with crashing surf or a harbor beach with gently lapping waves, don't miss the opportunity to savor the Nantucket seaside.

Take time to learn the existing swimming conditions before you head for the beach. Currents can be very strong along the entire south side of Nantucket, including Cisco, Madaket and Surfside beaches. The Parks and Recreation Department, 228-7213, recommends that people swim only at lifeguarded beaches; beaches are closed when conditions warrant it. Free parking is available at all beaches, and you can usually find a space even in the busy summer months. All of Nantucket's beaches are lovely; here are some of our favorites.

In-town

Children's Beach

Harbor View Way

Families naturally gravitate toward this pleasant beach, where a lifeguard is on duty, restroom facilities are available and there is a snack bar. And as you might expect, it has a nice play area for children, complete with a big wooden Jeep that one little boy we know found hard to leave.

Brant Point

Easton St.

This beach right by the lighthouse has no lifeguards or facilities, but the view of the harbor is always entrancing. An easy walk from town, it's a great place to just sit and watch the boats rounding the point.

Jetties Beach

N. Beach St.

This large, popular beach is within a short

INSIDERS' TIP

End-of-season poetry outside a Nantucket business:
No more lobsters, no more beach,
Closed for three weeks, can't be reached.
Going to San Fran to drink some wine.
Play some golf
And dine, dine, dine.

walk of town. It has lifeguards, restrooms, bathhouses, a restaurant, tennis courts and towels and chairs for rent. The town's Park and Recreation Department, 228-7213, offers swimming lessons here for children ages 6 and older from July 4 through Labor Day.

Out of town

Dionis Beach
Dionis Beach Rd.

The beach that bears the name of Tristram Coffin's wife, Dionis is 3 miles out of town, west of Jetties. Sheltered by dunes, this beach has calm waters, so it's a good one for children. The beach has lifeguards and restrooms.

Madaket Beach
Madaket Rd.

The currents here are strong and can be dangerous depending on weather conditions. Still, it's a popular spot for surf swimming, and lifeguards are on duty. The West Ender restaurant is about a five minutes' walk from the beach. Madaket is known for its spectacular sunsets.

Cisco Beach
Off Hummock Pond Rd.

Travel southwest about 4 miles out of town to reach this stretch of shore, which is a popular place for surf-casting. A lifeguard is on duty.

Surfside Beach
Surfside Rd.

Surfside is on the south end of the island and is one of the most popular Nantucket beaches. The beach is wide — perfect for kite-flying — and has a bathhouse, restrooms and lifeguards. It's accessible by bus and bike.

Natural Areas

The Nantucket Conservation Foundation owns many properties that can be used by the public for recreation such as hiking. Other properties are owned by the Nantucket Land Bank or other conservation organizations. The Conservation Foundation owns and manages more than 8,348 acres, about 28 percent of all the land on Nantucket. We've listed a few of our favorite properties; for others, look for their maroon concrete posts decorated with the Foundation's gull and waves logo. For a complete map of all Foundation properties and regulations, visit the Foundation office at 118 Cliff Road or call 228-2884. Remember, vehicles on these properties are strictly regulated or prohibited.

The Sanford Farm, Ram Pasture and The Woods

These properties total 767 acres of wetlands, grasslands and forests in the southwest portion of the island. With more than 6.6 miles of roadways and trails to explore, the area includes a panoramic view of Nantucket's south shore from the barn in Ram Pasture. Ambitious hikers can follow a 6-mile round trip trail that leads to the ocean and travels alongside Hummock Pond. You'll find a variety of wildflowers and may spot such wildlife as ring-necked pheasant, osprey, red-tailed hawk, rabbits and deer. The land is accessible from a parking area off Madaket Road, near the intersection of Cliff Road.

Long Pond

Owned by the Nantucket Land Bank, this 64-acre property is especially good for bird-watching. It features a 1-mile walking path that runs along the pond, past meadows and a natural cranberry bog. To reach the area, take Madaket Road and look for a dirt road on the left across from the sign to Hither Creek, near Madaket. Cross the bridge to reach a parking area and the entrance to the trail.

Eel Point

A spit of sand on the western end of the island, just north of and bordering Madaket Harbor, Eel Point is a Nantucket Conservation Foundation property that attracts great numbers of birds. The 100-plus acre property abounds in goldenrod, roses, wild grapes, bayberries and other vegetation. To get there, take Eel Point Road off Cliff Road and park on the dirt road. If you're biking, take a right off the Madaket bike path onto Eel Point Road.

Coskata-Coatue Wildlife Refuge

This barrier beach that stretches across Nantucket Harbor is actually several protected

Photo: Michael Gavin, The Inquirer & Mirror

An artist captures on canvas a scene from a street on Nantucket.

areas in one: Coatue Wildlife Refuge and The Haulover, 476 acres owned by the Nantucket Conservation Foundation; Coskata-Coatue Wildlife Refuge, 792 acres owned by the Trustees of Reservations; and Nantucket National Wildlife Refuge at Great Point, owned by the U.S. Fish and Wildlife Service. Great Point, which is home to the lighthouse of the same name that's a replica of the one lost in a severe storm in 1994, is the island's northernmost point, slicing up between Nantucket Sound and the Atlantic Ocean. Remote and wild, the barrier beach offers breathtaking views and the opportunity to observe nature first-hand. In spring, it's a nesting place for piping plovers, least terns, northern harriers and other shorebirds.

The area as a whole includes not just beaches and sand dunes, but salt marshes and wind-sheared oak and cedar forests. Vehicles are strictly controlled here; a pass is required to drive a four-wheel-drive vehicle, and officials advise inexperienced beach drivers not to drive in the very soft sand. This is a place for serious nature-lovers who don't care about frills or modern amenities. There are no lifeguards, and some of the beaches are particularly dangerous for swimming. There are no rest rooms, concessions or public buildings within the refuge; come here only if you want to be one with nature and are willing to respect her.

Recreation

Boating and Watersports

Watersports are big here, and it's a great place to finally learn how to sail or windsurf or try kayaking. Whether you're an old hand or just starting out, look to the following places for equipment and advice.

Nantucket Boat Rental

Slip 1 Boat Basin at the end of Main St., • 325-1001

If the sight of all those beautiful boats in the harbor makes you want to take one out yourself, contact Nantucket Boat Rental. They rent power boats by the day, week or month.

Nantucket Harbor Sail

Swain's Wharf • 228-0424

This operation rents sailboats during the season.

Force 5 Watersports

37 Main St. • 228-0700

Jetties Beach Rd. • 228-5358

Both locations offer lessons in windsurfing, kayaking and sailing for both children and adults from May through October. You can also rent equipment, small boats and Sunfish and hire guides. The Main Street location is open year round, while the Jetties Beach store is open May to October.

Sea Nantucket Kayak Rentals

Washington St. Ext. • 228-7499

This seasonal shop offers rentals, lessons and guided trips.

Fishing

Fishing has been a way of life for Nantucketers for generations and still provides a healthy and popular form of recreation, not to mention a delicious meal. If you want to go for bluefish or striped bass, you can pick up equipment, bait, and a guide with a four-wheel-drive and head for Great Point, Smith Point or Surfside Beach.

A four-wheel-drive vehicle is needed for access to Great Point and Smith Point, but you can walk onto Dionis, Surfside and Pebbles beaches. These are perhaps the best-known beaches, but keep in mind that Nantucket is rimmed by beaches, so finding a fishing spot is not difficult. Of course, as any angler knows, finding fish is another matter. We highly recommend that you contact local tackle shops for current information about fishing (we suggest several, below), since obviously the location of fish and conditions at sea change day to day.

The Nantucket Anglers Club, 228-2299, sponsors the Annual Billfish Tournament for offshore fishing. Open to the public, this weeklong tournament takes place around the last week in July and the first week in August.

If you don't own a boat, you can go fishing in a head boat (charges by the person) or a charter boat (charges for the boat). Head boats always provide fishing equipment, and you generally do not need reservations, but it is always best to check ahead. The cost is in the vicinity of $25 per person. There are not many big-game fish charters out of Nantucket. We recommend the ***Priscilla J***, 228-4225, and ***Monomoy Charters***, 228-6867, for serious fishermen.

If your kids want to do a little bottom fishing off the wharves, they might catch some scup or flounder, but most people head out to the beaches. Nine to 11-foot spinning rods are prevalent for surf fishing. According to Bill Pew at Bill Fisher Tackle, 90 percent of fishing here is done with artificial lures rather than live bait, and he sees growing interest in fly-fishing.

Tackle Shops

Barry Thurston Fishing Tackle

Nantucket Marina • 228-9595

With two decades of experience, this fishing shop outfits for deep-sea fishing, surf-casting, freshwater fishing and shellfishing. It's a licensed Orvis dealer and sells equipment and clothing, offers daily or weekly equipment rentals and does repairs.

Bill Fisher Tackle

14 New Ln. • 228-2261

Open year round, this shop has a full line

INSIDERS' TIP

The best place to get a bird's-eye view of Nantucket is from the tower of the First Congregational Church at 62 Centre Street. It's a climb but well-worth it, and the 94-step journey to the top is interrupted by a display of old photographs and history of the Old North Church, as it is known. The public can tour the church on weekdays from June through September.

of conventional freshwater and saltwater tackle, spinning tackle and fly-fishing tackle. It also offers freshwater bait, rental equipment, referrals for guide service and maintenance and repairs.

Golf

Miacomet Golf Club
Off Somerset Rd. • 325-0335

Owned by the Nantucket Land Bank since 1985, this is the island's only publicly owned course. It has nine holes, a par of 37, a driving range, pro shop and both pull and electric carts. Reservations for tee times are required at least a week in advance; the course turns away about 100 people a day in summer. Rates in 1996 were $22 for 9 holes and $40 for 18, but were expected to rise for 1997.

Sankaty Head Golf Club
Sankaty Rd., Siasconset • 257-6391

This year-round course is open to the public only from October 1 until the first Friday in June, excluding Memorial Day weekend when, as in summer, it's reserved for members. The 18-hole, par 72 course, developed in 1920 and still recognized as one of the country's finest links courses, enjoys water views from just about every hole. Carts are available, and an on-site pro shop offers everything a golfer may need. Greens fees are $90 a day, and reservations are required.

Tennis

Brant Point Raquet Club
48 N. Beach St. • 228-3700

This club has nine clay courts open to the public. You can pay hourly for court time or opt for instruction to improve your game. The club offers both private and group lessons. It also has a fully equipped pro shop, rental raquets and equipment.

Tristram's Landing Tennis Center
440 Arkansas Ave., Madaket • 228-4588

This center has five hard-surface courts available for play at hourly rates.

Jetties Beach Public Tennis Courts
North Beach St., Jetties Beach • 325-5334

These courts are free and open to the public, and available on a first-come, first-served basis.

Annual Events

There's a lot going on here, and not just in summer. Besides the annual events, there are dozens of concerts, craft fairs and other events to watch for when you come to the island. Check with the Chamber of Commerce, 228-1700, for a current guide.

April

The Daffodil Festival
Sconset • 228-1700

The Daffodil Festival heralds in spring as the island's thousands of yellow daffodils come to life in late April. The road to Sconset is lined with millions of the brilliant blooms, which the Garden Club and townspeople started planting in 1974. The highlight of the festivities is the gathering of 100 or so antique and classical cars on Main Street and the parade and giant tailgate party at Sconset.

May

Figawi Race
Hyannis to Nantucket • 771-1691

Now in its 26th year, this sailboat race from Hyannis to Nantucket and back generates as much excitement here as it does on the Cape. It takes place on Memorial Day weekend (see our Cape Cod Annual Events chapter for details).

June

Annual Nantucket Harborfest
Nantucket • 228-1700

Activities include the Blessing of the Fleet and Boat Parade, a chowder festival, the Pirate and Mermaid Parade, races and competitions, special music, historic and maritime displays, exhibits and activities, many of which are geared to children.

July

Independence Day

Nantucketers do it up on the Fourth, with a riotous fire hose contest on Main Street, pie-eating contests, face painting and more. In the evening, a gala celebration with music and children's games takes place at Jetties Beach, followed by a fireworks display.

August

Sandcastle & Sculpture Day

Jetties Beach, Nantucket

For nearly a quarter of a century, Sandcastle & Sculpture Day on Jetties Beach has given Nantucketers of all ages a chance to express their creativity in the island's most plentiful art material: sand. The event is always held on the third Saturday in August. Entries are judged in five divisions, ranging from Family to Under 7. You can use tools, but you cannot add any supporting or form devices to the sculpture.

September

Nantucket County Fair

Tom Nevers Navy Base • 325-4748

Set for the third weekend in September, this is a real old-fashioned tradition started six years ago. Baked goods, jams and jellies vie for ribbons, and an animal tent, tractor, hay rides, pet show and square dancing are some of the lively activities.

October

Cranberry Harvest Festival

Nantucket • 228-1700

Held right after Columbus Day, this festival gives folks a chance to compete in the annual cranberry cookery contest — only Nantucket-grown cranberries allowed! The day also includes a tour of the town's inns and a flurry of activities in the Cranberry Harvest Marketplace, including demonstrations of cranberry-wreath making and the sale of edible delights starring the celebrated fruit.

November

Nantucket Noel

Nantucket • 228-1700

A Christmas-tree lighting ceremony and caroling the day after Thanksgiving launch weeks of special events that end New Year's Eve. Throughout the holidays, you can join in lots of activities such as house tours, ice sculpting and wreath decorating contests.

December

Nantucket Christmas Stroll

Nantucket • 228-1700

During the first weekend in December, the Christmas Stroll draws tens of thousands of people to Nantucket with the town-wide celebration of Christmas. Some 274 Christmas trees are placed throughout the town and decorated by local businesses, services and students in a decorating contest. At noon on Saturday, a U.S. Coast Guard cutter (not Rudolph and Company) delivers Santa, who is then transported to the Stroll in a horse-drawn carriage. School children, carolers and bell-ringers in period costume create a joyful atmosphere with holiday song. And everywhere you look you'll find wonderful food, hot chocolate and beautiful decorations — even a talking Christmas tree!

Note: Make your holiday hotel reservations way in advance — a year ahead is strongly advised. And bring those Christmas lists (and wallets); Nantucket shops have the most exquisite gifts!

Healthcare

Nantucket Cottage Hospital

57 Prospect St., Nantucket • 228-1200

The only medical facility on the island, this hospital offers 24-hour emergency care, home-health care, chemotherapy, x-rays, mammography, physical therapy, dialysis and laboratory services.

Important Numbers

For medical, fire or police emergencies, dial **911**.

A Safe Place, 24-hour hotline, 228-2111
AIDS Awareness/Information, (800) 235-2331
Alcoholics Anonymous, (800) ALCOHOL
Children at Risk, (800) 792-5200
Missing Persons, (800) 622-5999
Alzheimer's Information, (800) 351-2299
Cancer Information, (800) 422-6237

Media

Newspapers

The Inquirer & Mirror
Milestone Rd. • 228-0001

The Inquirer & Mirror is Nantucket's oldest newspaper, established in 1821. The publication started as *The Inquirer* and merged with the competing paper, *The Mirror*, in 1865. This newspaper operated as an independent until 1990 when it was sold to Ottaway Newspapers Inc., a subsidiary of Dow Jones. Marianne Giffin Stanton is the publisher.

The Inquirer & Mirror, affectionately known on the island as The Inky, is published every Thursday and has a circulation of about 10,000. It has the largest classified ad section on the island and also publishes the "Nantucket Holiday" and a monthly vacation guide. Mailed subscriptions reach far and wide, including towns and cities in every state. You can request a mailed copy of the paper for $4.

The Nantucket Beacon
64 Old South Rd. • 228-8455

The Nantucket Beacon was founded in March 1989 by Island developer Bruce Poor. Edward R. (Ted) Leach of Hancock, New Hampshire, bought the paper six months later and then sold it in October 1995 to Ottaway Newspapers Inc.

In a short time, *The Beacon* has developed a reputation for outstanding journalism. During 1993 and '94, The New England Press Association recognized it as New England's Weekly Newspaper of The Year.

The Beacon is printed off-island at the plant of its sister paper, the *Cape Cod Times*; Scott Himstead, former publisher of the *Cape Cod Times*, is publisher. *The Beacon* is a Wednesday publication with a peak summer season distribution of about 8,000 (circulation and size of the paper vary due to Nantucket's resort character).

Martha's Vineyard

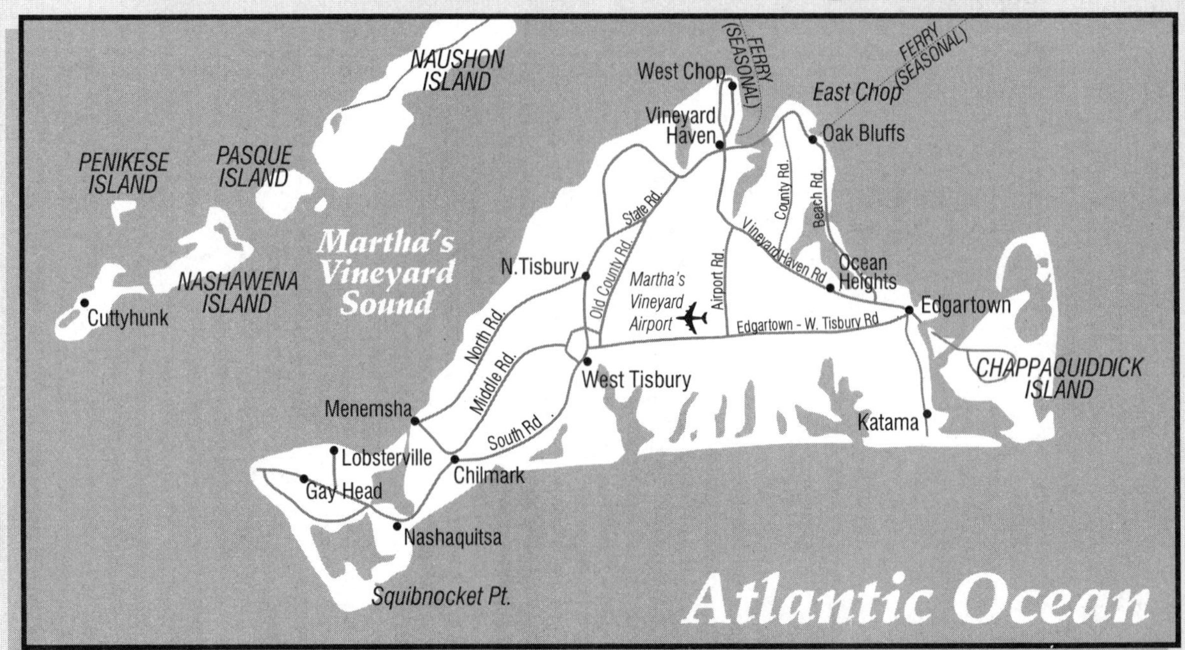

Martha's Vineyard

To visit the island of Martha's Vineyard is to fall in love with her. Her grasp is inescapable. You fall, willingly, into her arms, swept up in her spectacular views, her quaint villages, her charming gingerbread cottages and her rich sea captains' homes.

She is an island who is what she is and isn't what she doesn't wish to be. It may sound like gibberish, but the imbedded message is quite true. So easy it would be for the island to fall victim to the tourist traps that have infested many seasonal communities, reaching and grabbing for that fleeting tourist dollar. Yet, that is not what Martha's Vineyard is all about. She refuses to sacrifice her unique personality or compromise her ever-present beauty to increase net profit. Be thankful for what she is — and equally thankful for what she is not.

New England's largest island, Martha's Vineyard lies about 7 miles south of Cape Cod. The island is 20 miles long and 9 miles wide and consists of six towns, each with its own distinct personality. Some 14,000 year-round residents call the island home, but during the busy summer months that population swells to nearly 100,000. Together with the town of Gosnold on Cuttyhunk Island (the only public island of the Elizabeth Island chain) and No Man's Island (an uninhabited island off Gay Head), the six towns of Martha's Vineyard are part of Dukes County. FYI: You can get to Cuttyhunk Island from the Vineyard, see the Excursions section of this chapter.

The Vineyard's six towns have memorable names. When referring to Vineyard Haven locals are in reality talking about the town of Tisbury. The northernmost tip of Tisbury is called West Chop. Directly across the harbor is East Chop, which is the northernmost point of the town of Oak Bluffs. Southeast of Oak Bluffs is the town of Edgartown, which includes the island of Chappaquiddick, known locally by its nickname, Chappy. Up island refers to the much more rural towns of West Tisbury, Chilmark and Gay Head. Chilmark includes the fishing village Menemsha. The term "up island" can be confusing to visitors because you go up island by actually traveling down island or, rather, southwest. Up, in this case, refers to up in terms of longitude. The further west one travels, the higher the longitude . . . it's a nautical thing.

Famous stars of stage and screen call this island home. Some of the more popular islanders include singer Carly Simon, political humorist Art Buchwald, actress Patricia Neal, retired news anchor Walter Cronkite and Blues Brother Dan Ackroyd (his comedic partner, the late John Belushi, lies in an unmarked grave on the island). A certain princess who was formerly married to the Prince of Wales has visited the Vineyard, as has a certain U.S. President in recent years. But name-dropping is not what Martha's Vineyard is about either. There is something about the island that transcends all of these front-page stories, something that sets it apart as something truly wonderful, a gift handed to us by either the giant Indian god named Maushop or else by a half-mile thick sheet of ice many thousands of years ago.

History

Though the legend of Maushop creating Martha's Vineyard with the sand from his moccasin is fun to relate, Martha's Vineyard was in fact created during the last ice age when the Laurentide ice sheet deposited the boulders and gravel it had carried along in its slow journey southward. As the ice sheet receded, the southernmost deposits became the islands of Nantucket and Martha's Vineyard. The oceans began to rise with the melting ice, thus forming Nantucket Sound between these lovely islands and the equally lovely peninsula to the north known as Cape Cod.

As the climate warmed, Native Americans

began to migrate to the island, settling here some 5,000 ago. These Indians of Nantucket called themselves Pokanocket and named their island No-epe, which translates as "amid the water."

Legend has it that Viking explorers discovered the island back around A.D. 1000, but that story is very hard to prove, or disprove for that matter. What is known for sure is that in March 1602, English navigator Bartholomew Gosnold set off in his vessel *Concord* across the Atlantic to arrive months later along the coast of Maine. Farther south, he discovered Cape Cod and, on May 22, he arrived at Martha's Vineyard (Edgartown, to be more exact, Cape Poge, Chappaquiddick to be even more exact), which he named for his daughter, Martha, and for the multitude of grapes he found on the island. Gosnold later attempted to establish a settlement on nearby Cuttyhunk Island, but abandoned the attempt, citing unfavorable living conditions.

FYI

Unless otherwise noted, the area code for all phone numbers in this guide is 508.

Though there is a story of white settlers arriving as early as 1632, the official settlement of Martha's Vineyard, by Thomas Mayhew Jr., would not occur until 1642. During the previous year, his father, also named Thomas Mayhew, had purchased the islands of Martha's Vineyard, Nantucket and even the neighboring Elizabeth Islands for 40 pounds (less than the cost of a room on the island today). Thomas Mayhew Jr.'s group of 80 settled at Great Harbor, later incorporated as Edgartown in 1671. The settlement was renamed by New York Governor Lovelace to honor Edgar, the son of the Duke of York, and was no doubt done to earn the favor of the royal family. Edgar was the 3-year old nephew of King Charles, and because the King did not have children of his own, Edgar appeared to be heir to the throne. Unbeknownst to Lovelace, poor little Edgar died a month before the town's incorporation.

White settlers and Native Indians quickly learned to live together in this island paradise. As they had at the Plymouth colony, the Indians shared their farming and fishing skills with the settlers. Hostilities between the two groups were nonexistent, and even during the King Philip War of 1676-77 (which saw white settlers and Indians battling on the mainland) relations on the island remained friendly. Yet, this island paradise turned to disaster for the Natives as they began to fall in great numbers to the diseases brought with the white settlers. Some 3,000 Indians lived on Martha's Vineyard when Mayhew and his group first arrived. Within 30 years, the Indian population had been cut in half due to diseases. Many of the surviving Indians were converted to Christianity as they attempted to stave off elimination by praying to the white man's god as the white settlers seemed unaffected by the diseases that swept through the Native Indian numbers.

Very soon white residents outnumbered the dwindling Native Indians. By the middle of the 18th century there were perhaps only 500 Native Indians remaining, while the white population swelled to more than 2,000. Fortunately, pockets of Indians survived and today half the population of the town of Gay Head consists of Wampanoag Indians.

The Towns

The history of each of the Vineyard's towns is as varied as their differing personalities. Though settlement began in Edgartown, people began to settle in different parts of the island. Farming and fishing provided the staples of life early on, but very soon each town was built on what it had to offer.

Edgartown prospered as a whaling port during the early to mid-1800s. More than 100 whaling captains hailed from this town, and today their stately homes, a majority of them built between 1830 and 1845, line the main roads of Edgartown as reminders of the fortunes made harvesting whale oil. The last half of the 19th century saw a rapid decline in whaling as the discovery of petroleum made the pursuit of the leviathan an obsolete profession. Edgartown's prosperity stagnated until tourism restored the town and its many beautiful buildings to their 18th- and 19th-century splendor.

Vineyard Haven, known early on as Holmes Hole, is the island's second-oldest town, incorporated in 1671 as Tisbury. Its excellent harbor made it an important port town where the wares of the Vineyard could be readily sold to off-islanders. Oceangoing traffic was so busy in the area that Nantucket and Vineyard sounds were considered second to only the English Channel in terms of number of vessels passing through. The sea played a large part in the town's development as her sons would serve as sailors and fishermen upon local and not-so-local vessels. Today, Vineyard Haven maintains its port status, providing a busy harbor which connects the island to the mainland and to the rest of the world, for that matter.

The town of **Oak Bluffs**, incorporated in 1907, was once part of Edgartown. Its development as a seasonal community was begun by an Edgartown man back in 1835. In that year, Jeremiah Pease selected the area of Oak Bluffs to hold a Methodist camp meeting. The idea caught on, and each summer the camp meeting grounds were visited by religious folk who pitched tents to spend time worshiping and relaxing beneath the oaks which grew abundantly in the area. Very soon the tents were replaced by cottages. So many cottages were built that when Oak Bluffs broke away from the town of Edgartown in 1880 it was named Cottage Town (until 1907 when it was renamed). Residents decorated the cottages with ornate woodwork, and today their gingerbread flavor dictates the personality of this quaint resort town.

Up island lie the towns of West Tisbury, Chilmark and Gay Head. **West Tisbury** was largely a farming community and maintains its rural personality. It was formally a part of the town of Tisbury until it broke away as a separate town in 1892. Meanwhile, **Chilmark**, with its fishing village of **Menemsha**, earned its living from both the sea and the land. Chilmark was incorporated in 1694. **Gay Head**, which became an independent town in 1870, is a geological wonder with its cliffs of clay displaying the fingerprint of the last ice age. The town's roots stem from an Indian settlement, and today Gay Head is home to more than 100 members of the Wampanoag tribe.

Presently, Martha's Vineyard survives largely off tourism. Tourism began with Oak Bluff's mid-19th century Methodist campground that attracted thousands, many from New York, to the island for spiritual relaxation. In fact, the tourism so prevalent in Oak Bluffs, and then in neighboring Vineyard Haven, helped to resurrect Edgartown years after the whaling boom of the mid-1800s had gone bust. Potential was seen in renovating the old sea captains' houses, turning them into inns, bed and breakfasts, shops and restaurants. Thankfully, magnificent architecture and irreplaceable history has been preserved, and Edgartown stands today as an upscale vacation town where you can stay and dine in buildings that speak volumes of a century when men went to sea to hunt whales, and many did not return.

Tourist Information

To learn more about all that Martha's Vineyard has to offer, stop by, call or write the **Martha's Vineyard Chamber of Commerce**, 24 Beach Road, Vineyard Haven 02568, 693-0085. The chamber is open Monday through Friday, 9 AM to 5 PM, year round. From Memorial Day to Labor Day the chamber's satellite office, located on the Vineyard Haven pier as you come off the ferry, is open on Saturdays and Sundays.

If you are interested in visiting Edgartown, you can contact the **Edgartown Visitors Center** at 29 Center Street, Edgartown 02539 (no phone). The center is open seven days a week from Memorial Day through Labor Day.

Getting Here

From Woods Hole, Martha's Vineyard appears as if just a good swim away, it seems that close! Well, not quite. It takes a bit more than a brisk breaststroke to get to the island.

More than once we've heard a visitor to Cape Cod asking a native of the peninsula for directions to "the bridge to Martha's Vineyard." If you happen to be flipping through the pages of this guide searching for such directions, we're sorry to tell you that there is no such bridge. Therefore, there are only two ways of getting to the island: by air and by sea.

By Sea

Journeying to the island by water, you get a feel for what Gosnold saw and felt upon that May day in 1602 when he first made his discovery. Yet, for a singular treat, make the journey after nightfall and watch as Nobska Light of Woods Hole, West Chop Lighthouse of Vineyard Haven and East Chop Lighthouse of Oak Bluffs call out across the waves to one another like a triangle of lovers.

Once you've decided that you're going to travel to the island via water, you then have to decide how. Here are your options.

The Steamship Authority

Railroad Ave., Woods Hole
• 548-3788, (800) 352-7144 (Mass. only)

The lifeline to the Vineyard, The Steamship Authority has been making the run between Woods Hole and Martha's Vineyard for more than three decades. The line's large ships provide daily, year-round service to the ports of Oak Bluffs and Vineyard Haven. The trip across takes about 45 minutes — it seems as soon as you leave Woods Hole you're arriving at the Vineyard. The ride for passengers (no cars) costs only $10 round-trip for adults and $5 for children (1997 prices). Children younger than 5 travel for free.

The Steamship Authority is the only ferry service that can transport your car to the island, but make your reservation as early as possible by calling the number above. Space fills up quickly, especially in summer. The 1997 price for a round-trip car reservation is $88, dropping to $54 in the off season. FYI: The one way fare to transport a bicycle is just $3.

If you decide to leave your car behind, which is actually a pretty good idea as the island has an outstanding shuttle service, The Steamship Authority has three parking lots available. The daily cost for parking is $7.50. Shuttle buses provide free transportation from the parking lot to The Steamship Authority pier.

Island Queen

Falmouth Height Rd., Falmouth • 548-4800

As their radio jingle says, you can "sail away from Falmouth" aboard the *Island Queen*. She departs from Falmouth Inner Harbor daily from Memorial Day through Columbus Day (October 12) and arrives at Oak Bluffs Harbor 35 minutes later. Round-trip fares are $10 for adults, $5 for children younger than 13 and no charge for children younger than age 3. You can bring a bicycle for $6, round-trip.

Falmouth Ferry Service

278 Scranton Ave., Falmouth • 548-9400

This ferry service is unique in that it runs from Falmouth directly to Edgartown (most other ferry services dock at either Vineyard Haven or Oak Bluffs, from which you must take a shuttle or other transportation to Edgartown). Round-trip fares run $22 for adults and $16 for children 12 and younger, while children 5 and younger sail for free. Bicycle rates are $3 each way. Falmouth Ferry Service runs daily from Memorial Day to Columbus Day. The trip takes exactly one hour.

Hy-Line Cruises

Ocean St., Hyannis • 778-2600

Hy-Line is the only line that provides daily service from downtown Hyannis to Oak Bluffs from early May through late October. The crossing takes 1¾ hours, and round-trip tickets cost $22 for adults and $11 for children. Children 4 and younger travel free with boarding pass. Your bicycle travels for $4.50 each way. From June to mid-September the line also offers the only daily interisland service between Martha's Vineyard (Oak Bluffs) and Nantucket. This sojourn takes 2¼ hours and, the round-trip fares are $22 and $11 for adults and children, respectively.

Schamonchi

Rodney French Blvd., New Bedford
• 997-1688

If you travel via the ferry *Schamonchi,* you can visit two of Massachusetts' three major whaling ports, New Bedford and Edgartown (Nantucket being the third), all in the same day. The vessel makes the daily run from New Bedford's Billy Wood's Wharf to Vineyard Haven Harbor in 1½ hours. The fare is $16 same day round-trip for adults, $7.50 for children. Children younger than 2 travel for free, and your bicycle makes the passage for $2.50 each way. *Schamonchi* runs from mid-May to mid-October. Heck, after you've seen Edgartown you might as well catch an interisland Hy-Line cruise to Nantucket to tour the third whaling port while you're at it! We're sure Melville would be thrilled if you did.

By Your Own Boat

For those of you who master your own vessel, the island offers four harbors where you can dock. **Menemsha** offers slips with electricity; the harbor master, 645-2846, can provide more details. **Edgartown Harbor** has moorings available by the day, week or season. None have plug-in facilities. One pump-out station and one pump-out boat are available. You can reach the harbor master at 627-4746.

Vineyard Haven offers moorings, launch service and dockage. The harbor master's number is 696-4200. **Oak Bluffs** has plug-in slips for sail and motorboats for rent; a small number of moorings are available in the harbor. The harbor master's number is 693-4355.

By Air

If you cross by sea you'll notice the sea gulls of Woods Hole following along, crossing with you in hopes of grabbing a morsel of food from the passengers. Large, powerful engines move the ferry forward, yet the gulls seem to coast along at the same speed with very little effort, their God-given aerodynamics accomplishing with ease what it takes man's mighty machines to do. Who has the evolutionary upper hand here?

The gull's graceful aerial passage reminds us that we too can fly to the island and causes us to consider what wondrous sights can be seen along the way. Several airlines service the island and can provide those incredible sights.

The island has two airports: **Martha's Vineyard Airport**, 693-7022, located in nearly the center of the island, and the smaller **Katama Airfield** in Edgartown, 627-9018, offering runways of grass (how quaint!). Katama is one of the original Curtiss-Wright Fields from back in the early airmail days and is one of the largest turf fields of its type remaining in the Northeast. The following airlines serve the Martha's Vineyard Airport.

Air New England

693-8899

As its name suggests, this airline provides charter service to the island from various cities throughout the northeast.

Cape Air

(800) 352-0714

Cape Air makes regular daily flights between the Vineyard and Hyannis, Boston, Nantucket and New Bedford. In fact, their summer schedule offers over a dozen flights a day from Boston to the Vineyard. The airline's joint ticketing and baggage handling allows passengers on other airlines to connect with Cape Air flights.

Direct Flight

693-6688

You can't get a more direct flight than with this appropriately named line. It offers charter flights directly to the Vineyard from various locations.

USAir Express

(800) 428-4322

If you are from the Boston area, you can take the direct route to the island onboard one of USAir's regularly scheduled flights.

Continental Express

(800) 525-0280

This airline operates during the summer months, providing access to the island from several locations.

Getting Around

By Car (or bike or moped)

Arriving at the island without your car? No problem. The island is prepared for your arrival in a big way. There are cars, mopeds, scooters and bicycles for rent. Buses run every 15 minutes during peak season. For less than $5 the buses will shuttle you to the three towns of Vineyard Haven, Oak Bluffs and Edgartown and back again! Sightseeing tours and taxis are available as well.

Depending upon your visit, you may not even need any of the above. For instance, if you arrive at Oak Bluffs or Vineyard Haven via ferry for a daytrip and don't plan to leave the town at all, your legs alone can get you to nearly all the hot spots. Or a shuttle can take you to an adjoining town for a couple of bucks and your legs can take care of the rest. We arrived for a daytrip recently and took in the towns of Vineyard Haven, Oak Bluffs and Edgartown via a $4.25 roundtrip shuttle pass and the strength of our calves. Our legs were a bit tired as we sipped a beer on the ferry that night on our way back to Woods Hole, but it was a good kind of tired.

This is probably as good a point as any to give you an idea of distances between the island towns. Vineyard Haven and Oak Bluffs are side by side; it's a 10 minute car ride (if that) from the ferry dock of one, around Vineyard Haven Harbor, to the ferry dock of the other. From Oak Bluffs to Edgartown is a good 10 minutes along Beach Road. Across island from Edgartown west to the point where Edgartown-West Tisbury Road, State Road and South Road meet in West Tisbury is about 10 miles, or about a 15- to 20-minute scenic drive. From that point in West Tisbury to Beetlebung Corner in Chilmark is about 4 or 5 miles, less than 10 minutes of driving. Another 6 miles (10 minutes, perhaps 12) along State Road brings you to Gay Head. Then, to get from Gay Head back up north to Vineyard Haven, allow perhaps 35 to 40 minutes for the 18-mile trip. There, you just traveled the island in one paragraph's time!

Rentals

Auto rentals during peak season are offered at, of course, peak prices. It seems the average rate for an average car runs about $50 to $60 on an average day. Larger cars cost more. Jeeps and off-road vehicles cost even more. In Vineyard Haven is **Thrifty Car Rental**, 693-1959 or 693-8143, and **Holmes Hole Car Rentals**, 693-8838 or (800) 696-8838. **Budget Rent A Car**, 693-1911, is located near the harbors at Vineyard Haven and Oak Bluffs and at the main terminal at Martha's Vineyard Airport. Budget offers free customer pickup at Edgartown.

For about $35 you can rent a moped for the day; add about $5 to $10 for a double moped that allows two adults to ride on the same two wheels rather than renting two mopeds. Daily bicycle rates run from about $10 to $15 for a three-speed and $15 to $20 for a mountain bike. As you come off the boat at either Vineyard Haven or Oak Bluffs these rental outfits are everywhere. In fact, we challenge you to swing a striped bass without hitting a bike rental shop.

By Shuttle Bus

The island's bus shuttle service is superb. The drivers, who each probably answer the same dozen questions a couple thousand times a day, do so in such a courteous way that you'd think you were the first person ever to ask, "Does this bus go to Edgartown?" **Martha's Vineyard Transportation Service**, 693-1589 and 693-0058, offers daily service between Vineyard Haven and Oak Bluffs and between Oak Bluffs and Edgartown. From mid-May to mid-October the buses run every 15 minutes from 8 AM to 7:30 PM. Service is also provided to and from the airport and to the island's other three towns, West Tisbury, Gay Head and Chilmark. It's best to call ahead first for details.

In Edgartown, nothing can beat the **Edgartown Shuttle**, 627-7448, which you can ride for the cost of the change you might find buried in your sofa at home (about 50¢ one way, seniors and children travel for free). From mid-May to mid-September the shuttle runs throughout the historic streets of Edgartown. Edgartown also has an open-air trolley that carries passengers from the center of town to

INSIDERS' TIP

Martha's Vineyard was used as the setting for the fictitious town of Amity in Steven Spielberg's 1975 big-screen smash *Jaws*. Many other scenes were shot in Edgartown (even on the On Time ferry to Chappaquiddick), at Gay Head (in fact you can see the Gay Head Lighthouse in the background of a number of scenes) and of course, the fishing village of Menemsha. If you want to see a great white up close, plan to attend the Oak Bluffs Monster Shark Tournament, held every July.

South Beach every 30 minutes, mid-June to mid-September.

Accommodations

From the moment you step off the ferry you will feel welcome at Martha's Vineyard. The excitement that only an island can offer greets you, whether you are here for a daytrip, a night or an extended vacation.

If you are here for an overnight stay, or for several nights, you'll need to know your different options in the way of accommodations. By the way, if you happen to be glancing at this section on the boat ride over to the island, we hope you've already made reservations. Since Martha's Vineyard is an island, there are only a finite number of rooms available and they fill up very quickly. Even in September and October it is common to see the No Vacancy signs posted. Fall visitors are surprisingly many.

If your choice is to stay at an inn or bed and breakfast, you'll be happy to learn that there are many sprinkled throughout the island. Some are quaint places, others are majestic showplaces. All are beautiful in their own distinct way. Many of them are old sea captains' houses, or in the case of Edgartown, whaling captains. The history in these houses is omnipresent, it lulls you to sleep each tranquil evening amid dreams centuries old and gently awakens you again each morning with sunlight anew and yet a sunlight touched by the ages.

For those not in with the inn crowd, there are a number of fine hotels, some with spectacular views. More frugal travelers might opt for the hostel with rates starting around $12 a night. Also, there are two campgrounds; starting at around $27 per night for those who like to become one with nature.

The peak season generally runs from late May (Memorial Day) to late September, in some cases until Columbus Day in mid-October. During this peak season hotels, inns, bed and breakfasts, and guest houses charge peak prices. During the off-season, room rates are lowered, in some cases substantially. It is not uncommon to see rates cut in half after Columbus Day, and with the crowds gone you feel like you own the island!

Price Code

Our price code is based on the average cost of a night's stay in a double-occupancy room during peak season, minus tax and special charges. (State and local taxes add up to 9.7 percent of the bill.) Since this is an average, rooms may be had in some places for more or less than what's reflected in our code.

$	**Less than $75**
$$	**$76 to $110**
$$$	**$111 to $175**
$$$$	**$176 and more**

Unless otherwise noted, all accommodations are nonsmoking and welcome well-behaved children. We'll let you know which places accept pets. Most places accept major credit cards; we'll let you know those that don't.

We've also included a number of reservation services that can assist in your search for proper accommodations. The section following Accommodations lists real estate companies that handle rentals and sales.

Reservation Services

About the Beach

Box 269, Oak Bluffs • 693-1718

Owner Thea Hansen handles a variety of rentals, from bed and breakfasts to waterfront cottages. To give you a rough idea of what to expect, a five-bedroom beachside house runs about $2,000 per week. Meanwhile, a one-bedroom cottage facing the water can set you back about $3,200 per month. That's about $100 a day . . . rather reasonable considering the view.

House Guests Cape Cod and the Islands

Box 1881, Orleans • 896-7053, (800) 666-HOST

This company offers a varied selection of accommodations in bed and breakfasts and host homes at prices starting as low as $50 a night. They will also plan your Cape and islands itinerary. See the Accommodations chapter in the Cape Cod section of this book for more information. All properties are annually inspected; you'll pay a nonrefundable $15 booking fee for each reservation.

Martha's Vineyard and Nantucket Reservations

Box 1322, Vineyard Haven • 693-7200, (800) 649-5671

Since 1977, this company, the islands' oldest reservation service, has been booking rooms in inns, hotels, cottages, bed and breakfasts and guesthouses. You pay no fee.

Bed and Breakfasts and Country Inns

Vineyard Haven

The Hanover House

$$$ • 28 Edgartown Rd., Vineyard Haven • 693-1066, (800) 339-1066

Behind a row of large hedges hides the Hanover House, a cozy, quiet bed and breakfast inn located just steps from the harbor. This village inn offers 12 impeccably maintained rooms, each with a private bath, two double beds or a queen-size bed, air conditioning and cable TV. Many of the rooms feature entrances that open onto one of two spacious sun decks. In a separate carriage house are three suites, two of the which have kitchenettes. Each suite has a private deck or patio. Complimentary breakfast includes homemade breads and muffins and fresh-ground gourmet coffee. Innkeepers Ron and Kay Nelson keep a quiet home and ask that you inquire beforehand when bringing along infants or children. Hanover House is open year round.

Thorncroft Inn

$$$$ • 460 Main St., Vineyard Haven • 693-3333

Talk about elegance. The Thorncroft is one of the island's premier inns offering 14 guest rooms in two antique-appointed houses on 3° acres of private and beautiful land. Each room features a private bath and central air conditioning. Many have canopied four-poster beds and 10 have wood-burning fireplaces. Three rooms even offer two-person Jacuzzis, and two have private 300-gallon hot tubs.

A full country breakfast and afternoon tea and pastries are served daily in the dining rooms. This top-rated inn was recently cited as one of the 10 best handicapped accessible inns in the country as its private cottage was built with handicap access in mind. The entire inn and grounds are smoke-free. Special services include a fire-ready fireplace upon your arrival (just strike a match), a *Boston Globe* at your door in the morning and turndown service. Prepare to be pampered! Thorncroft Inn is open year round.

The Tisbury Inn

$$-$$$ • 9 Main St., Vineyard Haven • 693-2200, (800) 332-4112

The Tisbury Inn, located at the foot of historic Main Street and just two blocks from the ferry, has been serving guests since 1794. The inn has 30 rooms, each with a private bath, phone, air conditioning and cable TV. The inn also features a full-service health club that includes an indoor heated pool, a sauna and hot tub. A continental breakfast, included in the room rate, consists of bagels, pastries, juice and coffee and is served in the treetop sun room or porch overlooking Vineyard Haven. To satisfy a larger appetite, next door is the Cafe at the Tisbury Inn if you're in the mood for seafood, ribs or pasta. The Tisbury Inn is open year round.

The Tuckerman House

$$$-$$$$ • 45 William St., Vineyard Haven • 693-0417

Built in 1836 by seafarer Thomas Tuckerman, this inn is nestled amongst the historic sea captains' homes along William Street, just off Main Street. The five guest rooms are comfortable, air conditioned and feature canopy beds, fireplaces and Oriental rugs. The latticed veranda is a perfect place to sit and read or just sit and do absolutely nothing. Innkeepers Carolyn and Joe Mahoney serve an abundant continental-plus breakfast in the spacious dining room. They are adamant about their nonsmoking policy. The inn is open year round.

Photo: Peter Simon

Ferries transport thousands of visitors every summer.

Oak Bluffs

Beach House Bed and Breakfast

$$$ • Corner of Pennacook and Seaview Ave., Oak Bluffs • 693-3955

You couldn't ask for a better location: right across the street from the town beach on Vineyard Sound and within easy walking distance of all the sites in Oak Bluffs including the community of gaily colored gingerbread cottages. It is also within a five- to ten-minute walk from the ferry dock. This wonderful bed and breakfast, owned by Calvin and Pamela Zaiko, was converted to a year-round inn back in 1975 and has been owned by the Zaiko family since the 1940s. All nine rooms at the Beach House have private bathrooms. A complimentary continental breakfast buffet is served in the dining hall and on the front porch with magnificent views of the ocean. Children age 10 and older are welcome at the Beach House.

Dockside Inn

$$$ • Circuit Ave. Ext., Oak Bluffs • 693-2966, (800) 245-5979

The outside of this gaily colored inn is surely a feast for the eyes. A simply beautiful building to look at, it is painted a combination of cream, pink and soft pastel blue, as are the chairs that line its front porch. With its second-floor wraparound balcony and its proximity to the harbor, the place has a river boat feel to it. You almost expect to see Mark Twain sitting on the front porch.

It's hard to believe that this beauty, with architecture pointing to the mid- to late-19th century, was actually built in 1989. All 20 of the Dockside Inn's rooms have air conditioning, private baths and cable TV; most rooms have queen-size beds. Three fully equipped kitchen suites are also available. The Dockside, convenient to all that Oak Bluffs has to offer, is open from April to November.

Island Inn

$$$-$$$$ • Beach Rd., Oak Bluffs • 693-2002, (800) 462-0269

Along the road that connects Oak Bluffs and Edgartown lies the Island Inn. Overlooking the Farm Neck Golf Club, the Island Inn is a short walk to two of Oak Bluff's best beaches, Oak Bluffs Town Beach and Joseph Sylvia State Beach. The inn offers an assortment of 51 rooms, suites and even a cottage — all sporting fully furnished kitchens, private baths and cable TV. If you're into tennis you'll be happy to learn that there are three Har-Tru tennis courts on site. A full-time tennis pro is available to give you lessons. Families can take advantage of the 7 acres of grounds including a barbeque area, an outdoor pool and a playground for the kiddies. The Island Inn is open from mid-March to mid-December and has one handicapped-accessible unit available.

The Oak House

$$$-$$$$ • Seaview Ave. at Pequot Ave., Oak Bluffs • 693-4187

The Oak House truly lives up to its name. Throughout most of the guest and commons rooms oak is the rule. It's everywhere, rich, warm and inviting. This 1840s Governor's mansion, overlooking Nantucket Sound, has 10 rooms (two of which are suites), nearly all resembling oak-paneled ship cabins. All but three of the rooms offer water views; all have private baths. Some rooms have private balconies and some, air conditioning. You can relax in the sun porch or in a rocker on the wraparound veranda while you watch the waves chase each other toward shore. Or, you can settle down with a book in the elegant oak parlor. Innkeeper Betsi C. Luce, a professional pastry chef, serves a homemade continental breakfast and Victorian afternoon tea. Children older than the age of 10 are welcome. The Oak House is open from May through October.

The Ship's Inn

$$-$$$ • 14 Kennebec Ave., Oak Bluffs • 693-2760

The Ship's Inn is just a short five-minute walk from the island ferry and an even shorter two-minute stroll to Oak Bluffs Town Beach. All of Oak Bluffs, from her fanciful gingerbread cottages to her Flying Horses Carousel, is just around the corner. Each of the inn's 15 rooms are brightly decorated and include a private bath, air conditioning in some rooms and color TV. Several of the rooms also feature private entrances. The outdoor patio is a great place to socialize, and the on-premises Bohemian Cafe is convenient should you wish to grab a bite to eat after a day of touring the island. The DeBettencourt family are on hand to make sure your stay is both pleasant and comfortable. The inn is open from March to the end of November.

Edgartown

Ashley Inn

$$$ • 129 Main St., Edgartown • 627-9655, (800) 477-9655

This 19th-century sea captain's home features a spacious lawn with rose gardens and apple trees. Converted to an inn during the spring of 1983, it is convenient to the many shops of Edgartown. You can stroll the historic streets of the old whaling port, or else simply kick up your feet and relax in a hammock out in the lawn. Each of the inn's eight bedrooms and two suites has a private bath and period antiques. Innkeepers Fred and Janet Hurley invite you to enjoy a continental breakfast in the English tea room. Children age 11 and older are welcome at this year-round inn; younger children are welcome in the suites.

The Charlotte Inn

$$$$ • 27 S. Summer St., Edgartown • 627-4751

Like many of Edgartown's inns, The Charlotte Inn began life as a sea captain's home. Built in 1860, it is today one of the premier inns in Edgartown and on the island. Brick courtyards and flowerbeds accent the grounds. Inside, English antiques, fine furnishings and high ceilings convince you that you're in a very special place.

Each of the inn's 25 rooms is different and was individually decorated by innkeepers Gery and Paula Conover, who pride themselves on their meticulous attention to detail. Located within The Charlotte Inn is L'Etoile Restaurant, featuring French cuisine (see the Restaurants section of this chapter). The Charlotte Inn welcomes children older than the age of 14. Smoking is allowed, although heavy cigarette smoking is discouraged and guests are asked to refrain from smoking cigars and pipes in the guest rooms. Charlotte Inn is open throughout the year.

The Edgartown Inn

$$$, no credit cards • 56 N. Water St., Edgartown • 627-4794

You don't have to be a lover of history to stay at The Edgartown Inn, but it helps. Built in 1798 by Capt. Thomas Worth (Ft. Worth, Texas is named for his son, William, a hero of the Mexican War), this Colonial inn has had many distinguished guests over the past two centuries. Daniel Webster, Nathaniel Hawthorne, abolitionist Senator Charles Sumner and John F. Kennedy (while Senator from Massachusetts) have all stayed here. In fact, Hawthorne was writing his *Twice Told Tales* while a guest at the inn.

The 12 rooms in the main inn all have private baths; some have balconies offering harbor views. The Garden House has two spacious rooms with king-size beds, private baths and balconies overlooking the gardens below; a smaller room shares a bath. Two of the barn's five rooms have private baths; three share bath and shower. Children 6 years of age and older are welcome. The inn is open April through October.

Governor Bradford Inn

$$$ • 128 Main St., Edgartown • 627-9510, (800) 696-2723

Begin your day with a continental breakfast of freshly baked muffins, scones, breads, juice and coffee in the sunlit tea room. In the afternoon, enjoy a cup of tea and sample some tasty treats or else relax in the parlor or on the porch sipping complimentary sherry. The Governor Bradford Inn's 16 rooms all feature private baths, ceiling fans and king-size brass or four-poster beds. This wonderful Victorian is elegant and yet comfy all at the same time. Its convenient location along historic Main Street makes for a short stroll to the shops along Edgartown's waterfront. The inn is open year round.

Point Way Inn

$$$-$$$$ • 104 Main St., Edgartown • 627-8633

Beautiful high hedges, flower gardens, a vine-covered gazebo and a regulation croquet court spread across the manicured lawn welcome you to this very special inn. Innkeepers Ben and Linda Smith offer their brand of homey comfort, as well as their automobile for your use in getting around the island! Each of the inn's 15 rooms are luxurious yet comfortable. Most have double or queen-size beds, private baths, ceiling fans and a bedside decanter of sherry; many have four-poster beds and fireplaces. All rooms are air conditioned. A continental breakfast of popovers and granola is included, as are afternoon refreshments. Children are welcome, although they can't borrow the car! The inn is open 12 months of the year.

Shiverick Inn

$$$$ • 5 Peases Point Way, Edgartown • 627-3797, (800) 723-4292

This lovely inn was built in 1840 for the town physician Dr. Clement Francis Shiverick. It offers 11 guest rooms, many with fireplaces, two of which are suites. Innkeepers Denny and Marty Turmelle have blended American and English 18th- and 19th-century antiques in an attempt to transport you back to a time of tradition and elegance. Enjoy a complimentary breakfast of breads, cakes and freshly baked muffins in the garden room. Afterwards, stroll the immaculate grounds or else lounge on the terrace. The Shiverick Inn, which is open year round, welcomes children age 12 and older.

Tuscany Inn

$$$$ • 22 N. Water St., Edgartown • 627-5999

Innkeeper Laura Scheuer, a native of Tuscany, has succeeded in bringing a taste of Italy to Victorian Edgartown. She has combined her skills in art, interior design and culinary arts, and, along with husband, Rusty Scheuer, has transformed the Captain Fisher House into one of Edgartown's most unique lodging and dining experiences. Located in the very heart of the old whaling port, the inn's eight air-conditioned guest rooms are open from the middle of March to the end of December. (During the off-season Laura offers a cooking class at the inn).

In the morning you will awaken to the aroma of one of Laura's Italian breakfasts. In the afternoon, sample Laura's homemade biscotti while you sip a warm cappuccino in this unique blending of Italian and Victorian settings. The Tuscany Inn welcomes children older than age 7.

The Victorian Inn

$$$-$$$$ • 24 S. Water St., Edgartown • 627-4784

Directly across the street from the famous Edgartown Pagoda Tree is The Victorian Inn, built c.1820. Innkeepers Stephen and Karyn Caliri have carefully restored this whaling captain's home to its original elegance, and they cordially invite you to be their guest. All 14 guest rooms have private baths and are decorated with antiques and flowers. A number of rooms have four-poster beds and some have balconies. Some rooms overlook the historic harbor while others overlook the English garden below where a complimentary gourmet breakfast is served from 8 to 10 AM. An informal tea is also served in the afternoon. Children age 8 and older are welcome at the inn, and from November to April pets are allowed. The Victorian Inn is open year round.

Up Island

Lambert's Cove Country Inn

$$$ • Lambert's Cove Rd., West Tisbury • 693-2298

If you really want to get away from it all, this is the spot. Once a horticulturist's estate, Lambert's Cove is the kind of country inn you dream about. Off Lambert's Cove Road you take an unpaved path through wooded wilderness to this place hidden amid towering pines, 150-year-old vine-covered stone walls, lilting gardens and an old-fashioned orchard of apple trees.

Sixteen rooms comprise the inn, eight rooms in the original 1790 main building and the remainder in the restored carriage house and converted barn. Perhaps the most unique room is the Greenhouse Room that features a greenhouse sitting room complete with white wicker furniture. All rooms have private baths, air conditioning and some have private sun decks. A newly built gazebo rests in the yard beyond the inn, with a private tennis court just beyond that. Innkeepers Louis and Katherine Costable provide a full breakfast, and the inn is also home to one of the island's finest dining rooms (see the Restaurants section). Though Lambert's Cove is in a country setting away from the shoreline, guests are entitled to passes to the two private West Tisbury beaches.

Duck Inn

$$-$$$ • State Rd., Gay Head • 645-9018

At nearly land's end lies the Duck Inn with incredible views of the Gay Head Cliffs and Lighthouse. To get to this cozy five-room, 200-year-old farmhouse you must take a dirt road. The decor varies from Southwest to Japanese to some that is difficult to determine. The Southwest room has pink stucco walls while the Japanese room is filled with silks. Only one room has a private bath, as well as a fireplace, all others share bathrooms. There's also a hot tub and a licensed masseuse available for facials and body work. Oh, and we almost forgot to tell you, miles and miles of the most secluded beaches lie outside the door. Duck Inn is open all year long and children are welcome. Pets are welcome during the summer.

Hotels

Oak Bluffs

Wesley Hotel

$$$ • 1 Lake Ave., Oak Bluffs • 693-6611

The Wesley Hotel, built in 1879, is the last of the grand hotels of Oak Bluffs — and what a grande dame she is. Open from May to October, she seems to watch over the town from her knoll facing the harbor. How many changes she has seen all around her over the past century.

Renovations have restored the Wesley to her former greatness. You will feel yourself being transported back in time as you climb the steps to the veranda, enter the dark oak lobby and walk up to the old-fashioned registration desk. The main building contains 62 rooms, many with outstanding views of the harbor. These rooms include private baths. Twenty more rooms with shared baths are in the Wesley Arms Building behind the main building. There are handicapped-accessible rooms located on the first floor of the main building.

Edgartown

Edgartown Heritage Hotel

$$$ • 227 Upper Main St., Edgartown • 627-5161, (800) 922-3009

Those looking for a modern hotel just a 10 to 15 minute walk from Edgartown's historic waterfront will want to look into the Edgartown Heritage Hotel, built in 1985 as part of the Clarion chain. Each of the hotel's 34 rooms offer queen or king-size beds, a private bath, cable TV, a radio, air conditioning and a telephone. A complimentary continental breakfast is provided, while the on-site Beeftender Restaurant and Lounge offers a full menu for dinner. The Heritage can accommodate groups of up to 50 people for business meetings, social functions and private parties. This year-round hotel has two handicapped-accessible rooms available. Children younger than 18 stay free with an adult.

The Harborside Inn

$$$-$$$$ • 3 S. Water St., Edgartown • 627-4321, (800) 627-4009

A complete waterfront resort located right at Edgartown's historic harbor, The Harborside Inn offers seven buildings (some are former 19th-century whaling captains' homes) housing 89 rooms. About half of these rooms have exceptional views of the harbor, and some have huge private balconies. A large heated outdoor pool is just steps from the waters of the harbor.

You can relax in the whirlpool or in the sauna after a "stressful" day of shopping, swimming or bike riding. Rooms include color TV, a refrigerator, a private bath and air conditioning. The resort is open year round and provides full-service banquet facilities. If you have children you'll be happy to learn that children younger than 12 stay at the Harborside Inn free with an adult.

The Harbor View Hotel

$$$$ • 131 N. Water St., Edgartown • 627-7000, (800) 225-6005

Wow, what a place. At land's end it rests like a princess from another age, commanding your attention and getting it. Meanwhile, the windows command incredible views of Edgartown Lighthouse, Edgartown Harbor and Chappaquiddick Island beyond.

Dating to 1891 as two separate buildings, today the Harbor View Hotel is one large gem of a grand hotel, accented by a magnificent 300-foot veranda. A recent multimillion dollar renovation restored all her 124 rooms and suites to their former Victorian splendor.

Guests are pampered by the accommodating staff. Comfort is the rule. Concierge, room service and the daily newspaper are just some of the extras that set this hotel apart. Seven townhouses on site feature cathedral ceilings, kitchens and outside decks. The 12-acre complex includes two swimming pools, a private beach and all-weather tennis courts. Guests have privileges at Farm Neck Golf Course. Also, there are a restaurant and lounge on site, Starbuck's and Breezes, respectively.

Kelley House

$$$$ • 23 Kelley St., Edgartown • 627-7900, (800) 225-6005

Over the past two and a half centuries, since 1742 to be exact, the Kelley House has been open for travelers and vacationers alike. Formerly a tavern where whalers and sea captains raised their pints, today all of the inn's 59 rooms maintain the colonial charm that guests a century ago would have enjoyed. Of course, today's guests also enjoy all modern-day amenities.

Period antiques, quilts and an overall early American personality will make you think you're staying back in 19th-century Edgartown. Some rooms have kitchens and private balconies. A complimentary breakfast awaits you, as does afternoon tea. Bedtime arrives with homemade cookies and milk. A refreshing outdoor pool offers views of Edgartown Harbor. After a swim you can wander into the Newes From America, an American pub at the Kelley House that offers casual fare (see the Restaurant section). Kelley House is open from mid-May through mid-October.

Cottage Colonies

Edgartown

Edgartown Commons

$$$ • 20 Peases Point Way, Edgartown • 627-4671

Scattered among seven buildings are 35 units comprising Edgartown Commons. Included are studios and one- and two-bedroom apartments, all with full kitchens, private baths and cable TV. A family spot, the grounds include a swimming pool, shuffleboard, swings, a sandbox and slides. Edgartown Commons is open from mid-May to mid-October.

Deerfield Cottages

$$, no credit cards • State Rd., West Tisbury • 693-1467

Deerfield offers one- and two-bedroom cottages for rent during the spring, summer and fall months (May through October). The private cottages feature fully equipped kitchens, a Franklin fireplace, outside grills and picnic tables. Guests receive a pass to nearby Lamberts Cove beach. Weekly summer rates range from $580 for a one-bedroom cottage to $680 for a two-bedroom; September rates are $430 and $480, respectively.

Hostel

Manter Memorial AYH Hostel

$ • Edgartown-West Tisbury Rd., West Tisbury • 693-2665

If you weren't paying just $12 a night ($15 for non-AYH members), you'd think you were staying at the quaintest of country inns. This cedar-shake saltbox, which celebrated its 40th year as a hostel in 1995, sits at the edge of Manuel E. Correllus Forest. The hostel has a fireplace in the common room, a volleyball court, a sheltered bike rack out back and a spacious kitchen that awaits budding gourmets. Five dorms house 80 bunk-beds; lockout is from 9:30 AM to 5:30 PM. The hostel fills up quickly; we suggest you make reservations (especially during the season) at least two weeks in advance. The hostel is open from mid-March to mid-November.

Condominiums

Vineyard Haven

Harbor Landing Condo Trust

$$ • 15 Beach Rd., Vineyard Haven • 693-2600, (800) 545-4171

For families who want to spend an extended period of time on the island, Harbor Landing offers 38 very affordable condo units with a full, private bath, color TV, air conditioning and heating and a refrigerator. The efficiency units have a fully equipped kitchen. A large sundeck on the third floor offers great views of the harbor while a 5-acre park borders the rear of the building. Complimentary coffee is served each morning. If you're interested in visiting the Island during the off-season, check out Harbor Landing's incredibly low $45 rates. Harbor Landing is open year round.

Campgrounds

Martha's Vineyard Family Campground

$ • Edgartown-Vineyard Haven Rd., Vineyard Haven • 693-3772

Families who enjoy camping will enjoy the time they'll have at the Martha's Vineyard Family Campground, located just a mile or so away from Vineyard Haven center. Each camp site is allowed one motor vehicle and either one large tent or two small tents. Trailer sites are also available. Both types of sites include electric and water hookups; the trailer sites also include sewer. Rates for 1996 were $26 per night for a camp site and $29 for a trailer site. These rates are for 2 adults and any children younger than 18. Additional adults are charged $9 per night. Also, there are one- and two-room cabins and even tent trailers available. The grounds include plenty to keep the family busy: table tennis, billiards, biking, baseball, a store and a playground. Cable TV is available.

There are some 180 sites; open mid-May through mid-October.

Webb's Camping Area

$ • Barnes Rd., Oak Bluffs • 693-0233

If you're looking for seclusion, this is the place to make your camp. Offering some 80 acres of woodland, some of which overlook Lagoon Pond in Oak Bluffs, Webb's Camping Area has 150 sites from which to choose. Some sites have electric and water hookups, all have tables and stone fireplaces. Cyclists and backpackers are also accommodated with a special section of the campgrounds to cater to their needs. On the grounds is a general store, recreation hall, dumping station, laundry, showers and a playground for the kiddies. Sites cost a mere $27 per night per family (1996 rates) and for $2 more you can get a site with water view or a private site. By the way, the definition of "family" means two adults and any children younger than age 5. Extra adults cost $8 per night while children older than 5 are $1. The campground is open from mid-May through mid-September.

Vacation Rentals and Real Estate

There are a number of real estate companies on the island, and unfortunately space does not permit listing them all. Besides selling properties, many of these companies also handle vacation rentals. Below are a handful that do handle rentals. We encourage you to shop around, but don't wait too long to decide, as it's best to reserve a rental at least 10 months in advance. Otherwise there may be nothing left.

Photo: Peter Simon

Sunbathers sprinkle the sands and waters of the Vineyard.

Vineyard Haven

Island Real Estate

51 Beach Rd., Vineyard Haven • 693-4800, Massachusetts only (800) 287-4801

Living up to its name, Island Real Estate offers rentals throughout the island. Weekly rentals start at $700 for a small cottage, while waterfront and water view beach homes can run as high as $7,000 plus. Island Real Estate offers more than 400 properties from which to choose.

Bayberry Real Estate

236 Edgartown-Vineyard Haven Rd., Edgartown • 627-6646

This real estate company has a selection of properties island-wide, from $700-a-week two-bedroom cottages to $8,500-a-week five-bedroom waterfront houses.

Edgartown

American Real Estate

21A N. Water St., Edgartown • 627-3734

This company offers weekly and monthly rentals of cottages and homes just a short walk or bike ride to the beach. American represents about 400 properties with an average weekly rate of $1,500.

Conover Real Estate

19 S. Summer St., Edgartown • 627-3757

Conover Real Estate only represents waterfront properties and in-town historical homes for rent. The 150 properties they handle are rather pricey. For instance, a water-view home with at least four bedrooms can run anywhere from $16,000 to $18,000 a month. These prices decrease by around 50 percent from September 15 through June 15.

Linda R. Bassett Real Estate Sales and Vacation Rentals

201 Upper Main St., Edgartown • sales 627-3366, (800) 661-6626; rentals 627-9201, (800) 338-1855

Located in Edgartown, this company handles both the sale of properties and vacation rentals throughout the entire island of Martha's Vineyard. In the area of sales, it deals primarily in private year-round homes, cottages, condominiums and estates with many of its properties being either waterfront or waterview. On the rental side, Linda R. Bassett offers more than 800 properties from around the Vineyard. Weekly rentals run from $800 to $10,000, but the average is $1,200 to $1,600. With a dozen real estate agents, Linda R. Bassett is one of the largest outfits on the island. A West Tisbury office opened in spring 1997.

Sandpiper Rentals

60 Winter St., Edgartown • 627-6070

Whether you're in the market for a small seaside cottage or a sprawling 200-acre waterfront estate, Sandpiper Rentals can fulfill your order from their list of more than 600 rental properties. To give you an idea, a three-bedroom house runs from $1,800 to $2,200 a week.

FYI

Unless otherwise noted, the area code for all phone numbers in this guide is 508.

Restaurants

If you're hungry, you're in luck. Martha's Vineyard offers a variety of excellent restaurants to satisfy your every culinary desire.

As you might expect, the Vineyard offers the fare one would expect from an island — plenty of seafood. But the offering does not end there . . . no, no, no! Man and woman do not live by lobster alone, although it might be fun trying! Across the island there are a number of specialty restaurants preparing the finest in Italian, French, Indian, Chinese and Mexican dishes. There are also plenty of casual dining establishments serving your basic chow. Yet, even basic chow tastes so much better when you have an ocean view. Heck, even a cheeseburger takes on a whole new meaning when Vineyard Sound is staring back at you.

Half the fun of vacationing is trying out different eateries, and not just because someone else has to clean up the dishes. Below is a listing of some of the restaurants located throughout the towns, but we encourage you to be like Bartholomew Gosnold and explore.

You'll be fascinated at the wonderful discoveries you'll make. For instance, there are a number of fine dining experiences in Edgartown, but sometimes there is nothing better than wandering into a local pub and ordering the special off a chalkboard along with a pint of beer to wash it down. What these places lack in cloth napkins and unpronounceable entrees they make up for in honest, down-home Yankee cooking and atmosphere.

Something to keep in mind: only restaurants in the towns of Edgartown and Oak Bluffs are allowed to serve liquor. The other island towns are termed "dry," but you can bring your own bottle.

Price Code

The price code used here is intended as a guide in helping you decide where to dine and is based on the average price of dinner entrees for two, excluding appetizers, alcoholic beverages, dessert, tax and tip. Most restaurants accept major credit cards; we note the ones that do not.

$	**Less than $20**
$$	**$21 to $35**
$$$	**$36 to $50**
$$$$	**$51 and more**

Now, go ahead out there and explore. And don't come back until you discover something wonderful!

Vineyard Haven

The Black Dog Tavern

$$$ • Beach St. Ext., Vineyard Haven • 693-9223

The Black Dog Tavern rests just yards from the waters of Vineyard Haven Harbor during low tide and just feet away when the tide is high. Approaching the place, you feel like you're down along the docks of some old whaling port — rusted iron chains and anchors, weathered wooden barrels, a "Tavern" sign swaying in the salty breeze all providing the wharf atmosphere. As for the Black Dog itself, it's a rustic wooden building decorated with quarter boards and other nautical items and windows providing the most spectacular views of the harbor. You'll want to arrive early — we arrived minutes before the restaurant opened for dinner and just managed to get the last window table! No reservations are accepted.

Besides seafaring ambiance and great views, this year-round Vineyard Haven landmark serves up some tasty dinners. It is mighty tough to be this close to the water without a hankering for some seafood, and there's plenty on the menu to choose from, although we somehow opted for the gnocchi instead (landlubbers!). Have dinner while you watch the harbor traffic come and go. Also on the grounds are The Black Dog General Store and the Black Dog Bakery (see the Shopping section of this chapter).

Le Grenier

$$$$ • 96 Main St., Vineyard Haven • 693-4906

If you're going to open a French restaurant on Martha's Vineyard, it helps to hail from France. Le Grenier chef/owner Jean Dupon is a native of Lyon who excels at keeping his menu steeped in such traditional French cuisine as shrimp Pernod, escargots, frog legs Provençale and vichyssoise. The desserts are made at La Patisserie Francaise, the more casual eatery located downstairs where take-out is also available. Le Grenier is open for dinner nightly from the beginning of March through New Year's Eve, while La Patisserie serves three meals a day year round.

Oak Bluffs

Giordano's

$$, no credit cards • 107 Circuit Ave., Oak Bluffs • 693-0184

On summer weekend evenings patrons line up to get into Giordano's. It is worth the wait, for inside will be found an Italian dinner like your grandma used to make, that is, if your grandma was Italian. People have been waiting in line to get in ever since the Giordano family opened the Italian restaurant in 1930 (not the same line, of course). The food here is hearty and wholesome; expect heaping plates of cutlets and cacciatore, pizza, pasta, fried clams and seafood. There is a noisy ambiance about the place, but it's all part of the charm of this family dining experience. Children's meals are offered at substantially lower prices. Lunch and dinner are served daily from mid-May through mid-September. Reservations are not accepted.

Jimmy Seas Pan Pasta

$$, no credit cards • 32 Kennebec Ave., Oak Bluffs • 696-8550

Expect to receive your food in large portions and expect to receive it served right in the pan in which it was cooked. The restaurant has a comfortable atmosphere, and the staff is very friendly. Jimmy Seas is a favorite spot of the First Family when they are on the island. The restaurant does not accept reservations (although, for some reason we can't see the Clintons waiting in line for a table). Dinner is served nightly except Tuesday mid-April through mid-December.

Linda Jean's

$, no credit cards • 124 Circuit Ave., Oak Bluffs • 693-4093

If breakfast is your bag then you'll definitely want to check out Linda Jean's on Circuit Avenue. Fluffy pancakes made from scratch are as good a way as any to start the day on the island. A year-round family-owned restaurant, it is a favorite spot for locals and visitors alike. The President, First Lady and their daughter have been known to eat here after services at the Tabernacle, so don't be surprised if secret service agents are eyeing your pancakes with suspicion. Linda Jean's also serves lunch and dinner, check out the seafood platter with a full plate of clams, scallops, shrimp, haddock, fries and cole slaw. Good stuff! Open year round, it has been an Oak Bluffs fixture for nearly 20 years.

Mad Martha's

$ • 117 Circuit Ave., Oak Bluffs • 693-9151

If madness is contagious, then you too are sure to catch Mad Martha's ice cream-mania. With more than two dozen flavors from which to chose, there's something here for even the most picky tastes. Established in 1971, Mad Martha can be found at several other locations throughout the island: Dockside Market Place in Oak Bluffs, Lake Avenue in Oak Bluffs, Union Street in Tisbury and N. Water Street in Edgartown. Besides serving ice cream, Mad Martha's also offer burgers and grinders from early June to Columbus Day.

Ocean View

$$ • Chapman Rd., Oak Bluffs • 693-2207

As its name suggests, the Ocean View restaurant serves up peeks of the ocean, or rather, Oak Bluffs Harbor, from its front-facing windows. The Ocean View also serves up great tasting food at very reasonable prices. Its menu features everything from pizza to prime rib and lobster. Shrimp is a local favorite, and you'll definitely want to try the fillet of sole Français. The lounge has a large hearth with a fire crackling on cooler days as well as a popcorn maker built into the hearth. There are two dining rooms complete with a mural of the harbor and a large fish tank. The clientele is a mix of locals and visitors. Lunch and dinner is served daily year round. If you're on the island for New Year's, check out their New Year's buffet.

Oyster Bar

$$$$ • 162 Circuit Ave., Oak Bluffs • 693-3300

Once upon a time the building that now houses the Oyster Bar was a grocery store. Today it is a stylish restaurant complete with 14-foot-tall tin ceilings, faux-marble columns and a 40-foot mahogany and brass wine and raw bar. Open seven nights a week during July and August, the Oyster Bar opens for the season on Mother's Day and closes the day before Columbus Day. Between those dates, the restaurant serves the finest in seafood and land food. Reservations are accepted. The Oyster Bar offers off-season prices.

Season's Restaurant

$$ • 124 Circuit Ave., Oak Bluffs • 693-7129

Located halfway down the much-happening Circuit Avenue and right next to the rocking Atlantic Connection, is Season's Restaurant. The menu contains some 70 moderately prices items, such as scallop and shrimp plates for the seafood eaters, and chicken or shrimp stir-fry for those who can't make up their minds. During the summer there is acoustic entertainment, or for something a bit louder you can slip next door to the Atlantic Connection. Season's takes part in the Chili-Fest in January and holds a Halfway to St. Patrick's Day Party in September complete with corned beef and cabbage (and of course, live Irish music). Season's is open year round.

Edgartown

David Ryan's Restaurant Cafe

$$$ • 11 N. Water St., Edgartown • 627-4100

As you're hitting all the shops along North Water Street in Edgartown, you may want to hit the brakes and stop in for a bite at David Ryan's. How about Menemsha swordfish, blackened or grilled with citrus herb butter. Or perhaps Vineyard crab cakes with Jonah crab served with remoulade. Nothing like native seafood to give you a real feel for the island. David Ryan's also serves pasta dishes. After dinner you can either continue shopping or mosey on down to the wharf and just take in the sights. David Ryan's is every month of the year except January.

Espresso Love

$ • 2 S. Water St., Edgartown • 627-9211

After a night out on the ol' whaling town, you'll want to step into Edgartown's own Espresso Love for a cup of espresso, a cup of coffee or a late-night dessert before returning to your inn. It also serves breakfast and lunch. Espresso Love is open 10 months of the year; it's closed during January and February. Catering to locals, visitors, even the First Family when they are on the island, Espresso Love specializes in satisfying your sweet tooth. The scones alone are worth a visit. Don't let the crowds deter you — good things truly come to those who wait.

L'Etoile

$$$$ • 27 S. Summer St., Edgartown • 627-5187

Located at the elegant Charlotte Inn, L'Etoile is an exquisite French restaurant featuring the culinary artistry of chef/owner Michael Brisson. Begin with an appetizer of bacon and leek mashed potatoes with cognac cream sauce or perhaps sauteed fresh duck foie gras on sugar pea tendrils with seared plums and green ginger muscat and ginger sauce.

Your choice of entrees includes sauteed fresh dover sole fillets with fried green tomatoes and saffron-poached potato batons, or perhaps roasted spice-rubbed Australian lamb with artichoke, goat cheese, sunflower seed, cous cous melange. The incredible desserts are sure to break even the most determined diet. Dinner is served nightly from June through September; Wednesday through Sunday for the remainder of the year. L'Etoile is closed in January. Smoking is prohibited, and reservations are required.

Main Street Diner

$ • 65 Main St., Edgartown • 627-9337

This is your classic, right out of a Norman Rockwell print, diner. It's a bit hard to find, but the journey is well-worth it. You approach it from Main Street by following a long, well-lit, flower wallpapered hallway. Just keep going, the diner is down there, believe us! Along the way you'll pass American memorabilia. On the wall at the end is an American flag with 36 states. Turn left and then a quick right and there you are. Open the door and you enter a museum of early 20th-century stuff. What a place!

The food is good old-fashioned American chow, and the smells are delicious. The entrees are about $5. As you look at some of the pictures on the walls you'll be amazed at who else has found this spot: Kevin Costner, Patricia O'Neal, Bill Pulman, even a Kennedy or two. Main Street Diner serves breakfast, lunch and dinner year round.

The Navigator

$$$ • 2 Main St., Edgartown • 627-4320

If your idea of island dining is fresh lobster while enjoying the views of Edgartown Harbor, this is the place for you. Besides offering plenty of seating inside, the Navigator also offers outside tables complete with umbrellas and, of course, the harbor waters just yards away. This is a perfect place to enjoy a late-afternoon cocktail and a spectacular view. Open for lunch and dinner from mid-May though Columbus Day, it is located at the very foot of Main Street. The Navigator is a nonsmoking establishment.

Newes From America

$-$$ • 23 Kelley St., Edgartown • 627-4397

You almost expect to see Captain Ahab limp through the door into this classic whaling port pub. Brick walls and rustic wood planking on the walls and ceiling provide its character. Housed in an 18th-century building, the Newes is a famous gathering place for visitors and locals in search of good food at a good price. The beers served here have become legendary. If you can't make up your mind over which beer to have, why not order the Rack of Beers, which allows you to sample five different brews. Regulars who consume in the neighborhood of 1,000 short drafts, or 500 talls, receive their own personal bar stool for a full year! (Now's there's something to put on your resume!)

The food served here is good old American pub chow — hamburgers, grilled sandwiches and hot soups to burn away the thickest fog. (We had the veggie piago sandwich.) It's the kind of food that tastes great with a pint of beer and a salty sea tale, especially if you happen to be sitting on a barstool with your name on it! The Newes is open for lunch and dinner year round and is beside the Kelley House (see the Accommodations section).

Starbuck's

$$$ • 131 N. Water St., Edgartown • 627-7000

Located at the sprawling Harbor View Hotel (see the Accommodations section), Starbuck's is open year round for breakfast, lunch and dinner. Situated at land's end, across from the picturesque Edgartown Lighthouse, it is the ideal location for a bite to eat after you've shopped Edgartown. The atmosphere here is relaxed, and the lunch prices are rather relaxed as well. You'll find many tasty sandwiches and salads to stave off those hunger pangs so you can get right back out there hitting the shops. Offering one the largest selections of seafood on the Vineyard, Starbuck's serves dinner seven nights until Columbus Day; it's closed for dinner on Sundays, Mondays and Tuesdays after Columbus Day.

Up Island

Lambert's Cove Country Inn

$$$ • Lambert's Cove Rd., West Tisbury • 693-2298

Housed in a 1790 building, this restaurant offers a romantic country setting featuring beautiful pastoral views far removed from the hustle and bustle of the more populated town centers. Located at the end of a magical path through enchanted woodlands, this restaurant is contained within the beautiful Lambert's Cove Country Inn (see the Accommodations section).

Besides offering an elegant dining room, an outside deck is also available if you wish to look out over the apple orchard. Seafood lovers will want to try the salmon. Land lubbers may wish to sample the smoked duck breast or the peppered pork tenderloin. The restaurant is open year round; seven days a week during the summer months. During the offseason you should call ahead for days and hours of operation. Reservations are suggested, though walk-ins are always welcome. Lambert's is a nonsmoking establishment.

The Feast of Chilmark

$$-$$$ • State Rd., Chilmark • 645-3553

The Feast of Chilmark is accurately named, for it is in Chilmark and does serve up quite a feast. Open from mid-May until the end of October, this restaurant at Beetlebung Corner features a dining room with vaulted ceilings, a mezzanine and spacious seating. Also within the unassuming building is a photo gallery containing the works of island photographer Peter Simon, the brother of singer Carly Simon. Though the Feast serves up plenty of seafood, you may wish to try the roasted rack of lamb served with spinach and cognac glaze. If you do plan on dining here, leave your cigarettes behind as the nonsmoking policy applies throughout the restaurant. During the months of May, June, September and October, the restaurant is closed on Monday. Reservations are suggested.

Homeport Restaurant

$$-$$$ • 512 North Rd., Menemsha • 645-2679

Since 1931 the Homeport Restaurant has

been offering spectacular views along with the great seafood they serve. It is located right at the Menemsha fishing port with its weathered shanties lining the harbor, the very fishing port used as Quint's homeport in the movie *Jaws*. In fact, as you dine on lobster here you can look out across the water and see the remains of Quint's boat *ORCA* on the opposite shore. The Homeport is open from mid-April to mid-October.

The Aquinnah

$$ • Gay Head Cliffs, Gay Head • 645-9654

The views from the restaurant's open porch are incredible, courtesy of Gay Head Cliffs and the ancient glaciers that created them. A Gay Head landmark since 1949, the Aquinnah features plenty of great seafood and plenty of crowds. Patrons are offered both inside and outside seating, with take-out windows catering to those sitting out of doors to enjoy the awesome views. You can also buy clams and scallops by the pint and quart. Breakfast and lunch are served spring, summer and fall; dinner during the summer months only.

Shindigs

$ • Gay Head Cliffs, Gay Head • 645-3443

Open from May to the end of October, Shindigs offers fried seafood for those hungry tourists who have come to view the cliffs of Gay Head. Though small and unassuming, the view from Shindig's three or four window seats is absolutely incredible. Only in Gay Head can you eat a clam roll for $7.50 and enjoy a million dollar view for free.

Shopping

Can a Martha's Vineyard vacation truly be called a vacation without a little shopping along the way? How will you be able to prove to your friends back home that you were on the island without purchasing a Black Dog T-shirt before you leave? Ours is not to question why, ours is to do the tourist thing and shop.

Thankfully, there are many fine shops dotting the island's main roads to satisfy this essential vacationer's prerequisite. Most of these shopping experiences can be found in the towns of Vineyard Haven, Oak Bluffs and especially Edgartown where you can kill an entire day browsing and buying. The offerings are varied and the treasures you'll find are many. Like most things in life, the pursuit is half the fun, and on Martha's Vineyard you are afforded many opportunities to enter into the pursuit.

Besides individual shops, you'll also find a handful of what can best be called mini-malls (very mini, and "mall" isn't even the proper term). Tisbury Marketplace on Beach Road in Vineyard Haven is such a place. Another spot is Dockside Market Place on Oak Bluffs Harbor along Circuit Avenue Extension, which is a superb spot to do a little gift shopping, have a bite to eat or just grab a beer or glass of wine and watch the boats go by. Not to be outdone, Edgartown has a number of shops clustered at the Colonial Inn on North Water Street, just across from the harbor.

What follows is a smattering of the island's shops — our short list of what we consider required stops. You'll find that many of these shopping experiences, as well as many more not listed here, are a short walking distance from each other. For instance, Circuit Avenue in Oak Bluffs provides an easy walking tour of what we estimate at 75 percent of the shops in that town, while Main and North Water streets contain perhaps well over half (if not three quarters) of all the shops in Edgartown.

Unless otherwise noted, all the shops listed accept major credit cards and are open year round.

Vineyard Haven

All Things Oriental

57 Beach Rd., Vineyard Haven • 693-8375

You'll think you've left the island for the Far East when you visit All Things Oriental, located right down there in the old Yankee port of Vineyard Haven. This store is brimming with the most stunning furniture and porcelain, including rare hutches and armoires, hand-carved fans, rugs, jewelry, lamps, and a host of other things too numerous to name. The name of the place says it all. All Things Oriental is open mid-May through Christmas.

The Black Dog General Store

Water St., Vineyard Haven • 696-8182

This is *the* place, the place where all those

Black Dog T-shirts, sweatshirts and caps come from. You've seen them everywhere we're sure, as they've almost become the calling card for the island. The General Store is a must-visit (in fact, we don't think you can legally leave the island without stopping there first). All the Black Dog souvenirs you could ever think of are here, even some for your own pooch at home. Sweaters, coffee mugs, key chains, even mouse pads for your computer emblazoned with that famous black dog. There are even some sweets here: brownies, espresso-bean brittle and human-shape dog biscuits. Whatever you can't find at the store you may find in their 26-page oversized catalog (by the way, 1996 was their 25th anniversary). Also on the grounds is the Black Dog Bakery serving the finest in baked goods (and Black Dog T-shirts) and the Black Dog Tavern (see our Restaurants section). The store is open year round.

Bowl & Board

35 Main St., Vineyard Haven • 693-9441

Wind chimes fill your ears with the sounds of the invisible island breezes as you enter this airy building. The place is filled with wooden items, everything you could ever need for the home. Wooden baskets abound. And if you ever need a candle, there are plenty here.

Bramhall & Dunn

19 Main St., Vineyard Haven • 693-6437

This store, just up the road from the ferry, is a shopper's delight. Here you'll find hand-knit wool caps and sweaters, hand-hooked and woven rugs, elegant picture frames, English pine antiques, beautifully crafted ceramic bowls and so many other perfect gifts. Interestingly, all the furniture in the store is for sale. Upstairs we found an American Pencil Post Bed for sale. They also have an antique furniture showroom next door. Owners Emily Bramhall and Tharon Dunn personally choose the items they sell, and in fact, they travel to England once a year to make their selections. Bramhall & Dunn also have a store on the island of Nantucket. Both stores are open year round.

Bunch of Grapes Bookstore

44 Main St., Vineyard Haven • 693-2291, (800)693-0221

Bunch of Grapes? This place should have been called Bunch of Books. Lots and lots of books, two floors of books in a rustic, barn board of a building. As you go up the stairs there is a stained-glass window of yellow and red and orange — mesmerizing. With an endless array of best sellers and island-related titles (more than 38,000 titles spread throughout 5,000 square feet), it is one of the premier bookstores on the island. We're told that the late Jackie O shopped here — Oh boy! Browsers are especially welcome.

C. B. Stark

126 Main St., Vineyard Haven • 693-2284

In 1996 C.B. Stark celebrated its 30th anniversary, and you might want to celebrate your island visit with one of its uniquely Martha's Vineyard charms. The artists here create jewelry in the form of familiar island sites, such as the Chappaquiddick Ferry, the Flying Horses Carousel, town and village signs, the Gay Head, West Chop, East Chop and Edgartown Lighthouses, a Chilmark scallop, Menemsha lobster, the Island ferries, the Black Dog and just about any other Vineyard thing you can think of. C.B. Stark is best known for its grapes design. All charms are available in sterling or 14-karat gold. C.B. Stark also sells six lines of watches with, of course, Martha's Vineyard on its face.

C. W. Morgan Marine Antiques

Tisbury Wharf, Vineyard Haven • 693-3622

If you're one of those people who like things nautical, you'll like what you'll see at C.W. Morgan Marine Antiques. Collector Frank

INSIDERS' TIP

The Chilmark Cemetery is the final resting place of writer Lillian Hellman who penned the story *Julia*. The movie version of *Julia* earned both Vanessa Redgrave and Jason Robards Academy Awards.

M. Rapoza has put together such an impressive display of marine antiques you'll think you're in a maritime museum. Yet the great thing about this display is that it's all for sale. Here you will find centuries-old chests, models, paintings, compasses and seafaring equipment. The shop is open mid-May through Christmas Day and other times by appointment.

Midnight Farm

18 Water St. and Cromwell Ln., Vineyard Haven • 693-1997

The great thing about being on an island is that even the shops have a view of the water. Such is the case with Midnight Farm, which has windows overlooking Vineyard Haven Harbor. Inside the store you'll find a wide assortment of items, from clothing to a $595 wooden tree bed to honeys and jams to old fashioned leather photo albums to books, toys, candles, antique furniture to shampoos and bath oils. This is the store to visit if you're looking for that unique gift idea . . . how about antique Victorian beach boxes, pottery, cashmere throws, baskets or a CD or book autographed by Carly Simon, one of the owners of Midnight Farm. It's open year round.

Robins Fudge and Candy

10 Main St., Vineyard Haven • 693-6188

Hey, every once in a while you have to sin a little. Robins Fudge and Candy offers the greatest temptations: homemade fudge and candy, chocolates, truffles, taffy, caramels are all here just a short walk up from the ferry. You'll think you've died and gone to jellybean heaven for every conceivable flavor is here — from island punch to toasted marshmallow and everything in between. The store also offers a tasty selection of sugar-free goodies, and they do mail order.

Oak Bluffs

Hilliard's Kitch-in-vue

158 Circuit Ave., Oak Bluffs • 693-2191

Another great place to indulge in a sugar rush: David Hilliard has been carrying on the tradition his grandparents started back in 1945 of making homemade chocolates and candies, salt-water taffy, buttercrunch, truffles and turtles. The smell alone will make even the staunchest dieter's knees buckle, and belt unbuckle. If you opt for mail order, the yummies are sent on the same day they are ordered. Hilliard's is open year round.

Laughing Bear

138 Circuit Ave., Oak Bluffs • 693-9342

There's nothing like a bear with a sense of humor, but we can't figure out the name. Regardless, the Laughing Bear specializes in clothing — bright, colorful clothing. You'll find chenille and cotton fashions, velvet scarves and satin gowns. We still don't get the name. The store also sells plenty of interesting jewelry. Laughing Bear is open from the beginning of May through mid-January. Can someone please explain the name?

The Secret Garden of Martha's Vineyard

148 Circuit Ave., Oak Bluffs • 693-4759

This delightful store is full of great ideas for gifts, or better yet, for yourself. There is a selection of books, many island-related, as well as jewelry and Vineyard-related items. We particularly enjoyed the miniature wooden gingerbread cottages. The Secret Garden is open year round.

Take It Easy Baby

142 Circuit Ave., Oak Bluffs • 693-2864

Take It Easy Baby offers a great selection of some of the baddest clothing on the island (baddest in the sense of being real, real hip, if you know what we mean). Leather is the emphasis, but there's much more here than just leather. You really have to check it out to understand the full scope of the thing, baby. And while you're at it, ask them about the significance of that 1950s B-movie-looking flying saucer in the front window. Take It Easy Baby is open mid-May through Christmas.

Edgartown

Bickerton & Ripley Books

Main St., Edgartown • 627-8463

With more than 20,000 titles, Bickerton & Ripley Books is one of the Island's top bookstores, and certainly *the* bookstore of Edgartown. Established 17 years ago, it features regional books and author signings. Some of the authors who have been here are pictured on the wall leading upstairs to the second level. Whether you are looking for a serious read, a paperback for the beach or something for the kiddies, this store is sure to fill your bill. It closes January through March.

Edgartown Hardware

47 Main St., Edgartown • 627-4338

Built in 1946, this place personifies small-town Americana: a super-friendly staff, shelves overflowing with things you may need and an ambiance right off a *Saturday Evening Post* cover. It's worth a stop. Edgartown Hardware is open year round.

Essence

38 N. Water St., Edgartown • 627-3840

Opened in 1983, this exquisite perfumery is just one of a number of shops situated at the Colonial Inn. You can select from more than 350 natural scents and 150 fragrant oils. Or if that's not enough, they'll create a fragrance just for you. Essence also sells aromatherapy and spa products, island-made skin-care products and a myriad of scented products for body and home. It's open mid-May through Christmas.

The Fligors

27 N. Water St., Edgartown • 627-4722

This store has been on the island since 1960 and has a little bit of everything. You'll find kids' clothing, toys, collectibles, Vineyard artwork, ties, clocks, lamps and interesting seasonal items for Halloween, Thanksgiving and Christmas. If you're looking for a gift this is the spot to find one. The Fligors, which is owned by Richard and Carol Fligor (in case you're wondering about the name), is open year round.

In the Woods

55 Main St., Edgartown • 627-8989

What was once a former supermarket now houses a collection of impressive handmade wooden gadgets, everything from wooden kitchen utensils to wooden kids' toys to wooden bowls and wooden doodads with mysterious purposes. There's even a wooden canoe for sale. Did we mention all the wood? Then there are the homemade jams and jellies, rugs and birch bird houses. In The Woods is open from mid-March to early January.

Island Pursuit

Main St., Edgartown • 627-8185

Stop by the Island Pursuit to pursue Vineyard sweatshirts and hats. Or to really prove that you were on the island, get one of those cool oval MV stickers for your car. Island Pursuit also has some waterproof jackets to repel the most foul weather the island can dish up. Besides the Edgartown store, there is also an Island Pursuit in Vineyard Haven and on Nantucket.

Mariposa

12 N. Summer St., Edgartown • 627-9332

Mariposa owner Nancy Antik lives up to her name. Her store offers the finest in antiques on shelves, racks and tables and in the display window. Here you will find hand-painted pottery, linens, picture frames, chests, even hanging wrought-iron candle holders from India and Mexico. Step into a world of perfect, albeit unusual, wedding or anniversary gifts. Mariposa is open mid-May through Christmas.

Morning Glory Farm

West Tisbury Rd., Edgartown • 627-9003

Far from downtown Edgartown is the Morning Glory Farm, alive with all that grows from the island soil. We visited in October and the store was decorated with an autumn display of corn stalks and pumpkins resting on bales of hay. Inside, autumn-colored corn hung from wooden beams. Rustic barn board walls hold posters of Martha's Vineyard Agricultural Fairs of the years past. It's the perfect country farm store to pick up some native produce and perhaps a jug of cider, and to reflect on a simpler, more agrarian lifestyle.

Murdick's Fudge

21 N. Water St., Edgartown • 627-8047

This island fudge factory has locations in Edgartown, Vineyard Haven and Oak Bluffs, so you'll know you're never very far from your next chocolate fix. Peanut butter fudge, double

Photo: Peter Simon

Jetties offer something for everyone — fruitful fishing and beautiful scenery.

chocolate fudge, butter pecan fudge, Cape Cod cranberry fudge . . . it's just fudge, fudge, fudge everywhere you turn! Murdicks ships daily to 48 states, so now all your friends and relatives can join in too. Don't wait too long to order, though, as the Vineyard Haven and Oak Bluffs stores (on Main Street and Circuit Avenue, respectively) close around Columbus Day. The Edgartown store is open from April 1 to December 20.

Willow

4 Kelley St., Edgartown • 627-6674

This new shop, opened in 1995, showcases an incredible display of sterling silver jewelry, semiprecious stones and wondrous ethnic pieces from Mexico, Africa and Indonesia. Willow also has museum-quality geodes, amethysts and crystals. The shop is open from the beginning of May through the end of October and on weekends only through the second week of December.

Alley's General Store

State Rd., West Tisbury • 693-0088

You can almost hear Aaron Copland's "Appalachian Spring" playing in the background as you step up onto the front porch of this general store that dates to 1858. The sign hanging out front says, in true Yankee form, "dealers in lost everything." Believe it. You can buy most everything from fresh fruit and cookware to native jams and hiking boots. The West Tisbury post office used to be located here, but moved out years ago although it left behind a good many post office boxes that are still in use. The antique scale out on the front porch will tell your weight for a penny; 5¢ for your horoscope as well. A few years back it looked as if this landmark was going to be forced to close its doors, but the Martha's Vineyard Preservation Trust stepped forward to save this treasure from history's trash heap. Today you can still come here to get your mail or a gallon of milk, or to simply sit upon the bench out front and watch the world go by.

Up Island

Allen Farm

South Rd., Chilmark • 645-9064

Once a year, the 70 or so resident sheep are shorn at Allen Farm, and the Allens use the wool to knit the most beautiful shawls, sweaters, scarves and hats. This is a different kind of shopping experience out in the pastures of Chilmark, far removed from most everything else. The scenery is truly spectacular here; each direction offers a different picture with green rolling hills or the big blue sky crushing flat a distant blue-green sea. The operating hours are sporadic or by appointment; it's best to call ahead although it appears to be open every afternoon from Memorial Day through October.

The Granary Gallery

Old County Rd., Chilmark • 693-0455, (800) 468-2787

Established in 1954, The Granary is one of the premier galleries on the island. The showcase here is on the photographs of illustrious *Life* photographer and Vineyarder Alfred Eisenstaedt, who died in 1995. Also on display are a varied range of original art in oil, pastel and acrylic complemented by antiques. The photographs on display here are incredible, not only because they are pieces of art but also because they are a chronicle of the 20th century as seen through the lens of the great Mr. Eisenstaedt. Other local artists and photographers exhibit works here, including Alison Shaw, named Photographer of the Year by the New England Press Association, and the McAdoo family, who have created heirloom-quality hooked wool rugs for five generations.

FYI

Unless otherwise noted, the area code for all phone numbers in this guide is 508.

Peter Simon Photography

Tabor House Rd., Chilmark • 645-9575, (888) PS-FOTOG (off island)

Photographer Peter Simon has been capturing on film the wonderful images of Martha's Vineyard for years now — from special island events to its famous landmarks and everything in between. He snaps many island weddings as well as portraits depicted against the Vineyard's beautiful natural settings. He likes to capture his subjects in spontaneous, casual situations and many of his portraits are taken at the beach or against some equally wonderful Martha's Vineyard scene. Besides covering many island weddings and events for the local newspapers, he also offers a line of gift items such as calendars, large prints, note cards and posters graced with his photography as well as a series of compact discs and cassettes entitled "Vineyard Sound," which include music by nationally known artists such as Jonathan Edwards, Tom Rush, Orleans and sister Carly Simon as well as a number of local bands.

Entertainment and Nightlife

When you think of Martha's Vineyard you probably think of her during daylight hours — sunbathed beaches, outdoor activities, golf, tennis and sailing. But she is also an island with a dark side, and within this darkness she is twinkling with entertainment and nightlife. You just need to know where to look.

Two of the most memorable events on the island featured live entertainment from resident Carly Simon. The first was a 1987 concert filmed for HBO. The second was an August 1995 concert that reunited Simon and her former husband, James Taylor, for the first time in 16 years for Livestock '95 — The Concert. This concert, drawing some 10,000 fans, benefitted the Martha's Vineyard Agricultural Society's newly constructed barn. The duet even performed "Mockingbird," just like in the old days. At different spots around the island you see reminders of that legendary concert, mostly in the form of photographs and newspaper clippings on walls of stores and restaurants. It was the Woodstock of MV.

Yet, Carly and James aren't the only act in town (although they are one heck of a tough act to follow!). There are quite a few establishments on the island offering live entertainment. Again, you just need to know where to look. Your best bet is to grab one of the island newspapers. The *Vineyard Gazette* will do nicely or you can check the *Martha's Vineyard Times*' free "Vineyard Visitor" supplement for a calendar of events. For starters, though, you can check out at the information we've compiled below.

Vineyard Haven

The Vineyard Playhouse

10 Church St., Vineyard Haven • 693-6450

The Vineyard Playhouse is a nonprofit community center professional theater that puts on shows throughout the year. Tickets cost anywhere from $10 to $25 during the summer season. The Playhouse offers educational programs for both adults and children as well as children's shows with tickets around $5.

Island Theater Workshop

P.O. Box 2245, Vineyard Haven • 693-4060, 693-5290

This is the island's oldest year-round theater company presenting original plays as well as musicals and dramas. The group presents several shows a year at various venues. They also offer classes for children and adults. It is associated with the Young Director's Studio, Apprentice Players, The Theatre Guild and Children's Theatre.

Tashommo Overlook

State Rd., Vineyard Haven • 693-6450

Summer Shakespeare takes the stage at the natural Tisbury amphitheater. Ticket prices run anywhere from $5 to $10 for adults and $3 to $5 for children. A helpful hint: It's Shakespeare out of doors so you may want to bring along a blanket and plenty of mosquito repellent . . . perhaps we should call it OFFello.

Owen Park

off Main St., Vineyard Haven

Ocean Park

Seaview Ave., Oak Bluffs

Music fans will appreciate the free Sunday night summer concerts alternately given at Owen Park off Main Street in Vineyard Haven and at the gazebo in Ocean Park on Seaview Avenue in Oak Bluffs. The events are quite festive and as you lie back on your blanket the music provides the starry night sky with a soundtrack.

Oak Bluffs

Tabernacle

Campgrounds, Oak Bluffs • 693-0525

The Tabernacle on the campgrounds in Oak Bluffs often hosts band concerts and shows by big-name performers. Also, if you like sing-alongs, tune up your vocal chords and set aside an evening or two for communal music-making. Every Wednesday at 8 PM in season, the Tabernacle hosts a community sing-along. A songbook is provided for a small donation.

The Atlantic Connection

124 Circuit Ave., Oak Bluffs • 693-7129

This is the place on the island to hear live bands or to just hang out after hours. Peter Wolf, formerly of the J. Geils Band, has performed here. The hot band these days is EN-TRAIN, which performs world beat rock and has been rated the No. 1 dance club band in the Boston Music Awards (by the way, the Atlantic Connection was voted No. 1 dance club).

When there isn't a live band performing the music is provided via DJ who hosts a dance party. Besides providing the hottest rock and rhythm and blues, the Atlantic Connection also provides some non-rock selections, such as country line dancing and Celtic bands. There is also comedy. The dance floor here is quite large and is always packed. Playing the best in music year round, it is open all seven nights a week from Memorial Day to Labor Day and Wednesday through Saturday nights in the off-season.

Season's Pub

124 Circuit Ave., Oak Bluffs • 693-7129

Located right next to (and adjoining) the Atlantic Connection is its more mellow companion, the Season's Pub. This very busy pub offers acoustic guitar and favorite rock and folk music nightly from 9:30 PM to 12:30 AM. There is a Sunday afternoon happy hour, and in mid-September they hold the Annual Halfway to St. Patrick's Day party featuring live Irish music.

Lola's

Beach Rd., Oak Bluffs • 693-5007

This hot spot is at the Island Inn on Beach Road on your way to Edgartown (or if you're coming from Edgartown, it's on your way to Oak Bluffs). It's jazz and blues Wednesday through Saturday night.

Edgartown

The Old Whaling Church

89 Main St., Edgartown • 627-4442

The Old Whaling Church is often used for live performances. The day we stopped by there was an organ recital and high tea to benefit the restoration of the 1855 Simmons & Fisher organ. Performers such as Livingston Taylor visit regularly.

Federated Church

S. Summer St., Edgartown • 627-4421

At the Federated Church of Edgartown there is a free recital on an 1840 organ every Friday afternoon at 12:10.

The Seafood Shanty

Dock St., Edgartown • 627-8622

The Seafood Shanty on Edgartown Harbor is one of several Vineyard restaurants which feature piano and classical music. Entertainment in provided in the Shanty Pub Wednesday through Sunday evenings.

Up Island

The Yard

Middle Rd., Chilmark • 645-9662

This is a 100-seat theater in a renovated barn off in the woods of Chilmark. A professional dance troupe, The Yard stages various theatrical events and dance previews throughout the summer season. Designed to sharpen the skills of professional artists, The Yard supports original works. Located near Beetlebung Corner, it is culture out amongst the trees.

Chilmark Community Center

Beetlebung Corner, Chilmark • 645-9484, 645-3100

Beetlebung Corner's Chilmark Community Center is often a spot where outside concerts take place. The Center also holds dances and other social events for all ages including a family folk dance.

Martha's Vineyard Chamber Music Society

P.O. Box 4189, Vineyard Haven • 696-8055

Various summer and winter concerts take place around the island courtesy of the Martha's Vineyard Chamber Music Society; call for a schedule. A number of concerts are held at Edgartown's Old Whaling Church and the Chilmark Community Center.

Wintertide Coffeehouse

Beach Rd. Ext. (Five Corners), Oak Bluffs • 693-8830

This nonprofit year-round eatery and club founded in 1978. It features some of the best up-and-coming (and established) folk, jazz and blues performers, including Tom Paxton and Patty Larkin. A Singer/Songwriter's Retreat and Concert Series is held every September at Wintertide allowing audiences to meet and greet great musicians and to hear their music.

Hot Tin Roof

Martha's Vineyard Airport, West Tisbury • 693-1137

Blues and rock are served in large portions here in this hot club located on the road leading to the airport. Local and nationally known artists perform here. The Hot Tin Roof was built in 1974 and was rebought in 1996 by original owner Carly Simon.

David's Island House

120 Circuit Ave., Oak Bluffs • 693-4516

Monday through Friday from May through September, David's Island House features a piano bar along with seafood, pasta and cocktails.

Lampost

111 Circuit Ave., Oak Bluffs • 696-9352

This is a hot club for the younger than 30 crowd. Local bands perform here two nights a week until midnight or so, April to October. Cocktail hour is from 4:30 to 7:30 PM every day.

Rare Duck

111 Circuit Ave., Oak Bluffs • 696-9352

Another happening hotspot on Circuit Avenue is the Rare Duck, located next to the Lampost. The Rare Duck attracts the younger than 30 crowd as well, offering an assortment of local entertainment nightly from April to October.

Movies

For the latest cinematic releases, check out the **Capawock Theatre** on Main Street in Vineyard Haven, which is open year round. Seasonal theaters are the **Island Theatre** at

The Island of Martha's Vineyard...

...The Perfect Getaway

For our free vacation kit, write or call:

Martha's Vineyard
Chamber of Commerce
P.O. Box 1698 01G
Vineyard Haven, MA 02568
(508) 693 0085

For instant information on Martha's Vineyard by Fax, call the Martha's Vineyard InfoLine, (508) 696 0433 • http://www.mvy.com

Smart Travelers Head to the Harbor View

Located on Martha's Vineyard, the Harbor View Hotel is an example of Victorian heritage. A year round retreat offering spacious accommodations, a waterview seafood restaurant, casual cafe, heated pool, tennis, cycling and a private beach. Walk to the stores, galleries and harbor of historic downtown Edgartown. Experience life at a leisurely pace at the Harbor View Hotel. For reservations call 1-800-225-6005.

A Colony Resort

131 North Water Street, P.O. Box 7 • Edgartown, Martha's Vineyard, MA 02539
(508) 627-7000 • FAX (508) 627-7845

Make this a memorable summer with

Peter Simon Photography

Featuring:

- **Natural Family & Individual Portraits**
- **Weddings**
- **Birthday Parties**
- **Family Reunions**
- **Anniversaries**

Taken At Special Island Locations

Call 508.645.9575
for more information

Martha's Vineyard

Circuit Avenue in Oak Bluffs and **The Strand** across the street (and across the street from the Flying Horses Carousel). All theaters can be accessed by calling the Martha's Vineyard Moviehouses phone at 696-7469.

Attractions

Martha's Vineyard is an island rich in history. Settled just decades after the Pilgrims arrived in Plymouth, the island has grown, prospered and suffered just as the country has.

The Vineyard is a natural playground with its miles and miles of beaches and beautiful country settings, which might make you forget that colonists, patriots, whaling ship captains and Civil War soldiers once called this sandy island home. Today, their homes and churches and even gingerbread cottages stand as reminders of the grand lives they lived, lives that helped put Martha's Vineyard on the map as an important American port.

Many of the attractions listed below are historical sites that have, over the years, played a role in the island's development. We feel strongly that you would be amiss if you left these shores without first learning a bit about the history behind the beauty. The island's five lighthouses are listed according to location.

Vineyard Haven

Old Schoolhouse Museum

110 Main St., Vineyard Haven • 693-3860

Owned by the Martha's Vineyard Preservation Trust, the island's first schoolhouse dates back to 1829. In 1776 a Liberty Pole stood in front of this building. When the British decided they would take it down for use as a spar on one of their vessels, three Vineyard Haven women blew up the pole with gunpowder rather than let the patriotic symbol fall into enemy's hands. To commemorate their patriotism, a new pole was erected in 1898.

West Chop Lighthouse

Main St., Vineyard Haven

Follow Main Street westward to its end and there you will discover West Chop Lighthouse, the island's very first lighthouse site. The light was initially constructed of wood in 1817. This was replaced, in 1838, by the present brick structure. In 1848 it was moved back from the eroding 60-foot cliff, only to be moved again in 1891. It stands 84-feet tall and emits a white light that can appear either red or pinkish depending upon your vantage point due to red-tinted glass on one side of the tower.

Sea Captains' Houses

William St., Vineyard Haven

The largely residential William Street boasts many sea captains' houses, some of them now inns. Spared by the great fire of 1883 that engulfed much of the waterfront, William Street is now part of the Historic District, which protects the buildings in the area from alterations.

Seamen's Bethel

15 Beach St., Vineyard Haven

Catering to the needs of visiting sailors since 1893, this bethel houses a display of maritime artifacts including carved ivory and old photographs.

INSIDERS' TIP

Martha's Vineyard architecture is both beautiful and varied. On the island you can see colonial saltboxes dating from the early 18th century; Federal-style sea captains' houses complete with widows walks; Greek revivals dating from 1820 to 1850; and grand shingled-style summer cottages with wide curved porches, steeply pitched roofs and turrets dating from 1880 to 1910. Of course, you can also see late-19th century Queen Anne-style cottages with towers, turrets and even fish scale shingles. These grew from the Camp Ground Gothic Revivals of 1830 to 1870 which were based on 11th- to 14th-century European medieval architecture.

Association Hall and Cemetery
Spring St., Vineyard Haven

Originally a Congregational and Baptist Church built in 1844, this building is now the town hall and is also home to the Katherine Cornell Memorial Theater. Behind the building is an old cemetery with stones dating back to the 18th century.

Oak Bluffs

Flying Horses Carousel
Circuit Ave., Oak Bluffs • 693-9481

This is the oldest operating platform carousel in the United States. It features 20 wooden horses sporting real horse hair and glass eyes. It was constructed in New York City in 1876 and arrived at Oak Bluffs in 1884. Open from mid-April through mid-October, it is listed as a National Historic Landmark. Rides are only $1.

Tabernacle
Trinity Park, Oak Bluffs

At 100-feet high, 130-feet wide and with seating for more than 3,000, this open-air auditorium is considered one of the largest wrought-iron structures in the United States. A uniquely beautiful piece of architecture combining the seemingly unlikely mixture of stained-glass windows and corrugated metal, it was built in 1879 amidst the Oak Bluffs campground community. It replaced a one-ton tent used by the Methodists who congregated at this spot for their religious summer gatherings. The Martha's Vineyard Camp Meeting Association, 693-0525, offers a free schedule of events open to the public, including concerts (James Taylor has played here), flea markets and interdenominational services.

The Cottage Museum
1 Trinity Park, Oak Bluffs • 693-0525

This museum allows you a rare glimpse at the inside of a gingerbread cottage. It is representative of the more than 300 fancifully designed and painted cottages that line the narrow streets of the greater than 30-acre campground community. The architecture of these cottages was modeled after the Newport, Rhode Island, Victorian style, but these have special (could we say, revolutionary) touches and colors that helped to create a style unique to Oak Bluffs. Plan to take a good part of an hour just to stroll through the cottage community and examine the architecture and the many colors. The whole place is a 30-acre museum in itself!

Union Chapel
Kennebec Ave., Oak Bluffs • 693-9010, 693-2426 in summer

When it was built in 1872, this was a nondenominational church. The octagonal-shaped building is now used for summer concerts and a jazz series as its acoustics are quite good. This church building features some interesting architecture, including a three-tiered roof.

East Chop Lighthouse
Oak Bluffs

Tall atop a bluff it stands, some 80 feet above the sea, casting its lonely beam across the waves of Nantucket Sound below. This cast-iron lighthouse was built in 1876, replacing a wooden light erected in 1828 that burned down. Originally brown-red in color, it was known as the Chocolate Lighthouse until it was painted white in 1988. It emits a green light, marking the port side of Vineyard Haven Harbor and balancing West Chop's red beam marking the starboard side.

Civil War Memorial Statue
Seaview, Lake and Ocean aves., Oak Bluffs

Located at the busy intersection across the street from the Oak Bluffs ferry stop is a peculiar monument, and like most things in Oak Bluffs, it's the color scheme that is its peculiar attribute. This Civil War memorial dating to 1892 reads: "Erected in honor of Grand Army of the Republic by Charles Strahan, Co.

INSIDERS' TIP

The highest peak on the island is Little Peaked Hill in Chilmark. At 311 feet, perhaps it should be renamed.

B. 21st Virginia Reg." Yes, you read correctly, it was erected by a Confederate soldier — way up here in Yankee territory! In 1980, the town of Oak Bluffs repainted the Union soldier atop the memorial in Confederate gray colors to pay homage to Strahan.

Edgartown

Old Whaling Church

89 Main St., Edgartown • 627-8017

This is an absolutely massive structure, with six gigantic wooden columns supporting the weight of the centuries and a 92-foot clock tower whose four pointed spires seem to challenge the heavens. Since 1843 this soaring tower has been a landmark for sailors approaching Edgartown by sea. Built as sturdy as the old whaling ships, with 50-foot hand-hewn pine beams joined with wooden pegs, today the church is a 500-seat performing arts center. Summer church service is still held here on Sundays, as are weddings and receptions.

Dr. Daniel Fisher Home

99 Main St., Edgartown • 627-4440

This fine example of Federal-period architecture was built in 1840 as the home of town physician and whaling mogul Dr. Daniel Fisher. Fisher was also the founder of the Martha's Vineyard National Bank. The building was recently restored by the Martha's Vineyard Preservation Trust. To arrange a guided tour call 627-8619 for information and reservations. The tour also includes the Old Whaling Church and the Vincent House; cost for all three buildings is $5. This building is also available for weddings and receptions; call 627-8017.

The Vincent House Museum

Off Main St., Edgartown • 627-8619

This gem of a full-Cape was built in 1672 and is considered to be Martha's Vineyard oldest residence. It is located behind the Old Whaling Church and the Fisher House. Interestingly, sections of the interior walls of this museum have been left open and unfinished so you can observe its original colonial construction. The cost to tour the museum alone is $3, so you may as well pay the additional $2 to tour the Old Whaling Church and Vincent House. Children tour the museum free of charge.

Edgartown Lighthouse

Off N. Water St., Edgartown

Originally constructed on a man-made island in Edgartown Harbor in 1828, sands have since built up to connect the site with the beach. Before the sands filled in, there was a long wooden walk that led out to the lighthouse. This was called the Bridge of Sighs because it was a popular spot for young whalers to bring their girlfriends or wives before heading out on a long journey. In 1938 the lighthouse was replaced by another floated to this spot from Ipswich.

Vineyard Museum

8 Cooke St., Edgartown • 627-4441

This museum complex consists of four buildings that form one square block. The 1765 Thomas Cooke House was once a customs house and now houses antiquities of the island including tools and folk art. Exhibits to honor the whaling industry, such as scrimshaw and ship models, can be found in the Foster Gallery while Native American and island geophysical exhibits can be found in the Pease Galleries. The Gale Huntington Library is a must for those interested in genealogy while the carriage shed houses a fire engine dating back to 1854 as well as a whaleboat. If you're a lighthouse enthusiast be sure to get a look at the original Fresnel lens from the Gay Head Lighthouse, now resting on the museum's front lawn. Installed in 1856 and removed from the lighthouse in 1952, the lens is illuminated a few hours each evening during the summer months.

Pagoda Tree

S. Water St., Edgartown

A visit to Edgartown would not be complete without a visit to the famous Pagoda tree along S. Water Street. The tree was planted during the mid-19th century by Capt. Thomas Milton who carried it as a seedling from China. As you stand beneath its reaching branches, just imagine the sailors who, upon a hot summer's day, dodged the sun within the shade of her spreading limbs. It is considered perhaps the oldest and largest specimen of its kind in America.

Whale Memorial
Across from Memorial Wharf, Edgartown

A fitting memorial to the whales and the whalers is the Whale Memorial located down near the harbor in Edgartown. The memorial features a sculptured whale diving into the ground with its flukes showing and a whaleboat in pursuit. It was erected in 1995 and says it is "Dedicated to the whales and the whalers who pursued them."

Ferry to Chappaquiddick
Edgartown Harbor, Edgartown

We don't know if you would actually consider this a point of interest, but it does meet the criteria for must-see when visiting Edgartown. Two simple ferries, *On Time II* and *On Time III*, make the daily runs between downtown Edgartown and Chappy, transporting you, your car, bicycle or moped in the process. By the way, the ferries have never been late, thus earning their names. Of course, there is no schedule, they just transport people and vehicles as they arrive, but regardless, they have never missed a deadline. Round trip fares are $5 for a car and driver, $1 for each passenger, $3 for a bicycle and rider and $4 for a moped.

Cape Pogue Lighthouse
Chappaquiddick Island

By far the toughest of the island's lighthouses to visit, the Cape Pogue Lighthouse is located at the northernmost tip of Cape Pogue on the island of Chappaquiddick. Built as a wooden lighthouse in 1801, it was destroyed by the sea and replaced in 1838. The second light lasted for about 50 years until it too was destroyed and was replaced by a third, which was replaced by a fourth in 1892 (do you see a trend developing here?). This fourth lighthouse, which stood 33 feet high, was replaced by the present structure in 1922. This present lighthouse has earned its place in the Lighthouse Hall of Fame by being the only one ever moved in one piece by a helicopter. It stands 55 feet tall. Located at the farthest reaches of Chappaquiddick, the lighthouse is not accessible by road.

Up Island

Mayhew Chapel and Indian Burial Ground
off Indian Hill Rd., West Tisbury

This area known as Christiantown, known to the Wampanoag Indians as Manitouwattotan, can be found off Indian Hill Road in West Tisbury. You follow a dirt road to this historic site hidden in the woods (just keep going, it's up there, believe us!). Here stands the small Mayhew Chapel, built in 1829, and the adjoining Indian Burial Ground. The chapel is scarcely 20 feet by 15 feet and yet it contains a dozen pews and a small alter! Early settler and minister Thomas Mayhew Jr. preached here, converting many Natives in this area to Christianity. In the nearby cemetery nameless stones, perhaps as many as a hundred following the hilly terrain, mark Indian graves. It is a unique historical location, moving in its simplicity.

Menemsha Fishing Village
North St., Menemsha

A classic fishermen's harbor, Menemsha was the site chosen to represent Quint's home port in the movie *Jaws*. There are some unforgettable shots of the harbor in the movie, notably as Quint's vessel *ORCA* is chugging out of the fishing port to hunt down the 25 foot great white shark. In fact, a local told us that until recently one of the fishermen's shacks still had the name "Quint" painted on the door from the days when the movie was shot here. Furthermore, another local told us that the *ORCA* itself lies wrecked across the harbor at the mercy of the elements two decades after she was stove by the mechanical beast.

Beyond Hollywood, Menemsha is everything you expect from a salty fishing port: piles of lobster traps, heaps of discarded quahog shells, men wearing yellow waders bathed in fish blood, their faces aged by years at sea. Along the docks are little weather-beaten fishing shacks with shingles either warped with salt breezes, painted with gull droppings or else missing altogether.

Gay Head Cliffs
State Rd., Gay Head

Travel up-island to Gay Head and you'll

think you've landed on an entirely different island. No visit to the Vineyard would ever be complete without a visit to the incredible Gay Head Cliffs, at the westernmost reaches of the island. Clearly the island's most popular and most photographed tourist attraction, its clay painted cliffs cause you to hold your breath in awe of that which only nature herself could possibly create.

These 150-feet-high clay cliffs were originally named Dover Cliffs by explorer Bartholomew Gosnold, who first discovered the island in 1602. The Native Indians of the area have their own name for this place unlike any other — Aquinnah. Gay Head, which is the more widely accepted name, came from British sailors who sailed past this distinctive geological formation during in the 17th century.

Today, the cliffs are owned by the Wampanoags Indians of the area. Formed during the ice age, the cliffs are a geological treasure chest as well as a paleontologic gold mine with the numerous fossils unearthed here. The cliffs also had some practical uses, for instance, early islanders used the cliff's clay to make paint and bricks. The high cliffs were also a prime vantage point, a high ground you might say, and a perfect place to place a lighthouse. The cliffs, now a national landmark, are protected in an attempt to reduce erosion. Only the Gay Head Wampanoag Indians are allowed to remove clay.

Gay Head Lighthouse
Gay Head

High atop the Gay Head Cliffs is the red brick Gay Head Lighthouse, built in 1844 to replace its wooden sister. The original lighthouse was built by order of President John Adams. Due to a mingling of two tides, one from the north and one from the west, this stretch of ocean is considered very treacherous. Devil's Bridge off Gay Head has wrecked many a ship over the centuries, including the *City of Columbus* in 1884 with the loss of 120 lives. The Fresnel lens of the second lighthouse, which for the better part of a century warned sea captains of the hazardous cliffs, was removed in 1952 and is now on display at the Vineyard Museum in Edgartown.

Tours and Excursions

Boating excursions are popular throughout the island. We'll let you in on a few of our favorites.

The Arabella
Menemsha Harbor • 645-3511

This 50-foot catamaran sails out of Menemsha Harbor twice a day in season. Captain Hugh Taylor will take you to Cuttyhunk (or the town of Gosnold) — the only public island in the isolated Elizabeth Islands chain. Or you can take a sunset cruise to the Gay Head Cliffs.

Ayuthia
Coastwise Harbor, Vineyard Haven • 693-7245

This yacht sails out of Coastwise Harbor offering half- and full-day sails and overnight trips to Nantucket and the Elizabeth Islands.

Laissez Faire
Town Dock, Vineyard Haven • 693-1646

The 54-foot Alden ketch will take you on half- or full-day cruises along the coastline. Trips include beverages. You can also take overnight trips to Cuttyhunk or Nantucket.

Gosnold Cruises
Vineyard Haven • 693-8900

These cruises leave Vineyard Haven for Gay Head Cliffs or Cuttyhunk Island in full catered comfort.

Mad Max
Edgartown • 627-7500

Mad Max leaves Edgartown to cruise along Chappaquiddick and past Oak Bluffs. A 60-foot-long by 25-foot-wide catamaran, it departs three times daily.

Shenandoah
Vineyard Haven • 693-1699

If you really want to splurge, consider a six-day cruise aboard this square topsail schooner. If you have the time and money, you'll enjoy life in various ports, including Newport, Rhode Island; Block Island, Rhode Island; and Nantucket. Meals are included, as are the memories.

Finally, there are a number of companies presenting narrated tours. **Gay Head Sightseeing**, 693-1555, **Island Transport**, 693-0058, and **Martha's Vineyard Sightseeing**, 627-8687 all have buses waiting as you come off the ferries at Oak Bluffs and Vineyard Haven. Tours run from mid-May through mid-October. All three tour companies offer 2½-hour tours of the six island towns; the cost is about $11.50.

Whale Watch Express

1 Toledo St., Teaticket (Falmouth)
• 548-3047

East Coast Tours of Cape Cod provides round-trip van service from the Woods Hole (Falmouth) ferry dock to either Barnstable Harbor or Plymouth Harbor to meet the Whale Watch boats. Reservations are required to take part in this service provided from mid-May through end of September depending on the weather. Costs are in the $33 range for adults and $25 for children.

FYI

Unless otherwise noted, the area code for all phone numbers in this guide is 508.

Beaches

We hope you brought along your bathing suit because Martha's Vineyard has 125 miles of coastline offering some of the most memorable beaches you'll ever encounter. And we hope you wear your swim suit because sunbathing in your birthday suit, or swimming in it for that matter, is against the law in all six Vineyard towns, even if you do happen to be the only bather for miles and miles and miles.

Many of the beaches on Martha's Vineyard are private, though. In fact, we only count a little more than a dozen public beaches out of all those 125 miles. The rest belong to the privileged few whose rights go down as far as the low-water mark, so you can't even swim by at high tide without being caught for trespassing!

Below we've listed our favorite public beaches. To use these beaches, you'll need to get a parking and/or beach permit, which can be obtained by contacting the local town hall. (Vineyard Haven/Tisbury, 696-4200; West Tisbury, 696-0100; Chilmark, 645-2107; Oak Bluffs, 693-5511; Gay Head, 645-2300; Edgartown, 627-6110.) Of the beaches below, all but Gay Head and East beaches are free. For current fees for these two beaches call the Gay Head Town Hall.

So, get your permit, pack a lunch, bring along a book and head off to the beach.

Vineyard Haven

Lake Tashmoo Beach

Herring Creek Rd.

Sunbathers, swimmers, surf casters and shellfish seekers flock to this beach on the island's north shore, where the lake meets the ocean. This teeny stretch of sand is also known as Herring Creek beach. You'll find lifeguards here, but no bathhouses or concessions.

Owen Park Beach

Off Main St.

Here you'll discover a small, sandy, quiet harbor beach that offers great sunbathing, swimming, boat-watching and lifeguards. It even has a separate kiddie play area. Bathhouses and concessions are nearby.

Tisbury Town Beach

Owen Little Way

Sitting on the sand at Town Beach is the closest thing to being on a yacht since this beach is right next to the Vineyard Yacht Club. Lifeguards are on duty here and concessions and bathhouses are close at hand.

South Beach

Off Edgartown-West Tisbury Rd.

The 633-acre Long Point Wildlife Refuge Center preserve boasts this half-mile-long deserted beach where swimming and surf fishing are allowed in freshwater and saltwater ponds. Better get there early; there are only 55 parking spaces available. South Beach has lifeguards and bathhouses but no concessions.

Edgartown

Lighthouse Beach

Starbuck's Neck

Lighthouse Beach is a perfect place to watch boats entering and leaving the harbor. From here you get a nice view of Chappy and Cape Pogue. At night, it's an ideal spot for sunsets and stargazing. There are lifeguards at this beach, but no bathhouses or concessions. By the way, it's called Lighthouse Beach because it's right there beside the Edgartown Lighthouse.

Fuller Street Beach

Fuller St., Edgartown

This section of beach, not far from Lighthouse Beach, is a popular hangout for the younger crowd. It looks out across the water at Cape Pogue and Cape Pogue Lighthouse. There are no lifeguards, concessions or bathhouses at the Fuller Street beach.

Katama Beach

Katama Rd., Katama

Also known as South Beach, this 3-mile-long barrier strand is the island's largest public beach. It's a favorite among surfers, who challenge heavy wave action of the mighty Atlantic pounding at its doorstep. (Watch for riptides, and check for swimming conditions!) In contrast to the Atlantic waves is a calm salt pond to the north of the beach. A shuttle bus runs between the beach and the center of Edgartown. Lifeguards are on patrol and bathhouses are available, although there are no concessions.

Joseph Sylvia State Beach

Beach Rd., Edgartown and Oak Bluffs

This lovely beach is framed with grassy dunes and wild roses and marked by calm, shallow waters. It is also known as the Edgartown-Oak Bluffs State Beach because it stretches along 2 miles of those towns. (The Edgartown section of the beach is known as Bend-in-the-Road Beach because of its unusual shape.) The beach, which has lifeguards and nearby concessions but no restrooms facilities, is quite popular. It was along this stretch that some of the beach scenes from *Jaws* were filmed.

Oak Bluffs

Oak Bluffs Town Beach

Seaview Ave., Oak Bluffs

Oak Bluffs Town Beach straddles both sides of the ferry wharf, and its calm surf makes it ideal for families with small kids. It's also a great spot to sit and wait for the ferry to come in. This beach has lifeguards on duty. Public restrooms are available nearby on the ferry dock, while various concessions are close-by as well.

Eastville Beach

Beach Rd., Oak Bluffs

If you're looking for a quiet stretch of shoreline along the harbor, you've found it. You can find Eastville Beach at the bridge between Oak Bluffs and Vineyard Haven. When you're not being lulled by the gently lapping surf, you can watch the sails billowing in the breeze as the boats go tacking by. There are no lifeguards, restrooms or concession stands. Just sit back, relax and enjoy the view.

Up Island

Menemsha Public Beach

Menemsha Harbor, Chilmark

Resting right beside the stone jetty at the entrance to Dutcher's Dock, Menemsha Public Beach is a quiet place with a gentle surf and surprisingly few people. Sit and watch the fishing boats go in and out, or just kick back and catch some rays. Lifeguards, restrooms and nearby concessions provide all the comforts.

Gay Head Beach

Off Moshup Tr., Gay Head

A wooden boardwalk winds alongside the famous cliffs, through cranberry bogs and beach plum bushes, down to the surf. Below is Gay Head Beach, a 5-mile-long stretch that is actually four beaches in one. From north to south they are: Gay Head, Moshup, Philbin and Zack's Cliffs. The last two beaches are private. The farther south you walk, the more isolated you find yourself. This truly feels like the ends of the earth. Fortunately, these ends of the earth have restrooms and concessions located at the head of the cliffs, though you won't find any lifeguards out here. Be careful in the tricky surf. Note: the parking out here is a bit expensive — up to $15 a day!

Chappaquiddick

East Beach
Chappaquiddick Rd.

Wasque Reservation and Cape Pogue Wildlife Refuge are adjoining beaches, known as East Beach, that run along the eastern coast of the Island of Chappaquiddick. Even on the hottest day, you may find yourself the only one basking in the unspoiled glory. Since the beach sits at the end of a bumpy dirt road, it's accessible only by boat or four-wheel-drive vehicle. There are no bathhouses, concessions or lifeguards. To get to Chappaquiddick Island, you'll need to take your car across on the On Time ferry.

Natural Areas and Walking Trails

In a sense, Martha's Vineyard is one big natural area brimming with beauty at every town and down every road. Each part of the island offers wonders so varied and so vast that you'll doubt if heaven could ever be an improvement.

The island offers a delicious mixture of settings, and as you travel through say, Chilmark, you will see a number of her settings all in the same eyeful. Turn a corner and you get a vista of rolling fields dampened by small ponds and ending in vast sweep of ocean blue. Look the other way and you see painstakingly erected stone walls vanishing off into the distance, beyond a swaying marshland carrying the island to the sea. Such natural beauty is hard to sufficiently appreciate in such generous doses.

Nature and humanity share the island, although in the Up Island area it seems that nature has the upper hand. Wildlife is ever apparent. Upon an autumn lane in Chilmark we had to stop our vehicle to allow a quorum of turkeys to cross. They gobbled as turkeys do and continued on their way, not the least bit deterred by our car nor the fact that Thanksgiving was just a short month away!

More than a fifth of the island is protected from development and there are several sanctuaries and parks you can explore. You may have to pay a nominal parking fee.

Felix Neck Wildlife Sanctuary
Off Edgartown-Vineyard Haven Rd. • 627-4850

Situated 3 miles outside of Edgartown and run by the Massachusetts Audubon Society, Felix Neck is a nature lover's dream come true — 350 acres of open fields, woods, beaches and marshlands inhabited by reptiles and other wildlife. In the summer, visitors can hike 6 miles of meandering, marked trails; be sure to look for the osprey nesting platforms. Throughout the year, professional naturalists offer various demonstrations and expeditions, including snake and bird walks, and stargazing and snorkeling sessions.

An exhibition center features displays of fish, snakes and turtles and also has a library and gift shop. Felix Neck also offers summer camps for kids during the season.

Cedar Tree Neck Wildlife Sanctuary
Off Indian Hill Rd. • 693-5207

This 300-acre natural habitat and living museum is tucked among the unspoiled woods of West Tisbury. It's a varied environment where freshwater ponds, brooks, scrub oaks and beech trees, bayberry bushes, rocky bluffs and bogs all compete for your attention. The wooded color-coded trails offer many a delight: One leads to secluded North Shore Beach, another to a bird refuge, still another (the one starting at the parking lot) to the sanctuary's summit and breathtaking views of the Gay Head Cliffs. It is open year round.

Cape Pogue Wildlife Refuge and Wasque Reservation
Chappaquiddick Island • 693-7662

These two adjoining parcels of land (509 acres and 200 acres, respectively) bordering Katama Bay on the southeastern corner of Chappaquiddick Island form the perfect escape from crowds. Even on the hottest summer day, you'll find few people here.

Salt marshes, tidal flats, ponds, cedars, barrier beaches and sand dunes are everywhere. A myriad of shorebirds such as osprey, snowy egret, kestrel, great blue heron and the endangered least tern and piping plover populate this haven. In the summer months, you can take a bird-spotting "safari" on Saturdays. Swimming, fishing and picnicking are permitted. The areas are open year round.

Mytoi

Off Dike Rd., Chappaquiddick • 693-7662

This 14-acre Japanese garden is an astounding profusion of azalea, dogwood, iris, daffodils, rhododendron, wild rose, Japanese maple, holly and sweet gum. We could sit all day and stare at the koi and goldfish, innocently swimming in their picturesque creek-fed pool beneath an ornamental bridge. Mytoi, which is open year round, is still undergoing restoration from damage done by 1991's Hurricane Bob. Parking is now available.

Long Point Wildlife Refuge

Off Waldron's Bottom Rd., West Tisbury • 693-7662

Long Point is the best spot for bird and duck watchers, provided, that is, you can deal with the very bumpy roads that take you here. This 633-acre area of open grassland and heath is bounded on the sides by salt and fresh water. The trails here wind their way through pine and oak forests and will take you to either idyllic Long Cove Pond (look for the river otters) or the lovely, but crowded, South Beach, where you can swim.

Manuel E. Correllus State Forest

Airport Rd. • 693-2540

This forest sits smack-dab in the middle of the island, a 5,146-acre spread of scrub oak and pine laced with paved bike, nature, horse and hiking trails. You can pack a picnic basket and bask in the cool shade of the majestic trees. A hostel is located at the southwest corner of the forest (see the Accommodations section). There is no parking fee.

Waskosim's Rock Reservation

North Rd., Chilmark • 627-7141

The Martha's Vineyard Land Bank Commission acquired this unique 185-acre property in 1990 from a developer who planned on building scores of houses on it. Now, it remains an unspoiled preserve of rolling hills, wetlands, oak and beetlebung woods; it even has the ruins of an 18th-century homestead. As for Waskosim's Rock: Deposited by a retreating glacier and said to look like a breaching whale (which it does, sort of), the rock sits

Photo: Peter Simon

Sunset marks the end of the day for these boaters.

on a ridge from which you can soak in panoramic views of the Vineyard Sound foothills and the Mill Brook Valley.

Recreational Activities

The island is really one big playground. Surrounded as it is by the sea and the sounds, watersports and fishing abound. Meanwhile, on land there is plenty to do and discover.

Bicycling

Perhaps the best way to explore Martha's Vineyard is by bicycle. Just waiting to be explored are several superb bike paths that transverse the island. The island terrain is not known for its smoothness. The east side of the island is more flat that the west side, which rises well above sea level in some places. The more level bike paths are those connecting Vineyard Haven to Oak Bluffs, Oak Bluffs to Edgartown to South Beach and State Road between North Tisbury and Vineyard Haven. Middle Road in Chilmark has little traffic and it is a wonderful country jaunt.

If you do enjoy scaling hills, follow the circular trial that begins at the Gay Head Lighthouse. The views are incredible. There are also several paved bike paths in the Manuel E. Correllus State Forest, off Edgartown-West Tisbury Road, in Oak Bluffs, West Tisbury and Edgartown.

Many people bring their own bikes across from the mainland on the ferry, but you can lease bikes and riding equipment at a number of rental shops throughout the island. Here are a few:

Martha's Bike Rentals, Vineyard Haven, 693-6593

Anderson Bike Rentals, Oak Bluffs, 693-9346

DeBettencourt's Bike Shop, Oak Bluffs, 693-0011

Edgartown Bicycles, Edgartown, 627-9008

Bowling

If you get the urge to knock things over, first get out of that expensive antiques shop you may be browsing through, and then head over to **Spinnaker Lanes**, State Road, Tisbury, 693-9691, for some candlepin bowling and billiards. It is open year round, 7 days a week.

Fishing

Swimming along the coastline of the Vineyard are fish just looking to be caught. You don't have to be Quint, or Ahab for that matter, to catch the big one. You just have to be at the right place at the right time with the right equipment.

Fishing is superb at any of the beaches so you'll notice plenty of surf casters. You'll also spot anglers casting their lines over the island's various bridges and stone jetties.

Insiders head to the Chappaquiddick shore at Cape Pogue and Wasque and to Lobsterville Beach in Gay Head to reel in bluefish and bonito. Scup is common in the waters almost everywhere. Cod and striped bass are best caught during the spring and fall; head over to the entrance of Menemsha Harbor to find them.

If you're into surf casting, try the beaches at Gay Head or any beach facing south. Remember, the tides in the Atlantic Ocean can be tricky; for instance, there is an eight-hour difference between high tides at Cape Pogue and Gay Head. The *Vineyard Gazette* prints a tide chart each Friday on the Fishing page.

Equipment

Several stores offer fishing rods, tackle, bait and other equipment. Tackle shops are the best places to find out about local limits on size and numbers of fish you can keep. Here are four of our favorites:

Dick's Bait and Tackle, New York Avenue, Oak Bluffs, 693-7669

Captain Porky's, Dock Street, Edgartown, 627-7117

Coop's Bait and Tackle, 147 W. Tisbury Road, Edgartown, 627-3909

Larry's Tackle Shop, 258 Upper Main Street, Edgartown, 627-5088

Charter Fishing

Looking for tuna, shark and white marlin? Consider taking a fishing expedition; you'll find them offered at all of the island's harbors. Here are several of the local tried-and-true charter services.

Banjo's Captain Robert Plante, 693-3154, offers half- and full-day charters out of Oak Bluffs.

The party boat ***Skipper***, 693-1238, leaves from Oak Bluffs for fluke and scup.

Slapshot II's Captain Rob Coab, 627-8087, offers charters out of Edgartown Harbor.

Big Eye Charters, 627-3649, offers charters out of Edgartown Harbor.

Flashy Lady Charters, 645-2462, at Menemsha Harbor, offers half- and full-day charters in search of the three Bs (bass, bonito and blues).

Conomok, 645-9278, out of Gay Head, offers half- and full-day charters. Captain Brian Vanderhoop offers spin or fly fishing.

Chantey III, 645-2127, out of Gay Head, goes out after big bass and blues.

Golf

Every vacation should include a little driving, chipping and putting. To help you out in that area, Martha's Vineyard has two fine public golf courses.

Courses

Farm Neck Golf Course

Farm Neck Way, Oak Bluffs • 693-2504

This challenging 18-hole, par 72 championship course is open from mid-April to mid-December. Greens fees are $75 in season, $48 during the interim season and a bargain at $35 in the off-season. Call ahead for reservations (though no more than 48 hours in advance). This beautiful course follows Sengekontacket Pond and overlooks the beach. It features a driving range and pro shop with rental equipment.

Mink Meadows

Golf Club Rd., Vineyard Haven • 693-0600

Mink Meadows is an intimate course with nine holes and simply unbeatable ocean views. In fact, the views are so awesome that you might not be able to keep your eyes on the ball. The facility also has a pro shop and driving range. In 1996, a round cost $42 in season, while off-season greens fees were about half of that. (Rates were still being determined for 1997.) Mink Meadows is open from April 1 to November 1.

Minigolf

Island Cove Miniature Golf Course

State Rd., Vineyard Haven • 693-2611

If you're not up to the challenge of a full 6000-plus yard course, then bring the kiddies over to Island Cove for some family adventure golf. This Vineyard Haven course offers 18 holes and waterfalls to boot. The first nine holes are handicapped-accessible.

Horseback Riding

Enjoy the scenery of the island while in the saddle of a horse trotting down a country lane.

Scrubby Neck Farm

Scrubby Neck Rd., West Tisbury • 693-3770

Scrubby Neck Farm, formerly South Shore Stables, is situated on Watcha Pond along the beautiful south side of West Tisbury. You'll receive breathtaking views of the Atlantic Ocean, you can even take a dawn, sunset or moonlight ride. Choose from indoor and outdoor rings and a number of scenic paths.

Misty Meadows Horse Farm

Old County Rd., West Tisbury • 693-1870

Misty Meadows is a trail farm that is only open during the summer months. It offers family-oriented trail rides in the forest behind the farm.

INSIDERS' TIP

In 1898, island resident Joshua Slocum became the first person to sail around the world alone. It took three years in his 36-foot sloop *Spray*.

Arrowhead Farm
Indian Hill Rd., West Tisbury • 693-8831

This farm provides lessons, boarding, an outdoor and indoor ring and offers pony rides. There are beautiful woods to ride in. Arrowhead Farm welcomes visitors and offers a day riding camp during the summer.

Ice-skating

Martha's Vineyard Ice Arena
Edgartown-Vineyard Haven Rd., Oak Bluffs • 693-5329

This arena is open for skating, lessons and hockey games from the beginning of August through mid-April.

Tennis

Public tennis courts are available at the following locations.

Town Courts, Church Street (off Main Street)

Vineyard Town Courts, Niantic Avenue (off Circuit Avenue)

Oak Bluffs Island Inn, Beach Road, Oak Bluffs

Oak Bluffs Town Courts, Robinson Road, (just beyond Trolley Stop parking lot)

Edgartown Mattakesett Tennis Club, RFD 270, Katama Road, Edgartown

West Tisbury Elementary School, Old County Road, West Tisbury

Chilmark Community Center, South Road, Chilmark

Watersports and Boating

Equipment Rentals

Vineyard Scuba
S. Circuit Ave., Oak Bluffs • 693-0288

The waters around the Vineyard were unlucky for many an 18th- and 19th-century sailor. With the help of Vineyard Scuba you can now visit these sunken ships and lost schooners. They offer equipment rentals so you can explore the Vineyard's undersea world.

Wind's Up
Beach Rd., Vineyard Haven • 693-4252, 693-4340

Windsurfers will find the waters around the Vineyard to their liking. Wind's Up offers lessons and rentals of windsurfers, wet suits, body boards, sailboats, surfboards, sea kayaks and canoes. Ask for a free copy of their brochure listing the best places to catch the wind. Wind's Up is open until Christmas, reopening in March. Brrr, the water must be cold that time of year!

Martha's Vineyard Parasailing, Waterskiing, Jet Skiing
Owen Park Dock, Vineyard Haven • 693-2838

Their name tells the whole story. This business rents jet skis and will take you out for an afternoon of waterskiing or for the ride of your life — parasailing. The instructors are Coast Guard licensed and insured. Call ahead for reservations.

Boat Rentals

If your plans include hoisting your own sail, then you'll be happy to learn that there are many boat rental establishments on the Vineyard. Here are a few of our favorites.

Wind's Up!
Beach Road, Vineyard Haven's • 693-4252

This is the place to go for catamarans, Sunfish, sailboats, Windsurfers and Boogie Boards.

Dockside Whaler Rentals
Oak Bluffs Harbor • 693-8476

Dockside rents the ever-popular Boston Whaler, among other boats.

Mad Max Boat Rentals and Sales
15 Dock St., Edgartown • 627-7500

Mad Max has electric boats for rent that are extremely quiet and seat four comfortably.

Boat Ramps

Those who bring their own boat to the island, or buy their own boat on the island, can launch it at several boat ramps.

In Vineyard Haven: Beach Road, on the Vineyard Haven side of the lagoon drawbridge, into the lagoon or at Lake Street into Lake Tashmoo.

In Oak Bluffs: At East Chop Drive, along the north side of the Harbor, into the harbor or at Medeiros Cove, on the west side of town, into the lagoon.

In Edgartown: Anthier's Landing into Sengekontacket Pond or at the south end of Katama Bay Road into Katama Bay.

In Gay Head: At the Gay Head-Chilmark town line at Hariph's Creek Bridge into Nashaquitsa Pond or at Lobsterville, West Basin, into Menemsha Pond.

Annual Events

There's always something happening on the island, especially during the summer months when the island seems to be bursting at the seams with visitors and excitement. Whether it's fireworks, fairs, festivals, road races, concerts or fishing tournaments, you are bound to find something of interest. And the events don't end when the bridge is raised at the conclusion of Columbus Day weekend. Edgartown celebrates an old-fashioned Christmas with a host of festivities, and there's even a First Night event on the first night of the new year. So, get out your calendar and prepare to pencil in some dates.

January

WMVY Annual Chili Contest

Atlantic Connection, Oak Bluffs • 693-5000

This fund-raiser sponsored by radio station WMVY is sure to warm you up. This contest strives to solve an important culinary question: Who has the best-tasting chili on the island? One category involves the island's top chefs, and the other is for amateurs, with ordinary islanders bringing out their best recipes. Bring your appetite; bowls and spoons are provided. A fee of $10 will get you in the door to sample all the chili you can eat.

April

Annual Lip-Synch Contest

Oak Bluffs • 693-0976

Not many of us can sing like Barbra Streisand, but we can certainly fake it! This annual lip-synch fund-raiser held at the Atlantic Connection draws big crowds and big laughs, and also helps support the Martha's Vineyard After School Program.

May

Memorial Day 5K Road Race

Oak Bluffs • 639-0085

Memorial Day weekend is regarded as the kickoff for the new tourist season here on the island. It is also the weekend for the annual Memorial Day 5K road race, held on the Sunday of that weekend. You can sign up at the Wesley Hotel.

Rotary Club Annual Flea Market

Oak Bluffs • 693-0085

Held over Memorial Day weekend at the Edgartown School, this annual sale includes many items donated by local folks who have caught the spring cleaning bug. Imagine the treasures that emerge from people's attics and garages!

Spring Plant Sale

Felix Neck Wildlife Sanctuary, Edgartown • 627-4850

The beauty of the sanctuary is a fitting setting for this fund-raiser, which is always held over Memorial Day weekend. Bring lots of green — the sales and varieties are outstanding!

June

Oak Bluffs - Inn Place to Be

Oak Bluffs • 693-3627

Oak Bluffs has plenty of charming inns, and they're on display this day only as part of this popular self-guided tour. Held in early June, the admission is free and there is a wine reception afterwards.

Oak Bluffs Annual Harbor Festival

Oak Bluffs • 693-0085

This is a festive waterfront celebration that attracts both locals and tourists in large numbers. Bands fill the air with joyful sounds while seafood fills the air with enticing aromas. There are games and craft booths to keep kids and adults entertained. Admission is free. This event takes place on the second Saturday in June.

A Taste of the Vineyard

Edgartown • 627-4440

This event allows you to sample food and drink from more than 60 island eateries and beverage merchants. It is held under a tent next to the Old Whaling Church. The evening climaxes with an auction featuring various goods and services. All money raised benefits the Martha's Vineyard Preservation Trust; 1996 ticket prices were $85 per person.

Farmers Market

West Tisbury • 693-0085

This is what we call an old fashioned farmers market. Held at the old Agricultural Hall on Saturdays from mid-June to mid-October and on Wednesdays from the end of June to the end of August, it offers fresh local-grown vegetables and homemade baked goods. There are even some artisans selling their arts and crafts.

July

Tisbury Birthday and Street Fair

Vineyard Haven • 693-4124

Tisbury is the second-oldest town on the island, incorporated in 1671 just after Edgartown. To celebrate its incorporation, the town throws itself a party in early July, and you are invited. Festivities include games, live entertainment and craft booths. Of course, food is available as well.

Band Concerts

Vineyard Haven and Oak Bluffs • 693-0085

Now this is an island vacation — music on a summer night! Sunday night is the night for band concerts, alternating between Owen Park in Vineyard Haven and Ocean Park in Oak Bluffs. You might want to bring your own lawn chair or blanket and soak up the sweet sounds under the summer stars. The band is always the Vineyard Haven Band Inc. and the admission is always free.

Monster Shark Fishing Tournament

Oak Bluffs • (610) 706-0301

Images of Quint standing upon the rocking bow of the *ORCA* with a harpoon gun in his hands come to mind when you consider this fishing tournament. Local charters and anglers alike vie to land the largest beast. Registration is held at Oak Bluffs Wesley Hotel. Call the Big Game Fishing Club at the number above for more about this event.

Portuguese Holy Ghost Feast

Oak Bluffs • 693-1564

Portuguese first arrived on the island in the early to mid-18th century. Many found employment as merchant seamen or on whaling vessels. Portuguese-American heritage is the focus at the Holy Ghost Feast — a festival of games, entertainment and some of the greatest food on the planet. It's held on the third Saturday in July.

Edgartown Fireworks

Edgartown Harbor • 693-0085

Fireworks over the harbor, need we say more? The Edgartown fireworks cap off the town's Independence Day celebration, and everyone seems to show up to witness the event. Get there early to claim your spot. Parking is a challenge but don't worry, you'll find a space somewhere.

Independence Day Parade

Edgartown • 693-0085

What would the Fourth be without a good parade? Edgartown comes through with the annual event featuring local high, school bands and floats which pass through the historic main routes of this old whaling port. You'll find yourself humming a Cohen song as you are swept up in the patriotic theme.

Seafood Festival

Edgartown • 693-0391

If you're a lover of great seafood you'll think you've gone to shellfish heaven. Eat your fill of oysters, clams, lobster and scallops. Admission is $1, food costs are additional. It all takes place at Memorial Wharf on Edgartown Harbor on the Saturday of July Fourth weekend and benefits the Martha's Vineyard Shellfish Group.

Edgartown Regatta
Edgartown Yacht Club • 627-4361

This regatta is one of the largest amateur sailing events in the area, usually beginning of the third Thursday in July and running throughout the weekend. This year, 1997, marks its 74th running. Races include many classes of boats, from smaller boats to larger cruising vessels. The race weekend attracts large crowds to Edgartown so you may want to make your room reservations months in advance to guarantee accommodations.

Vineyard Antique Show
Edgartown • 627-5121

In the heart of antiques country, you'd expect a stellar gathering of dealers and collectors, and this is it. Thirty-two dealers take part in this event held at the Edgartown Elementary School on Robinson Road.

August

In the Spirit Festival
Oak Bluffs • 693-0085

The In the Spirit Festival is a multi-cultural extravaganza that combines music, dance, food and merrymaking. It takes place in early August; an admission fee is charged.

All Island Art Show
Oak Bluffs • 693-0525

The famed Tabernacle at the Methodist campgrounds in Oak Bluffs is the site of this art show, which features island artists placing juried works on display. The event is well-attended as the work is of the highest caliber. Admission is free. It usually takes place on the first Monday in August.

Shark Shoot-Out Fishing Tournament
Oak Bluffs • 693-6611

You could possibly call this shark tournament JAWS 2 since it follows the Monster Shark Tourney in July. The goal of this mid-August event is quite simple: catch the biggest shark and avoid getting eaten in the process. You can register at the Wesley Hotel.

Fireworks at Ocean Park by the Sea
Oak Bluffs • 693-0085

Be prepared to "ooh" and "aah" at this traditional end-of-summer fireworks show. The event is free; bring along your own lawn chairs and blankets.

Illumination Night
Oak Bluffs • 693-0085

As its name suggests, this annual event involves luminescence. Tradition abounds as each of the gingerbread houses of Oak Bluff's old Methodist campgrounds twinkles with Japanese lanterns and candles as they have each year for the past centuries. Illumination night marks the end of yet another summer season. So popular is the event that those participating try to keep the date a secret to keep the crowds at bay . . . at Cape Cod Bay, that is.

Annual Antique Show
Edgartown • 627-4221

This large antiques show, now in its 26th year, features hundreds of vendors from Massachusetts, Connecticut and New York showcasing their treasures. Benefitting the Edgartown Public Library, this three-day event is held at the Edgartown School.

Possible Dreams Auction
Edgartown • 693-7900

Vineyarder Art Buchwald hosts this early August auction at the Harborside Inn gardens. It is a fund-raiser for Martha's Vineyard Community Services in which you can bid on everything from a sailboat ride with Walter Cronkite to a tour of CBS and the "60 Minutes" studios with Mike Wallace, even lunch with Carly Simon. Anything is possible, so bring your checkbook.

Vineyard Artisans Festival
West Tisbury • 693-8989

Local artists display their work amidst West Tisbury's country setting. Sounds like a fun afternoon to us. It all takes place at the New Agricultural Hall at the very end of August.

Agricultural Fair

West Tisbury • 693-4343

Tradition is the centerpiece of this grand, old-fashioned country fair. Pastoral West Tisbury is the perfect setting, complete with cotton candy and pie contests. This fair prompted Bonnie Raitt to write "Stayed Too Long at the Fair." (She probably had too much cotton candy.) Sponsored by the Martha's Vineyard Agricultural Society, it is held in mid-to late-August.

Chilmark Road Race

Chilmark • 693-0085

This is a series of 3-mile races for varying age groups. It benefits the Chilmark Community Center.

September

Jazzfest

Oak Bluffs • 693-0085

The Union Chapel on Kennebec Avenue is the site of the Jazzfest. Some of the best jazz musicians in the country show up. Tickets average $15, and the event is held over Labor Day weekend.

Vineyard Nursing Association Annual Golf Tournament

Vineyard Haven • 693-1960

The 9-hole Mink Meadows golf course is the site of this annual tournament. It is held in mid-September.

Tivoli Day Festival

Oak Bluffs • 693-0085

Tivoli is a city in Italy, just northeast of Rome. Closer to home, the Tivoli used to be the old dance hall in Oak Bluffs. Today, Tivoli Day is a festival of music, arts, crafts and food. Admission is free.

Martha's Vineyard Striped Bass and Bluefish Derby

Oak Bluffs • 627-8342

This fishing tournament is a month-long competition with more than $100,000 in prizes for those who catch the largest bass, bluefish, bonito and false albacore. Running from mid-September to mid-October, there are daily, weekly and grand prizes awarded. The year 1997 marks the 52nd annual Derby. The weigh station is at Oak Bluffs Harbor, although the Derby Headquarters can be reached by writing Box 2101 in Edgartown.

Vineyard Trade Show

West Tisbury • 693-0085

You'll have an opportunity to see goods and services produced on the island at this event, established in 1994. It is held in late September at the Agricultural Fairgrounds. Fine crafts, local food and entertainment, jewelry, handcrafted dolls and decorations and even appliance repair are on tap.

October

Annual Crop Hunger March

Vineyard Haven • 693-3930

This 10-kilometer walk from Vineyard Haven to Oak Bluffs (and back) raises awareness and money for the problem of hunger. The event, sponsored by the Clergy Association, is usually held on the third Sunday of the month. Anyone can join in; participants are asked to be sponsored. Since 1991 each march has raised about $10,000.

Columbus Day Road Race

Oak Bluffs • 693-0085

The air is a little cooler for this 5K endurance race. The event usually draws a good field of runners and an enthusiastic crowd of onlookers. Registration is at the Wesley Hotel.

Walkathon for AIDS

Oak Bluffs • 693-8868

Participants in this 5th annual walkathon travel from Oak Bluffs to Edgartown, a distance of 10 kilometers. The walkathon takes place in mid-October and benefits the AIDS Alliance of Martha's Vineyard.

Vineyard Craftsmen Fair

Edgartown • 693-8989

The talent found at this non-juried show will amaze you: intricate woodwork, delicate

Photo: Peter Simon

Everyone loves a parade, especially at Christmas.

dolls and exquisite one-of-a-kind collectibles created by island craftspeople as well as by artisans from off island. The fair takes place at the Edgartown School.

Happy Haunting Weekend

Edgartown • 627-4711

Ghosts and goblins and a devilishly good time come together in this traditional Halloween weekend, held closest to October 31 at the Colonial Inn. There is a pumpkin-carving contest, face painting and trick or treating at participating stores. After dark all the pumpkins are illuminated. Spooky!

November

Annual Martha's Vineyard Figure Skating Club Open Competition

Oak Bluffs • 693-0085

Is there another Carol Heiss, Tenley Albright or Peggy Fleming out there waiting to capture Olympic gold? Come find out for yourself at the Martha's Vineyard Arena in mid-November when the figure skating club open competition is held.

Vineyard Artisans Festival

West Tisbury • 693-8989

Local artists display their work amidst West Tisbury's country setting (a reprise of the August show). This festival takes place at the New Agricultural Hall on Thanksgiving weekend.

Tisbury's Come Home for the Holidays

Tisbury • 693-0085

From Thanksgiving through the First Night Celebrations the town of Tisbury holds a variety of events. There are horse-and-buggy rides, chowder festivals and performances at the Vineyard Playhouse. For a listing of all the events, check the calendar section of either the *Vineyard Gazette* or *Martha's Vineyard Times*, or call the Chamber of Commerce at the above number.

December

Annual Chowder Festival

Vineyard Haven • 693-0085

There's nothing like a good chowder (pronounced chow-da) to keep you warm on a brisk December day. Your taste buds will be dancing as you sample the many delicious chowders by the various area restaurants competing for the coveted title of "Best Chow-da on the Island." Held at The Tisbury Inn, the event raises money for the Red Stocking Fund, a charity that buys gifts for families in need.

An Old-Fashioned Christmas in Edgartown

Edgartown (various locations) • 693-0085

It's the Christmas season in Edgartown and the old whaling port is celebrating in a big way. What a grand event, or rather, series of events, this is! This old-fashioned Christmas celebration, chock-full of fun and festivities is held over three days, typically on the second weekend of the month. There's so much to do that you need three days to do it all.

There are bah humbug walking tours, free trolley tours, festival of lights tours, hayrides, horse-and-buggy rides, musical events and holiday concerts at the Old Whaling Church. There's a Christmas parade, and you can even have breakfast with Santa. An annual craft fair is held at the bedecked Victorian Inn. And of course, all the shops are open for business to cater to all your Christmas shopping needs, and many offer free eggnog and tea to get you warm and toasty as you walk the brick sidewalks of the perfect Christmas village. Many of the inns and hotels offer special rates for the weekend, but be sure to call ahead for reservations. Christmas in Edgartown — it's the perfect way to get into the holiday spirit!

First Night Celebration

Island-wide • 693-0085

The first First Night was held in 1994, and in such a short time it has become (many say) The Island Event. Activities abound, including lantern-making classes for kids, steel drum concerts, ballet performances, dancing and a fireworks display over Vineyard Haven Harbor. The majority of activities are held in Vineyard Haven. Last year's First Night celebrations attracted 2,500 people who participated in 47 events featuring more than 200 performers. For a complete listing of events, call the Chamber of Commerce at the number above.

Healthcare

Martha's Vineyard Hospital

Linton Lane, Oak Bluffs • 693-0410

This full-service hospital has an emergency room, in patient/out patient service, operating rooms, a day surgical suite, a radiology department, a three-bed dialysis unit, a psychiatry department and a cardiac rehabilitation program — basically all the services available at the mainland hospitals. Hopefully you won't need any of these services, but they're all there just in case. There are 22 staff physicians available at the hospital.

Important Numbers

Emergency? Call **911**. For support and crisis services, call the numbers below.

Alcoholics Anonymous	**693-2150**
Narcotics Anonymous	**693-7155**
Overeaters Anonymous	**693-3703**
Co-dependent Anonymous	**693-8798**
AIDS Alliance	**693-8868**
Elder Abuse Hotline	**(800) 922-2275**
Rape Hotline	**696-SAFE**
Child Abuse/Teen Crisis Hotline	**(800) 352-0711 or (800)792-5200**

Media

Coming to the island for a vacation is no excuse to lose complete touch with the outside world. Besides being able to pick up the *Boston Globe,* the *Cape Cod Times* and many of the other mainland newspapers, the Vineyard has a couple of newspapers of their own. You'll be able to pick up the many Cape radio stations as well as those from Providence, Rhode Island and Boston stations, but everyone knows that WMVY is all you'll really need.

Newspapers

Vineyard Gazette

34 South Summer St., Edgartown • 627-4311

The *Vineyard Gazette* recently celebrated its 150th year on the island (and throughout the anniversary year sold *Gazette* T-shirts, tote bags and coffee mugs to commemorate the event). It publishes twice a week from Memorial Day to Columbus Day (on Tuesday and Friday) and once a week throughout the winter (Fridays only).

Martha's Vineyard Times

30 Beach Rd., Vineyard Haven • 693-6100

The island's other newspaper, the *Times*, keeps you up to date on all the island happenings from Vineyard Haven to Edgartown and from East Chop to Gay Head. Started in 1984, it is a weekly paper that comes out on Thursdays and has the largest circulation of any paper on the island — 13,000 off-season and 16,000 in the summer. It is free to residents and on sale at newsstands.

Radio

WMVY Radio

57 Carrolls Way, Tisbury • 693-5000

WMVY at 92.7 FM plays adult-oriented rock (AOR as they call it in radio station talk). You can hear local news and weather as well as entertainment, concert reports and steamship sailing updates along with great music.

Television

Channel 8

Carroll's Way, Vineyard Haven • 693-5943

This local station is owned by Adelphia Cable, 7 Merchant's Mart, State Road, Vineyard Haven, 693-6644. Channel 8 offers a comprehensive high school sports schedule as well as other shows geared to the island.

Index of Advertisers

Index

B

C

D

F

G

H

N

O

S

Y

Z

Any Suggestions?

We want to know what you think of the Insiders' Guide to Cape Cod, Nantucket and Martha's Vineyard:

Additions? ____________________

Changes? ____________________

Comments? ____________________

Ideas for Insiders' Tips? ____________________

How did you find out about this book? ____________________

Thank you for your time in filling out this response form. Return this card before December 15, 1997 and your name will be entered into a drawing for a gift certificate for a two night stay at an Inn or Bed & Breakfast on Cape Cod. No purchase necessary, entry blanks are available at the *Cape Cod Times*. For a complete set of contest rules write: Insiders' Guide Cape Cod, 319 Main St., Hyannis, MA 02601.

I hereby give permission to use my comments in promotional material along with my initials,town and state.

Name: (please print) ____________________

Address: ____________________

City: ____________________ State: __________ Zip: __________

Phone: (______) ______-______

Signature ____________________

☐ Check here if you are interested in receiving information about Cape Cod real estate opportunities

BUSINESS REPLY MAIL

FIRST-CLASS PERMIT NO. 23 HYANNIS, MA 02601

POSTAGE WILL BE PAID BY ADDRESSEE

Cape Cod Times

INSIDERS' GUIDE
P.O. BOX 550
HYANNIS, MA 02601-9947